Tartaria
Mongol.
Cathaio
ASIA
China.
EVROPA
Turcheltan
Mar de Bachu
Coraſan
Perſia
Natolia
Barbaria.
Aegyptus
Arabia.
India orien talis.
Guzarate
AFRICA.
Agi ſymba
Nubia
Abiſſini
Manicongo.
Melinde.
Iapan
OCEANVS AETHIOPICVS.
MAR DI INDIA
Lantchidol mare
Pſitacorum regio, ſic à Luſitanis appellata ob incredibilẽ earum auium ſtudem magnitudinem.
NONDVM COGNITA

# New Jersey

## ADVENTURES IN TIME AND PLACE

James A. Banks

Barry K. Beyer

Gloria Contreras

Jean Craven

Gloria Ladson-Billings

Mary A. McFarland

Walter C. Parker

NATIONAL GEOGRAPHIC SOCIETY

COVER: GOLDFINCH (STATE BIRD), CARVING BY BRUCE HUFFORD; VIOLET (STATE FLOWER), MODERN GLASS FLOWER BY KATHRYN H. DAVIS, ALLEY KAT'S GLASS; BACKGROUND MAP OF NEW JERSEY COPYRIGHT © MAPQUEST.COM, COLUMBIA, MD. PHOTOGRAPHY MHSD.

McGraw-Hill School Division

New York Farmington

## PROGRAM AUTHORS

**Dr. James A. Banks**
Professor of Education and Director of the Center for Multicultural Education
University of Washington
Seattle, Washington

**Dr. Barry K. Beyer**
Professor Emeritus, Graduate School of Education
George Mason University
Fairfax, Virginia

**Dr. Gloria Contreras**
Professor of Education
University of North Texas
Denton, Texas

**Jean Craven**
District Coordinator of Curriculum Development
Albuquerque Public Schools
Albuquerque, New Mexico

**Dr. Gloria Ladson-Billings**
Professor of Education
University of Wisconsin
Madison, Wisconsin

**Dr. Mary A. McFarland**
Instructional Coordinator of Social Studies, K–12, and Director of Staff Development
Parkway School District
Chesterfield, Missouri

**Dr. Walter C. Parker**
Professor and Program Chair for Social Studies Education
University of Washington
Seattle, Washington

Washington, D.C.

## CONSULTANTS FOR TEST PREPARATION

The Princeton Review is not affiliated with Princeton University or ETS.

## HISTORIANS

**Dr. Delight Wing Dodyk**
Adjunct Professor of American Women's History
Drew University
Madison, New Jersey
President, Women's Project of New Jersey, Inc.

**Dr. Herbert Kraft**
Professor of Anthrolopogy; Director of the Seton Hall University Museum
South Orange, New Jersey

**Dr. James McPherson**
George Henry Davis Professor of American History
Princeton University
Princeton, New Jersey

**Dr. Jennifer Morgan**
Assistant Professor of History and Women's Studies
Rutgers University
New Brunswick, New Jersey

**Dr. Peter Wacker**
Professor of Geography
Rutgers University
New Brunswick, New Jersey

**Giles Wright**
Historian of Black Studies
Willingboro, New Jersey

## ECONOMICS CONSULTANT

**Jane Blakely**
Council on Economic Education
Trenton, New Jersey

## GRADE-LEVEL CONSULTANTS

**Paul Cohen**
Member, New Jersey Geographic Alliance
Supervisor of Social Studies
East Brunswick School District
East Brunswick, New Jersey

**Robert Davis**
Social Studies Supervisor
Newark Public School District
Newark, New Jersey

**Dr. Joseph DiBiase**
Supervisor of Social Studies
Trenton School District
Trenton, New Jersey

**Shirlene Gibbons**
4th grade teacher
Newark Public School District
Newark, New Jersey

**Sandy Haftel**
Supervisor of Social Studies
Allendale School District
Allendale, New Jersey

**Carolyn Hughes**
4th grade teacher
Trenton School District
Trenton, New Jersey

**Pamela Lewis**
4th grade teacher
New Jersey Avenue School
Atlantic City, New Jersey

**Normita Quemuel**
4th grade teacher
Franklin Elementary School
Trenton, New Jersey

## CONTRIBUTING WRITER

**Linda Scher**
Raleigh, North Carolina



**Acknowledgments**

The publisher gratefully acknowledges permission to reprint the following copyrighted material:

From "Digging the Ditch" by Christopher Cook Gilmore in *New Jersey Monthly*, March 1997. Copyright © Christopher Cook Gilmore. From *A Geography of New Jersey* by Charles A. Stansfield, copyright © 1998 Rutgers University Press. From "Manville after the Flood" by David Learn in *Packet OnLine*, September 22, 1999. From *Delta Wedding* by Eudora Welty, copyright © 1945, 1946 and renewed 1973, 1974 by Eudora Welty. Reprinted with permission of Harcourt Brace & Company. From *The Pine Barrens* by John McPhee, copyright © 1968, 1988. Reprinted with permission of Farrar, Straus, and Giroux. From *Words That Make New Jersey History* edited by Howard L. Green. Copyright © 1995 New Jersey Historical Commission. From *The Indians of Lenapehoking: Resource and Activities Supplement* by Herbert Kraft. Copyright © 1986 by Herbert Kraft, Archeological Research Center, Seton Hall University Museum. From *The Delaware Indians: A History*. Copyright © 1972 by


*(continued on page R54)*


*McGraw-Hill School Division*
*A Division of The McGraw-Hill Companies*





McGraw-Hill School Division
Two Penn Plaza
New York, New York 10121

Printed in the United States of America

ISBN 0-02-149164-X

4 5 6 7 8 9 071 04 03

Teacher's Multimedia Edition

ISBN 0-02-149165-8

3 4 5 6 7 8 9 071 04 03

# Handbook for Reading Social Studies

One important thing you will do this year is *read* this textbook. In order to understand important facts and ideas it is necessary to read in a certain way. This Reading Handbook will show you some helpful ways to read Social Studies.

**Lesson Overview**

Actual passages from the student text are used to demonstrate the strategy of identifying main idea and details.

**Lesson Objectives**

★ Identify the main idea of a paragraph or selection.

★ Recognize and state the supporting details.

## 1 PREPARE

**MOTIVATE** Ask students:

- ***How would you find out what a social studies selection is about?***
- ***How can you remember the important parts of a passage?***

**SET PURPOSE** Read the title of the lesson to students. Ask them what they think it means. Explain that they will read passages from their books to learn how to find the main idea and supporting details.

## 2 TEACH

**Identifying the MAIN IDEA and SUPPORTING DETAILS** Guide students to see that the main idea is the most important part of a selection. Explain that the supporting details tell more about the main idea.

Read the sample paragraph aloud. Point out that it is from the lesson titled "Waters of New Jersey" in Chapter 1. Using the bubble call-outs, guide students to state the main idea of the paragraph and the details that support it.



# Main Idea and Supporting Details

As you read, look for the **main idea** and **supporting details**. The main idea is what a paragraph or section is mostly about. The details support or expand the main idea. Keeping track of the main idea and supporting details will help you remember what you read.

- The first sentence or two of a paragraph often—but not always—contains the main idea.
- Use the titles and subheads in your book as a guide in identifying the main idea.
- Make an outline of the main ideas and supporting details of a lesson to help you review.

**To Find the Main Idea**
Ask yourself:

- What is this paragraph or section mostly about?

**To Find the Supporting Details**
Ask yourself:

- What words give more information about the main idea?

In your book, you will read about the waterways of New Jersey and their importance to our state. Rivers, streams, and tributaries are some examples of waterways. Read this paragraph to find the main idea and details.

> Our state's waterways are like the branches of a tree. Small creeks flow into larger streams and rivers. Streams and rivers flow into even larger rivers or empty into the ocean. Waterways connect communities to one another. They connect our state to other states—and even to other countries.
>
> *from page 14*

Main Idea: *Our state's waterways are like the branches of a tree.*

Details: *creeks, streams, and rivers flow into larger waterways or the ocean; connect people to other communities, states, and countries.*



**USING A GRAPHIC ORGANIZER**

Draw a main idea and details graphic organizer like the one below to help students identify the main idea and details.

| | | |
|---|---|---|
| **Main Idea** | Our state's waterways are like the branches of a tree. | |
| **Details** | creeks, streams, and rivers flow into larger waterways | connect people to other communities, states, and countries |

## TRY IT!

Read the paragraph below about the climate of the Southwest region in the United States. Then copy and complete the chart below to find the main idea and supporting details.

The climate of the Southwest is varied. The Coastal Plain along the Gulf of Mexico is warm and rainy. High up in the Rocky Mountains, the temperature can drop far below freezing. Much of the Southwest, however, is hot and dry. Many parts of the region are covered by deserts—dry land where little rain falls. A desert gets less than 10 inches of precipitation each year.

*from page 32*

**Main Idea**: The climate of the Southwest is varied.

**Details**:
- coastal plain is warm and rainy
- Rocky Mountains can drop below freezing
- many parts of the region are covered by deserts

- How did you find the main idea and details?

### Practice Activities

1. **READ** Read the first paragraph under "Hard Times in New Jersey" on page 213. Copy the chart above and record the main idea and supporting details.
2. **WRITE** Write a paragraph describing your neighborhood or school. Include a main idea and supporting details.

READING SOCIAL STUDIES

## Keep in Mind...

*For more help in reading social studies, try these strategies:*

☑ **Reread**
Review each sentence carefully. Make sure you understand what each sentence means before you read further.

☑ **Look up unknown words**
Use a dictionary or the glossary in your book to find the meaning of any words or terms you do not know.

☑ **Form a mental picture**
As you read, think about what your reading would look like.

HANDBOOK 3

## TRY IT!

Ask students to silently read the selection on this page. Point out that this paragraph is also from their textbook. Have them copy and complete the graphic organizer to identify the main idea and details.

Direct students to the *Tip!* section on the preceding page to help them complete the main idea and details diagram.

- **How did you find the main idea and details?**

Encourage students to explain the procedure they used to find the main idea and details.

## 3 CLOSE

Discuss the importance of identifying the main idea and supporting details when reading social studies. Point out that using this reading strategy can help them remember the important information in this subject.

Direct students to the *Keep in Mind...* tab for general help in reading social studies.

### Practice Activities

1. **READ Main Idea:** The Great Depression hit New Jersey hard. **Supporting Details:** New Jerseyans lost their jobs; factories, stores, and businesses shut down; salaries decreased

Additional selection for practicing this skill includes:

- page 117, first paragraph under "Hard Times for New Jerseyans"

2. **WRITE** Have students apply what they have learned about main idea and details to their own writing.

**The Reading Social Studies Practice Book** provides students with additional practice in identifying main ideas and supporting details.

### EXTENDING BEYOND THE TEXTBOOK

- Have students listen to a news report on the radio or television. Have them tell what the main idea of the report was and at least three supporting details.
- Have students read an article in one of their favorite magazines. Have them draw a graphic organizer to show the main idea and supporting details of the article.

READING SOCIAL STUDIES

**Lesson Overview**

Actual passages from the student text are used to demonstrate the strategy of using context clues.

**Lesson Objectives**

★ Recognize context clues.

★ Use context clues to understand unfamiliar terms.

★ Give the meaning of the unfamiliar words based on context clues.

## 1 PREPARE

**MOTIVATE** Ask students:

- ***What do you do when you read a word or term you do not understand?***
- ***How can you learn new words and terms when reading your social studies book?***

**SET PURPOSE** Read the title of the lesson to students. Ask them what the word clues means. Explain that as they read the following selections they will look for clues to help them figure out meanings of words or terms that are unfamiliar.

## 2 TEACH

**USING CONTEXT CLUES** Guide students to read the sentences surrounding the unfamiliar term to find context clues.

Read the sample paragraph aloud. Point out that it is from the lesson titled "Working for a Better Life" in Chapter 6. Using the bubble call-outs, guide students to identify the context clues they can use to help them find the meaning of the word *efforts*. Then have volunteers tell what they think the word means based on the clues.



# Context Clues

As you read your book, you may find a word or term that you do not know. One way to find the meaning of a new word is to look for **context clues**. Context clues are the words and sentences around the unfamiliar term. Using context clues helps you become a better reader.

**To Use Context Clues**

Ask yourself:

- What word is new to me?
- What might the word mean?
- What other words, phrases, and sentences help me figure out the meaning of the new word? What information do these other words provide?

**TIP!**

- Have you heard this word before? How was it used?
- Write down the context clues you used to find the meaning of the new word.
- Use the new word in a sentence of your own to help you remember it.

In your book, you will read about how people worked to improve life for others in New Jersey during the late 1800s. Read the paragraph below about one of them. What context clues would you use to identify the meaning of *efforts*?

> The reformers of our state were people who worked for all kinds of changes. Some fought to improve public schools. Others spoke out for rights for all Americans, including women and African Americans. Some wanted to help the poor, the sick, and children. The reformers' efforts helped make New Jersey better for all its people.
>
> ***from page 154***

*Context Clue:* ***spoke out for rights***

*Context Clue:* ***fought to improve schools***



**USING A GRAPHIC ORGANIZER**

Draw a context clues graphic organizer like the one below to help students identify context clues.

| fought to improve schools | | spoke out for rights |
| --- | --- | --- |
| | **efforts** | |

## TRY IT!

Read the paragraph below about one of the ways in which New Jersey's forests are a resource. Copy and complete the chart below to find context clues for *harvested*.

> Trees are a renewable resource because they can be replanted. Trees that are harvested from New Jersey forests are used for lumber, paper, and Christmas trees. After workers cut down an area of forest, they often plant new trees. Ten or more years later this new crop of trees can be harvested. In this way, the forest is always "renewed."
>
> *from page 43*

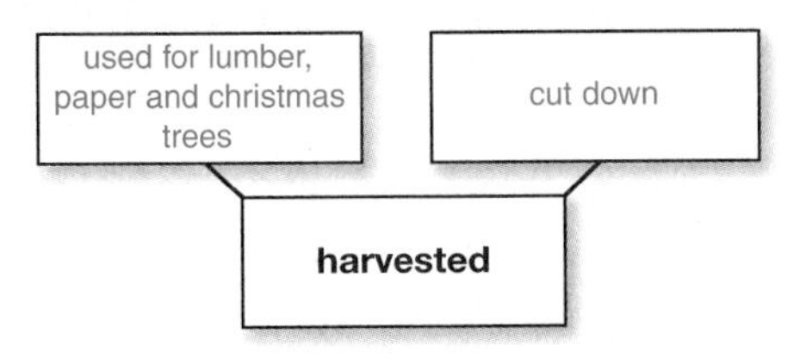


- How did you find the meaning of *harvested*?

## Practice Activities

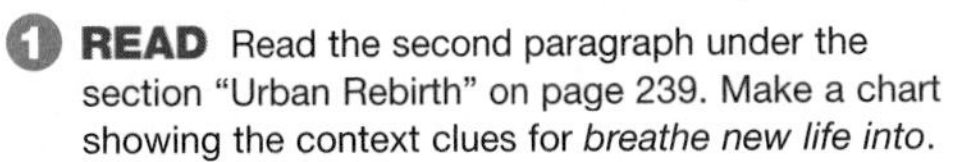

1. **READ** Read the second paragraph under the section "Urban Rebirth" on page 239. Make a chart showing the context clues for *breathe new life into*.
2. **WRITE** Look in the dictionary for the definition of the word *sagacious*. Write a paragraph using this word.

### Keep in Mind...

*For more help in reading social studies, try these strategies:*

- **Reread** Review each sentence carefully. Make sure you understand what each sentence means before you read further.
- **Form the big picture** As you read, think about the topic and the most important information in each paragraph or section.
- **Make predictions** As you read, think about what might happen next in your reading.



### EXTENDING BEYOND THE TEXTBOOK

Have students find a word they are not familiar with from a story in their literature book or another book they are reading.

- Read the sentences surrounding the new word.
- Have students use context clues to help them understand the meaning of the word.

## TRY IT!

Ask students to silently read the selection on this page. Point out that this paragraph is also from their textbook. Have them copy and complete the graphic organizer to find the meaning of *harvested*. Then have students write the meaning for *harvested*.

Direct students to the *Tip!* section on the preceding page to help them complete the context clues diagram.

- **How did you find the meaning of *harvested*?**

Encourage students to explain how they identified the context clues and how they used them to figure out the meaning.

## 3 CLOSE

Discuss the importance of using context clues when reading social studies. Point out that this strategy can help them find the meaning of unfamiliar words when they do not have a dictionary available to help, such as when they are taking a test.

Direct students to the *Keep in Mind...* tab for general help in reading social studies.

### Practice Activities

1. **READ Word:** breath new life into **Context Clues:** brought jobs, stores, and restaurants; rebirth; turned waterfront to a busy tourist site

Additional selection for practicing this skill includes:

- page 140, first paragraph under "The Big Picture." Use context clues to tell the meaning of *rose*.

2. **WRITE** Have students use what they have learned about context clues in their own writing.

**The Reading Social Studies Practice Book** provides students with additional practice in using context clues.

**Lesson Overview**

Actual passages from the student text are used to demonstrate the strategy of sequencing.

**Lesson Objectives**

★ Recognize and identify the sequence of events.

★ Recognize and identify the sequence of steps in a process.

## 1 PREPARE

**MOTIVATE** Ask students:

- ***How can you remember when important events occurred?***
- ***Why is it important to understand the correct sequence of events in social studies?***

**SET PURPOSE** Read the title of the lesson to students. Ask them what they think it means. Explain that they will read passages from their books to learn how to identify the sequence or order of events.

## 2 TEACH

**SEQUENCING** Guide students to see that sequence can mean the order of events or the order of steps in a process. Help them recognize clue words that show time order. Point out that in their social studies books, time clues are often given as dates as well as words.

Read the sample paragraph aloud. Point out that it is from the lesson titled "Early Peoples of New Jersey" in Chapter 3. Using the bubble call-outs, guide students to identify the order of events that are described in the paragraph.



# Sequencing

As you read, look for the order in which things happen. **Sequencing** events is listing them in the order in which they happen. Sequencing events helps you understand and remember what you read.

**TIP!**

- Look for dates—years, months, or centuries—that tell when events happened.
- Look for words like *first, next, then, followed, finally, last, before,* and *later* to identify the order of events.
- Use chapter time lines to help you remember the sequence of events.

**To Use Sequencing**

Ask yourself:

- Which event happened first?
- Which event happened next?
- Which order of events makes sense?

In your book, you will read about prehistoric New Jersey and the Ice Age. Read the paragraph below about how the Ice Age ended. Pay attention to the sequence of events.

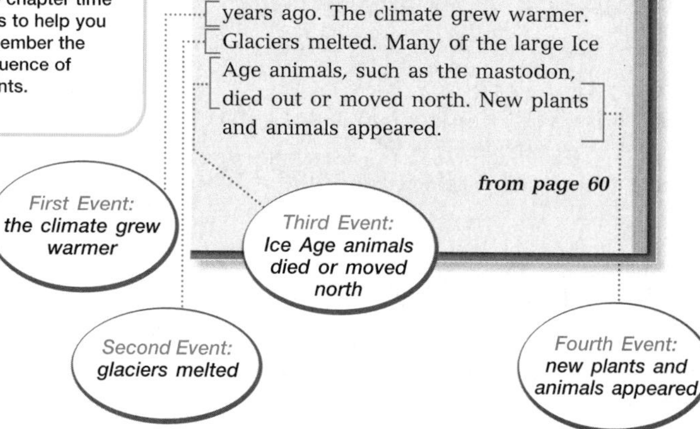




**USING A GRAPHIC ORGANIZER**

Draw a sequencing graphic organizer like the one below to help students identify sequencing.

**First Event:** The climate grew warmer.

↓

**Second Event:** Glaciers melted.

↓

**Third Event:** Ice Age animals died or moved north.

↓

**Fourth Event:** New plants and animals appeared.

READING SOCIAL STUDIES

## TRY IT!

Read the paragraph below about the changes in New Jersey's population druing the 1700's. Copy and complete the chart with events in sequence.

> During the 1700's, New Jersey's population grew quickly. At the beginning of the century, about 14,000 people lived in New Jersey. By 1750, this number had jumped to 71,000. By 1800 the population of New Jersey would swell to more than 211,000.
>
> ***from page 98***

At the beginning of the century, about 14,000 people lived in New Jersey.

↓

By 1750, the number had jumped to 71,000.

↓

By 1800 the population was more than 211,000.

• How did you determine the sequence of events?

### Practice Activities

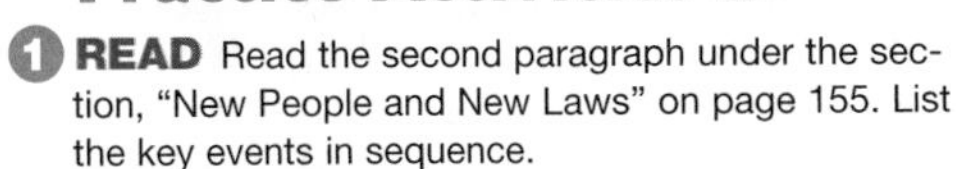

**1 READ** Read the second paragraph under the section, "New People and New Laws" on page 155. List the key events in sequence.

**2 WRITE** Write about the events of your day. Include words such as *first, then, next,* and *finally*.

### Keep in Mind...

*For more help in reading social studies, try these strategies:*

☑ **Look up unknown words**
Use a dictionary or the glossary in your book to find the meanings of any unfamiliar words.

☑ **Reread**
Review each sentence carefully. Make sure you understand what each sentence means before you read further.

☑ **Summarize**
In your own words, briefly describe what your reading is about. Look for topic sentences that contain the main ideas.

HANDBOOK 7

## EXTENDING BEYOND THE TEXTBOOK

- Have students watch their favorite television program and make a list of important events in correct sequence.
- Have students list in correct sequence the steps they follow to play their favorite game.

## TRY IT!

Ask students to silently read the selection on this page. Point out that this paragraph is also from their textbook. Have them copy and complete the graphic organizer to find the sequence of events.

Direct students to the *Tip!* section on the preceding page to help them complete the sequencing diagram.

- **How did you find out the sequence of events?**

Encourage students to explain how they identified the order of events.

## 3 CLOSE

Discuss with students the importance of understanding the sequence of events when reading social studies. Point out that this strategy can help them remember important events and how they are related.

Direct students to the *Keep in Mind...* tab for general help in reading social studies.

### Practice Activities

**1 READ First Event:** In 1776, the state constitution allowed any citizen with a certain amount of property to vote. **Second Event:** In the 1790s some women took part in elections but few African Americans voted. **Third Event:** In 1807, legislature passed a law stating that only free, white, adult males who paid a state tax could vote.

Additional selections for practicing this skill include:

- page 33, second paragraph under "The West"
- page 265, first paragraph under "A Trip Through Cyberspace"

**2 WRITE** Have students apply what they have learned about sequencing to their own writing.

**The Reading Social Studies Practice Book** provides students with additional practice in sequencing.

**Lesson Overview**

Actual passages from the student text are used to demonstrate the strategy of making predictions.

**Lesson Objective**

★ Combine background knowledge and what has already been read to make predictions about what comes next.

## 1 PREPARE

**MOTIVATE** Ask students:

- ***As you read, how do you get an idea of what might happen next?***
- ***What knowledge can you use to make a prediction?***

**SET PURPOSE** Discuss the title of this lesson with students. Ask them what they think it means. Explain that they will be reading passages from their textbooks to make predictions.

## 2 TEACH

**MAKE PREDICTIONS** Guide students to understand that they can identify clues in a passage that will help them make an educated guess about what might happen next. Their own background knowledge can also help them make predictions.

Read aloud the sample paragraph. Point out that it is from the lesson titled "Native Americans of New Jersey" in Chapter 3. Using the bubble call-outs, guide students to predict what will happen next.



# Make Predictions

As you read a paragraph or section in your book, think about what might come next. This is your **prediction.** A prediction does not have a correct or incorrect answer. Making predictions helps you to carefully consider what you are reading.

**To Make a Prediction**

Ask yourself:

- What happened in this section?
- What background knowledge do I already have?
- What similar situations do I know of?
- What do I think might happen next?

**TIP!**

- Think about other things you know that will help you make an "educated guess."
- Test your prediction: read further to see if you are correct.
- Revise your prediction: read further to see if more information changes your prediction.

In your book, you will read about the Lenape Indians of New Jersey. Read this paragraph about what they did during the spring, summer, and fall months. Then read the prediction about the winter. Do you agree or disagree with this prediction?

> In the spring, the Lenape planted their crops. Once the planting was done, some Lenape left the village. They traveled to the Jersey shore in the summer to collect clams and oysters. By the fall, everyone would return to the village to help harvest corn, beans, and squash.
>
> *from page 65*

Text Information: *planted crops in the spring; collected clams and oysters from the shore in summer; harvested corn, beans, and squash in the fall*

Background Information: *I know that winters are cold and long in New Jersey.*

Prediction: *In winter, the Lenape stayed in the village, living off of foods gathered earlier in the year.*



**USING A GRAPHIC ORGANIZER**

Have students fill in a make predictions graphic organizer like this to help students make predictions.

**Text Information**

Planted crops in the spring; collected clams and oysters from the shore in the summer; harvested corn, beans, and squash in the fall.

**Background Information**

I know that winters are cold and long In New Jersey.

**My Prediction**

To prepare for winter they stored food, gathered nuts and berries, and dried meats and fish to last through the winter.

## TRY IT!

In your book you will read about the incredible increase in New Jersey's population after World War II. More homes had to be built quickly. Read the passage below about the response to the need for housing. Copy and complete the prediction chart below.

> After the war thousands of soldiers returned home. They needed places to live. Businesspeople responded quickly to this need for housing. Builders created whole new communities, complete with schools and stores. William J. Levitt was one such builder. He turned the small farming village of Willingboro, with a population of 600, into a suburb of 40,000 people. How did Levitt do this?
>
> *from page 223*

**Text Information**
Builders turned small villages into suburbs or built whole new communities.

**Background Information**
I know that to build a house you need a lot of people and time.

**Prediction**
Levitt was able to build so many homes in a short amount of time because of mass production.

- How did you make your prediction?

### Practice Activities

1. **READ** Read the section titled "A New Government" on page 128 of your book. On a sheet of paper, predict what the outcome might be.
2. **WRITE** Write a paragraph predicting what you will do after high school. Give reasons why.

### Keep in Mind...

*For more help in reading social studies, try these strategies:*

- **Sequencing** As you read, think about the order in which things happened.
- **Form the big picture** As you read, think about the topic and the most important information in the paragraph or section.
- **Relate to personal experience** Think about how what you are reading about relates to your own life.



## EXTENDING BEYOND THE TEXTBOOK

Direct students to read about a local election or school issue and make predictions about the outcome. Note that:

- there will be a limited number of possibilities;
- reading about the issue or candidates will give students background information that can help them make predictions.

## TRY IT!

Ask students to read the selection on this page. Remind them that the passage is also in their textbook. Have them copy and complete the graphic organizer to record their predictions.

Encourage students to refer to the *Tip!* section on the preceding page if they are unsure of how to complete the make predictions diagram.

- **On what did you base your prediction?**

Invite students to discuss how they made their predictions.

## 3 CLOSE

Discuss with students the importance of being able to make predictions when reading social studies. Explain that when they make predictions they pay more attention to details as they read. As predictions are proved or disproved, students can use their new knowledge to make more predictions.

Direct students to the *Keep in Mind...* tab for general help in reading social studies.

### Practice Activities

1. **READ Text Information:** Larger states liked The Virginia Plan form of government. Smaller states liked The New Jersey Plan form of government. **Background Information:** Answers will vary depending on experience. **My Prediction:** Large and small states compromise.

Additional selections for practicing this skill include:

- page 185, section titled "Journey to a New Home"
- page 201, third paragraph under "Strike at Paterson"

2. **WRITE** Ask students to apply what they have learned about making predictions to their own writing.

**The Reading Social Studies Practice Book** provides students with additional practice in making predictions.

**Lesson Overview**

Actual passages from the student text are used to demonstrate the compare and contrast strategy.

**Lesson Objectives**

★ Recognize similarities and differences in order to compare and contrast elements in a text.

## 1 PREPARE

**MOTIVATE** Ask students:

- ***As you read, how can you decide how two things are similar?***
- ***How can you decide how things are different?***

**SET PURPOSE** Ask students what they think the title of this lesson means. Explain that they will be reading passages from their textbook in order to compare and contrast people, places, or events.

## 2 TEACH

**COMPARE and CONTRAST** Guide students to understand that they can compare things to see how they are alike and contrast things to see how they are different. Comparing and contrasting both help in understanding relationships between things.

Read aloud the sample paragraph. Point out that it is from the lesson "Life in the New Jersey Colony" in Chapter 4. Using the bubble call-outs, guide students to compare and contrast the lives of colonial boys and girls.



# Compare and Contrast

This book often **compares** and **contrasts** people or events. To compare things is to see how they are alike. To contrast things is to see how they are different. Comparing and contrasting helps you understand the relationships between things.

- To compare, look for clue words such as *like*, *similar*, *in common*, *same*, and *resemble*.
- To contrast, look for clue words such as *before*, *after*, *different from*, *unlike*, and *by contrast*.

**To Compare**

Ask yourself:

- What are the things being compared?
- How are they alike?

**To Contrast**

Ask yourself:

- What are the things being contrasted?
- How are they different?

In your book, you will read about the lives of the English settlers in New Jersey. Read the paragraph below to compare and contrast the lives of colonial boys and girls.

> Girls and boys began every day with chores. For girls, this meant sewing, preparing food, and washing pots. Girls also took care of younger children. Boys cut firewood, cared for animals, or led the horse or ox that pulled the plow. With all of this work to do, most children attended school only a few weeks each year. Some learned to read at home.
>
> ***from page 99***

Contrast: *Girls sewed, prepared food, washed pots, took care of younger children*

Compare: *Both began every day with chores, many attended school only a few weeks a year, some learned to read at home*

Contrast: *Boys cut firewood, cared for animals, led the animal that pulled the plow*



**USING A GRAPHIC ORGANIZER**

Draw a compare and contrast graphic organizer like the one below to help students practice comparing and contrasting.

| Colonial Girls | Both | Colonial Boys |
| --- | --- | --- |
| girls sewed, prepared food, washed pots, took care of younger children | both began everyday with chores, many attended school only a few weeks a year, some learned to read at home | boys cut firewood, cared for animals, led the animal that pulled the plow |

## TRY IT!

Read below about the differences between east and west New Jersey in the 17th century. Copy and complete the diagram below to compare and contrast them.

East and West Jersey were different. East Jersey looked like New England, with its small farms and towns, such as Newark and Shrewsbury. People worshipped in many different churches. West Jersey had larger farms, set farther apart. Many of the people who lived there were Quakers. Over time, the city of New York came to have a great influence over East Jersey. Philadelphia became important to West Jersey.

*from page 92*

| East New Jersey | Both in New Jersey | West New Jersey |
|---|---|---|
| Small farms and towns; many different churches; influenced by New York | | Large farms, set farther apart; mostly Quakers; influenced by Philadelphia |

- What steps did you take to compare and contrast?

### Practice Activities

1. **READ** Read the section titled "The Big Picture" on page 302 of your book. List the differences between education 300 years ago and today.
2. **WRITE** Compare and contrast the weather in your community for the months of July and December.

READING SOCIAL STUDIES

### Keep in Mind...

*For more help in reading social studies, try these strategies:*

- **Look up unknown words** Use a dictionary or the glossary in your book to find the meaning of any unfamiliar words.
- **Form the big picture** As you read, think about the most important information of the paragraph or section.
- **Summarize** In your own words, briefly describe what your reading is about.

HANDBOOK 11

## EXTENDING BEYOND THE TEXTBOOK

- Have students compare and contrast two sports, discussing ways in which the rules and manner of play are different and similar.
- Have students compare and contrast two (or more) seasons. If they prefer one season over another, they could give reasons for preferring it.

## TRY IT!

Ask students to silently read the selection on this page. Point out that the paragraph is also in their textbooks on page 92. Have students copy and complete the graphic organizer to compare and contrast East and West New Jersey.

If students are unsure of how to complete the compare and contrast diagram, direct them to the *Tip!* section on the preceding page.

- **What steps did you take to compare and contrast?**

Invite students to discuss the similarities and differences they identified.

## 3 CLOSE

Discuss with students the importance of using the compare and contrast strategy as they read social studies. Explain that to understand relationships between people and events in history they will need to identify similarities and differences often as they read.

Direct students to the *Keep in Mind...* tab for general help in reading social studies.

### Practice Activities

1. **READ Contrast:** 300 years ago schoolhouses had one room and students became farmers, homemakers, and craftworkers; today, more than a million students go to schools with computers, science labs, and art studios **Compare:** types of education in New Jersey

Additional selections for practicing this skill include:

- page 99, second and third paragraph under "Life on the Farm"
- page 162, second paragraph under "The Big Picture"

2. **WRITE** Ask students to apply what they have learned about the compare and contrast strategy to their own writing.

**The Reading Social Studies Practice Book** provides students with additional practice in using the compare and contrast strategy.

**Lesson Overview**

Actual passages from the student text are used to demonstrate the strategy of summarizing.

**Lesson Objectives**

★ Recognize the important ideas in a selection.

★ Write a brief, organized summary.

## 1 PREPARE

**MOTIVATE** Ask students:

- ***How can you tell others what a selection is about?***
- ***Do you need to remember every detail of a selection? Why or why not?***

**SET PURPOSE** Read the title of the lesson to students. Ask them what they think it means. Explain that they will read passages from their books to learn how to summarize what they read.

## 2 TEACH

**SUMMARIZE** Guide students to see that writing a summary involves several different skills. Explain that in order to write a summary, students must choose the most important ideas or information, organize them in a logical way, and use their own words to briefly write them.

Read the sample paragraph aloud. Point out that it is from the lesson titled "Early Peoples of New Jersey" in Chapter 3. Using the bubble call-outs, guide students to summarize the selection.



# Summarize

After you read a paragraph or section of this book, you can **summarize** what you have read. In a **summary**, you briefly tell in your own words about the most important information in the section. Summarizing is a way to help you understand what you read.

**To Summarize**

Ask yourself:

- What is this paragraph or section about?
- What information is most important?
- How can I say this in my own words?

**TIP!**

- Look for titles, headings, and key words that identify important information.
- Keep your summary brief, and organize the information in a clear way.
- Don't include information and facts that are not the most important.

In your book you will read about the early people of prehistoric New Jersey and how they survived. Read the paragraph and sample summary below.

Animals were important for more than food. They provided clothing and shelter as well. Early people dressed in animal furs and wore boots made from animal skins. They probably also used animal skins to make tents.

Hunting was not their only source of food. They also gathered fruits and nuts from the forest and fish from rivers. We call these people hunter-gatherers because they hunted and gathered their food.

*from page 60*

*Sample Summary:* *Hunters-gatherers hunted animals for food, shelter, and clothing. They also fished and gathered fruits and nuts.*

*Important information is underlined*



### USING A GRAPHIC ORGANIZER

Draw a summarizing graphic organizer like the one below to help students make a summary.

| Important Information | Summary |
|---|---|
| Animals provided clothing and shelter. | Hunter-gatherers hunted animals for food, shelter, and clothing. They also fished and gathered fruits and nuts. |
| They used animal skins to make boots and tents and dressed in animal fur. | |
| They gathered fruits and nuts from the forest and fish from the rivers. | |

## TRY IT!

Read the paragraph below about the time after World War I that was nicknamed "The Roaring Twenties." Copy and complete the summary diagram.

> The decade of the 1920s was an exciting time. Business boomed. Inventions such as vacuum cleaners and refrigerators made life easier. New ideas were changing the way people wrote, painted, sang, and danced. In New Jersey and all over the United States, this decade was rightly called "The Roaring Twenties."
>
> *from page 210*

**Important Ideas**

- Business boomed, more people had jobs.
- New inventions made life easier.
- New ideas were changing the way people created their art.

**Summary**

The Roaring Twenties was a period with new and exciting ideas, inventions and jobs.

- How did you choose what to include in the summary?

### Keep in Mind...

*For more help in reading social studies, try these strategies:*

**Reread**
Review each sentence. Make sure you understand what each sentence means before you read further.

**Form the big picture**
As you read, think about the topic and the main ideas of the paragraph or section.

**Make an outline**
As you read, write an outline of the topic and the main ideas of the reading.

### Practice Activities

1. **READ** Read the section titled "Labor Unions" on page 178. Summarize the section in your own words.
2. **WRITE** Write a summary of a book you have recently read.



## TRY IT!

Ask students to silently read the selection on this page. Point out that this paragraph is also from their textbook. Have them copy and complete a graphic organizer to make a summary.

Direct students to the *Tip!* section on the preceding page to help them complete the summarize diagram.

- **How did you choose what to include in the summary?**

Encourage students to explain the procedure they used to write and organize their summaries.

## 3 CLOSE

Discuss the importance of being able to summarize when reading social studies. Point out that this strategy helps students both understand what they read and provides notes they can use to study for tests.

Direct students to the *Keep in Mind...* tab for general help in reading social studies.

### Practice Activities

1. **READ Important Information:** workers formed labor unions, held strikes, 137 strikes took place in Paterson between 1881 and 1900, by 1900 workers made few gains, still worked long hours for low wages.
**Summary:** Workers held many strikes in the late 1800s to improve working conditions, but by 1900 they still worked long hours for little pay.

Additional selections for practicing this skill include:

- page 46, second paragraph under "Conservation and Recycling"
- page 252–253, section titled "How a Business Works"

2. **WRITE** Have students apply what they have learned about summarizing to their own writing.

**The Reading Social Studies Practice Book** provides students with additional practice in summarizing.

### EXTENDING BEYOND THE TEXTBOOK

- Have students write a summary of a story they enjoyed reading.
- Have students write a summary of a movie they saw. Have them share and compare summaries with the class.

READING SOCIAL STUDIES

**Lesson Overview**

Actual images from the student text are used to demonstrate the strategy of using visuals.

**Lesson Objectives**

★ Clarify and supplement information in the main text by using visuals.

## 1 PREPARE

**MOTIVATE** Ask students:

- ***How can a visual help you understand what you read?***
- ***How can you use a map to find information about a place?***

**SET PURPOSE** Ask students what they think it means to use visuals. Explain that they will use visuals in their textbooks to better understand what they read.

## 2 TEACH

**USE VISUALS** Guide students to understand that they can use visuals to better understand the main text. Visuals such as captions, photos, graphs, charts, maps, and diagrams can give additional information that is not included in the main text.

Have students study the diagram and read the captions silently. Point out that the photo is from the lesson titled "Daily Life of the Lenape" in Chapter 3. Using the bubble call-outs, guide students to understand how the visuals help to explain lunch tray recycling.



# Use Visuals

One way to learn is to use **visuals.** Visuals are charts, pictures, and maps in your book. They give information in an easy-to-study form.

- Read the caption and labels for information they give.
- Be sure to find the meanings of special symbols.

**To Use Visuals**

Look closely at the visual. Ask yourself:

- What does the graph, chart, picture, or map show?
- How does it help me to understand what I have read?
- How does it add to the information I have read?
- What information does the visual's caption provide?

In your book, you will read about the daily life of the Lenape Indians. Study the picture below of a Lenape village.

This Lenape village has been re-created to show how the Lenape lived in the 1600s.

*The caption tells us that this is a recreation of a Lenape village from the 1600s.*

*Women cooked outdoors. They used tools made of wood and stone to cook and pots made of clay.*

*from page 70-71*



### USING A GRAPHIC ORGANIZER

Draw a using visuals graphic organizer like the one below to help students use visuals.

**Caption:** This is a recreation of a Lenape village from the 1600s.

**Visual:** Women cooked outdoors.

**Visual:** They used tools made of wood and stone to cook and pots made of clay.

READING SOCIAL STUDIES

## TRY IT!

Study the pictures below from the silk workers strike at Patterson in 1913. Copy and complete the chart below to use visuals.

The International Workers of the World union supported the Patterson Strike. It arranged a march (below) and a play (right) so workers could tell their story.

*from page 201*

*Caption: I.W.W. marched in support of strikers; strikers held a play*

*Visual: tickets for the play were between 10¢ and $2.00*

*photograph, poster*

*Visual: People dressed differently. Most are wearing hats.*

*Visual: some women carry flags, others wear I.W.W. banners*

### Practice Activities 

1. **READ** Read page 182–183 in your book. How does the photograph add to the information on the page?
2. **WRITE** Create a visual illustrating something you like. Write a caption for it.

### Keep in Mind...

*For more help in reading social studies, try these strategies:*

- **Use Visuals** Review captions and labels carefully. Make sure you understand what each sentence means before you read further.
- **Study the charts and graphs** Charts and graphs provide information in an easy-to-understand form.
- **Study the unit and chapter openers** The first page of a unit or chapter often summarizes what you will read about. It also may contain useful maps and pictures.

HANDBOOK 15

## EXTENDING BEYOND THE TEXTBOOK

Direct students to a newspaper story with photos to apply their understanding of using visuals. Note that:

- the photos show people or events referred to in the news story;
- captions identify the photos and relate them to the text.

## TRY IT!

Ask students to study the visual on this page. Point out that the visual is also in their textbooks on page 201. Have students copy and complete a graphic organizer to record their responses.

Direct students to the *Tip!* section on the preceding page to help them complete the use visuals diagram.

- **How did you use the visual to get more information?**

Invite students to discuss how they used details in the visual to get information.

## 3 CLOSE

Discuss with students that it is important to be able to use visuals while reading social studies because this strategy will help them better understand the text. Also, visuals sometimes include details that are not in the text.

Direct students to the *Keep in Mind...* tab for general help in reading social studies.

### Practice Activities

1. **READ Visual Information:** The photograph shows immigrants arriving at Ellis Island. The people in the photo are dressed differently than today, seem tired and scared, and are carrying many bags.

Additional selections for practicing this skill include:

- page 16, visual called "How an Aquifer Works"
- page 88, visual of a Dutch "groot kamer"

2. **WRITE** Ask students to apply what they have learned about using visuals to their own writing.

**The Reading Social Studies Practice Book** provides students with additional practice in using visuals.

# CONTENTS

**UNIT TWO** 52

# The Settlement of a New Land



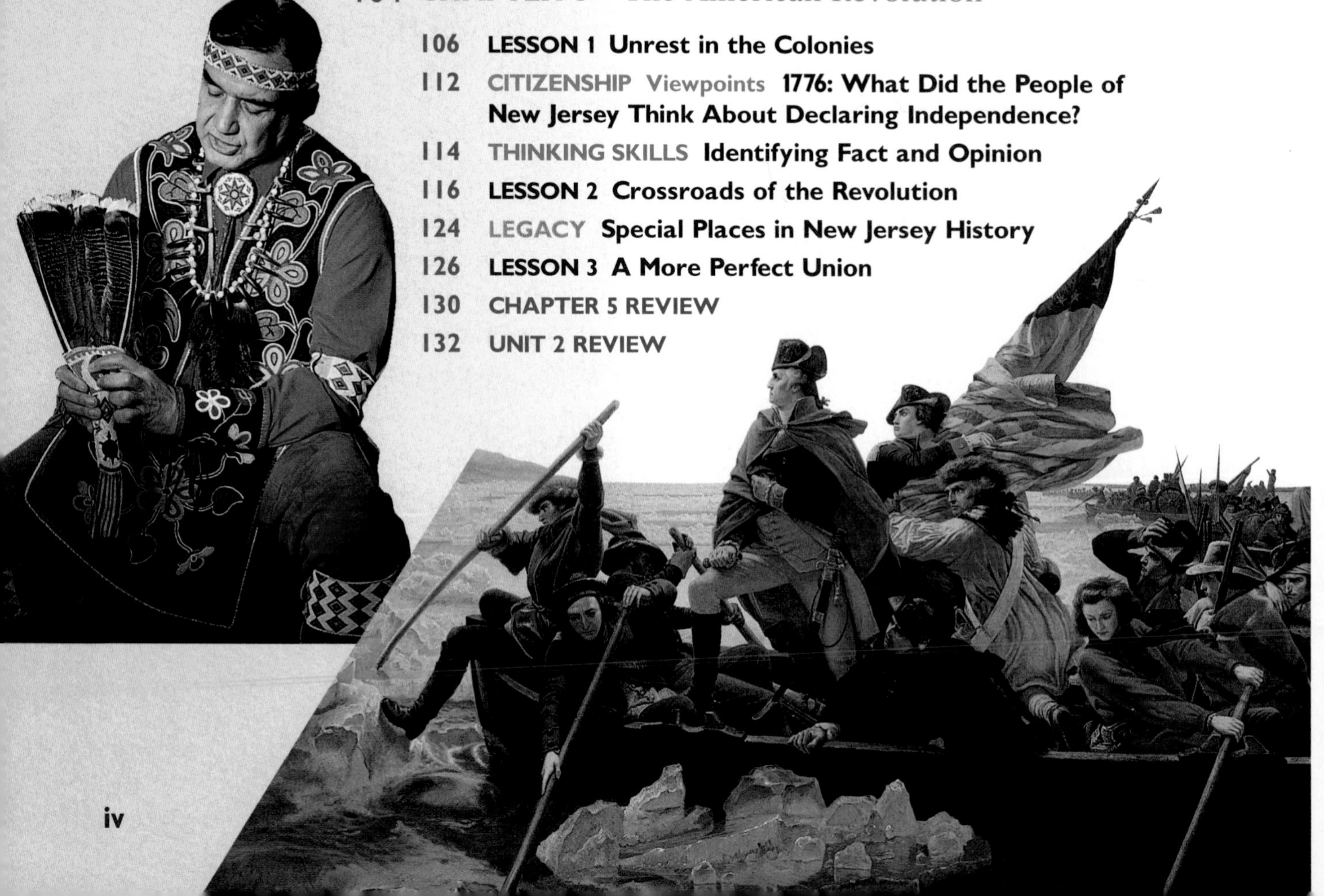

# UNIT THREE A Growing State

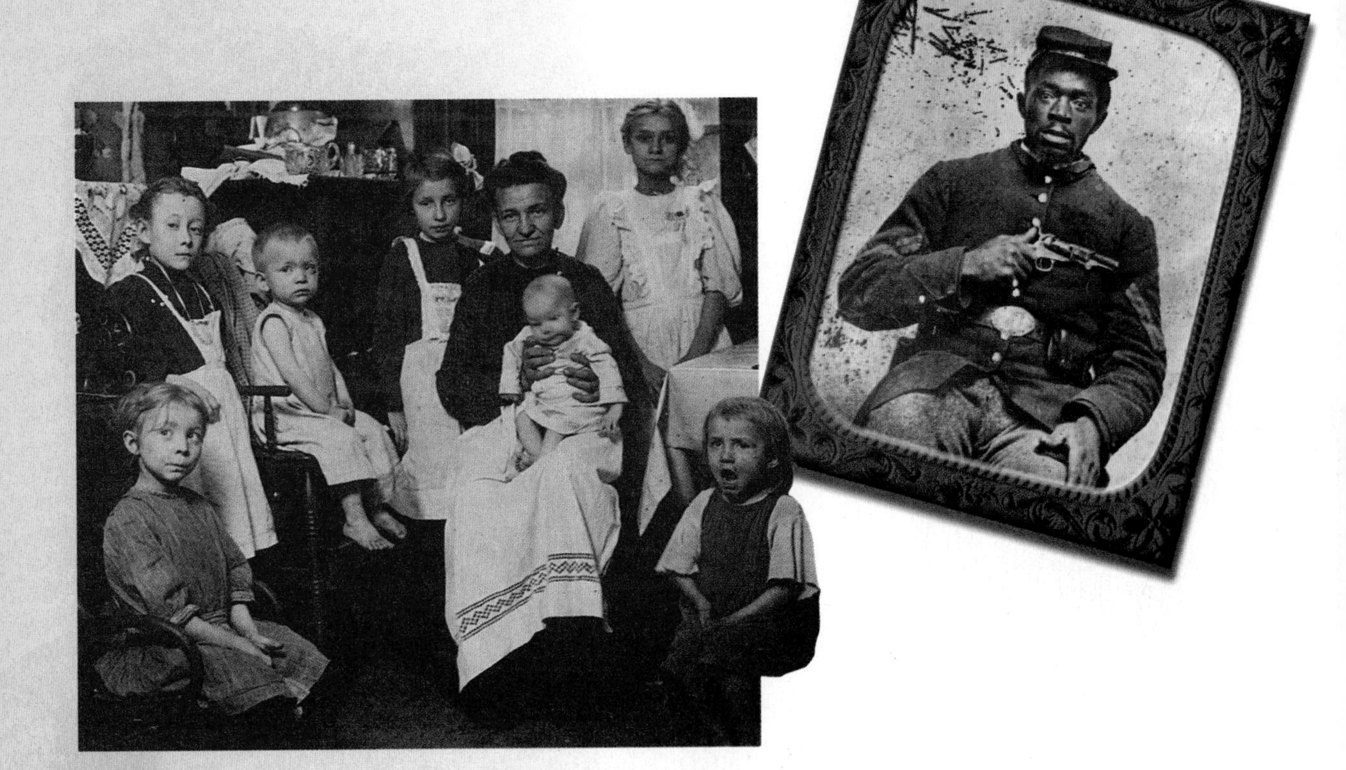

## UNIT FOUR New Jersey Comes of Age

UNIT FIVE
244

# New Jersey in the Twenty-First Century

# REFERENCE SECTION



# STANDARDIZED TEST SUPPORT

# FEATURES

## SKILLS LESSONS



## CITIZENSHIP



## LEGACIES

## Many Voices

### Primary Sources



### Literature



### Art



### Music



## INFOGRAPHICS



## LINKS



## DID YOU KNOW?

# CHARTS, GRAPHS, & DIAGRAMS



# TIME LINES

# MAPS



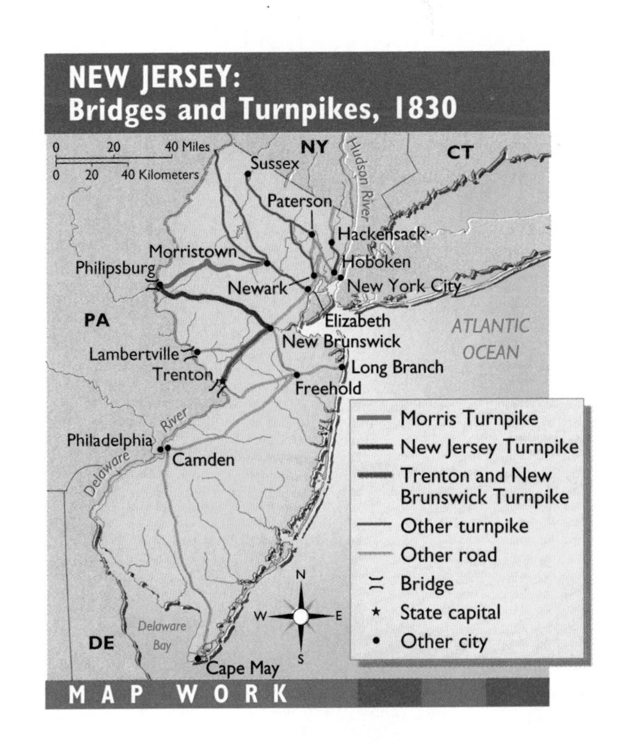
NEW JERSEY:
Bridges and Turnpikes, 1830
0 20 40 Miles
0 20 40 Kilometers
NY
CT
PA
DE
Sussex
Paterson
Hudson River
Hackensack
Morristown
Hoboken
Philipsburg
Newark
New York City
Elizabeth
New Brunswick
ATLANTIC OCEAN
Lambertville
Trenton
Long Branch
Freehold
Philadelphia
Camden
Delaware River
Delaware Bay
Cape May
N
S
E
W
Morris Turnpike
New Jersey Turnpike
Trenton and New Brunswick Turnpike
Other turnpike
Other road
Bridge
State capital
Other city
MAP WORK

# YOUR TEXTBOOK at a glance

**Your book is called *New Jersey: Adventures in Time and Place*. It has twelve chapters and a special section. Each chapter has three or more lessons. There are also many special features for you to study and enjoy.**

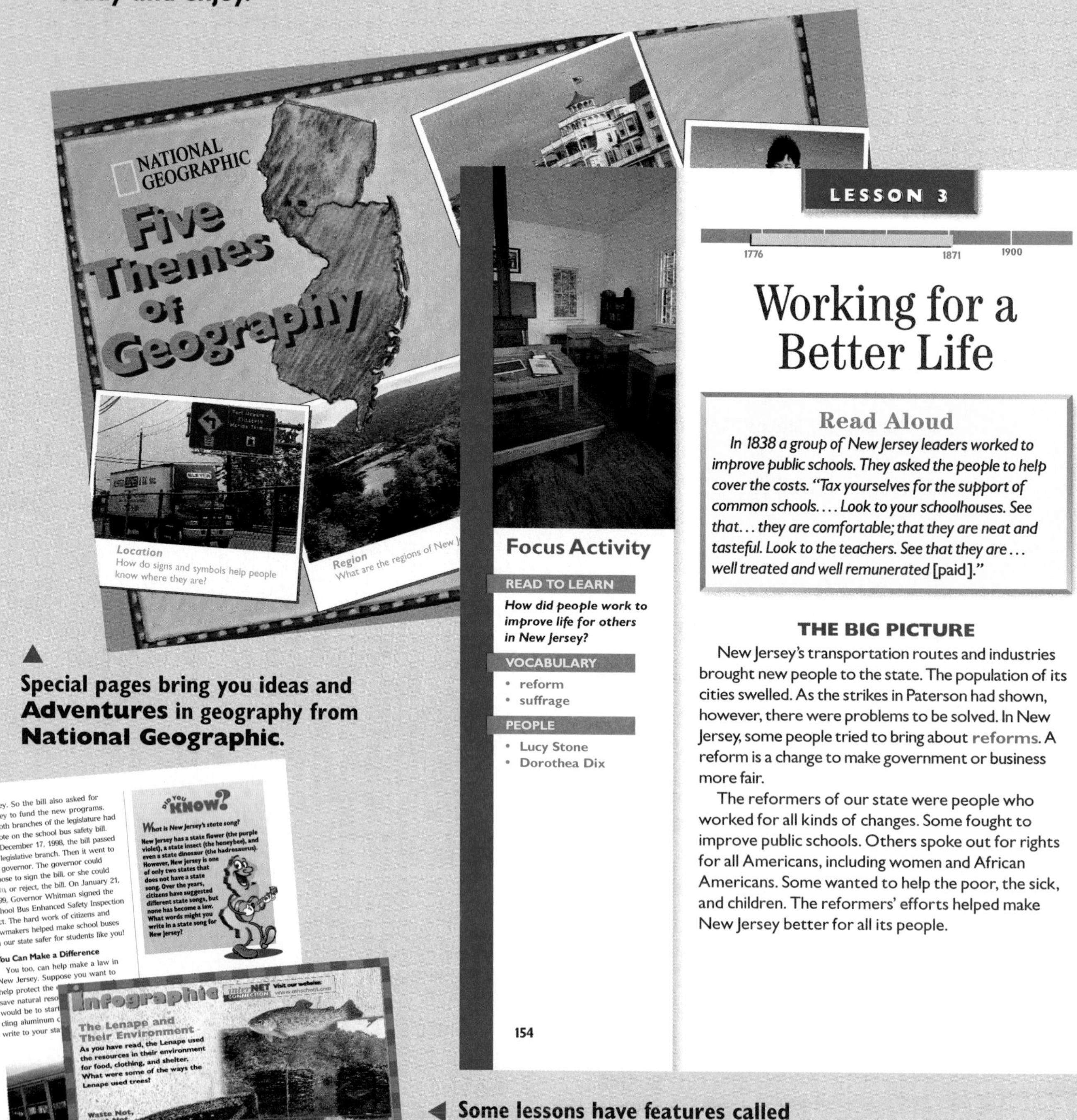


**Special pages bring you ideas and Adventures in geography from National Geographic.**

**Some lessons have features called Did You Know. They offer you interesting information to share. Infographics inform you with pictures and maps.**

Look for a variety of lessons and features. **Links** are activities to try. You will build **Skills**, learn about **Legacies** that connect us to the past, and meet people who show what **Citizenship** is.

## NEW PEOPLE AND NEW LAWS

From about 1820 to 1860, many immigrants came to the United States. Many of these immigrants came from England, Ireland, and Germany. New Jersey had a lot of jobs to offer, so many immigrants settled here. The graph on this page shows how New Jersey's population grew.

Not all of the people who lived in New Jersey had the same rights. State laws about who could vote changed several times. In 1776 the state constitution allowed any citizen with a certain amount of property to vote, including women and African American men. In the 1790s some women took part in elections, but few African Americans voted. Then, in 1807, the legislature passed a new law. It said that only free, white, adult males who paid a state tax could vote.

In 1844 New Jersey held a Constitutional Convention to improve the state constitution. The new constitution allowed any white male over the age of 21 who had lived in the state for one year to vote. However, all women and African American men were still unable to vote.

Some women became part of a growing suffrage movement. Suffrage means the right to vote. Lucy Stone was an important leader in the struggle for women's rights. In addition to suffrage, she also struggled for women's equality in jobs and education. After she moved to Orange in 1857, she refused to pay her taxes. Here is part of a letter she wrote explaining her reasons. Do you think she expected her protest to be successful?

**MANY VOICES**
PRIMARY SOURCE

**Excerpt from a letter from Lucy Stone to the tax collector of Orange, New Jersey, 1858.**

*Enclosed I return my tax bill, without paying it. My reason for doing so is that women suffer taxation and yet have no representation, which is not only unjust to one half of the adult population, but is contrary to [against] our theory of government. . . .*

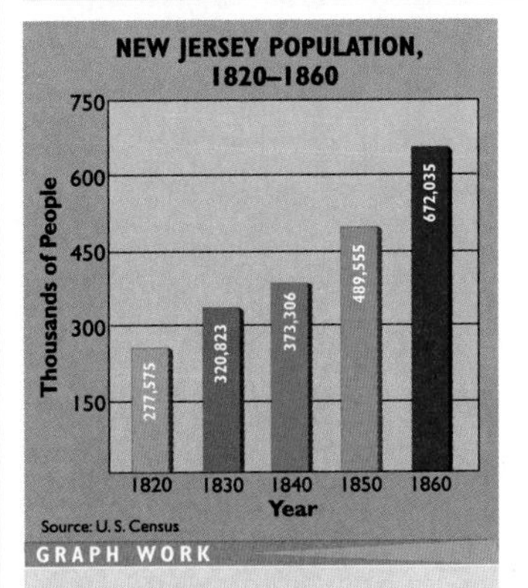


GRAPH WORK

Immigration to New Jersey began to increase after 1840.

1. During which years shown on the graph did our state's population grow fastest?

155

The end of your book has a **Reference Section** with many types of information. Use it to look up words, people, and places.

Lessons begin with a **Read Aloud** selection and **The Big Picture**. Study with the **Read to Learn** question and a list of words, people, and places. Enjoy **Many Voices**—writings from many sources.

**Location**
How do signs and symbols help people know where they are?

**Region**
What are the regions of New Jersey?

**Place**
How do places like Cape May make New Jersey special?

**Human/Environment Interaction**
Why is New Jersey known as the Garden State?

**Movement**
How do people—and goods—travel from one place to another?

Reviewing

# GEOGRAPHY SKILLS

## PART 1
## Using Globes

**VOCABULARY**

ocean
continent
hemisphere
equator

### *What does a globe show?*

- A globe is a small copy of Earth. Like Earth, a globe is a round object, or sphere.
- Globes show the parts of Earth that are land and the parts that are water. Earth's largest bodies of water are called **oceans**. There are four oceans—the Arctic, Atlantic, Indian, and Pacific Oceans. Look at the globe shown here. What color is used to show oceans?*
- Globes also show the seven large bodies of land called **continents**. The continents are Africa, Antarctica, Asia, Australia, Europe, North America, and South America. Find North America and South America on the globe below. Which oceans do you see bordering these continents?**

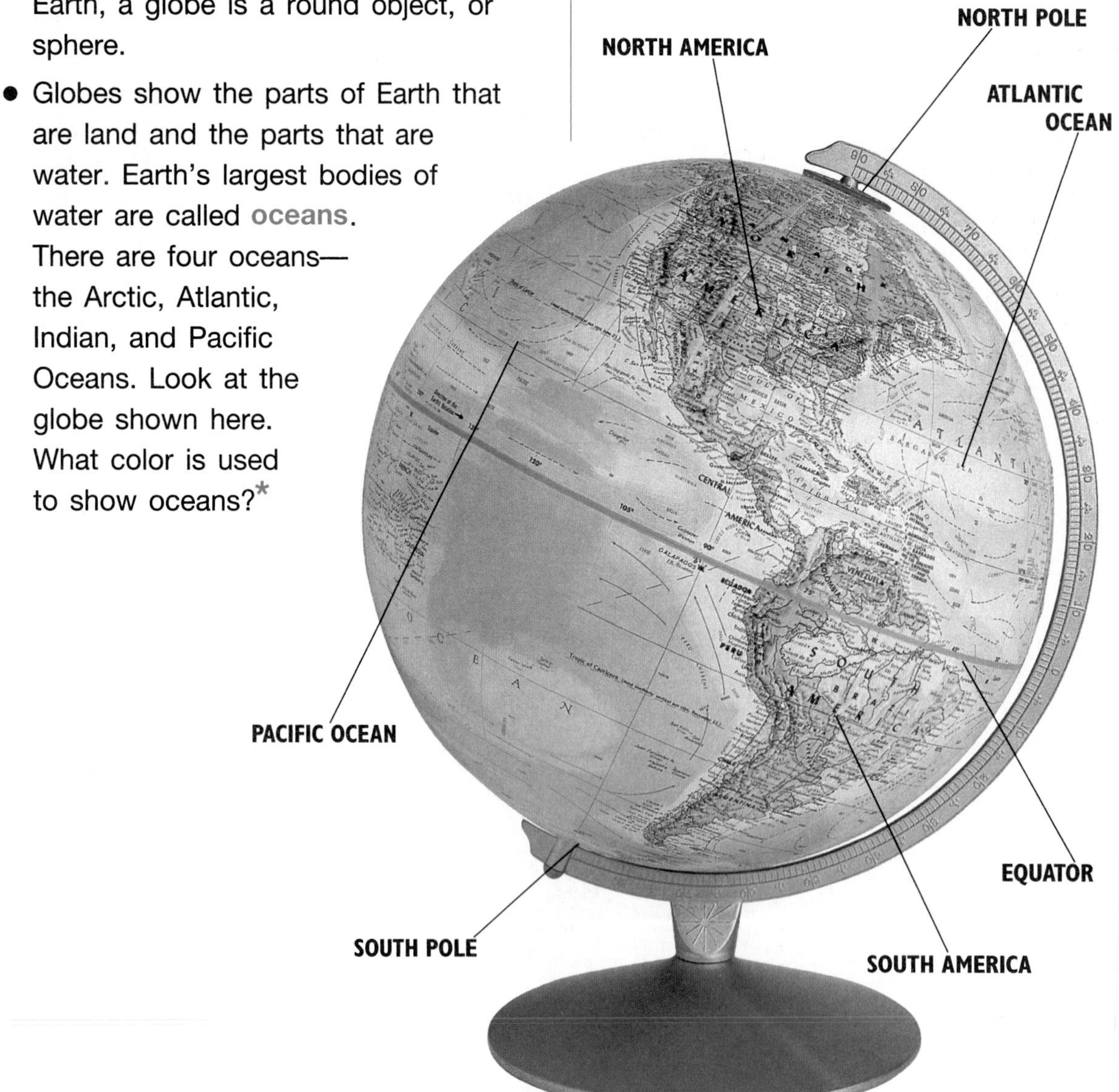


*blue
**Atlantic Ocean, Pacific Ocean

### *What are the four hemispheres?*

- Look again at the globe on page G4. Can you see the whole globe? You can see only half of a globe from any one direction. A word for half a globe or sphere is **hemisphere**. The word *hemi* means "half." Geographers divide Earth into four different hemispheres.
- Earth is divided into the Northern Hemisphere and Southern Hemisphere by the equator. The **equator** is an imaginary line that lies halfway between the North Pole and the South Pole. Look at the maps of the hemispheres below. What continents are located on the equator? On which continent is the South Pole shown?*
- Earth can also be divided into two other hemispheres. What are the names of these hemispheres? In which hemisphere do you live?**

## More Practice

There are more maps in this book that show the equator. For examples, see pages 59, 82, 84, and R4.

*South America, Africa, Asia; Antarctica
**Western Hemisphere, Eastern Hemisphere; probably Northern and Western Hemispheres, but answers may vary depending on location

*east
**south ***SE, SW, NW; southeast

PART 2
# Using Maps

### VOCABULARY

cardinal directions
compass rose
intermediate directions
symbol
map key
scale
locator

### *What are cardinal directions?*

- Directions describe the way you face or move to get somewhere. North, east, south, and west are the main directions, or cardinal directions.
- If you face the North Pole, you are facing north. When you face north, south is directly behind you. West is to your left. What direction will be to your right?*

### *How do you use a compass rose?*

- A compass rose is a small drawing on a map that can help you find directions.

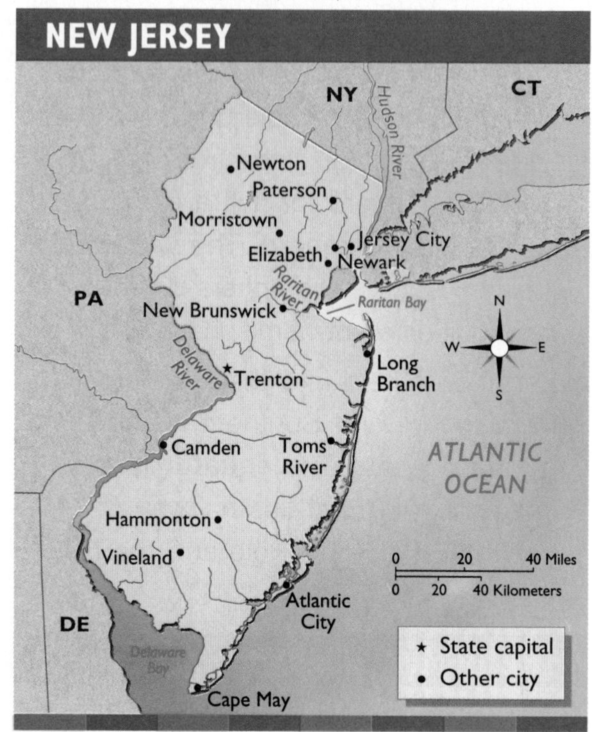


- The cardinal directions are written as **N, E, S**, and **W**. Find the compass rose on the map on this page. In which direction is Atlantic City from New Brunswick?**

### *What are intermediate directions?*

- Notice the spikes between the cardinal directions on the compass rose. These show the intermediate directions, or in-between directions.
- The intermediate directions are northeast, southeast, southwest, and northwest. Northeast is often written as **NE**. What letters are used for the other intermediate directions? Which intermediate direction is between south and east?***

### More Practice

You can practice finding directions using a compass rose on most maps in this book. For examples, see pages 19, 59, and 87.

*Southern New Jersey: State Parks; Trenton
**cities

***airport
****green square; place of interest; city

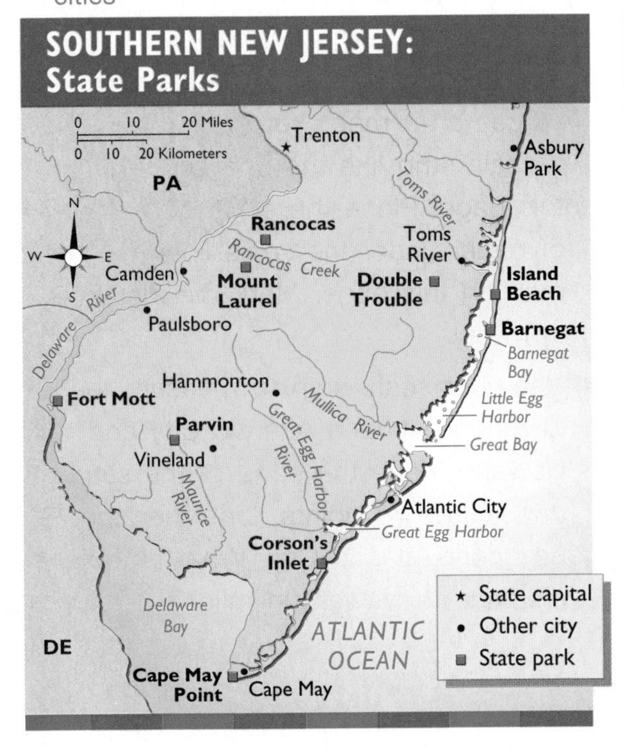


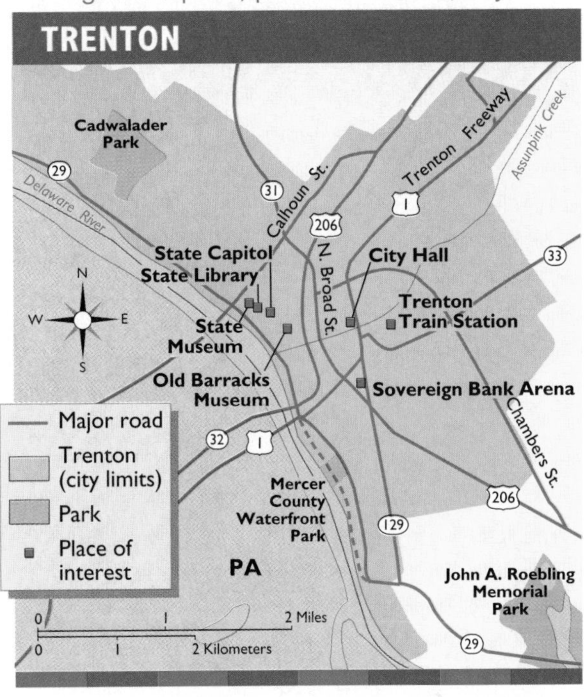


### *Why do maps have titles?*

- When using a map, first look at the map title. The title names the area the map shows. It may also tell you the kind of information shown on the map. Look at the maps on this page. What is the title of each?*

### *Why do maps include symbols?*

- A **symbol** is something that stands for something else.
- On a map common symbols include dots, line, stars, and colors. Many maps use the color blue to stand for water, for example. What do dots sometimes stand for?**
- Maps also often use symbols that are small drawings of the things they stand for. A drawing of a tree, for example, might stand for a forest. What do you think an airplane might stand for?***

### *How can you find out what map symbols stand for?*

- Often the same symbol stands for different things on different maps. For this reason many maps include a **map key**. A map key gives the meaning of each symbol used on the map.
- When you look at a map, you should always study the map key. Look at the maps on this page. What symbol marks the state parks on the map of Southern New Jersey? What does the same symbol stand for on the map of Trenton? What do the dots stand for on the map of Southern New Jersey's state parks?****

## More Practice

There are many maps with symbols and map keys in this book. For examples, see pages 35, 107, and 228.

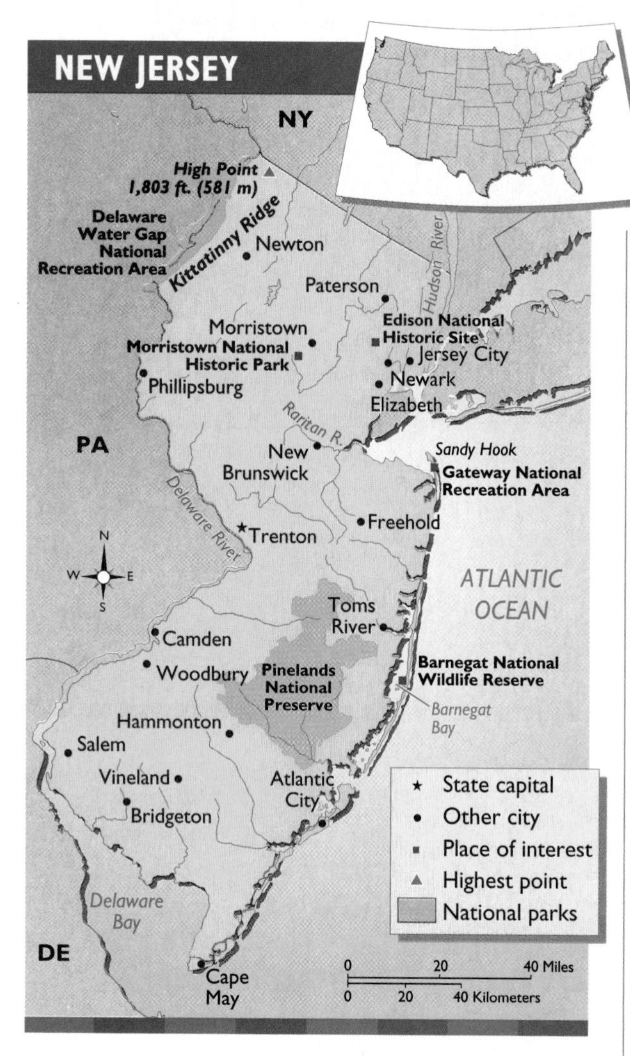


### *What is a map scale?*

- All maps are smaller than the real area they show. So how can you figure out the real distance between places? Most maps include a **scale**. The scale shows the relationship between distance on a map and real distances.
- The scales in this book are drawn with two lines. The top line shows distance in miles. What unit of measurement does the bottom line use?*

### *How do you use a map scale?*

- You can use a ruler to measure distances on a map. You can also make a scale strip like the one shown on this page. Place the edge of a strip of paper under the scale lines on the map on this page. Mark the distances in miles.
- Use your scale strip to measure the distance between Atlantic City and Newark. Place the edge of the strip under the two points. Line the zero up under Atlantic City. What is the distance to Newark in miles?**

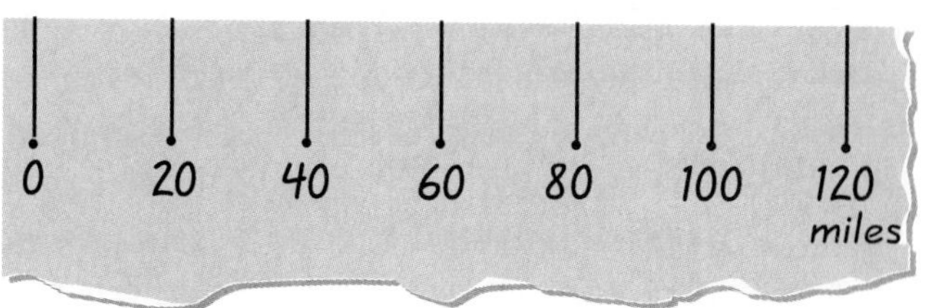


### *What do locators show?*

- A **locator** is a small map set onto the main map. It shows where the area of the main map is located. Where on the map on this page is the locator?***
- Most of the locators in this book show either the United States or New Jersey. Look at the map on this page. What area does the locator show?****

## More Practice

For examples of scales, see pages 15, 79, and 164. For examples of locators, see pages 79, 164, and 208.

*kilometer **about 100 miles
***in the upper right-hand corner of the map
****the United States

PART 3

# Different Kinds of Maps

**VOCABULARY**

political map
physical map
landform map
transportation map
historical map

### *What is a political map?*

- A **political map** shows information such as cities, capital cities, states, and countries. What symbol is used to show state capitals on the map below? What city is the capital of our state? What is the symbol for our national capital?*
- Political maps use lines to show borders. The states or countries are also shown in different colors. Look at the map below. What color is used to show our state? How many different colors are used to show the states? What countries are shown?**

## More Practice

There are other political maps in this book. For examples, see pages R4 and R6.

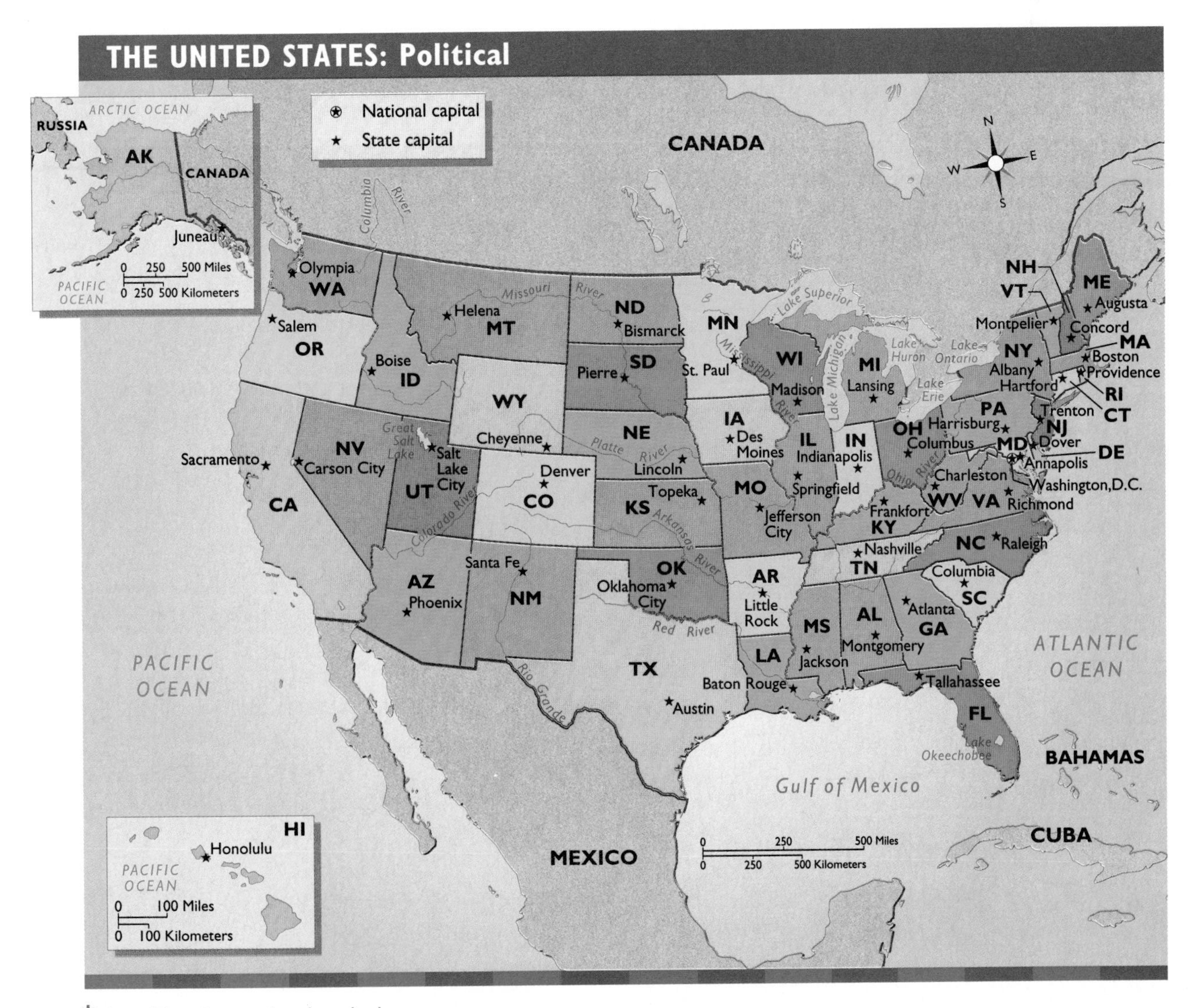


*star; Trenton; star in circle
**red; six; United States, Russia, Canada, Mexico, Cuba, Bahamas

### *What are physical maps?*

- Maps that show the natural features of Earth are called **physical maps**. There are different kinds of physical maps in this book.
- One kind of physical map shows landforms, or the shapes that make up Earth's surface. These maps are called **landform maps**. Mountains, hills, and plains are all examples of landforms. Landform maps also show bodies of water such as lakes, rivers, and oceans.
- Look at the map above. What kinds of landforms are found in the United States? What is the name of the plains area that is to the east of the Rocky Mountains? Which ocean borders the Coast Ranges?*

### *What is a transportation map?*

- A **transportation map** is a kind of map that shows you how you can travel from one place to another.
- Some transportation maps show roads for traveling by car, by bike, or on foot. Other transportation maps may show bus, train, ship, or airplane routes. What kinds of routes are shown on the map of Newark?**

## More Practice

There are other physical and transportation maps in this book. For examples of physical maps, see pages 9, 15, and 35. For an example of a transportation map, see page 228.

*mountains, hills, plateaus, and plains; Great Plains; Pacific Ocean **major roads, subways, railroads

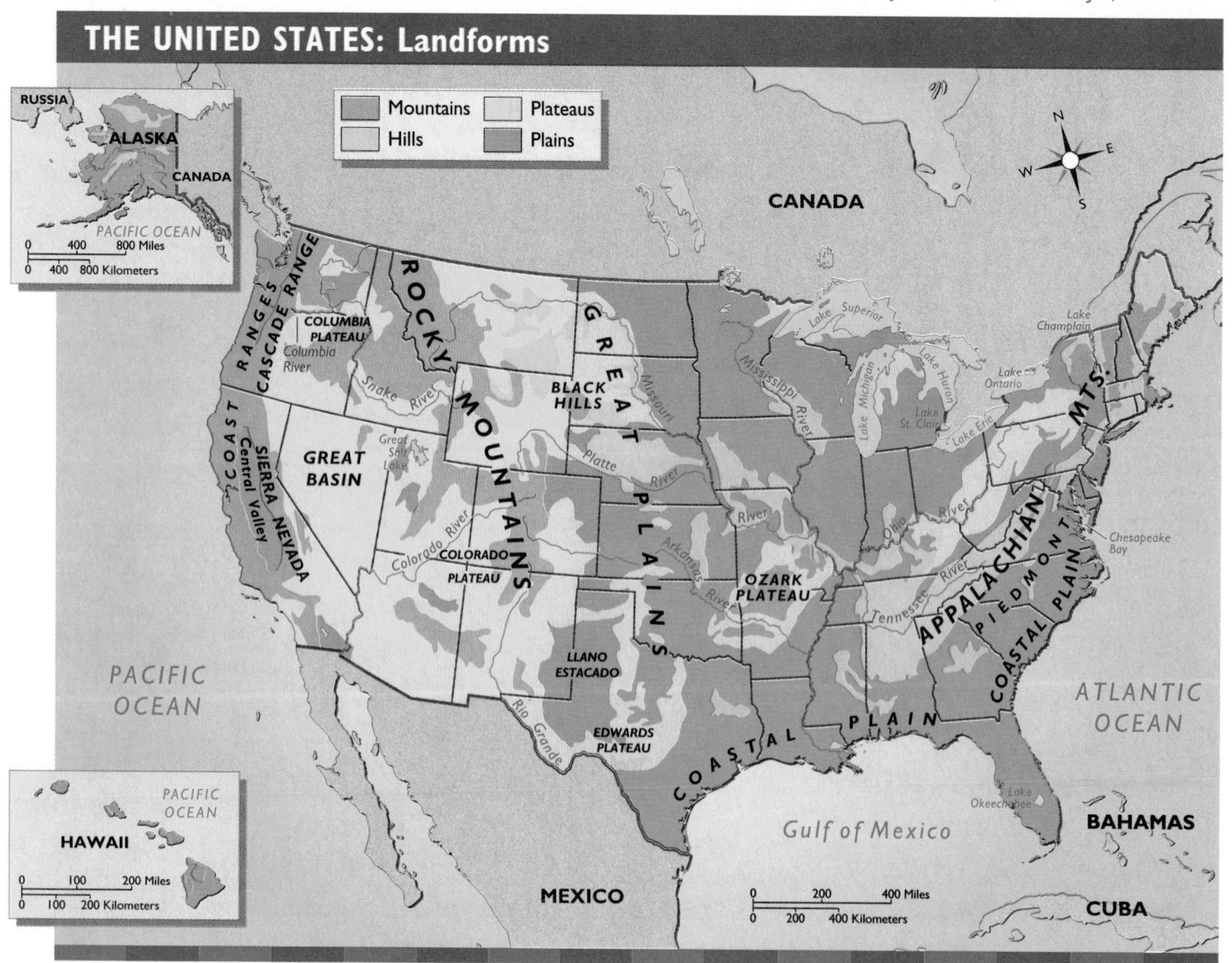

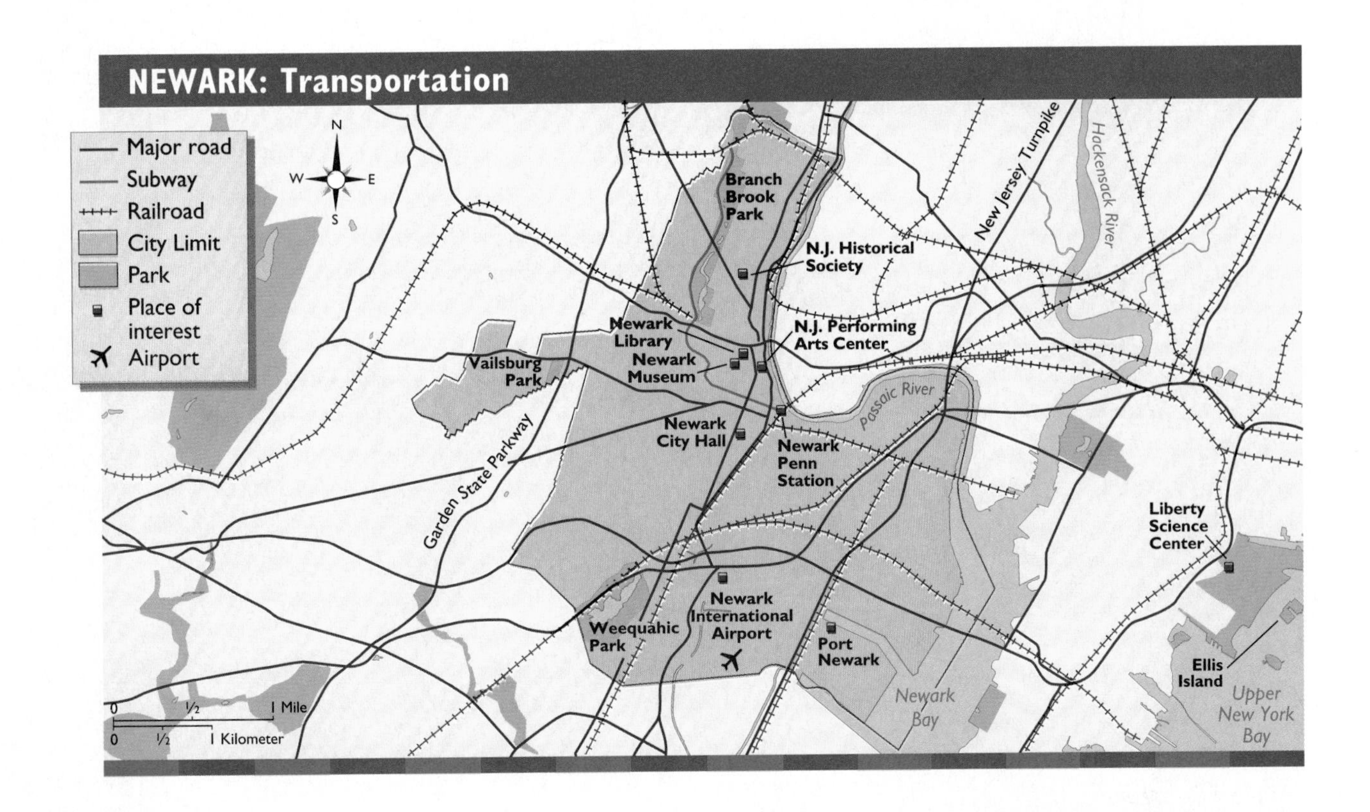


*What is an historical map?*

- An **historical map** is a map that shows information about past events and where they occurred.
- When you look at an historical map, first study the map title. What does it tell you about the historical map on this page?*
- Historical maps often show dates in the title or on the map. Study the map of the Jockey Hollow Encampment in New Jersey. What historical dates does it show?**
- Next look at the map key. The map key tells you what the symbols stand for on the map. Which symbol shows headquarters?***

## More Practice

There are other historical maps in this book. For examples, see pages 79, 107, and 164.

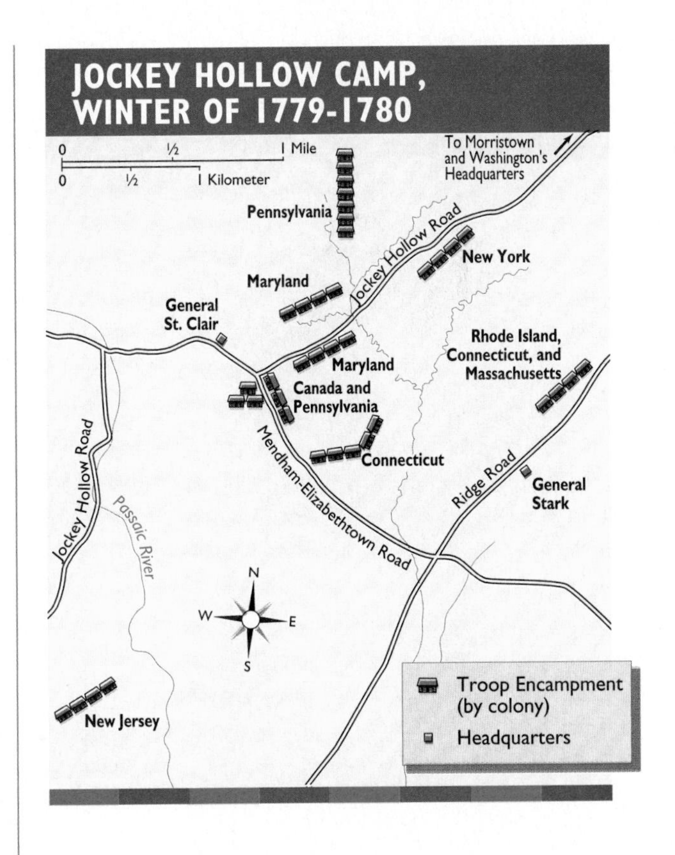


*The map shows the Jockey Hollow Encampment in the winter of 1779–1780
**1779–1780 ***a square

PALISADES PARK (RIGHT); EDWIN B. FORSYTHE NATIONAL WILDLIFE REFUGE (BELOW)

CHILDREN AT ISLAND BEACH STATE PARK

UNIT ONE

# The Geography of New Jersey

*"Each region has features that make it special."*

Geographer Michelle Goman
See page 34.

## Why Does It Matter?

Where is New Jersey? What does New Jersey look like? Are all parts of New Jersey the same? Our state offers great riches both in land and in resources. How does the land affect the way people live? How do people change the land? Read on. Unit 1 introduces the geography of New Jersey and some of the people who make it a special place.

HOLSTEIN COW

**FIND OUT MORE!**
Visit our website:
www.mhschool.com
interNET CONNECTION

Adventures with
NATIONAL
GEOGRAPHIC
25

# The Pinelands

New Jersey has more people per square mile than any other state. But it has its wild side, too. In the southern part of the state, for example, the Pinelands National Reserve stretches across more than a million acres. Here you can find large forests of pine and cedar trees, as well as swamps, bogs, lakes, and rivers. The Pinelands Reserve is home to many types of plants and animals, including the endangered Pine Barrens tree frog (above) and the rare arethusa orchid (below). People depend on the Pinelands, too. They use this area for recreation (far left) and for growing cranberries (bottom left) and blueberries. The Pinelands is a wilderness we can all enjoy.

**GEO JOURNAL**

*If you could spend a day in the Pinelands, what would you see and do?*

CHAPTER 1

# The Geography of New Jersey

## THINKING ABOUT GEOGRAPHY AND CULTURE

New Jersey has mountains, hills, plains, and a long shoreline. Thousands of miles of rivers and streams flow through our state. Look at the photographs on the next page. Using the colored squares, match each photograph to its location on the map. What do they tell you about New Jersey?

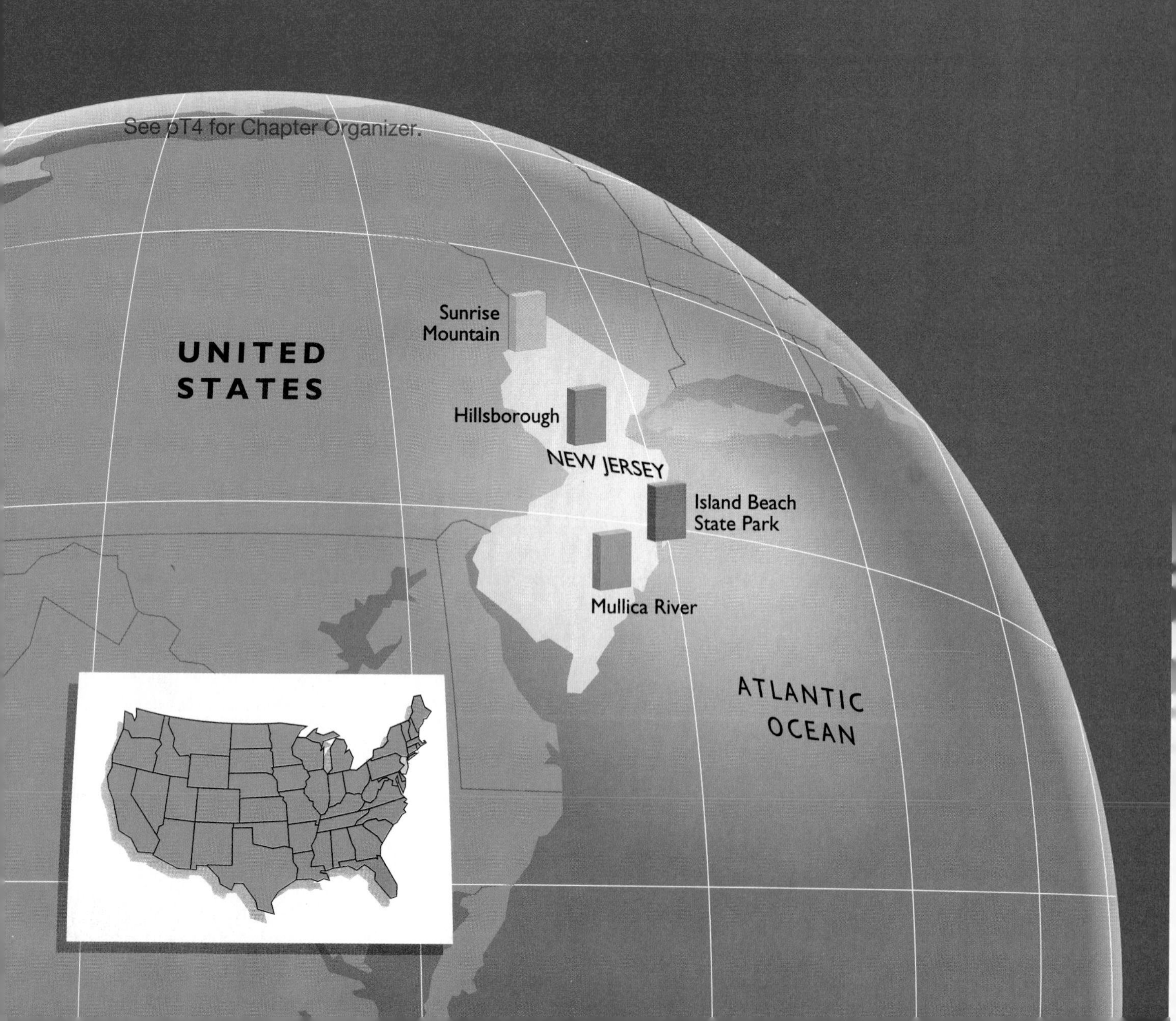

## Island Beach State Park

New Jersey has 127 miles of coast along the Atlantic Ocean. This state park is just one of many places people go to relax and have fun.

## Hillsborough

Farming in New Jersey is important to our state and country. New Jersey is a leading producer of tomatoes, spinach, and peaches.

## Sunrise Mountain

This mountain is part of the Kittatinny Ridge that is in the northwestern part of our state. Melting snow from this ridge flows into some of New Jersey's rivers.

## Mullica River

The Mullica River is one of the many important waterways in our state. New Jersey's rivers, streams, and lakes provide water for drinking, farming, factories, and recreation.

## LESSON 1

See p. T5 for Lesson Teaching Strategies.

# Landscape of New Jersey

### Focus Activity

**READ TO LEARN**

***What would you see on a trip across our state?***

**VOCABULARY**

- landforms
- geography
- border
- coast
- wetland

**PLACES**

- High Point State Park
- Delaware Water Gap National Recreation Area
- Delaware River
- Great Swamp
- Sandy Hook
- Pinelands
- Cape May

### Read Aloud

*"It's great to be a New Jerseyan," says Eleanor Hero. "I was born in Hopewell, and I have lived in New Jersey all my life. We have the ocean, mountains, lakes, forests—anything you could ever want. We're close to so much. It's all right here."*

### THE BIG PICTURE

Compared to other states, New Jersey is not very big. In fact, it is the fifth smallest state in the United States. At its widest point, New Jersey stretches only 65 miles across. A car could travel this distance in a little more than an hour.

Within its small area, however, New Jersey packs a rich variety of **landforms**. Landforms are the shapes that make up Earth's surface. Mountains, hills, and plains are all examples of landforms. New Jersey has plenty of each, ranging from the mountains of the northwest to the plains along the Atlantic Ocean in the southeast.

New Jersey is more than just its landforms. It is also home to thousands of different kinds of plants and animals and over 8 million people. One of the best ways to describe our state is to talk about its **geography**. Geography is the study of Earth and the way people, plants, and animals live on it and use it. In this lesson, you will begin to read about New Jersey's geography.

*Pennsylvania and Delaware; Delaware River; New York

MAP WORK: 1. High Point 2. Raritan Bay

## FINDING NEW JERSEY

Suppose you wanted to tell a pen pal in another country about the location of our state. What would you say? You could start by asking your friend to look at a map of North America. The map shows that New Jersey is part of the United States and that it shares a **border** with three other states. A border is a line people agree on to separate one place from another.

To the east of our state lies the Atlantic Ocean. The land that lies along an ocean is known as a **coast**. Cool ocean breezes make our state's coast a favorite spot for people to go on their summer vacations.

Look at the map on this page. It shows New Jersey in more detail than a map of North America would. You can use it to give your friend a better idea of our state's location. Which states border New Jersey to the west? What body of water forms this border? What other state shares a border with New Jersey?*

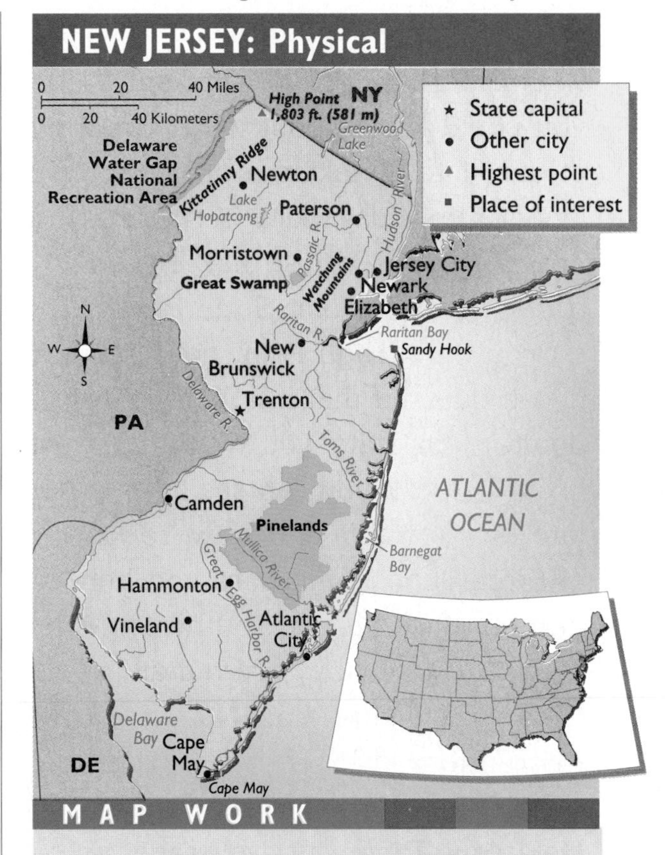


**MAP WORK**

This map shows the features of the land in New Jersey.

1. What is the highest point in our state?
2. The Raritan River empties into which bay?

**Sand dunes at Island Beach State Park help protect the beach against damage from wind and surf.**

## A TRIP AROUND OUR STATE

You probably never thought that you could learn about the geography of our state by taking a drive across it. One summer day, Sara Garner and her grandmother did just that. Their trip began at **High Point State Park**. How do you think High Point got its name? If you guessed that it is the highest point in our state, you would be right. From its peak you can see all the way into Pennsylvania and New York!

From High Point, Sara and her grandmother headed southwest. After about an hour, they arrived at the **Delaware Water Gap National Recreation Area**. Here, over the course of millions of years, the **Delaware River** cut a passage, or gap, through the Kittatinny Ridge.

Next, Sara and her grandmother drove eastward to the **Great Swamp**. A swamp is a type of **wetland**. A wetland is an area that is covered by water at least part of the year. The Great Swamp was formed when a large lake 30 miles long and 10 miles wide began to dry up over 10,000 years ago. It has not finished drying up yet!

At **Sandy Hook**, Sara and her grandmother stood on the beach and looked out at the Atlantic Ocean. How do you think this peninsula got its name? The shoreline of Sandy Hook, like the rest of our state's coast, is always changing. Ocean waves wash sand away in one place and pile it up in other places.

### South to the Land of Pines

Turning south, Sara and her grandmother drove through a mostly flat area. Millions of years ago, this area of plains was on the bottom of the ocean.

One feature of these plains is a large area of pine tree forest known as the **Pinelands**. Hundreds of years ago, people began burning some of these forests to create open areas for hunting and farming. Pine trees, which thrive in open space and sandy soil, grew up in many of these places. Today there are fewer fires, and other trees, such as oaks and maples, grow up in the shade and thicker soil of the pine forests.

**The walls of the Delaware Water Gap soar over 1,000 feet high.**

See p. T5 for Answers to Think About It.

Hundreds of birds and animals such as the greater yellowlegs and raccoon (above) make their home in the Great Swamp. The oldest working lighthouse in the United States (below) can be found at Sandy Hook.

The last stop on the trip was Cape May. Cape May was the first place in our country built just so people could visit it on their vacations. The people of Cape May like to say that once visitors get sand in their shoes at Cape May, they will never leave.

Sara did not get sand in her shoes, but her tour of our state had come to an end. She gave her grandmother a big hug and said, "I never knew there was so much to see in New Jersey."

## WHY IT MATTERS

New Jersey has a variety of landforms, including mountains, hills, and plains. Our state's geography has shaped the ways people have used the land for many thousands of years. In the lessons to come you will read more about how this all happened, and how special our state is.

## Reviewing Facts and Ideas

### SUM IT UP

- Geography is the study of Earth and everything on it.
- Landforms are the shapes that make up Earth's surface.
- As you go from one part of New Jersey to another, you see many different kinds of landforms.

### THINK ABOUT IT

1. What is a wetland?
2. What are landforms?
3. **FOCUS** What landforms would you see on a trip around our state?
4. **THINKING SKILL** If you were to travel south from High Point, in what *sequence* would you pass the following places: Great Egg Harbor River, the Pinelands, the Passaic River, Lake Hopatcong? Look at the physical map on page 9 for help.
5. **GEOGRAPHY** Describe the landforms near where you live.

See p. T6 for Legacy Teaching Strategies.

Legacy

LINKING PAST AND PRESENT

# State and National Parks of New Jersey

Look at your things at home. Is there anything there you would like to keep for a long time? It might be a picture that you drew or a favorite toy. It probably reminds you of something or someone special.

Now look ahead to the future. Would you like to give this special thing to your children or grandchildren? If you do, it will be a legacy. A legacy is something we have received from the past that we want to pass on to the future.

The state and national parks of New Jersey are a legacy. They are special places that preserve our state's natural wonders, wildlife, and history. People visit them to experience nature, learn about the past, and just to have fun. Many special places in our state have been changed by humans. Wetlands, for example, have been drained to build farms and houses. That is why we save what we have left. They are a beautiful and important legacy for all Americans.

**Sun and shadow, wind and water make Island Beach State Park a popular place to visit in the summer.**

**The knobbed whelk, usually called the conch shell, is the official state shell of New Jersey.**

The Appalachian Trail winds through Wawayanda State Park (above) for more than 19 miles. Exploring the park's natural features, visitors might see wildlife such as deer (right).

Hiking is a popular activity in High Point State Park. There are more than 13 miles of trails, as well as a portion of the Appalachian Trail, in the park.

LESSON 2

See p. T7 for Lesson Teaching Strategies.

# Waters of New Jersey

## Focus Activity

**READ TO LEARN**

***How are waterways important to our state?***

**VOCABULARY**

- waterway
- transportation
- source
- tributary
- mouth
- recreation
- aquifer
- port

**PLACES**

- Raritan River
- Hudson River
- Musconetcong River
- Newark
- Elizabeth

### Read Aloud

*The writer Christopher Cook Gilmore has written of the plant and animal life he found in the waters off Cape May. "The tide was all the way out. I saw gulls, terns, and oyster catchers. I watched a long "V" of ducks flapping and honking south down the wine-dark bay."*

### THE BIG PICTURE

Our state's **waterways** are like the branches of a tree. Small creeks flow into larger streams and rivers. Streams and rivers flow into even larger rivers or empty into the ocean. Waterways connect communities to one another. They connect our state to other states—and even to other countries. Is there a stream or creek near your home or school?

The longest river in our state is the **Raritan River**. It drains over 1,100 square miles of land. Two other important rivers, the Delaware River and the **Hudson River**, start in mountains outside of New Jersey. They have been important pathways of trade and **transportation**. Transportation is the movement of people or goods from one place to another. Our state's long shoreline on the Atlantic Ocean connects it to places around the world.

*Atlantic Ocean

MAP WORK: 1. New Brunswick 2. The Great Egg Harbor River

## IMPORTANT RIVERS

All rivers have a beginning called a **source**. The source of the Delaware River is north of our state in the Catskill Mountains. There, in a small stream near a place called Hancock, New York, the Delaware River begins its 280 mile journey.

As the Delaware River moves south, it grows wider and deeper. Why does this happen? First, the river cuts through softer ground, letting it dig deeper into Earth's surface. Second, smaller rivers and streams called **tributaries** (TRIB yoo tair eez) join the Delaware, adding water to its flow. The **Musconetcong River** is one of the main tributaries of the Delaware in our state.

The **mouth** of the Delaware River forms Delaware Bay. The mouth is the place where a river empties into a larger body of water. Look at the map on this page. You can see that the Delaware River flows into Delaware Bay. Into what body of water does the Delaware Bay empty?*

Another important waterway of our state is the Hudson River. We share the Hudson River with New York state. For hundreds of years, ships from all over the world entered New Jersey on the Hudson River.

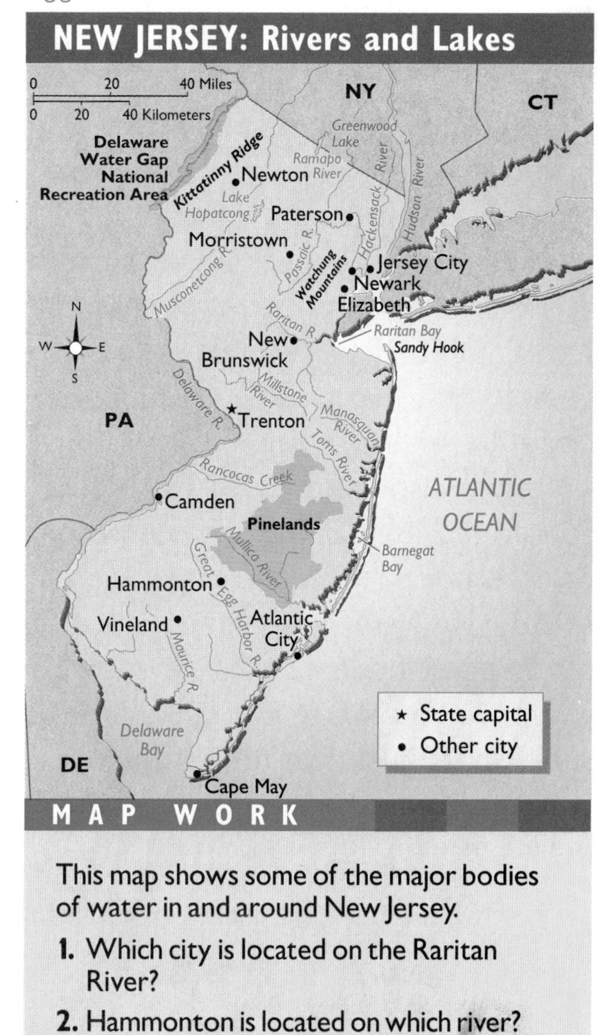


MAP WORK

This map shows some of the major bodies of water in and around New Jersey.

1. Which city is located on the Raritan River?
2. Hammonton is located on which river?

**Searching for food, a Great Blue Heron explores a tributary of the Delaware River.**

## WATER WATER EVERYWHERE

People, plants, and animals must have water to live and grow. Rivers, streams, and lakes provide most of the fresh water we use for drinking. These rivers also provide water for farming and factories. That is why it is important that we keep our water clean and safe.

People also enjoy using water for **recreation**. Recreation is what people do in order to relax and enjoy themselves. The New Jersey landscape offers many opportunities for recreation. Do you like to swim, water-ski, sail, fish, or just float on a raft? You couldn't do any of these things without water.

**DID YOU KNOW?**

***How did thousands of ships sink off the New Jersey coast?***

**Our state's waterways provide a link to the world, but they also are home to more than 5,400 sunken ships. Most lie on the floor of the Atlantic Ocean, under 30 to 300 feet of water. Storms, wars, and bad luck have sent all kinds of boats to the bottom. They serve a useful purpose by providing a protected place for fish and sea animals to nest. New Jersey is one of the only states in the country that allows divers to keep what they find on sunken ships.**

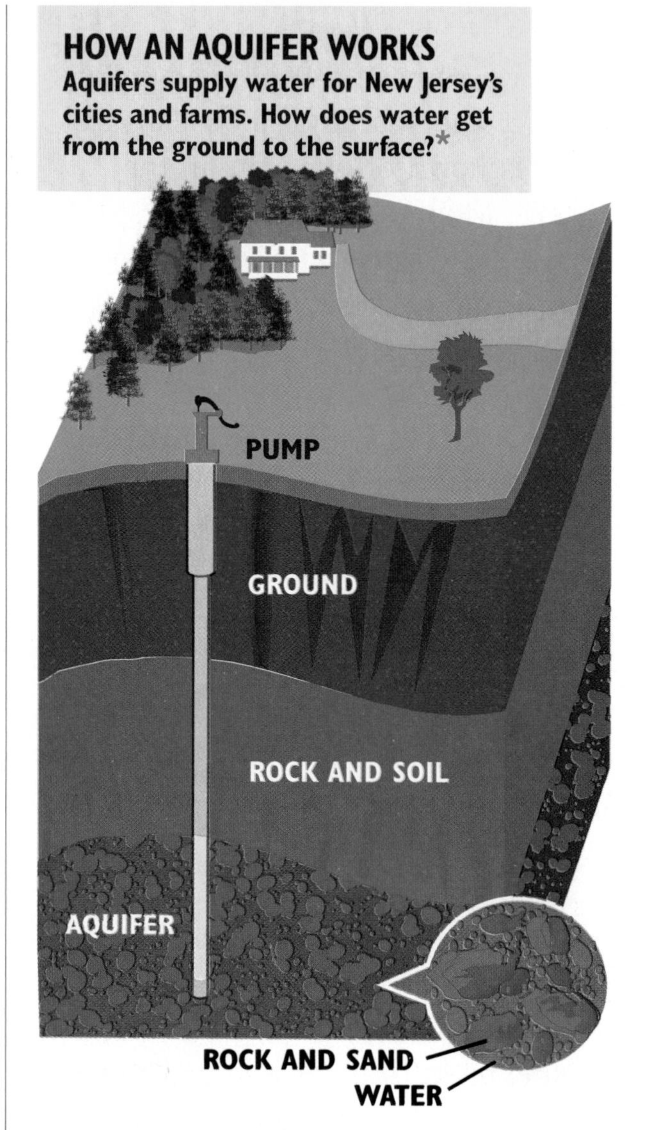


**HOW AN AQUIFER WORKS**
**Aquifers supply water for New Jersey's cities and farms. How does water get from the ground to the surface?***

*the water is pumped

### Aquifers

Some of New Jersey's water is not on the surface. It flows underground. Beneath parts of New Jersey are layers of rock and sand that absorb water like a sponge. These layers are called **aquifers** (AK wuh furz). People dig wells and pump this water to the surface. Look at the diagram on this page to see how aquifers are formed.

The Cohansey Aquifer lies under much of the Pinelands. Aquifers like the Cohansey and the Elizabethtown Aquifer supply water to almost half of the people in our state.

See p. T7 for Answers to Think About It.

### A Link to the World

As you have read, our state's waterways connect New Jersey to people and places around the world. The port at Newark, when it is joined with its neighbor New York City, handles the third-largest amount of cargo in the country. A port is where ships load and unload their goods. Port cities usually are protected from the ocean or the main course of the river by islands.

The port at Elizabeth, which is near Newark, became the first container port in the world in 1962. This modern system makes it easy for large ships to load and unload containers that are the size of trucks.

## WHY IT MATTERS

New Jersey has many rivers and lakes. Some of these waterways are important transportation routes. Some provide water for drinking. Many of them are great places for swimming and boating. We must take care of our state's waterways if we want to continue to use and enjoy them.

### Reviewing Facts and Ideas

#### SUM IT UP

- Ships from all over the world carry goods to and from the ports of our state.
- Rivers, streams, and lakes provide water for drinking, farming, factories, and recreation.
- Taking care of New Jersey's waterways is important if we want to keep enjoying them.

#### THINK ABOUT IT

1. What is the difference between the mouth of a river and its source?
2. What makes the Musconetcong River a tributary?
3. **FOCUS** How are waterways important to our state?
4. **THINKING SKILL** Suppose you want to travel from Trenton to Atlantic City by water. *Decide* which route you would take and explain why.
5. **WRITE** Write a letter to a friend, describing a body of water near where you live.

**A container ship unloads at the port at Elizabeth.**

See p. T8 for Skill Teaching Strategies.

# Reading Elevation Maps

**VOCABULARY**

elevation

### WHY THE SKILL MATTERS

Suppose you take an airplane ride from Newark, New Jersey, to Chicago, Illinois. Soon after you take off, you see the low rolling hills of our state. As you cross into Pennsylvania, the land becomes more rugged and the hills steeper. Soon, you are above the Pocono Mountains. Suppose you want to know how high you must fly to safely pass over these mountain peaks. How can you find out?

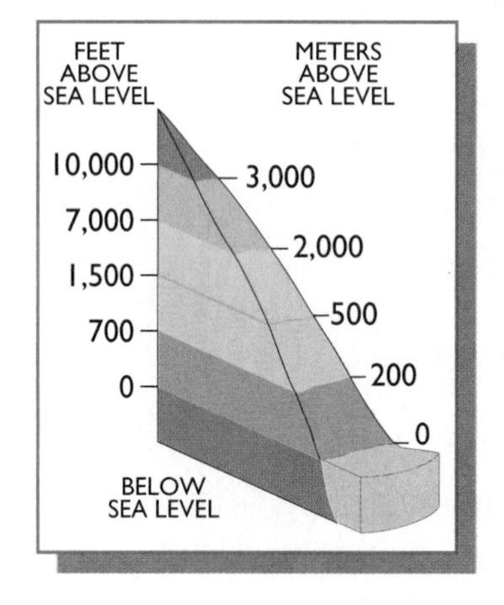


For this kind of information, you need an **elevation** (el uh VAY shun) map. Elevation is the height of the land above sea level. Elevation at sea level is 0 feet.

An elevation map uses colors to show elevations. Look at the map key on this page. You can see that all the places shown on the map in dark green are between 0 and 700 feet above sea level. The other colors show different elevations.

### USING THE SKILL

Of course, elevation maps tell us about many things besides mountains and plains. For example, they give us important information about rivers.

Have you ever wondered why the water in a river flows in one direction? The answer is simple: water runs downhill. The elevation where a river begins is higher than where it ends. Gravity pulls the water downhill toward a lower elevation. Let's say the land slopes downhill toward the east. Then the river will flow from west to east. That's how an elevation map can help you understand a river's course.

Try using an elevation map to trace the path of

**High in New York's Adirondack Mountains, several small lakes, including Lake Tear-of-the-Clouds, form the source of the Hudson River.**

*orange

**lower; south; gets lower

See p. T8 for Answers to Reviewing the Skill.

the Delaware River. Locate the river on the map on this page. Find the source of the river in the Catskill Mountains. What color is this area? Check the map key to find out what elevation this color represents. You can see that the Delaware River starts at an elevation more than 1,500 feet above sea level.*

Follow the river's main path. It flows through an area of lower elevation moving from north to south. For many miles the Delaware River forms the border between New Jersey and Pennsylvania. Then the river empties into the Delaware Bay, which is at sea level.

## Helping yourself

- **Elevation maps show you how high the land is above sea level.**
- **Study the map key to match the colors with the different elevations on the map.**

### TRYING THE SKILL

You have just used the elevation map to trace the path of the Delaware River. Now trace the path of the Hudson River. It starts in the northeastern part of New York.

Does the Delaware River begin at a higher or lower elevation than the Hudson River? In which direction does the Hudson River flow? What does that show you about the elevation in that direction?**

### REVIEWING THE SKILL

Now use the elevation map to answer the following questions. Use the Helping Yourself box for hints.

1. What is elevation?
2. What is the elevation of the highest point in New Jersey? What is the elevation along the coast?
3. In what color would this map show a hill that is 800 feet above sea level?
4. How does an elevation map help us learn about geography?

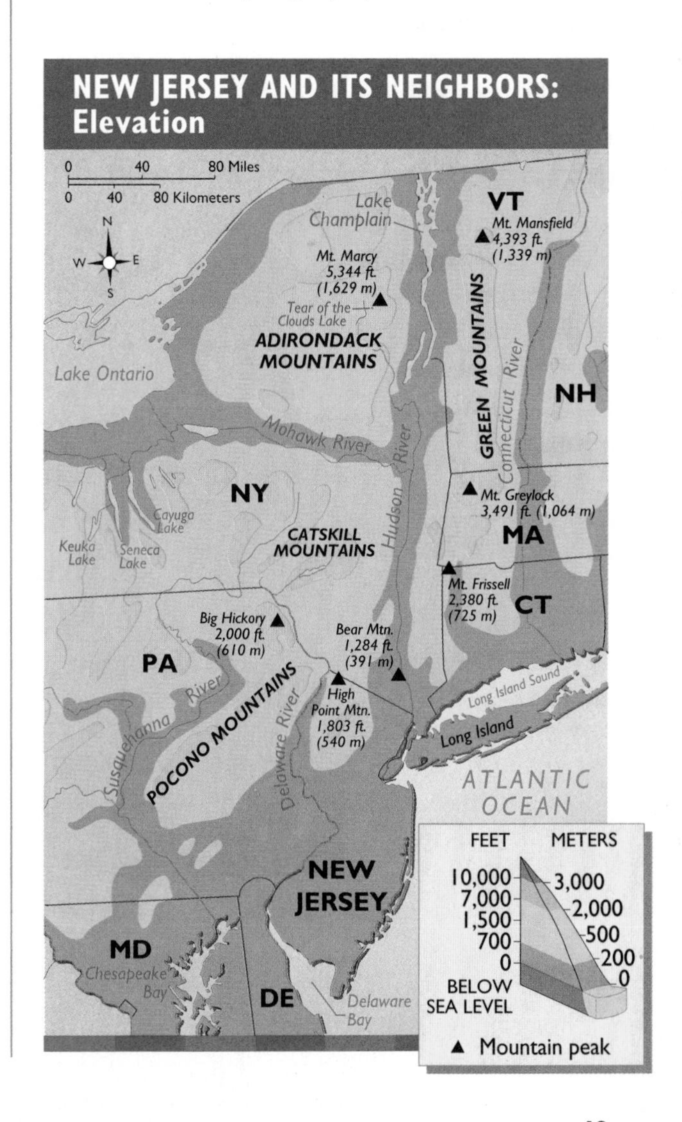

LESSON 3

See p. T9 for Lesson Teaching Strategies.

# Our State's Climate

## Focus Activity

**READ TO LEARN**

***What affects the climate of our state?***

**VOCABULARY**

- weather
- climate
- temperature
- precipitation
- blizzard
- hurricane

**PLACES**

- Secaucus
- Trenton
- Morristown
- Atlantic City
- Camden

### Read Aloud

*"The changes of weather* [in New Jersey]*," wrote Jedidiah Morse in 1807, "are great and frequently sudden. It has the moisture of Ireland in spring; the heat of Africa in summer; the snow and cold of Norway in winter; the tempests* [storms] *of the West Indies in every season; and the variable* [changing] *wind and weather of Great Britain in every month of the year."*

### THE BIG PICTURE

This description of New Jersey was written almost 200 years ago, but it still describes the **weather** of our state today. Weather is the condition of the air at a certain time and place. The weather changes from day to day, sometimes from hour to hour.

Every place has a pattern of weather over many years. That pattern is called **climate** (KLĪ mit). What is the difference between weather and climate? Weather affects how you live day to day. For example, will you need to take an umbrella to school today? Climate affects long-range plans and plays a big role in our lives. It affects the foods we eat, how we enjoy ourselves, what type of work we do, and even the clothes we wear. For example, will you buy a light jacket or a heavy coat for the winter?

## TWO PARTS OF CLIMATE

What questions would you ask to find out about the climate of our state? You might ask, "How hot are the summers? How cold are the winters?" These questions ask about **temperature** (TEM pur uh chur), which is an important part of climate. Temperature measures how hot or how cold the air is.

Storm Field thinks about temperature every day. He is a weather reporter for a television station in **Secaucus**. He studies information from weather satellites and other instruments to predict the weather.

He uses maps like the ones on this page to understand what the weather will be like. The map below shows you average temperatures for New Jersey in July. The afternoon temperature in **Trenton** may be 76°F in July. In January, the afternoon temperature may reach only 36°F.

Another important part of climate is **precipitation** (prih sip ih TAY shun). Precipitation is the moisture that falls to the ground in the form of rain, snow, sleet, or hail. Some places in New Jersey get a lot of precipitation. The precipitation map below shows how much precipitation to expect during one year. For example, the city of **Morristown** gets more than 48 inches of precipitation each year—but **Atlantic City** gets less than 44 inches of precipitation a year—at least 4 inches less.

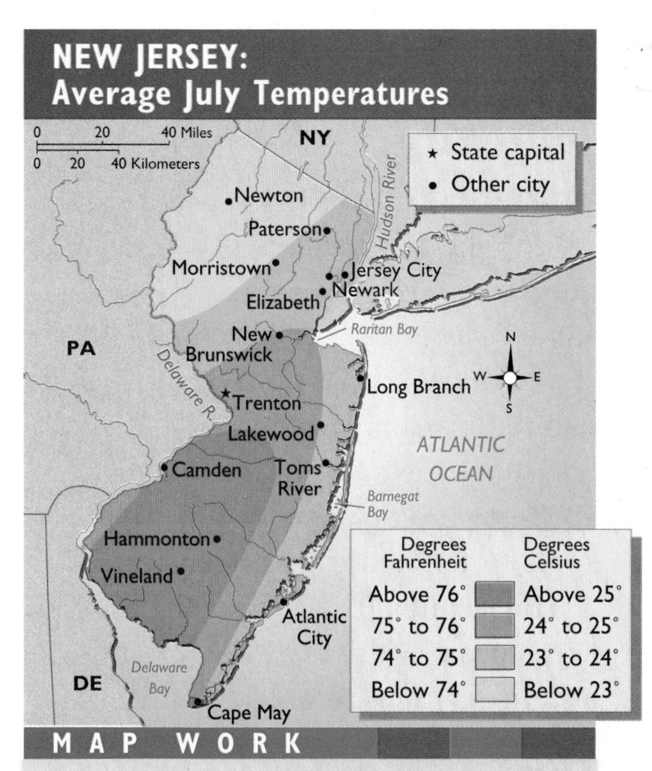


July **temperatures** vary in New Jersey.

1. Which city is hotter in July—Newton or Cape May?

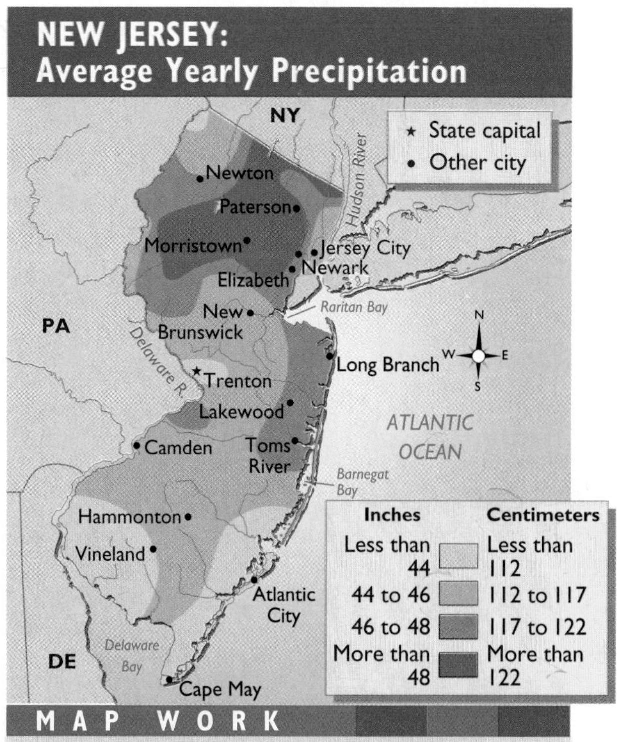


**Precipitation** in our state does not vary much.

1. Where is the driest part of New Jersey?

MAP WORK: 1. Cape May

MAP WORK: 1. southeast, southwest, Trenton, northwest corner

## WHAT AFFECTS CLIMATE

"Many factors affect climate," explains weather reporter Field. "One is elevation. Another is the nearness of the land to a large body of water like the Atlantic Ocean. A third is the direction of the wind flow and the direction storms come from."

### Cool Ocean Breezes

Take a look at the weather map below. It is the weather for a spring day. You can see that the temperature in Atlantic City is cooler than the temperature in Camden.

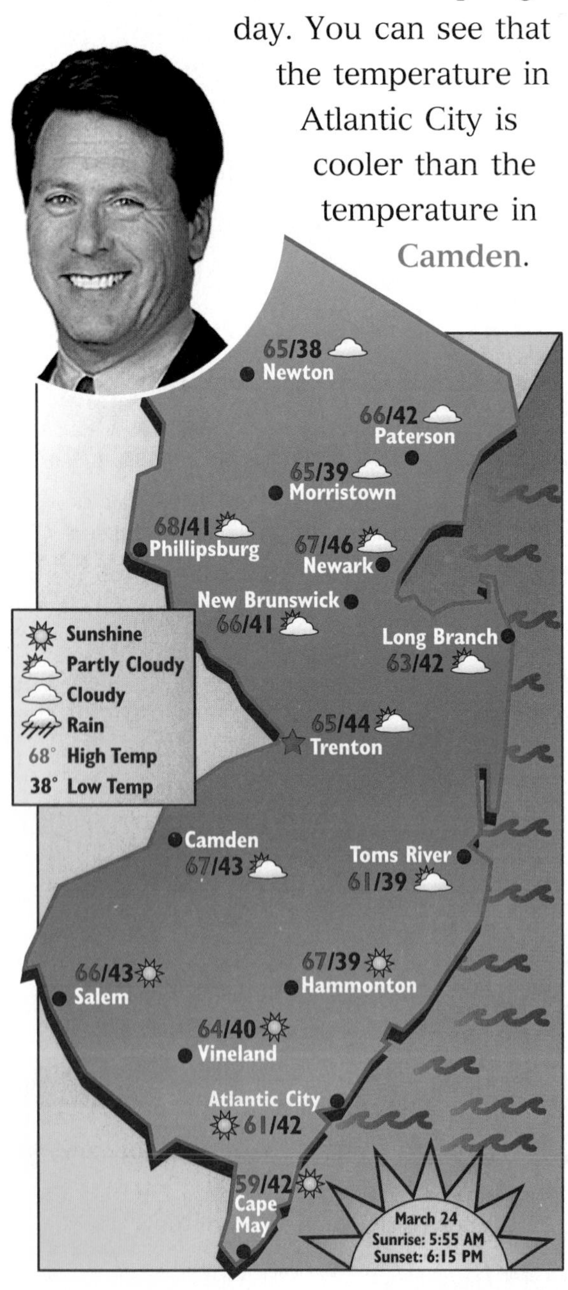


There's a reason for this. Water warms up more slowly than air during spring and summer. As a result, the Atlantic Ocean stays cooler than the land all through summer. Breezes from the ocean cool the land near the coast. The ocean also stays warmer than the land during fall and winter. In winter, ocean breezes bring warmer air to the land along the coast.

### How Far From the Equator?

Another thing that affects climate is how far away a place is from the equator. Places closer to the equator usually have warmer climates than places far away. New Jersey lies about halfway between the equator and the North Pole. Therefore, our state has a temperate climate, which means that it is neither too hot nor too cold.

### Extreme Weather

Our state's climate is usually mild, but Storm Field says, "We do get some severe weather here in New Jersey." A blizzard is a heavy snowstorm with very strong winds that can strike our state in winter. In the blizzard of 1888, for example, snow "piled up in spots to ten and even fifteen feet."

Hurricanes [HUR ih kaynz] are violent storms with very strong winds and heavy rains. They form in the ocean and smash into the coast with

**Storm Field (above, left) uses maps like this one to forecast the weather.**

winds from 75 to 200 miles per hour. They often cause heavy flooding. In September 1999 Hurricane Floyd struck New Jersey. Many towns along the Raritan and Passaic Rivers suffered from floods. How did the mayor of Manvillle respond to this disaster?

**MANY VOICES**
**PRIMARY SOURCE**

**Excerpt from an interview with Manville Mayor Angelo Corradino, 1999.**

***We—the borough police chief and I—did a tour of the town at 7:30 p.m. Thursday, the night of the flood. Bound Brook was already underwater . . . The flooding had already started. The only way I can describe this is like a tidal wave. Cleanup isn't going to finish for six months or seven months. We'll rebound. We always do. It's going to take a lot longer than other times, but we're going to recover.***

See p. T9 for Answers to Think About It.

## WHY IT MATTERS

New Jersey's varied climate makes it a great place to live. New Jerseyans can snowboard in winter and surf in summer. The climate lets farmers grow many kinds of crops and attracts many visitors to our state's beaches. As you read about New Jersey, think about the many ways climate affects how people live in our state.

## Reviewing Facts and Ideas

### SUM IT UP

- Climate is the pattern of weather a place has over time. Temperature and precipitation are two key parts of climate.
- New Jersey's nearness to the Atlantic Ocean and its distance from the equator affect its climate.
- Severe weather in New Jersey can include blizzards and hurricanes.

### THINK ABOUT IT

1. What is the difference between climate and weather?
2. As you move away from the equator, what usually happens to the climate?
3. **FOCUS** Name two factors which affect the climate of New Jersey.
4. **THINKING SKILL** Compare the weather today with the weather six months ago. Is it the same or different? What does this say about the climate in your area?
5. **GEOGRAPHY** Describe the climate of your area. Include how the distance from the equator and the nearness of the Atlantic Ocean affect it.

See p. T10 for Answers to Chapter 1 Review.

# CHAPTER 1 REVIEW

## THINKING ABOUT VOCABULARY

Number a sheet of paper from 1 to 10. Next to each number write the word from the list below that best completes the sentence.

| | |
|---|---|
| port | precipitation |
| transportation | wetland |
| geography | climate |
| hurricane | tributary |
| landform | border |

1. The movement of people or goods from one place to another is called _________.
2. A _________ is a river or stream that flows into a larger river.
3. A place where ships load and unload goods is called a _________.
4. Rain, snow, sleet, and hail are all forms of _________.
5. The study of Earth and the way people, plants, and animals live on and use it is called _________.
6. A _________ is a line that people agree on that divides one place from another.
7. The pattern of weather in one place over many years is called _________.
8. A _________ is a violent storm with very strong winds and heavy rains.
9. A _________ is an area covered by water at least part of the year.
10. When you see a mountain, hill, or plain, you are looking at a type of _________.

## THINKING ABOUT FACTS

1. What is New Jersey's highest point?
2. What body of water forms part of the western boundary of our state?
3. The beginning of a river is called its source. What is the end called?
4. Name two important waterways in New Jersey.
5. Why does the Delaware River grow wider and deeper along its course?
6. What is the difference between weather and climate?
7. Name two parts of climate and tell why they are important.
8. What does it mean if a climate is temperate?
9. Is the temperature warmer in Camden or Atlantic City in winter? Why?
10. Explain why ocean breezes cool the land along the coast in the summer.

## THINK AND WRITE

### WRITING A LETTER
Severe weather can include hurricanes, blizzards, and even bad thunderstorms. Write a letter to a friend telling about some severe weather that you have experienced.

### WRITING A DESCRIPTION
Read Eleanor Hero's description of New Jersey in the Read Aloud on page 8. Then write your own description of our state.

### WRITING AN EXPLANATION
Explain how tributaries make a river larger.

## APPLYING GEOGRAPHY SKILLS

### ELEVATION MAPS

Answer the following questions about the map on this page to practice your skill at reading elevation maps.

1. How do you know that this is an elevation map?
2. What area of New Jersey has the highest elevation?
3. In what color would this map show a hill that is 400 feet above sea level?
4. At about which elevation is the city of Vineland?
5. Does the Great Egg Harbor River flow northwest or southeast? How can you be sure?

## Summing Up the Chapter

Use the following word map to organize information from the chapter. Copy the word map on a sheet of paper. Then write at least one piece of information in each blank circle. When you have filled in the map, use it to write a paragraph that answers the question "How do the land, water, and climate of New Jersey affect how you live?"

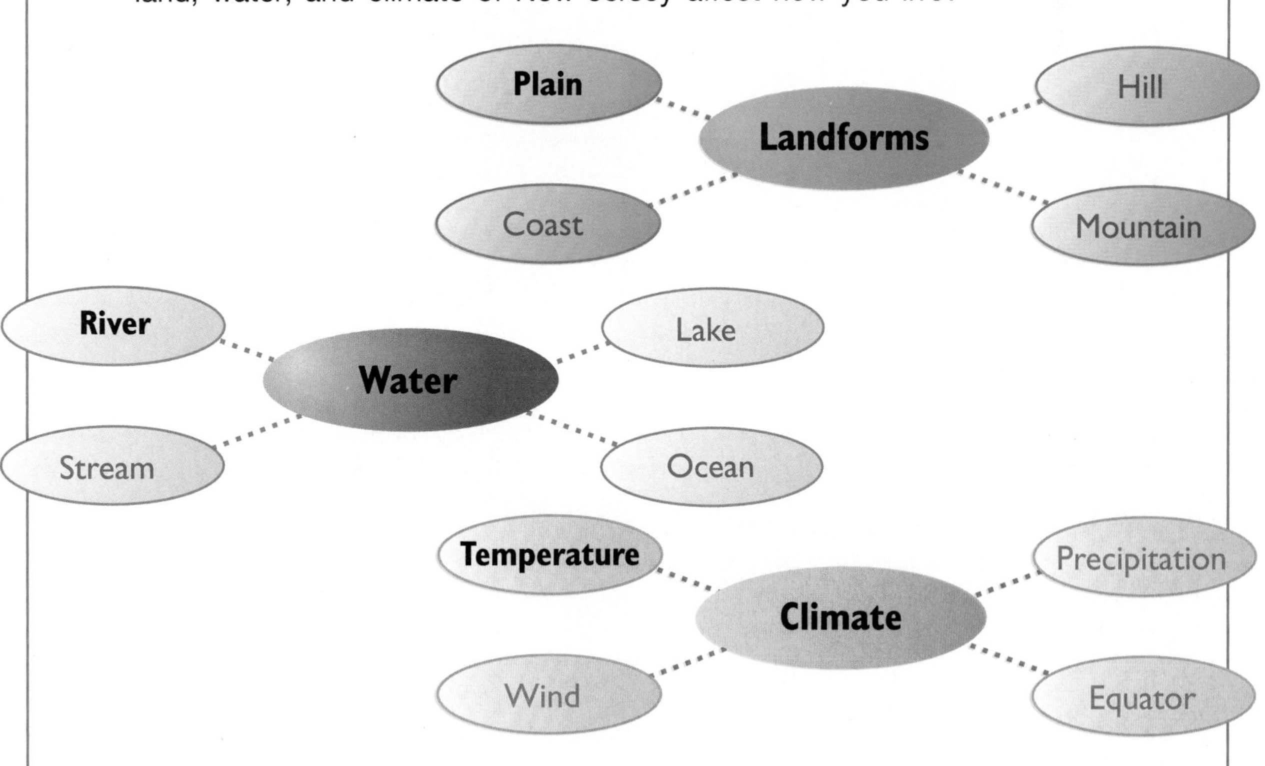

CHAPTER 2

# Regions and Resources

## THINKING ABOUT GEOGRAPHY AND ECONOMICS

You know that New Jersey is located in the Northeast region of the United States. Did you know that New Jersey is divided into different regions, too? Each of these regions is unique, with land, water, and resources that make it special. Read on to learn how the people of our state use its geography to create a great place to live.

See pT11 for Chapter Organizer.

**Docks and Shoreline LAKE HOPATCONG**

Lakes in New Jersey provide recreation, beautiful scenery, and drinking water for the people of our state.

**City Neighborhood HOBOKEN**

New Jersey has more people per square mile than any other state in the United States.

**State Highway PINELANDS**

A forest of more than a million acres, the Pinelands has been preserved by the government for the use of future generations.

**River Scene DELAWARE WATER GAP**

Located at the point where the Delaware River cuts through the surrounding mountains, the Delaware Water Gap has been an important transportation route for hundreds of years.

LESSON 1

See p. T12 for Lesson Teaching Strategies.

# One Country, Five Regions

## Read Aloud

*In the late 1800s poet Walt Whitman celebrated America in this poem:*

*Land of coal and iron! land of gold! land of cotton, sugar, rice!*
*Land of wheat, beef, pork! land of wool and hemp! land of the apple and the grape!...*
*Land of ocean shores!*

## Focus Activity

**READ TO LEARN**

***What is special about each region of the United States?***

**VOCABULARY**

- region
- swamp
- marsh
- bayou
- desert
- rain shadow

**PLACES**

- Appalachian Mountains
- Mississippi River
- Davis Bayou
- Interior Plains
- Central Plains
- Great Plains
- Rocky Mountains
- Grand Canyon

### THE BIG PICTURE

As Walt Whitman wrote, the United States is a country of great variety. Geographers find it useful to divide our country into five main **regions**. A region is an area with common features that set it apart from other areas. New Jersey is in the Northeast region of the United States. The other regions are the Southeast, the Southwest, the Middle West, and the West. Find these regions on the map on the next page.

Landforms are one of the features that set regions apart from each other. Mountains, plains, and hills are all examples of landforms. Use the Atlas map on page R10 to find the landforms of our country. Climate and bodies of water are other special features. In this lesson you will read how these different features combine to form the five regions of our country.

## THE NORTHEAST

Look at the map on this page and find the Northeast. One landform that can be found in the Northeast is the Coastal Plain—a flat lowland along the edge of the Atlantic Ocean. It begins in Massachusetts and stretches south and west into Texas.

Among the oldest mountains in the world are the **Appalachian** (ap uh LAY chee un) **Mountains**. They are found in most of the states in the Northeast. Some scientists think they once rose miles into the sky. Yet today the Appalachians are not very high. Over many years wind, water, and ice have worn them down.

### Four Seasons

In the Northeast, winter, spring, summer, and autumn bring different kinds of weather. Autumn is the favorite season of many Northeasterners. In the fall the days grow shorter and the temperature drops. These changes have an effect on the colors of the leaves of many trees.

For a few weeks the leaves turn from green to bright red, gold, and orange. Then the leaves drop off the branches. These trees are preparing for winter when there is less sunlight and lower temperatures.

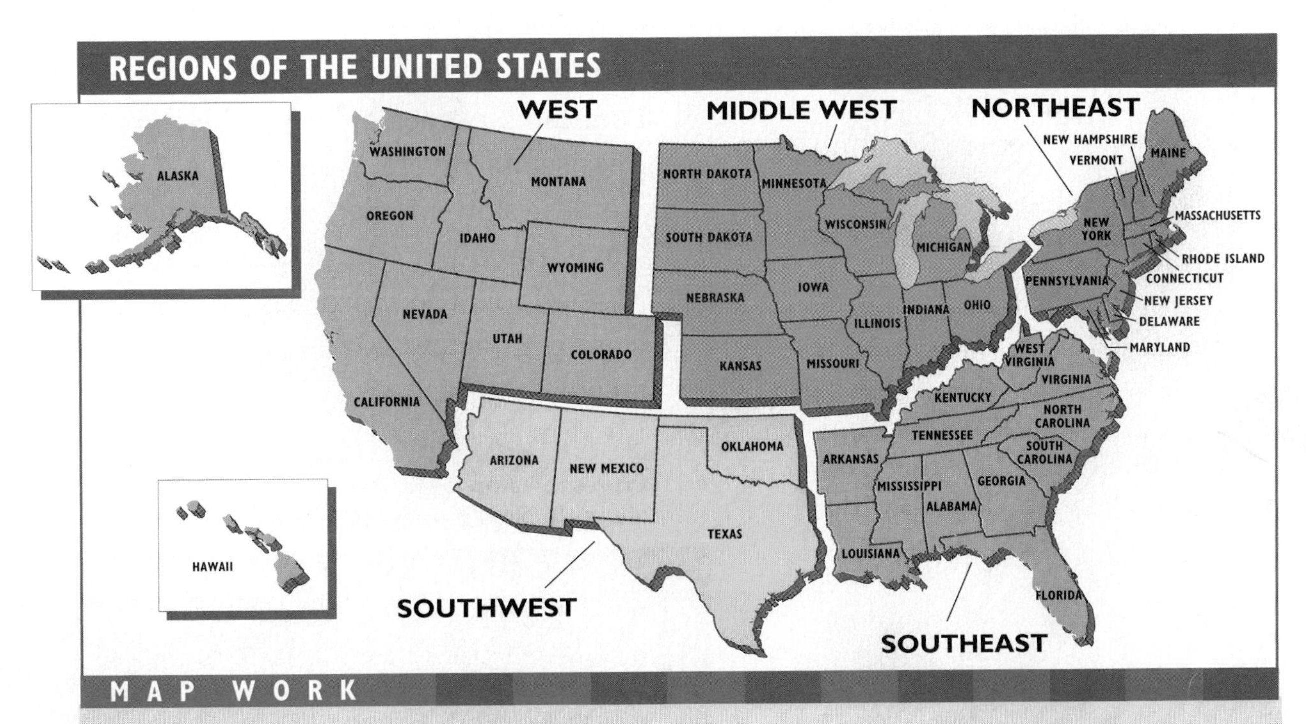


**MAP WORK**

New Jersey is part of the Northeast **region**.

1. How many states make up the Northeast region?
2. Which two regions border the Northeast region?
3. Find Nebraska. In which region is it?
4. Have you ever visited another state? What region is it in? What differences did you notice between that state and New Jersey?

**MAP WORK:** **1.** eleven **2.** Southeast, Middle West **3.** Middle West **4.** Encourage students to think about differences between or within regions.

## THE SOUTHEAST

Like the Northeast, the Southeast includes part of the Coastal Plain of the United States. The Appalachian Mountains run through the Southeast too.

The Southeast is a warm region that is crisscrossed with rivers. Most rivers in the Southeast start in the Appalachian Mountains. However, the region's biggest river, the **Mississippi River**, begins in the Middle West. It flows into the Gulf of Mexico.

Along the Mississippi River lies the Yazoo Delta. Eudora Welty describes the Delta in one of her books. What is the insect that she compares the Delta to?

**Excerpt from *Delta Wedding* written by Eudora Welty in 1946.**

***In the Delta, most of the world seemed sky. . . . The land was perfectly flat and level, but it shimmered like the wing of a lighted dragonfly. It seemed strummed, as though it were an instrument and something had touched it.***

### Wetlands

Many coastal and lowland areas in the Southeast are dotted with wetlands. Wetlands are areas that are covered by shallow water for at least part of the year.

**Swamps** and **marshes** are two types of wetlands. Swamps usually have many trees. Marshes are wetlands covered with tall grasses. You can find many swamps and marshes near rivers that flood at certain times of the year.

The Everglades in southern Florida is one of the largest wetlands in the United States. Other Southeastern wetlands include the Okefenokee Swamp located in Georgia and Florida and the Great Dismal Swamp in North Carolina and Virginia.

There are hundreds of **bayous** in Louisiana, especially along the lower Mississippi River. A bayou is a marshy, slow-moving stream. The **Davis Bayou** is one of several in Mississippi. The word bayou comes from a Choctaw Indian word that means "sluggish stream."

**Cypress Swamp is just north of Jackson, along the Ross Barnett Reservoir.**

The corn grown on the Central Plains (left) and the wheat grown on the Great Plains (below) help feed our growing country.

## THE MIDDLE WEST

The Middle West is part of a landform of the United States called the Interior Plains. There are really two parts to the Interior Plains. They are the Central Plains in the east and the Great Plains in the west. There is no sharp dividing line between them. Yet the geography of these two areas is different. Find them on the Atlas map on page R8.

### Different Kinds of Plains

The Central Plains are low in elevation, not much higher than sea level in some places. Gently rolling hills cover much of the land. Corn is one of the main crops on the Central Plains. Farmers in Iowa can produce 900 million bushels of corn in a year. This is enough corn to give each person in the United States more than 100 quarts of corn! Can you imagine eating that much? Some of the corn is shipped to markets across the country and around the world.

The climate of the Middle West can be extreme. Writer Neal Peirce called the Great Plains "a land of fiercely cold winters and furnace-like summers." This region also experiences harsh storms and tornadoes, and the wind is often blowing.

The Great Plains are mostly dry grassland. Not enough rain falls for most types of trees to survive there.

Wheat is the major crop on the Great Plains. In fact, the dry climate is perfect for growing it. The states of Kansas and North Dakota are the biggest wheat producers in the United States.

## THE SOUTHWEST

The Southwest has only four states—Texas, Oklahoma, Arizona, and New Mexico. Except for Arizona, the states of the Southwest all share the Great Plains of the Middle West.

Like the Northeast and the Southeast, the Southwest includes part of the Coastal Plain. But Texas is the only state of the Southwest that has this landform. Much of the Southwest is made up of high plateaus and plains.

Farther west the geography is very different. The Rocky Mountains appear. This mountain range stretches from Canada through many states of the United States and into Mexico.

The climate of the Southwest is varied. The Coastal Plain along the Gulf of Mexico is warm and rainy. High up in the Rocky Mountains, the temperature can drop far below freezing. Much of the Southwest, however, is hot and dry. Many parts of the region are covered by deserts—dry land where little rain falls. A desert gets less than 10 inches of precipitation each year.

### The Grand Canyon

One of the most famous landforms of the Southwest is the Grand Canyon. A canyon is a deep valley with steep sides.

The Grand Canyon was carved over many, many centuries by the Colorado River and stretches 217 miles through northern Arizona. In some places this gigantic canyon is more than one mile deep! At its widest, the canyon measures 18 miles from one rim, or edge, to the other. If there were a footbridge across the canyon, someone could walk across in about six hours.

**The Grand Canyon is vast—whether you are at the top looking down or riding into it.**

See p. T12 for Answers to Think About It.

**The redwood trees in California make people look very small.**

## THE WEST

Among the different landforms in the West are mountains, plateaus, and valleys. The high elevations of the mountains affect temperature and precipitation.

Winds from the Pacific Ocean push warm, wet air over the land. This air cools as it moves up the mountains, forming clouds. The cooled clouds drop most of their moisture in the form of rain or snow. When the air reaches the top of the mountains, most of the moisture is gone. Little water is in the wind-driven air that reaches the other side of the mountains. This eastern side of the mountains stays much drier. The dry side lies in the **rain shadow**. Much more rain falls in the western part of the region than in the eastern part.

Thick forests of tall trees cover parts of the Pacific Coast. The redwood trees that grow in California and Oregon are the tallest trees in the world. Many are over 300 feet tall.

## WHY IT MATTERS

Our country is one of the largest in the world, with a great variety of landforms. Geographers sometimes divide the United States into five regions because of the common features found in a region.

In the next lesson you will read about the regions in New Jersey and how each region's geography affects the way people live and work there.

### Reviewing Facts and Ideas

#### MAIN IDEAS

- The five regions of the United States are the Northeast, Southeast, Middle West, Southwest, and West.
- The Coastal Plain is found in the Northeast, the Southeast, and the Southwest.
- Corn and wheat are the main crops of the Middle West.
- The mountains of the West have an effect on rainfall.

#### THINK ABOUT IT

1. Name the major landforms of the United States.
2. What is a region?
3. **FOCUS** Describe the region in which New Jersey lies.
4. **THINKING SKILL** What _questions_ would you ask someone to learn about his or her region?
5. **GEOGRAPHY** What landforms does the Northeast region share with other regions of the United States?

See p. T13 for Lesson Teaching Strategies.

# Regions of New Jersey

## Read Aloud

*"Even on bright days, rivers can be dark and almost sunless," wrote John McPhee of the rivers of the Pinelands in 1967. "Then, all in a moment, [the rivers] run into brilliant sunshine where the banks rise higher and the forest of oak and pine is less dense."*

## Focus Activity

**READ TO LEARN**

***What is special about each of the four regions of New Jersey?***

**VOCABULARY**

- culture
- population
- urban
- rural
- fall line
- commute
- glacier
- reservoir

**PLACES**

- Atlantic Coastal Plain
- Piedmont
- Highlands
- Ridge and Valley
- Franklin

## THE BIG PICTURE

In the last lesson, you read about the regions of the United States. New Jersey can also be divided into regions. Our state has four. Geographer Michelle Goman explains, "Each region has features that make it special." Some of the features that make a region special are its landforms, its history, and its **culture**, or way of life. Language, music, food, and holidays are all part of culture.

Take a look at the map on page 35. What is the largest region of New Jersey? What are the names of the other regions in our state? In this lesson, you will read about the four regions of our state and how the land and the people make each one special.*

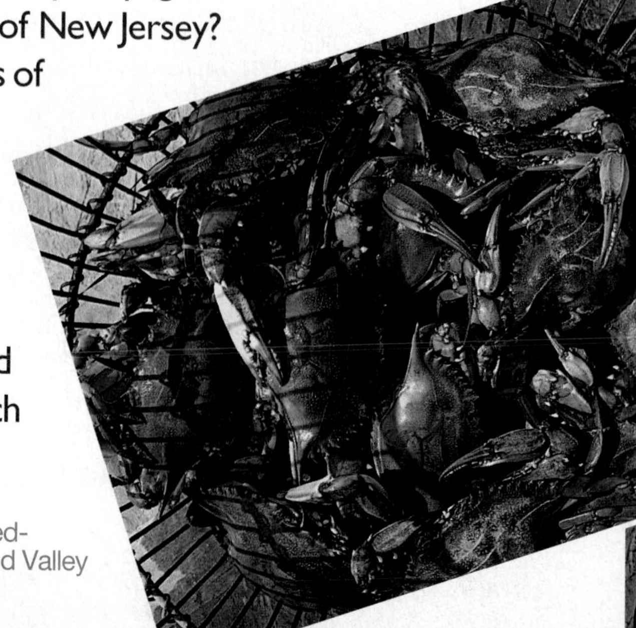

*Atlantic Coastal Plain; Piedmont; Highlands; Ridge and Valley

*The Atlantic Coastal Plain

## PEOPLE AND THE LAND

Geographers like Michelle Goman study the land and how people change it over time. One way people change the land is by their choice of where to live.

Take another look at the map on this page. Which region of our state do you think has the largest number of people or **population**? You might think the answer is the **Atlantic Coastal Plain** region, because it is the largest in size. Actually, the **Piedmont** (PEED mahnt) region has the greatest population. About two out of five New Jerseyans live there.

**Each region of New Jersey has features that make it special. Which region do you think provides us with crabs and other seafood?***

MAP WORK: **1.** The Ridge and Valley region **2.** The Atlantic Coastal Plain region

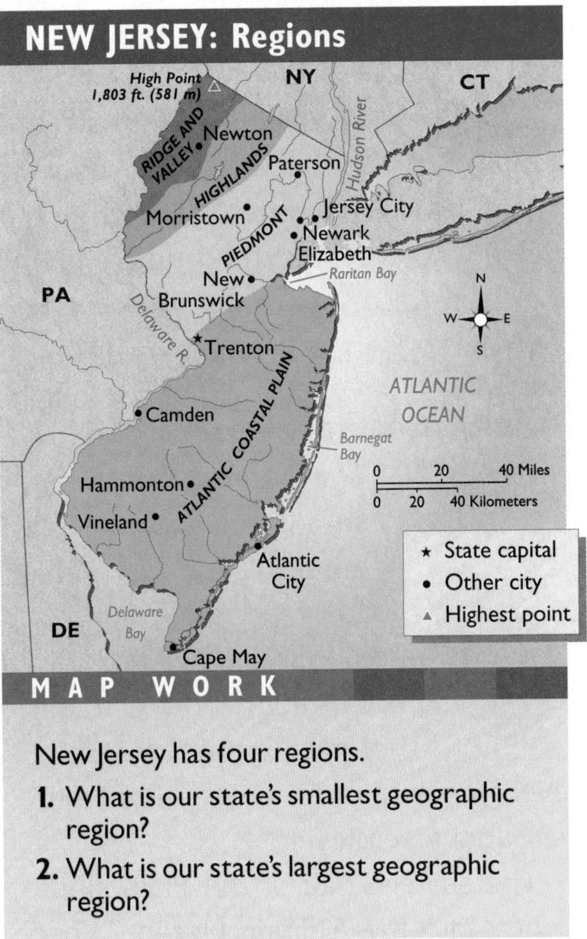


**MAP WORK**

New Jersey has four regions.

1. What is our state's smallest geographic region?
2. What is our state's largest geographic region?

### Where We Live

As you read in Chapter 1, New Jersey has more than 8 million people. Most of them live in **urban** areas. Urban means "of a city." An urban area includes a city and the communities that surround it. Newark and Camden are two of the urban areas in our state.

Most of our state is **rural**. Rural means "of the countryside." Rural areas include farms, villages, or unsettled land. Fewer people live there. As Professor Goman says, "People think New Jersey is urban, but about two-thirds of it is farmland or forests."

## FROM COAST TO FOOTHILLS

Most New Jerseyans live in one of two regions, the Atlantic Coastal Plain or the Piedmont. Together, these two regions extend up from the southern tip of our state into central New Jersey.

### Atlantic Coastal Plain

The Atlantic Coastal Plain covers more than one-half of our state. Millions of years ago, this area was part of the ocean floor. Today, it is not very high above sea level. The highpoint is less than 400 feet above sea level.

The eastern half of the Plain slopes gently into the Atlantic Ocean. Where the land meets the sea, there are sandy beaches and marshy wetlands. Everyone knows about our state's famous beaches. However, fewer people know the important role wetlands play. They are home to a rich variety of plant and animal life. According to geographer Goman, "About 200 to 300 types of plants, birds, and other animals come together in New Jersey's wetlands."

Much of the Atlantic Coastal Plain is made up of farmland. The low plains and rich soil of this region helped New Jersey earn its nickname as "the Garden State." The farmers of this region grow fruits and vegetables, including blueberries, cranberries, and the famous Jersey tomato.

The Atlantic Coastal Plain is also home to the Pinelands. The area is known for its forests and rivers. You read John McPhee's description of the waters of the Pinelands in the Read Aloud at the beginning of this lesson.

**Amusement parks (above) attract many visitors to the New Jersey shore each summer, but some people prefer to relax by watching the waves roll in (right).**

**The Great Falls mark the fall line of the Passaic River.**

Trenton is located near the fall line. The fall line is the place where the Piedmont meets the Atlantic Coastal Plain. At this line, rivers drop from highlands to lowlands. The change in height is a good source of water power. About 200 years ago, power from river water helped factories develop in this region.

Today, many people who live in the Piedmont region commute, or travel, to jobs in other cities, such as New York City.

### The Piedmont

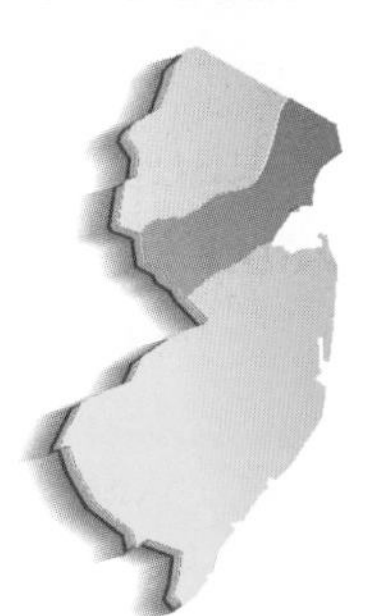

New Jersey's Piedmont region stretches across the northcentral part of the state. *Piedmont* means foothills, or low hills at the bottom of mountains.

The Piedmont region is a strip of land only 20 miles wide. It sits beneath tall ridges in the northern part of our state. The Palisades form its eastern border. These cliffs are located along the Hudson River and stand as high as 540 feet tall. The Palisades were formed more than 200 million years ago from molten, or liquid rock. About 3 million people live in the Piedmont. Several of New Jersey's largest cities can be found here, including Trenton, our state capital.

**DID YOU KNOW?**

***What is a flyway?***

**Each year thousands of ducks, geese, and other birds come to New Jersey to nest and feed. They follow a bird "highway," called a flyway, into our state. There are four such flyways in North America. The Atlantic Flyway extends from Canada and follows the shore of the Atlantic Ocean to Florida and into the Gulf of Mexico and South America. Before winter sets in, birds leave the north to find warmer weather in the south. In the spring, they return north. Birds travel the flyway to many areas in New Jersey. They visit the beaches of the Atlantic Coastal Plain, the Great Swamp in the Piedmont, and other regions in our state.**

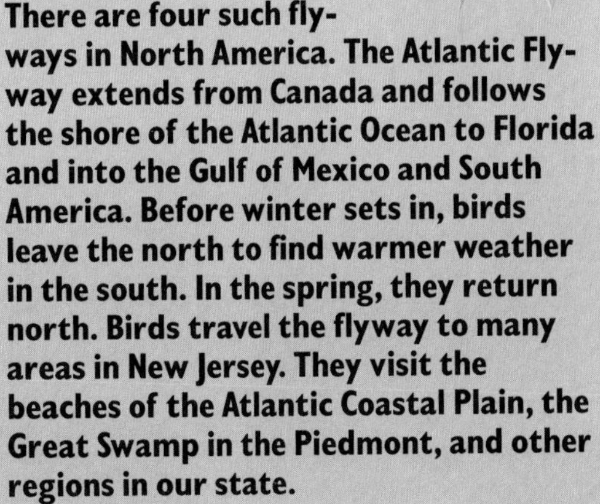

## HILLS AND VALLEYS

New Jersey's other two regions lie in the northern part of our state. They are the Highlands and the Ridge and Valley regions. The population in these two areas is much smaller than in the rest of our state.

### The Highlands

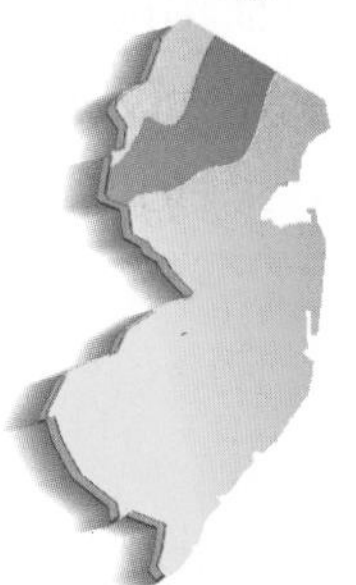

Just north and west of the Piedmont region is the Highlands region. It is a land of long, thin valleys that run north to south. Forests of hardwood trees line the hard mountaintops.

Many rocks in the Highlands are found nowhere else on earth. Some even glow in the dark! Franklin, a town in the region, is famous for its glowing rocks.

Most of our state's lakes are found in the Highlands region. Lake Hopatcong is the largest. It was formed thousands of years ago. Huge moving sheets of ice called glaciers [GLAY shurz] dug holes in the ground. When the ice melted the holes filled with water.

Some of the lakes in the Highlands are reservoirs [REZ ur vwahrs]. A reservoir is a natural or human-built lake used to store water.

The Highlands region provides a good example of how people use land differently over time. Until about 30 years ago, few people lived there. The land was poor for farming, and it was difficult to travel from the Highlands to the cities.

As more people began to commute to jobs in cities, they built homes in the Highlands region. Explains Michelle Goman, "People are beginning to see that they can have the beauty of the Highlands and still be close to more urban areas."

**The rushing rivers and streams of the Highlands region let some early settlers set up mills. Michelle Goman (right) explains how land use in the region has changed.**

See p. T13 for Answers to Think About It.

**Holstein cows are one variety that help the Ridge and Valley region's farms supply dairy products to our tables.**

## WHY IT MATTERS

New Jersey can be divided into four regions. Each has features that make it special. Together they make our state a nice place to live and work.

### Ridge and Valley

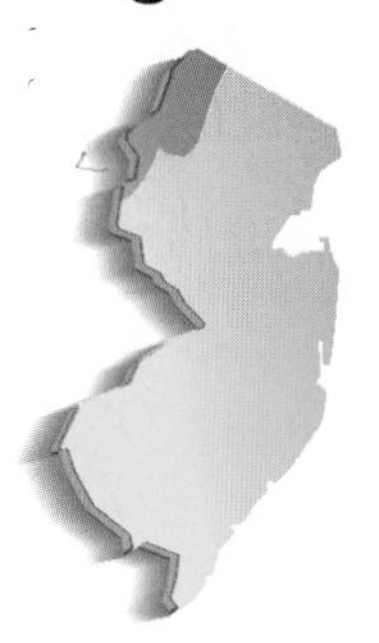

The Ridge and Valley region cuts across the northwestern corner of our state. It is part of the Appalachian Mountains, which run from Maine to Alabama.

It is difficult to grow crops in the region's rocky soil. However, grassy slopes in the valleys are perfect for grazing cows. As a result, dairy farming is an important business in the region. More than 25,000 cows provide milk, butter, and cheese for our state.

In fact, if you get milk at school with your lunch, you can be sure it came from a New Jersey cow. A state law says that only New Jersey dairies can sell milk to our state's schools. Many of those dairies are located in the Ridge and Valley region.

Much of the Ridge and Valley is set aside as parks and recreation areas. The Appalachian Trail, Delaware Water Gap, High Point State Park, and other sights attract visitors to the area.

## Reviewing Facts and Ideas

### MAIN IDEAS

- The Atlantic Coastal Plain is our state's largest region.
- The Piedmont has the most people of any New Jersey region.
- The Highlands region has most of our state's lakes and reservoirs.
- The Ridge and Valley region offers recreation and good land for dairy farms.

### THINK ABOUT IT

1. Define *urban* and *rural.*
2. Which region of New Jersey has the largest population?
3. **FOCUS** Name one feature that is special for each of the four regions of New Jersey.
4. **THINKING SKILL** Compare and contrast the Atlantic Coastal Plain and Ridge and Valley regions.
5. **WRITE** Write a letter to a friend describing the features that make the area where you live special.

# Thinking Skills

See p. T14 for Skill Teaching Strategies.

## Decision Making

**VOCABULARY**
decision

### WHY THE SKILL MATTERS

Decision making is a skill people use every day. Making a decision is the same as making a choice. You have to make up your mind what to do. Decisions may be simple, such as deciding what clothes to wear, or very difficult, such as deciding where to live. To make a good decision, you have to know what your goal is.

When people move to New Jersey, they must make many decisions. They have to decide where they want to work and where they want to live. Do they want to live in a city, or would they rather live in the country? Do they want to rent an apartment or buy a house?

### USING THE SKILL

Today most of New Jersey's people live in urban areas. The two largest cities are Newark and Jersey City. Some people in our state live in rural areas. They might own small farms and drive to work in nearby towns and cities.

Let's read about one newcomer from India who has just moved to our state. Her name is Deepa Moghul and she is staying with relatives in Princeton in central New Jersey while she makes her plans. Deepa has lived in India all of her life and wants to learn what life in New Jersey is like. Her relatives would like her to stay in Princeton. However, Deepa hopes to find a place to stay on the New Jersey coast because she wants to be near a beach. She is thinking about moving near Sandy Hook or to Cape May.

Here are some possible results of each choice.

- Deepa may find it difficult to live in a new location where she has no family.
- Deepa may learn to like living in Princeton.
- Deepa may enjoy being on the coast because she has always wanted to live near a beach.

See p. T14 for Answers to Reviewing the Skill.

## Helping yourself

- **A decision** is a choice about what to do.
- **Identify the choices you can make, and predict the results of each choice.**
- **Make the choice that helps you reach your goal.**

### TRYING THE SKILL

Suppose your family is planning to take a summer vacation. Your family wants to find a place where you can go swimming. You can choose High Point State Park in the Ridge and Valley region, or a place on the Atlantic Coastal Plain, such as Long Beach Island.

If you decide to go to High Point State Park, you can camp out near one of the many lakes in the park. There you can swim or canoe. This area is also a good place to go hiking. You can join other campers on a "learning trail" along the Appalachian Trail to find out about the plants and animals that live in this park's forest.

On the other hand, if you decide to go to Long Beach Island on your vacation, you can spend your time at the beach. Here your parents can relax and lie in the sun. You can swim, build sand castles, and search for seashells. You can also visit Island Beach State Park, where you can see how the forest has been "pruned" by salt spray from the ocean or visit Barnegat lighthouse. You can learn to sail on the bay or try to spot herons, egrets, and osprey at the Spizzle Creek Bird Blind.

How would you decide which vacation to take? Use the Helping Yourself box for hints. What is your goal for the vacation? What do you think the results of either choice might be?*

**Some people choose to live in busy urban areas like Trenton (left), while others enjoy the natural beauty of the New Jersey coast (above).**

### REVIEWING THE SKILL

1. What is a decision?
2. Look at the section called Trying the Skill. If your goal were to go canoeing, which vacation would you choose?
3. How will predicting possible results help you to make a good decision?
4. Why is it important to know how to make a good decision?

*Answers should reflect setting of goals and predicting results of choices.

LESSON 3

See pp. T15–16 for Lesson Teaching Strategies.

# Our State's Resources

## Focus Activity

**READ TO LEARN**

***In what ways are natural resources important to New Jersey?***

**VOCABULARY**

- environment
- natural resource
- economy
- renewable resource
- agriculture
- nonrenewable resource
- mineral
- pollution
- conservation
- recycle

**PLACES**

- Sparta
- Linden

### Read Aloud

*"We know that open land is at a premium* [scarce], *and we must preserve it. We know that clean air is invaluable* [precious], *and we must safeguard it. We know that clean water is priceless, and we must do all we can to protect [it]." This is how New Jersey Governor Christine Todd Whitman described her concern for the land, air, and water of New Jersey in her yearly message to the people of our state for 2000.*

### THE BIG PICTURE

The surroundings in which people, animals, or plants live is called an **environment**. We depend on our environment for clean air, water, food, and countless other things.

We also use and shape our environment. For example, we cut down forests for wood. In time, we use that same land for farms and towns. We grow food in the soil and drink water that comes from lakes and rivers. Something in the environment that people can use is called a **natural resource**. Through the years, people have fed their families, built their homes, and earned their livings with our state's natural resources. Every natural resource in New Jersey creates jobs. Jobs help create a strong **economy**. An economy is the way a community uses resources to meet people's needs and wants.

*forests, water

## RENEWABLE RESOURCES

Many different natural resources are found in our environment. Some of these are **renewable resources**. Renewable resources are ones that can be replaced.

### Forests

Trees are a renewable resource because they can be replanted. Trees that are harvested from New Jersey forests are used for lumber, paper, and Christmas trees. After workers cut down an area of forest, they often plant new trees. Ten or more years later this new crop of trees can be harvested. In this way, the forest is always "renewed."

Forests can be a resource even when they are not harvested. They provide homes for animals and places of recreation for people. Today, 

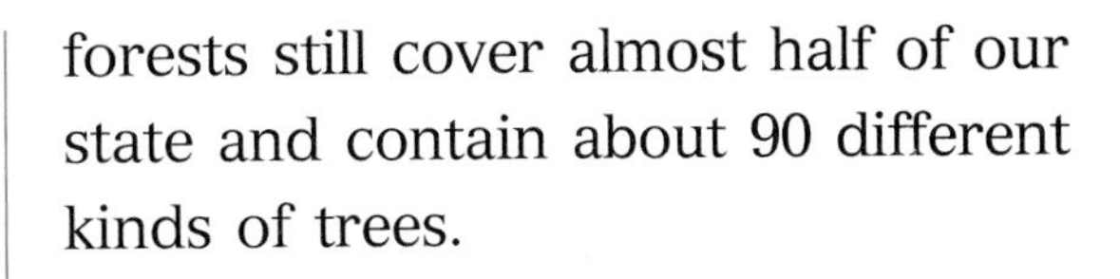

forests still cover almost half of our state and contain about 90 different kinds of trees.

### Soil

Soil is another important resource. It is necessary for **agriculture**. Agriculture is the business of growing crops and raising animals. Soil wears out from growing the same crops in a field year after year. One way farmers renew the soil is by adding fertilizer, the "food" that helps plants grow. Farmers also help keep the soil healthy by changing, or "rotating," the crops grown on an area of land. A farmer might grow beans on land one year and tomatoes on it the next.

### Water

Nothing can live without water. Think about all the ways people use water. Drinking, washing, watering crops, and making electricity are all activities that use water. Every time rain or snow falls in New Jersey, water returns to our state's land, rivers, aquifers, and lakes. That means water also is a renewable resource.

**What renewable resource is the person in each photograph using?***

## NONRENEWABLE RESOURCES

Some resources are available in a limited supply. These are called nonrenewable resources. When we have used them up, they will be gone forever. They cannot be replaced.

### Minerals

Minerals are nonrenewable resources. A mineral is a natural substance that is found in the ground that does not come from plants or animals. All rocks on Earth are made up of different minerals.

Iron has been an important mineral in our state. For many years it was mined both in the marshy areas of the south and the hilly regions to the north. Early factories turned iron into tools and building materials. Today most iron mining has stopped in our state. The iron is found in such small amounts, it is not worth mining.

Limestone, sandstone, and granite are other important minerals found in our state. They are often used as building materials. They are also used to make roads. A large limestone quarry, or place where stone is cut, is located near Sparta. It is shown in the photo below.

### Fuels

Most fuels [FYoo ulz] are nonrenewable resources. A fuel is something that is burned to make energy. Petroleum, or oil, is a liquid fuel that is found underground. Although our state produces no oil, millions of gallons of this "black gold" come to our state by ship and train.

In factories in Elizabeth and Linden, this raw oil is changed into gasoline, plastic, and other useful products.

Other fuels that provide energy to our state are natural gas and uranium. Uranium is a mineral that is also a fuel. The power from uranium, called nuclear power, creates electricity at four factories in our state. Although these fuels come from other places, they help keep our houses warm, our factories humming, and our economy strong.

Take a look at the Infographic on page 45. You can read more about the natural resources found in our state. You can also read about our state's most important resource—its people.

**Limestone is a nonrenewable resource.**

# Infographic

interNET CONNECTION Visit our website: www.mhschool.com

## NEW JERSEY'S RESOURCES

**New Jersey has many natural resources. Fish and shellfish are important resources along the shore. Farmland covers a large part of the state. What other resources are found in New Jersey?**

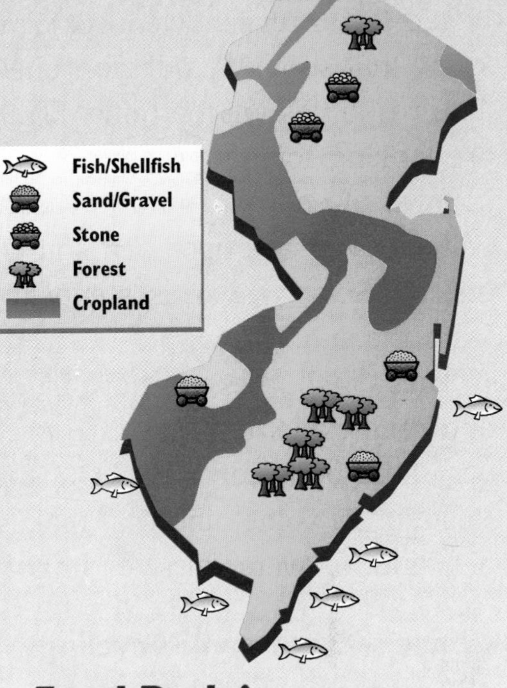

### Everyday People

People are New Jersey's most important resource. One out of five New Jersey workers, for example, has graduated from college.

### Food Dude!

Our state has about a million acres of cropland. New Jersey farmers grow crops ranging from asparagus to zucchini.

### Into the Woods

New Jersey's forests are home to many plants and animals. People use trees from our forests to build homes and make furniture.

### From Sand to Glass

People have been making glass using New Jersey sand since the 1700s. A jar in your refrigerator may have been made with New Jersey sand!

### We're Number One

Seafood is an important New Jersey resource. Two out of three clams harvested in the United States come from our state!

*paper, glass, plastics, and metal

## ENERGY FOR THE FUTURE

People used to think our resources would last forever. Scientists now know that someday our nonrenewable resources will be gone. So they are looking for new renewable sources of energy. Wind power and water power are two such sources of energy. Solar power uses energy from the sun.

These resources are not only free and renewable, but they also produce very little pollution (puh LOO shun). Pollution is something that makes the air, land, or water dirty or unhealthy.

### Conservation and Recycling

Conservation (kahn sur VAY shun) is the careful use of our natural resources. When people use only as much of a resource as they need, they are practicing conservation. Which resources can you conserve in your daily life?*

Another way to use our resources wisely is to recycle (ree SI kul) them. To recycle something is to use it again. All communities in New Jersey recycle newspapers, paper, glass, plastics, and metal. In fact, every year we recycle more than three billion aluminum cans. If you stacked these cans together, they would reach more than halfway from Earth to the moon! Our old car tires are also recycled. They come back to life as rubber balls, bike tires, and even skateboard parts. Who knows? Next time you are at recess you could be kicking around a recycled tire.

See p. T16 for Answers to Think About It.

## WHY IT MATTERS

There is one more resource that is very important in New Jersey—people. Only people like you can conserve our state's natural resources. By conserving our resources, we can all make sure that New Jersey has a bright, clean, and healthy future. As you read "Helping the Environment" on the next page think about what you can do to help conserve resources in your area.

## Reviewing Facts and Ideas

### MAIN IDEAS

- Natural resources are things in the environment that people can use.
- Renewable resources include trees, soil, and water. Nonrenewable resources include minerals, oil, and natural gas.
- Conservation helps to protect our state's resources.

### THINK ABOUT IT

1. List three examples of natural resources.
2. How can farmers renew soil when they plant crops?
3. **FOCUS** Why is it important for New Jerseyans to conserve our natural resources?
4. **THINKING SKILL** What are two reasons people might *decide* to use renewable sources of energy?
5. **GEOGRAPHY** Name one natural resource that is important to the area in which you live. How do people use this resource?

See p. T17 for Citizenship Teaching Strategies.

CITIZENSHIP

# MAKING A DIFFERENCE

## Helping the Environment

Morristown, New Jersey—Just a few years ago, members of the Lafayette 4-H Club did not know much about trash. Now they are experts. "We learned about it the hard way," says club member Jordan Anderson. "We have picked up hundreds of candy wrappers, popsicle sticks, and soda cans."

The Lafayette Club is made up of 40 boys and girls who range in age from 6 to 14. They often play sports or make craft projects. The club started working on the environment when their advisor suggested that they team up with a neighborhood community group.

The adults were cleaning up the Whippany River, which was badly polluted. Adults took canoes into the river and fished out most of the heavy objects, such as couches and chairs. Lafayette Club members picked up trash along the riverbank and in the Abbett Avenue Park alongside the river.

"We found bottles, car parts, tires, and old bikes," says Matthew King, age 13. "You really see how much garbage piles up if you just leave it on the ground."

Club members divided into groups for the cleanup. Some looked for glass or aluminum; others collected paper or plastic objects. They sorted the recyclables and put the trash by the curb for garbage and pick-up. It was hard and dirty work, but Matthew said club members liked it. "It makes you feel good," he said, "because you are helping the community and the environment. It is not just cleaner, but it is also a safer place for kids to play."

Club members next cleaned up a second park and playground, the Jersey Cottage Park. They keep it clean, plant shrubs in the park, and trim the bushes. Jordan Anderson, age 10, is glad the club has taken on this project. "Someone has got to do it. If no one cleans it up, it's just going to turn into a waste dump." With a little help from the Lafayette Club, maybe it won't.

See p. T18 for Answers to Chapter 2 Review.

# CHAPTER 2 REVIEW

## THINKING ABOUT VOCABULARY

Number a sheet of paper from 1 to 10. Beside each number write **C** if the underlined word or phrase is used correctly. If it is not, write the word or phrase that would correctly complete the sentence.

1. Rainwater refilling a lake describes a renewable resource.
2. An area with features that set it apart from other areas is called a region.
3. The place where rivers drop from highlands to lowlands is called the fall line.
4. A natural or human-built lake used to store water is called a reservoir.
5. Many jobs help to create a strong economy.
6. The side of a mountain that is usually dry because precipitation falls on the other side is called the desert.
7. The careful use of our natural resources is called environment.
8. An area that includes small towns and farms is called a rural area.
9. A swamp is a marshy, slow-moving stream.
10. The business of growing crops and raising animals is called agriculture.

## THINKING ABOUT FACTS

1. Which landforms are found in the Northeast region of the United States?
2. List three features that help to form a region.
3. How are the Central Plains and the Great Plains of the Middle West different?
4. How do people help shape a region?
5. Name the four regions of New Jersey.
6. How does the Highlands region show how land use changes over time?
7. Name the region with mountains that is bordered by the Highlands region.
8. What are some of the ways people use natural resources?
9. What is New Jersey's largest region?
10. What are some materials that we can recycle?

## THINK AND WRITE

### WRITING A DESCRIPTION
Write a description of the marshes and bayous in the Southeast.

### WRITING A TRAVEL BROCHURE
Write a travel brochure for your town or community. Describe the land and resources of the area and explain why people should visit there.

### WRITING A SUMMARY
Describe the importance of New Jersey's resources, such as soil and water, to the state's agriculture.

## APPLYING THINKING SKILLS

### DECISION MAKING

Suppose you want to visit a cousin in Camden. You plan to spend as much time as you can watching fish and other sea creatures at the nearby State Aquarium. Answer the following questions to practice your skill at making decisions.

1. What is your goal?
2. What are the choices you can make to reach your goal?
3. What do you think the results of each choice you make might be?
4. Which choice will you make?
5. Do you think you made a good decision? Why?

## Summing Up the Chapter

Use the horizontal organization chart below to organize information from the chapter. Copy the chart on a sheet of paper. Use the words in the box below to fill in the blanks in the columns. When you have filled in the chart, use it to help you write a paragraph that answers the question "How do New Jersey's resources provide jobs for New Jerseyans?"

| | UNITED STATES | NEW JERSEY |
|---|---|---|
| REGIONS | 5 Regions—Northeast, Southeast, Middle West, Southwest, West | 4 Regions—Atlantic Coastal Plain, Piedmont, Highlands, Ridge and Valley |
| MOUNTAINS | Appalachian Mountains, Rocky Mountains | The Appalachian Mountains run through the Ridge and Valley Region. |
| RIVERS | The Southeast has many rivers. The Mississippi River is its largest. | The Pinelands, in the Atlantic Coastal Plain, is known for its rivers. |

See p. T19 for Answers to Unit 1 Review.

# UNIT 1 REVIEW

## THINKING ABOUT VOCABULARY

Number a sheet of paper from 1 to 5. Next to each number write the letter of the definition that best matches the word.

1. transportation
   - **a.** A river that connects two states
   - **b.** Moving goods or people from one place to another
   - **c.** Long waterways inland
   - **d.** A small river or stream
2. landform
   - **a.** An area where plants and animals live
   - **b.** One of the shapes that makes up the surface of Earth
   - **c.** An area affected by climate
   - **d.** An area of high elevation
3. fall line
   - **a.** A wetland made up mainly of grasses
   - **b.** Gently rolling hills
   - **c.** The place where a river drops from highlands to lowlands
   - **d.** A slow-moving stream
4. history
   - **a.** People who were born before you
   - **b.** The study of everything on Earth
   - **c.** The story of what happened in the past
   - **d.** The story of a region's past
5. conservation
   - **a.** The surroundings in which people live
   - **b.** The use of something again and again
   - **c.** The careless use of resources
   - **d.** The careful use of our natural resources

## THINK AND WRITE

### WRITING A LETTER

Suppose you have a pen pal in another state. Your pen pal knows very little about New Jersey. Write a description of our state. Be sure to include information about the environment, the people, and the climate of New Jersey.

### WRITING A PARAGRAPH

Choose two regions of our state and write a paragraph comparing them. Include statements about how they are alike and how they are different.

### WRITING A LIST

Write a list of five vocabulary words from Unit 1. Then write a paragraph with five sentences, using each of the vocabulary words in a sentence.

## BUILDING SKILLS

1. **Elevation maps** Suppose you are planning a hiking trip to Wawayanda State Forest. Explain why it would be important to have an elevation map with you on your trip.
2. **Elevation maps** Using the elevation map on page 25, find the approximate elevation of the area where you live. Then find the approximate elevation of the Kittatinny Ridge.
3. **Decision making** What is a good first step to take when making a decision?
4. **Decision making** Describe one decision you have made today. What steps did you take to make it?
5. **Decision making** Why do you think it is important for you to learn how to make decisions?

## YESTERDAY, TODAY & TOMORROW

**People used to think that our natural resources would last forever. Now we know that many of these resources can be used up or polluted. Do you think that conservation efforts will be able to preserve our state's resources? Why or why not?**

## READING ON YOUR OWN

These are some of the books you might find at the library to help you learn more.

*RESOURCES*
**by Brian Knapp**
Explore the history of natural resources such as coal and water.

*WEATHER FORECASTING*
**by Gail Gibbons**
This book describes how people predict the weather and why weather forecasting is important.

*WATER, WATER EVERYWHERE*
**by Mark J. Rauzon and Cynthia Overbeck Bix**
Read about how the movement of water affects Earth's geography and people.

## UNIT 1 REVIEW PROJECT

### Make a Natural Resources Mobile

1. Think about the geography and the natural resources of New Jersey.
2. Work in a group. Have each group member choose one natural resource or feature.
3. Cut a shape from a piece of construction paper. You might draw a square, circle, star, or other shape.
4. On each shape draw a picture of the natural resource that you chose.
5. Color each picture and write a caption beneath it.
6. Punch a hole in the top of each shape and attach it to a piece of string.
7. Cut three rectangles of cardboard. Punch holes at the ends and tie the rectangles together to form a triangle.
8. Next, punch a hole in the center at the top of each piece of cardboard. Attach a piece of string to each one and tie the strings together at the top.
9. Finally, tape each natural resource picture to the cardboard.

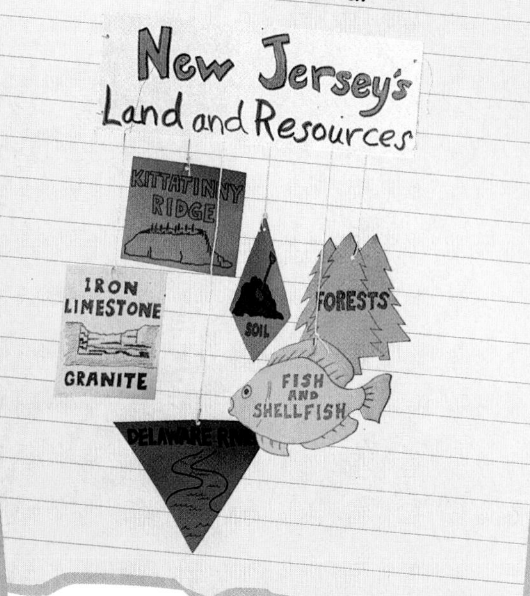

EARLY UNITED STATES FLAG

DUTCH SPOON RACK (LEFT); HENRY HUDSON (RIGHT)

# UNIT TWO

# Settlement of a New Land

*"We are thankful to the East because everyone feels good in the morning. . ."*

Lenape belief, as told to historian M.R. Harrington
See page 73.

## Why Does It Matter?

Who were the first people to live in our state? Why did they come here? What do we know about their ways of life? What other people made journeys to New Jersey?

In Unit 1 you studied New Jersey's geography. Unit 2 begins our study of New Jersey's history. You will find out about the Native Americans who were the first people to live in the land we now call New Jersey. You will also read about the European people who came to this land in the 1600s.

LENAPE BOWL

**FIND OUT MORE!**
**Visit our website:**
www.mhschool.com
*inter*NET CONNECTION

# Adventures with NATIONAL GEOGRAPHIC

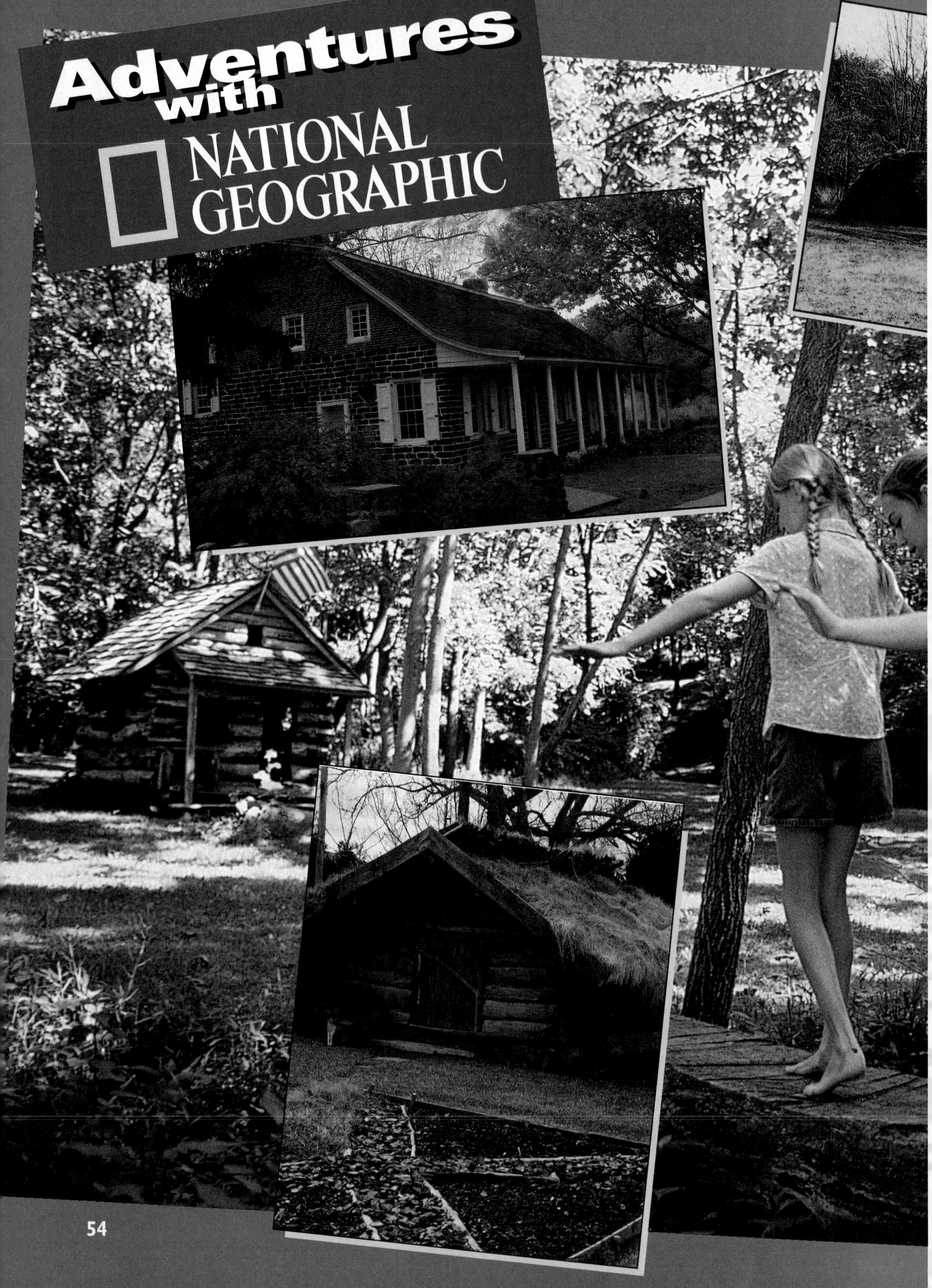

# Stepping into the Past

Ever wonder what life was like way back when? Maybe that is what these children are wondering as they head for a log cabin playhouse in Mendham, New Jersey. Houses of the past help us enter another world—the world of our ancestors. Native Americans were New Jersey's first inhabitants. They used saplings to build longhouses (top) and covered them with large pieces of bark. Early European settlers also used materials found in the area to build homes. Swedes settling along the Delaware River introduced the log cabin to America. This one-room log cabin (opposite, bottom), in Salem, New Jersey, is a copy of one built in the early 1700s. The oldest part of this stone house (above, left) was built by Dutch settlers about 1713. Its walls were made from fieldstone. For shelter and protection—and for learning about the past—there is no place like home.

## GEO JOURNAL

*Are there any historic houses in your area? What do they tell you about the past?*

CHAPTER 3

# The First People of New Jersey

## THINKING ABOUT HISTORY AND GEOGRAPHY

Did you know that the place where we live has been called "New Jersey" for only about 300 years? However, people have lived on this land for thousands of years. Who were these early people? Where did they come from? How did they live? What resources did they use? Read on to learn the answers to these questions and to find out what life was like long ago.

**40,000 YEARS AGO**

ALASKA

**People travel from Asia to North America.**

**12,000 YEARS AGO**

ABBOTT FARM SITE

**Early people gather around a campfire at the Abbott Farm site.**

**1,000 YEARS AGO**

NEAR SALEM

**Native Americans gather their fall harvest of corn, beans, and squash.**

40,000 B.C. | 10,000 B.C. | 2,000 B.C.

See pT22 for Chapter Organizer.

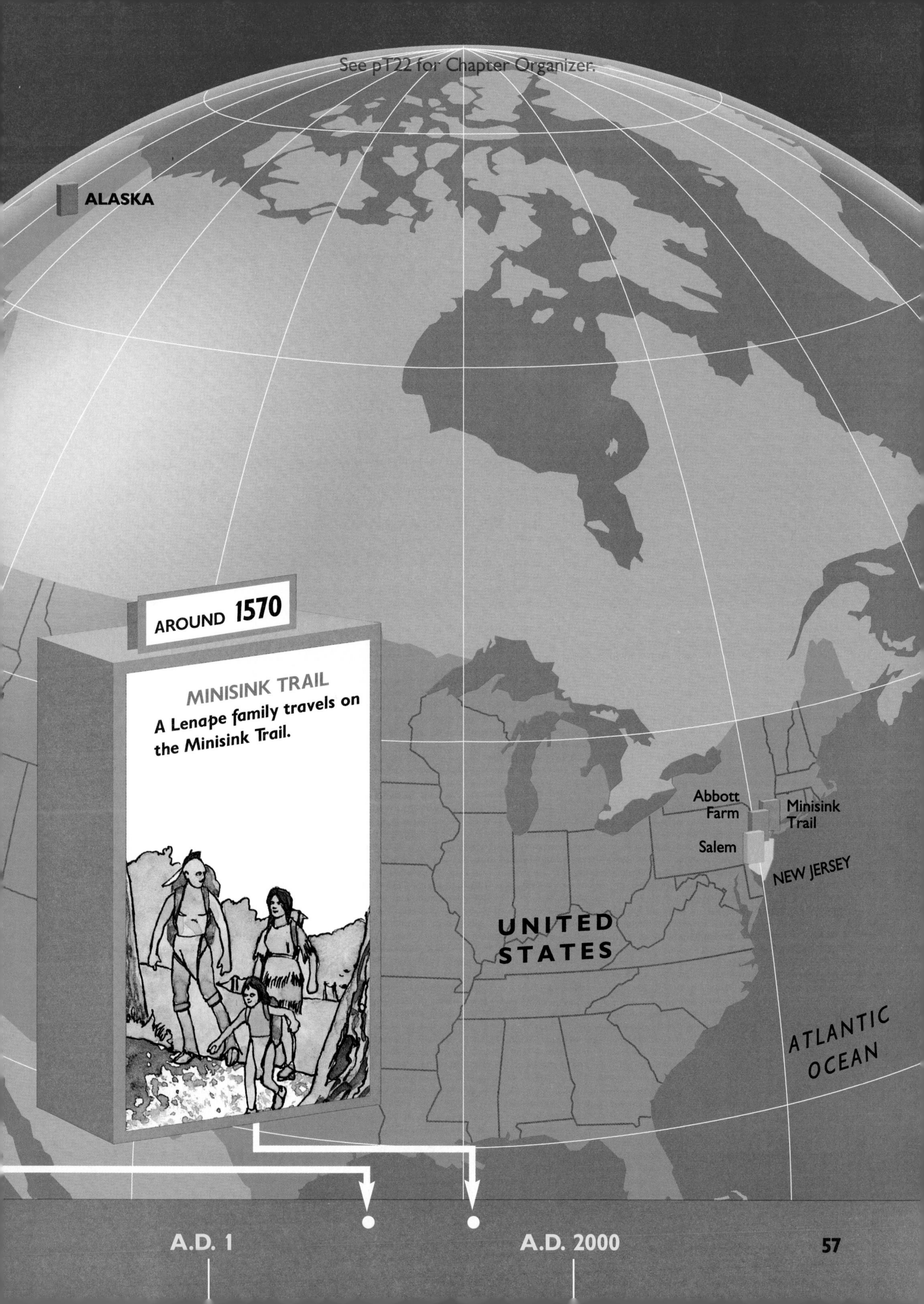

LESSON 1

40,000 YEARS AGO — 1,000 YEARS AGO

See p. T23 for Lesson Teaching Strategies.

# Early Peoples of New Jersey

## Read Aloud

*Hallie Borstel is a fourth grader in Maplewood, New Jersey. Her father is a scientist who studies objects from the past. "He brings home arrowheads, tools, and pieces of pottery," she says. "I like to picture how people used them and lived a long time ago."*

## Focus Activity

**READ TO LEARN**

***Who were the first people to live in New Jersey?***

**VOCABULARY**

- Ice Age
- artifact
- archaeologist
- prehistory
- hunter-gatherer
- ancestor

**PEOPLE**

- Charles C. Abbott

**PLACES**

- Beringia
- Bering Strait
- Abbott Farm

## THE BIG PICTURE

How and when did people first come to North America? Many scientists believe that people first arrived from Asia about 40,000 years ago. This was during the **Ice Age**. The Ice Age was a time when Earth's climate was much colder than it is now. Glaciers, or huge sheets of ice, covered much of Earth's surface. So much water froze into glaciers that the level of the oceans dropped!

Look at the map on the next page. Scientists believe that for about 2,000 years during the Ice Age a strip of land connected Asia with what is today Alaska. They call this strip of land **Beringia** (buh RIHN jee uh). People could have crossed from Asia to North America on this land bridge. When the Ice Age ended, the ocean levels rose once more, covering the land bridge. Today the **Bering Strait**, a body of water 56 miles across, separates Alaska from Asia.

**MAP WORK: 1.** Asia and North America

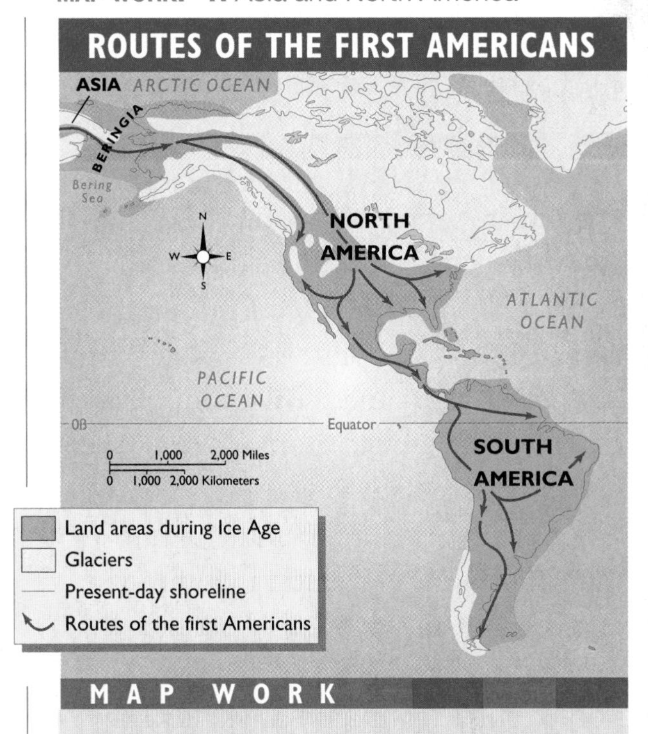


**MAP WORK**

People first came to America about 40,000 years ago.

1. Which continents did Beringia connect?

## CLUES FROM THE PAST

People were living in the land that is now New Jersey by about 12,000 years ago. How do we know this? Scientists have found **artifacts** left behind by people of that time. An artifact is an object made by people in the past. Tools, such as stone axes, knives, and arrowheads, are examples of artifacts.

A scientist who studies artifacts to learn about the past is called an **archaeologist** (ahr kee AHL uh jihst). Chris Borstel, Hallie's father, is an archaeologist. He has found artifacts in many different places in New Jersey, including parking lots and construction sites.

Sometimes artifacts are the best clues we have about how people lived in **prehistory**. Prehistory is the time before people left written records. "Each arrowhead or stone," explains Chris Borstel, "may provide a little more information that solves some of the mysteries of the past."

### An Exciting Find

One of New Jersey's first archaeologists was Dr. **Charles C. Abbott**. In 1867 Abbott found some stone tools on his farm near Trenton. He thought these tools dated to the Ice Age. It turned out Abbott was right! Since Abbott's find, archaeologists have studied objects from **Abbott Farm** and other places. In this way, they can piece together what life was like in New Jersey thousands of years ago.

**Dorothy Cross Jensen (right) worked as an archaeologist at Abbott Farm (below).**

## LIFE IN PREHISTORIC NEW JERSEY

The early people of New Jersey spent much of their lives moving around in search of food. They traveled in groups of about 20 people. These first people hunted big animals like caribou (KAR ih boo), which are a type of large deer. They may also have hunted giant elephant-like animals called mastodons.

Animals were important for more than food. They provided clothing and shelter as well. Early people dressed in animal furs and wore boots made from animal skins. They probably also used animal skins to make tents.

Hunting was not their only source of food. They also gathered fruits and nuts from the forest and fish from rivers. We call these people hunter-gatherers because they hunted and gathered their food.

Life was not easy for these early people. The large animals they hunted were dangerous. Diseases easily cured today often ended in death for early people. Scientists believe that these people lived no more than 35 years.

### Changing Environment

The Ice Age ended about 10,000 years ago. The climate grew warmer. Glaciers melted. Many of the large Ice Age animals, such as the mastodon, died out or moved north. New plants and animals appeared.

In New Jersey the retreating ice left behind a changed landscape. Lakes that had been formed when glaciers trapped river water began to dry up. This is how the Great Swamp, which you read about in Chapter 1, was formed.

**The early peoples who lived in New Jersey may have hunted mastodons and other large animals for food and furs.**

See p. T23 for Answers to Think About It.

## Agriculture

By about 1,000 years ago, people in New Jersey had developed agriculture. They raised corn, beans, squash, and pumpkins. People still hunted and gathered, but farming allowed them to stay in the same area rather than move from place to place.

These farming people were probably the ancestors of the people now known as Native Americans. Ancestors are people in your family, starting with your parents, who were born before you. The word *native* means "one of the first people to live on a land." Many Native Americans, however, believe their people have always lived here. They do not believe their ancestors crossed Beringia.

## WHY IT MATTERS

The first people of New Jersey were hunters and gatherers. In time people learned how to grow crops. Even today, our lives depend on these ancient skills.

**Links to SCIENCE**

### The Dating Game

**Did you know that you have something called carbon 14 inside you? All living things do. When something dies, however, the amount of carbon 14 starts to decrease. An archaeologist can measure how much carbon 14 is left in a very old object and figure out the age of the object. This method, called carbon dating, works for objects up to 50,000 years old!**

**Suppose a stone blade is found near an ancient campfire. Stone does not contain carbon 14, but the campfire wood does. Carbon dating shows that the wood is 9,000 years old. If the same people made the blade and the fire, how old do you think the stone blade is? Explain.***

## Reviewing Facts and Ideas

### MAIN IDEAS

- Many scientists think that people from Asia crossed Beringia to Alaska about 40,000 years ago.
- Archaeologists use artifacts to learn about people who lived thousands of years ago.
- Early New Jerseyans got food by hunting and gathering.
- About 1,000 years ago, people in New Jersey started farming.

### THINK ABOUT IT

1. What is prehistory?
2. What is an artifact?
3. **FOCUS** How do we know about the first people of New Jersey?
4. **THINKING SKILL** Compare and contrast the lives of hunter-gatherers with the lives of early farmers.
5. **GEOGRAPHY** Why do you think that archaeologists often look for artifacts in caves and near rivers?

*about 9,000 years old; the blade is probably close to the same age as the fire

See p. T24 for Skill Teaching Strategies.

# Identifying Cause and Effect

**VOCABULARY**
cause
effect

### WHY THE SKILL MATTERS

You read in the last lesson that people may have crossed a land bridge called Beringia about 40,000 years ago to reach North America. Scientists believe that these early people were following large animals across the land bridge to hunt them. The movement of the animals was a cause. A cause is an event that makes something else happen. The journey of these early people across the land bridge was an effect. An effect is what happens as a result of something else.

Understanding cause and effect allows you to put facts together in a meaningful way. It helps explain *why* things happen. It shows connections between one event and another. Use the Helping Yourself box for some clue words that may help you find causes and effects.

### USING THE SKILL

We learned in the last lesson that archaeologists study prehistoric New Jersey. In the following passage, an archaeologist describes the Ice Age. Try to find a cause and an effect. Look for clue words that can help you identify the effect.

*At that time, the weather was very cold. Thick Ice Age glaciers covered large parts of North America and Asia. Because it was so cold, the snow and ice did not melt off the land, and frozen water could not return to the seas. As a result, oceans became shallow, and beaches that were once under water became dry land. In these prehistoric times, Asia was connected to North America by a land bridge that was over one thousand miles wide.*

The land bridge was the effect of the Ice Age glaciers. Some of the clue words that helped you figure out the cause and effect were *because* and *as a result.*

*cause; they were cut off from their relatives on the Asian side and gradually drifted south; *therefore*

See p. T24 for Answers to Reviewing the Skill.

### TRYING THE SKILL

Now read another passage written by an archaeologist. Look for any causes and effects. Remember to watch for clue words.

*Later, when the glaciers melted, the icy waters returned to the oceans. Therefore, the land bridge once again became flooded. People on the Asian side were cut off from their relatives on the North American side who thus became the first Americans. Gradually, these people drifted south. Many generations later, about 12,000 years ago, their descendants reached the Atlantic coast.*

Was the melting of the glaciers a cause or an effect? How did the flooding of the land bridge lead to people reaching the Atlantic coast? Did you use clue words in the passage to help you to figure out cause and effect? What were the clue words?*

- **A cause is an event that makes something happen. An effect is what happens because of it.**
- **Look for clue words that show causes—*because, since, as a result.***
- **Look for clue words that show effects—*so, therefore, as a result.***

### REVIEWING THE SKILL

1. What is a cause? What is an effect?
2. What caused the early people in North America to be cut off from Asia?
3. How can the appearance of the land bridge be seen as an *effect* of one thing and a *cause* of something else?
4. What was an effect of the glaciers melting?
5. How might identifying cause and effect help you to understand history?

LESSON 2

1000 1200 1400 1500 1700 1800

See p. T25 for Lesson Teaching Strategies.

# Native Americans of New Jersey

## Read Aloud

*In 1698, a visitor to a Lenape village described the ways of the people he found there. "[The men spend their time] in hunting, fishing, making canoes and bowls, in all which arts they are very [skillful]. [The women work in] planting corn and pounding it to meal to make bread. They also make Indian mats, hats, and baskets. . . ." The people he described called themselves the Lenape.*

## Focus Activity

**READ TO LEARN**

***How did the Lenape use resources in their environment?***

**VOCABULARY**

- Lenape
- heritage
- religion
- manetu

**PLACES**

- Lenapehoking
- Raritan River

## THE BIG PICTURE

By the 1600s the **Lenape** (LEN nah pee) lived throughout New Jersey. They also lived in parts of Delaware, Pennsylvania, and New York. Some archaeologists call this area **Lenapehoking**, which means "where the Lenape dwell."

About 12,000 people lived in Lenapehoking by 1600. They were spread out in small villages located by streams or rivers. The Lenape used the resources in their environment for food, clothing, and shelter. When resources ran low, the Lenape moved their villages to newer areas. That way they made sure never to overuse the resources of their land.

# THE LENAPE

By the 1600s there were two main groups of Lenape in New Jersey. They were the Munsee and the Unami (woo NAH mi). The two groups spoke similar languages and shared a common culture. However, they lived in different areas.

The **Raritan River** formed a rough dividing line between the two groups. The Munsee lived north of the river, in the Ridge and Valley, the Highlands, and the Piedmont regions. Their name means "people of the stony country." The Unami lived south of the Raritan River. Their name means "people down the river." Look at the map on this page to see where these two groups lived.

## The Cycle of the Seasons

As you have read, the Lenape used the resources in their environment to provide food, clothing, and shelter. Their lives were tied to the cycle, or pattern, of the seasons.

In the spring, the Lenape planted their crops. Once the planting was done, some Lenape left the village. They traveled to the Jersey shore in the summer to collect clams and oysters. By the fall, everyone would return to the village to help harvest corn, beans, and squash.

In late fall, the Lenape worked hard to store up enough food for the winter. Lenape women and children stayed close to the village. They collected nuts and berries in the forest and packed them away in baskets.

**MAP WORK: 1.** the Munsee

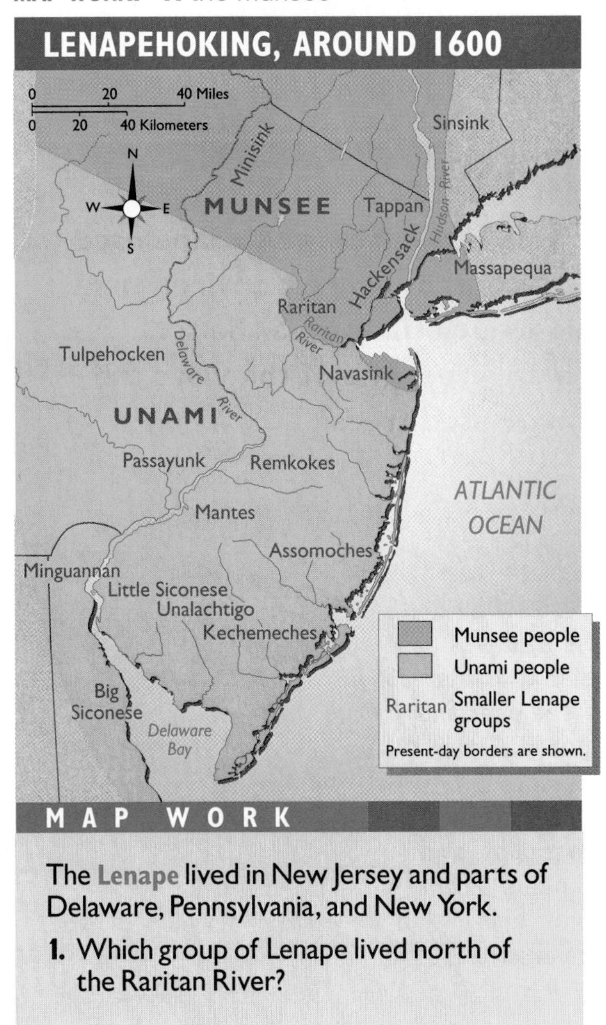


**MAP WORK**

The **Lenape** lived in New Jersey and parts of Delaware, Pennsylvania, and New York.

1. Which group of Lenape lived north of the Raritan River?

They also dried meat and fish. Lenape men often went on hunting trips in the forests. They could be gone for many weeks at a time.

**Even today you can see large piles of shells like these along the Maurice River, left behind by the Lenape.**

# Infographic

interNET CONNECTION Visit our website: www.mhschool.com

## The Lenape and Their Environment

**As you have read, the Lenape used the resources in their environment for food, clothing, and shelter. What were some of the ways the Lenape used trees?**

### Waste Not, Want Not

The Lenape used all parts of the deer they hunted. From deerskin they made clothing, moccasins, and blankets. From bones and antlers they made tools.

### Fishing

Fish were an important source of food for the Lenape. One way they caught fish was to use a weir (WEER), or V-shaped wall set in a stream. The wall had an opening into which a fisher herded the fish. At the opening, other fishers speared the fish or else used a net made from vines to catch them.

### Medicines from the Forest

The Lenape used certain plants to cure illnesses. To reduce fevers, for example, they created tea by boiling the inner bark of dogwood trees (below).

### Dugout Canoes

The Lenape made canoes from trees. They burned out the center of a log, removed the burned part, then shaped the inside of the log for seating.

See p. T25 for Answers to Think About It.

## LENAPE BELIEFS

The people who lived in Lenapehoking shared a common **heritage**. Heritage is the history, beliefs, and way of life that a group of people share. One important part of this heritage was the Lenape **religion**. Religion is the way people worship the god or gods they believe in.

The Lenape believed that many different spirit forces controlled the world. The Lenape called these spirits **manetu**. A Lenape woman named Touching Leaves, also known as Nora Thompson Dean, described these beliefs.

> *Spirits are everywhere. [For example,] each of the trees has a spirit we call a manetu, and each of the plants has a lesser manetu.*

Most manetu were good and helpful. They brought rain, good harvests, and safe hunting. However, some manetu were bad. They created trouble for people, such as stinging insects, thorns on berry bushes, and illness.

Before leaving on a journey or beginning a hunt, people prayed to the manetu for protection. The Lenape also held many ceremonies to honor the manetu. One of the most important ceremonies was the corn festival, which happened during the fall harvest. The Big House ceremony occurred when the Lenape gave thanks to the Creator, the most important manetu. This festival lasted 12 days and included music, dancing, and singing.

**Lenape carvings like this one watched over ceremonies.**

## WHY IT MATTERS

For hundreds of years the Lenape lived throughout New Jersey. They used the natural resources of the region to live. You will read more about their daily lives in the next lesson.

### Reviewing Facts and Ideas

#### MAIN IDEAS

- The Lenape of New Jersey were divided into two main groups—the Munsee and the Unami.
- Lenape lives followed the cycle of the seasons.
- Religion was an important part of Lenape life.

#### THINK ABOUT IT

1. What is a manetu?
2. Name five resources from their environment that the Lenape used.
3. **FOCUS** Why did the Lenape travel with the seasons?
4. **THINKING SKILL** What was one *effect* of a bad manetu?
5. **GEOGRAPHY** Look at the map on page 65. Which bodies of water did each Lenape group use?

See p. T26 for Legacy Teaching Strategies.

Legacy

LINKING PAST AND PRESENT

# In the FOOTSTEPS of the LENAPE

If you take a drive on Route 27 in central New Jersey, you will find yourself on a busy highway with several lanes. However, hundreds of years ago Route 27 was known as the Assunpink Trail, named for a Lenape group.

Many people traveled on this and other trails. As the years passed, the footpaths changed into horse trails, then dirt roads, and finally paved highways.

Trails tended to go around mountains and lakes, and crossed rivers at their shallowest points. Today's roads and bridges follow these same patterns.

The map on the next page shows some of the original trails the Lenape followed from their villages to the ocean. It also shows some of today's highways. Of course, a Lenape hike took a lot longer than a car ride today. But try telling that to the people stuck in rush hour traffic on Route 27!

**Hiking trails like these (above) might be a legacy of the Lenape. Many rural roads (right) in our state follow old Native American paths.**

From foot trails to wagon trails to super highways, New Jersey has always been an important transportation corridor.

| 1000 | 1200 | 1400 | 1500 | 1700 | 1800 |
|---|---|---|---|---|---|

See p. T27 for Lesson Teaching Strategies.

# Daily Life of the Lenape

## Read Aloud

*Music and dance were important parts of Lenape life. One visitor to a Lenape village more than 200 years ago described a dance. "The women [follow] the men, dancing in a circle . . . . They have no other music than the drum. When one dance has been finished, the one who beats the drum sings and beats until another begins."*

## Focus Activity

**READ TO LEARN**

***What was daily life like for the Lenape?***

**VOCABULARY**

- longhouse
- wigwam
- sakima
- oral tradition

## THE BIG PICTURE

Lenape children did not go to school. There were no schools. Instead, Lenape girls and boys learned by working with their parents. They also listened to the stories of the older members of their group. This taught them all kinds of useful and interesting things. They learned how to trap a beaver, how to sew moccasins, how to cure illness with special plants, and how to sing and dance.

For Lenape children, the whole environment was a classroom. The trees in the forest, the stars in the sky, and the waves in the ocean all taught important lessons to young Lenape. Just as computers and books help you prepare for today's world, learning from nature helped young Lenape prepare for theirs.

## GROWING UP LENAPE

If you were born in a Lenape village, your first memory might have been watching the women of the village tending the crops. Mothers strapped their babies onto "cradleboards" and took them into the cornfields. The women wore the cradleboard on their backs as they worked. Sometimes they would hang it in a tree. After a few years, the small children would help their mothers hoe, weed, and collect the crops.

As children grew older, girls and boys had different jobs. Girls helped the women grind corn, cook, make baskets, and care for younger children. Boys learned to hunt and fish and to make tools.

Boys dressed like their fathers, wearing breechcloths in the summer. A breechcloth is a piece of deerskin worn between the legs and held up by a belt. Girls wore short deerskin skirts. In winter everyone dressed in warm deerskin leggings, fur robes, and feather robes.

### Mealtime

The Lenape ate only two meals a day, in the morning and late afternoon. Food was served in wooden bowls or turtle shells. Knives were made from chipped stone, forks from sharp animal bones, and spoons from clam shells.

The main food of the Lenape was corn. They ate it fresh from the cob, roasted, baked into bread, or boiled in water. In addition to the corn, beans, and squash that they grew, the Lenape also lived off wild foods. They gathered strawberries, raspberries, crab apples, onions, and nuts of all kinds in nearby forests and fields.

The Lenape ate meat from many animals, especially deer, elk, and bear. Since they had no refrigerators, the Lenape cooked and then dried meat and fish. This way it could be eaten months later. No matter what food they brought home, the Lenape always shared it with others in the village.

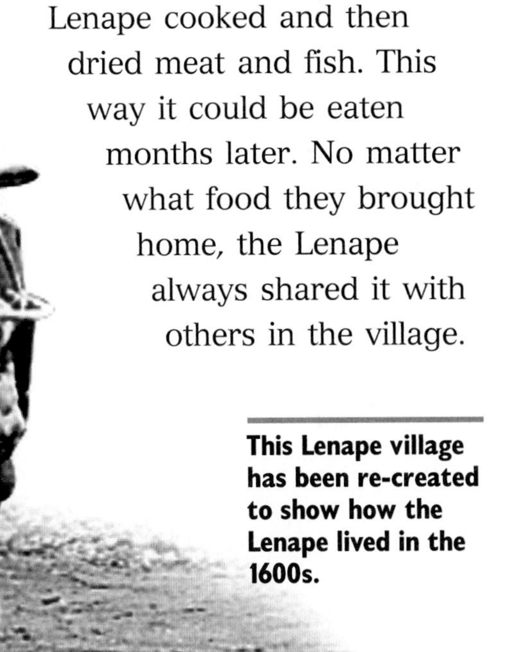

**This Lenape village has been re-created to show how the Lenape lived in the 1600s.**

## VILLAGE LIFE

The Lenape had two kinds of houses in their villages. **Longhouses** measured about 60 feet long and 20 feet across. Several families—as many as 25 people—lived together in one longhouse. **Wigwams** were smaller houses that had a round shape. Usually just one family lived in a wigwam. Look at the diagram below to see how a wigwam was built.

Since these houses had no windows, it was always dark inside. A fire burned in the middle and smoke escaped through a hole in the roof.

The Lenape built benches into the sides of their longhouses and wigwams. These benches were used for sitting during the day and for sleeping at night. The Lenape stored food in baskets and pots on shelves along the walls.

The longhouse was also used as a meeting place for the people of the village. Men and women would meet to discuss important matters, such as when to begin a hunt. Some villages had a **sakima**, a wise man or woman, who would settle any arguments that came up. The sakimas could not give orders, but everyone respected their opinions.

### Fun and Games

Although there was always work to be done in the village, the Lenape found time for fun and recreation. Children played many different games. One game was played with four moccasins and a nut. A child would hide the nut inside one of the moccasins and then move them all around. The other players would try to guess which moccasin hid the nut.

Music and dancing were other popular types of entertainment. Also, children loved to hear older people tell the legends of monsters and

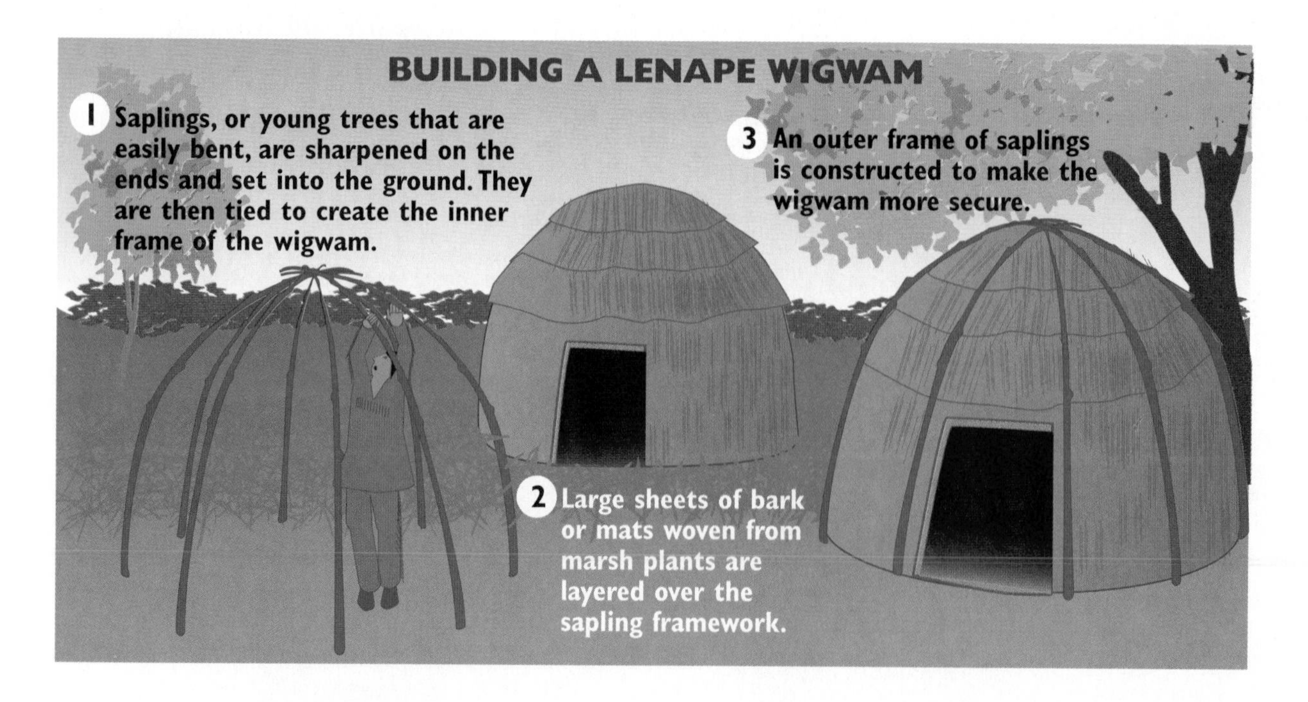

heroes from the past. Since the Lenape had no system of writing, they preserved their culture through oral tradition. This means that information was passed along by word of mouth. In the following passage, a Lenape explained some of his customs to a historian, M. R. Harrington. Why did the Lenape feel thankful to the Earth?

**MANY VOICES**
**PRIMARY SOURCE**

**Excerpt from *Religion and Ceremonies of the Lenape*, written by M. R. Harrington in 1921.**

*We are thankful to the East because everyone feels good in the morning when they awake, and see the bright light coming from the East, and when the Sun goes down in the West we feel good and are glad that we are well; then we are thankful to the West. . . . And we thank our mother, the Earth, whom we claim as mother, because the Earth carries us and everything we need.*

See p. T27 for Answers to Think About It.

## WHY IT MATTERS

The Lenape lived peacefully for hundreds of years. Some Lenape live and work in New Jersey today. In the next chapter you will read about Europeans who came to this land, changed its name to New Jersey, and changed life for the Lenape forever.

## Reviewing Facts and Ideas

### MAIN IDEAS

- Lenape boys and girls had different tasks and learned different skills.
- The village was the center of Lenape life. The people built longhouses and wigwams to live in.
- Lenape passed down customs through oral tradition.

### THINK ABOUT IT

1. Name three foods that were part of the Lenape diet.
2. What is an oral tradition?
3. **FOCUS** How did Lenape children learn the skills they needed?
4. **THINKING SKILL** *Compare* and *contrast* your daily life with that of a Lenape child.
5. **WRITE** Write a story describing the construction of a longhouse or a wigwam.

See p. T28 for Answers to Chapter 3 Review.

# CHAPTER 3 REVIEW

## THINKING ABOUT VOCABULARY

Number a sheet of paper from 1 to 10. Next to each number write the word or phrase that best matches the definition.

| | |
|---|---|
| ancestor | manetu |
| archaeologist | hunter-gatherer |
| artifact | longhouse |
| sakima | heritage |
| prehistory | oral tradition |

1. Information passed down by word of mouth
2. The time before people left written records
3. People in your family, starting with your parents, who were born before you
4. A person who studies artifacts to learn about the past
5. A person who travels from place to place in search of food
6. Spirit forces that the Lenape believed controlled the world
7. An object made by people in the past
8. A long building made of wood poles and covered with sheets of bark
9. The history, beliefs, and way of life that a group of people share
10. A wise Lenape man or woman who would settle arguments

## THINKING ABOUT FACTS

1. What is the Bering Strait? Where is Beringia?
2. When did the earliest people first reach New Jersey? How do many scientists believe they got there?
3. What kinds of food did the early hunter-gatherers eat?
4. How long ago did people in New Jersey develop agriculture?
5. What were the two groups of Lenape that lived in New Jersey?
6. Describe some of the chores Lenape children did.
7. What was the Big House ceremony?
8. Instead of going to school, how did Lenape children learn?
9. What was the main food of the Lenape?
10. How did the Lenape make decisions about important matters in their village?

## THINK AND WRITE

### WRITING A SUMMARY
Write a summary about life in a Lenape village.

### WRITING A JOURNAL
Suppose you are an archaeologist working at the Abbott Farm. Write a journal entry describing some of the things you find there.

### WRITING A COMPARISON
Write a paragraph comparing the lives of the earliest people of New Jersey to the lives of the Lenape.

## APPLYING THINKING SKILLS

### CAUSE AND EFFECT

1. What is a cause? What is an effect?
2. What caused the disappearance of Beringia?
3. Was learning to farm a cause or an effect of Native Americans staying in the same area and traveling less?
4. What do you think was an effect of modern archaeologists discovering carbon dating?
5. How does studying cause and effect help you understand history?

## Summing Up the Chapter

Use the following cause-and-effect chart to organize information from the chapter. Fill in the blank spaces and use the information to write a paragraph that answers the question "How did the lives of New Jersey's Native Americans change from the Ice Age to the 1600s?"

| CAUSE | EFFECT |
|---|---|
| Ice Age glaciers cause ocean levels to drop. | Land bridge appears between Asia and North America. |
| People begin to develop agriculture. | They can stay in the same area rather than move from place to place. |
| The Lenape used the environment for food, clothing, and shelter. | The Lenape traveled to different locations in different seasons. |
| The Lenape had no way to refrigerate food. | The Lenape dried meats and stored nuts and berries. |

CHAPTER 4

# Colonial New Jersey

## THINKING ABOUT HISTORY AND GEOGRAPHY

In the year 1492 three small ships sailed across the Atlantic Ocean from Europe to the Americas. After this journey, life would never be the same for Europeans or for Native Americans. What did these people think of one another? How did they learn from one another? What happened next? Read on to learn how this contact changed both peoples and how our state got its name: New Jersey.

**1609**

NEWARK BAY

**Henry Hudson lands near Sandy Hook and meets the Lenape.**

**1630s**

BERGEN

**Enslaved African Americans are brought to New Netherland.**

**1660s**

HACKENSACK

**Sarah Kiersted translates for Dutch settlers and Lenape people.**

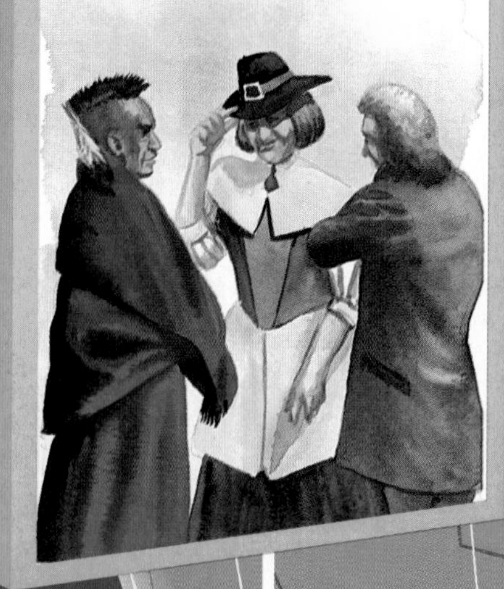

1600 1625 1650

See pT29 for Chapter Organizer.

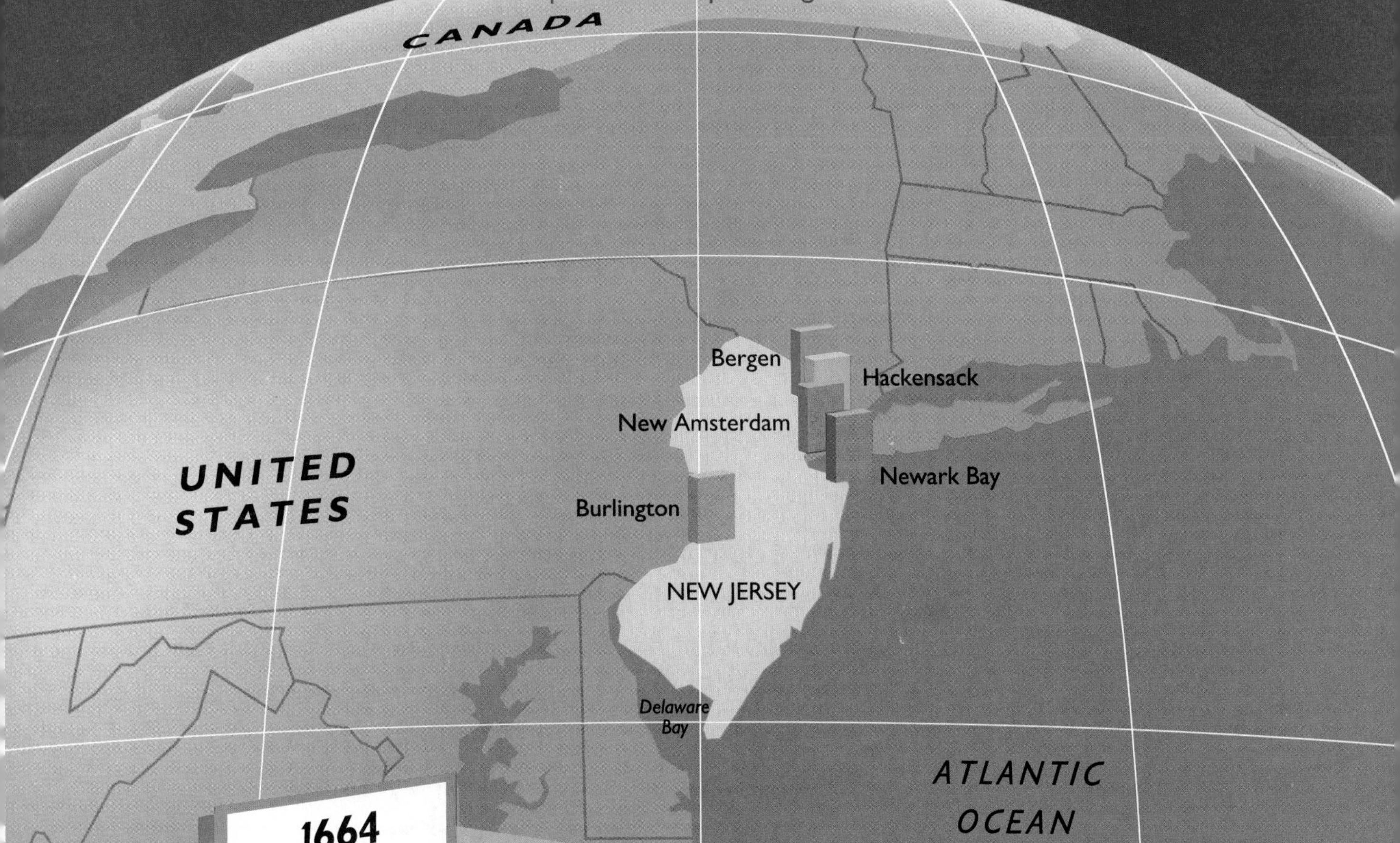

CANADA

UNITED STATES

Bergen

Hackensack

New Amsterdam

Newark Bay

Burlington

NEW JERSEY

Delaware Bay

ATLANTIC OCEAN

1664

NEW AMSTERDAM
Peter Stuyvesant surrenders New Netherland to English soldiers.

1702

BURLINGTON
Delegates hold the first assembly meeting of the English royal colony of New Jersey.

1675

1700

1492 | 1609 | 1650 | 1725 | 1800

See p. T30 for Lesson Teaching Strategies.

# The Arrival of the Europeans

## Focus Activity

**READ TO LEARN**

***Who were the first Europeans to come to New Jersey?***

**VOCABULARY**

- explore

**PEOPLE**

- Christopher Columbus
- John Cabot
- Giovanni da Verrazano
- Henry Hudson

**PLACES**

- Sandy Hook
- Newark Bay

### Read Aloud

*Three days after setting sail across the Atlantic Ocean, Captain Christopher Columbus wrote, "This day we completely lost sight of land. Many of the men sighed and wept for fear they would not see it again for a long time." Five weeks later, Columbus "saw a light to the west. . . . Then . . . [the ship]* Pinta *fired a cannon, my signal for the sighting of land."*

### THE BIG PICTURE

In 1492, **Christopher Columbus** sailed west from Spain, a country in Europe. He wanted to find a new water route from Europe to the Indies, a group of islands in Asia. There he hoped to trade for gold, silks, and spices. Columbus never reached Asia, however. Instead, he landed on islands in the Caribbean Sea. He called the people he met there "Indians" because he thought he was in the Indies. The islands he landed on became known as the West Indies.

Later many Europeans said that Columbus had found a "New World." To the Native Americans who were living there, this world was not "new" at all. Their people had been there for thousands of years before Columbus.

MAP WORK: 1. Cabot

## TWO WORLDS MEET

After Columbus's trip, other European countries sent ships across the Atlantic Ocean. In May 1497, the king of England sent an Italian sailor named John Cabot to explore a westward water route to Asia. To explore is to travel in unfamiliar places in order to learn about them.

Cabot reached North America's eastern coast in June 1497. He returned the following year. On his voyages, Cabot sailed past what is now New Jersey. As a result of Cabot's visit, the English later claimed ownership of much of this land. They did not think it mattered that people already lived there.

Cabot and other European explorers soon realized that they had found a continent unknown to them. Still, they thought they might find a water route that cut through North America. We know today that there is no such route.

**These are replicas of the three ships Columbus guided to North America.**

**ROUTES OF EUROPEAN EXPLORERS, 1498-1609**

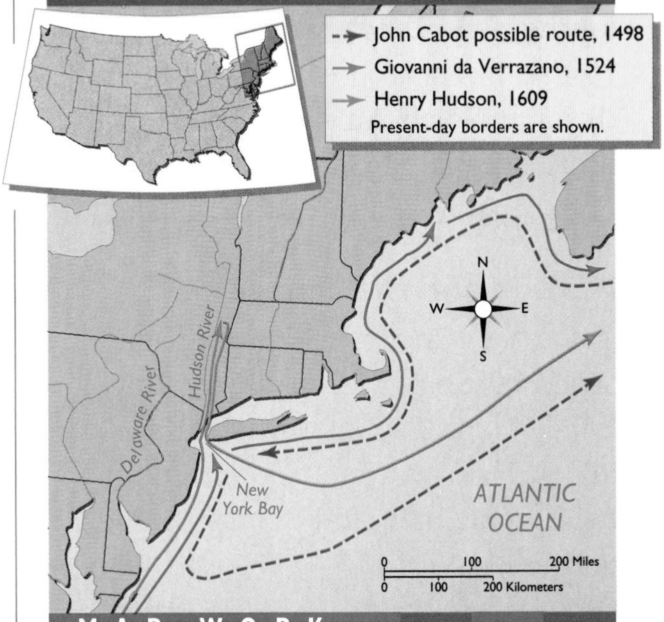

**MAP WORK**

The early explorers came to New Jersey from two different directions.

1. Which explorer came from the north?

### Verrazano Reaches New Jersey

In 1524, the king of France sent an Italian sailor named Giovanni da Verrazano (joh VAHN nee duh vair uh ZAHN oh) to look for a water route to Asia. You can see his route on the map on this page. Along New Jersey's shore, Verrazano met the Lenape people. He wrote that:

> *They came without fear aboard our ship. This is the goodliest* [best] *people and of the fairest conditions that we have found in this our voyage* [trip].

When Verrazano reached what is now Sandy Hook, New Jersey, he anchored his ship. In a small boat he explored New York Bay.

## EXPLORING NEW JERSEY

Almost 100 years after Verrazano's journey, the Dutch sent Henry Hudson in search of a water route through North America. The Dutch are the people from the Netherlands. This country is also called Holland.

### Hudson and the Lenape

On September 4, 1609, Hudson sailed his ship, the *Half Moon,* into Sandy Hook Bay and dropped anchor. When Hudson went ashore, he found the Lenape men and women friendly and eager to trade.

The Dutch and the Lenape each had goods that the other wanted. The Native Americans offered animal furs and skins. Hudson's sailors offered beads, knives, mirrors, clothing, kettles, and jewelry.

Despite trading with them, the Dutch sailors did not always treat the Lenape well. This angered some Lenape. Fighting broke out between the two groups. One day Native Americans in two canoes attacked a small Dutch boat exploring Newark Bay. A Dutch sailor was killed. Early in October, sailors on the *Half Moon* killed several Lenape.

### New Jersey's Riches

Before returning to the Netherlands, Hudson and his crew sailed up the river that would later be named

**Henry Hudson and his crew traded items such as tools and mirrors to the Lenape for furs.**

**The furs of North American animals like the beaver (above) were valued in Europe for clothing and hats.**

the Hudson River. They traveled north as far as what is now Albany, New York. They found no passage to Asia.

Even so, the Dutch had learned that Native Americans could provide furs and other goods that people in Europe would want to buy. When the *Half Moon* returned to the Netherlands, Robert Juet, one of Hudson's sailors, published his journal. How did this sailor describe the Lenape?

**Excerpt from the journal of Robert Juet, September 9, 1609.**

***This day the people of the country came aboard of us, seeming very glad of our coming. . . . They go in deer skins loose, well dressed. They have yellow copper. They desire clothes, and are very civil.***

**civil:** polite

See p. T30 for Answers to Think About It.

Juet's journal spread the word of the many "good furs [and] skins of diverse [different] sorts" that could be found in North America. Soon, trade with the Lenape brought more Dutch ships to New Jersey's shores.

## WHY IT MATTERS

Cabot, Verrazano, and Hudson failed to find a water route to Asia. Instead they found Native Americans and a rich supply of resources. In the next lesson you will read how Europeans began to settle this region, take advantage of its resources, and come into conflict with its people.

## Reviewing Facts and Ideas

### MAIN IDEAS

- Columbus reached North America in 1492.
- European explorers searched for a water route to Asia.
- Giovanni da Verrazano and Henry Hudson explored New Jersey, meeting with the Lenape.

### THINK ABOUT IT

1. Who was Columbus?
2. Why did European countries send explorers to North America?
3. **FOCUS** Who were the first Europeans to explore New Jersey?
4. **THINKING SKILL** Predict what might have happened if Columbus turned back before he reached land.
5. **GEOGRAPHY** How could explorers sailing west from Europe have reached Asia? Use the Atlas map on page R4 for help.

# Geography Skills

See p. T31 for Skill Teaching Strategies.

# Using Latitude and Longitude

**VOCABULARY**
latitude
parallel
degree
longitude
prime meridian
meridian
global grid

### WHY THE SKILL MATTERS

In the last lesson you read about how Henry Hudson looked for a water route to Asia. Suppose you want to trace his exact route. Your only clue is an old map. The writing on the map is faded, but you can just make out some lines that cross each other like a tic-tac-toe grid. Each line has a number on it.

You discover that these lines were invented by mapmakers long ago. The lines describe the location of particular places. They provide an "address" for every place on the map, even for places in the middle of an ocean.

This grid of imaginary lines is still used today. It helps ship captains and airline pilots keep track of where they are and where they are going. Out at sea or up among the clouds it is often hard to figure out a location. Ship captains and airline pilots also need an exact way to explain where they are going. However, these lines work anywhere on Earth.

You can always locate a place on a map by looking up its "address" in a gazetteer (ga zuh TEER) like the one on page R30.

### USING LATITUDE

Let's study these imaginary lines. Look at the map on this page, and place your finger on the equator. This is the starting point for measuring latitude. Latitude is a measure of how far north or south a place is from the equator.

Geographers also call lines of latitude parallels because they are parallel lines. Parallel lines always remain the same distance apart.

Each line of latitude has a number. You can see on the map below that the equator is labeled 0°, meaning zero degrees.

**LINES OF LATITUDE (PARALLELS)**

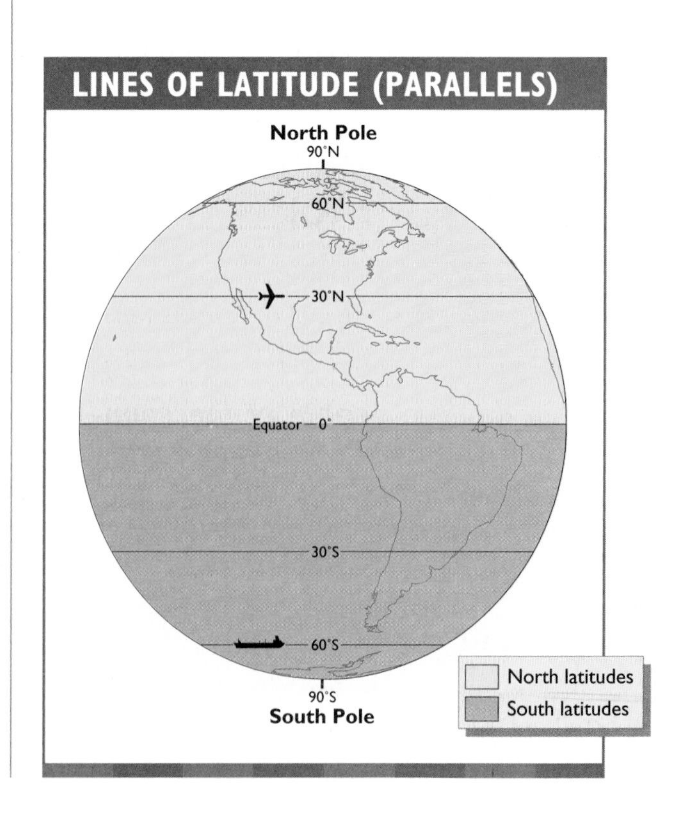

Degrees are used to measure the distance on Earth's surface. What is the latitude of the equator on this map?*

Now look at the lines of latitude north of the equator. Notice that these parallels are labeled N for "north." The North Pole has a latitude too, which is 90°N. The parallels south of the equator are labeled S for "south." The latitude of the South Pole is 90°S.

Find the ship on the map. The ship is sailing west. It is located at 60°S. Now find the small airplane on the map. Along which parallel is it flying? In which direction is it traveling?**

## USING LONGITUDE

Now look at the map on this page. It shows lines of **longitude**. Like parallels, these are imaginary lines on a map or globe. Instead of measuring distance north or south, they measure distance east or west of the **prime meridian.** Prime means "first." Lines of longitude are also called **meridians**. The prime meridian is the first line, or starting place, for measuring lines of longitude. That's why the prime meridian is marked 0° on the map. Put your finger on the prime meridian. It runs through the western parts of Europe and Africa.

Look at the meridians to the west of the prime meridian. These lines are labeled W for "west." The lines to the east of the prime meridian are labeled E for "east." Longitude is measured up to 180° east of the prime meridian and up to 180° west of the prime meridian.

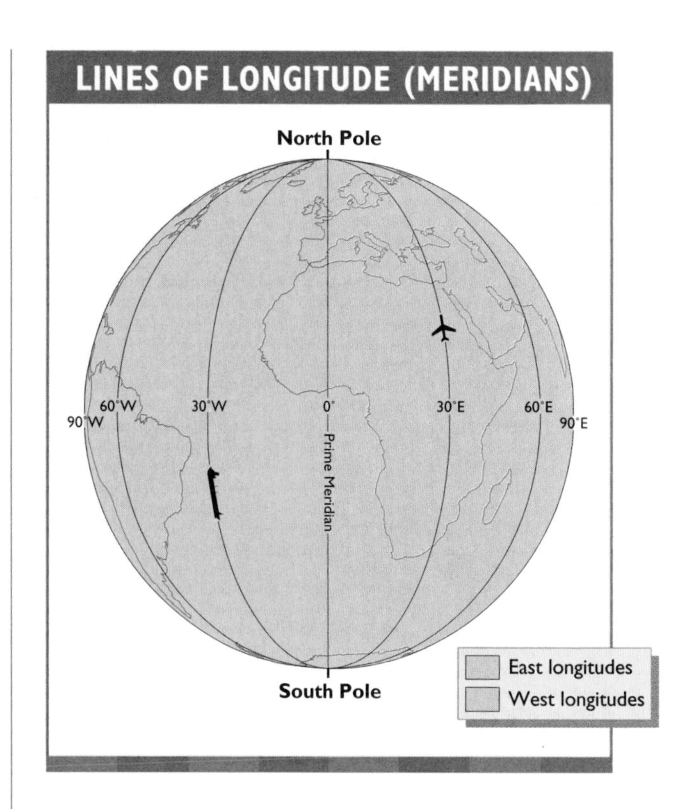


Since 180°E and 180°W fall on the same line, this line is marked neither E nor W. The line labeled 180° runs through the Pacific Ocean.

Unlike lines of latitude, meridians are not parallel to one another. Since Earth is round, meridians divide Earth into pieces like the sections of an orange. Look again at the map on this page. As you can see, the meridians are far apart at the equator. They meet, however, at the North Pole and the South Pole.

Lines of longitude measure degrees east and west. Look at the ship on the map. It is sailing along the meridian known as 30°W. Now look at the airplane on the same map. It is flying over the continent of Africa. Along which meridian is it flying? In which direction is the airplane traveling?***

*0° **30°N; east

***30°E; north

# Geography Skills

## GLOBAL GRID

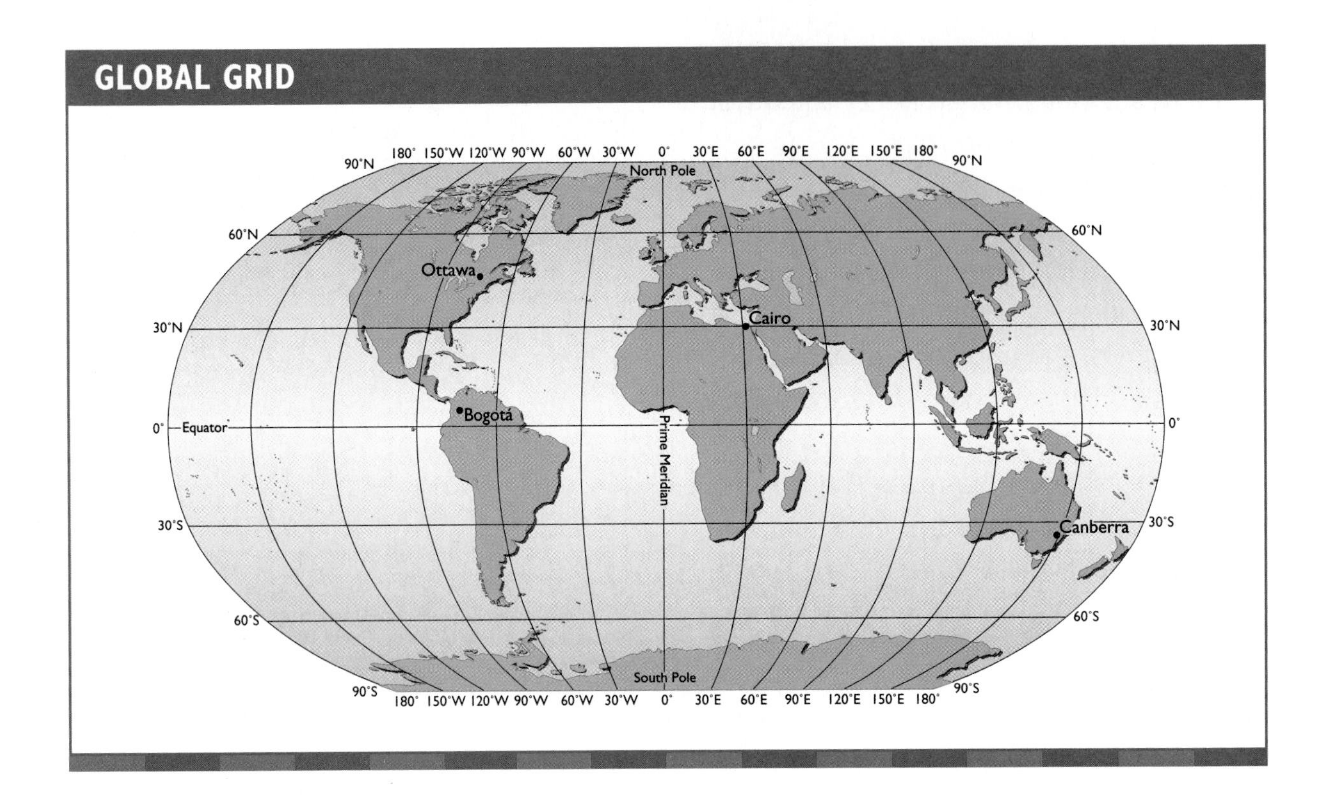


### FINDING PLACES ON A MAP

In order to use latitude lines and longitude lines to find places, you must combine them on the same map. Look at the map of the world on this page. You can see that the lines of latitude and the lines of longitude cross to form a grid on the map.

The grid on this map is called a **global grid** because it covers the entire Earth. By using the global grid, you can locate the "address" of any place in the world.

Look at the map again. Find Canberra, Australia, and Bogotá, Colombia. Which of these two cities is closer to the equator? How can you tell?*

Now find Ottawa, Canada. Is this city east or west of the prime meridian? Find Cairo, Egypt. Is Cairo east or west of the prime meridian? Is Cairo north or south of the equator?**

Look at the latitude and longitude map of New Jersey on the opposite page. Find the city of Palmyra. As you can see, it is located at 40°N latitude. It is also located at about 75°W longitude. So we say that the location, or "address," of the city of Palmyra is about 40°N, 75°W.

Remember that when you locate a place on a map, you always give the latitude first and the longitude second. You also must remember to give north or south for the latitude and east or west for the longitude. To describe a place that is not exactly at the point where two lines cross, you must use the closest lines.



*Bogotá; It is fewer degrees away from the equator.

**west; east; north

See p. T31 for Answers to Reviewing the Skill.

## TRYING THE SKILL

Try to find a city in New Jersey by its "address." This city is located near 41°N, 74°W. What is the name of the city? Now describe the location of Blairstown using latitude and longitude.*

Imagine that you have found a map showing buried treasure. It points the way to a huge chest of gold. The map has an X near the following numbers: 40°N, 74°W. What town is closest to the buried treasure? Start digging!**

## Helping yourself

- **Latitude is the distance north or south of the equator. Longitude is the distance east or west of the prime meridian.**
- **Find the latitude line you are looking for on the global grid. Follow the line across until you reach the right longitude line.**

## REVIEWING THE SKILL

Use the map below to answer these questions.

1. What are lines of latitude and longitude? What are they used for?
2. Name three cities on the map located exactly on 40°N.
3. What two cities share the same line of longitude?
4. How did you find the answer to the last question?

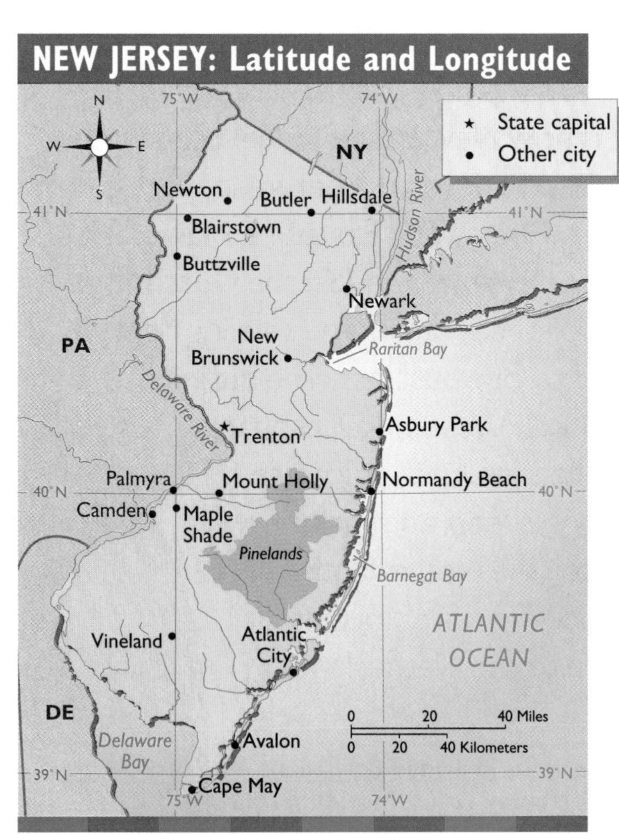


*Hillsdale; 41°N, 75°W. **Normandy Beach

1500 1575 1609 1660 1725 1800

See p. T32 for Lesson Teaching Strategies.

# New Netherland

## Read Aloud

*In 1634 a Dutch explorer on the Delaware River wrote, "The river abounds* [is full] *with beavers, otters, and other [less valuable] furs, which are taken . . . on the banks." Dutch traders hoped that these furs would make them rich when they were sold in Holland.*

## Focus Activity

**READ TO LEARN**

***Why did the Dutch settle New Netherland?***

**VOCABULARY**

- colony
- governor
- immigrant
- patroon
- slavery

**PEOPLE**

- Cornelius Mey
- Peter Minuit
- Sarah Kiersted
- Peter Stuyvesant

**PLACES**

- New Netherland
- Fort Nassau
- Bergen

## THE BIG PICTURE

Soon after Henry Hudson's voyage at the beginning of the 1600s, the Netherlands, England, Sweden, France, and Spain began to settle colonies in North America. A **colony** is a place ruled by another country.

The Dutch were the first Europeans to start a colony in what is now New Jersey. In 1614 the Dutch government claimed a huge area between what is now Barnegat Bay, New Jersey, and Eastport, Maine, and called it **New Netherland**. In 1621 the Dutch government gave control of all trading and settling rights in New Netherland to one business. The business was called the Dutch West India Company. The company sent the Dutch colonists cows, hogs, horses, sheep, and various food supplies from the Netherlands. In return, the colonists sent furs plus tobacco and corn to the Netherlands.

**Native Americans provided European settlers with many crops, including tobacco and corn.**

## A NEW DUTCH COLONY

In 1623 Cornelius Mey became the first governor of New Netherland. A governor is an official appointed to rule a colony. Mey decided to build permanent settlements to protect and support trading. In 1624, 30 Dutch families came to live in New Netherland. Some sailed up the Delaware River. They built Fort Nassau near what is now Gloucester City, New Jersey. This small Dutch settlement was found empty when a Dutch ship sailed there eight years later. Even today no one knows what happened to the settlers.

In 1626 Peter Minuit, New Netherland's third governor, bought Manhattan Island from the Lenape for some inexpensive trade goods. A village was built, and this became the center for the Dutch West India Company.

MAP WORK: 1. Fort Orange

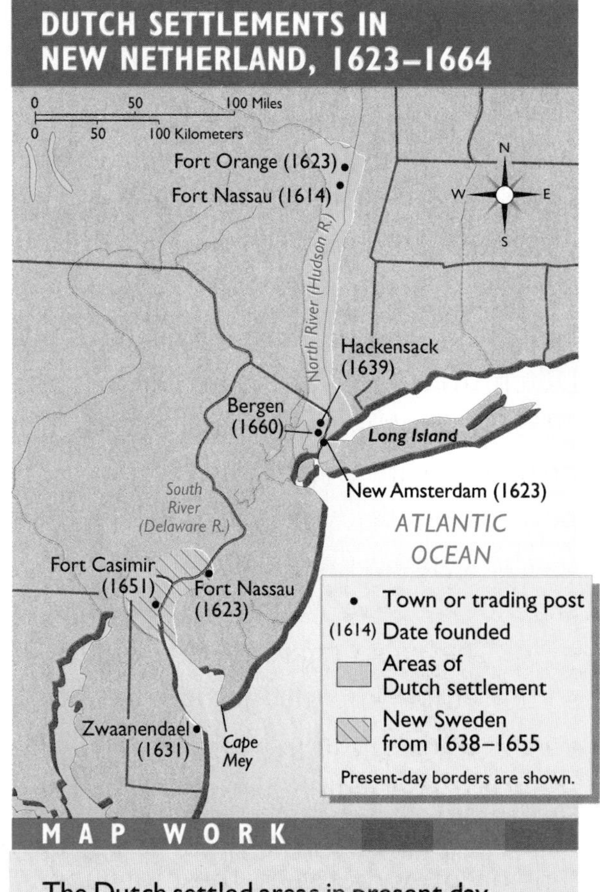


MAP WORK

The Dutch settled areas in present-day New Jersey, New York, and Delaware.

1. What was the northernmost settlement?

### Newcomers to the Colony

The company wanted to increase settlement without spending money. They offered a large piece of land to anyone who would bring 50 or more immigrants to farm the land. An immigrant is a person who comes to a new country or place to live. The person who became the landowner was called a patroon. However, most patroons had trouble finding immigrants. To get more workers to the colony, the company forced Africans into slavery. Slavery is the practice of making one person the property of another. The Dutch brought many enslaved workers from their homes in Africa to the colonies in North America.

The Dutch West India Company worked to control all of New Jersey's fur trade. Settlers from Sweden had set up a small colony along the Delaware. They were trading with the Lenape. In 1655, the Dutch took over the small colony, making it part of New Netherland.

## LIFE IN NEW NETHERLAND

When the Dutch settlers arrived in New Netherland they got right to work building houses and farms. The environment of this colony, however, was very different from the one in Holland. The Dutch were lucky to get help from the Lenape. Sarah Kiersted, a Dutch housewife, tried to help. She learned the Lenape language and helped Lenape Chief Oratam work out peaceful treaties with the Dutch.

The Lenape taught the Dutch their skills of hunting, fishing, and trapping. They also shared with Dutch settlers their knowledge of growing corn, squash, pumpkins, beans, and tobacco. The Dutch also grew their own crops, such as wheat. However, tension grew between these groups because their cultures were very different. Also, the Dutch brought diseases with them. Many Lenape caught these diseases and died.

### Home Life

The Dutch built houses similar to the ones they lived in back in Holland, but they used local materials, such as stones and trees. A typical Dutch house in New Netherland had two rooms. There was a large fireplace in the kitchen, where the family cooked, ate, relaxed, and even slept. The other room was called the *groot kamer* [grot KA mur], or "big room." This room held the family Bible, the best furniture, and special things they brought from Holland.

### New Jersey's First Town

By the 1640s, misunderstandings between Indians and Dutch colonists had become fights. Peter Stuyvesant, the governor of New Netherland, warned colonists to keep their "houses, goods, and cattle" inside of settlements and villages. He was concerned that the Lenape would attack houses and farms that were not protected.

**Dutch colonists used their kitchen (below) for cooking, eating, visiting with friends, and even sleeping. In winter they used footwarmers made of metal and wood that held small cans of hot coals (below left).**

See p. T32 for Answers to Think About It.

In 1660 the Dutch built the first permanent town in New Jersey. They called it Bergen. The town of Bergen was built around a square that was 800 feet long on each side. Tall wooden walls surrounded the village. Outside the walls, villagers grew their gardens and tended their cows. At night, the cattle came back inside and the villagers locked the gates. Bergen is now part of Jersey City, but you can still see its outlines today in the shape of Bergen Square.

### A Mix of Cultures

Life for the Dutch settlers in New Jersey became a mix of Europe and the new world of America. Pinkster was an old Dutch festival that was celebrated every spring. Colonists dressed in their best clothes. They ate old-fashioned Dutch food like colorful hard-boiled eggs, and new food like corn and squash. There was music and dancing. As the years went by, Africans in the colony joined in the celebration, too. They brought their own style of dancing and drum music to the festival. Eventually, Pinkster became a colorful mix of many different cultures.

## WHY IT MATTERS

As the Dutch became settled in New Netherland, the fur trade became less important. Farming became more important. Fewer fur animals and bigger Dutch farms meant that the Lenape had to move farther west to keep their way of life.

**Links to LANGUAGE ARTS**

### Dutch Words

**There are many words in the English language that were borrowed from the Dutch. In Dutch a "yacht" is a boat. If you like to have a "cruller" or a "cookie" for a treat, give the Dutch credit for the word. If you sit on your front "stoop," you can also thank the Dutch for that name.**

**Write an English sentence that uses at least two of these Dutch words.**

## Reviewing Facts and Ideas

### MAIN IDEAS

- The Dutch first came to New Jersey to trade for furs with the Lenape.
- The Dutch West India Company controlled trade in New Netherland and brought new settlers from Europe and Africa.
- Dutch settlers learned skills from the Lenape and built New Jersey's first permanent town, Bergen.

### THINK ABOUT IT

1. What is a colony?
2. What was a patroon?
3. **FOCUS** Why did the Dutch decide to settle New Netherland?
4. **THINKING SKILL** *Predict* what might have happened if the Lenape had not taught the Dutch skills for farming and hunting.
5. **GEOGRAPHY** Look at the map on page 87. The Dutch called the Hudson the North River. What did they call the Delaware River?

1500 1575 1664 1738 1800

See p. T33 for Lesson Teaching Strategies.

# English New Jersey

## Read Aloud

*Dutch governor Peter Stuyvesant was shocked when he heard the news in 1664. English ships had arrived to take over New Netherland. When Stuyvesant surrendered to the English, a settler reported that the old governor said, "I had rather be carried to my grave."*

## Focus Activity

**READ TO LEARN**

***How did English rule change life in New Jersey?***

**VOCABULARY**

- proprietor
- constitution
- assembly
- delegate

**PEOPLE**

- Richard Nicolls
- Sir George Carteret
- Lord John Berkeley
- Philip Carteret
- William Penn

**PLACES**

- West Jersey
- Burlington
- East Jersey
- Perth Amboy

### THE BIG PICTURE

Both England and Holland looked at North America as a source of land and furs. The English believed that they had the right to own most of North America. They said that explorer John Cabot had claimed this area for England more than 150 years earlier. In 1664 England's King Charles gave his brother, James, the Duke of York, all of the land between the Connecticut and Delaware Rivers. This huge land grant, or gift, included the Dutch colony of New Netherland.

The Duke of York sent Colonel **Richard Nicolls** to defeat the Dutch and take over New Netherland. Nicolls sailed with four warships and several hundred soldiers. New Netherland governor Peter Stuyvesant wanted to put up a fight. Many Dutch citizens urged him to surrender. "Let it be so," he agreed.

## A COLONY CALLED NEW JERSEY

The Duke of York divided the land he owned in America, giving part of it to two good friends. The land that lay between the Hudson and Delaware Rivers, today's New Jersey, he gave to Sir George Carteret and Lord John Berkeley.

The Duke of York named New Jersey to honor his friend, Sir George Carteret. Carteret was born on the island of Jersey, off the coast of England. He had defended Jersey during a recent war.

### Running the New Jersey Colony

Berkeley and Carteret became the proprietors of New Jersey. A proprietor was a person who owned land and had the right to start a colony. New Jersey's proprietors chose to stay in England. They appointed Philip Carteret, a relative of Sir George Carteret, to govern in their place. The new governor arrived in the colony in July 1665.

Philip Carteret had two jobs as governor. He was the ruler of the colony. He was also responsible for collecting rents for the proprietors.

### A Divided Colony

The proprietors hoped that New Jersey would produce a great deal of money in rent and trade. However, they knew they could be successful only if many men and women came to live in New Jersey. When Carteret arrived, fewer than 1,000 colonists lived there.

To attract settlers, the governor tried a different plan from the Dutch. He offered low rents and many freedoms, including religious freedom. Many colonists from New England and Long Island liked Carteret's offer enough to move to New Jersey. The colony's population began to grow. Settlers bought their land from the Lenape and paid rent to the proprietors. The Lenape, who believed that the land belonged to all people, thought the settlers were just paying for the use of the land. They became angry as the settlers cleared more and more of their hunting lands for farms.

**Philip Carteret (center) served as New Jersey's first English governor.**

## CHANGES IN THE COLONY

In 1674 Lord Berkeley sold his part of New Jersey to two men. The new proprietors were English Quakers. The Quakers were members of a group known as The Religious Society of Friends. Some people called them Quakers because they sometimes quaked, or shook, with feeling when they prayed. Among their beliefs was the equality of all people in the sight of God. Quakers also rejected the use of violence, refusing to go to war.

Quakers in England and in the English colonies suffered harsh treatment because of their religious beliefs. In New Jersey they finally found a place that promised them freedom to follow their religion.

### East and West

In 1676 New Jersey was divided into two sections, East and West Jersey, shown on the map on this page. **West Jersey** was America's first Quaker colony, with **Burlington** as its capital. A group of 24 people, including 12 Quakers, owned and governed **East Jersey**. Their capital was **Perth Amboy**.

East and West Jersey were different. East Jersey looked like New England, with its small farms and towns, such as Newark and Shrewsbury. People worshiped in many different churches. West Jersey had

**MAP WORK: 1.** West Jersey

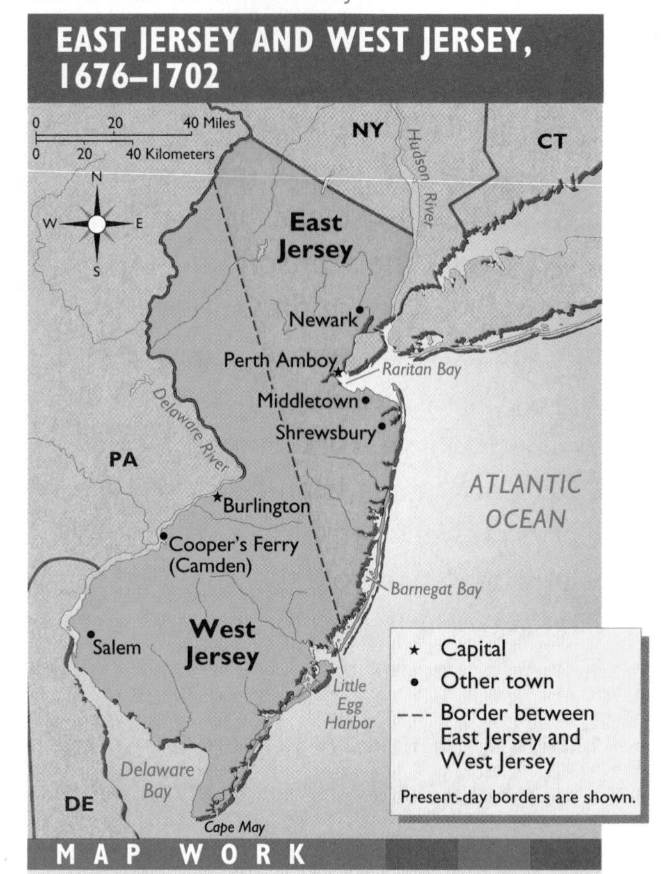


**MAP WORK**

In 1676, the colony of New Jersey was divided into two sections, East Jersey and West Jersey.

**1.** Which colony bordered Delaware Bay?

**The Meeker homestead in Lyons Farm was a typical Quaker farm in West Jersey.**

larger farms, set farther apart. Many of the people who lived there were Quakers. Over time, the city of New York came to have a great influence over East Jersey. Philadelphia became important to West Jersey.

### Jersey Assemblies

Before New Jersey was divided into two colonies, it had a **constitution**. A constitution is a document that contains the basic rules for governing a colony or country. This 1665 constitution was New Jersey's first. It guaranteed freedom of religion to all people in the colony.

The colony's government included an **assembly**, or group of lawmakers, which met for the first time in 1668. A member of the assembly was known as a **delegate**. A delegate is a person chosen to speak or vote for others.

Many of the delegates argued that the colonists, and not the proprietors, owned the land. After all, the colonists had bought the land from the Lenape. These delegates also felt that the settlers should have the right to govern themselves. Some even refused to pay rent to the proprietors and elected their own president of the colony.

After 1676 the assemblies of the split colony met separately. West Jersey's assembly first met in 1681. Several Quakers in the assembly, including **William Penn**, wrote a constitution for West Jersey. Called "The Concessions and Agreements of West Jersey," this constitution greatly limited the power of the proprietors. It allowed colonists to vote every year for their own delegates. Settlers charged with a crime were guaranteed a trial by jury. When arguments with the Lenape arose, a jury of six Lenape and six colonists would decide how they should be settled.

Read the following short section from "The Concessions." What important freedom did it give to the people?

**MANY VOICES**

**PRIMARY SOURCE**

**Excerpt from "The Concessions and Agreements of West Jersey," probably written by William Penn and Edward Byllynge in 1677.**

***No men . . . upon earth have power or authority to rule over men's* consciences *in religious matters . . . no person or persons whatsoever within the said Province . . . shall be any way . . . called in question or in the least punished or hurt . . . for the sake of his opinion, judgment, faith or worship towards God, in matters of religion. But that each and every such person and persons may . . . at all times freely and fully have and enjoy . . . the exercise of their consciences in matters of religious worship.***

The Concessions and Agreements of the Proprietors Freeholders and Inhabitants of the Province of West New Jersey in America:
Chapter I

---

**conscience:** feeling of right and wrong

Infographic

interNET CONNECTION Visit our website: www.mhschool.com

## A Diverse Colony

**Colonial New Jersey was home to a diverse group of people. Each brought valuable skills and a rich culture. Together they made the New Jersey colony a special place to live.**

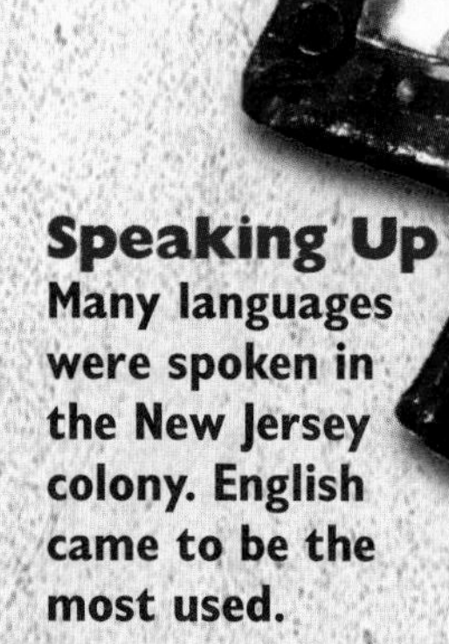

### Speaking Up

Many languages were spoken in the New Jersey colony. English came to be the most used.

### Dutch Games

Along with donuts, Dutch colonists to New Jersey brought skittles, a game similar to bowling.

### New Sounds

Africans settled throughout colonial New Jersey. Musical instruments like the banjo were just part of the rich culture that they brought with them.

### Across the Water

The Lenape used canoes to travel and transport goods. Some Lenape canoes held as many as 20 people.

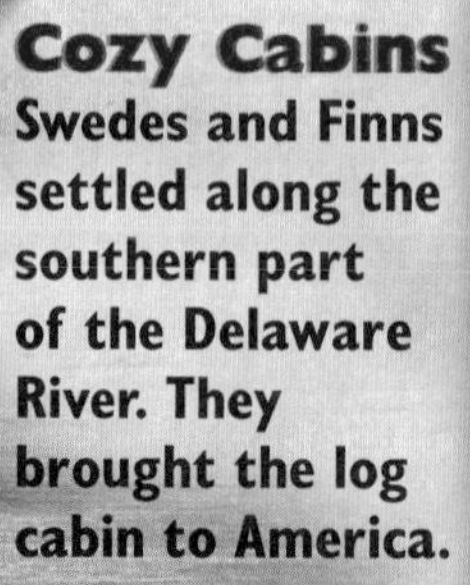

### Cozy Cabins

Swedes and Finns settled along the southern part of the Delaware River. They brought the log cabin to America.

See p. T33 for Answers to Think About It.

## A UNITED COLONY

Even though they had many rights, the colonists of East and West Jersey were unhappy with the rule of the proprietors. Many of the proprietors lived in faraway England. They showed little concern for the colonists' problems. The government had trouble keeping order in the colonies.

The proprietors knew they had lost control. They agreed to give up their rule. On April 15, 1702, England's Queen Anne reunited East and West Jersey as the royal colony of New Jersey. Becoming a royal colony meant changes for New Jersey colonists. From 1702 until 1738 the royal governor of New York also ruled New Jersey. This governor could approve or deny any new laws.

**Queen Anne reunited East Jersey and West Jersey in 1702.**

Still, New Jersey had a General Assembly, and its elected representatives continued to meet. One year they met at Perth Amboy. The next year they met at Burlington. However, only white men who owned property were allowed to vote.

## WHY IT MATTERS

English rule in New Jersey began some traditions that are important even today. Freedom of religion is one. A government of delegates of the people is another. These ideas would play an important part in the birth of New Jersey as one of the first states of the United States 80 years later.

### Reviewing Facts and Ideas

**MAIN IDEAS**

- The English defeated the Dutch and took over New Netherland.
- The English attracted settlers to New Jersey from England and from other colonies.
- East Jersey and West Jersey developed differently. The Quakers played an important role in West Jersey.
- East and West Jersey were reunited in 1702 and became a royal colony.

**THINK ABOUT IT**

1. Why did England want to take over New Netherland?
2. What important freedom did New Jersey's first constitution guarantee?
3. **FOCUS** Describe two ways the English changed New Jersey after they took over from the Dutch.
4. **THINKING SKILL** What were some of the *causes* for New Jersey colonists to be unhappy with the proprietors?
5. **WRITE** Suppose you lived in East Jersey in the late 1600s. Write a letter to a friend in England describing what life is like there.

# Study Skills

See p. T34 for Skill Teaching Strategies.

## Reading Time Lines

**VOCABULARY**

time line

### WHY THE SKILL MATTERS

In Lesson 1 you read that Christopher Columbus reached North America in 1492. This marked the beginning of European exploration and settlement of this continent. You also read that John Cabot first explored North America's coast in 1497. This event, too, played an important role in America's early history.

Understanding history means knowing when things happened. In addition, you need to know which things happened first and which things happened next. For example, the Duke of York gave New Jersey to Berkeley and Carteret. In a different year, Bergen was founded. Which event happened first?*

You can answer a question like this by using a **time line**. A time line is a chart showing when events happened. It also shows how much time passed between events. A time line helps give a sense of order to history. The time line below shows some important events in the history of colonial New Jersey.

### USING THE SKILL

Look at the time line of Events in Colonial New Jersey. As you can see, the name of each event appears above or below the date when it happened. Hudson's exploration of the river, the earliest event, is on the left side. The opening of a glass factory in Salem, which is the latest event, is on the right.

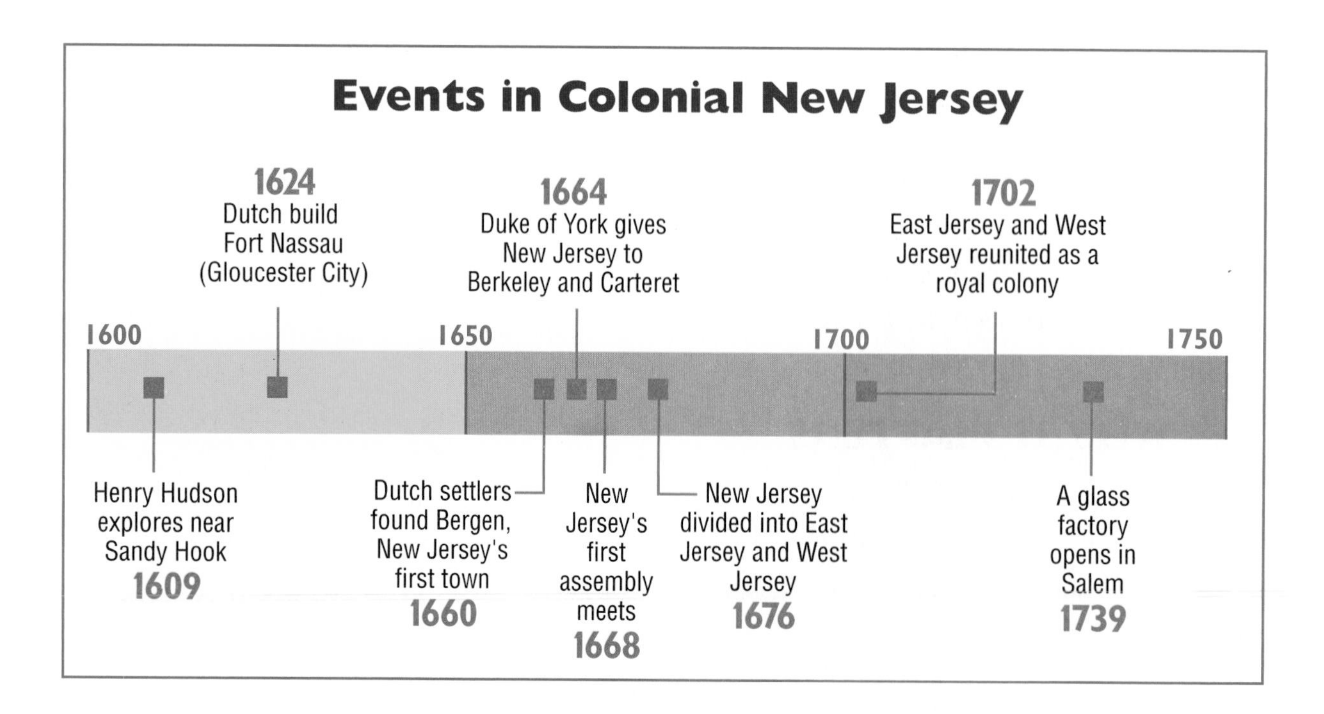




*Founding of Bergen was first

See p. T34 for Answers to Reviewing the Skill.

Like most time lines, this one is divided into equal parts. Each part stands for a certain number of years. Each part of the Events in Colonial New Jersey time line stands for 50 years.

Now read the time line from left to right. Which two events took place after 1600 but before 1650?*

## Helping yourself

- **A time line is a chart that shows when events took place.**
- **Note how much time is shown by each part of the time line.**
- **Read the events from left to right.**

### TRYING THE SKILL

Now read the time line of Events in British Colonial North America. Use the Helping Yourself box for hints.

What period of history does the time line cover? Which event on the time line happened first? When did the English take New Netherland from the Dutch? How many years passed between the landing of the Pilgrims at Plymouth and William Penn receiving a charter for Pennsylvania?**

### REVIEWING THE SKILL

Look again at both time lines. Use them to answer the following questions.

1. How does a time line help you to place events in the right order?
2. Which occurred first: England reuniting East and West Jersey or taking New Netherland from the Dutch?
3. How much time passed between the founding of the Jamestown colony and the chartering of Pennsylvania?
4. What event took place in 1623?
5. In what other subjects would a time line be useful?

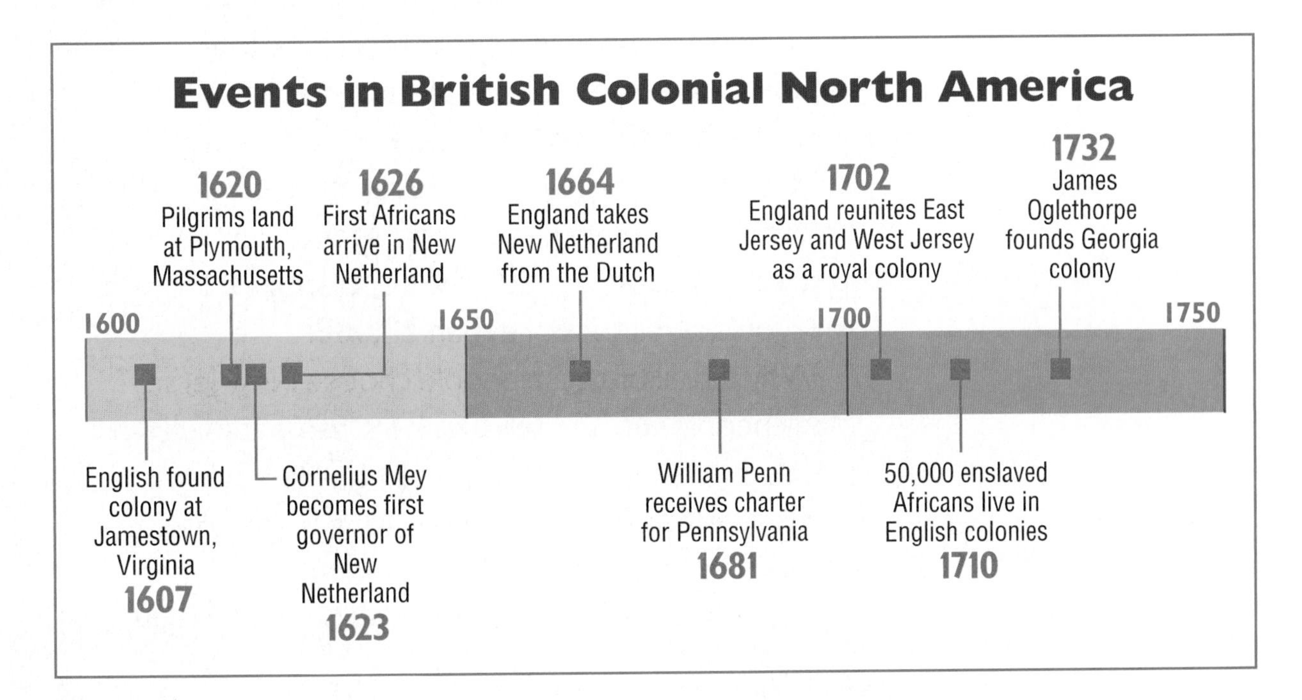


*Hudson explores near Sandy Hook; Dutch build Fort Nassau
**1600–1750; English establish Jamestown colony; 1664; 61 years

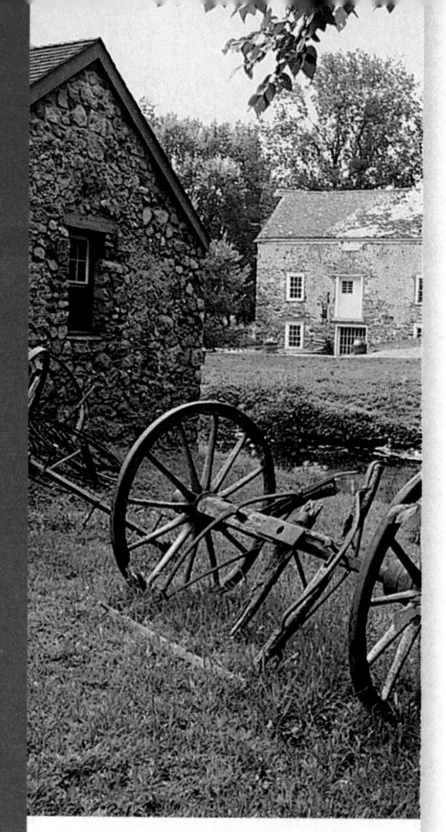

## Focus Activity

**READ TO LEARN**

***What was life like in the New Jersey colony?***

**VOCABULARY**

- industry
- indentured servant

**PLACES**

- Middle Colonies
- Salem

**LESSON 4**

1500 1575 1650 1700 1801

See p. T35 for Lesson Teaching Strategies.

# Life in the New Jersey Colony

### Read Aloud

*"The country through which we passed was for the greatest part level . . . some parts were covered with trees, but far the greater part of the country was without woods; on the other hand, I never saw any place in America, the city excepted, so well peopled." This is how a visitor to New Jersey described the colony in 1747.*

### THE BIG PICTURE

During most of the 1700s, England ruled the east coast of North America, from Maine to Georgia. New Jersey was one of England's **Middle Colonies**. The other Middle Colonies were New York, Pennsylvania, and Delaware. New Jersey's central location made it an important pathway for people and supplies.

During the 1700s, New Jersey's population grew quickly. At the beginning of the century, about 14,000 people lived in New Jersey. By 1750 this number had jumped to 71,000. By 1800 the population of New Jersey would swell to more than 211,000.

Why did all of these people choose New Jersey? Many people, such as the Quakers, came for religious freedom. Others came because New Jersey's rich farmland offered opportunities for a better life. Still others had no choice. Enslaved Africans were brought against their will to this colony to work in the fields and homes of other colonists.

## A GROWING COLONY

The English settlers who came to New Jersey greatly expanded the settlement begun by the Dutch. Farms and towns spread across the colony in the early 1700s, especially in East Jersey. West Jersey had a smaller population and most of its people lived near the Delaware River.

### Life on the Farm

Most colonists who lived on farms in New Jersey in the 1700s were self-sufficient. This means that they were able to provide for their own needs. They raised their own food, sewed their own clothes, and even built their own houses.

Women and men had different jobs in colonial times. Women took care of the family home and farm, which meant much more than cooking and cleaning. Colonial women had skills that ranged from weaving cloth on a loom to making candles and soap from animal fat. They also took care of the chickens and milked the cows. They made butter and cheese. Women were often doctors for their families. Sometimes they grew plants for medicine in their gardens.

Men spent much of their time farming and hunting. In addition to raising crops such as corn, beans, squash, wheat, potatoes, and carrots, they also raised animals.

Girls and boys began every day with chores. For girls, this meant sewing, preparing food, and washing pots. Girls also took care of younger children. Boys cut firewood, cared for animals, or led the horse or ox that pulled the plow. With all of this work to do, most children attended school only a few weeks each year. Some learned to read at home.

If a farmer managed to grow extra crops, he might sell them in town. He could use the money to buy things that could not grow in the New Jersey climate, such as tea or sugar.

A butter churn was used to turn milk into butter.

### New Jobs in the Colony

Not everyone lived or worked on a farm. Some people began to work in **industry** at this time. Industry is the making of things on a large scale, especially by people and machines working together.

Iron mining was one such industry. Colonists used iron for tools, weapons, and kitchen items. Some men found jobs working in sawmills. In 1739 a glass factory opened in **Salem**, in the southern part of the colony. Along the coast, in Cape May County and Long Beach Island, whaling and fishing provided work for many.

## NEW JERSEY SOCIETY

In spite of the small industries that sprouted up, farming was still the most important part of New Jersey's economy. Since farming required large areas of land, the people who owned the most land were the richest in the colony.

### Land and Labor

The biggest landowners in the colony were the proprietors. Some of their farms covered more than 1,000 acres. Many of the people who worked on these huge farms were **indentured servants**. Indentured servants agreed to work for a landowner in exchange for a trip from Europe to the colonies. *Indenture* means "written agreement." These people usually signed a paper agreeing to work for between three and seven years. After that time they were free to start their own farms or find other work.

Seven-year-old John Morris became an indentured servant for Pell and Huma Teed in Newark. Morris's agreement stated that "he shall behave himself as a good and faithful servant." His master and mistress, in turn, had to provide Morris "suitable and sufficient meat, drink, washing, lodging, and apparel, and learn him the weaver's trade and to read, write, and cipher [arithmetic]."

Many other workers on the large farms were enslaved Africans. By the mid-1700s, about 1 in 13 people in New Jersey was an enslaved African. Like indentured servants, enslaved Africans worked long hours in the fields, houses, and barns of the colony. However, most Africans worked with no promise of freedom. They were enslaved for life. A few Africans did gain their freedom and were able to start small farms or work at other jobs for money.

Some people, including many Quakers, spoke out against slavery. Quaker minister John Woolman of Mount Holly said, "I believe slave keeping to be a practice inconsistent to [not in agreement with] the Christian religion."

**Indentured servants used plows (right) to prepare fields for planting. Corn (below) was an important crop in the colonial economy.**

## Freedom for Some

Many people moved to New Jersey because they could have more freedom here than in other places. Women had fewer rights than men. When women married, many of these rights were passed on to their husbands. For example, a married woman's job earnings belonged to her husband.

Only white men who owned land had full rights. They were the only people who could vote or serve in the assembly. Enslaved people and indentured servants could not vote or own property. For a few years in the 1700s women were allowed to vote, but soon they, too, were denied this right.

The Lenape could not vote either. As the colonists' farms grew, the Lenape lost their lands. By 1758 the Lenape people owned only 3,000 acres. By 1801, almost all the Lenape had left New Jersey. They headed west, hoping to preserve their culture far away from European settlers.

See p. T35 for Answers to Think About It.

## WHY IT MATTERS

The New Jersey colony grew rapidly in the 1700s. Some of the people in this colony began to think of themselves as separate from England. They began to think of themselves as Americans. You will read about what happened next in Chapter 5.

### Reviewing Facts and Ideas

#### MAIN IDEAS

- Most people in colonial New Jersey lived on farms, but some worked in industries, too.
- Most farms were small family farms. Larger farms were worked by indentured servants and enslaved Africans.
- Only white men who owned property had full rights in the New Jersey colony.

#### THINK ABOUT IT

1. What different jobs did men and women do in colonial New Jersey?
2. What were three industries that started in New Jersey in colonial times?
3. **FOCUS** Why was farming so important in colonial New Jersey?
4. **THINKING SKILL** Compare and contrast the life of a colonial child with that of a Lenape child as described in Chapter 3.
5. **WRITE** Imagine that you were a 10-year-old indentured servant in New Jersey. Write a letter home to your family describing your experience.

See p. T36 for Answers to Chapter 4 Review.

# CHAPTER 4 REVIEW

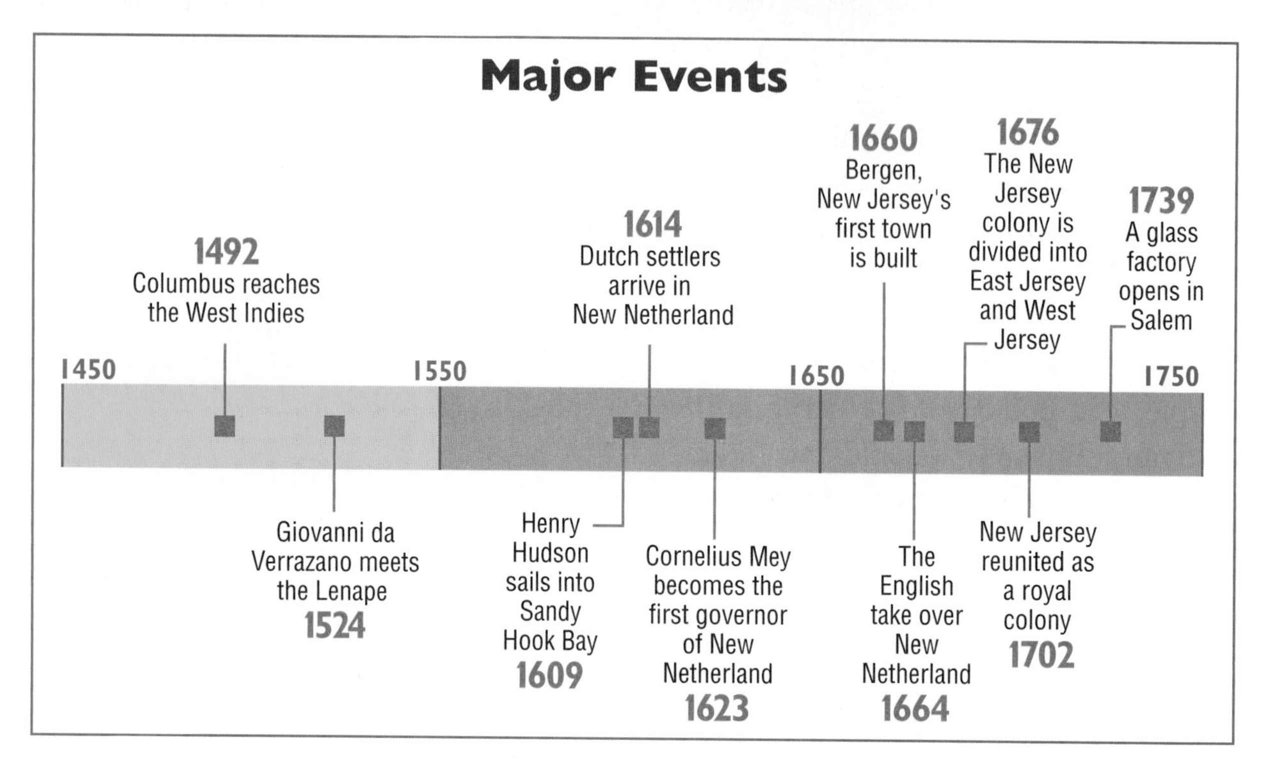


## THINKING ABOUT VOCABULARY

Number a sheet of paper from 1 to 5. Next to each number write the word or term that best completes the sentence.

colony · proprietor · constitution · slavery · delegate

1. People brought to this country under __________ had no rights.
2. New Netherland was a Dutch __________.
3. Lord John Berkeley was a __________ of New Jersey.
4. A member of the assembly was called a __________.
5. New Jersey's first __________ guaranteed freedom of religion.

## THINKING ABOUT FACTS

1. How did the earliest explorers in New Jersey describe the Lenape?
2. Why did most of the first Dutch settlers come to New Jersey?
3. What caused tension between early settlers and the Lenape?
4. What part of New Jersey's first town can you still see?
5. How did Governor Peter Stuyvesant feel about surrendering New Netherland to the English?
6. How did New Jersey get its name?
7. How did New Jersey's first proprietors attract immigrants?
8. In which section of New Jersey did Quakers have the most influence?
9. How much time did most colonial children spend in school?
10. What was life like for most Africans who lived in colonial New Jersey?

### THINK AND WRITE

**WRITING A JOURNAL**
Imagine that you are one of the early European explorers. Write a journal describing the sights and people that you might see on one day of your journey.

**WRITING A MENU**
Write a menu for the meal that a Dutch family in New Netherland might eat at dinnertime.

**WRITING A CHART**
Make a chart to show how power was shared in colonial New Jersey. Someone who looks at your chart should be able to see who had the most power, who had some power, and who had the least power.

### APPLYING STUDY SKILLS

**TIME LINES**
Use the Major Events time line on the opposite page to answer the following questions.

1. How many years does the time line cover?
2. When did Henry Hudson sail to the area that became New Jersey?
3. How many years later did the Dutch settle in New Netherland?
4. Was Bergen established before or after New Jersey was reunited as a royal colony?
5. How are time lines useful for studying history?

## Summing Up the Chapter

Use the following table to organize information from the chapter. Copy the table on a sheet of paper. Then list the differences between New Netherland and New Jersey. When you have filled in the table, use it to write a paragraph that answers the question "How did life change for European colonists when England took over New Jersey?"

| | NEW NETHERLAND COLONY | NEW JERSEY COLONY |
|---|---|---|
| LANGUAGE | Dutch | English |
| ECONOMY | fur trade | farming, some factories |
| LAND OWNERSHIP | patroons | proprieters |
| GOVERNMENT | governor | governor, assembly |

CHAPTER 5

# The American Revolution

## THINKING ABOUT HISTORY AND GEOGRAPHY

This chapter begins in the 1700s, when New Jersey was ruled by a king in faraway Great Britain. By the end of the 1700s, however, a new country had risen to power in North America. This country was called the United States of America. Read on to learn how New Jerseyans struggled to break free from Great Britain and played an important role in forming this new country.

**1759**

TRENTON

**British soldiers train during the French and Indian War.**

GREENWICH

**Colonists dressed as Lenape take part in the Greenwich Tea Party.**

**1778**

MONMOUTH COURTHOUSE

**Mary Ludwig Hays helps the Continental Army against the British.**

1760 1770 1780

See pT37 for Chapter Organizer.

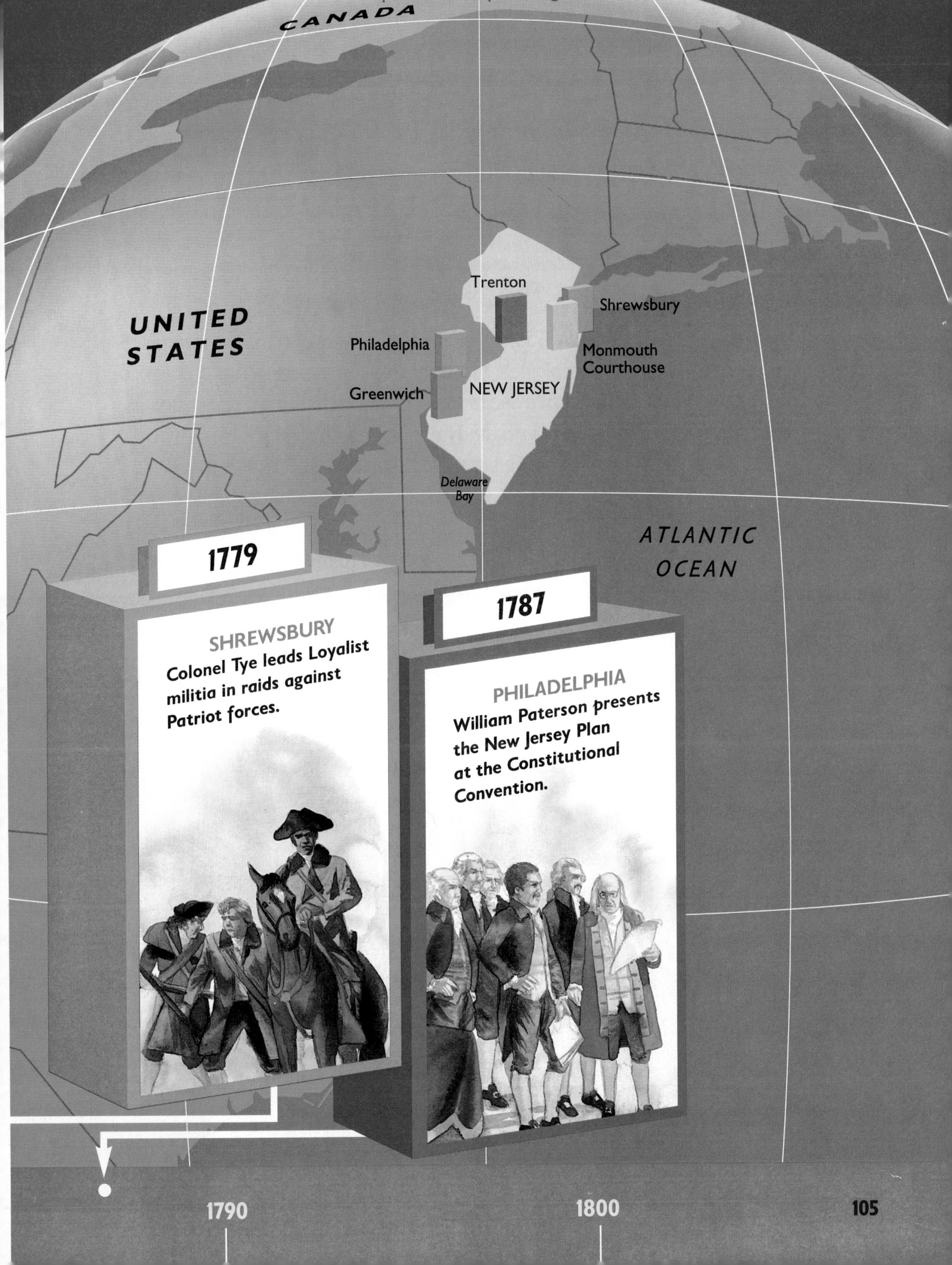

CANADA

UNITED STATES

Trenton

Shrewsbury

Philadelphia

Monmouth Courthouse

Greenwich

NEW JERSEY

Delaware Bay

ATLANTIC OCEAN

1779

SHREWSBURY

Colonel Tye leads Loyalist militia in raids against Patriot forces.

1787

PHILADELPHIA

William Paterson presents the New Jersey Plan at the Constitutional Convention.

1790

1800

1720 1740 1754 1776 1800

See p. T38 for Lesson Teaching Strategies.

# Unrest in the Colonies

## Focus Activity

**READ TO LEARN**

***What events led the colonists to break with Great Britain?***

**VOCABULARY**

- French and Indian War
- ally
- tax
- Stamp Act
- militia
- American Revolution
- Declaration of Independence

**PEOPLE**

- George Washington
- William Franklin
- Thomas Jefferson
- Abraham Clark
- Richard Stockton
- John Witherspoon

**PLACES**

- Greenwich

### Read Aloud

*In 1754 the Duke of Newcastle, an English leader, complained: "The French claim almost all North America except a line to the sea, to which they would confine all our colonies, and from whence they may drive us whenever they please." To this he added, "That is what we must not, we will not suffer." One thing both the British and the French seemed to forget, of course, was that the land both claimed belonged to the Native Americans.*

### THE BIG PICTURE

France and Britain had been fighting in Europe for centuries. By the middle 1700s, France and Britain were once again headed for conflict, this time in North America. Both countries claimed land west of the Appalachian Mountains. Both believed they had a right to be in that region. The French built forts to protect their territory. The British did the same.

The stage was set for war. It came in 1754. This war is known as the **French and Indian War**.

**Some British soldiers trained for the French and Indian War at the barracks in Trenton.**

# THE FRENCH AND INDIAN WAR

The British colonies were growing rapidly. The French colonies had far fewer settlers. Over time, British colonists began moving west.

## The French and British Clash

The French built forts, fearing that the British would take control. The British sent George Washington, a young officer from Virginia, into the area. In 1754 Washington's forces clashed with French soldiers. This marked the beginning of the French and Indian War.

Both European powers wanted the support of Native Americans. Many Native American groups fought as allies of the French. An ally is a friend with whom one is united for a common purpose.

**MAP WORK: 1.** The Appalachian Mountains

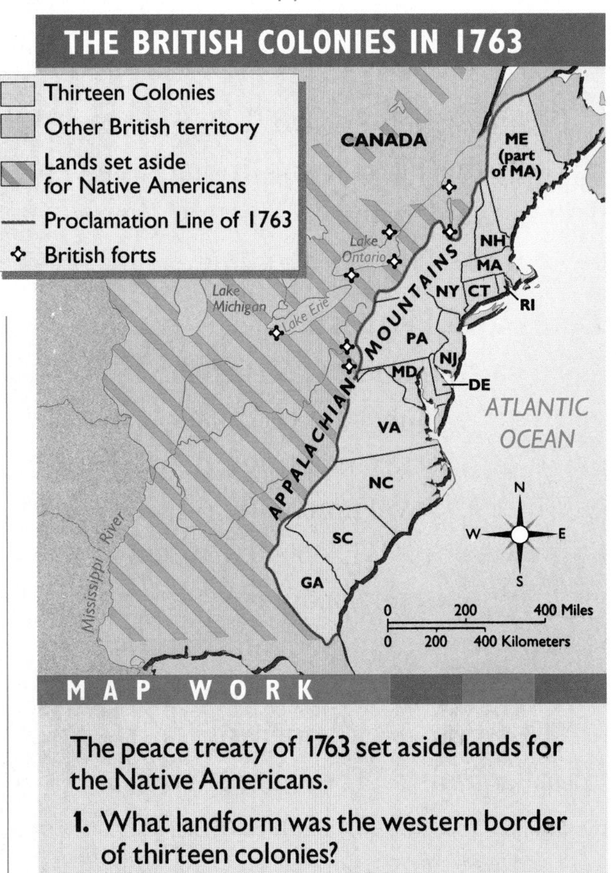


**MAP WORK**

The peace treaty of 1763 set aside lands for the Native Americans.

1. What landform was the western border of thirteen colonies?

## British Victory

At first, New Jersey had little interest in the war because its lands were not in danger. After time, the colony provided soldiers for the British army. Many of these soldiers lived and trained at buildings called barracks in Trenton.

The last major battle of the war took place in 1759 at Quebec, a city in Canada. The British victory there put an end to France's power in North America. A peace treaty was signed in 1763. As the map on this page shows, France gave Canada and lands east of the Mississippi River to Britain. The British set aside lands between the Appalachian Mountains and the Mississippi for Native Americans.

## CONFLICTS IN THE COLONIES

Great Britain spent much money fighting the French and Indian War. Britain wanted the colonists to help pay for the costs of the war.

### Taxes and Protests

To raise money, the British decided to make the colonists pay a tax. A tax is money people pay to the government. The Stamp Act of 1765 placed a tax on items like newspapers. A stamp on an item showed that the tax had been paid.

The Stamp Act angered many colonists. They were used to paying taxes to their colonial assemblies. However, this tax was different. Colonists could vote for representatives to their assemblies. They were not allowed any representatives to the British government in faraway London.

Soon the cry of "no taxation without representation" was heard throughout the colonies. In New Jersey three lawmakers sent a letter to Britain about taxes:

> *We look upon all taxes laid upon us without our consent* (agreement) *as a [way of keeping us from having our] rights . . . as English subjects.*

The British ended the tax in 1766 because of colonial protests. However, new taxes and the presence of soldiers in the colonies sparked new rounds of protests.

**American colonists (above) protested the Stamp Act by burning British tax stamps (above, right) in a bonfire.**

### The Greenwich Tea Party

Many colonists were upset about a tax on tea. Some people avoided the tax by refusing to drink tea. Others took direct action. In December 1773, about 100 colonists in Boston held what became known as the Boston Tea Party. They disguised themselves as Native Americans, boarded a British ship, and threw boxes of tea into the water. The British punished Boston. They closed its port and sent soldiers there to keep order.

A year later, New Jersey had its own "tea party" in the town of Greenwich. One night about 40 young men dressed as Lenape. They broke into a building in town where the tea was stored. They seized the tea and burned it in a big fire in the center of town.

### Important Meetings

People in New Jersey were divided about the problems with Great Britain. The royal governor, William Franklin, was a firm supporter of Great Britain. He feared that matters could get out of control. He refused to call the colonial assembly to meet. On July 21, 1774, concerned colonists called their own meeting in New Brunswick.

They declared the tax laws unfair. They voted to send five men to the meeting of the First Continental Congress, to be held in Philadelphia on September 5. Many delegates hoped to patch up the quarrel with Great Britain. They wanted the British government to take away unfair laws and agree that the colonists had certain rights.

The delegates voted to stop all trade with Great Britain unless their demands were met. They also called on the colonies to prepare to defend themselves by forming militias. A militia is a group of citizens trained to fight and help in emergencies.

New Jersey's delegates returned home. Governor Franklin urged the colony's assembly to reject the plans formed at the Continental Congress. The assembly refused.

**Colonists dressed as Native Americans destroyed British tea in Greenwich (below). A bill of credit (below, left) was often used in place of cash.**

## A BREAK WITH BRITAIN

Before the Continental Congress met again, colonists in Massachusetts battled British troops at Lexington and Concord. In April 1775, British soldiers in Boston fought with members of a local militia. People on both sides died. These battles marked the start of the **American Revolution**.

Word of the battles traveled quickly to New Jersey. Jemima Condict of Morristown wrote in her diary:

> *As every day brings new trouble, so this day brings news that yesterday very early in the morning they began to fight at Boston.*

### Declaring Independence

One month after the fighting broke out, leaders of the colonies met in Philadelphia for the Second Continental Congress. They sent a letter to Britain's King George III. It asked him to end the new taxes. Just in case, they also chose George Washington to lead the new Continental Army.

The king refused to change the laws. By June 1776, the delegates had decided that the colonies should become independent, or free, from British rule. **Thomas Jefferson** of Virginia wrote a statement explaining the decision. This statement, known as the **Declaration of Independence**, says "all men . . . are created equal."

On July 4, 1776, Congress approved the Declaration of Independence. **Abraham Clark**, **Richard Stockton**, and **John Witherspoon** of New Jersey signed the declaration. After the signing, Abraham Clark wondered how Britain would respond. In a letter to a friend, he wrote "a few weeks will . . . determine our fate—perfect freedom or Absolute Slavery."

**Abraham Clark (right) was a New Jersey delegate to the Second Continental Congress (below).**

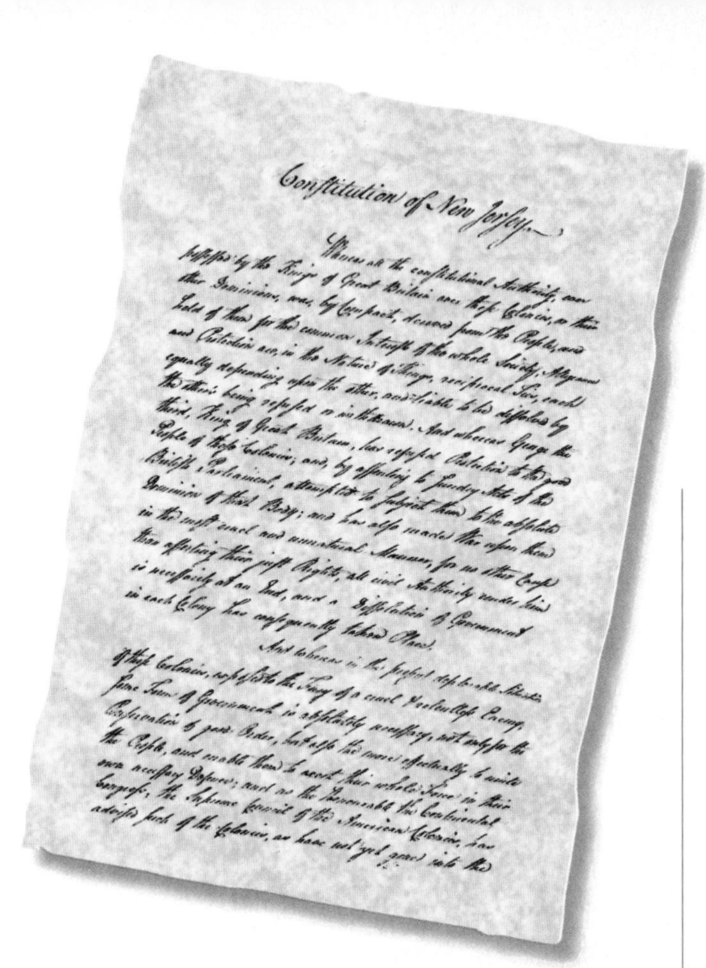
Constitution of New Jersey

See p. T38 for Answers to Think About It.

**New Jersey's Constitution of 1776 allowed for a return to British rule.**

The declaration and this statement both ignored one fact. Even with freedom from Great Britain, most of New Jersey's 10,000 enslaved African Americans remained unfree.

### A Constitution for New Jersey

New Jersey's leaders gathered to write a state constitution. Only 26 of the 65 delegates actually voted in favor of the document. Many others had doubts about separating from Britain. They left the meeting before the vote was taken. By a vote of 26 to 9, the state constitution was passed. It left open the chance for a return to British rule. It said that if Britain and the colonies worked out their problems, the constitution was no longer in effect.

## WHY IT MATTERS

Problems between the colonists and the British grew and grew. The 13 colonies were about to become the United States of America. You will read about the American Revolution in Lesson 2.

## Reviewing Facts and Ideas

### MAIN IDEAS

- The British fought the French and Native Americans in the French and Indian War.
- Many colonists became angry with British laws and taxes that they thought were unfair.
- Leaders of the colonies declared independence in 1776.

### THINK ABOUT IT

1. Why did Britain want the colonists to pay more taxes?
2. What was one way the people of New Jersey protested the taxes?
3. **FOCUS** Name two events that led the colonists to break away from Great Britain.
4. **THINKING SKILL** Put these events in the correct *sequence:* the Declaration of Independence, the Stamp Act, the French and Indian War, and the Greenwich Tea Party.
5. **WRITE** Imagine that you live in New Jersey at the time of the Greenwich Tea Party. Write a letter to a friend explaining how you feel about it.

See p. T39 for Citizenship Teaching Strategies.

# CITIZENSHIP VIEWPOINTS

Declaring independence and forming a new country was an important decision for British colonists.

## 1776: What did the people of New Jersey think about declaring independence?

In New Jersey, people had different ideas about separating from Britain. Some favored continuing British rule in the 13 colonies. Many who felt this way agreed with New Jersey's royal governor, William Franklin. He believed that declaring independence would be a terrible mistake. He was certain that the colonies would lose any war with Britain.

Some in New Jersey were uneasy about what might follow an attempt at independence. Jonathan Elmer of Cumberland County was one. Even so, after reading the Declaration of Independence, Elmer was ready to support the cause.

Still others in New Jersey were strong supporters of independence. William Livingston argued that the colonies would have much greater economic and political freedom if they were independent. He felt that this freedom would lead Americans to greater wealth.

Consider these three viewpoints on this issue and answer the questions that follow.

See p. T39 for Answers to Building Citizenship.

# Three DIFFERENT Viewpoints

1 **WILLIAM FRANKLIN**
Governor of the New Jersey colony
Excerpt from a letter to the New Jersey Legislature, 1776

No independent state ever was or ever can be so happy as we have been under the government [of Britain]. . . . Should [the Patriots succeed in] their baneful [deadly] purpose, . . . their government will not be lasting.

---

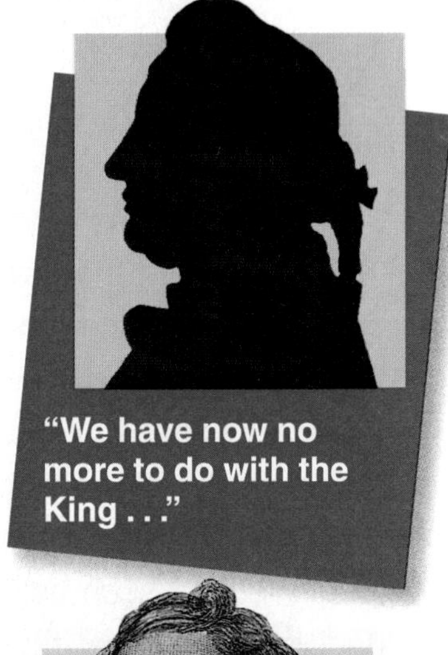


2 **JONATHAN ELMER**
Chairman of the Cumberland County Inspection Committee
Excerpt from an address after the reading of the Declaration of Independence, August 28, 1776

From what has now been read, you see the long wished for, but much dreaded [feared] period has arrived, in which the connection [link] between Great Britain and America is totally dissolved [broken], and these colonies declared free and independent states. . . . We have now no more to do with the King and people of England than we have with the King and people of France or Spain.

---

**WILLIAM LIVINGSTON**
Lawyer and first governor of the state of New Jersey
Excerpt from a letter written May 6, 1778

What a miserable and despised [hated] people should we be, if we were to make peace with England. . . . Our trade would be confined [limited] more than ever. . . . How happy shall we be if independent! . . . Then we shall make our own laws . . . have only our own governments. . . . We shall trade with England as much as we find it in our own interest [to our advantage] and no further. . . . A free trade will make us rich.

## BUILDING CITIZENSHIP

### THINKING ABOUT VIEWPOINTS

1. Which person opposes independence? Which person strongly favors it?
2. How would you summarize each of the viewpoints in one sentence?
3. What viewpoints might Native Americans or African Americans have had on this issue?

### SHARING VIEWPOINTS

Discuss what you agree with or disagree with about these and other viewpoints. Then, as a class, write three statements that all of you can agree with about the conflict over British rule.

See p. T40 for Skill Teaching Strategies.

# Identifying Fact and Opinion

**VOCABULARY**

fact

opinion

## WHY THE SKILL MATTERS

In the last lesson you read about the events that led the colonists to declare independence from Great Britain. Suppose somebody told you that the Declaration of Independence was approved by the colonies in 1776. This statement is a fact. You can check the information in a reference source, such as an encyclopedia. A fact is a statement that can be proven true.

Suppose, however, that somebody told you that she thinks Abraham Clark would have been a better commander of the Continental Army than George Washington. This statement cannot be proven, and so it is not a fact. It is an opinion. An opinion is a statement of a person's belief or feeling. One person might believe that George Washington would make a good military leader. Another might say that someone else would do a better job.

Facts and opinions are very different kinds of statements. It is important to be able to tell them apart because good decisions are based on facts.

## USING THE SKILL

Read the following passage. Then identify which statements are facts and which are opinions.

*William Franklin was the son of Benjamin Franklin. He took office as royal governor of New Jersey in 1763. I believe he was one of the best leaders of the time. But by the time he took office, the power of Great Britain had begun to fade.*

Which statements in the passage are facts? Which are opinions? The first two sentences in the passage are facts. They could be proven true. You could check the information in a reference source.

**Continental soldiers arrested Governor Franklin in 1776 because he sided with the British.**

*Facts: Fleets and armies are preparing; facts can be looked up in reference sources. Opinions: All hopes of peace are at an end, troublesome times are coming, war must come; opinions can be identified by the words *I think, I fear.*

See p. T40 for Answers to Reviewing the Skill.

Sometimes you can tell opinions by the use of such word clues as *I think, I believe, the best,* or *should.* Two of these word clues appear in the passage. The statement "I believe he was one of the best leaders of the time" cannot be proven true. However, opinions do not always have word clues.

**Helping yourself**

- **Facts are statements that can be proven true. Opinions are statements of beliefs or feelings.**
- **Opinions can sometimes be recognized by such word clues as I think, I believe, the best, or should.**

### TRYING THE SKILL

You have just identified facts and opinions in a passage about Governor Franklin. Now read this passage adapted from the diary of Jemima Condict, a colonist who supported the break from Britain. When you are done, figure out which statements are facts and which express opinions. Use the Helping Yourself box to guide you in identifying these two kinds of statements.

> *I have just now heard that all hopes of peace between Britain and her colonies are at an end. Fleets and armies are preparing for our destruction. I think we have troublesome times a coming, and they say it is the tea that caused it. If they will quarrel about such a trifling thing as that, what must we expect but war? I think it will be so. At least I fear that war must come.*

Which of these statements could be proven true? How? Which statements do you think are opinions? What did you do to identify these facts and the opinions?*

### REVIEWING THE SKILL

1. In what ways is a fact different from an opinion?
2. Why does a word clue like *the best* often tell you that the speaker is expressing an opinion?
3. How would the reference section of the library help you to decide if certain statements were facts or opinions?
4. Why is it useful to be able to tell a fact from an opinion?
5. Write down a statement that provides both a fact and an opinion.

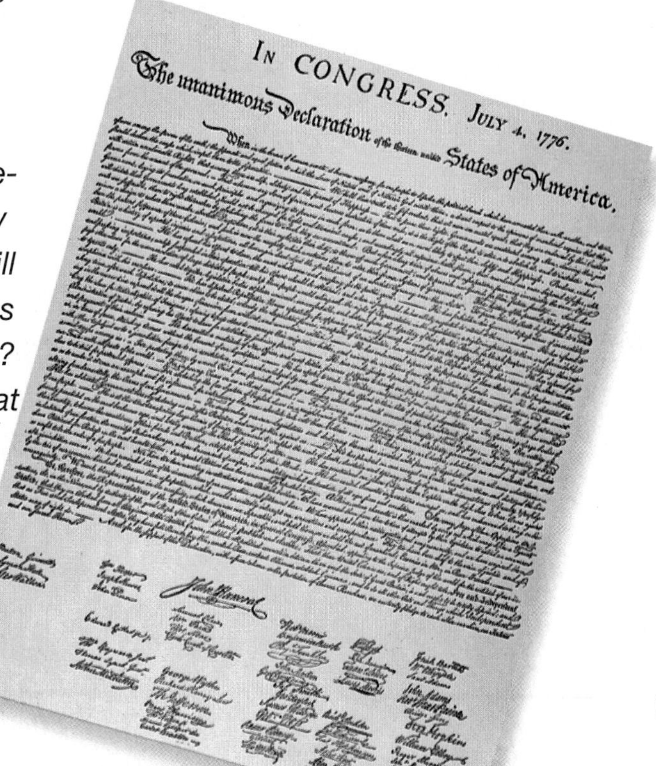


**The Continental Congress approved the Declaration of Independence on July 4, 1776.**

**LESSON 2**

| 1720 | 1740 | 1760 | 1776 1783 | 1800 |
|---|---|---|---|---|

See p. T41 for Lesson Teaching Strategies.

# Crossroads of the Revolution

## Focus Activity

**READ TO LEARN**

***What important role did New Jersey play in the American Revolution?***

**VOCABULARY**

- Patriot
- Loyalist
- Hessian

**PEOPLE**

- William Livingston
- Mary Ludwig Hays

**PLACES**

- Princeton
- Monmouth Courthouse
- Morristown
- Short Hills

### Read Aloud

*In August 1777, Ebenezer Hazard was traveling through New Jersey and wrote the following: "Great devastation [ruin] was made by the enemy at Somerset Court House: the Dutch and Presbyterian churches . . . were stripped of their pulpits and pews, their doors and windows were broken, and the boards torn off the outside. . . . Several houses were destroyed." Located at the "crossroads of the Revolution," New Jersey felt the terrible effects of the war.*

### THE BIG PICTURE

New Jersey was a key state in the American Revolution. Its location between New England and the Southern states made it important to both sides. If the British took control of New York, New Jersey, and Pennsylvania, then New England would be separated from the South. The Americans would find it much harder to work together in fighting the war.

The war was also especially painful in New Jersey because it was a divided state. New Jerseyans who supported the king fought bitterly against those eager for independence. Many years would pass before the angry feelings died away.

## WAR COMES TO NEW JERSEY

As you will see, people in New Jersey were divided in their feelings about separating from Britain. New Jerseyans caught in the middle tried to protect their homes and families.

### Patriots and Loyalists

One in three New Jerseyans was a Patriot, a supporter of the cause of revolution. Another one in three was a Loyalist. Loyalists, also called Tories, were people who remained faithful to Britain. The rest of the people of the state tried not to take sides. Many of these people were Quakers. Their religious beliefs led them to oppose wars.

Citizens who wanted to join the British army slipped past Patriot guards along the New Jersey border to get to British forces in New York. Also, some enslaved African Americans saw a chance for freedom. They fled their homes to join the British army.

William Livingston, the state's first governor, ordered the New Jersey militia to capture any Loyalists caught trading with the British or trying to join the British army. Many Loyalists hated Livingston. His enemies tried to kill him at least four times. To protect himself, Livingston did not sleep in the same place more than two nights in a row.

### Hard Times for New Jerseyans

New Jerseyans suffered from the war in many ways. Loyalists and Patriots burned down each other's homes and destroyed businesses, farms, and crops. The British and American armies also caused great damage. New Jersey's Joseph Reed, who helped General Washington, wrote to his wife:

> *It is of little consequence* [matter] *which army passed. It is equally destructive* [damaging] *to friend or foe.*

**A group of boys who sided with the Patriot cause make fun of a Loyalist, or Tory. The question of separating from Britain divided many communities.**

## MARCHING ACROSS NEW JERSEY

The war was going poorly for the Americans. Their attempt to invade Canada failed. Washington and his men were forced out of New York. British soldiers chased the American troops south through New Jersey into Pennsylvania.

### A Daring Plan

With these defeats, many Americans began to lose faith in the Continental Army. Washington looked over his troops and wrote in mid-December 1776: "I think the game is pretty near up. . . . No man, I believe, ever had a greater choice of difficulties, and less means to extricate [remove] himself from them."

General Washington needed a bold plan. He had one. On the snowy night of December 25, 1776, Washington and his ragged soldiers crossed the icy Delaware River back into New Jersey.

Some British soldiers were camped at Trenton just across the river. Washington's troops surprised them and captured more than 900 **Hessians**, soldiers from the German state of Hesse. They were paid to fight for Britain.

Victories at Trenton and a week later at **Princeton** helped restore confidence in Washington and his army. They also showed Americans that the British could be beaten.

### Hot Day at Monmouth

In June 1778, the British army left Philadelphia and marched to New York City. Once there they planned to board ships that would take them to the Southern states.

**General George Washington surprised the British by crossing the Delaware River. His bold action led to victories at Trenton and Princeton.**

Washington saw a chance to strike as the British marched across New Jersey. He chose General Charles Lee to lead the attack. Washington's troops were to meet Lee's army at Monmouth Courthouse. As the battle began, Lee thought he was outnumbered and ordered a retreat. Washington took charge. He rallied Lee's confused troops. In almost 100-degree heat, the British and American armies fought hard. Neither side was driven back.

The British counted on strong Loyalist support at Monmouth. One place they got it was from a former slave named Titus. He captured a New Jersey militia officer and delivered him to the British. Titus earned the rank of colonel from the British for his daring and became known as Colonel Tye.

Finally the British general ordered his army off the field. Both sides suffered losses. About 250 British soldiers died, many from the heat. The Continental Army reported 58 killed and 161 wounded. The British headed for New York City. Washington's exhausted troops did not try to follow. He wrote to his brother, "from an unfortunate and bad beginning, [it] turned out a glorious and happy day."

**Mary Ludwig Hays helped the Continental troops at the Battle of Monmouth.**

### A Hero at Monmouth

The Battle of Monmouth gave us a hero named Mary Ludwig Hays. Like many soldiers' wives, Hays traveled with her husband, William, when he joined the army. In the army camp she washed soldiers' clothing and cared for the wounded. On the day of the battle, she carried pitchers of water to the tired and wounded American soldiers. That's how she earned her nickname Molly Pitcher. When her husband was wounded, Hays even took his place firing a cannon!

Infographic

interNET CONNECTION Visit our website: www.mhschool.com

# The Revolutionary War in New Jersey

**About one of every three battles during the American Revolution was fought in New Jersey. That is one reason why our state is known as the "Crossroads of the Revolution." What were some of the battles that took place here?**

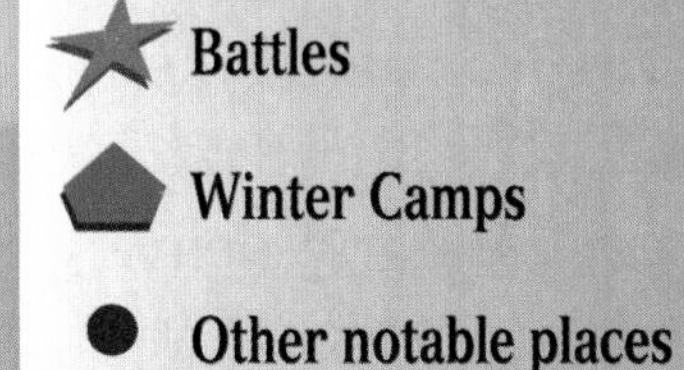

## At Sea

**New Jersey sailors used whaleboats to raid British shipping and outposts around New York City, Long Island, and along the Delaware River.**

## Army Dress

**Continental Army soldiers often provided their own uniforms. Few soldiers ever had the correct uniforms, as worn here by reenactors.**

**Capital City**

When Congress fled from Philadelphia in 1783, it moved to Princeton, and Nassau Hall became the new country's capitol for a short time.

**Winter Quarters**

The Continental Army spent three hard winters in New Jersey. The soldiers' cabins at Middlebrook (shown here in a reconstruction) were "but one room [with] 10 or 12 men."

**On Land**

On Christmas night in 1776, Continental soldiers led by George Washington (below) surprised the Hessians soldiers at Trenton.

## CAMP AT MORRISTOWN

After the Battle of Monmouth, the main action of the war shifted to the Southern states. However, the war was not over in the North. The British continued to control New York City. In 1779 General Washington decided to spend the winter nearby, where he could watch the moves of the British. He chose the town of Morristown, which was close to New York but also protected by hills. This was the second winter that Washington's troops spent in Morristown.

### A Harsh Winter

The winter of 1779–1780 was the coldest of the century. The Raritan River and Delaware River froze solid. Heavy carriages could be pulled across the ice.

About 12,000 troops struggled to survive the cold winter at Morristown. The Continental Congress ran out of money. The Army could not buy food or pay troops. On April 12, 1780, Washington wrote: "We have not this day one ounce of fresh meat or salt."

As the war dragged on, some soldiers simply went home. However, many stayed on in the hope that the war would soon turn in the Americans' favor. They kept their spirits up as best they could. Songs like the one on the next page helped them through these troubled times. Why might singing have made the soldiers feel better?

# YANKEE DOODLE

## THE WAR ENDS

In the spring of 1780, word came to New Jersey that France would give help in the war against Britain. Victory seemed closer than ever.

In June 1780 one last battle took place in New Jersey. The British wanted to capture Washington's camp at Morristown. About 6,000 British troops landed in Elizabethtown, which today is called Elizabeth. As they came ashore, 500 American soldiers were there to meet them.

Although outnumbered, the American soldiers prepared to fight. Patriots fired guns to sound an alarm in the town of Short Hills. They also lit signal fires on towers to bring in New Jersey militias. Washington's army at Morristown was on the march, too.

New Jerseyans held off the British until Washington arrived. The British did not invade New Jersey again. Governor Livingston praised the New Jerseyans, saying, "Never did troops, either Continental or militia, behave better than ours did."

**Cannons were used to attack the enemy, and to sound the alarm in times of danger.**

See p. T41 for Answers to Think About It.

With the signing of a peace agreement in 1783, many Loyalists left the state for Canada or Britain. At home, Patriots celebrated the war's end.

## WHY IT MATTERS

The American Revolution gave birth to a new country. Americans could now make their own laws. They began to build a country based on ideas of freedom. New Jersey played an important role in the war. In the next lesson you will read about its part in shaping this new country.

### Reviewing Facts and Ideas

#### MAIN IDEAS

- Because of its location, New Jersey played an important part in the American Revolution.
- The battles of Trenton and Princeton gave Americans hope in the Continental Army.
- Washington's army struggled through a harsh winter at Morristown.

#### THINK ABOUT IT

1. What is a Loyalist?
2. How did New Jerseyans suffer during the war?
3. **FOCUS** Name three important battles of the American Revolution that were fought in New Jersey.
4. **THINKING SKILL** Predict what might have happened if Washington had not defeated the British at Trenton and Princeton.
5. **GEOGRAPHY** Look at the map on page 120. How did New Jersey's location affect its role in the war?

See p. T00 for Legacy Teaching Strategies.

Legacy

LINKING PAST AND PRESENT

# Special Places in New Jersey History

You have just read about the hard winter the Continental Army spent in Morristown. Did you know that you can visit the house where General Washington stayed during that snowy winter? New Jersey has many special places that have been set aside to preserve New Jersey history. Some are buildings or parks that remind us of important New Jerseyans or major events in history. Some show us how New Jerseyans lived and worked 100 or even 200 years ago. Some, like the battleship *New Jersey,* honor the contributions of all Americans during wartime.

New Jerseyans are proud of their history and they work hard to preserve it. Historic sites help to keep memories of our past alive. The special places shown on these pages will continue to remind New Jerseyans of the people and events that contributed to our state's history.

**The Peter Mott house (top right) in Lawnside was once a hiding place for enslaved African Americans escaping from slavery. Today, it is being restored for visitors. The U.S. battleship *New Jersey* (lower right) was launched in 1942. It helped to protect the United States for almost 40 years. Today it is a floating museum in Camden.**

Step back in time and visit the Ford mansion in Morristown. George Washington lived here during the harsh winter of 1779–1780.

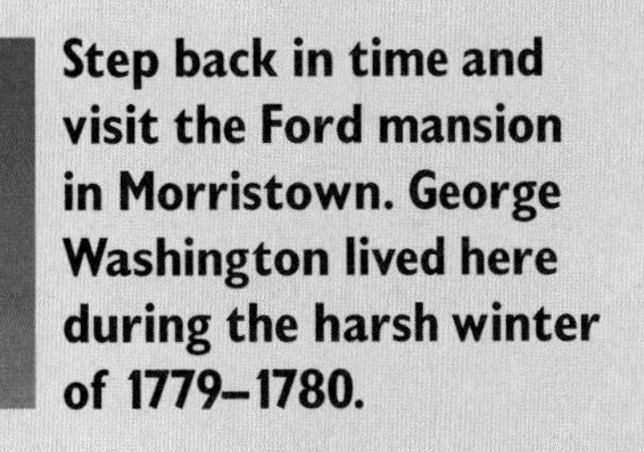

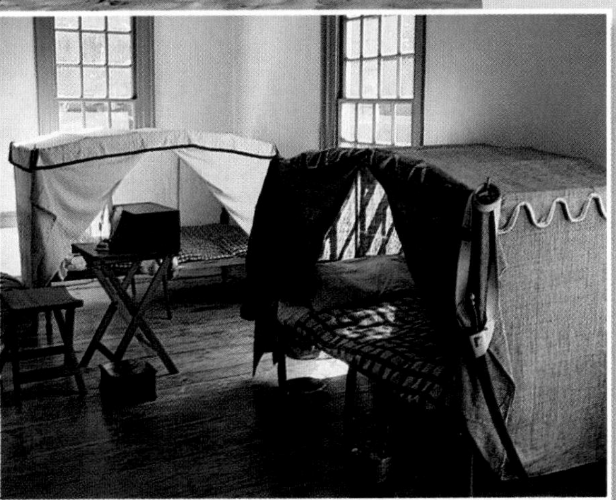

The history of glassmaking in New Jersey is explained at Wheaton Village. You can watch glass being made and shaped (above).

At the Howell Living History Farm, you will see what life was like on a New Jersey farm in 1900.

1720 1740 1760 1783 1790 1800

See p. T43 for Lesson Teaching Strategies.

# A More Perfect Union

## Focus Activity

**READ TO LEARN**

***How did New Jersey become part of the new country of the United States?***

**VOCABULARY**

- convention
- New Jersey Plan
- compromise
- ratify
- Bill of Rights

**PEOPLE**

- William Paterson

**PLACES**

- Trenton

### Read Aloud

*The war was over. Independence had been won. But a question remained: could the 13 separate states that had united for war against Britain unite for their common good? In June 1783, George Washington sent a letter to the governors of the 13 states. He urged them to take hold of "a fairer opportunity for political happiness than any other nation has ever been blessed with." However, not even George Washington was sure how one country could be forged out of 13 different states.*

### THE BIG PICTURE

Many citizens of New Jersey may have been asking the same question: what would become of the new nation of the United States? The people of New Jersey faced new challenges after the war. It was a time of uncertainty.

The problems of New Jersey and other states pointed to an important task: to create a strong national government. At first Americans chose a form of government that gave most of the power to the states. As a result, the new national government was weak. It could not raise taxes and had no way to enforce the laws it made. People felt a change was needed. New Jersey leaders played a key role in bringing this change about.

## A STATE IN CRISIS

New Jersey was in bad shape at the end of the war. Fighting and raiding by the armies of both sides had caused much damage. The clashes between Patriots and Loyalists had left homes and public buildings in ruins.

### An Appeal to Congress

After the war, Congress had asked each of the 13 states to contribute money to support the new government. New Jersey's share of this money was $166,716.

The request came at a time when New Jersey's economy was weak. On top of everything else, New York began charging New Jersey high taxes on any goods passing through New York. Most New Jersey goods did so on their way into or out of the country.

New Jerseyans turned to the Congress of the new national government for help. However, the Congress had little power over trade between states. It could not tell New York what to do.

### New Jersey Stands Up

In protest, New Jersey refused to pay the amount of money that Congress had asked for. Lawmakers wrote a letter explaining their decision. The New Jerseyans called the national government "weak and unjust," and complained that New Jersey had to pay "more than her share of expenses."

The Congress sent three men to New Jersey to ask the lawmakers to think over their decision not to pay the money owed by the state. The lawmakers agreed to take back their demands, but they never paid the money.

New Jersey's problems were just one example of why the national government had to be made stronger. The Articles of Confederation were no longer enough. A new document was needed to hold the young nation together.

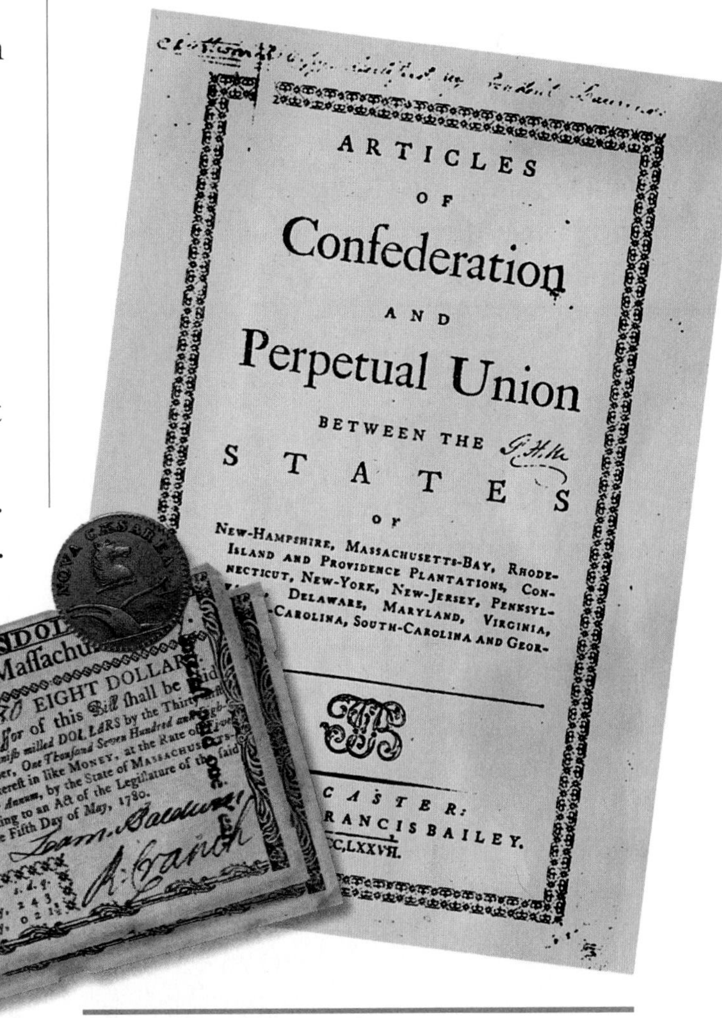


Under the Articles of Confederation (above right), states did not accept paper money or coins (above left) from other states.

## A NEW GOVERNMENT

In 1787 leaders of the states called for a constitutional **convention**. A convention is a formal meeting held for a special purpose. In Philadelphia, a new constitution would be written.

Big states and small states had different ideas. The Virginia Plan expressed the ideas of the larger states. It called for a national legislature, or Congress, divided into two houses. Voters in each state would elect members of Congress based on the size of the state's population. Larger states would have more representatives than smaller ones.

**William Paterson** of New Jersey suggested the **New Jersey Plan**, which called for Congress to have one house. Each state would have the same number of representatives.

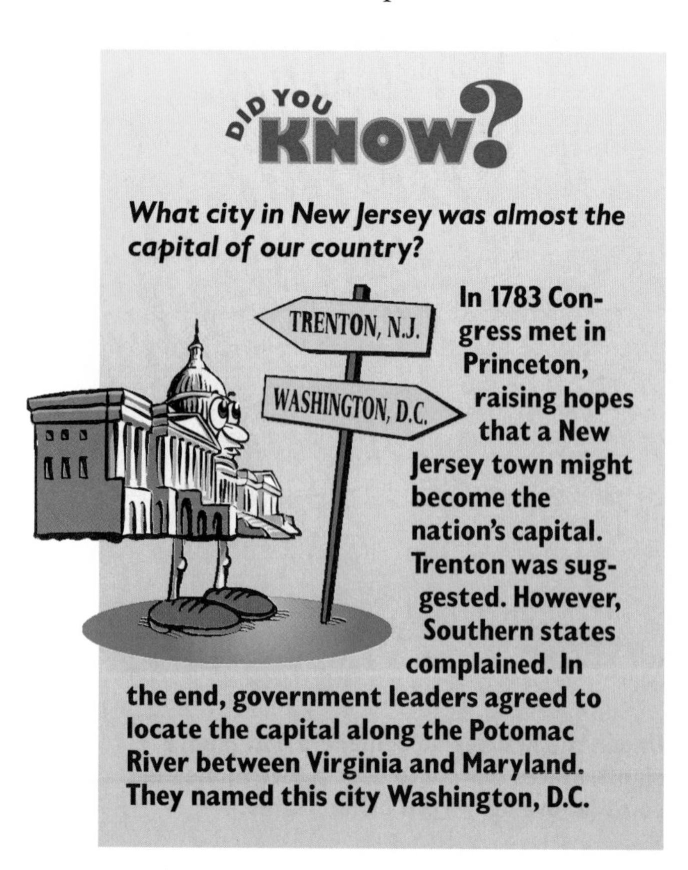


***What city in New Jersey was almost the capital of our country?***

**In 1783 Congress met in Princeton, raising hopes that a New Jersey town might become the nation's capital. Trenton was suggested. However, Southern states complained. In the end, government leaders agreed to locate the capital along the Potomac River between Virginia and Maryland. They named this city Washington, D.C.**

### The Great Compromise

Supporters of the two plans reached a **compromise**. In a compromise, each side gives up some of its demands to reach an agreement. The delegates agreed that Congress would have two houses. In the House of Representatives, the number of each state's representatives would be chosen based on the population of the state. In the Senate, each state, big or small, would have two representatives. This agreement is known as the Great Compromise. This pleased New Jersey and the other small states.

## A New State Government

The people of New Jersey strongly supported the new Constitution. New Jersey became the third state to ratify, or approve, it on December 18, 1787. The Constitution allowed for additions or changes. The first ten additions are known as the Bill of Rights. These laws promise basic rights to citizens, such as freedom of religion and freedom of speech. However, the Constitution did not end slavery. Also, it did not give women many of the rights promised to men.

Changes also took place in New Jersey. In November 1790, lawmakers chose Trenton to be our state's capital.

**Delegates to the Constitutional Convention met at Independence Hall in Philadelphia (left). An early flag (above) had thirteen stars, one for each of the first thirteen states.**

See p. T43 for Answers to Think About It.

## WHY IT MATTERS

The Constitution is the foundation of the United States government. The delegates to the Constitutional Convention created a strong government that has lasted more than 200 years. New Jersey played an important role in creating the Constitution.

### Reviewing Facts and Ideas

#### MAIN IDEAS

- Quarrels between the states pointed to the need for changes in our country's government.
- Leaders from each state met in Philadelphia in 1787 to write a new constitution for the United States.
- The New Jersey Plan led to a compromise about Congress.

#### THINK ABOUT IT

1. What issue did New Jersey and New York quarrel about after the war?
2. Why did Americans decide they needed a new constitution?
3. **FOCUS** List one way in which New Jersey influenced the forming of the government of the United States.
4. **THINKING SKILL** *Compare* and *contrast* the Virginia Plan and the New Jersey Plan.
5. **WRITE** Suppose you were a New Jersey delegate to the Constitutional Convention. Give your opinion of the Virginia and New Jersey Plans.

See p. T44 for Answers to Chapter 5 Review.

# CHAPTER 5 REVIEW

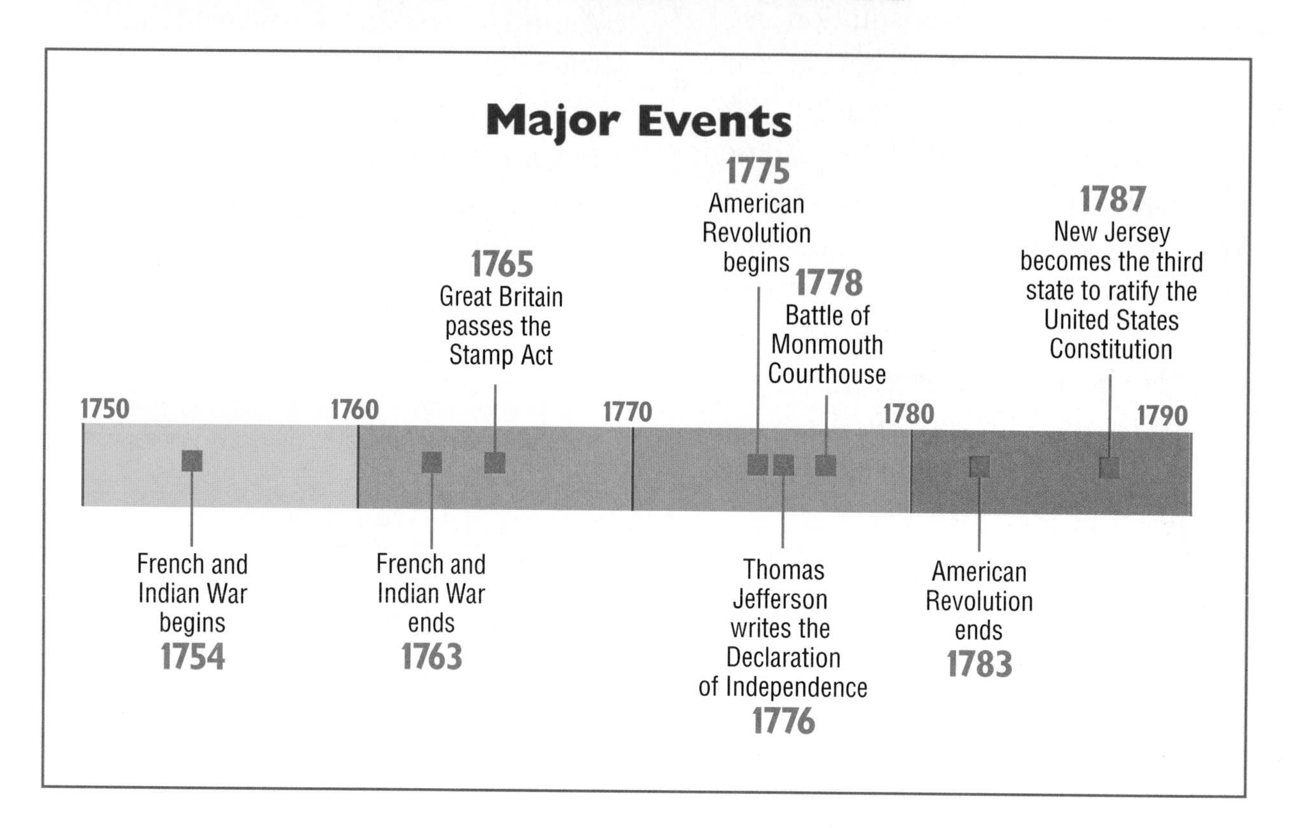


## THINKING ABOUT VOCABULARY

Write a sentence for each pair of words below. Include details that give clues to the meaning of the terms in each pair.

1. Loyalist, Patriot
2. Stamp Act, tax
3. militia, American Revolution
4. Battle of Trenton, Battle of Princeton
5. New Jersey Plan, Great Compromise

## THINKING ABOUT FACTS

1. Why did the British government tax the colonists following the French and Indian War?
2. How were Patriots different from Loyalists?
3. What did the American colonists think about the Stamp Act?
4. What New Jersey town held a tea party?
5. What problems were discussed at the First Continental Congress in 1774?
6. Why was New Jersey called "the crossroads of the Revolution?"
7. Why were the Battles of Trenton and Princeton important?
8. Why did Washington's troops have such a difficult time during the second winter at Morristown?
9. What did the states of New Jersey and New York disagree about after the American Revolution?
10. Why did states with smaller populations support the New Jersey Plan?

## THINK AND WRITE

### WRITING A LETTER
Write a letter from the colonies to King George explaining why you think the Stamp Act of 1765 is unfair.

### WRITING AN ESSAY
Write an essay that explains why you are a Patriot or a Loyalist.

### WRITING A PARAGRAPH
Write a paragraph that explains how the Great Compromise contains parts of both the Virginia Plan and the New Jersey Plan.

## APPLYING THINKING SKILLS

### IDENTIFYING FACT AND OPINION
1. What is the difference between a fact and an opinion?
2. What are some clue words that help you recognize opinions?
3. Identify the fact and the opinion in the following statement: *The Stamp Act was passed in 1765. Many colonists believed it was unfair.*
4. Write a statement of your own including a fact *and* an opinion.
5. Why is it important to learn how to tell a fact from an opinion?

## Summing Up the Chapter

Use the vertical organization chart below to order information in the chapter. When you have filled in the blank spaces, use the chart to write a paragraph that answers the question "How did New Jersey change from a colony to one of the United States?"

**Unrest in the Colonies**

**EVENTS:** Greenwich Tea Party; First and Second Continental Congress; Declaration of Independence; New Jersey Constitution

**IMPORTANCE:** New Jersey and other colonies were on the road to independence.

**The American Revolution**

**EVENTS:** Patriots and Loyalists; battles of Trenton, Princeton, and Monmouth; Mary Ludwig Hays; hard winter at Morristown

**IMPORTANCE:** The 13 colonies became an independent country.

**A New Nation**

**EVENTS:** Constitutional Convention; Virginia and New Jersey Plans; The Constitution; Bill of Rights; the Great Compromise.

**IMPORTANCE:** New Jersey played an important role in the creation of the Constitution—the foundation of our government.

See p. T45 for Answers to Unit 2 Review.

# UNIT 2 REVIEW

## THINKING ABOUT VOCABULARY

Number a sheet of paper from 1 to 5. Next to each number write the letter of the definition that best matches the word.

**1.** Ice Age
- **a.** A time before there were any people
- **b.** A time when glaciers covered much of Earth's surface
- **c.** A cold winter after the arrival of European colonists

**2.** ally
- **a.** a friend with whom one is united for a common purpose
- **b.** an enemy
- **c.** a person who refuses to help anyone

**3.** colony
- **a.** a settlement ruled by another country
- **b.** an independent country
- **c.** a settlement that rules itself

**4.** sakima
- **a.** a Native American house constructed of saplings and animal skins
- **b.** how far north or south a place is from the equator
- **c.** a wise Native American man or woman who settled arguments

**5.** slavery
- **a.** a group of people who join together to help one another
- **b.** the practice of making a person the property of another
- **c.** a group of people ruled by one person

## THINK AND WRITE

### WRITING A DESCRIPTION
Write a paragraph that describes an artifact shown in Chapter 3. Tell what material it is made from and how the item may have been used.

### WRITING AN INTERVIEW
Write an interview with a farmer who lived in English New Jersey.

### WRITING A NEWSPAPER ARTICLE
Suppose you are a newspaper reporter in New Jersey during the American Revolution. Write a news report about one of the events. You might choose the Greenwich Tea Party, the Declaration of Independence, or the Battle of Trenton.

## BUILDING SKILLS

1. **Cause and effect** Name two word clues or phrases that show cause and two that show effect.
2. **Cause and effect** Name one cause and one effect of the Stamp Act.
3. **Latitude and longitude** Look at the map on page 85. Name the city closest to 75°W and 40°N.
4. **Time lines** Draw a time line that goes from 1600 to 1800. Place five events that you read about in Unit 2 on the time line.
5. **Fact and opinion** What are some clue words that tell you a writer is expressing an opinion?

## YESTERDAY, TODAY & TOMORROW

**You have read about how Europeans explored and settled New Jersey. Today explorers are learning more about remote parts of the world, such as places north of the Arctic Circle in Alaska. What might be some results of these explorations? What might happen if people lived in these cold places?**

## READING ON YOUR OWN

These are some of the books you might find at the library to help you learn more.

*A RIDE INTO MORNING: THE STORY OF TEMPE WICK*
**by Ann Rinaldi**
When unrest spreads among the soldiers at Morristown, a young woman cleverly hides her horse.

*A HISTORICAL ALBUM OF NEW JERSEY*
**by Frank Topper**
The story of our state from its earliest settlement by Native Americans to modern times.

*THE 18 PENNY GOOSE*
**by Sally M. Walker and Ellen Beier**
Eight-year-old Letty attempts to save her pet goose from British soldiers.

## UNIT 2 REVIEW PROJECT

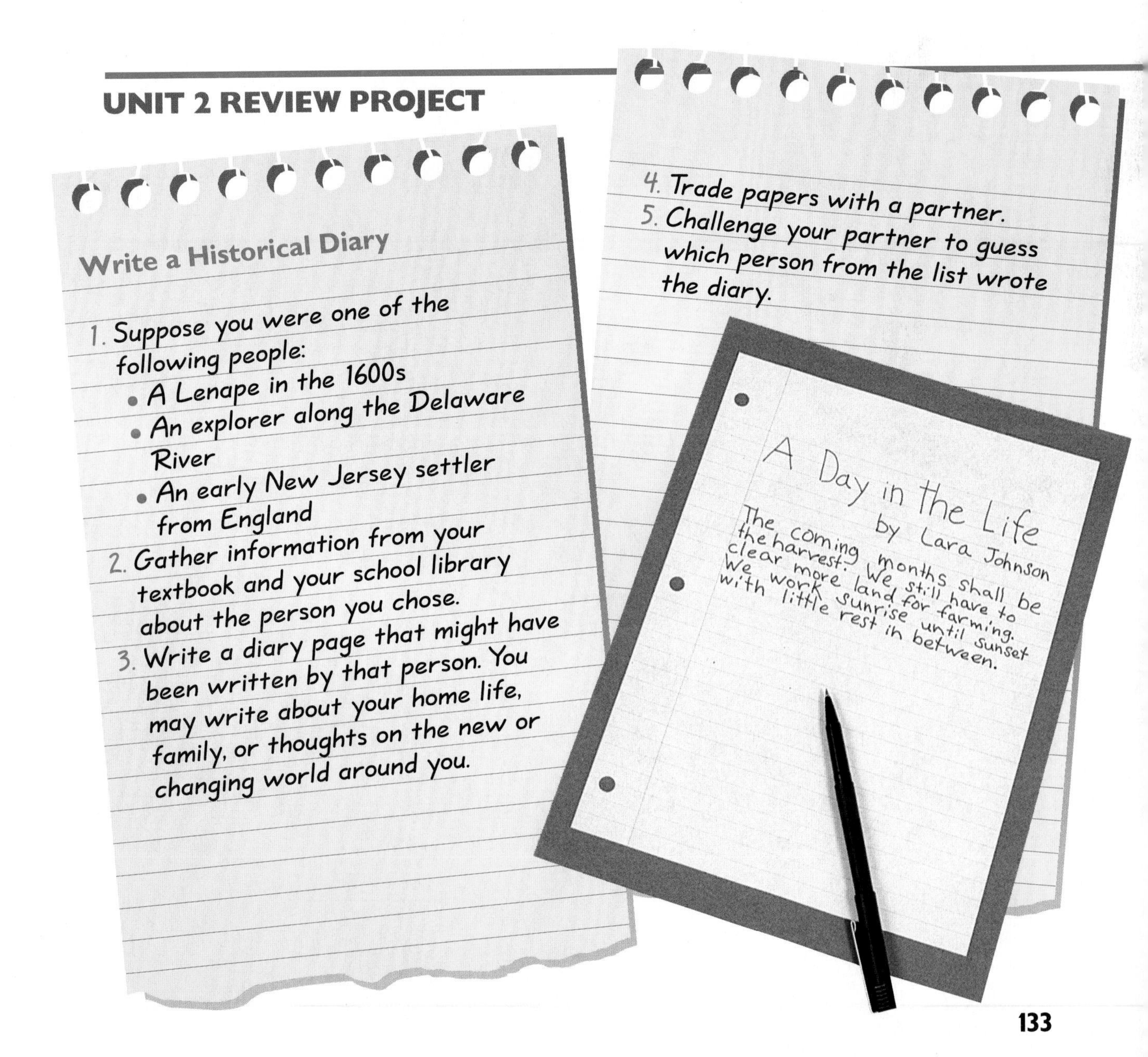

CITIZEN OF RED BANK (RIGHT)

STATUE OF LIBERTY (RIGHT); STAGECOACH TOLL BOARD (BELOW)

UNIT THREE

# A Growing State

*"...if we are not free and equal, we are not men..."*

from a statement by John S. Rock

See page 162.

## Why Does It Matter?

Our young state faced many challenges in the 1800s. Growing cities and industries brought about great change. New forms of transportation helped the state keep up with these changes. People disagreed about slavery. New Jerseyans were called to fight in a war that tore our country apart. In Unit 3 you will also read how new inventions and new people helped our state grow.

EDISON'S PHONOGRAPH

**FIND OUT MORE!**
**Visit our website:**
www.mhschool.com

interNET CONNECTION

## Adventures with NATIONAL GEOGRAPHIC

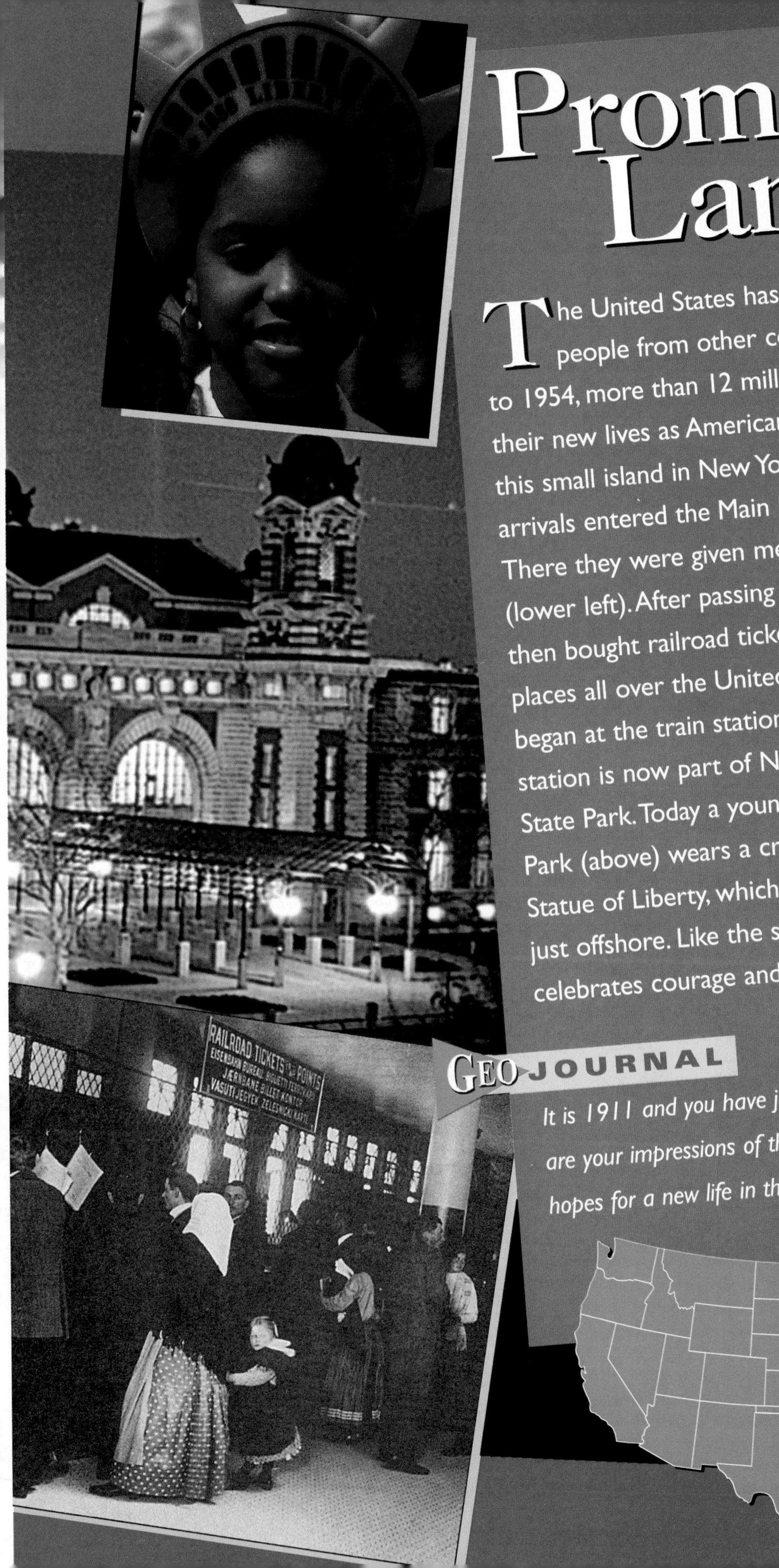


# Promised Land

The United States has always welcomed people from other countries. From 1892 to 1954, more than 12 million people began their new lives as Americans at Ellis Island. On this small island in New York Harbor, the new arrivals entered the Main Building (background). There they were given medical and other tests (lower left). After passing the tests, many people then bought railroad tickets (lower right) to places all over the United States. Many trips began at the train station in Jersey City. The station is now part of New Jersey's Liberty State Park. Today a young visitor to Liberty State Park (above) wears a crown like that of the Statue of Liberty, which stands in the harbor just offshore. Like the statue itself, the park celebrates courage and opportunity.

**GEO JOURNAL**

*It is 1911 and you have just arrived at Ellis Island. What are your impressions of this busy depot? What are your hopes for a new life in the United States?*

CHAPTER 6

# Building the Garden State

## THINKING ABOUT GEOGRAPHY AND HISTORY

New Jersey was now part of the new, independent country of the United States. What would happen next? The people of this young state faced many challenges. How could new roads and waterways be built? How would women and African Americans gain the same freedoms as white men? How would factories begin to replace farms across our state? Read on to learn how New Jerseyans began to meet these challenges.

**1787**

**BURLINGTON**

**John Fitch launches the first steamboat.**

**1791**

**PATERSON**

**Alexander Hamilton helps found the first planned industrial city in the United States.**

**1825**

**HOBOKEN**

**John Stevens demonstrates the first railroad in the United States.**

1780 1800 1820

See pT48 for Chapter Organizer.

1780 1787 1834 1840 1860

See p. T49 for Lesson Teaching Strategies.

# Changes in a New State

## Read Aloud

*On May 12, 1825, the first locomotive in the United States set off on a trial run. A reporter for the* New York Evening Post *wrote, "It traveled around the circle of the Hoboken Hotel... at the rate of about six miles an hour." From this simple beginning, a new form of transportation was born. New Jersey was on the move.*

## Focus Activity

**READ TO LEARN**

***How did people and goods move across New Jersey in the early 1800s?***

**VOCABULARY**

- charter
- toll
- turnpike
- canal
- monopoly
- Joint Companies

**PEOPLE**

- John Fitch
- John Stevens

**PLACES**

- Bordentown

## THE BIG PICTURE

After the American Revolution, the United States grew quickly. Between 1790 and 1830, our country's population rose from about 4 million people to almost 13 million. New Jersey also grew, but not as fast. Its population rose by only 137,000 people from 1790 to 1830. In contrast, Ohio, which was not even a state until 1803, added more than 900,000 people.

During this time, New Jersey's economy remained mostly agricultural. Most people lived and worked on farms. In the north, farmers shipped their crops to New York City. In the south, they sent their crops to Philadelphia. By the early 1800s, those cities were two of the main ports in the United States. Located right in the middle, New Jersey was an important link between the two cities.

## SLOW TRANSPORTATION

Moving goods and people around New Jersey was not easy. In the late 1700s and early 1800s, there were no cars, buses, or trains. These forms of transportation had not yet been invented. Instead, most people walked wherever they needed to go. Others traveled by horse, carriage, or boat.

### Rough Roads for Travel

Roads in New Jersey also made travel difficult. One problem was that some areas did not have roads at all. Hills or swamps, for example, made it difficult to build roads. In other places, rivers or streams blocked the way.

Areas that did have roads faced other problems. The roads were often in awful shape. In the winter, ice could make them dangerous. In the spring, they became muddy. In the summer, they were full of deep ruts.

Poor roads made getting around difficult. Henry Wansey, a visitor from England, traveled across New Jersey by stagecoach in 1796. He wrote that the road between Trenton and New Brunswick was full of "loose stones and deep holes, in going over which, we were so violently shook, that when we got down, many of us could scarcely stand."

Bad roads also made travel slow. For example, in 1750 the trip across New Jersey from New York City to Philadelphia took two days. A new road made the trip shorter, but by the early 1800s it still took about 12 hours. Today, that trip takes about two hours!

NEWARK AND
ELIZABETH TOWN
LINE OF STAGES.

THE subscriber informs his friends and the public in general, that he is running a LINE OF STAGES between the above places:—Leaves Elizabeth Town every day at 8 and 1 o'clock, and leaves Newark at half past 10 and 5 o'clock. This line will run to meet the Morristown, Rahway, and Somerville lines of Stages to and from ElizabethTown, every day. Passengers will be called for or put down at their own dwellings, by leaving their names at Roff's & Drake's Hotels in Newark, and at David Sanderson's Hotel in Elizabeth Town.
AARON BENNET, Agent.
july 2 tf

**Bad roads and bad weather (below) made travel by stagecoach slow. Many companies advertised their routes in newspapers (right).**

## ON THE MOVE

Why was transportation so bad? Today most roads are built and taken care of by governments. In the early 1800s, governments did not collect taxes to build and repair bridges and roadways. Instead, they granted a charter to a person or company. A charter is an official document giving a person permission to do something. Charters gave people permission to build and run a road or a bridge as a business.

### Bridges and Roads

In the 1790s, the New Jersey legislature granted charters for the building of bridges over several rivers. However, the charter did not provide money to cover the costs. Instead, companies were allowed to charge a fee, or toll, from the people who crossed the bridge. Tolls helped pay for building and repair. The largest bridge chartered at this time was over the Delaware River at Trenton in 1798.

Charters were also used to build turnpikes in our state. Turnpikes are a kind of toll road. They got their name from the pole, or pike, that was used to stop travelers until they paid a toll. When travelers paid their toll, the pike was turned, allowing them to go on their way.

Between 1801 and 1829, 51 new turnpike companies were chartered in New Jersey. About 550 miles of toll roadways were created. The map on this page shows some of the important turnpikes and bridges built at this time.

**MAP WORK: 1.** the Morris Turnpike

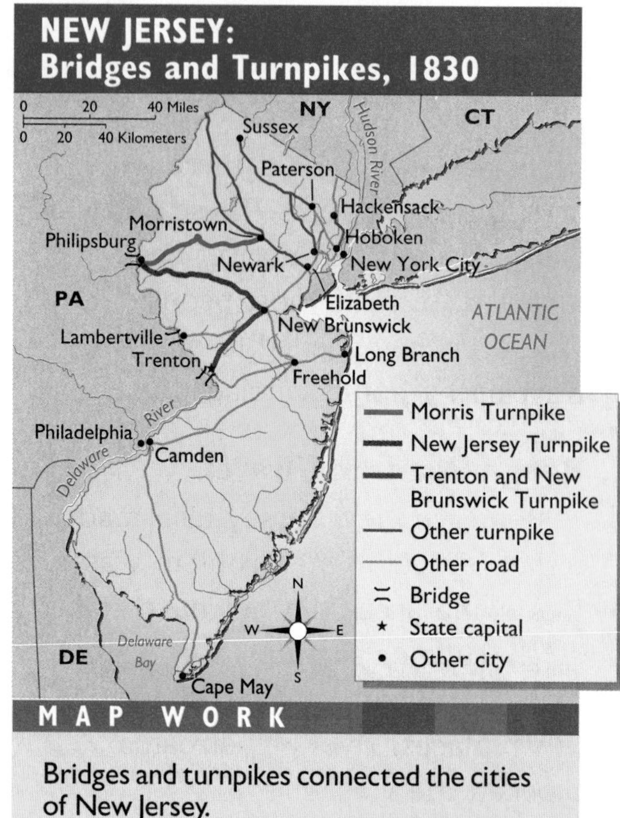


**MAP WORK**

Bridges and turnpikes connected the cities of New Jersey.

1. Which turnpike ran from Philipsburg to Morristown?

### New Water Routes

New Jersey also created canals in the late 1820s and 1830s. A canal is an inland waterway built by people for transportation. Canals usually connect other bodies of water.

Two large canals were built in our state. The Morris Canal was started in 1825. Six years later, the first boats passed along it. More than 100 miles long, the canal brought coal from mines in Pennsylvania to New Jersey factories. Part of the Delaware and Raritan Canal connected New Brunswick and Trenton. It was about 40 miles long. People compared this canal to a belt running across the "waist" of New Jersey.

# Infographic

**interNET CONNECTION** Visit our website: www.mhschool.com

## THE MORRIS CANAL

**The Morris Canal was one of the two major canals of New Jersey. It was located in the north. The Delaware and Raritan Canal crossed the middle of the state. Both canals were completed in the 1830s.**

## CANAL BOATS

"Section" or "hinge" boats were the type of boat used most often on the Morris Canal. They were made of two boats connected with a hinge. They were pulled by teams of mules and could carry up to 60 tons of cargo.

## HOW A LOCK WORKS

A canal lock is a kind of water elevator that moves boats to higher or lower levels. The diagram below shows how a lock works.

Higher level

Closed lock

Lock gates being opened

Lower level

Mules tow boats along canal

Canal towpath

## CONSTRUCTION FACTS

- **Most canal workers were Irish immigrants. They worked sunup to sundown, six days a week.**
- **Pay was good and housing was provided.**
- **Work was dangerous. Cave-ins or flying boulders blasted loose by dynamite sometimes killed or injured workers.**

Morris Canal Cargo in Peak Year (1866)

*bar and pig iron, brick, sand, flour, lumber

**Links to READING**

**Since they first appeared in the United States, railroads have been the subject of many poems and songs. One early example was written by John Pierpont, the grandfather of the famous banker J.P. Morgan. Pierpont expressed sadness at the change from horsepower to steampower:**

> ***We hear no more the clanging hoof,***
> ***And the stage-coach rattling by,***
> ***For the steam-king [railroad] rules the traveled world,***
> ***And the old pike's left to die.***

**In your school library, find some examples of poems or songs about railroads, such as "Casey Jones" and "Wabash Cannonball." Then write a railroad poem of your own.**

## STEAM POWER

For a long time, humans or animals provided the power for transportation. The final years of the 1700s brought a new kind of power: the power of steam.

### Dreams of Steam

John Fitch, who lived in Trenton, launched the first steamboat in the country at the Constitutional Convention in Philadelphia in 1787. Unfortunately, there was little interest in this new form of transportation.

Fitch's invention did manage to catch the attention of Colonel John Stevens of Hoboken. In 1808 Stevens launched his steamboat, the *Phoenix*. He hoped to use the *Phoenix* to carry goods and people along the Hudson River. However, Robert Fulton already had a steamboat running on the Hudson. His boat the *Clermont* was a big success. That is why Fulton, not Fitch, became known as the inventor of the steamboat.

Fulton's company had a monopoly on the steamboat trade in New York waters. A monopoly is a business that has total control of one kind of good or one kind of service. Fulton's monopoly kept Stevens from operating in New York.

### Railpower

Beaten on the water, Stevens turned to the land. In 1814 he walked across the entire state from Lower Landing near New Brunswick to Trenton. Stevens did this to plan a route for a railroad.

The state legislature gave Stevens a railroad charter in 1815. In 1825 he ran the first American locomotive on a track he built himself. You read about this event in the Read Aloud.

It was hard for Stevens to get people to support his ideas. Many still thought canals were the best way to transport goods. Also, canal owners were trying to stop railroads from

See p. T49 for Answers to Think About It.

being built. They feared that railroads would take away canal traffic.

Robert Stevens, John's son, continued his father's work. In 1830 the state legislature granted Robert Stevens a charter for the Camden and Amboy Railroad. The next year, in Mile Hollow at Bordentown, Stevens showed off his locomotive, the *John Bull.* Many important people came to ride the train that day. They were amazed at the high speed of 30 miles an hour. In 1833 the *John Bull* began making regular trips. It ran from Bordentown to South Amboy.

By 1834 Stevens and his workers finished building the railroad. It now ran from South Amboy all the way to Camden. That was part of the same route as the Delaware and Raritan Canal. The canal owners decided to come to an agreement with Stevens. The two businesses were combined as the Joint Companies.

As more lines were built, railroads brought several changes to our state. Towns and cities developed along the tracks. Also, the economy began to shift from farms to factories. New Jersey was truly on the move.

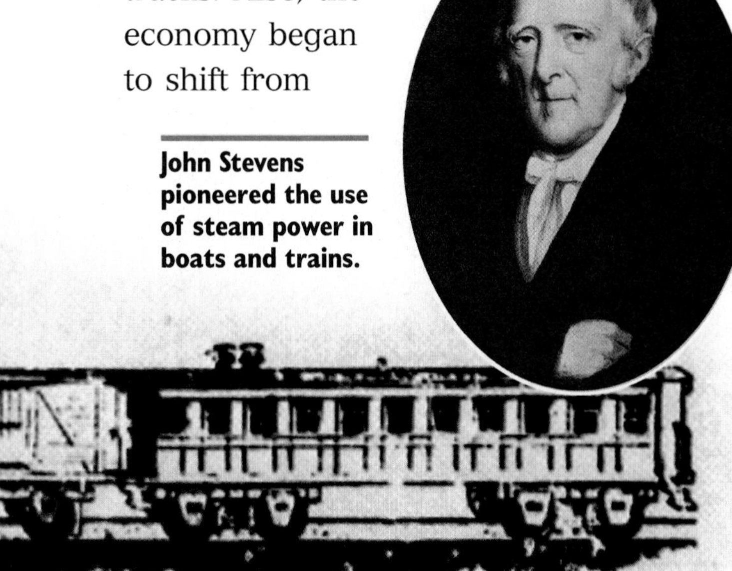

**John Stevens pioneered the use of steam power in boats and trains.**

## WHY IT MATTERS

New methods of transportation in the early 1800s changed the way that people lived, worked, and moved from one place to another. Today New Jersey's transportation routes link the state to the rest of the country and the world.

### Reviewing Facts and Ideas

#### MAIN IDEAS

- New bridges and turnpikes improved transportation in New Jersey.
- Canals provided a water link between cities and brought coal from Pennsylvania.
- John Fitch built the country's first steamboat in New Jersey.
- Railroads came into use in the 1830s and soon controlled transportation in our state.

#### THINK ABOUT IT

1. Why was travel in New Jersey difficult in the early 1800s?
2. What is a monopoly?
3. **FOCUS** Name three new ways people traveled in New Jersey in the early 1800s.
4. **THINKING SKILL** Place the following events in the correct sequence: John Stevens builds the first American locomotive; John Fitch launches his steamboat in Philadelphia; the *John Bull* begins regular trips.
5. **GEOGRAPHY** How was New Jersey a crossroads in the early 1800s?

See p. T50 for Skill Teaching Strategies.

# Using Map Scales

**VOCABULARY**

scale

## WHY THE SKILL MATTERS

Imagine that you live in Trenton in 1850 and hope to travel by railroad to New Brunswick to visit your aunt. This is your first train trip, and you want to find out how far away these cities are. How can you discover this? A scale on a map can tell you the answer. Scale is the relationship between the distance shown on a map and the real distance on Earth.

A map has a scale because it is not the same size as the area it shows. By reading a map scale, you can figure out how far apart places are. This will help you plan travel time.

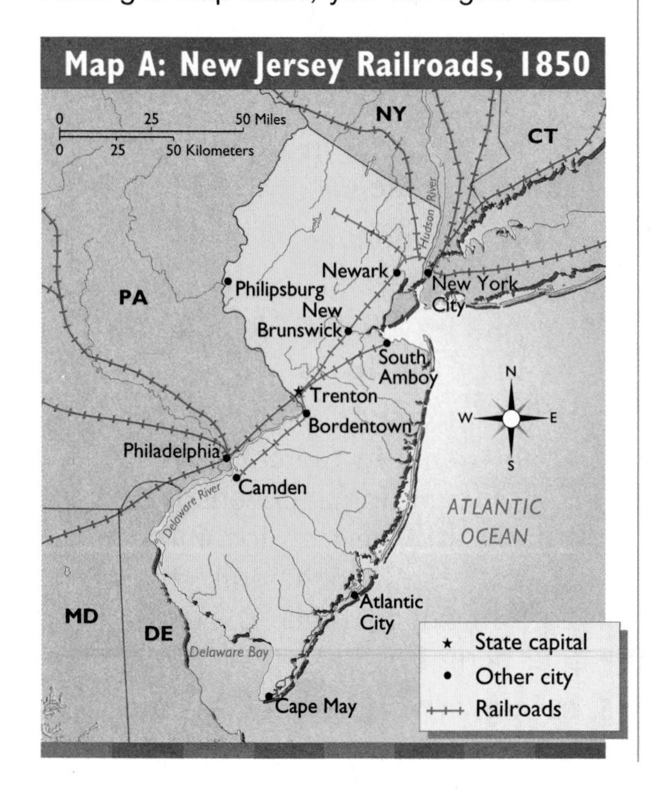


Look at Map A on this page. Then look at Map B on page 147. The two maps have different scales. Why are the maps here drawn to different scales? Some maps need to show a lot of details, such as buildings and streets. In order to include these details, the map cannot show a large area. A map with fewer details can show a much bigger area. Different size areas need different scales.

## USING THE SKILL

Look at Map A of New Jersey Railroads in 1850. Find the map scale. The top line tells how many miles on Earth are shown by one inch on the map. One inch stands for 50 miles. The bottom line tells how many kilometers on Earth are shown by one and one-half centimeters.

Suppose you wanted to measure the distance from Newark, New Jersey, to Philadelphia, Pennsylvania. You could guess by looking at the map scale, but you could make a more accurate measurement using a scale strip.

Use the scale on Map A to make a scale strip. Place a piece of paper below the scale and mark the distances. Move the paper along and continue marking distances. Your scale strip should look like this:

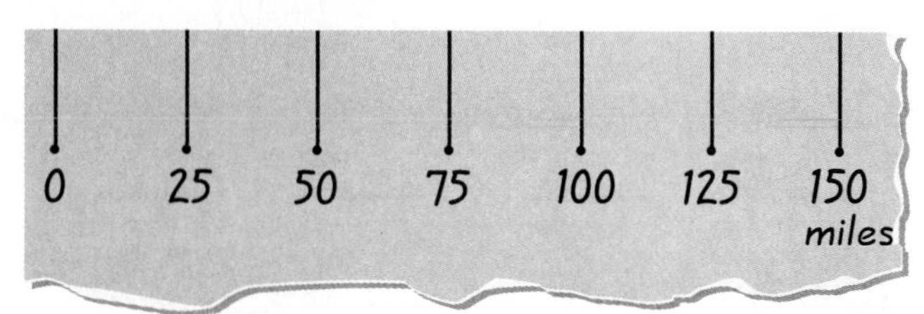

*100 miles; about 2 inches
**Map B; Map A
***about 200 miles; about 320 kilometers

See p. T50 for Answers to Reviewing the Skill.

Place the edge of the scale strip on the symbols for the two cities. Make sure the zero is lined up with the symbol for Newark. Then read the number closest to Philadelphia. You can see that the distance is about 75 miles. How far is Cape May from South Amboy? What is the distance in inches on the map?*

**Helping yourself**

- **Different scales allow maps to show either more detail or a larger area.**
- **Study the scale on the map.**
- **You can make a scale strip to find out the real distance between points on a map.**

### TRYING THE SKILL

Now look at Map B: Northeast Railroads, 1850. This map shows some of the same area of land as Map A. As you can see, however, the areas are different sizes. If you compare the two scales, you will see that they are different. On which map does one inch stand for a greater distance? Which map shows more detail? Use the Helping Yourself box for hints.**

Make a scale strip for Map B following the example on page 146. Using your scale strip, measure the distance between Trenton and Albany, New York. What is the distance in miles? What is the distance in kilometers?***

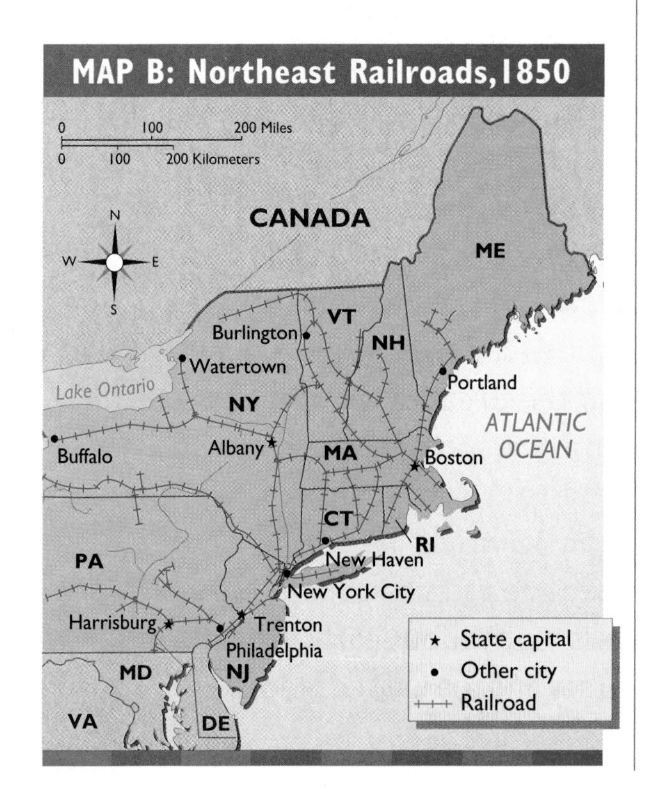


### REVIEWING THE SKILL

1. What is a scale on a map?
2. Why is it helpful to use a scale strip?
3. Which map would you use to find the distance between Camden and Atlantic City? What is the distance between the two cities in miles? What is the distance in kilometers?
4. What information is shown on Map A that is not shown on Map B?
5. When might it be helpful to use maps drawn to different scales?

LESSON 2

1780 1787 1850 1860

See p. T51 for Lesson Teaching Strategies.

# The First Factory Town

## Read Aloud

*In 1778 George Washington traveled with aides through New Jersey. They stopped for lunch at the Great Falls of the Passaic River. Alexander Hamilton, one of Washington's aides, gazed up in wonder at the power of the falls. With great force, the water plunged 70 feet between rocky cliffs. Thirteen years later, Hamilton had a vision of a city powered by rushing water. Paterson, New Jersey, would become that city.*

## Focus Activity

**READ TO LEARN**

***How did the city of Paterson change the way people lived and worked in New Jersey?***

**VOCABULARY**

- manufacturing
- War of 1812
- strike

**PEOPLE**

- Alexander Hamilton
- John Colt

**PLACES**

- Paterson
- Weehawken

## THE BIG PICTURE

In 1789 **Alexander Hamilton** held an important job in the United States government. He believed that for our country to grow strong, it had to develop **manufacturing**. Manufacturing means making large amounts of goods in factories.

One of Hamilton's ideas was to build a planned city. He suggested New York, Pennsylvania, or New Jersey as possible locations for the city. Seven hundred acres of land near the Great Falls of the Passaic River was chosen as the spot. The new city was called **Paterson**, after William Paterson, New Jersey's governor. It would be a long time before this city became a success. But the story of its growth tells much about early manufacturing in New Jersey and the United States.

## A CITY BY THE FALLS

Alexander Hamilton believed that government had to take the lead in building the economy. New Jersey's leaders agreed. You have already read how they encouraged economic growth by chartering bridges and turnpikes. They also worked to build industry.

In November of 1791, Governor William Paterson signed a charter to found the Society for Establishing Useful Manufactures, or S.U.M. The purpose of S.U.M. was to develop manufacturing. Paterson was to be S.U.M.'s first factory town.

The Society worked out a special deal with the state legislature. S.U.M. was given almost a monopoly on manufacturing in Paterson and would pay no taxes. It was given control of the waters of the entire Passaic River, including the power of the mighty falls. In fact, S.U.M. was the real government in the city.

In 1793 S.U.M. built a cotton mill in Paterson. By the following year, the population had shot up from about 50 people to about 500 people. Even with government help, however, manufacturing had a shaky start. The mill failed in 1797, and soon there were only about 50 people living in Paterson again. The city later came back to life when new factories were built.

Alexander Hamilton did not live to see this success. For years, Hamilton and Aaron Burr, the Vice President of the United States, had been enemies. On July 11, 1804, they fought a duel at Weehawken. Burr shot Hamilton, who died the next day.

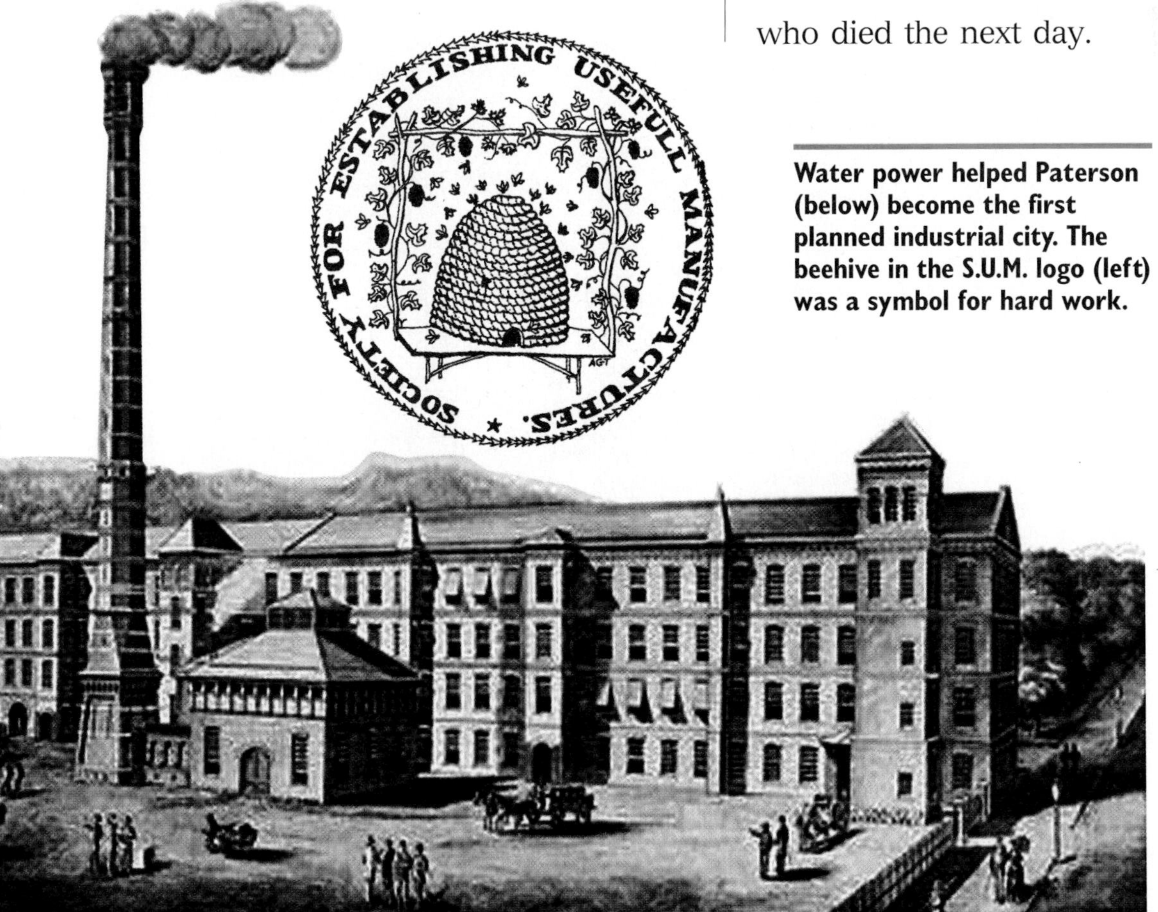


**Water power helped Paterson (below) become the first planned industrial city. The beehive in the S.U.M. logo (left) was a symbol for hard work.**

## PATERSON TAKES OFF

In 1812, war broke out between the United States and Great Britain. This conflict is known as the War of 1812, though it lasted until 1815. During the war, British ships prevented European goods, such as cotton cloth, from reaching American ports.

### Made by Machine

During this time, industry was growing in Paterson. Many factories and smaller shops had opened. By 1814 the population had reached about 1,500 people. The town was on its feet and could manufacture supplies for the war.

John Colt convinced the United States Navy to use cotton cloth for its ships' sails instead of linen. Colt also convinced them that Paterson could make the fabric. Its cotton mills began to turn out yards and yards of cloth. The town became known for cotton cloth manufacturing.

The diagram on this page shows the steps in producing cotton cloth. The first cotton factories performed all of these tasks in one place. Paterson would become even more famous for manufacturing a different cloth, silk. In 1838 Christopher Colt, John's brother, made the first silk manufactured in town. Other mill owners followed. Soon Paterson was known as "Silk City." By 1860, its population had grown to almost 20,000.

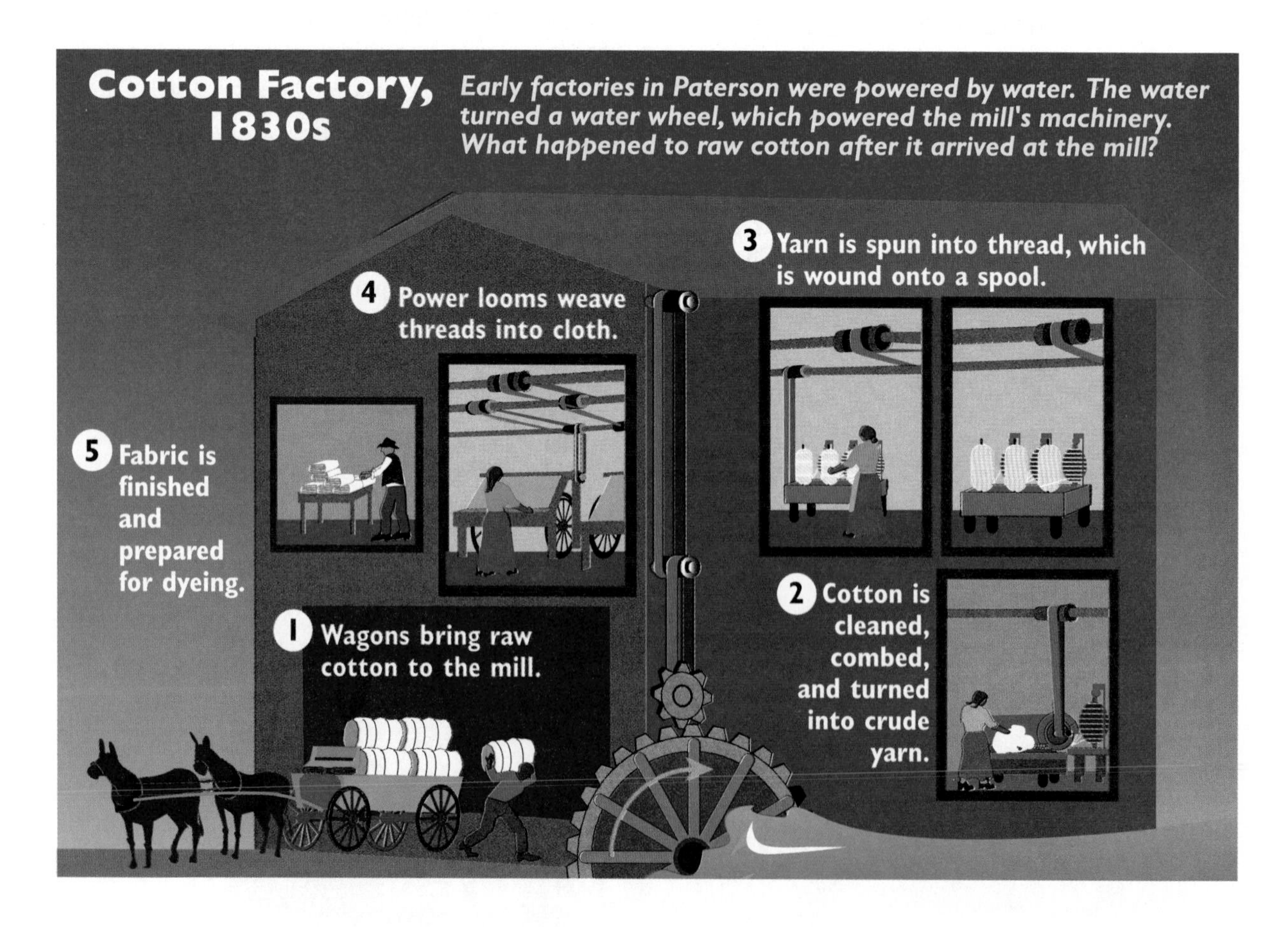


**Cotton Factory, 1830s** *Early factories in Paterson were powered by water. The water turned a water wheel, which powered the mill's machinery. What happened to raw cotton after it arrived at the mill?*

See p. T51 for Answers to Think About It.

## Factory Towns

Industry developed in other cities in New Jersey as well. Great iron mills were built in Trenton. Factories in Jersey City and the southern part of our state produced glass. By 1850, paper mills near Paterson, Whippany, Millburn, and Trenton made New Jersey an important paper-producing state. Orange was known for manufacturing fine hats.

What was good for business, however, was not always good for workers. They had to work long hours. In Paterson the S.U.M. owned everything in the town, and the people could not even vote for a town government.

In the summer of 1828 the Paterson factory owners tried to change workers' lunch hour from 12 o'clock to 1 o'clock. As a result, many child workers, some younger than 12, went on strike. A strike happens when all the workers in a business refuse to work until the owners meet their demands. One observer said, "The children would not stand for it, for fear if they agreed to this, the next thing would be to deprive them of eating at all." Many other workers joined the strike to support the children. When the owners agreed to keep the 12 o'clock lunch hour, the strike ended.

As industry grew in Paterson and throughout New Jersey, many workers went on strike for shorter work days, better pay, and safer working conditions. Often the strikes failed. However, workers continued to band together and gradually improved their conditions.

**Today you can visit the Paterson historic district and tour the old factories.**

## WHY IT MATTERS

Alexander Hamilton's plans for Paterson came true in some ways. Today Paterson is called the "cradle of American industry." Manufacturing became an important part of New Jersey's economy—and still is today.

### Reviewing Facts and Ideas

#### MAIN IDEAS

- The Great Falls of the Passaic River provided power to run factory machines.
- Paterson became a center for making cotton cloth and silk.
- Factory work was hard, and workers struggled to gain rights.

#### THINK ABOUT IT

1. Who founded Paterson?
2. What is manufacturing?
3. **FOCUS** Name two ways Paterson changed the way people lived and worked in New Jersey in the 1800s.
4. **THINKING SKILL** Name one *cause* and one *effect* of factories coming to Paterson.
5. **GEOGRAPHY** What natural resources made Paterson a good location for a factory city? Why?

# Study Skills

See p. T52 for Skill Teaching Strategies.

## Reading Circle and Line Graphs

**VOCABULARY**

graph
circle graph
line graph

### WHY THE SKILL MATTERS

In the last lesson you read about the growth of industry in New Jersey in the years after the American Revolution. One way to understand this growth is to read a graph. Graphs are special diagrams that show a lot of information in a clear way. They can help you make conclusions. By presenting facts in a picture, they tell you a lot with only a few words.

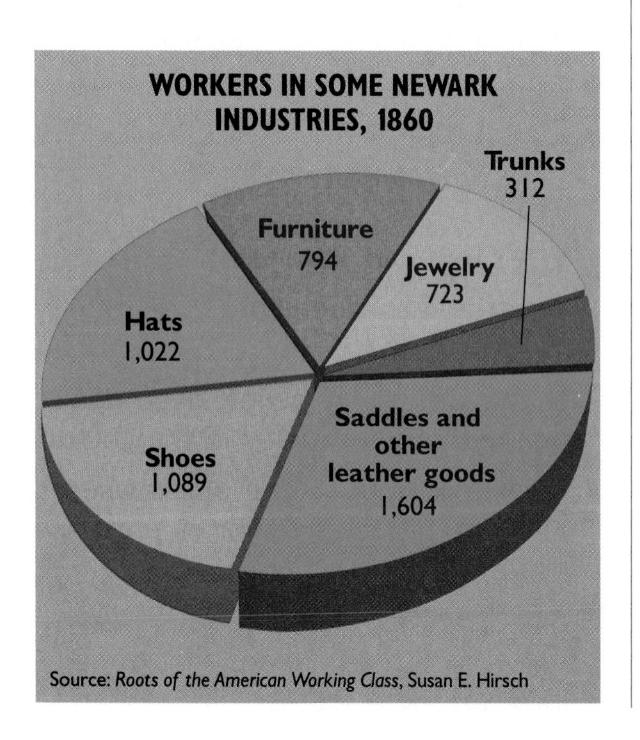


### USING A CIRCLE GRAPH

Look at the graph on this page. It is a circle graph. This kind of graph can show you how the parts of something make up or fit into the whole. Because each part may look like a slice of pie, a circle graph is sometimes called a pie graph or pie chart.

Read the title of the graph. The circle graph shows the number of workers in several Newark industries in 1860.

The "slices" show the number of workers in each industry. You can tell that the largest number of workers made saddles and other leather goods because this is the largest "slice" on the graph.

### USING A LINE GRAPH

Unlike a circle graph, a line graph shows you how a piece of information changes with time. A line graph often shows an increase or decrease in number over time.

Look at the line graph on page 153. Start by reading the title. The title tells you that this is a graph that shows the number of people who lived in Newark in the years 1820 to 1860.

Read the label at the left side of the graph. This gives you the number of people. The dates at the bottom of the graph tell you the years during which the population was measured.

Trace the line with your finger. Each dot on the line stands for the number of people who were living in Newark during a particular year. As you can see, the population of Newark was smallest in 1820.

*shoes; trunks
**10,953; 71,941

See p. T52 for Answers to Reviewing the Skill.

### TRYING THE SKILL

Look again at the circle graph of Workers in some Newark Industries in 1860. What industry had the second-highest number of workers in Newark? What industry had the smallest number? Use the Helping yourself box for hints.*

Now look at the line graph of the population of Newark from 1820 to 1860. How many people lived in Newark in the year 1830? How many lived in that city in 1860?**

### Helping yourself

- **Circle graphs show you how the parts fit into the whole.**
- **Line graphs show how a piece of information changes over time.**
- **Study the title, key, and labels.**
- **Use the graphs to compare facts or figures.**

### REVIEWING THE SKILL

1. Did more people work in Newark's furniture industry or its leather-making industry? How did you get your answer?
2. What can you conclude from the line graph about the number of people in Newark between 1820 and 1860?
3. How do line and circle graphs differ? How do graphs make it easier for you to understand information?

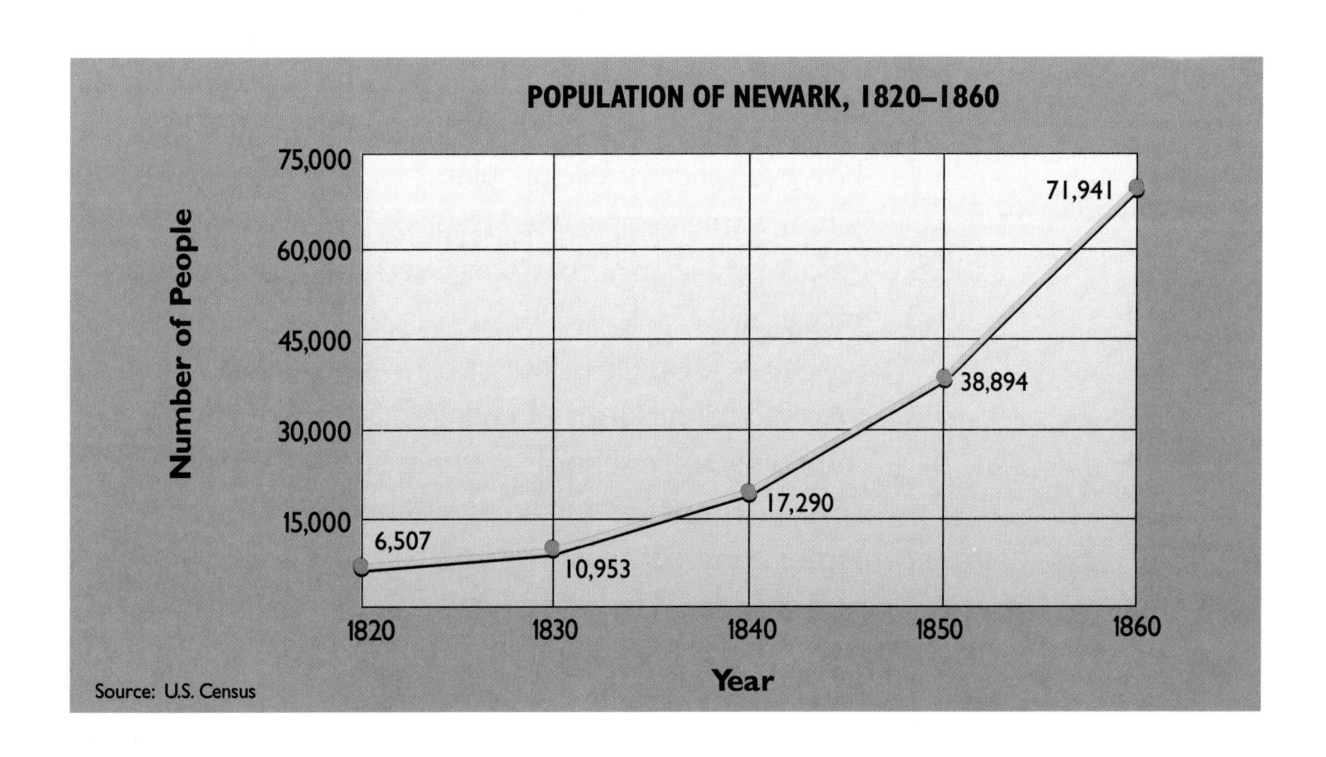

LESSON 3

1780 1800 1807 1845 1860

See p. T53 for Lesson Teaching Strategies.

# Working for a Better Life

## Focus Activity

**READ TO LEARN**

***How did people work to improve life for others in New Jersey?***

**VOCABULARY**

- reform
- suffrage

**PEOPLE**

- Lucy Stone
- Dorothea Dix

### Read Aloud

*In 1838 a group of New Jersey leaders worked to improve public schools. They asked the people to help cover the costs. "Tax yourselves for the support of common schools.... Look to your schoolhouses. See that... they are comfortable; that they are neat and tasteful. Look to the teachers. See that they are... well treated and well remunerated* [paid]."

### THE BIG PICTURE

New Jersey's transportation routes and industries brought new people to the state. The population of its cities swelled. As the strikes in Paterson had shown, however, there were problems to be solved. In New Jersey, some people tried to bring about **reforms**. A reform is a change to make government or business more fair.

The reformers of our state were people who worked for all kinds of changes. Some fought to improve public schools. Others spoke out for rights for all Americans, including women and African Americans. Some wanted to help the poor, the sick, and children. The reformers' efforts helped make New Jersey better for all its people.

## NEW PEOPLE AND NEW LAWS

From about 1820 to 1860, many immigrants came to the United States. Many of these immigrants came from England, Ireland, and Germany. New Jersey had a lot of jobs to offer, so many immigrants settled here. The graph on this page shows how New Jersey's population grew.

Not all of the people who lived in New Jersey had the same rights. State laws about who could vote changed several times. In 1776 the state constitution allowed any citizen with a certain amount of property to vote, including women and African American men. In the 1790s some women took part in elections, but few African Americans voted. Then, in 1807, the legislature passed a new law. It said that only free, white, adult males who paid a state tax could vote.

In 1844 New Jersey held a Constitutional Convention to improve the state constitution. The new constitution allowed any white male over the age of 21 who had lived in the state for one year to vote. However, all women and African American men were still unable to vote.

Some women became part of a growing suffrage movement. Suffrage means the right to vote. Lucy Stone was an important leader in the struggle for women's rights. In addition to suffrage, she also struggled for women's equality in jobs and education. After she moved to Orange in 1857, she refused to pay her taxes. Here is part of a letter she wrote explaining her reasons. Do you think she expected her protest to be successful?

**Excerpt from a letter from Lucy Stone to the tax collector of Orange, New Jersey, 1858.**

*Enclosed I return my tax bill, without paying it. My reason for doing so is that women suffer taxation and yet have no representation, which is not only unjust to one half of the adult population, but is contrary to* [against] *our theory of government. . . .*

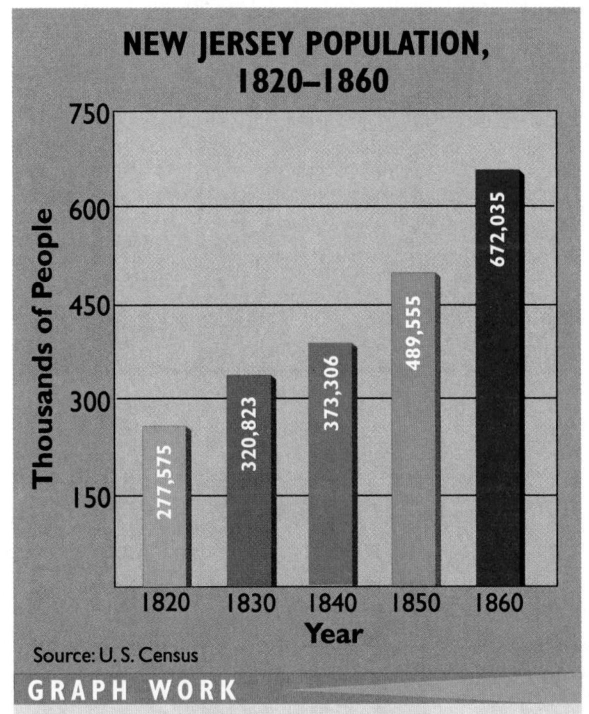


Source: U. S. Census

**GRAPH WORK**

Immigration to New Jersey began to increase after 1840.

1. During which years shown on the graph did our state's population grow fastest?

**GRAPH WORK: 1.** Between 1850 and 1860

## NEW SCHOOLS AND HOSPITALS

Some New Jersey reformers worked to create free public schools. Others hoped to improve care for mentally ill people.

### School Days in New Jersey

In the 1820s, there were no public schools in New Jersey. Wealthy children received an education. They attended private schools. By law, poor children also received some schooling. However, many children did not go to school at all.

The idea for founding public schools gained support. The schools would be paid for by state funds. As you read in the Read Aloud, state leaders later asked the people to contribute with taxes.

In 1836 the city of Newark opened free public schools. Jersey City and Paterson soon followed. By 1871 education was free all over the state.

### Dorothea Dix

In the 1800s mentally ill people were often sent to prison. There were few hospitals to care for them properly. These unfortunate conditions came to the attention of **Dorothea Dix**. Dix was a reformer who helped mentally ill people in her home state of Massachusetts. She decided to come to New Jersey to bring about changes here.

For eight weeks in 1844, Dix visited prisons, poorhouses, and other places where mentally ill people stayed. Conditions were terrible. For example, Dix found that in Newark, men, women, and children who were mentally ill were locked up with those who were well. In one poorhouse, she saw a man in chains. In another, people with mental illnesses were kept in a filthy basement.

**How does this early classroom (below) compare to yours? Dorothea Dix (right) worked to reform hospitals.**

On January 23, 1845, Dix gave a report to the New Jersey legislature. She said, "I come to ask justice . . . for those who [cannot plead] their own course." The lawmakers acted quickly. They immediately set aside $150,000 to build the New Jersey State Asylum in Ewing Township. People with mental illnesses would be cared for with respect in the asylum.

Due to the efforts of reformers, New Jersey made important changes. However, more work needed to be done. Some African Americans in New Jersey and many throughout the United States remained enslaved. In the next chapter, you will read about the fight to end slavery and bring freedom to all people.

### DID YOU KNOW?

**What were schools like in the early 1800s?**

**Schools in the 1800s were very different from those you attend. Children of all ages shared the same classroom. Older students helped the younger ones with the main subjects—reading, writing, spelling, and arithmetic. The school year was short because children had to help out in shops and on farms. In fact, the school calendar used today was designed to let children be away from school during the busy planting and harvesting seasons. That's why you have a summer vacation.**

CLOSED FOR HARVEST

PUBLIC SCHOOL 43

See p. T53 for Answers to Think About It.

## WHY IT MATTERS

Some of the problems from the 1800s are with us today. Women still struggle for the same rights as men. Americans still argue about the way schools are run. Proper health care for everyone remains a challenge. Fortunately, the reformers taught us that we can make changes if we work together.

## Reviewing Facts and Ideas

### MAIN IDEAS

- New Jersey's laws in the 1800s denied women and African American men the right to vote.
- New Jersey leaders created free public schools.
- Dorothea Dix worked to improve the treatment of people with mental illnesses.

### THINK ABOUT IT

1. What is suffrage?
2. Why were public schools needed in New Jersey in the 1820s?
3. **FOCUS** Name two ways in which New Jersey reformers worked to improve the lives of others in the state.
4. **THINKING SKILL** What *effect* did Dix's report to the legislature have on health care for people with mental illnesses?
5. **WRITE** Imagine that you are a woman who lives in New Jersey in 1855 and you want to vote. Write a letter to the governor explaining why you should have this right.

See p. T54 for Answers to Chapter 6 Review.

# CHAPTER 6 REVIEW

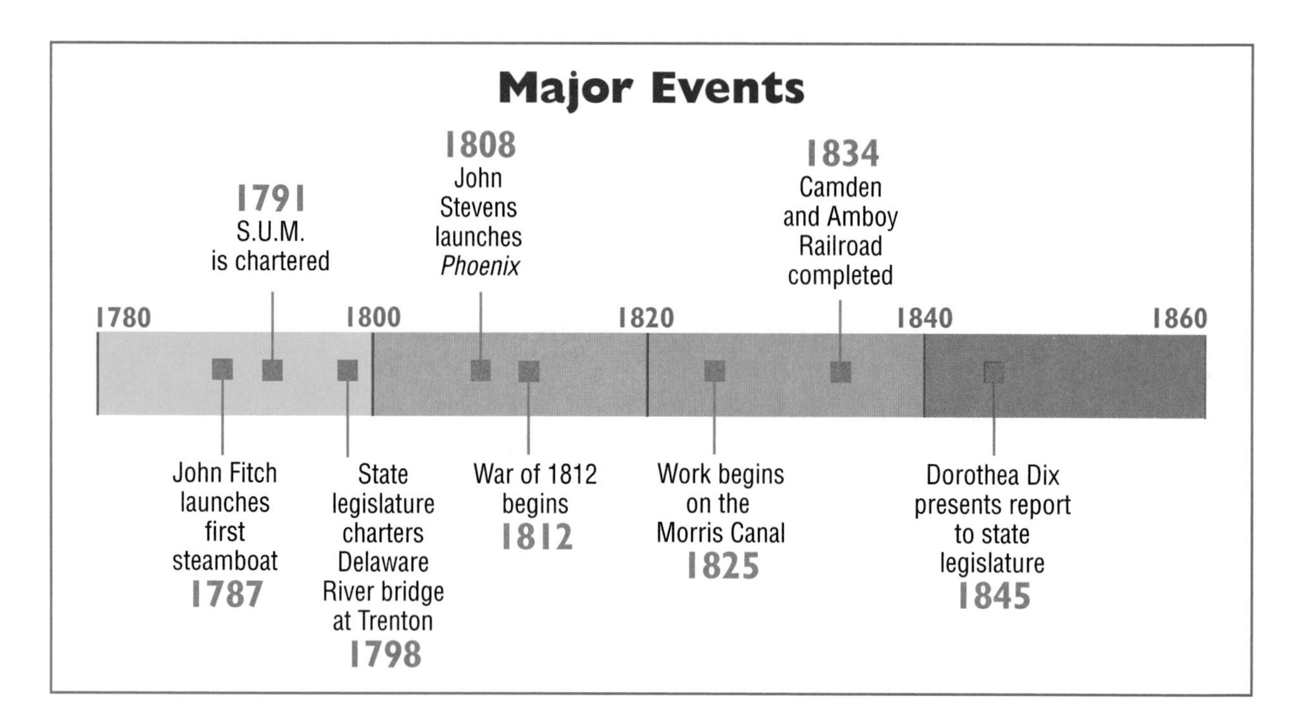


## THINKING ABOUT

### VOCABULARY

Number a sheet of paper from 1 to 5. Next to each number write the word or phrase from the list below that best matches the definition.

canal
suffrage
reform
toll
strike

1. A fee charged for the use of a bridge or road
2. A change to make government or business more fair
3. The right to vote
4. An inland waterway built by people for transportation
5. Refusal to work until demands are met

## THINKING ABOUT FACTS

1. What were the two major canals in New Jersey in the 1830s?
2. What was the purpose of the Society for Establishing Useful Manufactures (S.U.M)?
3. List three goods manufactured in New Jersey in the 1800s.
4. Who was Lucy Stone?
5. What was the result of Dorothea Dix's report on the treatment of the mentally ill in New Jersey?

## THINK AND WRITE

### WRITING A SUMMARY

Write a summary of transportation improvement in New Jersey in the 1800s.

### WRITING AN ADVERTISEMENT

Write an advertisement for Paterson in the 1800s that would tell immigrants why they might want to move there.

### WRITING AN EXPLANATION

Write an explanation of why Dorothea Dix thought there should be changes in the way mentally ill people were treated.

## APPLYING GEOGRAPHY SKILLS

### USING MAP SCALES

Refer to the maps on pages 146 and 147 to answer the following questions.

1. What is a map scale?
2. How does a scale strip help you to measure distances accurately?
3. Use a scale strip to measure the distance between Philipsburg and Newark. About how many miles is it from Camden to Bordentown?
4. Which cities are closer—Boston and Philadelphia, or Burlington and Trenton?
5. Why it is useful to have maps drawn at different scales?

## APPLYING STUDY SKILLS

### READING CIRCLE AND LINE GRAPHS

1. How are circle and line graphs different?
2. Look at the circle graph on page 152. Which industry had about the same number of workers as the hat-making industry?
3. Look at the line graph on page 153. How many people lived in Newark in 1820?
4. Which kind of graph, circle or line, would you use to show how many miles of railroad track were laid in New Jersey from 1835 to 1905?
5. How do graphs make some information easier to understand?

## Summing Up the Chapter

Use the following word maps to organize the information from Chapter 6. Copy the word maps on a sheet of paper. Then write at least one piece of information in each blank circle. When you have filled in the maps, use them to write a paragraph that answers the question "How did New Jersey change in the early 1800s?"

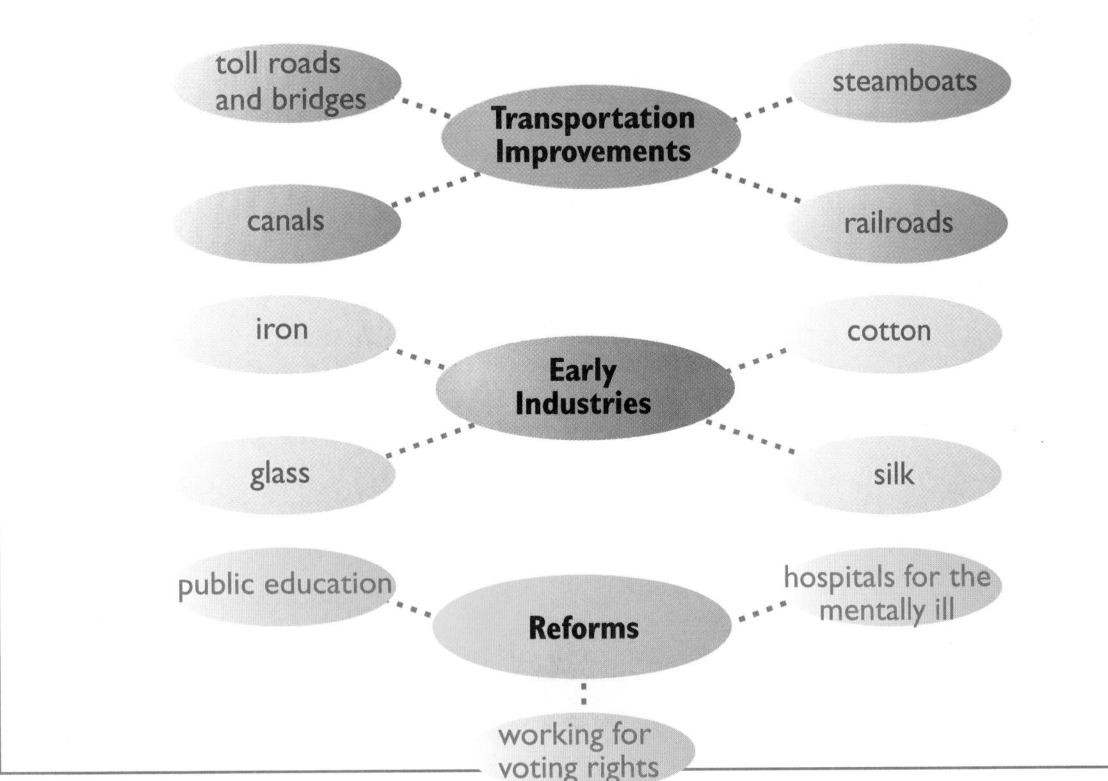


3. about 50 miles; 25 miles 4. Boston and Philadelphia

CHAPTER 7

# Challenge and Growth

## THINKING ABOUT GEOGRAPHY AND HISTORY

The United States was not yet 100 years old, and a terrible war threatened to tear the young nation apart. People in the North and South disagreed about slavery. This disagreement had also divided people in our state for many years. Read on to learn how the war changed life for New Jersey's African Americans. You will also read how industry grew and new immigrants arrived in the years after the war.

**1863**

GETTYSBURG

**Cornelia Hancock nurses Union soldiers wounded at Gettysburg.**

**1870**

PERTH AMBOY

**Thomas M. Peterson is the first African American in New Jersey to vote under the 15th Amendment.**

**1876**

MENLO PARK

**Thomas Edison opens his "invention factory."**

1860 | 1870 | 1880

See pT55 for Chapter Organizer.

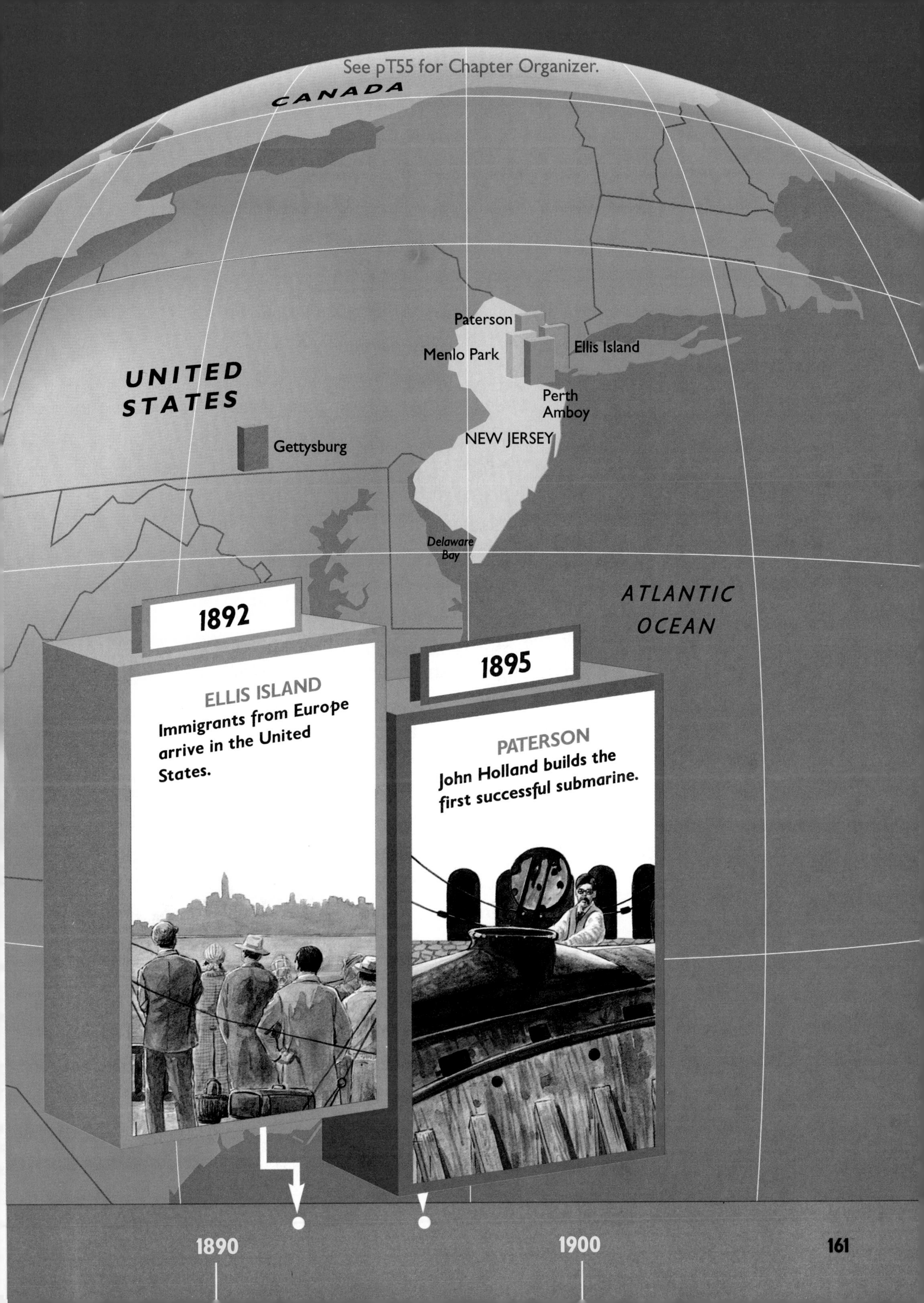

LESSON 1

1800 1860 1875 1900

See p. T56 for Lesson Teaching Strategies.

# A Divided Country

## Focus Activity

**READ TO LEARN**

***How did people in New Jersey work to oppose slavery?***

**VOCABULARY**

- abolition
- Underground Railroad
- Fugitive Slave Act

**PEOPLE**

- John S. Rock
- Angelina Grimké
- Sarah Grimké
- Harriet Tubman
- Charity Still

**PLACES**

- Fort Lee
- Cape May

### Read Aloud

*"I still see before me a life of toil* [hard work] *and trials* [hardships]," *wrote Frederick Douglass. He knew the fight against slavery would be difficult. "But justice must be done, the truth must be told. . . . I will not be silent."*

### THE BIG PICTURE

In the 1840s and 1850s, many people in New Jersey and throughout the country joined Frederick Douglass to call for the **abolition**, or the complete end, of slavery. **John S. Rock** of Salem used the words of the Declaration of Independence to make his case. "You say that all men are created free and equal, and at the same time you deny that equality, which is nothing more nor less than denying our manhood. If we are not free and equal, we are not men."

Disagreements about slavery divided the entire country. Most slaveholders and enslaved African Americans in the United States lived in the South. Most abolitionists lived in the North. Slavery also divided the people of New Jersey. Many New Jerseyans wanted to end slavery, but many also had strong ties to the South. The problem of slavery could not be solved with words—it would take a war.

## FIGHTING SLAVERY

During colonial times, slavery was common in New Jersey. In 1737 there was 1 enslaved person for every 12 free persons in New Jersey. In 1790 New York was the only Northern state that had more enslaved people than New Jersey. However, even in colonial times, some New Jerseyans thought slavery was wrong and worked to end it.

### Abolition, Slow but Sure

In 1786 New Jersey lawmakers passed a law making it illegal to bring any more enslaved persons into the state. In 1788 another New Jersey law made it illegal for a slaveholder to move an enslaved person out of the state without that person's consent.

In 1804 New Jersey lawmakers passed a law that slowly abolished slavery in our state. This law said that all children born to enslaved parents should be free. However, the process was very slow. Boys had to work for their mother's owner until they were 25 years old. Girls had to work until they were 21. Only then would these people be free.

By 1860 there were still 18 enslaved African Americans in New Jersey. There were 25,318 free African Americans. Some of them owned farms or ran stores. Communities of free African Americans began to develop, and many of them built churches and schools.

Many important abolitionists lived in New Jersey. They included **Angelina Grimké** and **Sarah Grimké**, Quaker sisters who were writers and speakers. Angelina married Theodore Weld, also an abolitionist. They moved to **Fort Lee** with Sarah. Here the three wrote a powerful antislavery book, *American Slavery as It Is: Testimony of a Thousand Witnesses.*

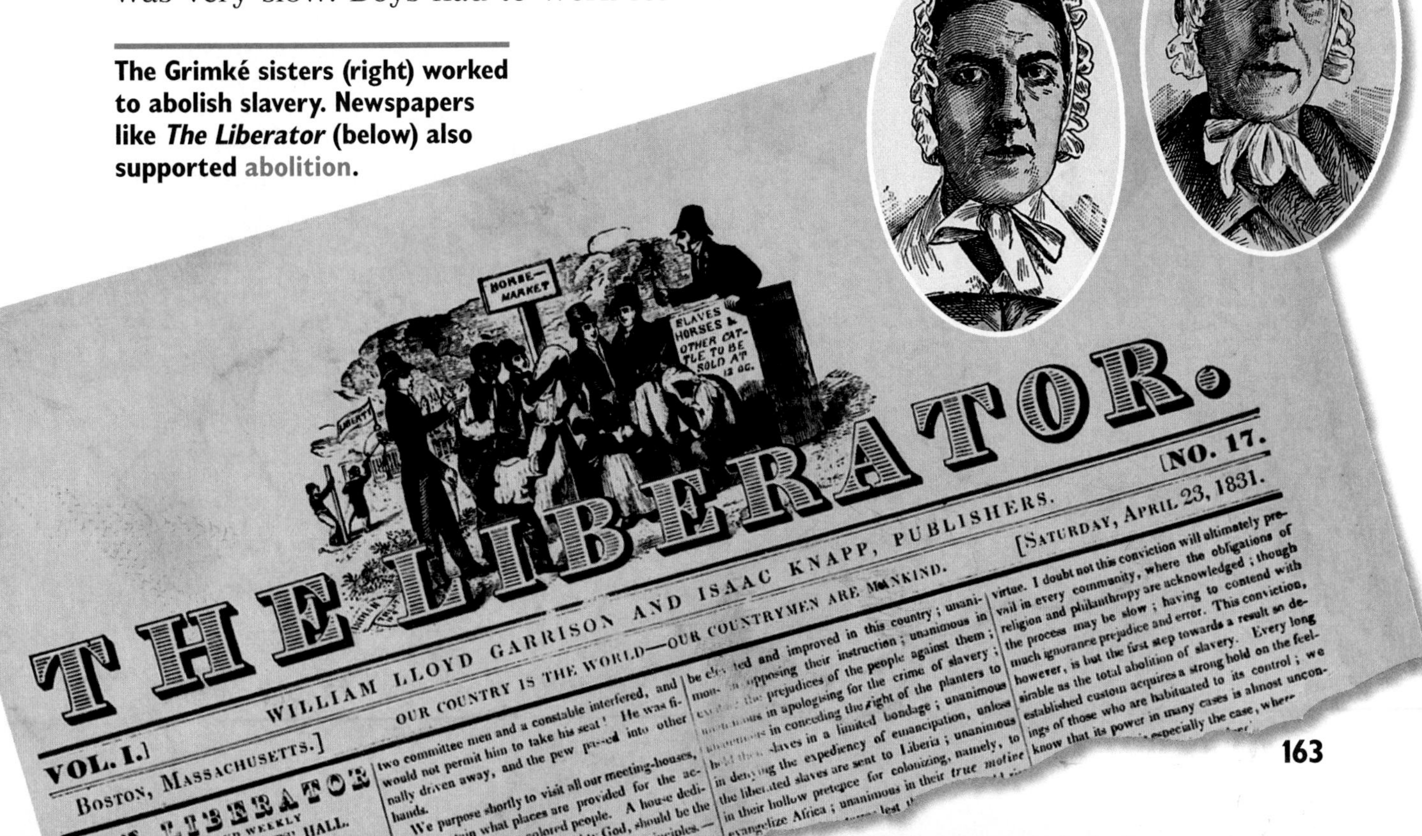
THE LIBERATOR.

WILLIAM LLOYD GARRISON AND ISAAC KNAPP, PUBLISHERS.

VOL. I.] BOSTON, MASSACHUSETTS.] OUR COUNTRY IS THE WORLD—OUR COUNTRYMEN ARE MANKIND. [SATURDAY, APRIL 23, 1831. [NO. 17.

**The Grimké sisters (right) worked to abolish slavery. Newspapers like *The Liberator* (below) also supported abolition.**

## THE UNDERGROUND RAILROAD

Many enslaved African Americans in Southern states sought to escape to free states or to the country of Canada. Starting in the 1830s, some made their way North along what is known as the **Underground Railroad**.

### Path to Freedom

The Underground Railroad was not a tunnel, nor was it a train. It was a community of helpful people, or "conductors," and safe hiding places, or "stations." People who opened up their houses to hide people were called "station masters."

As many as 40,000 people may have escaped slavery by traveling on the Underground Railroad. Take a look at the map on this page. It shows the routes escaping people followed through New Jersey. One of the most famous conductors on the Underground Railroad was **Harriet Tubman**. Tubman, who escaped from slavery herself, worked in **Cape May** hotels to earn money to help pay for her rescue raids.

**THE UNDERGROUND RAILROAD IN NEW JERSEY, 1830–1860**

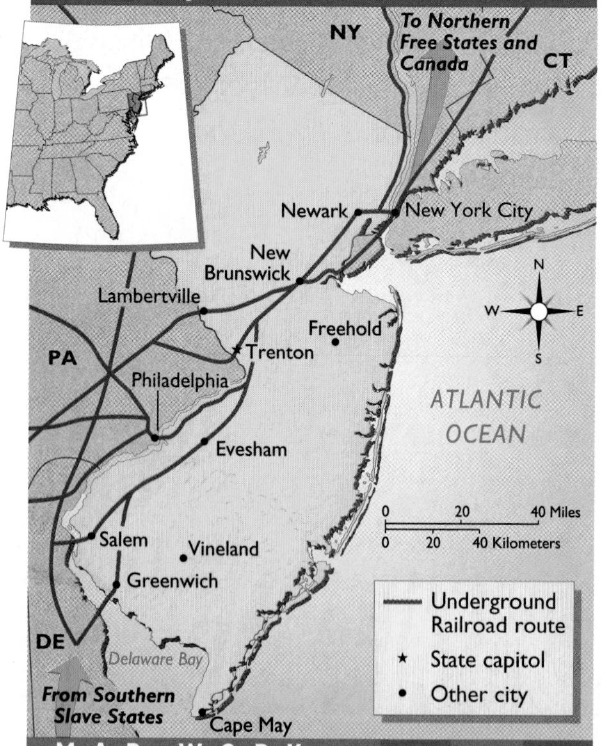

**MAP WORK**

New Jersey was an important part of the **Underground Railroad.**

1. Which New Jersey Underground Railroad stop is the farthest south?

**MAP WORK:** 1. Greenwich

### Follow the Stars

Some African Americans seeking freedom slept in hiding during the day and traveled at night. The stars in the night sky helped them find their way. The North Star pointed the way to freedom. The constellation known as the Big Dipper, also called the Drinking Gourd, helped these travelers locate the North Star. You can read a song about these stars on page 166.

When they reached the Delaware River, the freedom seekers looked for blue and yellow signal lights across the water in Salem and Cumberland Counties. These lights meant that it was safe to cross and that a conductor would meet them. Once they reached New Jersey, some newly free African Americans settled in towns such as Lawnside. Others continued on the Underground Railroad to the New England states. Still others went further north to Canada.

**"Stations" along the Underground Railroad often contained secret hiding places in out-of-the-way spots.**

## One Family's Story

Charity Still was born into slavery in Maryland. When New Jersey outlawed slavery in 1804, Still decided to seek freedom here. Her husband was able to buy his freedom and travel to New Jersey. He said, "I will die before I submit [give in] to the yoke." A yoke is a wooden frame that farmers put on oxen to pull a plow.

Several weeks after her husband left, Charity Still made her escape. Traveling at night with her four small children, she made her way north. Still and her husband were reunited near the New Jersey border. However, their joy did not last long. Slave hunters captured Charity and her children and dragged them back into slavery.

Determined to be free, Charity escaped again. She left two of her sons behind, hoping to purchase their freedom later. This time Still made it to the Pinelands. One of the sons she left in slavery died before she had a chance to see him again. The other son, Peter, was reunited with his mother when he bought his freedom 40 years later.

Another son, William, became an abolitionist and a conductor on the Underground Railroad. He is sometimes called the "Father of the Underground Railroad." How does William Still describe the situation of those families who have just reached freedom in New Jersey?

**MANY VOICES**
**LITERATURE**

**Excerpt from *The Underground Railroad*, written in 1871 by William Still.**

***The following day, they reached their much desired haven, the Jersey shore. The relief and joy were unspeakably great, yet they were strangers in a strange land. They knew not which way to steer. True, they knew that New Jersey bore the name of being a Free State; but they had reason to fear that they were in danger.***

**haven:** place of safety
**steer:** go
**bore:** had

## MANY VOICES
MUSIC

How did escaping slaves find their way in the dark? They had no maps or flashlights. How did they know which way was north?

They followed the stars. A star called the North Star always points the way north. To find the North Star, escaping slaves were told to look for a constellation called the Drinking Gourd.

African Americans sang a song about the Drinking Gourd. It guided many people to freedom. You can read the words below.

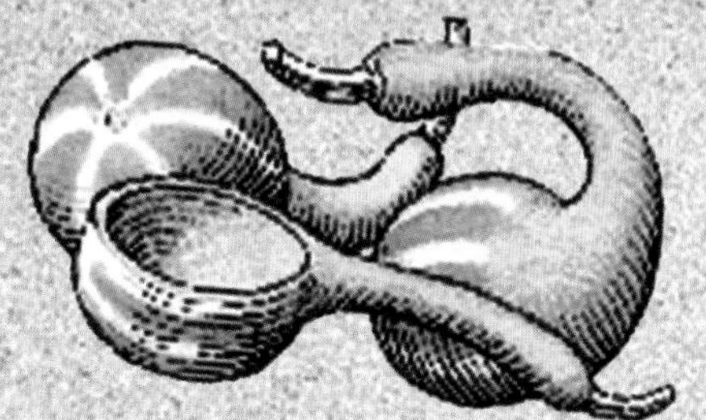

A gourd is a hard-shelled fruit. Its shell was used as a cup. A group of stars shaped like a cup was known as the Drinking Gourd, or the Big Dipper.

# Follow the Drinkin' Gourd

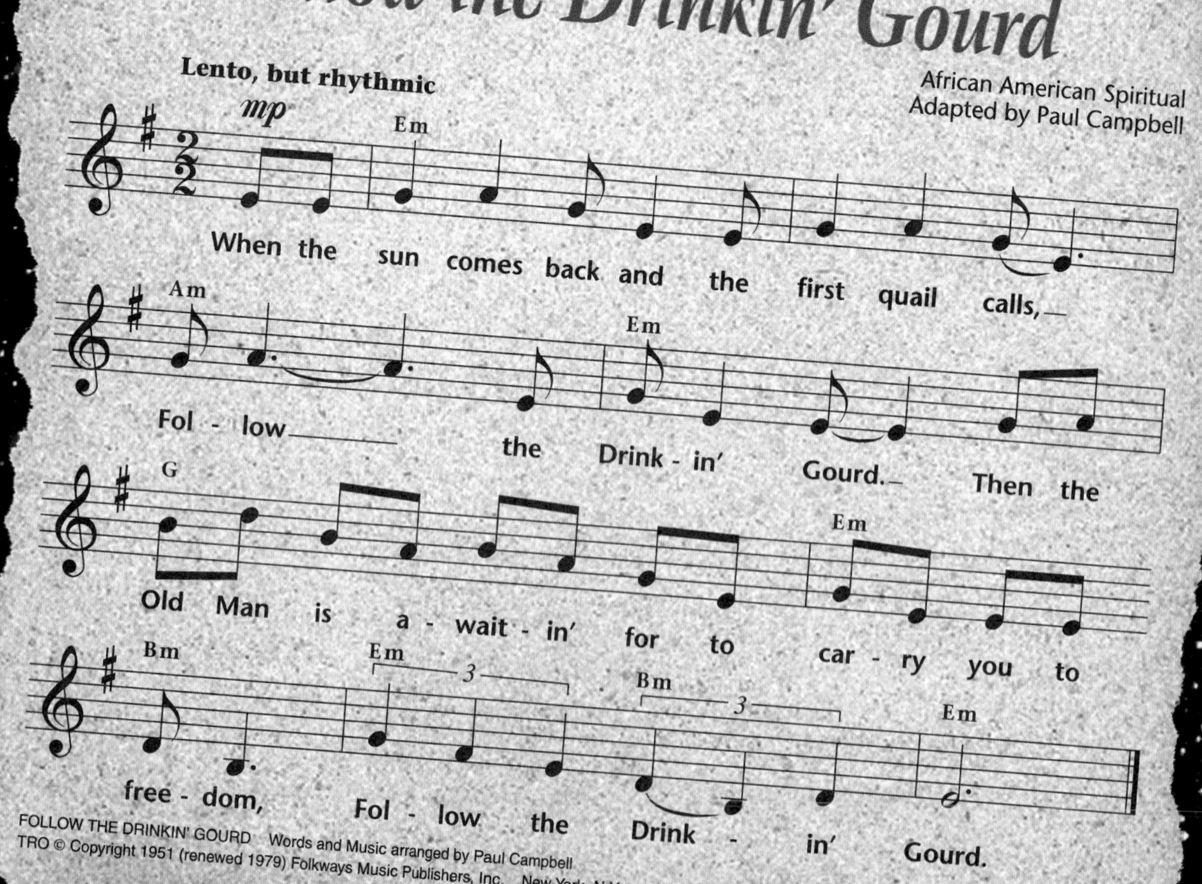

See p. T56 for Answers to Think About It.

## A DIVIDED STATE

Although New Jersey lies in the northeastern part of our country, our state had many ties to the South in the middle 1800s. Textile mills such as those in Paterson depended on Southern cotton. Many New Jersey products, such as shoes, clothing, and carriages, were sold to customers in the South. As our country edged closer to war, people began taking sides. In New Jersey even friends and family sometimes had different views on slavery.

The Fugitive Slave Act, passed in 1850, said that enslaved people who had escaped to the North had to be returned to their owners in the South. Many Northerners found ways to avoid this law, but most people in New Jersey never questioned it. They thought that peace between the North and the South was more important than the abolition of slavery.

25 Dollars

*REWARD!!*

RANAWAY from the residence of the Subscriber, in *Manalopan*, on Sunday the 21st inst., a Colored Boy, named BILL MILLER, aged about 18 years—five feet five or six inches high—with a large Scar over one of his eyes, occasioned by the kick of a horse, from which he can be easily recognized. He had on when he went away a tight-bodied coat of olive brown cloth, a black silk hat, velvet vest, and corderoy pantaloons.

The above reward, together with all reasonable charges, will be paid to any person taking up said Runaway, and bringing him to the Subscriber, in Manalopan, Monmouth county, New Jersey, or by giving information where he may be had.

PETER S. CONOVER.

January 23, 1838.

**Newspaper advertisements were used to capture people who had escaped to freedom in the North.**

## WHY IT MATTERS

The disagreement between the North and the South on the subject of slavery would only grow stronger. It would finally end in a long and bloody war.

## Reviewing Facts and Ideas

### MAIN IDEAS

- Some New Jerseyans opposed slavery, but our state also had strong ties to the South.
- In 1804 New Jersey passed a law that slowly abolished slavery.
- By 1860 there were still 18 enslaved people in our state.
- Thousands of African Americans escaping from slavery followed the Underground Railroad through New Jersey.

### THINK ABOUT IT

1. What is abolition?
2. Name two reasons why New Jersey had ties to the South.
3. **FOCUS** When and how did New Jerseyans work to abolish slavery?
4. **THINKING SKILL** *Contrast* the views of New Jerseyans on the subject of slavery.
5. **GEOGRAPHY** What river would a person fleeing from slavery in Delaware have to cross to reach New Jersey?

LESSON 2

1800 1825 1860 1865 1900

See p. T57 for Lesson Teaching Strategies.

# New Jersey and the Civil War

## Focus Activity

READ TO LEARN

***What role did New Jersey play in the Civil War?***

VOCABULARY

- states' rights
- secede
- Confederacy
- Union
- Civil War
- draft
- Emancipation Proclamation

PEOPLE

- Abraham Lincoln
- Philip Kearny
- George B. McClellan
- Cornelia Hancock
- Ulysses S. Grant

PLACES

- Gettysburg
- Appomattox Courthouse

## Read Aloud

*People in New Jersey had different opinions about the growing split between the North and the South, but they soon rallied to the Northern cause. Soldiers from New Jersey who joined the Union Army sang this song:*

The brave volunteers of New Jersey,
All patriots, noble and true;
Aroused at the call of our country,
We'll stand by the red, white, and blue,
To tyrants we can never give in;
Rebellion shall have its just due,
For Union and liberty live, in
The hearts of the true Jersey Blue.

## THE BIG PICTURE

In 1860 more than three million African Americans were enslaved in the South. These workers grew most of the world's cotton. White Southerners thought slavery was necessary for their way of life. They called for **states' rights**. This meant that states should make their own laws about slavery and other issues.

In the North, however, the push to abolish slavery was growing stronger. When **Abraham Lincoln** ran for President in 1860, he did not support abolition, but he was strongly against the spread of slavery. Many people in the free states voted for Lincoln. New Jersey was the only free state not to vote for Lincoln.

## WAR BREAKS OUT

After he was elected President, Lincoln traveled through eight Northern states on his way to Washington, D.C. One witness said New Jerseyans greeted Lincoln with "wild delight."

Leaders in the Southern states had a different view of Lincoln. They were afraid he would abolish slavery everywhere in the country. Soon after Lincoln's election, 11 Southern states voted to **secede**, or withdraw, from the United States. These states formed a new government called the Confederate States of America, or the **Confederacy**. The United States was called the **Union**. You can see the Union and the Confederacy on the map on this page. Notice that part of New Jersey extends as far south as the Confederacy.

On April 12, 1861, Confederate soldiers fired on Union troops at Fort Sumter in Charleston, South Carolina. This started the **Civil War**, or the "War Between the States."

### Comparing North and South

The Union was stronger than the Confederacy in most ways. It had a population of about 22 million, compared to the Confederacy's 9 million people. Northern factories could produce goods worth ten times as much as Southern factories. The Union had almost three times more railroad tracks. The Confederacy, however, had many trained military leaders.

**THE UNION AND THE CONFEDERACY, 1861–1865**

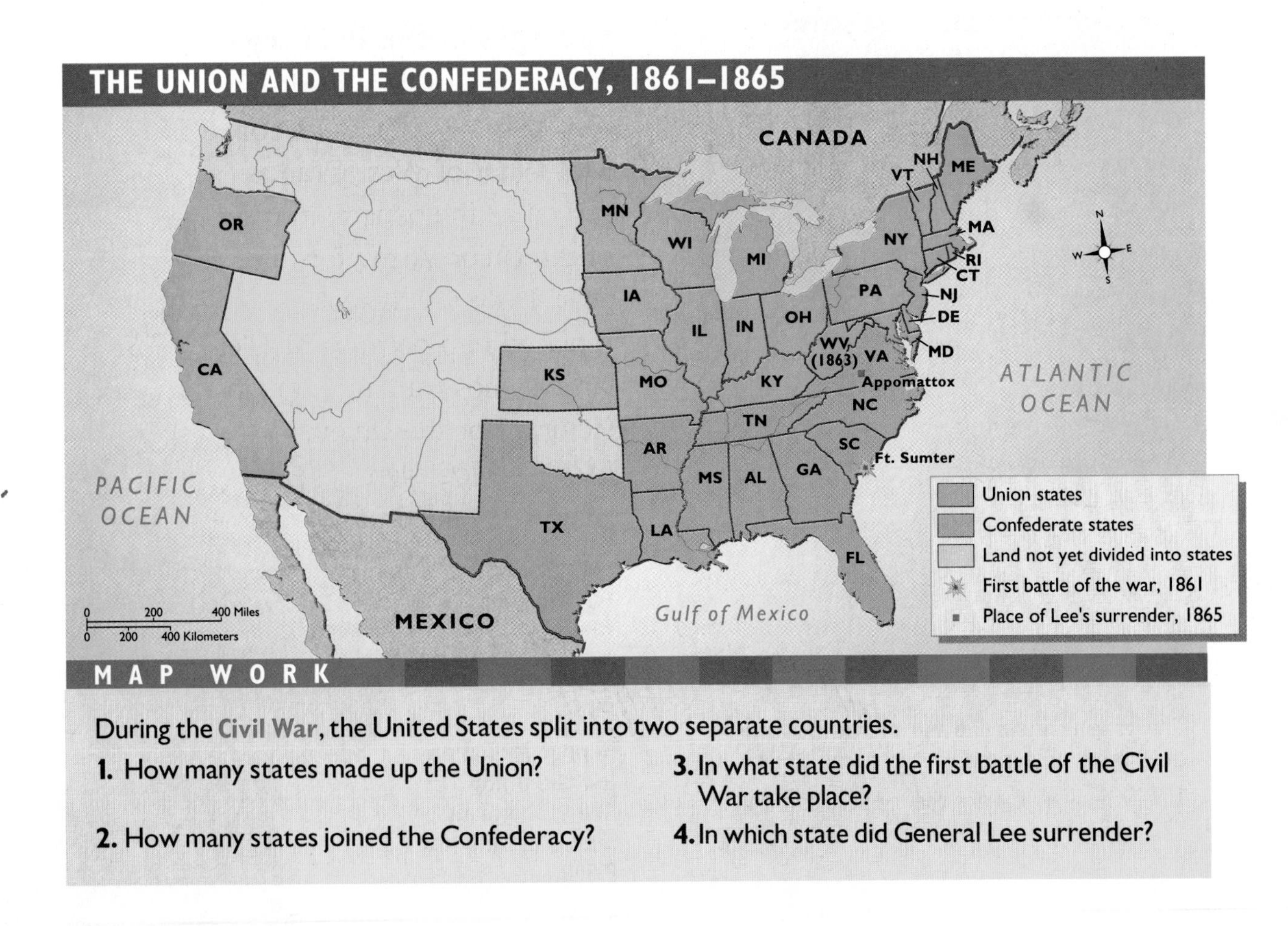


**MAP WORK**

During the **Civil War**, the United States split into two separate countries.

1. How many states made up the Union?
2. How many states joined the Confederacy?
3. In what state did the first battle of the Civil War take place?
4. In which state did General Lee surrender?

**MAP WORK:** **1.** 24 **2.** 11 **3.** South Carolina **4.** Virginia

## NEW JERSEY AND THE UNION

After the attack on Fort Sumter, Lincoln asked New Jersey's governor to send about 3,000 soldiers to fight for the Union. In less than a week, almost 10,000 had signed up.

Most troops had to bring their own supplies. Few weapons were ready for battle. Most had been in storage since the American Revolution. One captain bought ammunition in New York City. He hurried by train through our state to give it to soldiers as they sailed across the Chesapeake Bay. New Jerseyans made up the first unit of Union soldiers to reach Washington, D.C., on May 6, 1861.

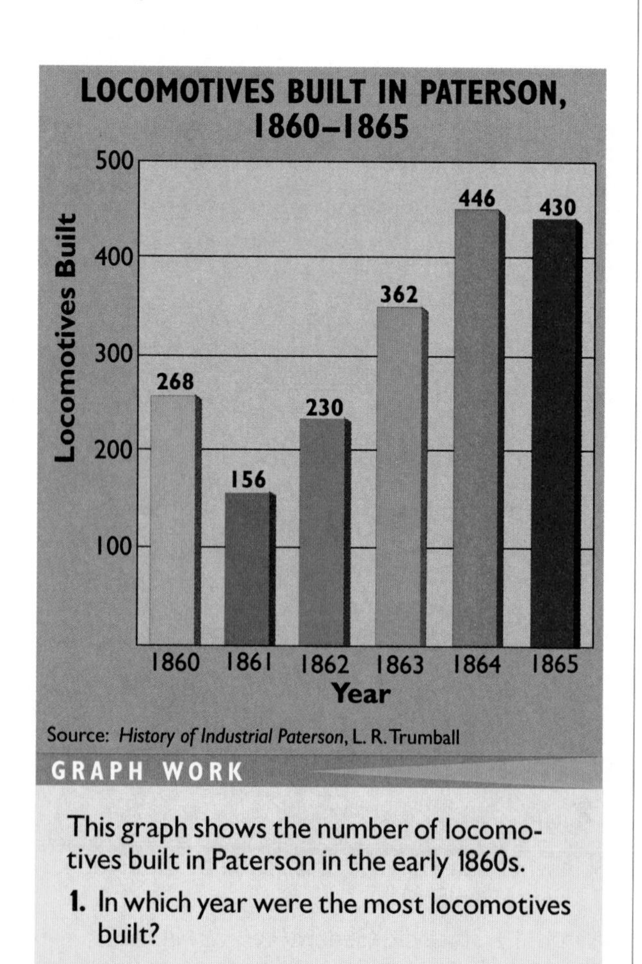


GRAPH WORK

This graph shows the number of locomotives built in Paterson in the early 1860s.

1. In which year were the most locomotives built?

GRAPH WORK: 1. 1864

### New Jersey Goes to War

Right after the war started in 1861, New Jersey factories and farms were hurt by the loss of Southern business. However, by the end of 1861, factories were busy turning out rubber, gun barrels, woolen uniforms, locomotives, and rails for train tracks. Farmers sent crops to the Union Army and to factories. A Newark newspaper editor boasted in 1863: "We can get along even without the Southern trade."

Many of New Jersey's soldiers fought bravely. Philip Kearny, a skilled general, became the leader of the First New Jersey Brigade. He was killed on September 1, 1862, at a battle in Virginia.

### Changes in the Military

Another military leader from New Jersey, Major General George B. McClellan of West Orange, served as the general-in-chief of the Union Army for one year. However, Lincoln replaced him because McClellan was not winning enough victories for the Union. In 1864, McClellan ran for President against Lincoln. While most

**George McClellan led the Union Army, then ran unsuccessfully for President.**

Some Civil War units chose their own uniforms. These Union soldiers are wearing uniforms similar to those worn in Morocco.

New Jersey voters chose McClellan, Lincoln won the election easily.

As time passed, the need for soldiers grew so great that the Union Army created a draft. A draft is a plan to select people and force them to serve in the army. New Jersey did not have to draft soldiers until 1864, because enough had volunteered. Now they had no choice. Many people disliked the draft.

### A Volunteer Nurse

One of the women who helped the war effort was Cornelia Hancock. A volunteer nurse with the Union Army, she served at the Battle of Gettysburg in Pennsylvania. Hancock wrote many letters asking her family and friends in New Jersey for supplies. How do you think Hancock felt about serving as a Civil War nurse?

**MANY VOICES**
**PRIMARY SOURCE**

**Excerpt from a letter from Cornelia Hancock to her mother, July 21, 1863.**

*I like to be here very much, am perfectly used to the suffering and the work just suits me. . . . Food we are scarce of sometimes but it is generally plenty. I received, a few days ago, a Silver Medal worth twenty dollars. . . . on one side [it said] "Miss Cornelia Hancock, presented by the wounded soldiers 3rd Division 2nd Army Corps." On the other side is "Testimonial of regard for* **ministrations** *of mercy to the wounded soldiers at Gettysburg, PA.—July 1863." You need not fear for me, I am all right.*

**ministrations:** giving aid or service

## THE WAR CONTINUES

In September 1862 President Lincoln announced the Emancipation Proclamation (ee man suh PAY shun prahk luh MAY shun). The word *emancipation* means "freedom." This official announcement said that on January 1, 1863, all enslaved people in the Confederate states would be "forever free." Confederate leaders did not accept this rule, and the war continued for two more years.

After the Emancipation Proclamation, more than 180,000 freed African Americans fought for the Union in the Civil War. About 2,800 African American men from New Jersey served in the Union Army. Some were freed slaves. Others were African Americans who were already free.

### The Final Surrender

In 1865 Union forces under the command of Ulysses S. Grant drove deep into Virginia. The soldiers knew that the war was almost over. "We saw THE END shining . . . through the battle smoke," wrote one New Jersey soldier.

The Confederate forces surrendered at Appomattox Courthouse in Virginia on April 9, 1865. An officer in the 2nd Jersey Brigade described the scene: "Officers and men were perfectly wild . . . shoes and hats flew high in the air."

By the end of the war, more than 88,000 New Jersey men—about one of every ten people who lived in New Jersey—had served in the Union forces.

**African American soldiers helped the Union win the Civil War.**

**A great parade of Union troops in Washington, D.C. celebrated the end of the war.**

About 6,300 of them lost their lives. The Medal of Honor was awarded to 25 people from our state. One of them was 15-year-old Willie Magee of Newark. Magee entered the war as a drummer boy at age 13. Two years later, he led an Ohio regiment in a successful attack near Murfreesboro, Tennessee.

The sorrows of the country did not end with the war. On April 14, 1865, President Lincoln was shot by an actor named John Wilkes Booth at a theater in Washington, D. C. Lincoln died the next day. Thousands of New Jerseyans watched his funeral train as it passed through the state on its way to Lincoln's home in Illinois.

See p. T57 for Answers to Think About It.

## WHY IT MATTERS

The Civil War divided the country. Almost 600,000 lives were lost to the fighting and disease. The war saved the Union and freed enslaved African Americans. After the war, African American men gained the right to vote. In 1870 Thomas Mundy Peterson of Perth Amboy became the first black New Jerseyan to vote under this new law. However, New Jersey women, both black and white, were still denied this right.

## Reviewing Facts and Ideas

### MAIN IDEAS

- The Civil War began in 1861 and ended in 1865.
- New Jersey sent more than 88,000 men to fight in the Union Army.
- New Jersey factories and farms supplied the war effort.
- The Emancipation Proclamation abolished slavery.

### THINK ABOUT IT

1. Why were New Jerseyans divided before the Civil War began?
2. What event started the Civil War in 1861?
3. **FOCUS** What role did New Jersey play in the Civil War?
4. **THINKING SKILL** Compare and contrast the Union and the Confederacy at the start of the Civil War.
5. **WRITE** Imagine that you were a New Jersey soldier fighting for the Union. Write a paragraph about how you would feel about the end of the war.

# Thinking Skills

See p. T58 for Skill Teaching Strategies.

## Making Conclusions

**VOCABULARY**

conclusion

### WHY THE SKILL MATTERS

In the last lesson, you read about the Civil War. You read that one out of ten New Jerseyans fought in the war. You also learned that New Jersey's farms and factories helped provide supplies for the Union Army. You might think about these facts and decide that New Jersey was an important part of the Union's success in the war.

When you put together several pieces of information and decide what they mean, you are making a conclusion. A conclusion does not repeat specific facts. Instead, it adds up these facts and shows how they are connected.

**This corporal in the Union Army posed for a photograph to send home to loved ones.**

### USING THE SKILL

In Lesson 2, you read that many African Americans fought in the Civil War. Read each of the following statements:

- Enslaved people could not serve in the Union Army.
- The Emancipation Proclamation freed enslaved African Americans.
- More than 180,000 African Americans joined the Union Army.

First ask yourself, "What do all of these statements have in common?" The three statements have the common theme that the Emancipation Proclamation brought African Americans into the Union Army. Now, state this theme in your own words. A conclusion you might make is "The Emancipation Proclamation made it possible for African Americans to fight for the Union's cause." This conclusion connects all three statements. It finds a common idea behind the statements and says it in one sentence.

### TRYING THE SKILL

You have practiced drawing a conclusion about the Emancipation Proclamation. Now read the following statements about Cornelia Hancock, the army nurse you read about in Lesson 2. Then make a

*Cornelia Hancock's efforts as a nurse; they point to how Cornelia Hancock made sure her patients received the proper care; Cornelia Hancock was an excellent nurse because she took good care of the soldiers at Gettysburg.

conclusion from the statements. Use the Helping Yourself box for hints.

- In 1863 Cornelia Hancock nursed hundreds of wounded soldiers at Gettysburg.
- Hancock knew that there were not enough medical supplies for her patients.
- She asked her friends and family to send bandages, sheets, blankets, and other supplies.
- The soldiers gave Cornelia Hancock a silver medal to show their thanks for her work.

What common theme or meaning did you find in all four statements? How do they "add up" to a conclusion? What conclusion can you make about Cornelia Hancock as a nurse?*

**Helping yourself**

- **When you make a conclusion, you add up several facts or statements to see how they are connected.**
- **Skim through the information for a common idea.**
- **State the meaning in your own words.**

See p. T58 for Answers to Reviewing the Skill.

## REVIEWING THE SKILL

1. How did you reach your conclusion?
2. What did the four statements suggest about Cornelia Hancock? How do you know?
3. How might making conclusions help you to learn about history?
4. Name some occasions in school when you might find it useful to make conclusions.

**Cornelia Hancock was among the nurses of the Second Corps Hospital, shown here, at the Battle of Gettysburg.**

LESSON 3

| 1800 | 1825 | 1850 | 1869 | 1900 |
|---|---|---|---|---|

See p. T59 for Lesson Teaching Strategies.

# Inventions and Industry

## Focus Activity

**READ TO LEARN**

***How did new industries change the way people lived and worked in New Jersey?***

**VOCABULARY**

- patent
- labor union

**PEOPLE**

- Thomas Alva Edison

**PLACES**

- Menlo Park
- Roselle

### Read Aloud

*"I have it now!" said the young inventor Thomas Alva Edison as he worked on a new electric light. "I have obtained it through an entirely different process than that from which scientific men have ever sought to secure it. . . . Everybody will wonder why they never thought of it, it is so simple."*

### THE BIG PICTURE

After the Civil War, New Jersey industry grew rapidly. Existing industries expanded, such as the potteries of Trenton and the jewelry shops and leather factories of Newark. Paterson continued as a leading manufacturing city, now producing silk and locomotives. Camden became an important site for furniture making. New Jerseyans made cloth and produced iron in many parts of our state.

New inventions sparked many new industries. **Thomas Alva Edison** set up an "invention factory" in **Menlo Park**. He became famous around the world with new products such as the electric light bulb, the phonograph, and the motion picture camera.

**Edison's "invention factory" in Menlo Park produced thousands of new products and ideas.**

GRAPH WORK: **1.** 1888

## THE WIZARD OF MENLO PARK

As a young man, Edison worked as a telegraph operator. However, he was an inventor at heart. By selling his ideas about improving the telegraph, Edison made enough money to work full-time on his inventions.

In 1876 Edison opened a workshop in Menlo Park. He and his assistants worked on many inventions at the same time. In 1877 he improved the telephone invented by Alexander Graham Bell. His work with the telephone and the telegraph led to the invention of the phonograph, a machine to play recorded sound.

In 1879 Edison successfully developed the light bulb. In 1882 he built a dynamo, a machine that makes electricity. The following year, his dynamo brought light to the town of Roselle. Before long, Edison's inventions brought electricity across the country.

In 1886 Edison invented the motion picture camera. He wrote, "I am experimenting upon an instrument which does for the eye what the phonograph does for the ear."

In his lifetime, Edison was awarded 1,093 patents. A patent is a document issued by the government. It gives an inventor the right to make, use, or sell a particular invention. The chart on this page shows a few of Edison's many inventions. Perhaps his greatest contribution, however, was his invention factory. It was a model for many other research laboratories.

**MAJOR EDISON INVENTIONS**

| Year | Invention |
|---|---|
| 1878 | Typewriter |
| 1879 | Electric Lamp |
| 1881 | Electric Motor |
| 1888 | Phonograph |
| 1897 | Kinetoscope Projector |
| 1903 | Movie Film |

**CHART WORK**

Thomas Edison invented many things that changed our way of life.

1. In which year did Edison invent the phonograph?

## FACTORIES AND CITIES

New Jersey's growing population supplied workers for its many new factories. By 1880 more than a million people lived in the state. For the first time, more people lived in cities than in rural areas in our state.

Factory work was usually hard. Sometimes it was dangerous. The pay was low, and the hours were long. Workers often performed the same task over and over again.

In 1890 a newspaper reporter interviewed a woman named Joanna, who had immigrated from Ireland as a young girl. In this interview she describes her work in a textile mill in Paterson. What do you think was the hardest part of working in a textile mill?

**MANY VOICES**
**PRIMARY SOURCE**

**Excerpt from "Stories Told by Factory Girls," by Nell Nelson, *New York World*, February 10, 1890.**

***I went into the mill when I was about eleven and stayed there fifteen years off and on—off when I was too sick to work and on when I could get anything to do. I began at $1.25 a week, "picking" cotton . . . then I learned to wind. . . . At the silk work. . . . when it costs her all she earns for board and there's nothing left for clothes she has to go back to the hard work.***

### Labor Unions

To improve working conditions, workers joined together to form **labor unions**. A labor union is a group of workers united to gain better wages, or pay, and working conditions. Factory owners often fired workers who joined unions. However, workers continued to band together. They held strikes to make factory owners pay attention to their demands. Despite strikes, workers made few gains by 1900.

### New Industries, Growing Cities

During the 1800s many new industries began in New Jersey. In Camden, RCA Victor Company made phonographs. The Johnson & Johnson Company of New Brunswick made bandages and other medical supplies. In 1870 John Dryden started the company that became Prudential Insurance. Workers paid a small amount of money each month to the company. If they had an accident

See p. T59 for Answers to Think About It.

or lost property to a fire, they received money from the company.

New ideas helped turn food into big business. Thomas B. Welch started making Welch's Grape Juice in Vineland in 1869. That same year, Joseph Campbell produced the first cans of Campbell's Soup in Camden.

Electric streetcars allowed cities to expand outward. With faster transportation, people could now live far from their places of work. Streetcars even spurred the growth of early suburbs. Yet most workers and their families at this time continued to live in the cities.

### WHY IT MATTERS

The ideas of Edison and other inventors led to changes in the way people live and to important industries that are still part of New Jersey's economy. Many research laboratories continue to thrive in our state today.

**Young women often worked long hours at dangerous machines (left) in New Jersey's mills and factories (below right).**

## Reviewing Facts and Ideas

### MAIN IDEAS

- Following the Civil War, industry grew rapidly in New Jersey.
- Thomas Edison invented many new products and developed the first research laboratory.
- Workers formed labor unions to win better pay and better working conditions.

### THINK ABOUT IT

1. Name three inventions of Thomas Edison.
2. What is a labor union?
3. **FOCUS** Describe one way that new industries changed life in New Jersey after the Civil War.
4. **THINKING SKILL** Read the "Many Voices" on page 178. What is one *conclusion* you could make about the life of a child who worked in a factory?
5. **WRITE** Write a paragraph describing how some of the inventions of Thomas Edison affect us today.

See p. T60 for Legacy Teaching Strategies.

Legacy

## LINKING PAST AND PRESENT

# Innovations

*Innovation* means "introducing something new." Our fast-changing state has always been a place for new inventions and new ways of doing things. Thomas Edison was just one of many people who have made New Jersey a center for innovation. Among the new ideas that they have come up with are: air conditioning, picture postcards, and even saltwater taffy.

Take a look at some of the other amazing New Jersey innovations on this page. These innovations have changed life forever. They are some of our state's most important legacies.

**In the 1940s Les Paul of Mahwah invented a new musical instrument—the electric guitar!**

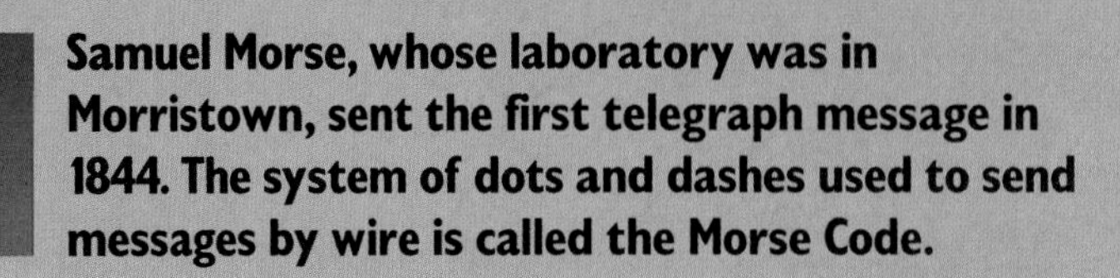

**Samuel Morse, whose laboratory was in Morristown, sent the first telegraph message in 1844. The system of dots and dashes used to send messages by wire is called the Morse Code.**

New Jerseyan Arthur Hill came up with the idea of a traffic cloverleaf (right) in 1916. It was 1928 before the first one was built, in Woodbridge, New Jersey.

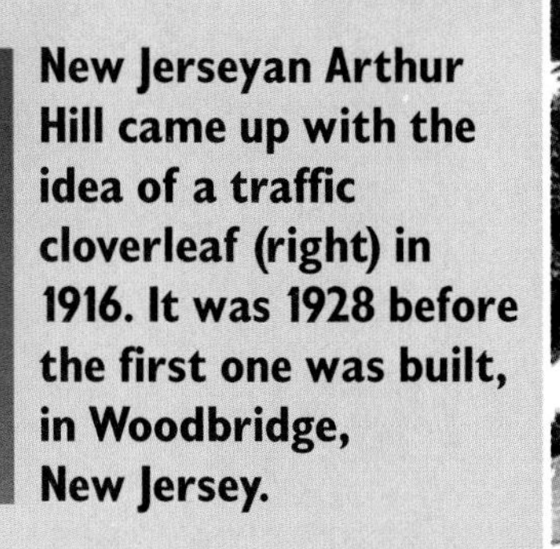

In 1916 Elizabeth C. White (left) and Frederick Coville created a new kind of blueberry plant with bigger and juicier berries. Today, our state's blueberry industry is one of the largest in the United States.

John Philip Holland, an Irish immigrant who settled in Paterson, built the world's first successful submarine in 1895.

1800 1825 1850 1870 1900

See p. T61 and T62 for Lesson Teaching Strategies.

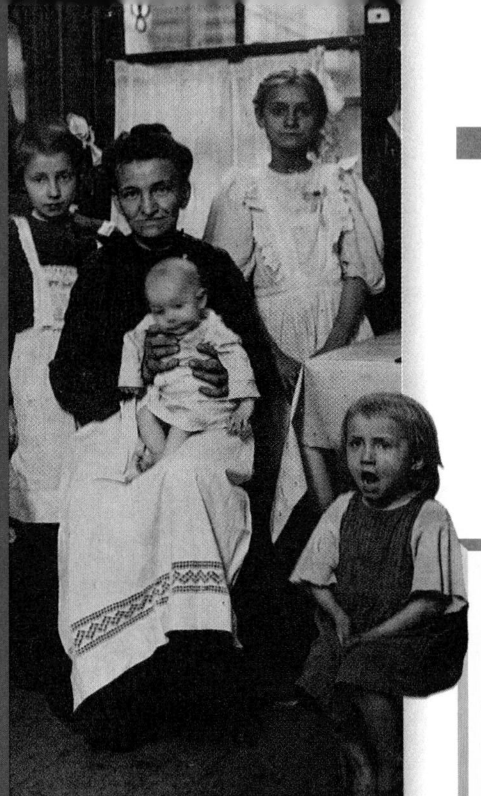

# Welcoming the World

## Read Aloud

*In the 1930s a Polish immigrant described his first experiences in the United States. "At the age of eighteen, I decided to go to the United States to get work because it couldn't be had in Poland. . . . A week after my arrival I got a job on a farm. . . . Next, I worked a summer in a brickyard at three dollars per ten-hour day. In the winter, brickyards are slow, and I went to work in coal mines in Pennsylvania for three months. . . . In 1916, I came to Newark and took a job in a spring-mattress factory and stayed there for ten years."*

## Focus Activity

**READ TO LEARN**

***Why did thousands of people leave their homes in other countries to settle in New Jersey?***

**VOCABULARY**

- discrimination

**PEOPLE**

- Grover Cleveland

**PLACES**

- Ellis Island

## THE BIG PICTURE

The first immigrants to New Jersey were the Dutch settlers who arrived in the 1620s. Immigrants from England, Germany, and other parts of Europe followed in the 1700s. Irish immigrants and more German immigrants poured into our state in the early 1800s. In the late 1800s and early 1900s, great numbers of people arrived from southern and eastern Europe—from Italy, Hungary, Russia, Poland, and other countries. By 1910 more than half of the people who lived in New Jersey were immigrants or had parents who had been born in another country.

## COMING TO AMERICA

The voyage by ship across the Atlantic Ocean from Europe to America was long and difficult. Many passengers became seasick. Diseases spread quickly in the crowded cabins. When the ship arrived in New York Harbor, people crowded on deck to catch a glimpse of the Statue of Liberty.

The Statue of Liberty was a gift from the people of France to the people of the United States. President Grover Cleveland, who was born in Caldwell, accepted this gift in a ceremony on October 28, 1886.

### Ellis Island

Ellis Island was the first stop for most immigrants. This island is located just off the shore of New Jersey, near New York City. In 1892 the United States government built an immigration station here. Until it closed in 1954, nine out of every ten immigrants passed through Ellis Island.

Sometimes, 5,000 people a day walked through these doors. Immigrants were asked where they came from and whether they could read and write. They waited in long lines to be examined by doctors. People who were not healthy enough to work were sometimes sent home. However, four out of five newcomers were given a landing card and allowed to stay.

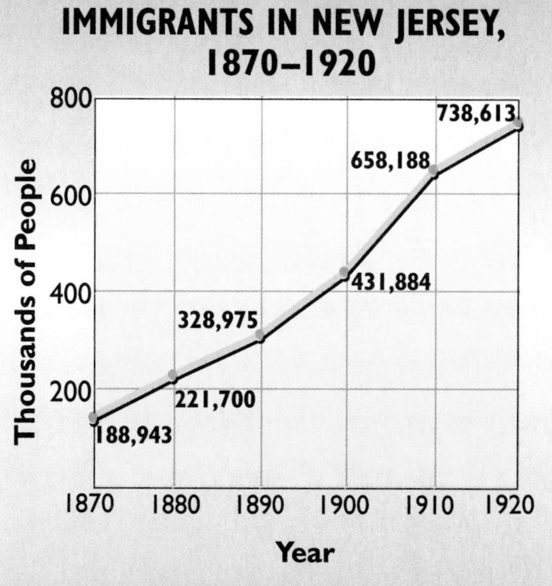


Source: *A Stone's Throw from Ellis Island*, Thomas Espinshade.

**GRAPH WORK**

The graph shows how the number of immigrants coming to New Jersey steadily grew.

1. How many immigrants lived in New Jersey in 1900?

**Immigrants arriving at Ellis Island faced an uncertain future. Still, the promise of freedom drew millions of people.**

# Infographic

**interNET CONNECTION** Visit our website: www.mhschool.com

## The Path of the Immigrant

**In the late 1800s and early 1900s, immigrants came from many countries to start new lives in New Jersey. They faced struggles and hardship. Yet their determination helped shape our state in years to come.**

### FINDING WORK

**Many immigrants found jobs in our state's factories.**

### Immigrants in New Jersey 1900*

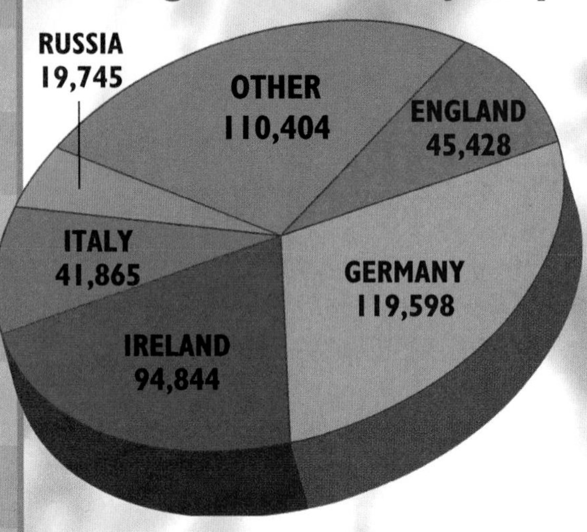


*By country of origin
Source: *A Stones Throw from Ellis Island*, Thomas Espinshade

### A NEW HOME

**Many immigrants' first homes were crowded city apartments.**

### AT SEA

**The sea journey from Europe could take many months.**

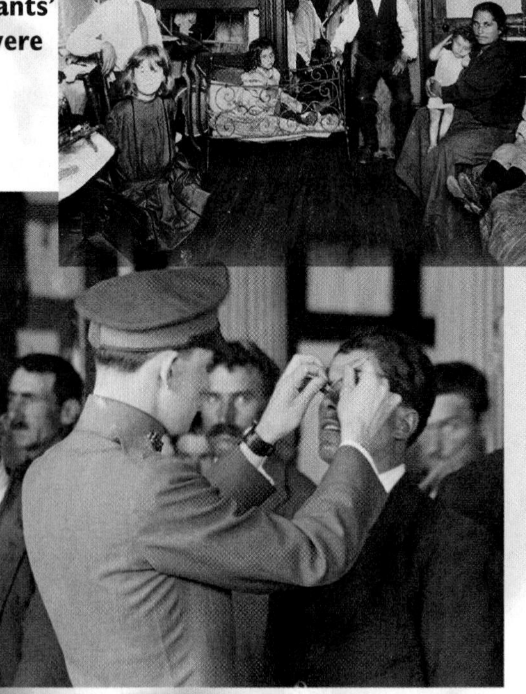

### ELLIS ISLAND

**Immigrants had to pass a health exam before being allowed to stay in the country.**

## JOURNEY TO A NEW HOME

Why did so many immigrants choose to come to the United States? Many came to find better jobs. For example, from 1845 to 1848 the potato crops in Ireland failed. Thousands of Irish came to New Jersey. Here men found work building railroads, digging canals, or working in factories. Women also worked in factories and as maids in other people's homes.

In the late 1840s, wars in Germany had left many people without jobs. As a result, many Germans immigrated to New Jersey. Later, in the 1880s, large numbers of Jews left Russia, where they were treated harshly because of their religion.

Many other immigrants were attracted to New Jersey by promises of freedom, fair treatment, jobs, and the chance to own land.

A. Losi, an immigrant from Oratina, Italy, first lived with his uncle in Newark. How would he earn enough money to have a home of his own?

**Excerpt from an interview with an Italian immigrant in the early 1900s.**

***When I arrived in Newark [in 1887], it was semi-country with plenty of trees and open fields. . . . Four days after my arrival, my uncle secured a job for me on the Erie Railroad . . . in three years' time my salary had gone up [from $6.25] to nine dollars per week. . . . Not long after that, when I was about to be married, I prepared a home for us—a six-room, cold flat. Not long after that, everyone wanted to board with us."***

---

**cold flat:** an apartment with only cold water

**Newly arrived immigrants often carried everything they owned with them.**

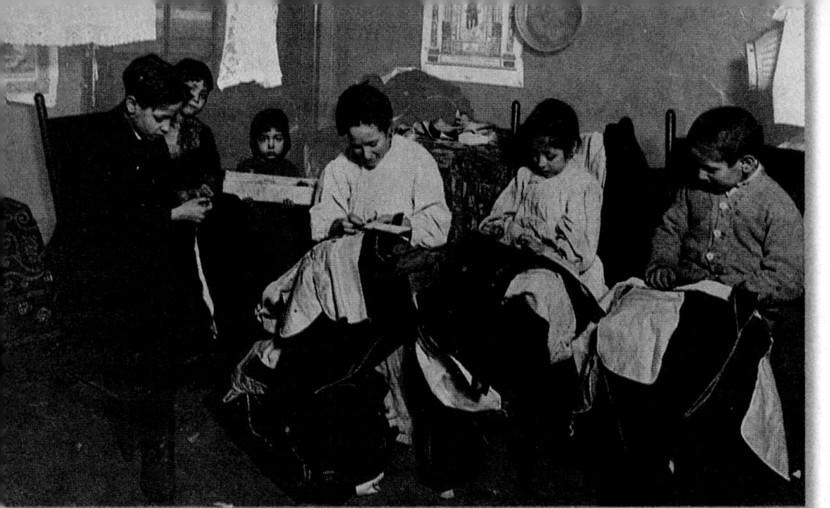

Immigrant women often found jobs they could do at home. Here, a woman's children help her with sewing.

## IMMIGRANT COMMUNITIES

Immigrants often settled in communities close to other people from their native country. This way, they could speak their native language, enjoy foods that were familiar, and worship together.

German immigrants built Egg Harbor City in the 1850s. Russian and Polish Jews founded the village of Alliance in 1881. By the 1900s, many of New Jersey's cities became patchworks of immigrant neighborhoods. For example, in one five-block area of West Hoboken, people from 18 different countries lived.

Not all Americans welcomed the newcomers. Immigrants suffered from **discrimination**, or unfair treatment based on their nationality or religion. Some native-born Americans were angry at immigrants for working for low wages. They felt this lowered the rate of pay for all workers. However, over time, most immigrants and native-born Americans learned to accept one another.

See p. T62 for Answers to Think About It.

## WHY IT MATTERS

Immigrants came to New Jersey for a better life. They helped the state to grow, and they added to the state's varied culture. Today, new immigrants are coming to New Jersey. You will read about some of these people in Chapter 12.

## Reviewing Facts and Ideas

### MAIN IDEAS

- Immigrants came to New Jersey to seek a better life.
- Large numbers of immigrants passed through Ellis Island when they entered the United States.
- Many immigrants settled in communities or neighborhoods with people from their homeland.
- Immigrants suffered discrimination from some native-born Americans.

### THINK ABOUT IT

1. Where did many of New Jersey's immigrants come from in the late 1800s and early 1900s?
2. Name the immigration station that lies off the New Jersey shore.
3. **FOCUS** Why did immigrants leave their homelands to settle in New Jersey?
4. **THINKING SKILL** Make a <u>generalization</u> about the kind of person who would risk immigrating to a new land.
5. **WRITE** Imagine that you are an immigrant to New Jersey in 1900. Write a letter to friends in your native country describing your new home.

See p. T63 for Citizenship Teaching Strategies.

# MAKING A DIFFERENCE

## Immigrants Help One Another

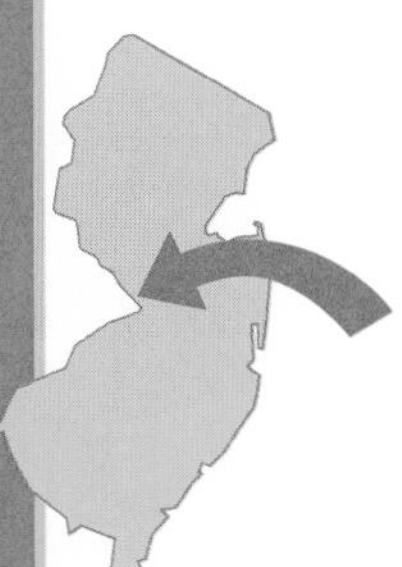

Trenton—Sasa Olessi Montano started a group called *Latinas Unidas,* which means "united Latin women." The group's goal is to give immigrants the skills and knowledge they need to succeed in their new country. "At the first meeting of our Friday group almost ten years ago, seven women came," says Montano. They were all immigrants from countries in Central or South America with hopes for new lives in the United States. Most of them spoke Spanish, but little English.

Meeting once a week in a local church, the women learned about getting medical care, how to budget, how to recycle, and how to apply for citizenship. As the months went by, more women came. "Latinas Unidas has always been a place for people to build partnerships and friendships with others," says Nidia Fernandez, director of Latinas Unidas. Soon, activities and classes were offered all week long. Men started coming, too. Soon the group had to move to a larger space.

Among the first programs to be added were English classes, parenting classes, and citizenship classes for immigrants studying to take the test to become citizens. Men and women can also get help finding a job. They learn how to fill out applications and go for interviews.

Fernandez is proud of how the group helps one another. "When people first come, they see a lot of barriers. They need to have someone to encourage them. Others who have been here longer tell them 'I did it, you can too.' It's great to see people moving along."

"a place for people to build . . . friendships."

See p. T64 for Answers to Chapter 7 Review.

# CHAPTER 7 REVIEW

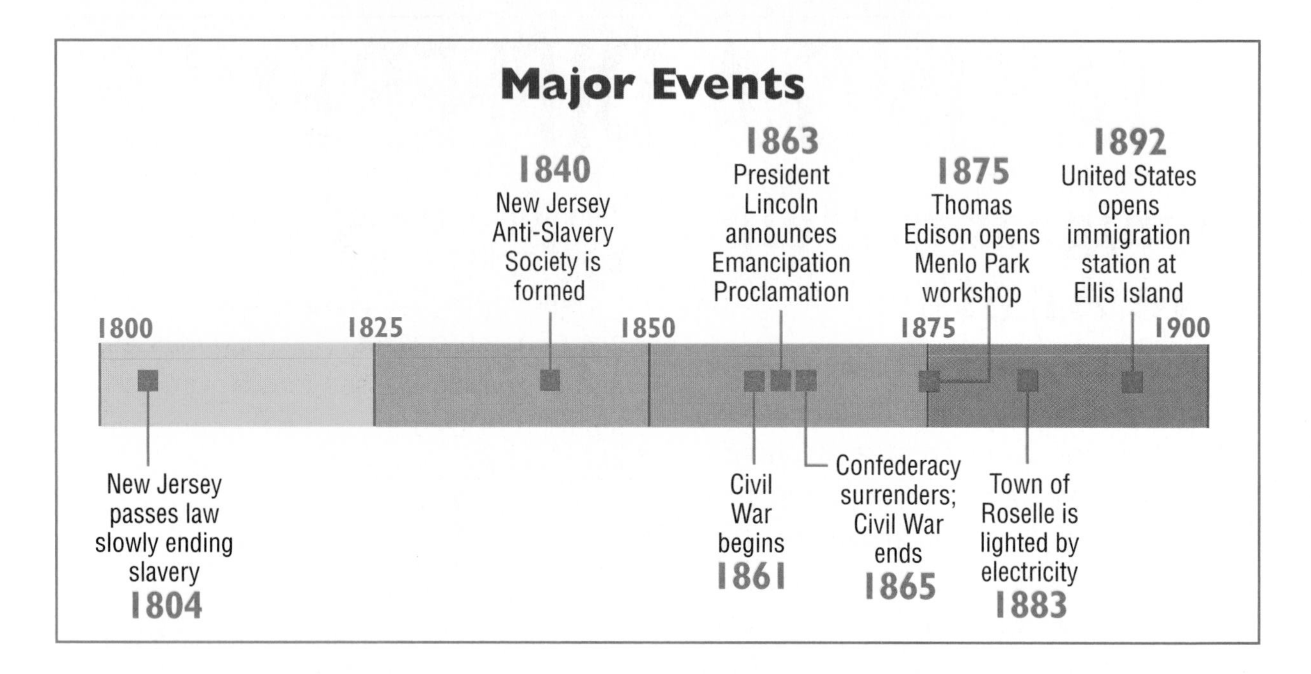


## THINKING ABOUT VOCABULARY

Number a sheet of paper from 1 to 5. Next to each number write the term from the list that best fits the description.

abolition

discrimination

Emancipation Proclamation

labor union

secede

1. To withdraw or leave an organization such as a government
2. A group of workers united to gain better pay and working conditions
3. The complete end or stop of something; often used in reference to slavery
4. The announcement by President Lincoln in 1863 that all enslaved people living in Confederate states were free
5. Unfair treatment based on nationality or religion

## THINKING ABOUT FACTS

1. Name two New Jerseyans who fought to abolish slavery.
2. What were two ways that New Jerseyans supported the Union?
3. In what year did New Jersey pass a law that did away with slavery?
4. What was the name of the new government formed by the Southern states that seceded from the Union?
5. What battle started the Civil War?
6. How did Cornelia Hancock help the Union cause in the Civil War?
7. In what town did Thomas A. Edison open his "invention factory"?
8. Name three new industries that started in New Jersey during the 1800s.
9. What was Ellis Island?
10. List two reasons immigrants came to America in the late 1800s and early 1900s.

## THINK AND WRITE

### WRITING A SPEECH
Suppose you are an abolitionist in New Jersey in the early 1800s. Write a speech saying why you think slavery should be ended.

### WRITING A DIARY
Suppose you are traveling on or helping people along the Underground Railroad. Write several diary entries that describe your activities.

### WRITING AN OPINION
Think about something in your community that you would like to improve. Write an opinion that explains why you think it is a problem and how you would go about changing it.

## APPLYING THINKING SKILLS

### MAKING CONCLUSIONS
1. What is meant by making a conclusion?
2. What steps should you follow when making a conclusion?
3. Read the sections under "The Underground Railroad" on pages 164–165. What conclusion could you make about people reaching freedom using the Underground Railroad?
4. Read the sections under "New Jersey and the Union" on pages 170–171. What conclusions could you make about New Jersey's role in the Civil War?
5. Why is it important to make conclusions about what you read?

## Summing Up the Chapter

Copy the following cause-and-effect chart on a sheet of paper. Fill in the blank spaces on the chart. Then use the information to write a paragraph that answers the question "How did life change in New Jersey during the time of the Civil War?"

| CAUSE | EFFECT |
|---|---|
| Abolitionists oppose slavery. | New Jersey passes law to abolish slavery slowly over time. |
| Confederate soldiers fire at Fort Sumter. | The Civil War begins. |
| Edison creates new inventions. | Home and work life in New Jersey change. |
| People face difficult conditions in their homelands. | Many immigrants come to New Jersey. |

See p. T65 for Answers to Unit 3 Review.

# UNIT 3 REVIEW

## THINKING ABOUT VOCABULARY

Number a sheet of paper from 1 to 10. Next to each number write the word or phrase from the list that best completes each sentence.

| | |
|---|---|
| abolition | manufacturing |
| canal | reform |
| charter | states' rights |
| immigrant | strike |
| labor union | suffrage |

1. The belief that each state should have the right to make its own laws about slavery and other issues is called ________.
2. A ______ is an official document giving a person or group of people permission to do something.
3. A person who comes to a new country or place to live is called an ________.
4. A ___________ helps workers unite to gain better pay and working conditions.
5. A change to make government or business work better is called a ______.
6. The right to vote is called ______.
7. Making large amounts of goods in factories is called ___________.
8. A ______ occurs when all the workers in a business refuse to work until the owners meet their demands.
9. An inland waterway built by people for transportation is called a ______.
10. ______ means to end or do away with completely.

## THINK AND WRITE

### WRITING A COMPARISON

Write a paragraph comparing forms of transportation used during the 1800s with transportation used today.

### WRITING A SONG

Suppose you are a Union soldier in 1863. Write words to a song about what it felt like to be in the Civil War.

### WRITING AN ADVERTISEMENT

Suppose you are the owner of a railroad company in the 1800s. Design and write an advertisement encouraging passengers and shippers to use your railroad.

## BUILDING SKILLS

1. **Making conclusions** In Chapter 7 you read about the Civil War. What is one conclusion you can make about this event?
2. **Circle and line graphs** Refer to the line graph on page 153. What happened to the population of Newark between 1830 and 1840?
3. **Circle and line graphs** Would you use a line graph or a circle graph to show how you spend your time after school?
4. **Circle and line graphs** Refer to the circle graph on page 152. If the numbers were removed from each "slice" of the circle graph, could you tell which industry had the most workers? If so, how?
5. **Map scale** When might it be useful to use maps drawn to different scales?

## YESTERDAY, TODAY & TOMORROW

**In this unit you have read about the expansion and development of New Jersey. Just 200 years ago, Europeans had settled only some areas of New Jersey. Today, our state is the most densely populated state in the country. How do you think New Jersey will change in the future?**

## READING ON YOUR OWN

These are some of the books you might find at the library to help you learn more.

*THE GADGET WAR*
**by Betsy Duffey**
Kelly Sparks must prove that her imagination is tops in an innovation contest.

*LETTERS FROM RIFKA*
**by Karen Hesse**
A Jewish girl describes her family's flight from Russia to the United States.

*THE JOURNAL OF EDMOND PEASE*
**by Jim Murphy**
The story of a 16-year-old orphan's experiences during the Civil War.

## UNIT 3 REVIEW PROJECT

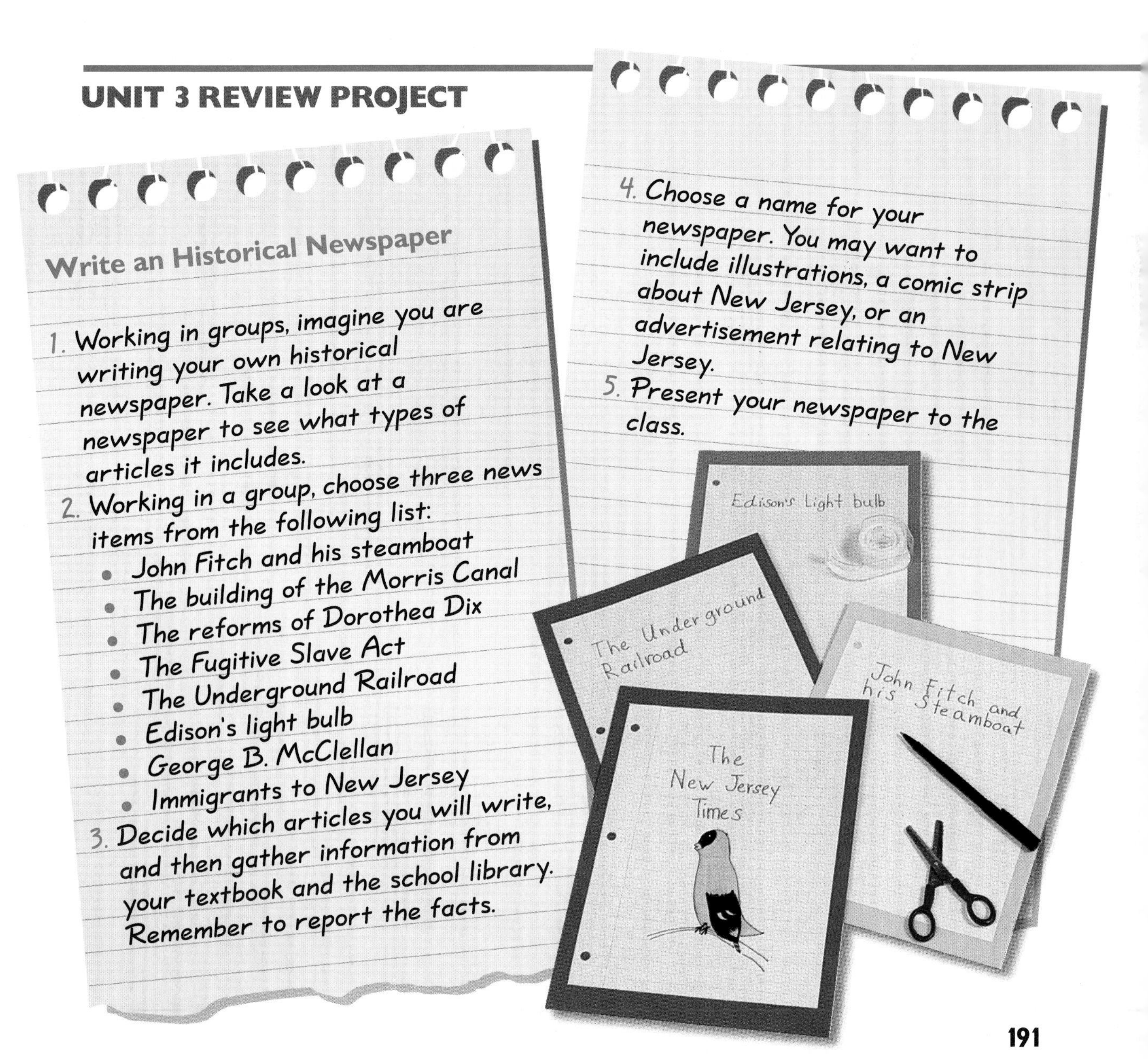

### Write an Historical Newspaper

1. Working in groups, imagine you are writing your own historical newspaper. Take a look at a newspaper to see what types of articles it includes.
2. Working in a group, choose three news items from the following list:
   - John Fitch and his steamboat
   - The building of the Morris Canal
   - The reforms of Dorothea Dix
   - The Fugitive Slave Act
   - The Underground Railroad
   - Edison's light bulb
   - George B. McClellan
   - Immigrants to New Jersey
3. Decide which articles you will write, and then gather information from your textbook and the school library. Remember to report the facts.
4. Choose a name for your newspaper. You may want to include illustrations, a comic strip about New Jersey, or an advertisement relating to New Jersey.
5. Present your newspaper to the class.

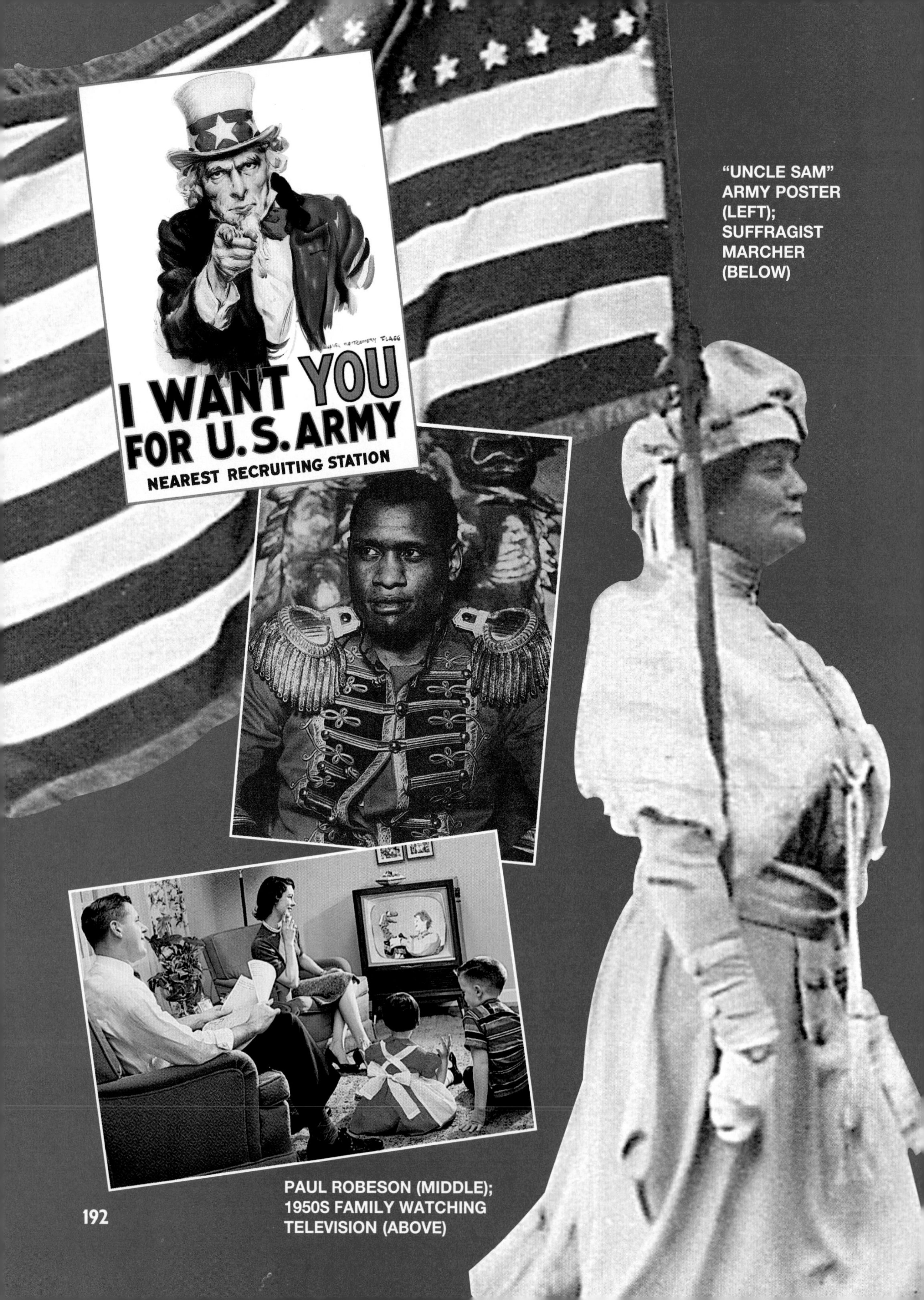


"UNCLE SAM" ARMY POSTER (LEFT); SUFFRAGIST MARCHER (BELOW)

PAUL ROBESON (MIDDLE); 1950S FAMILY WATCHING TELEVISION (ABOVE)

UNIT FOUR

# New Jersey Comes of Age

*"The economy is moving so fast. You always need. . .new skills."*

from a statement by Miriam Rios-Lebron
See page 237.

## Why Does It Matter?

The 1900s brought the promise of greater freedom and opportunity to more people in our state. Women won the right to vote after years of struggle. The protests of factory workers brought about better working conditions. African Americans gained better jobs and a fairer system of education.

In Unit 4 you will read about these struggles. You will also read about the Great Depression, two world wars, and a changing economy. How did these important events affect the people of our state? Read on to learn more.

PRESIDENT WOODROW WILSON

**FIND OUT MORE!**
Visit our website:
www.mhschool.com
interNET CONNECTION

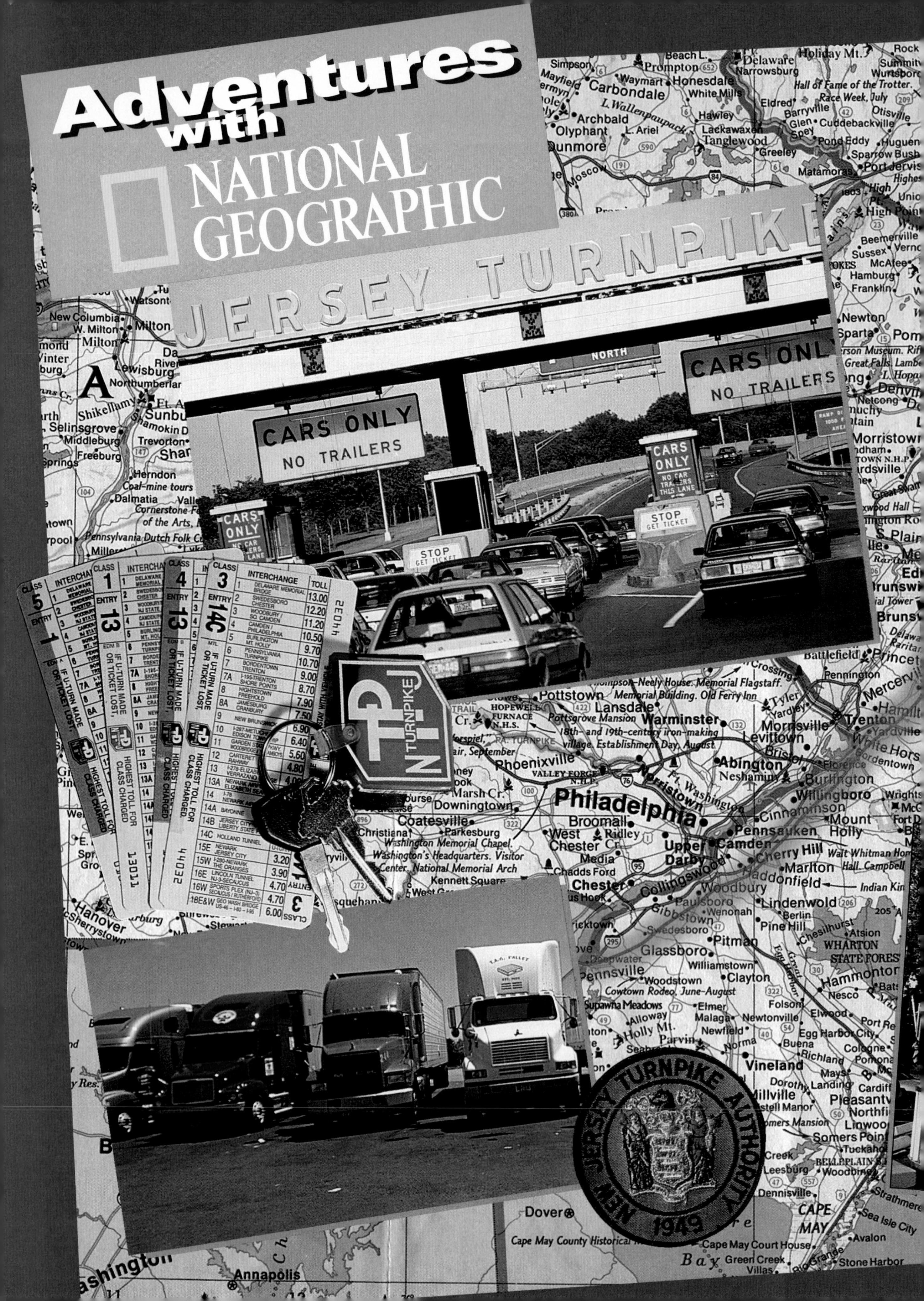
Adventures with
NATIONAL GEOGRAPHIC
JERSEY TURNPIKE
NORTH
CARS ONLY
NO TRAILERS
CARS ONLY
NO TRAILERS
CARS ONLY
NO CAR TRAILERS THIS LANE
STOP
GET TICKET
STOP
GET TICKET
N J TURNPIKE
NEW JERSEY TURNPIKE AUTHORITY
1949
Philadelphia

# The Road to Modern Life

It is as wide as a football field and extends 148 miles across our state. A concrete ribbon, the New Jersey Turnpike (shown in pink on the map) extends from the Delaware Memorial Bridge in the south to the George Washington Bridge (left) in the north.

The road opened in 1952. Each year about 200 million cars and trucks pay a toll and travel the turnpike—making it the busiest toll road in the United States. Run by a special organization called the Turnpike Authority, the highway links many of our state's farms, factories, cities, suburbs—and roadside diners (bottom)! From rural areas in the south to the urban north, the turnpike plays a key role in the life of New Jersey today.

## GEO JOURNAL

*Talk to family members and friends to learn how the turnpike affects your community.*

CHAPTER 8

# A New Century

## THINKING ABOUT GEOGRAPHY AND HISTORY

The 1900s brought good times and hard times to New Jersey. Citizens in our state struggled to make laws more fair and to improve conditions for workers. Women worked to gain rights. Our country entered a world war in Europe. By the 1930s, New Jerseyans faced another challenge: the Great Depression. Read on to learn how people survived these hard times only to face another terrible war in Europe.

**1901**

JERSEY CITY

**Mark Fagan brings "new ideas" as mayor of Jersey City.**

**1913**

PATERSON

**Hannah Silverman leads striking silk workers.**

**1917**

CAMP DIX

**Soldiers at Camp Dix train in World War I.**

1900 | 1910 | 1920

See pT68 for Chapter Organizer.

# LESSON 1

1880 | 1901 | 1924 | 1940 | 1960

See p. T69 for Lesson Teaching Strategies.

# The Reform Years

## Focus Activity

**READ TO LEARN**

***What changes came to New Jersey in the early 1900s?***

**VOCABULARY**

- **bribe**
- **New Idea**
- **political party**
- **primary**

**PEOPLE**

- **Mark Fagan**
- **Franklin Murphy**
- **Woodrow Wilson**
- **Hannah Silverman**
- **Mary Philbrook**
- **Alice Paul**
- **Mary T. Norton**

**PLACES**

- **Jersey City**

### Read Aloud

*In the early 1900s many Americans wanted to change how government was run. New Jersey Governor Woodrow Wilson was a leader of these people. He promised to "take the selection of candidates . . . out of the hands of small groups . . . and put it into the hands of the people."*

### THE BIG PICTURE

In the last chapter you read that many immigrants came to New Jersey in the early 1900s in search of a better life. Many of these immigrants found jobs in factories. By 1920, for example, nearly half of our state's workers had jobs in factories. Only 1 in 20 working people had jobs on farms.

More factories meant jobs and money for some people. But factories at this time could also be unsafe places to work. In addition, pay for workers was often so low that it was difficult for a family to make a living. Cities were often crowded, and housing conditions were poor or unhealthy. Many people believed it was time for change.

## CLEANING UP NEW JERSEY

In Chapter 6 you read about how the Joint Companies controlled the railroad and canal businesses during the mid-1800s. People often complained that Joint Companies charged high prices but paid low taxes. Despite these complaints, nothing happened.

Why not? The Joint Companies often gave a **bribe** to an official or a government worker. A bribe is money paid to an official to do something. Bribes are against the law. Once bribed, lawmakers made laws that helped the Joint Companies, and judges made decisions in the Companies' favor.

Big businesses like the Joint Companies often worked through a person known as a "boss" in order to get their way. A boss took money from big businesses and then used that money to bribe city and state officials. The officials then did what the boss said. Under this system, many bosses became rich and powerful.

### A New Idea

Bosses were a problem in many parts of the United States, and people were working for change. Many women, in particular, were concerned about the poor and unhealthy conditions in cities and work places.

In 1901 a man named **Mark Fagan** ran for mayor of **Jersey City**. Fagan and his supporters called for a **New Idea** in government. They wanted to defeat bosses and make businesses pay a fairer share of taxes.

Fagan also promised to improve schools, parks, and hospitals. When Fagan won the election, it surprised many people.

Many New Idea reforms were taken up by Governor **Franklin Murphy**. Murphy worked to make taxes and elections fairer. He also worked to pass laws making it illegal to hire children under 14 years old to work in factories.

**This political cartoon shows railroad monopolies taking over the New Jersey waterfront. Its title is "What Jersey Has Come To."**

## WORKING FOR CHANGE

Despite reforms, New Jersey bosses remained powerful. In 1910 they supported a man for governor whom they thought would fight against the New Idea. They chose the president of Princeton University, **Woodrow Wilson**. Wilson came out against the bosses instead!

### Wilson Works for Reform

Wilson promised to be honest. He challenged New Jersey "to set an example" for the country. Voters gave Woodrow Wilson a great victory. After his election, he noted that it would not be easy: ". . . to put right and fairness and public spirit in the saddle [in control] again."

Within a year Wilson had signed laws to correct unfair practices in business and government. Look at the chart on this page. It shows some of the reform laws passed in New Jersey. One important law changed how a candidate gets chosen by a **political party**. A political party is a group of people who share similar ideas about government. Before this time, a party's bosses chose candidates. The new law called for an election in which all the members of a political party choose a candidate. This election is known as a **primary**.

Wilson's success in New Jersey gained him national attention. In 1912, after only two years as governor, Wilson was elected President of the United States.

**NEW JERSEY REFORM LAWS, 1911–1913**

**1911**

- Primary law lets voters, not bosses, choose candidates
- Law toughens punishments for cheating in elections
- Law gives state government the power to set rates for gas and electricity
- Law makes employers pay workers hurt as a result of unsafe working conditions

**1913**

- Seven laws limit unfair business practices, such as forming monopolies

**CHART WORK**

From 1911 to 1913, New Jersey passed many reform laws.

**1.** Which law helped workers on the job?

### Strike at Paterson

People working in factories still faced difficult conditions. Paterson had become the center of the silk industry. It attracted skilled workers from England, Italy, and other countries to work in its factories. Yet it was also, in the words of a visitor:

> *a miserable* [unhappy] *place of factories, dye-houses,* [and] *silk mills, . . .* [without a] *place for the children to play in and no gardens where mothers can give their babies fresh air.*

Paterson's silk workers had few protections on the job. They worked

**CHART WORK: 1.** the law passed in 1911 that made employers pay workers who were hurt as a result of unsafe working conditions long hours, and the pay was often low. When business slowed down, factory owners cut their pay or even fired them. Many of the workers were women and children.

In the early 1900s, factory owners tried to replace the skilled workers with machines. In 1913, 25,000 silk workers in Paterson went on strike, refusing to go to work. They demanded an eight-hour workday and a wage of $12 a week. The Paterson strike was one of the biggest of its time. One of the leaders was a 17-year-old girl named Hannah Silverman. Hannah had worked as a silk weaver. Once the strike began, she joined workers in trying to close down a factory. Police arrested her. On the way to jail, she sang songs to show that she was not afraid.

Despite such determination, the factory owners refused to meet strikers' demands. The owners had seen many strikes in the past, and most had failed. After nearly six months, some strikers were almost starving. The strike ended. At least five people had died in the fighting. Some strikers won a shorter workday, but most did not.

**The International Workers of the World union supported the Paterson strike. It arranged a march (below) and a play (right) so workers could tell their story.**

## A LONG FIGHT FOR VOTES

In Chapter 6 you read about Lucy Stone. In 1867 she and others started the New Jersey Woman Suffrage Association. They wanted to change our state constitution so that women would once again have suffrage, or the right to vote.

In 1895 Mary Philbrook worked to get a special law passed. It allowed women to become lawyers. Philbrook became the first woman lawyer in our state. Now women could argue their case in court. The following words present an argument suffragists used. Why was a state not a true democracy if women couldn't vote?

**Excerpt from a circular prepared by the New Jersey Woman Suffrage Association, about 1915.**

***No state can be a true democracy in which one-half the people are denied the right to vote. . . . . Women need the vote for the same reasons that men need it. . . . Because laws regulate [control] a woman's life and the lives of her children, and because they tax her property, . . . she should have the right to share in the making of the laws.***

### The Nineteenth Amendment

By 1915 the work of Philbrook and others led to a special vote. Voters had to decide on an amendment, or change, to the state constitution. The amendment would have allowed women the right to vote. The voters, of course, were all men.

Suffragists worked tirelessly. They traveled thousands of miles, held 2,000 meetings, gave speeches, and wrote letters. Still, voters rejected the amendment. Similar amendments in other states were also defeated. Suffragists decided to try a different plan. If they could change the United States Constitution to allow votes for women, then the state laws against woman suffrage would no longer count.

Alice Paul was a leader in this drive. Born in Mount Laurel in 1885, Paul was willing to make sacrifices. She organized a parade in support of suffrage in Washington, D.C., in 1913.

**Suffragists spread their message at parades, picnics, and rallies like this one in Verona Park in 1914 (below left). Alice Paul (above) helped women get the right to vote.**

Angry crowds attacked the parade, but it drew attention to her cause.

Eventually, the hard work of the suffragists paid off. In 1919 Congress passed the Nineteenth Amendment. It gave women the right to vote starting in 1920.

In addition to voting, women also began to to run for government office. In 1924 Mary T. Norton of Jersey City became one of the first women elected to the House of Representatives in Washington, D.C.

### The Limits of Reform

Reformers made many changes in our state, especially in government. But bosses remained powerful. Also, some

See p. T69 for Answers to Think About It.

reformers ignored many of the needs of working people, like those in Paterson who went on strike.

## WHY IT MATTERS

In the early 1900s, reformers worked to make our state better. They improved the lives of many people. A war in Europe, however, soon overshadowed reform efforts.

## Reviewing Facts and Ideas

### MAIN IDEAS

- New Idea supporters, women's groups, and Woodrow Wilson worked for reforms.
- Workers in Paterson tried to improve their lives through a strike in 1913.
- Under the Nineteenth Amendment, women gained the right to vote in 1920.

### THINK ABOUT IT

**1.** What did New Idea supporters believe?

**2.** How did women from New Jersey work for woman suffrage?

**3. FOCUS** What were three reforms that came to New Jersey during the early 1900s?

**4. THINKING SKILL** How did the Nineteenth Amendment change women's lives in our country? Give reasons for your conclusion.

**5. WRITE** Imagine that you live in New Jersey at the time Woodrow Wilson is governor. Write a letter telling him how you feel about his reform ideas.

See p. T70 for Skill Teaching Strategies.

# Using Primary and Secondary Sources

**VOCABULARY**

primary source
secondary source

## WHY THE SKILL MATTERS

Suppose you wanted more information about strikes held by factory workers in the late 1800s and early 1900s. You could get this information from two different kinds of sources.

One is a **primary source**. A primary source is information that comes from someone who saw or took part in what he or she is describing. A primary source might be a journal, letter, pamphlet, oral history, newspaper report, or even a photograph. For example, in the last lesson you read a primary source from 1915 that gave an opinion on a woman's right to vote.

Most of the information in this textbook, however, is a **secondary source**. This kind of source is written by people who were not present at the events they describe. They got their information "secondhand."

Both kinds of information are important. A primary source can make us feel as though we were there. It can help us understand how one person thought about something. A secondary source may help us to see a broader view of events. It may give us more points of view on a subject.

## USING THE SKILL

Read the two passages below. Both give information about children working in New Jersey mills before the New Idea reforms. The first passage, Excerpt A, is from Teresa Cobianci, an Italian immigrant who had worked in a silk mill in Paterson as a ribbon weaver since the age of 13. Excerpt B, the second passage, is from a book written by Paul G.E. Clemens in 1992.

**EXCERPT A**

[The mill] is not a good place to work. . . . The air is bad. The windows are nailed down. . . . The floor is so rough great splinters stick into your shoes. It is very dirty too. . . . All the other weavers are young like me. . . . Most of the girls go before the year is up. . . . The bosses they holler and curse at you so. I hate to go back to the mill. . . . I hate always to be . . . screamed at.

**EXCERPT B**

What sort of work awaited immigrants? Men found work . . . everywhere: in factories, on the railroads and canals, along the docks. Women commonly worked as domestics *[servants]*, but unmarried females (often very young girls) could be found as well in factories. . . . Children either assisted their mothers at home tasks or entered the industrial labor force . . . as factory workers. Most children began working between the ages of 12 and 14.

*Excerpt A; Excerpt B.
**Excerpt A; Excerpt B; the primary source can make you feel as though you were there; the secondary source can help you see a broader perspective

## TRYING THE SKILL

Which of the two excerpts is a primary source? Which is a secondary source?* Now think about the differences between them. Which source tells you how a child felt about working in a factory? Which source tells you about the kinds of jobs children held during this time period? Which places child labor in New Jersey in a broader view? If you were writing a report about children working in factories, how would each kind of source be helpful to you?**

### Helping yourself

- **A primary source is an account of an event by a person who saw or experienced it.**
- **A secondary source is written by someone who was not present at the events he or she describes.**

See p. T70 for Answers to Reviewing the Skill.

## REVIEWING THE SKILL

1. What is the difference between a primary source and a secondary source?
2. If you wrote an article about child labor in the 1900s, would it be a primary source or a secondary source? Why?
3. Is a biography a primary source or a secondary source?
4. How can both primary and secondary sources help you understand history?

**Like Teresa Cobianci, this girl worked in a textile mill. She is taking care of a weaving machine.**

## Focus Activity

**READ TO LEARN**

***How did life change in New Jersey during World War I and the 1920s?***

**VOCABULARY**

- World War I
- Allied Powers
- Central Powers
- Great Migration

**PEOPLE**

- Walter G. Alexander
- Jacob Lawrence
- Jesse Redmon Fauset
- Paul Robeson

**PLACES**

- Hoboken
- Camp Dix
- Burlington

LESSON 2

1880 1900 1914 1929 1940 1960

See p. T71 for Lesson Teaching Strategies.

# World War I and the 1920s

## Read Aloud

*During the month of June 1914, war broke out in Europe. President Woodrow Wilson asked Americans to be "impartial* [not biased] *in thought as well as action." This soon became impossible. Before it was over, the war across the ocean would claim more than 320,000 American lives.*

### THE BIG PICTURE

**World War I** began in Europe in 1914. It was a war between the **Allied Powers**, made up of Britain, Russia, France, and Italy, and the **Central Powers**. This side included Germany and Austria-Hungary. At first the United States tried to stay out of the war.

The United States traded goods with both sides. The Central Powers believed, however, that this trade helped the Allied Powers. Soon German submarines began attacking United States ships. This angered many Americans. On April 6, 1917, the United States entered the war on the Allied side.

## NEW JERSEY IN WORLD WAR I

When the United States entered the war, the people of New Jersey jumped into action. Men and women signed up to serve in the armed forces. About 130,000 New Jerseyans served in the armed forces. The city of Hoboken bustled with activity. Nearly half of all United States soldiers who crossed the Atlantic passed through its port.

New Jersey factories shifted to making goods for the war. In Elizabeth, the state's largest sewing machine maker shifted to making cannon parts. Textile plants in Paterson and Passaic churned out blankets, tents, and uniforms to keep the troops warm. In Bayonne and Bayway, oil refineries produced the gas that powered many Allied cars and trucks. Shipyards at Camden and Newark built ships to carry soldiers and supplies across the Atlantic.

When the war cut off the supply of chemicals from Germany, the state responded. Twenty-three New Jersey chemical companies were started in 1917.

By the summer of 1917, thousands of soldiers were training in New Jersey. The biggest of the 16 military camps in our state was Camp Dix. This huge camp of 1,600 buildings was built in a pine forest near Burlington in less than a year!

### The Home Front

People at home made sacrifices during the war. Sugar, coal, and meat were in short supply. So the government declared different days of the week "sweetless, heatless, wheatless, and meatless" to save resources. The war, however, opened up job opportunities for women and African Americans. For the first time, they were able to get jobs as mechanics and shipbuilders.

In the fall of 1918, the war ended in an Allied victory. President Wilson had stated that the war would "make the world safe for democracy."

**New Jersey women played an important part in the war effort. Here, women weld bomb casings in a munitions factory.**

## THE GREAT MIGRATION

African Americans have lived in New Jersey since colonial times. Many African Americans moved to New Jersey during World War I. They were part of a much larger movement from the rural areas of the South to the cities of the North and Middle West. This movement, which began in the 1890s, is called the **Great Migration**. Look at the map on this page to see some of the routes of the Great Migration.

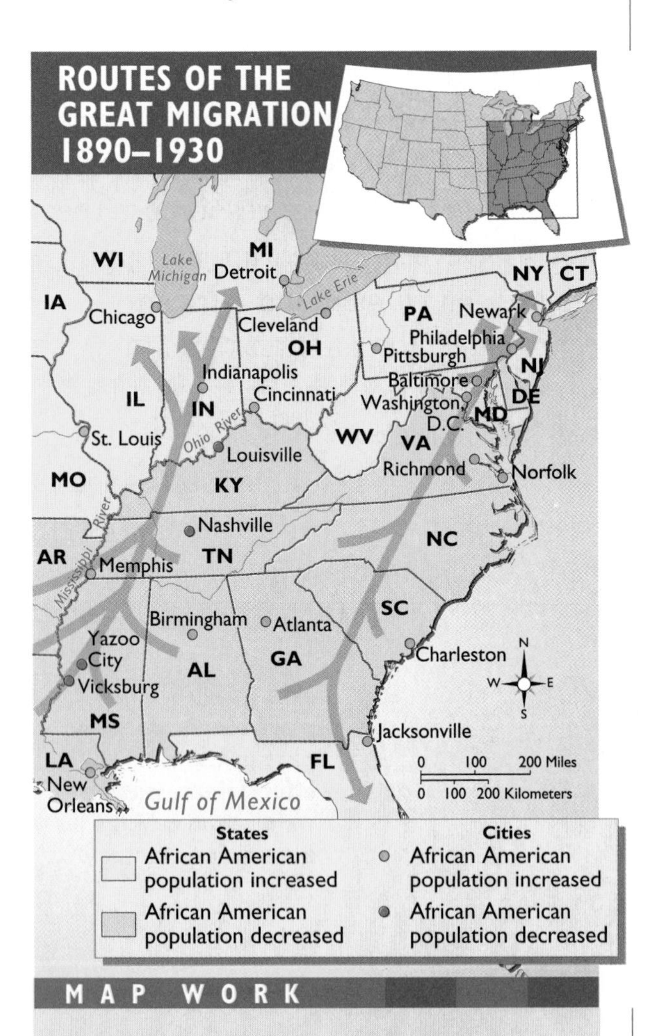


**MAP WORK**

This map shows the directions in which many African Americans migrated.

1. Name three cities in which the African American population increased.

### A New Start

By moving north, African Americans hoped to escape the poverty and discrimination they faced in the South. In 1924, African American Mildred Arnold traveled to Newark, New Jersey, from the small town of North in South Carolina. Her father had gone ahead. Arnold remembers,

> *My father and uncle met us at the Pennsylvania Railroad station and brought us up here to Newton street. . . . Everything was amazing. You had a lot of gaslights in Newark. When they come on in the nighttime, . . . the street lit up. We had never seen anything like that. Down South, when the sun went down there was only darkness.*

### Building Communities

Most of the people who took part in the Great Migration settled in cities, such as Newark and Trenton. Jobs were plentiful, especially during World War I. The graph on this page shows how the African American population of our state grew. Between 1900 and 1930, the African American population of New Jersey tripled.

The African Americans who settled in New Jersey helped build strong communities. Churches often acted as centers to support newcomers. African Americans formed organizations to help other migrants from the South get settled and succeed.

**MAP WORK: 1.** Any three of the following: St. Louis, Chicago, Indianapolis, Cleveland, Atlanta, Philadelphia, New York, Birmingham, Charleston, Jacksonville, Richmond, Newark, Norfolk, Memphis, New Orleans, Baltimore, Detroit, Washington, D.C., Cincinnati, and Pittsburgh

**GRAPH WORK: 1.** Between 1900 and 1910
**2.** Between 1920 and 1930

## Hopes and Disappointments

Gradually, African Americans began to gain political power. In 1921, Walter G. Alexander of Orange became the first African American elected to the state legislature.

As the African American population in New Jersey grew, some whites reacted by treating them badly. Some hotels and restaurants stopped serving African Americans. White leaders made schools and entire neighborhoods either all-white or all-black.

The Great Migration was a period of both hope and disappointment. Jacob Lawrence, an artist born in Atlantic City, examined these mixed feelings in a series of paintings. What feelings are expressed by the painting shown below?

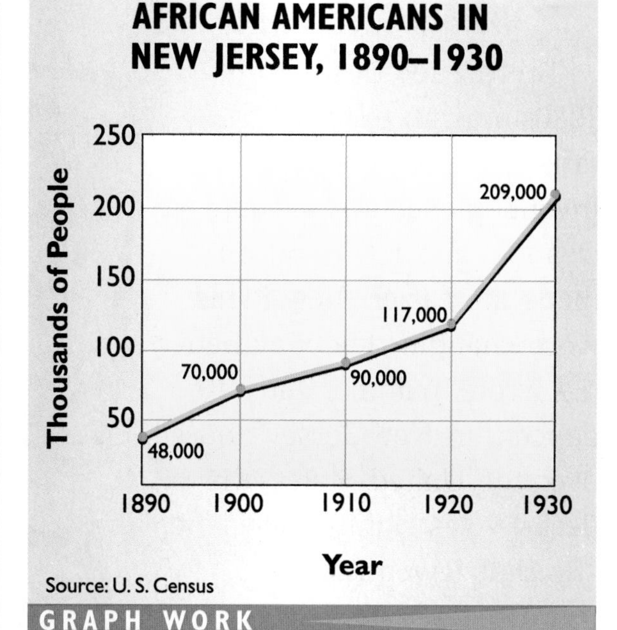

Source: U. S. Census

**GRAPH WORK**

Many African Americans moved to New Jersey during the Great Migration.

1. During which years shown on the graph did New Jersey have the smallest African American population growth?
2. In which years did it have the largest?

**MANY VOICES**
**ART**

**Painting by Jacob Lawrence. Part of a series made in 1941.**

*As the painting shows, African Americans traveled north by train to build new lives. Often the immigrants left behind family and friends.*

The Phillips Collection, Washington, D.C.

## ROARING TWENTIES

The decade of the 1920s was an exciting time. Business boomed. Inventions such as vacuum cleaners and refrigerators made life easier. New ideas were changing the way people wrote, painted, and danced. In New Jersey and all over the United States, this decade was rightly called the "Roaring Twenties."

### New Culture in Harlem

Perhaps no place was more exciting than Harlem. Harlem is an African American community in New York City. Harlem became the center of a new culture, and two New Jerseyans were at the center of it.

Jesse Redmon Fauset from Fredericksville was a poet, teacher, and newspaper writer. She also wrote many novels about the African American experience.

Paul Robeson became a famous singer and actor. He grew up in Princeton. His father had been enslaved, and his mother was a teacher. At Rutgers University, he was a star football player and the top student in his class.

Robeson's fame spread across the United States and Europe. He also worked to support the rights of African Americans and working people.

**Jesse Redmon Fauset (top) and Paul Robeson (left) helped make Harlem a center of African American culture. The Pulaski Skyway (below) was just one transportation improvement built in the 1920s. It sped cars from Jersey City to Newark.**

See p. T71 for Answers to Think About It.

## New Transportation

With businesses growing and hiring more workers, many people were able to buy automobiles for the first time. From 1918 to 1929, the number of cars in our state jumped from about 163,000 to over 800,000. Factories in New Jersey produced cars and car parts, such as seats, headlights, and horns.

The increase in cars and trucks led to a demand for more and better roads. In 1921 New York and New Jersey formed the Port of New York Authority. This group was responsible for improving the ports along the Hudson River and building roads and bridges. In 1927 it completed the Holland Tunnel under the Hudson River. The tunnel joined New York City and Jersey City and was the first underwater tunnel built just for cars. Before this, cars crossed the Hudson River on ferry boats.

Other important transportation links built at this time included the George Washington Bridge and the Pulaski Skyway. The Delaware River Bridge was also built at this time. Later renamed the Benjamin Franklin Bridge, it links Camden with Philadelphia. Together these new bridges and roads helped keep New Jersey an important transportation corridor.

## WHY IT MATTERS

World War I and the Great Migration brought many changes to our state. The new bridges and roads built in the 1920s are important transportation links we still use today.

### Reviewing Facts and Ideas

**MAIN IDEAS**

- The United States joined the Allied Powers in World War I.
- During the Great Migration many African Americans moved to New Jersey.
- The 1920s brought new ideas, new businesses, and improved transportation to New Jersey.

**THINK ABOUT IT**

1. What were some ways New Jerseyans helped the United States in World War I?
2. What was the Great Migration and why did African Americans come to the North?
3. **FOCUS** How did life change in New Jersey during World War I and the 1920s?
4. **THINKING SKILL** Identify one *cause* and one *effect* of the Great Migration.
5. **WRITE** Suppose you were writing a newspaper article about life in the 1920s. What would you describe?

## Focus Activity

**READ TO LEARN**

***How did the Great Depression and World War II change the way people lived and worked in New Jersey?***

**VOCABULARY**

- Great Depression
- New Deal
- Axis Powers
- World War II
- Allies

**PEOPLE**

- Franklin D. Roosevelt
- Frank Hague
- Albert Einstein

LESSON 3

1880 1900 1920 1929 1945 1960

See p. T72 for Lesson Teaching Strategies.

# The Depression and World War II

## Read Aloud

*In the spring of 1934, many families were suffering. These lines are from a letter written to the wife of the President by a girl from Port Morris: "I am a young girl of fifteen and I need a coat, so bad I have no money, nor any means of getting any. My father has been out of work for two years."*

## THE BIG PICTURE

The Roaring Twenties ended suddenly in 1929 with the collapse of the stock market. Stocks are shares, or parts, of ownership in a company. In the 1920s many Americans put their life savings into buying stocks. In October 1929 stock prices fell sharply. Americans rushed to sell their stocks. This caused stock prices to fall even more. The economy went from boom to bust.

The stock market crash was the beginning of the **Great Depression**. A depression is a time when many businesses fail and many people are out of work. For the next ten years, many Americans struggled just to survive.

## HARD TIMES IN NEW JERSEY

The Great Depression hit New Jersey hard. Many New Jerseyans lost their jobs when factories, stores, and businesses shut down. By the early months of 1932, as many as 400,000 people in New Jersey had lost their jobs. In New Jersey the average worker made $839 a year in 1929 but only $479 a year in 1932.

Factories that made machines and motors were hurt. People stopped buying cars, washing machines, and other expensive goods. Most people had little money for vacations, so resorts along the New Jersey shore suffered, too. Owners of fancy shops saw their business slow down as the rich lost their fortunes. Farmers and people working in oil refineries had better luck. People still needed to eat and to drive.

Many people stood in long lines to get free bread and soup from local governments and religious groups. People sold apples in the streets just to earn some money.

Family life was disrupted. One Maplewood woman describes her father's situation. He had risen from being a messenger at the age of 13 to an important businessman at 40. He lost this job in the crash. "About 1933 [my parents] traded our house for a smaller one in Newark . . . for the next few years we moved about five times to places with lower rents." New Jersey's African Americans suffered more than other groups. Often they were the first to be let go from jobs.

Some local governments tried to help. Bergen County was among the first to try to put people to work. More than 5,600 people lined up for the 1,000 road crew jobs the county could offer.

**Many people seeking work during the Great Depression waited in long lines.**

## A NEW DEAL FOR AMERICA

In 1932 Americans chose a new President, Franklin D. Roosevelt. Like the country, Roosevelt had faced hard times. In 1921 a disease called polio had caused him to lose the use of his legs. Yet he did not let the disability stop him from reaching his goals. FDR, as he was called, promised to get the country going again. His plan, called the New Deal, was designed to help those in need.

Two of FDR's New Deal programs were the Civilian Conservation Corps (CCC) and the Works Progress Administration (WPA). These programs put people to work on projects that helped everyone.

### The Boss of Jersey City

New Deal programs helped many New Jerseyans find work. They also boosted the career of one of the last bosses of New Jersey, Frank Hague.

Mayor Frank Hague ran Jersey City for more than 30 years.

As mayor of Jersey City for more than 30 years, Hague tightly controlled local government.

Hague found many different ways to stay in power. Not all of them were legal. For example, Hague's supporters helped their candidate to win by paying people to vote using the names of people who had long since moved away or died.

Hague grew rich through the money he took in from gambling, dishonest land deals, and other schemes. Efforts to remove him failed in 1929. In the following years, he was able to give out thousands of New Deal jobs and millions of dollars in relief money. Grateful voters reelected him year after year.

# Infographic

**interNET CONNECTION** Visit our website: www.mhschool.com

## The New Deal in New Jersey

**From public housing to conservation, there were many New Deal projects built by the WPA and the CCC in New Jersey. We can still see some of these projects today.**

### Housing

With money from the New Deal, workers such as these designed and built housing for senior citizens and the poor in our state.

### Conservation

The CCC planted millions of trees throughout our state. Shown here are new CCC workers arriving at Fort Dix.

### The Arts

Artists funded by the WPA created murals in public buildings. This mural by Ben Shahn (detail below) is in an elementary school in Roosevelt.

## WORLD WAR II

In 1939 Americans were still struggling through the Great Depression. In Europe, another war had begun. The **Axis Powers** led by Germany, Italy, and Japan started **World War II**. They fought against the **Allies**, led by Great Britain, France, and later the Soviet Union.

At first the United States tried to stay out of this conflict. Then on December 7, 1941, Japanese planes bombed the naval base at Pearl Harbor, Hawaii. The next day Congress declared war on Japan.

### New Jersey and the War

World War II gave a boost to the state's economy. People went back to work as factories turned out war supplies such as airplane motors, explosives, uniforms, medical supplies, and food. Training camps and the port of Hoboken again bustled with soldiers. The war brought a quick end to the Great Depression.

At home, there were shortages of tires, gasoline, fuel oil, sugar, meat, and butter. Families planted "victory gardens." Food from these gardens fed people at home so that farm products could be sent to soldiers. Even children helped with the war effort. Eileen Witte Treash, of Newark, remembers, "we knitted for Britain . . . and there were bandage rollings . . . we saved tin foil."

New Jersey women were proud to take a direct role in the war effort. Elizabeth Hawes worked in an airplane factory in Paterson. Yes, jobs were sometimes boring, but, she noted, "when you work the machine that makes the bit that turns the

**Soldiers learn paratrooping skills (left). Factory workers produced supplies for soldiers (right).**

motor that raises the plane that's going to soar in the clouds . . . you feel creative."

## An End to War

New Jersey scientists also helped the war effort. The discoveries of Albert Einstein of Princeton were used to create the most powerful weapon in history, the atomic bomb. After this weapon was dropped on two Japanese cities, the war ended on August 14, 1945. The Allies had won.

More than 560,000 New Jerseyans served in World War II. The soldiers were glad to be coming home. Many soldiers, however, were troubled by what they had seen. One described his thoughts: "I felt how horrible war is, and how inhumane war is. . . . "

See p. T72 for Answers to Think About It.

**Links to VISUAL ARTS**

**Margaret Bourke-White was a photographer who grew up in New Jersey. She was one of the four photographers chosen for the staff of *Life*, a weekly picture magazine started in 1936. One of her pictures appeared on its first cover. Bourke-White is best known for her powerful photographs of the Depression and of World War II. Locate some of Bourke-White's photographs and discuss how they help you understand the time in which she lived.**

## WHY IT MATTERS

The Great Depression and World War II were two of the greatest challenges faced by the United States in the 1900s. Determination and hard work helped New Jerseyans meet these challenges and prepare for growth and change ahead.

## Reviewing Facts and Ideas

### MAIN IDEAS

- The stock market crash of 1929 marked the beginning of the Great Depression.
- President Roosevelt's New Deal programs helped many people in New Jersey get jobs.
- The United States entered World War II in 1941. The war ended the Great Depression.
- New Jerseyans helped the war effort as citizens, soldiers, workers, and scientists.

### THINK ABOUT IT

1. What was the Great Depression?
2. How did the New Deal help the people of New Jersey recover from the Great Depression?
3. **FOCUS** How did the Great Depression and World War II change life in New Jersey?
4. **THINKING SKILL** Put these events in the correct *sequence:* attack on Pearl Harbor; New Deal programs; stock market crash; end of World War II.
5. **WRITE** Imagine that you are a writer hired by the WPA. Write a paragraph describing the special geography of your community.

See p. T73 for Answers to Chapter 8 Review.

# CHAPTER 8 REVIEW

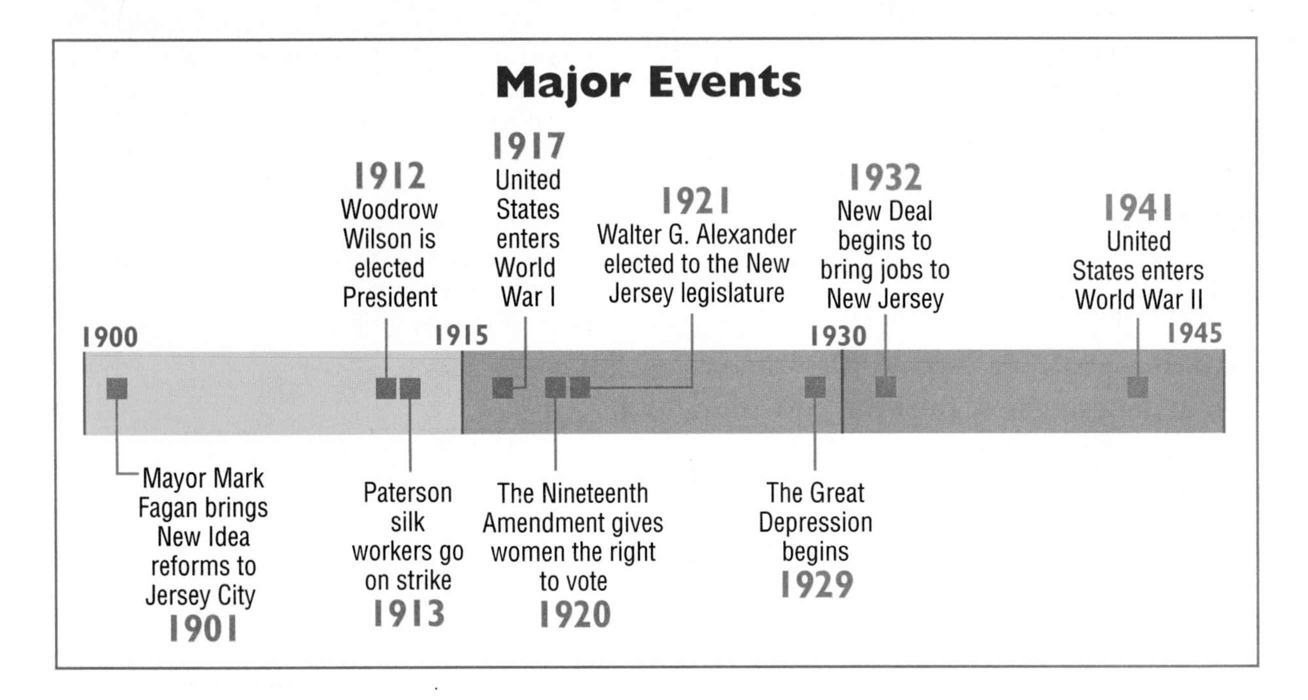


## THINKING ABOUT VOCABULARY

Number a sheet of paper from 1 to 10. Beside each number write **C** if the underlined term is used correctly. If it is not, write the term that would correctly complete the sentence.

1. The New Idea in government involved defeating bosses and making businesses pay a fairer share of taxes.
2. The Allies in World War II included Great Britain, France, and the Soviet Union.
3. A bribe is money paid unlawfully to an official to do something.
4. The United States entered World War II in 1917.
5. In World War I, the Central Powers were Britain, Russia, France, and Italy.
6. The Great Migration was a movement of African Americans from the rural South to the cities of the North and Middle West beginning in the 1890s.
7. The Axis Powers in World War II were led by Germany, Italy, and Japan.
8. A primary is a group of people who share similar ideas about government.
9. The Great Depression began with the stock market crash of 1929.
10. The New Deal was President Roosevelt's plan for recovery from the Great Depression.

## THINKING ABOUT FACTS

1. Describe two types of reforms that occurred in New Jersey in the early 1900s.
2. What was the Great Migration?
3. Why was there a demand for new and better roads in New Jersey in the 1920s?
4. List three types of New Jersey businesses that were hit hard by the Great Depression.
5. How did New Jerseyans help with the war effort during World War II?

## THINK AND WRITE

### WRITING A SPEECH
Imagine that you lived in New Jersey in the early 1900s. Write a speech telling why the bosses should have less power.

### WRITING A LETTER
Suppose that you are a fourth grader living in New Jersey during World War I. In a letter to a friend, describe how the war affects you.

### WRITING A DESCRIPTION
Write a description of how the Great Depression affected people in New Jersey.

## APPLYING STUDY SKILLS

### USING PRIMARY AND SECONDARY SOURCES

1. Explain the difference between a primary source and a secondary source.
2. Find two primary sources in the chapter.
3. Find two examples of information you think came from secondary sources.
4. Why are primary sources useful when studying history?
5. Why is it important to understand the difference between primary and secondary sources?

## Summing Up the Chapter

Copy the following cause-and-effect chart on a sheet of paper. Fill in the blank spaces on the chart. Then use the information to write a paragraph that answers the question "How did life change in New Jersey during the years 1900 to 1940?"

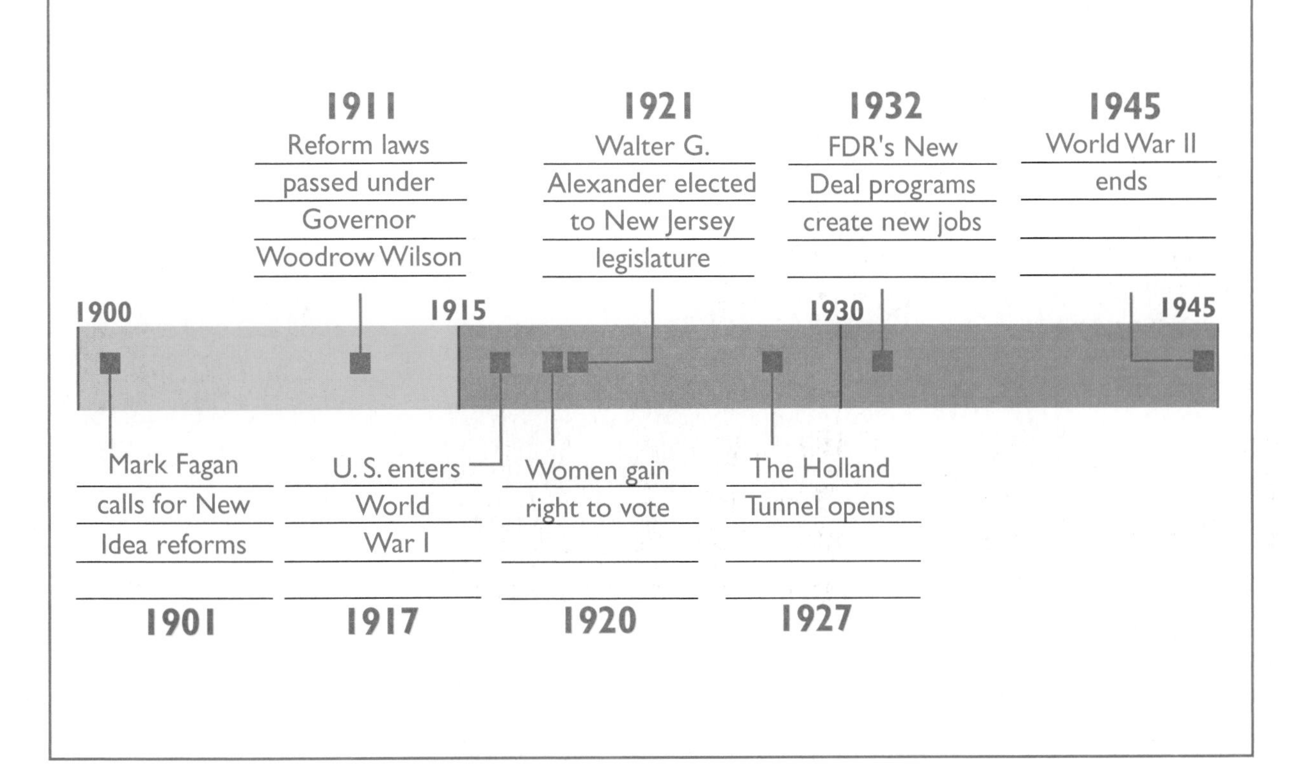

CHAPTER 9

# Growth and Change

## THINKING ABOUT GEOGRAPHY AND HISTORY

After World War II, suburbs grew, highways expanded, and the economy boomed. What did these changes mean for the people of our state? Not everyone enjoyed the same opportunities. African Americans and women continued a long struggle for equal rights. The growth had hurt our environment, and citizens worked to clean up and preserve our state. Read on to learn how these struggles helped to make our state a better place to live.

1950s

WILLINGBORO

New suburbs provide homes for a growing population.

1951

DEEPWATER

Workers begin construction on the New Jersey Turnpike.

1963

ENGLEWOOD

Students and parents protest segregated schools.

1950 | 1960 | 1970

See pT74 for Chapter Organizer.

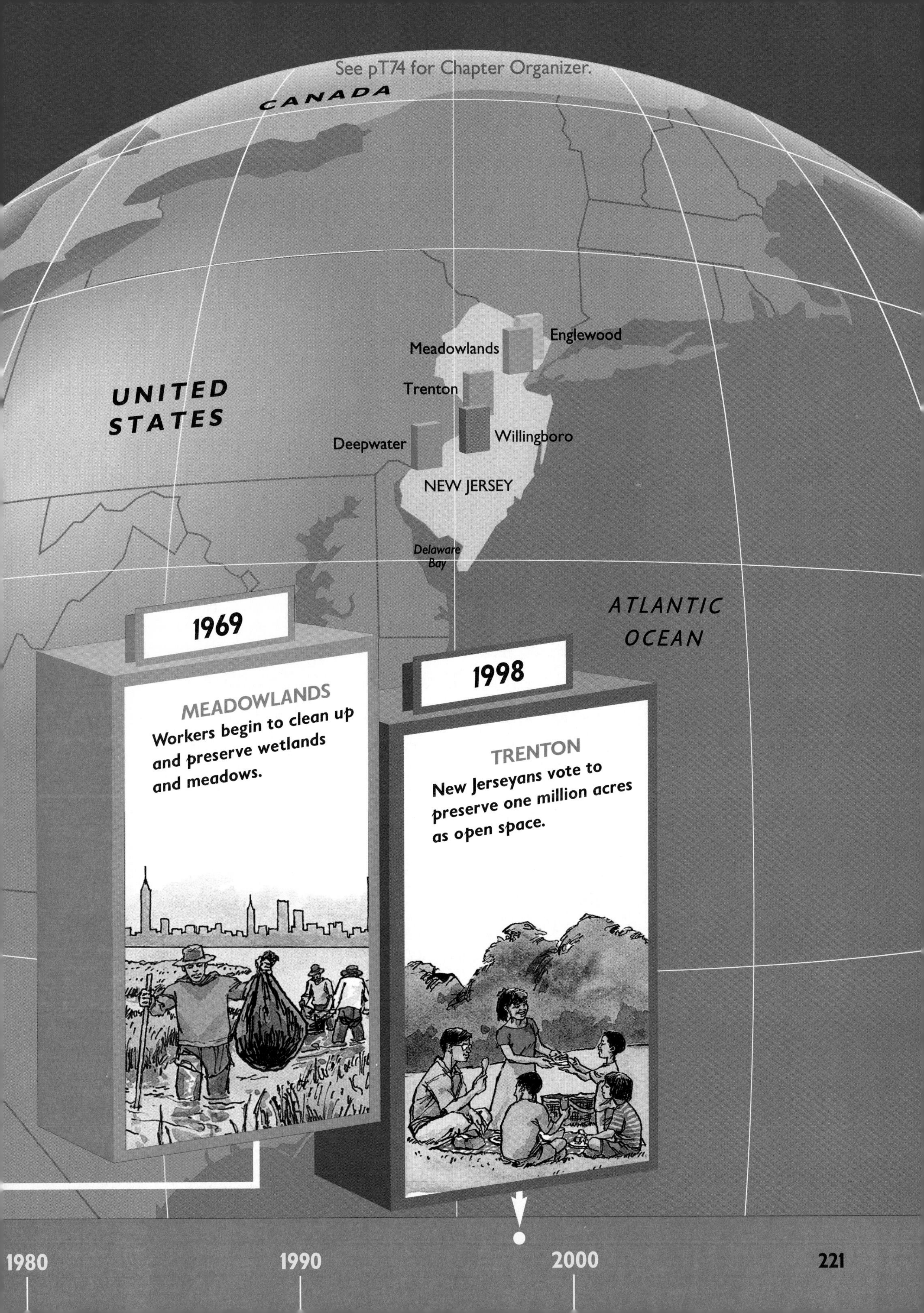

CANADA

UNITED STATES

Meadowlands

Englewood

Trenton

Deepwater

Willingboro

NEW JERSEY

*Delaware Bay*

*ATLANTIC OCEAN*

**1969**

MEADOWLANDS

**Workers begin to clean up and preserve wetlands and meadows.**

**1998**

TRENTON

**New Jerseyans vote to preserve one million acres as open space.**

1980

1990

2000

LESSON 1

1940 1945 1962 1970 1985 2000

See p. T75 for Lesson Teaching Strategies.

# Booming New Jersey

## Focus Activity

**READ TO LEARN**

***What changes took place in New Jersey after World War II?***

**VOCABULARY**

- **mass production**
- **transistor**

**PEOPLE**

- **William J. Levitt**
- **Charles Seabrook**

**PLACES**

- **Willingboro**
- **Mahwah**
- **Murray Hill**

## Read Aloud

*Like many soldiers during World War II, Harold B. Merritt of New Jersey wrote letters home to his family. In one letter he asked his wife about "our plans after the war. . . , particularly in connection with where we would live." New homes and new communities were on the minds of many New Jerseyans as the war came to a close in 1945.*

## THE BIG PICTURE

In the years following World War II, New Jersey grew as never before. From 1945 to 1955, for example, our state's population grew by more than 2 million people, from just over 4 million to more than 6 million people. The economy grew, too.

Returning soldiers married, started families, and looked for homes. African Americans from the South continued to migrate to our state. New immigrants from places such as Puerto Rico and Cuba moved here as well. Most of the new immigrants settled in cities like Newark and Paterson.

However, the fastest growing communities were suburbs, especially in areas close to New York City and Philadelphia. Many people moved from those and other cities to the new suburbs. These new communities changed the way people lived and worked.

## NEW COMMUNITIES

After the war, thousands of soldiers returned home. They needed places to live. Businesspeople responded quickly to this need for housing. Builders created whole new communities, complete with schools and stores. William J. Levitt was one such builder. He turned the small farming village of Willingboro, with a population of 600, into a suburb of 40,000 people. How did Levitt do this?

The secret to Levitt's success was mass production. Mass production means manufacturing large numbers of goods using identical parts. Levitt's workers moved from one house to the next doing just one job, such as roofing, painting, or plumbing. Workers in the first community built by Levitt completed an amazing 180 homes per week this way.

Some people called these houses "little boxes." However, most homeowners were thrilled with their new homes. In Willingboro, they even changed their town's name to Levittown. Later, it was changed back to Willingboro.

### Life in the Suburbs

The growth of suburbs like Willingboro changed life in our state. The automobile became even more important, since people often needed to drive to jobs in the cities. Meals changed, as homemakers cooked new foods, such as frozen TV dinners. Families changed, too. Before this time, grandparents often lived with families. Suburban households were usually just parents and children.

New Jersey's new suburbs gave thousands of people the chance to own homes and have more living space. However, not everyone had this chance. Many suburbs unfairly discriminated against African Americans and other nonwhites, refusing to allow them to buy houses.

**New communities, such as this one in Clifton (below), grew up all over the state. In the suburbs, families often gathered to watch television (left).**

## CHANGING INDUSTRY

The booming economy provided plenty of jobs for our state's growing population. In 1955, for example, the largest automobile factory in the United States opened in Mahwah. This factory, bigger than 34 football fields, employed 5,000 workers.

In southern New Jersey, Charles Seabrook built what was called the "biggest vegetable factory on earth." Workers used mass production to move crops from field to freezer in less than an hour.

In the 1940s many Japanese Americans had settled nearby and worked for Seabrook. Later, many workers in the factory and surrounding farms were migrant workers from Puerto Rico and Mexico. They worked half the year in New Jersey harvesting crops. During colder months, they traveled south to Florida to work on farms there. They worked long hours for low pay.

### Big Inventions in Small Packages

In the years after the war, our state's scientists and inventors continued the legacy of innovation begun by Thomas Edison. The new products they created, such as plastics, medicines, and rockets, also created jobs.

In 1947 New Jersey scientists at a company in Murray Hill invented the first transistor. A transistor is a tiny device that controls the movement of electricity. Transistors allow electronic items, such as radios and televisions, to be made very small. Without transistors, a mobile phone, for example, would need to be as big as the Washington Monument!

In 1962 New Jersey scientists invented the world's first communications satellite. Communications satellites orbit in outer space and send telephone or television signals from one place on Earth to another.

*Links to* **MATHEMATICS**

**As new technology improves, its price usually goes down. During the 1950s, the cost of a transistor went from $45 to $2. Today you could buy about a thousand for one cent! Suppose that you bought a transistor radio in 1959 that included 6 transistors. At $2 each, how much would the transistors for that radio cost? How much would they have cost at $45 each? What is the difference in cost?**

## Roads Across New Jersey

The new suburbs and factories were changing the New Jersey landscape. Perhaps the biggest change to our state's landscape in these years came in the form of new roads. From 1950 to 1960, our state's highway system added more than 500 miles of new roads.

The Garden State Parkway opened in 1954. The Atlantic City Expressway opened in 1962. The most important new highway, though, was the New Jersey Turnpike. It stretches 148 miles from Deepwater in southwestern New Jersey to the George Washington Bridge at the New York border.

The Turnpike opened in 1952, after only two years of construction! It proved an instant hit with drivers. So many people used the Turnpike on Thanksgiving Day in 1952 that toll collectors had to use wastebaskets to hold all of the extra toll money.

**New roads, including the New Jersey Turnpike (below), helped make the growth of suburbs possible.**

## WHY IT MATTERS

The years following World War II brought great changes to our state. Our population and economy grew. Whole new industries and towns sprang up. But not everyone shared equally in the growth. In the next lesson you will read how efforts to make life fairer for all people made our state a better place.

### Reviewing Facts and Ideas

#### MAIN IDEAS

- The population of New Jersey grew quickly after World War II and many people settled in suburbs.
- New Jersey's economy expanded after the war.
- New transportation routes were built in the 1950s, including the New Jersey Turnpike.

#### THINK ABOUT IT

1. How did the end of World War II affect homebuilding in New Jersey?
2. Why was the invention of the transistor important?
3. **FOCUS** Name two new industries that developed in New Jersey after World War II.
4. **THINKING SKILL** *Draw a conclusion* about why New Jersey grew after World War II.
5. **GEOGRAPHY** How did people moving to the suburbs affect transportation in New Jersey?

See p. T77 for Citizenship Teaching Strategies.

# CITIZENSHIP VIEWPOINTS

Cars take us to many places. But are too many cars clogging our roads?

## How can New Jersey solve its traffic problems?

Most people who live in New Jersey ride in a car or a bus to get where they're going. No matter where you live in the state, chances are that you know what it's like to be stuck in traffic. One reason for this is that New Jersey has more people and highways per square mile than any other state. Millions of cars and buses fill New Jersey's highways, bridges, and tunnels.

New Jerseyans agree that traffic is a problem. People have different viewpoints about how to solve this problem. Donna McDonough hopes more people will walk or ride bicycles whenever they are not traveling very far. She urges people to carpool or use mass transit when possible. Pam Fischer does not think car pooling will work. She says better planning is needed in many areas. Lynn Wilkins favors wider use of mass transit, such as trains and buses. Read and consider three different viewpoints on this issue. Then answer the questions that follow.

See p. T77 for Answers to Building Citizenship.

# Three DIFFERENT Viewpoints

"Biking or walking is just as good. . . ."

1

**DONNA MCDONOUGH**
RideWise, Somerville, New Jersey
Excerpt from Interview, 2000

Building more roads is only a temporary solution to our traffic problems. Some day we won't be able to build more roads. People don't need their cars for short trips to the grocery store, bank, or dry cleaners. Biking or walking is just as good for trips that are close to home. For longer trips, we favor car pooling or mass transit. But even if they only carpool two or three times a week, it can reduce traffic problems.

---

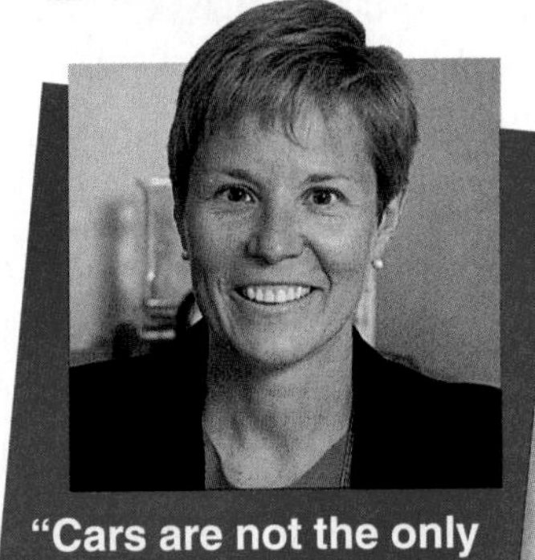

"Cars are not the only cause of traffic problems."

**PAM FISCHER**
AAA New Jersey Automobile Club, Florham Park, New Jersey
Excerpt from Interview, 2000

Cars are not the only cause of traffic problems. Everybody keeps pointing at cars as the problem, but the real problem is poor planning. We haven't given enough thought to where we put our business centers and housing developments. We haven't put them close to mass transit. We need to look at where people live and where they work.

---

"Use more mass transit."

**LYNN WILKINS**
Central Division Transportation Director, NJ Transit, Maplewood, New Jersey
Excerpt from Interview, 2000

Americans love the automobile. When we widen roads or build new ones, it encourages people to use their cars more. We have to find ways to get [more] people to take mass transit. We can keep the open spaces and green areas that we now enjoy if we use more mass transit.

## BUILDING CITIZENSHIP

1. What is the viewpoint of each person? What solution does each person favor?
2. In what ways do the viewpoints agree? How do they disagree?
3. What other viewpoints might New Jerseyans have on this issue?

**SHARING VIEWPOINTS**

Share with your classmates what you think about these and other viewpoints. Give reasons to support your opinions. Then, as a class, write three statements that all of you can agree with about solving our state's traffic problems.

# Geography Skills

See p. T76 for Skill Teaching Strategies.

## Reading Road Maps

**VOCABULARY**
road map
interstate highway

### WHY THE SKILL MATTERS

In the last lesson you read about changes in New Jersey transportation after World War II. As new suburban communities grew, new roads allowed people to commute to jobs in the cities. Many people in our state still commute to work. Some New Jerseyans take trains to work. Others ride buses. Many continue to drive cars to work. In New Jersey, this often means traveling on a highway. A highway is a main road and a major route of travel.

How do all of these people find out how to get where they are going? Many travelers use a road map. A road map is a map that shows people which roads to use to get from one place to another.

ROADS IN CENTRAL NEW JERSEY

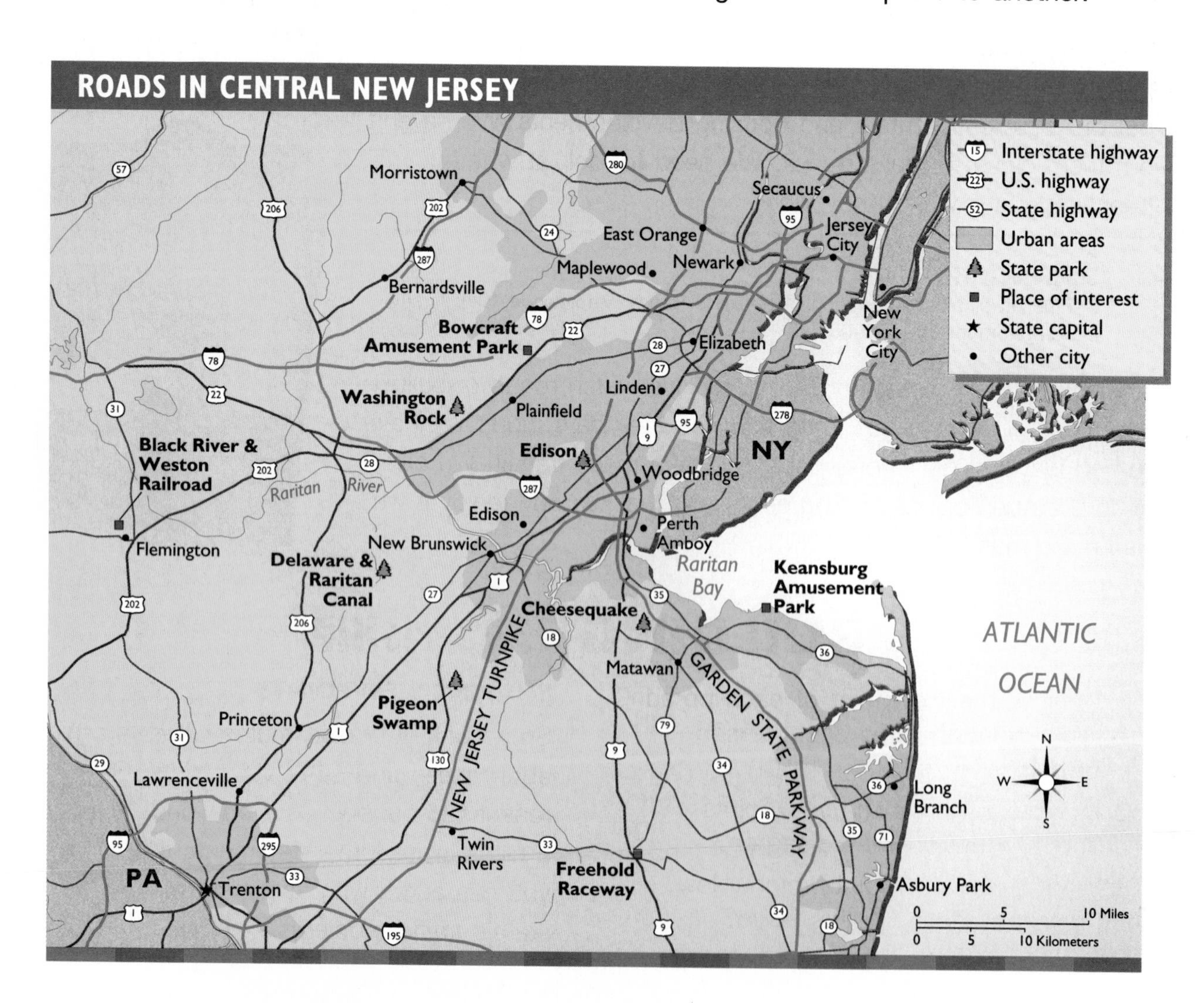

*state highway; U.S. highway
**Route 18
***Route 27; state highway; by the color of the line—red

- **A road map helps to guide travelers from one place to another.**
- **Road maps show highways and other information needed by road travelers.**
- **Study the map key to identify the symbols and colors used on the map.**

See p. T76 for Answers to Reviewing the Skill.

****33 to NJTP to 18; state and interstate highways
*****with a square symbol

## USING THE SKILL

Look at the road map of central New Jersey on page 228. It shows some of the important places to visit in this area and the roads that connect these places.

The map shows several different kinds of roads. Look at the map key. As you can see, a green line tells you that the road is an **interstate highway**. An interstate highway connects two or more states. Usually these roads have at least two lanes in each direction, with traffic flowing both ways.

Look back at the map key. What kind of road does a red line stand for? A brown line?*

You probably noticed that most roads on the map are labeled with numbers. The number of the road appears inside a special symbol. What is the number of the road that connects New Brunswick to the New Jersey Turnpike?**

If you follow some roads with your finger, you will see that they have more than one number. That is because sometimes more than one road will share a certain route.

You may have noticed something else, too. Most even-numbered roads tend to run east and west. Odd-numbered roads usually run north and south. This fact can help drivers know which way they are going.

## TRYING THE SKILL

Suppose you lived in Princeton and worked in New Brunswick. Which route would you take to get to work? What kinds of roads are on the route? How can you tell?***

Suppose you lived in Twin Rivers and were planning a trip to the Crossroads Theatre in New Brunswick. Which route would be the most direct? What kinds of roads are on this route? ****

The road map on page 228 also shows state parks, urban areas, and places of interest in central New Jersey. How are places of interest marked on this map?*****

## REVIEWING THE SKILL

1. What does a road map show?
2. According to the map, which interstate highway runs north and south? What did you do to find the answer? Look at the road map again. What route would you take to visit Edison State Park if you started from Long Branch?
3. What kind of road is Highway 27?
4. Why is it important to be able to read a road map?

LESSON 2

1941 1976 1985 2000

See p. T78 for Lesson Teaching Strategies.

# Times of Change

## Read Aloud

*In the summer of 1947 state leaders met at Rutgers University in New Brunswick to write a new constitution for New Jersey. Governor Alfred E. Driscoll led the meeting, telling the men and women delegates that "a great work is expected of you."*

## Focus Activity

**READ TO LEARN**

***How did African Americans work to gain rights in New Jersey?***

**VOCABULARY**

- segregation
- civil rights
- county
- apportionment
- income tax

**PEOPLE**

- Oliver Randolph
- Marion Thompson Wright
- Martin Luther King, Jr.
- S. Howard Woodson, Jr.
- Madaline Worthy Williams
- Ulysses S. Wiggins
- Kenneth Gibson
- Brendan Byrne

**PLACES**

- Englewood

## THE BIG PICTURE

In November 1947 New Jersey voters approved the new constitution that the leaders wrote. It replaced the old constitution of 1844. The new constitution was much shorter and clearer than the old one. It gave the governor more power. It also made our state's court system simpler.

The new constitution also tried to make life fairer for all New Jerseyans. By simply changing the word *men* to *persons*, for example, it gave women equal rights and protections in our state. The new constitution also made it against the law to discriminate against people because of their race, color, or the country they came from. Despite this change, African Americans had to struggle for their rights for many years. Women, also, continued to work for equal opportunities in education and jobs.

## SEPARATE BUT NOT EQUAL

Oliver Randolph was the only black delegate to the 1947 constitutional convention. He worked hard to make sure that racial discrimination would become against the law. He knew that discrimination was affecting the lives of most African Americans in our state every day.

In the 1940s, segregation occurred in many public places in our state, such as parks and restaurants. This means these places were separate for blacks and whites. Blacks were not allowed to buy houses in certain neighborhoods. There were even separate sports teams for blacks and whites.

### Life Under Segregation

African Americans also faced discrimination at work. Some businesses, for example, would not hire blacks. Some labor unions also would not allow blacks to become members.

Schools, too, were segregated by race. Historian Marion Thompson Wright, from East Orange, studied schools in our state in the early 1940s. Her study showed that in 1941 there were "at least seventy separate schools for Negro [African American] children." Schools for black children almost always had poorer classrooms and fewer supplies than schools for white children. Black teachers were often paid less than white teachers.

Helen Jackson Lee moved to Trenton in 1940. She recalled how segregation affected her life.

> *Black people could [not] eat in the better restaurants or hotel dining rooms downtown. And long lines of blacks waited to climb the steps to the peanut galleries [less costly seats] . . . of the theaters and first-run movie houses . . .*

When Helen Jackson Lee tried to get a job as a secretary in 1942, she was told:

> *I'm not going to hire you. . . . As long as I'm in charge. . . no colored [African American] women are going to work in these offices.*

**Protest marchers demanded an end to segregation in schools.**

## THE STRUGGLE FOR EQUALITY

African Americans throughout the United States, not just in New Jersey, faced unfair treatment. The situation was worse in the South. There, many African Americans were not even allowed to vote.

### Civil Rights Movement

In the 1950s and 1960s, many Americans began working for civil rights. Civil rights are the rights of all citizens to be treated equally under the law. Reverend Martin Luther King, Jr., from Georgia, was a leader in the movement for civil rights. His ideas and energy inspired millions across the country.

In New Jersey, the constitution of 1947 had outlawed discrimination but had not ended it. African Americans still faced unfair treatment. Civil rights leaders worked to end the system of segregation in schools, housing, and public places. Reverend S. Howard Woodson, Jr., Madaline Worthy Williams, and Dr. Ulysses S. Wiggins were three leaders of the civil rights movement in New Jersey.

Civil rights workers protested segregation in many different ways. For example, in 1963 African American students and their parents staged a "sit-in" at a mostly white school in Englewood. They sat down and refused to leave the school until school officials agreed to end segregation. Vincente Tibbs, the only African American on the town council, said "There are people here who don't even admit there's a problem."

The efforts of civil rights workers, both black and white, gradually paid off. In 1962, for example, blacks were finally allowed to buy homes in the all-white suburb of Willingboro. Schools throughout the state slowly ended segregation. In 1964, the United States Congress passed

**Reverend Martin Luther King, Jr., inspired many people to work for civil rights.**

the Civil Rights Act. It made discrimination against the law everywhere in the United States.

### Anger Boils Over

Many African Americans still faced great challenges. In many cities, jobs were scarce and living conditions were poor. In Newark, African Americans were angry that they had no power in the city government, even though they made up half the population. In 1967 a terrible riot began. The riot lasted for four days. Before it was over, 23 people had died. Hundreds more were injured, and the center of the city lay in ruins. Riots also took place in Plainfield, Atlantic City, Camden, Paterson, and other cities in the United States.

The riots shocked many people. Some whites moved away from Newark to suburbs. Slowly, however, the city began to rebuild. In 1970, **Kenneth Gibson** became the first African American mayor of Newark. Three years later, the Reverend S. Howard Woodson, Jr., became leader of the state General Assembly.

**In 1967 riots destroyed much of downtown Newark (above). In 1970 Kenneth Gibson (below right) became mayor of Newark. In 1973 Reverend S. Howard Woodson, Jr. (below) became leader of the General Assembly.**

## COURTS CALL FOR CHANGE

One of the most important changes brought by the new constitution in 1947 was a new court system. The Supreme Court became the most powerful court in New Jersey. The judges of this court had the power to order the government to follow laws. For example, the court ordered many towns to end segregation in their schools.

### One Person, One Vote

The 1947 constitution guaranteed that each **county**, or section of the state, had one representative in the State Senate and at least one in the Assembly. The **apportionment**, which means dividing according to a plan, of the Assembly seats was based on population. Counties with more people had more representatives. However, apportionment of Senate seats was different. A county with 50,000 people might have one senator, but so would a county with nearly a million residents. This gave people in rural counties much more power than people in urban counties.

In 1964 the Supreme Court declared that this system was illegal. The court argued that no citizen in the state should have more power than any other citizen. The court forced the legislature to make reforms. Under the new plan, the state's population would be counted every ten years. After each count, a committee would draw up districts that had equal numbers of people. Every district would have two assembly members and one senator.

### Dollars for Schools

In 1973 the state Supreme Court declared that the state government had not provided a "thorough and efficient" education for all students in the state. This was what the constitution required. The court said that students in rich towns and poor towns should have an equal opportunity for education.

In order to follow the court order, the government needed more money. Governor **Brendan Byrne** pushed a bill through the legislature in 1976 that

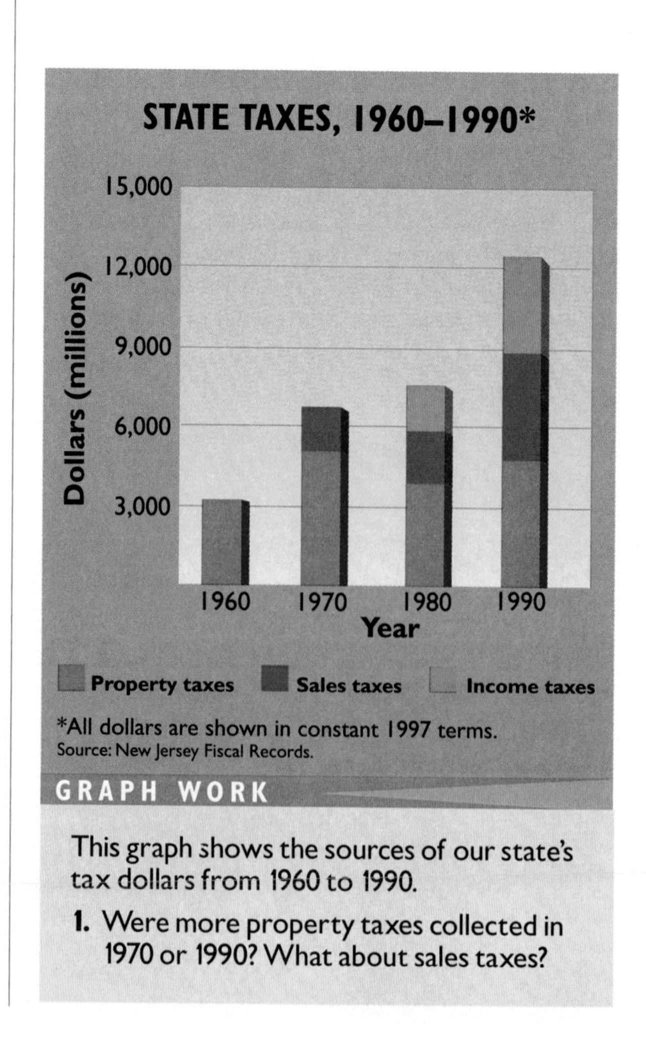


**GRAPH WORK**

This graph shows the sources of our state's tax dollars from 1960 to 1990.

1. Were more property taxes collected in 1970 or 1990? What about sales taxes?

**GRAPH WORK: 1.** more property taxes were collected in 1970; more sales taxes in 1990.

Brendan Byrne, who became governor in 1973, signed into law new taxes to pay for schools.

set up a state income tax. Income tax is money paid to the government on the money people earned. New Jersey was one of the last states in the country to have an income tax. Look at the graph on page 234 to see how our state's taxes have changed over the years.

## Equality in Education

Women, especially, struggled to bring more equality to schools in New Jersey. Princeton University first accepted women students in 1969, as did Rutgers in 1972. In 1972 girls in New Jersey schools gained the right to try out for all varsity sports. In 1975, the state government required that all state education programs be open to all people. Women, African Americans, and Hispanics began to get the same opportunities for education that white men had.

See p. T78 for Answers to Think About It.

## WHY IT MATTERS

New laws and the civil rights movement helped more citizens to realize the promise of equality in New Jersey. Still, changes were often slow in coming.

## Reviewing Facts and Ideas

### MAIN IDEAS

- In 1947 a new state constitution outlawed discrimination.
- Many New Jerseyans took part in the civil rights movement in an attempt to end segregation and discrimination.
- The apportionment of seats in the legislature was made more fair after 1964.
- The legislature created an income tax to support education in 1976.

### THINK ABOUT IT

1. What are civil rights?
2. What effect did the 1947 constitution have on discrimination in New Jersey?
3. **FOCUS** Name two ways African Americans worked for civil rights in the 1950s and 1960s.
4. **THINKING SKILL** Place the following events in the correct *sequence*: New Jersey approves a new constitution; New Jersey begins to tax income; African American students stage a sit-in; Kenneth Gibson becomes the mayor of Newark.
5. **WRITE** Imagine that you lived in the 1950s and were troubled by discrimination. Write a letter to a local newspaper that tells why this discrimination is wrong.

## Focus Activity

**READ TO LEARN**

***How did New Jersey's economy change from the 1970s to the 1990s?***

**VOCABULARY**

- service
- global economy
- interdependent

**PEOPLE**

- Christine Todd Whitman

**PLACES**

- South Brunswick
- Meadowlands
- Cherry Hill

LESSON 3

1940 1950 2000

See p. T79 for Lesson Teaching Strategies.

# A Changing Economy

### Read Aloud

*Singer Bruce Springsteen grew up in Freehold. His 1984 song "My Hometown" described some of the changes that hit New Jersey's economy in the 1980s.*

*They're closing down the*
*textile mill*
*across the railroad tracks.*
*Foreman says these jobs are going boys,*
*and they ain't coming back. . . .*

## THE BIG PICTURE

From the 1950s to the 1990s New Jersey's economy, like the economy of the United States as a whole, changed greatly. Manufacturing jobs, for example, became less important. Many factories closed or moved away. Older industries were replaced by newer ones. Look at the graphs on the next page to see some of these changes.

Many workers now had jobs in **service** industries. Service workers do not make things, but they fix things, help people, and create information. Mechanics, teachers, and writers are all service workers.

In addition, many more married women began to work outside the home. In 1960, for example, one out of three women worked outside the home. By 1990 more than half of all women worked outside the home.

## A NEW ECONOMY

Miriam Rios-Lebron, from South Brunswick, experienced many of these changes first-hand. For 23 years Miriam's mother worked in a belt factory in New York City. One day in 1987, her mother learned that the factory was going to close.

Miriam worried about her own job future. She was studying computer science at college at that time. She hoped her new skills would prepare her for a job in the changing economy.

Miriam was right! When she left college she programmed computers. Today she creates web pages for a newspaper.

Miriam knows that her working life will not be like her mother's. "The economy is changing so fast. You always need to be learning new skills."

### Economic Connections

As New Jersey's economy changed, it became more a part of the global economy. In the global economy, people, products, and resources move from one country to another. For example, an oil filter made in a factory in Rahway might be shipped to Mexico, where it is installed into a new car. That car may be shipped back to New Jersey to be sold.

The global economy shows how we are interdependent. This means that each of us depends on many people around the world for the things we want or need.

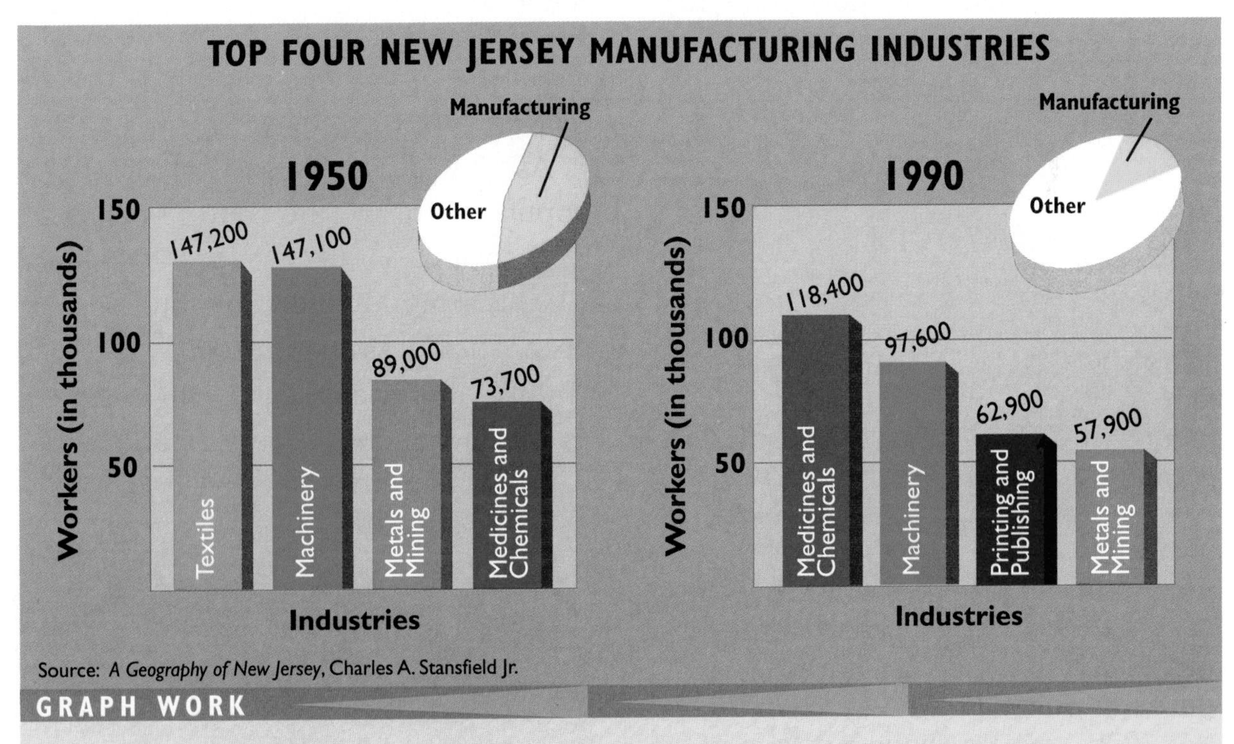


Source: *A Geography of New Jersey*, Charles A. Stansfield Jr.

**GRAPH WORK**

From 1950 to 1990, New Jersey's economy changed. The overall number of manufacturing jobs shrank. So did the number of manufacturing jobs in relation to other types of jobs.

1. In 1950, which two industries had nearly the same number of workers?
2. Between 1950 and 1990, which industry lost the most workers?

**GRAPH WORK:** **1.** textiles and machinery **2.** textiles

## RENEWING NEW JERSEY

As part of the global economy, New Jersey had to compete against other states and countries for jobs and businesses. Many people felt high taxes scared off businesses. Christine Todd Whitman, New Jersey's first woman governor, was elected in 1993 and responded by cutting taxes. This meant that some government services had to be cut, too.

The state government also worked to improve New Jersey's environment. Factories had dumped chemicals and other pollutants into our state's water, soil, and air. In the 1970s, the government spent millions of dollars to clean up the environment. For example, the wetland area known as the Meadowlands was a dumping ground for more than 10 million tons of waste. How did the area get many of its hills?

**Excerpt from *The Meadowlands* by Robert Sullivan published in 1998.**

*There are real hills in the Meadowlands and there are garbage hills. . . . Garbage hills are everywhere in the meadows, and they are filled with all different types of garbage. . . . For a long time the Meadowlands was the largest garbage dump in the world. In the 1970s, eleven thousand tons of garbage were dumped there every day—an amount that would just about fill Giants Stadium.*

**A cleaner environment lets everyone enjoy our state's natural beauty.**

After more than 25 years of clean-up, this area again became home to unique plants and animals, including herons, hawks, and muskrats. More than $1 billion has been spent to return the 32-square mile wetland to its natural condition.

### Saving Open Space

As New Jersey's economy and population grew, the state's open land shrunk. In 1920, New Jersey had 29,000 farms. By 1980 this number dropped to less than 10,000. Cherry Hill mayor Susan Bass Levin watched as the town's last farm was about to be sold for a housing development.

"Sometimes you have to say 'Enough already,'" said Mayor Levin. "To lose our last working farm was an emotional issue." The town stepped in and leased the land so that it continued to be used as a farm.

In the 1990s the state government pledged to preserve one million acres. Known as the Green Acres program, this law preserves farmlands and places where wildlife live.

### Urban Rebirth

New Jerseyans have also worked to preserve and rebuild urban areas. From 1960 to 1990, cities such as Newark, Camden, and Atlantic City lost one-quarter of their population. As factories and stores closed, many cities faced hard times.

During the 1990s city residents found ways to breathe new life into their communities. The New Community Corporation, also called NCC, has brought jobs, stores, restaurants, and new housing to Newark. Other cities are enjoying a rebirth, too. Camden has created many service jobs by turning its waterfront into a busy tourist site. Hoboken has added parks, shops, and homes.

**The New Jersey State Aquarium draws many people into Camden.**

See p. T79 for Answers to Think About It.

## WHY IT MATTERS

New Jerseyans have always been able to change with the times. This has made our state strong and will help its people meet future challenges.

### Reviewing Facts and Ideas

#### MAIN IDEAS

- From 1950 to 1990, New Jersey lost many manufacturing jobs and gained many service jobs.
- In the 1980s and 1990s, New Jersey became part of the global economy.
- New Jerseyans are working to preserve the environment and rebuild cities.

#### THINK ABOUT IT

1. What is a service job?
2. How is New Jersey part of the global economy?
3. **FOCUS** Name two ways New Jerseyans are working to rebuild their state.
4. **THINKING SKILL** _Predict_ whether or not our state's cities will continue to grow. Explain the reasons for your prediction.
5. **WRITE** Write a paragraph comparing the global economy to the economy of colonial New Jersey.

See p. T80 for Answers to Chapter 9 Review.

# CHAPTER 9 REVIEW

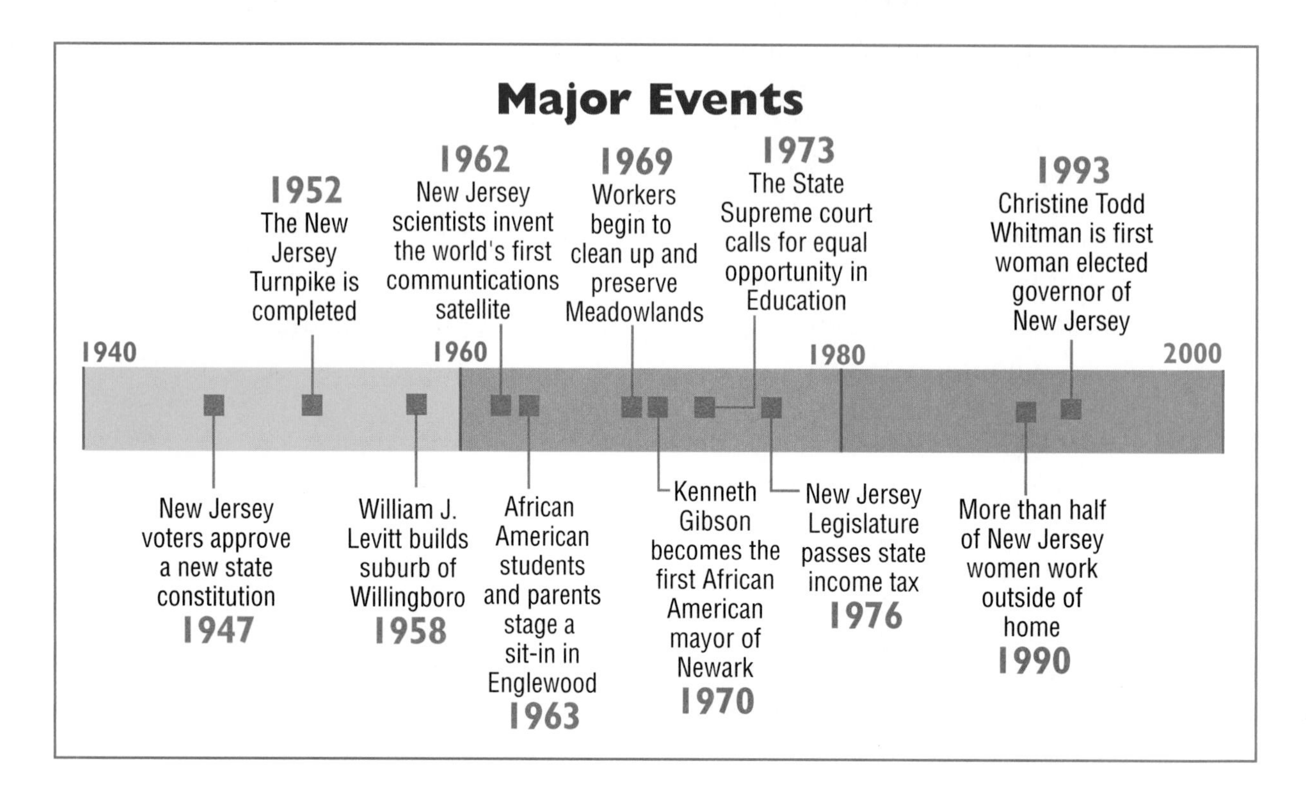


## THINKING ABOUT VOCABULARY

Number a sheet of paper from 1 to 10. Next to each number write C if the underlined word or phrase is used correctly. If it is not, write the word or phrase that would correctly complete the sentence.

1. A transistor is a tiny device that controls the movement of electricity.
2. Mass production is a tax on money people earn.
3. New Jerseyans who are interdependent depend on many people around the world for the things they need or want.
4. Global economy workers fix things, help people, and create information.
5. Segregation means separating people by race.
6. Dividing something, such as seats in a legislature, according to a plan is called communications.
7. An income tax is the manufacturing of large numbers of goods.
8. Civil rights are the rights of all people to be treated fairly under the law.
9. A county is a section of a state.
10. In a service people and products move from one country to another.

## THINKING ABOUT FACTS

1. How did William J. Levitt change the way houses were built?
2. Name two industries that grew in New Jersey after World War II.
3. How did transportation change in New Jersey in the 1950s?
4. What stopped segregation in New Jersey schools?
5. How are New Jerseyans working to prevent and clean up pollution?

## THINK AND WRITE

**WRITING A SUMMARY**

Write a summary describing the effort to clean up the Meadowlands.

**WRITE AN ADVERTISEMENT**

Write an advertisement for a suburban house in Willingboro.

**WRITING AN EDITORIAL**

Write an editorial for a newspaper about the need to end segregation in New Jersey public schools after the 1947 state constitution became law.

## APPLYING GEOGRAPHY SKILLS

**READING ROAD MAPS**

Use the map on page 228 to plan a trip using a road map.

1. What does a road map show?
2. How does the map show which roads are interstate highways?
3. On which interstate highway can you travel from east to west?
4. What highway would you travel from New Brunswick to Lawrenceville?
5. Why is it important to be able to read road maps?

## Summing Up the Chapter

Use the following table to organize information from the chapter. Copy the table on a sheet of paper. Complete the table by writing words that apply to each main topic. When you have filled in the table, use it to write a paragraph that answers the question, "What were the most important changes that took place in New Jersey after World War II?"

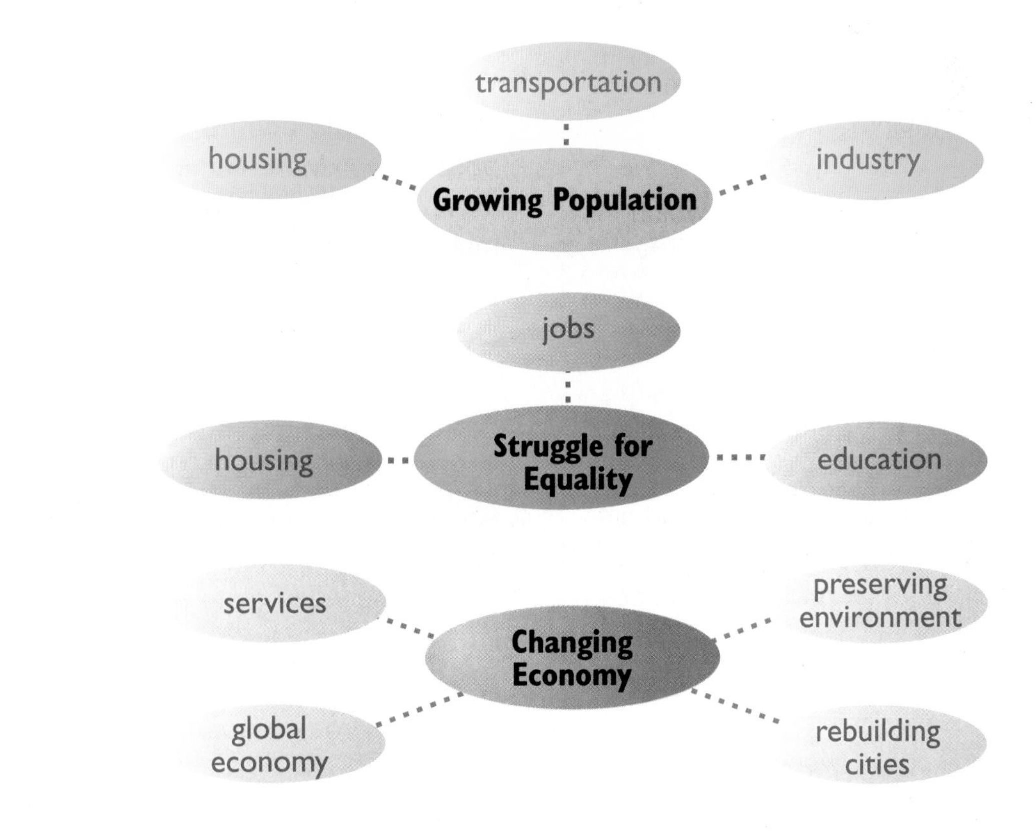

See p. T81 for Answers to Unit 4 Review.

# UNIT 4 REVIEW

## THINKING ABOUT VOCABULARY

Number a sheet of paper from 1 to 10. Next to each number write the word or phrase from the list that best matches the description.

| | |
|---|---|
| civil rights | mass production |
| county | political party |
| Great Depression | primary |
| Great Migration | service |
| income tax | transistor |

1. A ________ is a group of people who share similar ideas about government.
2. The right of all citizens to be treated equally under the law is called ________.
3. ________ is manufacturing large numbers of goods using identical parts.
4. A tiny device that controls the movement of electricity is called a ________.
5. A ________ is an election in which all the members of a political party choose a candidate.
6. A ________ is a section of a state.
7. Money paid to the government from workers' income, or salaries, is called ________.
8. ________ is the industry where workers do not make things, but they fix things, help people, and create information.
9. The ________ was a time when many businesses failed and many people were out of work.
10. The large movement of African Americans from rural areas of the South to the cities of the North and Middle West is called the ________.

## THINK AND WRITE

### WRITING A REPORT

Write a report comparing and contrasting New Jersey's major industries in the early 1900s with its major industries today.

### WRITING AN EXPLANATION

Write a paragraph explaining why people held a sit-in at Englewood High School in 1963.

### WRITING A SPEECH

Suppose you are the mayor of a New Jersey city during the Great Depression. Write a speech explaining how you will try to help people through hard times.

## BUILDING SKILLS

1. **Primary and secondary sources** Suppose Mayor Mark Fagan had written an autobiography. Would this be a primary or secondary source?
2. **Primary and secondary sources** How can both primary and secondary sources help us to understand history?
3. **Reading road maps** How is a road map different from an elevation map?
4. **Reading road maps** Look at the map on page 228. How can you tell the difference between state highways and interstate highways?
5. **Reading road maps** How can the skill of reading road maps help you in your own life?

## YESTERDAY, TODAY & TOMORROW

**You have read about some of the changes that took place in New Jersey. Many of these changes were related to technology. What kinds of new technology do you predict will become important in your life?**

## READING ON YOUR OWN

These are some of the books you might find at the library to help you learn more.

*BUD, NOT BUDDY*
**by Christopher Curtis**
During the hard times of the Great Depression, ten-year-old Bud searches for his father.

*OUT OF THE DUST*
**by Karen Hesse**
The Dust Bowl of the 1930s is the stage for this novel written as a cycle of poetry.

*THE DAY WOMEN GOT THE VOTE*
**by George Sullivan**
This book will tell you some of the history of woman's suffrage.

## UNIT 4 REVIEW PROJECT

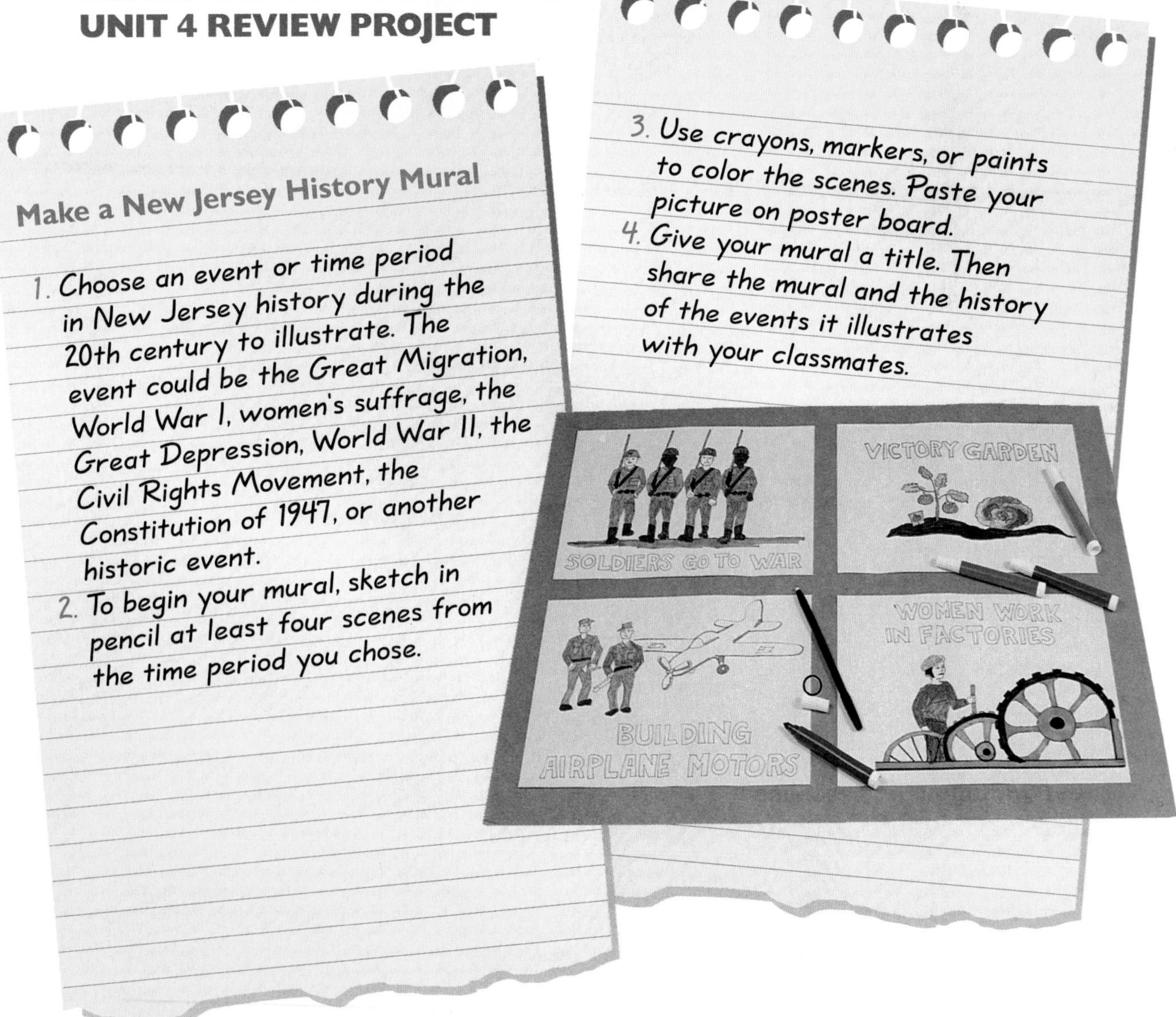


### Make a New Jersey History Mural

1. Choose an event or time period in New Jersey history during the 20th century to illustrate. The event could be the Great Migration, World War I, women's suffrage, the Great Depression, World War II, the Civil Rights Movement, the Constitution of 1947, or another historic event.
2. To begin your mural, sketch in pencil at least four scenes from the time period you chose.
3. Use crayons, markers, or paints to color the scenes. Paste your picture on poster board.
4. Give your mural a title. Then share the mural and the history of the events it illustrates with your classmates.

BELMAR POSTCARD, 1951 (RIGHT); WORKING WITH NEW TECHNOLOGY (BELOW)

KEITH VAN HORN (RIGHT); COLLEGE GRADUATES (BELOW)

UNIT FIVE

# New Jersey in the Twenty-First Century

*"By voting, our voice is heard."*

Mary Mazza Duffy, mayor of Monroe Township
See page 270.

## Why Does It Matter?

What do you think New Jersey will be like in the future? Do you think New Jerseyans will continue to work and play in the same ways they do now? What kinds of improvements and problems will tomorrow bring?

Learning about what our state is like today can help us imagine what it will be like tomorrow. So read on. In Unit 5 you will learn more about New Jersey's economy, government, arts, technology and schools. You will also read about the culture and diversity that makes our state special.

CHRISTINE TODD WHITMAN

**FIND OUT MORE!**
**Visit our website:**
**www.mhschool.com**

*inter*NET CONNECTION

# Adventures with NATIONAL GEOGRAPHIC

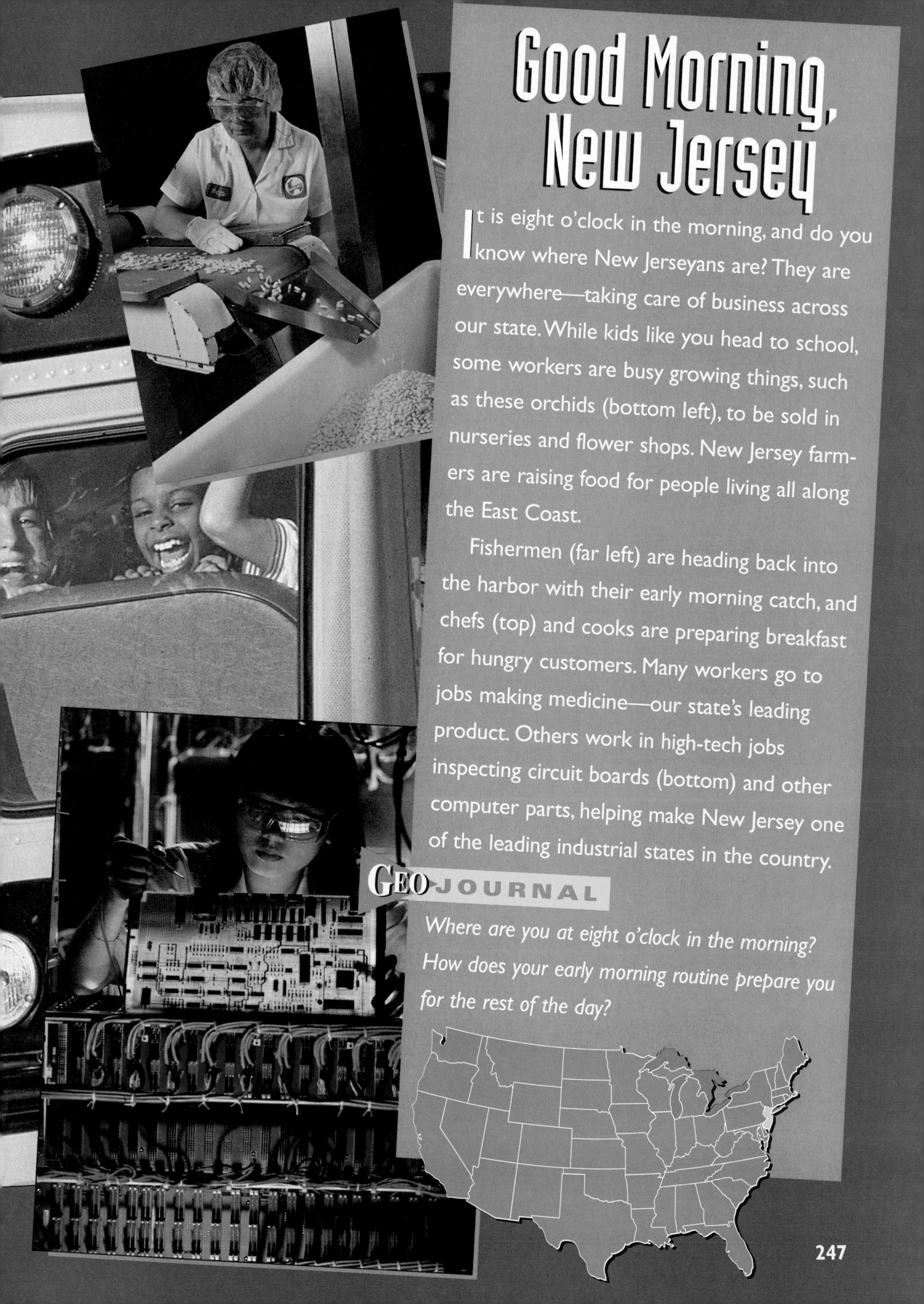

# Good Morning, New Jersey

It is eight o'clock in the morning, and do you know where New Jerseyans are? They are everywhere—taking care of business across our state. While kids like you head to school, some workers are busy growing things, such as these orchids (bottom left), to be sold in nurseries and flower shops. New Jersey farmers are raising food for people living all along the East Coast.

Fishermen (far left) are heading back into the harbor with their early morning catch, and chefs (top) and cooks are preparing breakfast for hungry customers. Many workers go to jobs making medicine—our state's leading product. Others work in high-tech jobs inspecting circuit boards (bottom) and other computer parts, helping make New Jersey one of the leading industrial states in the country.

**GEO JOURNAL**

*Where are you at eight o'clock in the morning? How does your early morning routine prepare you for the rest of the day?*

## CHAPTER 10

# New Jersey's Economy Today

### THINKING ABOUT GEOGRAPHY AND ECONOMICS

What kinds of work do people in your community do? How are these jobs different from 100 years ago? The workers of New Jersey today provide many different goods and services to the economy of the United States. We are lucky to have rich farmland, busy port cities, and many educated workers. Read on to learn about how these workers prepare to face the challenges of a fast-changing, global economy.

See pT84 for Chapter Organizer.

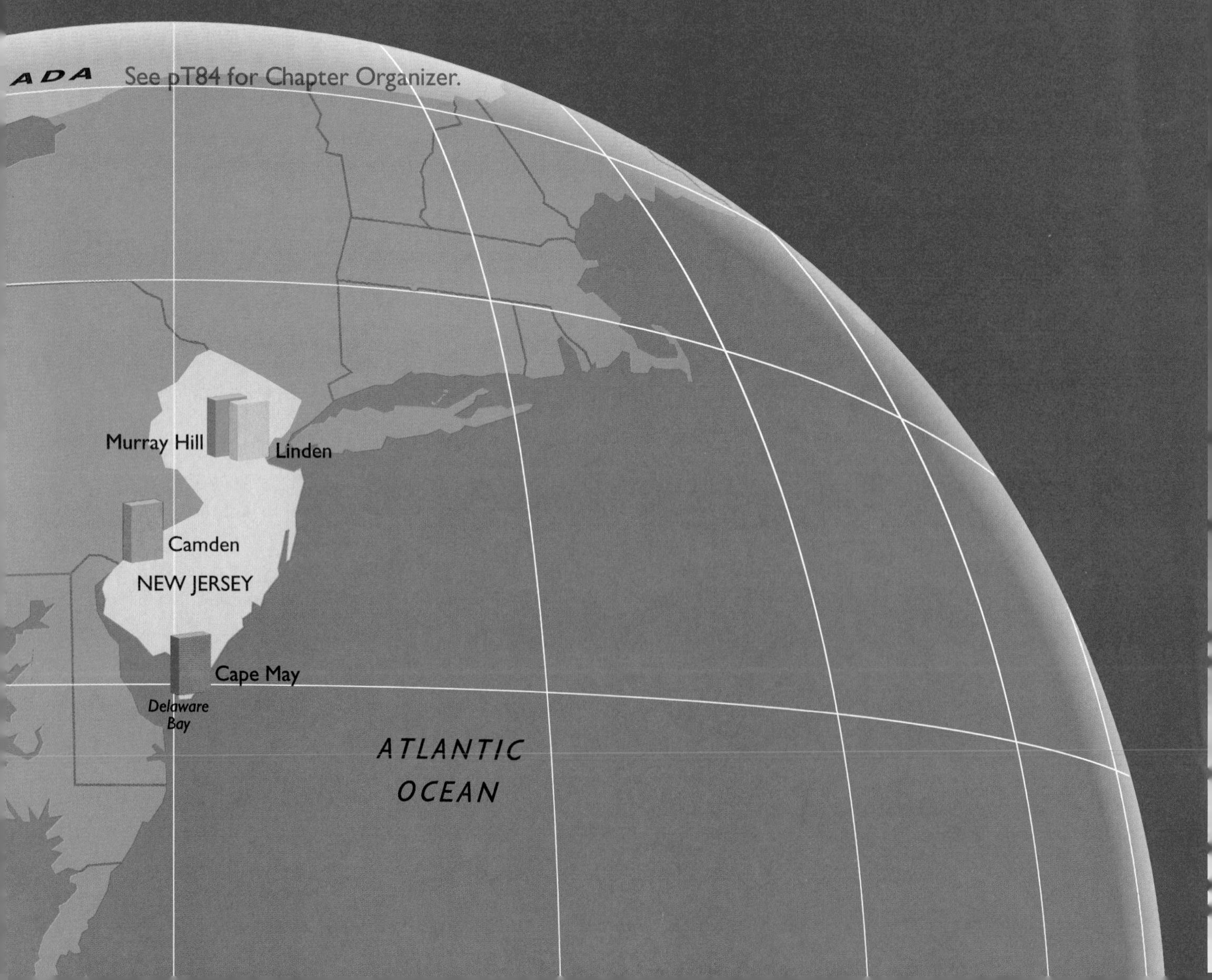

### Cape May

The Cape May ferry is one small link in New Jersey's huge transportation network. This ferry steams across Delaware Bay, carrying people between New Jersey and Delaware.

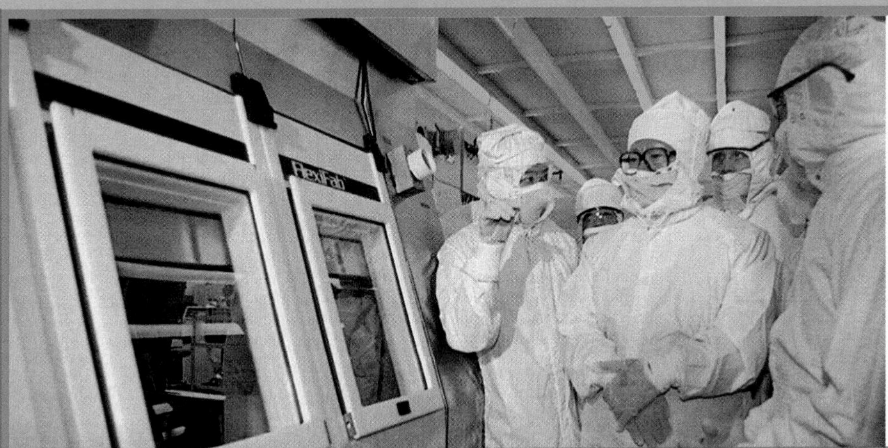

### Murray Hill

New Jersey's workers design and build some of the most advanced electronic equipment in the world. This "clean room" is used for creating tiny devices called "semiconductors."

### Linden

The automobiles built in New Jersey factories end up on roads and highways across the United States.

### Camden

New Jersey's public transportation system, which includes many trains and buses, moves thousands of workers to their jobs everyday.

## Focus Activity

**READ TO LEARN**

***How does the free enterprise system work?***

**VOCABULARY**

- entrepreneur
- profit
- consumer
- free enterprise
- investor
- competition

**PLACES**

- Mount Olive
- Mays Landing

LESSON 1

See p. T85 for Lesson Teaching Strategies.

# The Free Enterprise System At Work

## Read Aloud

*In the summer of 1998, the Wilcox family opened an ice cream shop. Business went well until winter. "It was rough," Jeanie Wilcox remembers. "I have had doubts about whether we will make it or not. . . . But we learned a lot from that first winter, and now it is satisfying to see the business take root and grow."*

## THE BIG PICTURE

Jeanie Wilcox is talking about JJ's Heavenly Delights, which sells ice cream and sweets in **Mount Olive**. Jeanie is an **entrepreneur**, a person who takes risks by creating products she or he thinks people will want to buy. When a business is successful, an entrepreneur makes a **profit**. Profit is the money a business earns after it pays for supplies, tools, salaries, and other costs. Businesses make profits by serving **consumers**, the people who buy products or use services.

A business like JJ's is possible only in an economy that is based on **free enterprise**. Free enterprise is the economic system that allows people to own and run their own businesses. In this lesson you will see what free enterprise means to the people of New Jersey.

## A BUSINESS BLOOMS

New Jersey is a great place for starting a small business. In recent years, many new jobs in the state have been created by companies with fewer than 50 employees.

JJ's Heavenly Delights is one New Jersey success story. Jeanie Wilcox's daughter, Jamie, works alongside her mother—that is how JJ's got its name. Like many entrepreneurs, Jamie wanted to take a chance with her own business. "I did have an office job where I was making a steady income," Jamie says, "but it was not going anywhere, and I wanted to be my own boss."

Being an entrepreneur involves many choices. When JJ's opened in the summer of 1998, the Wilcoxes sold only ice cream. They did well that first summer. With the coming of winter, however, business suffered. Most people do not want ice cream on a winter day. Now the Wilcoxes also sell chocolate and baked goods at their shop. Business is good all year.

Running a business, however, is very demanding. "Since we started this business, it has taken all my time," says Jeanie. "I do not see my family as much as I used to, and I do not have time for much else."

Entrepreneurs like the Wilcoxes must be willing to put in time and hard work. They also have to spend money on their business. Many businesses have **investors**, outside people who put money into the business and expect a share of the profit.

Profit is the payoff for investors. For entrepreneurs, there is even more. As Jeanie Wilcox points out, "I really like the interaction with people and it is great not going to an office job."

**An entrepreneur like Jeanie Wilcox must offer products that people want if she hopes to make a profit.**

## HOW A BUSINESS WORKS

Some students at Oakcrest High School in Mays Landing have learned first hand how the free enterprise system works. Three years ago, students worked with their teachers to start a snack bar called Falcon Express.

### First Steps

Falcon Express began with a plan in one of Karol Bucci's school-to-work classes. Six students in ninth through twelfth grades worked to get the business off the ground. They chose the name based on their school's mascot.

The school offered them part of a storage area as a business space. However, the students also needed money to get started. Soon, they found an investor. A flower shop called the Falcon Sprout—another student business—lent them $500.

Like any business, Falcon Express also needed tools and equipment. A local business owner provided a refrigerator. Students rescued some adding machines that had been thrown away. They also borrowed a wheeled cart from a nearby school.

Students chose different jobs at the snack bar. Some worked in sales. Others worked restocking shelves. One student worked as a manager, planning orders and keeping the books. Soon Falcon Express was serving hundreds of snacks each week.

**Falcon Express student-workers learned important lessons about free enterprise.**

## Hard Lessons

Before long, the students learned that no business is a sure thing. Like any other free enterprise business, Falcon Express had to face tough competition. Competition is other businesses offering consumers a similar product. One student describes some of the lessons they learned:

> *We've learned about business the hard way. Last year the cafeteria was taken over by a big company. They actually tried to run us out of business. The old cafeteria used to sell us their sandwiches at the end of the day for practically nothing. Then we could sell them to the athletes after practice. The new company tried to take over our space. They charged less money because they could buy large amounts at a discount. They offered a lot of junk food. We almost did go out of business.*

## Problem-Solving and Success

The students worked to figure out a solution. "They had to find new things to offer that the cafeteria was not offering," teacher Karol Bucci explains. The new ideas worked. Soon Falcon Express began making a profit. In its first three years in business, the snack bar made $7,000!

The students used some of this profit to repay the loan from their investor. They also lent money to another student start-up business, called Little Oak Sweets and Treats.

See p. T85 for Answers to Think About It.

Other profits are poured back into the school business program. If business classes want to attend an entrepreneur's conference, for example, Falcon Express helps pay the bill.

"Today, Falcon Express is thriving," Bucci says proudly. Falcon Express entrepreneurs have learned some valuable lessons along the way.

## WHY IT MATTERS

In a free enterprise system, people make their own economic decisions. These decisions make the economy stronger for everyone.

## Reviewing Facts and Ideas

### MAIN IDEAS

- The free enterprise system provides opportunity and choice.
- Competition between businesses means that consumers have a choice of products and services.
- Entrepreneurs and investors create jobs and help build the economy.

### THINK ABOUT IT

1. What is an entrepreneur?
2. How do investors help a business get started?
3. **FOCUS** How is Falcon Express an example of free enterprise?
4. **THINKING SKILL** What made Jeanie Wilcox decide to sell baked goods in addition to ice cream?
5. **WRITE** Suppose your class wanted to start a business. Write a paragraph describing a product you think consumers would buy. Explain why people would buy it.

LESSON 2

See p. T86 for Lesson Teaching Strategies.

# New Jersey's Workers

## Focus Activity

**READ TO LEARN**

***What are the important parts of New Jersey's economy today?***

**VOCABULARY**

- telecommunications
- tourism

**PLACES**

- Murray Hill

### Read Aloud

*New Jersey is a leader in many areas of business. Why? "There are many reasons," explains Barbara Hopper at the New Jersey Small Business Development Center. "New Jersey is located close to New York City and Philadelphia. There is plenty of easy access to transportation. We have a bright workforce, and the state helps encourage businesses to grow."*

### THE BIG PICTURE

Another reason for New Jersey's business success is that our state has kept up with the times. You have read about how New Jersey's economy shifted from agriculture to manufacturing. More recently the economy has shifted from manufacturing to services and high technology.

Today three out of four New Jersey employees are service workers. Almost all of the rest work in manufacturing. Today only 1 in every 100 workers makes a living from agriculture. All these workers make New Jersey's economy very strong. Although New Jersey is the fifth-smallest state in size, its economy is one of the biggest.

**Manufacturing provides many jobs for New Jerseyans. A worker loads videotapes on an assembly line (right).**

## MANUFACTURING IN NEW JERSEY

Manufacturing is still important in our state. Chances are that you use a product made in New Jersey every day. Look around your classroom. Some of your books, computers, and other materials were probably made in New Jersey. Whenever you take a shower or bath, you probably use soap or shampoo made in New Jersey. More soap is made in New Jersey than in any other state. If you have been sick, your medicine may have been developed in New Jersey. Our state ranks number one in the production of medicines.

You have probably eaten food grown, canned, or frozen in New Jersey. Food products are also a leading New Jersey industry. New Jersey factories produce soups, cookies, and tea.

New Jersey ranks tenth in the country in producing electronics equipment. More than 85,000 New Jerseyans work making televisions, VCRs, and other kinds of electronic equipment. Scientists in Murray Hill, for example, helped to create a new type of television. High-definition television, also called HDTV, has a much clearer picture than other types of televisions.

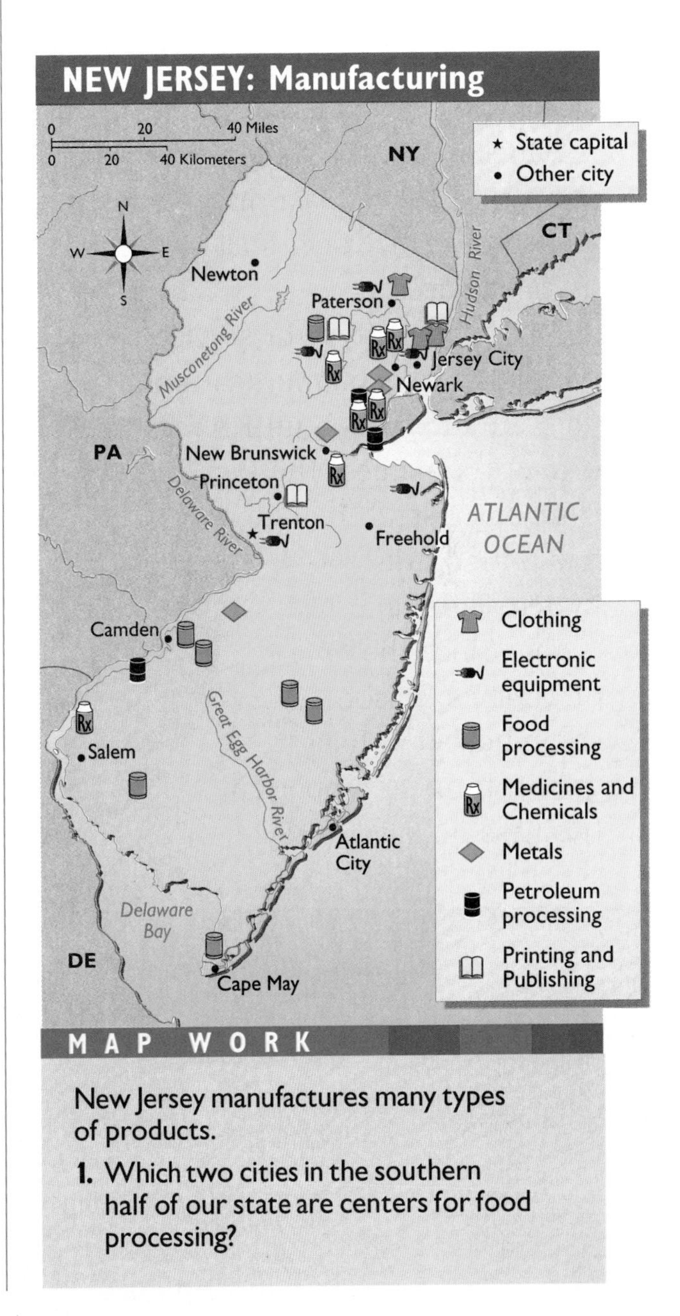


**MAP WORK**

New Jersey manufactures many types of products.

1. Which two cities in the southern half of our state are centers for food processing?

## AT YOUR SERVICE

Manufacturing is important, but services are by far the largest part of our state's economy today. You read about service workers in Chapter 9. Today more than one million New Jerseyans are service workers. Over half of these workers are employed by government.

Your teacher provides a service by giving you an education. Your mail carrier provides a service by bringing you the mail. Police officers keep your community safe. All of these workers are employed by the government.

Other service workers are in private industry. Bankers, taxi drivers, doctors, and restaurant workers all provide useful services.

One modern type of service is offered by telecommunications (tehl uh kuh myoon uh KAY shunz) companies. These companies send information long distances by telephone and television. Since the time of Thomas Edison, communication has grown to be an important business in New Jersey.

The health care industry employs more than 300,000 people in our state. Many of these people are service workers: from counselors, to x-ray technicians, to ambulance drivers. Another important service industry is called "financial services." This industry includes banks and insurance companies. Workers in financial services help people save money and invest in the stock market. Services are growing more and more important to New Jersey's economy. Can you think of other service workers in New Jersey?

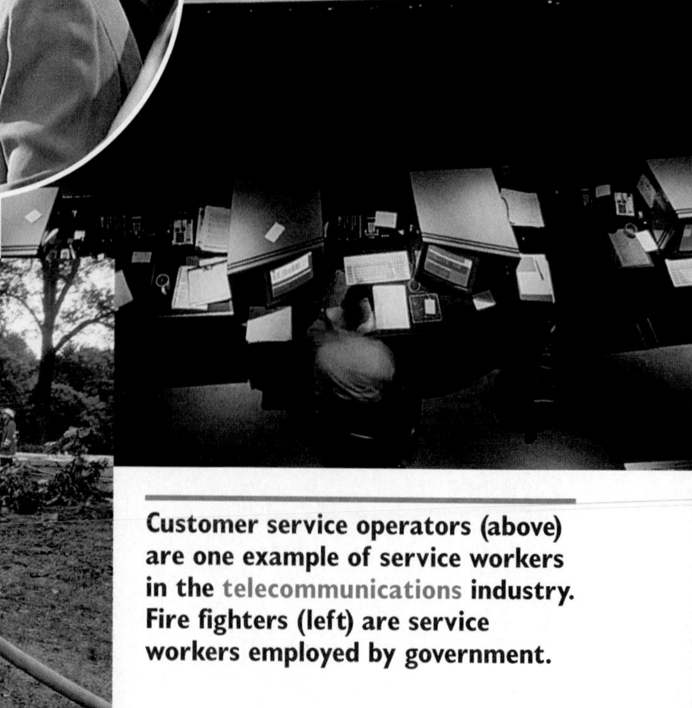

**Customer service operators (above) are one example of service workers in the telecommunications industry. Fire fighters (left) are service workers employed by government.**

## Taking in the Sights

One big part of the service economy is tourism. Tourism is the business of providing services for tourists, or people who travel for fun or to learn about new places. The many different kinds of businesses that sell goods and services to tourists make up the tourism industry.

People come to New Jersey to visit the shore, to enjoy our state's parks and recreation areas, or to see the many historical sites. Of course, many New Jerseyans also like to visit the beaches and parks of their home state. Maybe you'll want to take your next vacation in New Jersey!

Tourism helps our state's economy. "More visitors spending money year-round in New Jersey means more economic growth and job creation in the state," says New Jersey Commerce Secretary Gualberto Medina.

More than 400,000 people have jobs in New Jersey's tourism industry. They work in the hotels, restaurants, and amusement parks that serve tourists.

Tourists who visit our state spend a lot of money here—more than $22 billion every year. About $3 billion of this money comes from people visiting gaming casinos in Atlantic City. Although the casinos provide more than 50,000 jobs, many people in our state oppose them.

**Tourism is a big part of our state's economy. Visitors enjoy our parks and beaches.**

# Infographic

interNET CONNECTION Visit our website: www.mhschool.com

## New Jersey's Economy

**Suppose New Jersey were a country of its own. It would have the sixteenth largest economy in the world! What goods and services make New Jersey's economy strong?**

### High Tech Powerhouse

New Jersey employs more scientists, engineers and technicians than any other state. Together they help make our state a leader in medicines and chemicals.

### Jersey Fresh

Our state's farmers are leading producers of blueberries, cranberries, and peaches.

### New Jersey Makes, the World Takes

Almost half a million people in our state work in manufacturing. Rubber and plastics, clothing, computer parts, glass, and toys are some of the products they make.

### Crossroads of the World

With major airports, bustling ports, and miles of highways and railroad tracks, New Jersey's transportation network links it to places all over the world.

## Serving Your Needs

**Services make up the largest part of New Jersey's economy. More than one million people work in service industries such as healthcare, tourism, and postal services.**

## New Jersey Employment, 2000

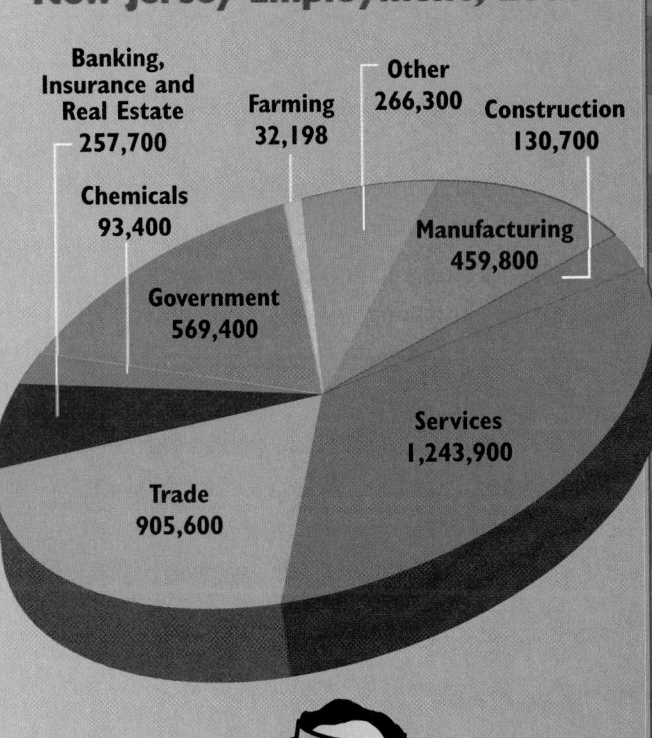

## Money Matters

**A large part of our state's economy deals with money. This industry includes banking, insurance, and real estate.**

See p. T86 for Answers to Think About It.

## WHY IT MATTERS

New Jersey has a strong economy that meets the needs of its people. Our state's economy has changed over time and continues to grow. The service industry provides jobs for many workers. New Jersey also leads the nation in manufacturing many different products. Our varied economy helps make New Jersey a great place to live.

## Reviewing Facts and Ideas

### MAIN IDEAS

- New Jersey's economy is one of the largest in the United States, despite the state's small size.
- New Jersey is a leader in manufacturing chemicals, medicines, soaps, and electronics.
- Many New Jerseyans today work in services.
- The tourist industry is an important part of our state's economy.

### THINK ABOUT IT

1. What are some of the products manufactured in New Jersey today?
2. What are some of the services provided in New Jersey today?
3. **FOCUS** Why are services the most important part of New Jersey's economy today?
4. **THINKING SKILL** *Predict* whether service jobs will continue to grow in importance.
5. **WRITE** Write a paragraph explaining why tourists should visit New Jersey. Give examples of two interesting places in our state and reasons why tourists should visit.

See p. T87 for Skill Teaching Strategies.

# Using Reference Sources

**VOCABULARY**

reference source
dictionary
guide word
encyclopedia
CD-ROM
Internet

## WHY THE SKILL MATTERS

In the last lesson you read about subjects such as manufacturing, tourism, and telecommunications. You might like to find out more about any of these topics—telecommunications, for example.

You could find the information you want in reference sources. These are books and other sources that contain facts about many different subjects. They can be found in a special part of the library called the reference section.

## USING A DICTIONARY

To begin, you might want to know the exact meaning of the word *telecommunications.* To find out, you would look in a dictionary. A dictionary gives the meaning of words. It shows how to pronounce and spell each word. Sometimes a dictionary explains where a word comes from or uses it in a sentence.

The words in a dictionary are arranged in alphabetical order. To make your work faster, you can refer to the guide words. These appear at the top of each page of the dictionary. They tell you the first and last words that are defined on that page.

Look at the guide words on the sample dictionary page. According to them, what is the last word to be defined on the page? Would the word *temperature* appear on this page? Now find the word *telecommunications.* What does this word mean? *

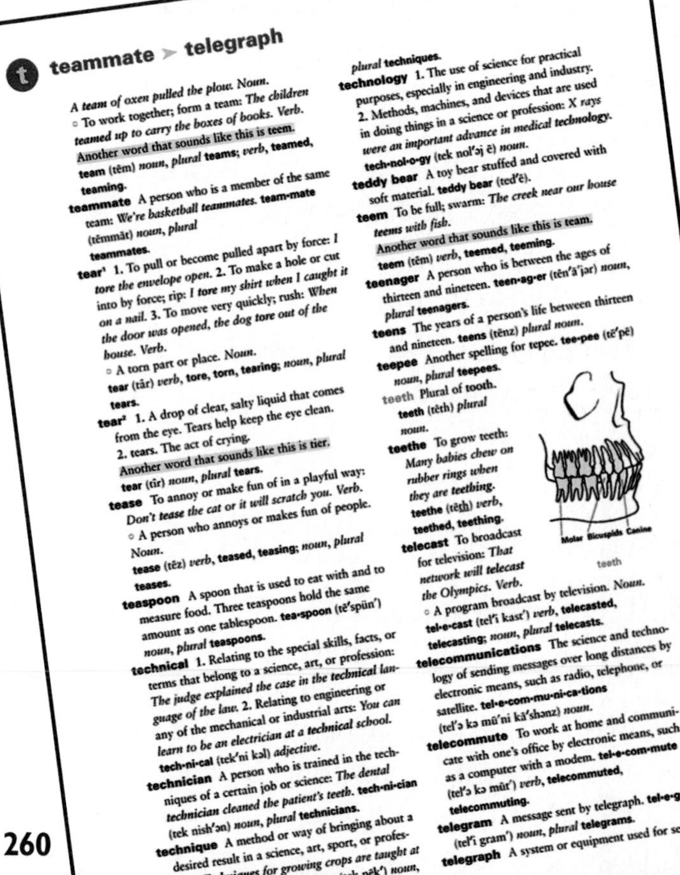

t **teammate ➤ telegraph**

*A* ***team*** *of oxen pulled the plow.* Noun.
◦ To work together; form a team: *The children* ***teamed*** *up to carry the boxes of books.* Verb.
Another word that sounds like this is teem.
**team** (tēm) *noun, plural* **teams;** *verb,* **teamed, teaming.**
**teammate** A person who is a member of the same team: *We're basketball* ***teammates.*** **team•mate** (tēmmāt) *noun, plural* **teammates.**
**tear¹** 1. To pull or become pulled apart by force: *I* ***tore*** *the envelope open.* 2. To make a hole or cut into by force; rip: *I* ***tore*** *my shirt when I caught it on a nail.* 3. To move very quickly; rush: *When the door was opened, the dog* ***tore*** *out of the house.* Verb.
◦ A torn part or place. Noun.
**tear** (târ) *verb,* **tore, torn, tearing;** *noun, plural* **tears.**
**tear²** 1. A drop of clear, salty liquid that comes from the eye. Tears help keep the eye clean. 2. tears. The act of crying.
Another word that sounds like this is tier.
**tear** (tîr) *noun, plural* **tears.**
**tease** To annoy or make fun of in a playful way: *Don't* ***tease*** *the cat or it will scratch you.* Verb.
◦ A person who annoys or makes fun of people. Noun.
**tease** (tēz) *verb,* **teased, teasing;** *noun, plural* **teases.**
**teaspoon** A spoon that is used to eat with and to measure food. Three teaspoons hold the same amount as one tablespoon. **tea•spoon** (tē'spün') *noun, plural* **teaspoons.**
**technical** 1. Relating to the special skills, facts, or terms that belong to a science, art, or profession: *The judge explained the case in the* ***technical*** *language of the law.* 2. Relating to engineering or any of the mechanical or industrial arts: *You can learn to be an electrician at a* ***technical*** *school.* **tech•ni•cal** (tek'ni kəl) *adjective.*
**technician** A person who is trained in the techniques of a certain job or science: *The dental* ***technician*** *cleaned the patient's teeth.* **tech•ni•cian** (tek nish'ən) *noun, plural* **technicians.**
**technique** A method or way of bringing about a desired result in a science, art, sport, or profession: ***Techniques*** *for growing crops are taught at agricultural schools.* **tech•nique** (tek nēk') *noun, plural* **techniques.**
**technology** 1. The use of science for practical purposes, especially in engineering and industry. 2. Methods, machines, and devices that are used in doing things in a science or profession: *X rays were an important advance in medical* ***technology.*** **tech•nol•o•gy** (tek nol'əj ē) *noun.*
**teddy bear** A toy bear stuffed and covered with soft material. **teddy bear** (ted'ē).
**teem** To be full; swarm: *The creek near our house* ***teems*** *with fish.*
Another word that sounds like this is team.
**teem** (tēm) *verb,* **teemed, teeming.**
**teenager** A person who is between the ages of thirteen and nineteen. **teen•ag•er** (tēn'ā'jər) *noun, plural* **teenagers.**
**teens** The years of a person's life between thirteen and nineteen. **teens** (tēnz) *plural noun.*
**teepee** Another spelling for tepee. **tee•pee** (tē'pē) *noun, plural* **teepees.**
teeth Plural of tooth. **teeth** (tēth) *plural noun.*
**teethe** To grow teeth: *Many babies chew on rubber rings when they are* ***teething.*** **teethe** (tē*th*) *verb,* **teethed, teething.**
**telecast** To broadcast for television: *That network will* ***telecast*** *the Olympics.* Verb.
◦ A program broadcast by television. Noun.
**tel•e•cast** (tel'i kast') *verb,* **telecasted, telecasting;** *noun, plural* **telecasts.**
**telecommunications** The science and technology of sending messages over long distances by electronic means, such as radio, telephone, or satellite. **tel•e•com•mu•ni•ca•tions** (tel'ə kə mū'ni kā'shənz) *noun.*
**telecommute** To work at home and communicate with one's office by electronic means, such as a computer with a modem. **tel•e•com•mute** (tel'ə kə mūt') *verb,* **telecommuted, telecommuting.**
**telegram** A message sent by telegraph. **tel•e•gram** (tel'i gram') *noun, plural* **telegrams.**
**telegraph** A system or equipment used for send-



742

## USING AN ENCYCLOPEDIA, A CD-ROM, OR THE INTERNET

Another useful reference tool is the encyclopedia. This book or set of books gives information about people, places, things, and events. Like a dictionary, the topics in the encyclopedia are arranged in alphabetical order. Most encyclopedias also use guide words.

*telegraph; no; the science and technology of sending messages over long distances by electronic means, such as radio, telephone, or satellite

## Helping yourself

- **Reference sources** have information about many subjects.
- **A dictionary** gives the meanings of words. An **encyclopedia** gives information on people, places, things, and events.
- Look up a subject using a **guide word** or title.

See p. T87 for Answers to Reviewing the Skill.

**the volume with *H* on its spine

Suppose you want to learn even more about telecommunications. You would look in the encyclopedia volume, or book, with *T* on the spine. Which volume would you look in to learn more about health care? **

Two newer kinds of reference sources are the **CD-ROM** and the **Internet**. A CD-ROM is a compact disc that you "read" with the aid of a computer. Like an encyclopedia, a CD-ROM contains facts about many subjects. It may also include sounds, music, and even short movies! The Internet is a computer network. With a computer that has an Internet connection, you can "visit" sources of information such as libraries, schools, or government offices. Your teacher or librarian will help you use these types of reference sources.

### TRYING THE SKILL

You have practiced using reference sources. Now suppose you want to write a report on pharmaceuticals. What are pharmaceuticals? What reference source would you use to find out? How would you find out more about pharmaceuticals? Use the Helping yourself box for hints.***

***medicines; a dictionary; look up *pharmaceuticals* in an encyclopedia, a CD-ROM, or the Internet

### REVIEWING THE SKILL

1. What is a reference source?
2. Which reference source would you use to find the meaning of the word *democracy?*
3. Some encyclopedias have guide words instead of letters. Suppose you had a volume covering everything from *machinery* to *Oklahoma.* Would it contain an article about oranges?
4. When are reference sources useful to students?

## Focus Activity

**READ TO LEARN**

***How does new technology change the way we live?***

**VOCABULARY**

- research and development
- biotechnology
- fiber optics
- cyberspace
- software
- e-mail

**PLACES**

- Totowa

LESSON 3

See p. T88 for Lesson Teaching Strategies.

# Cutting Edge in New Jersey

### Read Aloud

*Someday soon, trips to the mall might be very different. Shoppers will still choose new clothes or toys, then walk to the cash register to pay. But all the consumer will have to do is stare into the register and blink. Just as if the shopper had used a credit card, the store will have all the information it needs. This may sound like science fiction, but sales like this are not far off. A New Jersey company has invented a way to identify you by "reading" the information in your eyeball. "It is more unique than a fingerprint," the company explains.*

### THE BIG PICTURE

It is not surprising that New Jersey continues to lead the country with new technology. After all, New Jersey has long been home to creativity and innovation.

Over the last several decades, technology has been changing with lightning speed. Businesses that used typewriters 20 years ago, for example, now have computers at every desk. These computers are linked to other computers all over the world. Advances in chemistry, medicine, and telecommunications have also changed the ways people live and work in our state and the world.

## RESEARCH AND DEVELOPMENT

New Jersey is home to more research and development companies than any other state. Research and development involves coming up with new ideas and creating new products. Many people who do this work are scientists. In fact, more than 140,000 scientists and engineers work in our state today. One reason that New Jersey has so many scientists is that it has universities such as Princeton and Rutgers. Scientists can learn, teach, and do research at these schools.

The work these scientists and engineers do can effect our daily lives. For example, every time you make a phone call, you are using technology developed in our state. New Jersey scientists today are working in biotechnology to create new treatments for illness or injury. Biotechnology combines biology and technology to make scientific advances. The machine that identifies people by "reading" their eyes is an example of biotechnology.

You can hear the voice of a friend on a phone thousands of miles away thanks to fiber optics. Fiber optics is a technology that uses special glass cables to send light waves that carry information. Fiber optics allows television, telephone, and computer cables to carry more information at higher speeds.

New Jersey scientists are leaders in fiber optic and other sorts of research. Much of this research takes place in laboratories modeled after Thomas Edison's "invention factory," which you read about in Chapter 7.

**A scientist records results from an experiment (below).**

## THE CYBER ECONOMY

Al and Gary Potenzone (POH tinh zhon) are brothers who own Apollo Flag Company, Inc., in Totowa. Apollo sells the official flags of sports teams. The company also sells the United States flag, flags of other countries, and banners to hang outside homes. Al and Gary's grandfather started the company in 1912. Their father took over the business from him. "Now our sons are working here as well," says Gary.

Four years ago, Apollo moved to a larger building to meet growing demand. A year ago, the company made an even bigger change. "We went on the Internet," Gary explains. "We got a web site and it's really taken off. Now people from all over the country and all over the world can order our flags."

Gary notes that the new "cyber economy" is changing the way people shop. "We just sold some flags to Guam for their police offices, and some others to an Air Force base in California. Now people can go online and add their orders to a 'shopping cart' and we can ship their order out to them the next day. We're still a family business, but now we can do business without any borders."

The new web site allows customers to look at any one of Apollo's flags with the click of a mouse. More importantly, the Internet has opened the doors of the Totowa store to the entire world.

**A worker at Apollo Flag Company checks an on-line order.**

Apollo Flag Company is just one example of the Internet changing business in our state. Edmund DePalma works for a company that studies these changes. What does he say about how the Internet has changed the way people do business?

**MANY VOICES**
**PRIMARY SOURCE**

**Excerpt from a 1999 interview with Edmund DePalma, World Internet Resources, Woodbridge.**

***The way people do business is really changing. . . . It is about a lot more than just designing a website. It is streamlining operations* [making them simpler]*, distribution, selling products, and making money. We have seen a lot of change in a short period of time and we can expect to see much more. It is scary and exciting.***

See p. T88 for Answers to Think About It.

## A Trip Through Cyberspace

Let's take a journey into cyberspace, the on-line world of computer networks. Most computers have software that allows you to go on-line. Software is a program, or set of instructions, that tells the computer what to do. The first step into cyberspace is to connect the computer in your home or school to a "host" computer. You do this using a phone line or a cable. After your computer "shakes hands" with your host, you are on-line. Now, you can check your e-mail, or electronic mail, and explore the Internet.

The Internet is a huge network of computers throughout the world. The most popular part of the Internet is the World Wide Web. The Web is made up of millions of web sites, each containing unique information. Web sites are located in many different computers, called servers, in many different places in the world.

The easiest way to explore "the Web" is to use a search engine. This is a tool that helps you find your way through the huge network of web sites. You type in a few key words, perhaps "homework" and "help." Within seconds, the search engine finds web sites for these topics.

## WHY IT MATTERS

New Jersey has long been a leader in innovation. Today, New Jersey continues to lead the way with new technology and new ideas. You will see, and perhaps create, even greater changes as you get older.

*Links to* **MATHEMATICS**

### Think Digital

**Do you know what "01000001" means? To a computer, these numbers stand for the letter *A*. Computers read a code that uses only binary numbers. Binary numbers are made up of zeroes and ones. Each zero or one equals one "bit" of information. A string of eight bits—such as 01000001—is called a "byte." There are one million bytes in a megabyte. A personal computer can store thousands of megabytes of information. Such computers are called "digital" because they use numbers, or digits, to stand for any kind of information. Write your own digital message by creating a code in which numbers stand for letters.**

## Reviewing Facts and Ideas

### MAIN IDEAS

- New Jersey leads the nation in research and development.
- New Jersey scientists are creating new products that help us lead healthier lives.
- The Internet has changed the way New Jersey companies do business.

### THINK ABOUT IT

1. What is research and development?
2. What is biotechnology?
3. **FOCUS** In what ways is new technology important to how we live today?
4. **THINKING SKILL** *Predict* what new inventions might change our lives in the future.
5. **GEOGRAPHY** How does the Internet help New Jersey companies do more business?

See p. T89 for Answers to Chapter 10 Review.

# CHAPTER 10 REVIEW

## THINKING ABOUT VOCABULARY

Number a sheet of paper from 1 to 10. Beside each number write **C** if the underlined word or phrase is used correctly. If it is not, write the word or phrase that would correctly complete the sentence.

1. A free enterprise is the money a business earns after it pays for supplies, tools, salaries, and other costs.
2. Software is a set of instructions that tells the computer what to do.
3. Sending information over long distances by telephone and television is called telecommunications.
4. An investor is a person who takes risks by creating products she or he thinks people will want to buy.
5. Electronic mail sent through cyberspace is called biotechnology.
6. Tourism is the business of providing services for people who travel for fun or to learn about new places.
7. Fiber optics is a technology that uses glass cables to send light waves that carry information.
8. An entrepreneur is an outside person who puts money into a business and expects a share of the profit.
9. Competition combines biology and technology to make scientific advances.
10. A business's cyberspace is made up of other businesses offering a similar product that might attract their customers.

## THINKING ABOUT FACTS

1. What is the free enterprise system?
2. Who are consumers?
3. How do investors contribute to the free enterprise system?
4. What are three products manufactured in New Jersey?
5. What is telecommunications?
6. Provide three examples of businesses that would be involved in tourism.
7. What do research and development companies do?
8. How does fiber optics improve communication?
9. Describe how a company might use the Internet to do business.
10. How is the World Wide Web really "worldwide"?

## THINK AND WRITE

### WRITING AN EXPLANATION

Write an explanation of how the free enterprise system allows people to make choices about their businesses.

### WRITING A LIST

Write a list of items New Jersey manufactures and services it provides.

### WRITING AN ADVERTISEMENT

Write an advertisement for New Jersey that tells why our state is a good place to start a business.

## APPLYING STUDY SKILLS

1. What are reference sources? Name three different kinds.
2. Which reference source could you use to learn more about the free enterprise system?
3. Suppose the guide words on a dictionary page are *entire* and *envy.* Would the word *entrepreneur* be found on the page?
4. Suppose you wanted to watch a demonstration of how fiber optics works. What kind of reference source would you use?
5. How might reference sources be helpful when you are studying history?

## Summing Up the Chapter

Use the following word maps to organize information from the chapter. Copy the word maps on a sheet of paper. Then write at least one piece of information in each blank circle. When you have filled in the word maps, use them to write a paragraph that answers the question "What are some of the most important parts of New Jersey's economy today?"

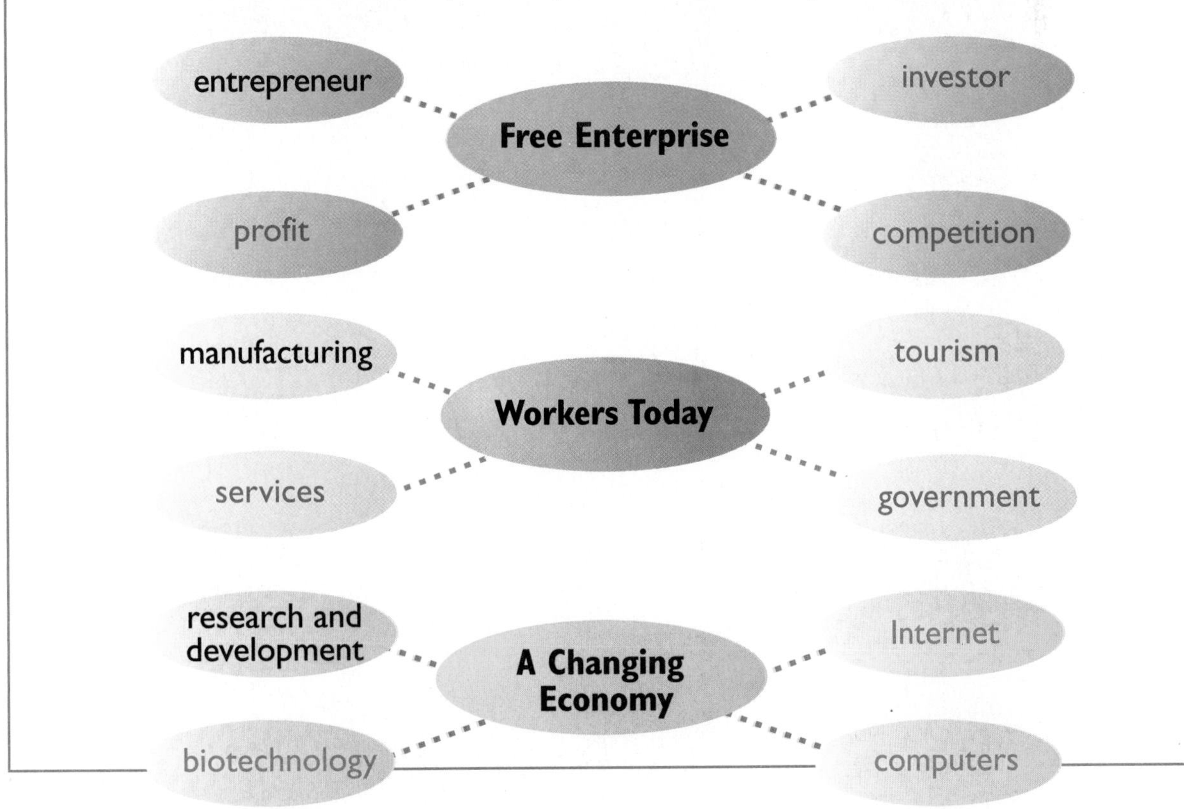

CHAPTER 11

# New Jersey's Government and You

## THINKING ABOUT GEOGRAPHY AND CITIZENSHIP

Have you ever wondered how you could help make changes in your community? Have you ever thought about ways you would like to help our state? Do you know what your responsibilities are as a United States citizen? This chapter is all about our government. Read on to learn how our local, state, and national governments work.

See pT90 for Chapter Organizer.

**TRENTON**

**The governor and other state leaders make decisions about our state in the state capitol building in Trenton.**

# Focus Activity

**READ TO LEARN**

***What role do citizens play in our local government?***

**VOCABULARY**

- elect
- municipality
- council
- mayor
- budget
- special district
- county seat
- Board of Chosen Freeholders

**PLACES**

- Monroe
- Maplewood
- Flemington



See p. T91 for Lesson Teaching Strategies.

# Your Local Government

## Read Aloud

*Mary Mazza Duffy is mayor of Monroe Township in Gloucester County. She explains what it means to be a citizen of the United States. "What's unique about our country's government is our ability to be part of our own government process. We choose leaders to represent us each time we vote. These leaders then pass the laws that affect our way of everyday life. By voting, our voice is heard."*

## THE BIG PICTURE

Voting is an important way for United States citizens to make their opinions heard. Voting is both a right and a responsibility. In the United States, citizens **elect**, or choose by voting for, their government leaders. The job of these leaders is to carry out the wishes of the people who elect them.

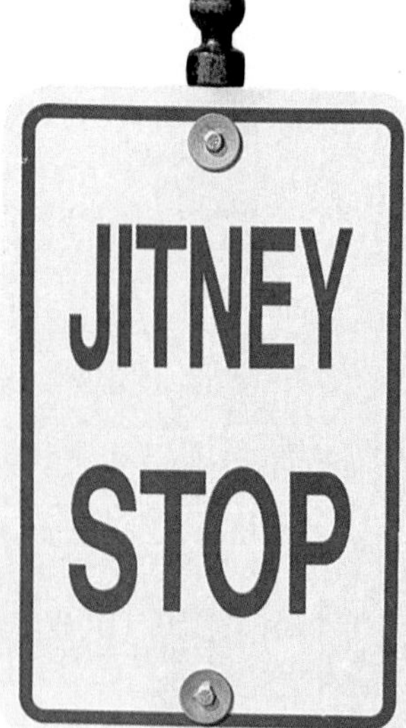

Mary Mazza Duffy is the mayor of **Monroe**. The mayor is the head of the local government. Local government has always been very important in New Jersey. In this lesson you will read about the ways in which this type of government helps the citizens of New Jersey.

## GOVERNMENT IN YOUR COMMUNITY

Why is it important to have a government in the community where you live? Community or local governments are needed to make decisions about things that affect all the people in a community. For example, a local government usually makes decisions about where and how a park in your community will be built.

Local government handles many things that affect you every day. It keeps the streets and parks clean, runs the public library, and pays the people in the police and fire department.

### Solving a Problem

Take a look at how local government serves the people who live in Maplewood. In 1996 residents were facing a problem. A new railroad line offered service directly into New York City. It became very hard for people to park their cars near the train station. The railroad company wanted to build a parking garage. However, many people in Maplewood did not want a building that would make the downtown area too crowded.

The local government formed a committee to find a solution. The committee decided to create a local jitney service. A jitney is a small bus that travels a special route. This jitney took people to the station in the morning and met the trains at the end of the day. The local government even raised enough money to offer jitney service for free!

Today, more than 350 people in Maplewood ride the jitneys every day. "I love the jitney," says Lorraine Storch. "It picks me up a half a block from my house. I see the same people every day. If someone isn't on the jitney for a few days, everyone asks, 'Is everything o.k.? I was worried about you!' It's been great for the community."

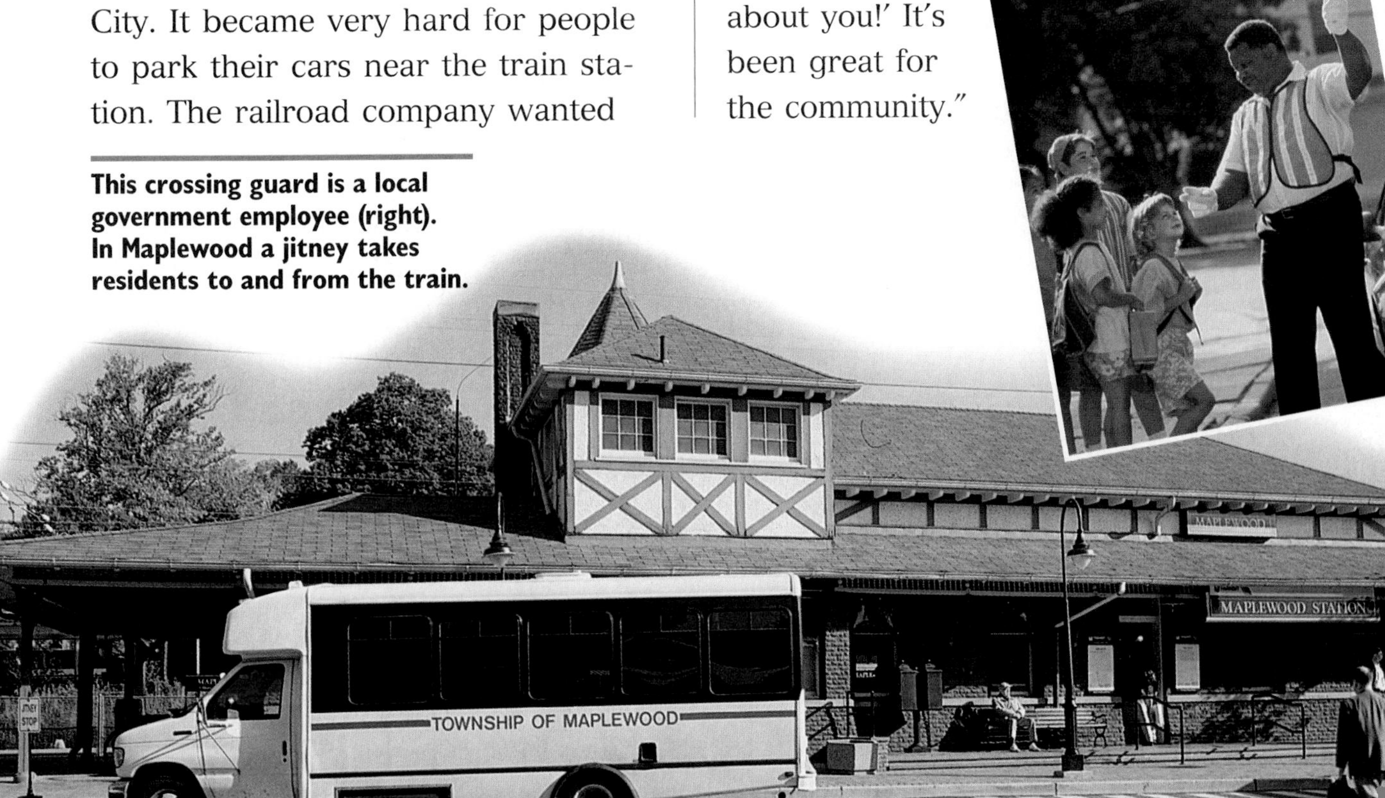


**This crossing guard is a local government employee (right). In Maplewood a jitney takes residents to and from the train.**

## HOW LOCAL GOVERNMENT WORKS

Each of the 566 local governments in New Jersey is called a **municipality** (myoo NIHS I pahl ih tee). There are five types of municipalities in our state: boroughs, townships, cities, towns, and villages. Each type of municipality has a slightly different form of government. These different municipalities have similar responsibilities. Boroughs and townships are the most common types. Villages are the least common. Look at the chart below. It shows two types of municipal government.

Most municipalities elect a group such as a **council**. The council is a group of people elected to make laws concerning issues such as crime, local taxes, and public safety. Most municipalities also elect a **mayor**. The mayor is the head of the local government. He or she is responsible for carrying out local laws. The mayor also works with the council to make a **budget**. The budget is the plan for spending the municipality's money.

**NEW JERSEY MUNICIPAL GOVERNMENT**

Mayor - Council — OR — Council - Manager

| | |
|---|---|
| Police Department | Health Department |
| Fire Department | Planning Department |
| Sanitation Department | Tax Collection Department |
| Building Inspection Department | |

**CHART WORK**

There are many departments in most municipal governments.

1. Name three departments in municipal government.

Citizens take part in government in many ways. For example, they vote in elections and pay taxes. They also serve on citizen groups that help to solve local problems.

### Special Districts

**Special districts** are an important part of local government in our state. A special district is an area in which a particular service is provided to the people who live there. For example, a municipality might be divided into several special districts for garbage pickup. Other special districts are created to provide fire protection or public road safety.

A school district is a special district set up to oversee schools. School board members are officials who run a school district. They make decisions about what students should learn and what kinds of equipment they need. They also decide whether there is a need to build new schools and how to spend the district's money. Special districts receive money through special taxes, voted on by the people who live in the district.

### County Government

Each municipality in the state is part of a larger community called a county. There are 21 counties in New Jersey. Look at the county map on page R13. Find your county. Each county has a **county seat**. That is

**CHART WORK:** **1.** any three of the following: police, fire, sanitation, building inspection, health, planning, tax collection

**Voting is an important role citizens play in our government.**

where the county government is located. Flemington, for example, is the county seat for Hunterdon County. Where is your county seat?

Counties are governed by a Board of Chosen Freeholders. The word *freeholder* comes from New Jersey's colonial days, when people who owned land were called *freeholders*. Only freeholders could vote or hold office. Today every county in New Jersey has a board with three to nine elected freeholders. The county government has many responsibilities. It runs the court system and keeps track of marriages, births, and deaths.

See p. T91 for Answers to Think About It.

## WHY IT MATTERS

Local government, elected by citizens, provides many services to its citizens. Some problems cannot be solved by local government alone. New Jersey's local government often works with the state government to solve these problems. In the next lesson, you will learn about the state government in New Jersey.

## Reviewing Facts and Ideas

### MAIN IDEAS

- Your local government makes decisions for your community.
- The five types of municipalities in New Jersey are boroughs, townships, cities, towns, and villages.
- A special district is an area where a special service is provided to the people who live there.
- County governments are run by a Board of Chosen Freeholders.

### THINK ABOUT IT

1. What are the five types of municipalities in New Jersey?
2. What are two services that local governments provide for their citizens?
3. **FOCUS** Name two ways in which citizens participate in local government.
4. **THINKING SKILL** *Compare* and *contrast* the roles of municipal governments and special districts.
5. **GEOGRAPHY** Look at the map on page R13. Make a list of the names of the counties that border your county.

# Study Skills

See p. T92 for Skill Teaching Strategies.

# Reading Newspapers

**VOCABULARY**

current event
news article
feature article
editorial
headline
byline
dateline

### WHY THE SKILL MATTERS

In the last section you read about citizens taking part in local government. Are you interested in learning more about your government? One good way to get information about government is by reading the newspaper.

Newspapers report on current events, or the things that happen every day. Some newspapers print only stories about the local events that go on in a city or town. Others write about events all over the country and around the world.

### USING A NEWSPAPER

Newspapers have different parts. The front part of a paper contains mostly news articles. These are stories based on facts about events that happened. Inside are feature articles. A feature article has many details about a person, subject, or event.

Newspapers also include sports articles, cartoons, and letters to the editor. Editors, the people who run the paper, write editorials in which they express their own ideas about an issue. They state their opinions, not just the facts. An editorial might make you think harder about an issue.

### USING A NEWS ARTICLE

Look at a newspaper. What is the thing that first catches your attention? You may notice the words printed in large letters at the top of each article. They form the headline of the article. It sums up the main idea of the story.

Now look at the news article on the next page. As you can see, the headline is "In Search of Fields of Dreams." One thing you might not notice at first is an article's byline. The byline tells the reader who wrote the story. The author of that story is David M. Campbell.

Another useful part of an article is its dateline. The dateline tells you when and where a story was written. As you can see, the dateline in the story tells that it was written in West Windsor on December 15.

A news article that gives you all the facts should answer five questions. They are: (1) *Who* was involved in the story? (2) *What* took place?

*It provides detailed information and facts about recent events; radio, television, magazines, the Internet
**news article; editorial; The first headline is factual, but the second states an opinion.

See p. T92 for Answers to Reviewing the Skill.

(3) *When* did or will the event happen? (4) *Where* did it happen? (5) *Why* did it happen?

Use the Helping Yourself box to guide you in reading the article below. Does the article answer the five questions? The answer to the first question, for example, might be "the West Windsor–Plainsboro Soccer Association." Can you sum up the article in your own words?

**Helping yourself**

- **Identify whether you are reading a news article, a feature article, or an editorial.**
- **Study the headline, byline, and dateline.**
- **Ask yourself the "five questions" about the article.**

## TRYING THE SKILL

You just read a news article about a soccer league trying to obtain more playing fields. Why, do you think, is a newspaper a good way to learn about events in your community? What other sources might give you information about the event?*

Now suppose you wanted to find out about a different topic: the construction of a new state highway. An article in the newspaper has the headline, "Highway Opening Delayed." What kind of article do you think this is? Another is called "New Highway Is a Step in the Right Direction." What kind of article do you think this is? How do you know?**

## REVIEWING THE SKILL

1. Name three different kinds of articles that appear in newspapers.
2. How can you tell that the article printed below is a news article and not an editorial?
3. Why is it important for some news articles to have a dateline?
4. How would a newspaper help you learn more about New Jersey?

### IN SEARCH OF FIELDS OF DREAMS

**by David M. Campbell**

WEST WINDSOR, December 15—The kids sitting in the back seats wear jerseys with names on them like Torpedos, Riptide, and Cyclones. The minivans that stream into community parks and fields each week are testament to soccer's growing popularity.

But as soccer rosters grow, so does the need for one other component: land.

In presentations made by the West Windsor–Plainsboro Soccer Association last week, the Township Council and the Recreation Board were asked to consider a proposal to acquire open-space parcels to develop a five-field soccer complex. Council Vice President Kristin Appelget was very much in favor of the proposal. "I think recreation is a very important part of our community. It's what makes a town a town."

LESSON 2

See p. T93 for Lesson Teaching Strategies.

# Our State Government

## Read Aloud

*In January, 2000, Governor Christine Todd Whitman talked to New Jersey legislators. She called on all New Jerseyans to "[make] this state—our home—the very best place in which to live, work, and raise a family."*

## Focus Activity

**READ TO LEARN**

***What are the roles of the three branches of New Jersey's state government?***

**VOCABULARY**

- checks and balances
- executive branch
- legislative branch
- bill
- veto
- judicial branch

**PEOPLE**

- James H. Coleman, Jr.
- Deborah Poritz
- Marie Garibaldi

**PLACES**

- Trenton

## THE BIG PICTURE

Governor Whitman was talking about the importance of making New Jersey a great place to live. The New Jersey Constitution was created with this purpose in mind. It is the guide lawmakers use to run our state government. The New Jersey Constitution describes the rights and responsibilities of our state's citizens. As you have read, the current constitution was written in 1947. It is our state's third constitution.

The Constitution divides the government into three branches so that no single person or group of people will have too much power. Each branch of government keeps watch over, or checks, the other two branches. This is called the system of **checks and balances**.

## OUR STATE AND YOU

Have you ever visited Trenton, our state capital? Many important decisions are made there every day. These decisions affect the lives of every New Jerseyan—including you! Our state government works to protect the health, safety, and jobs of New Jersey's citizens.

### The Executive Branch

The executive branch of government is responsible for carrying out the laws of the state. The governor is the head of the executive branch. The governor is elected by the people of our state to serve for a term of four years. He or she may be reelected for a second four-year term.

In New Jersey, the governor is the only person in the executive branch to be elected by the people. The governor then chooses the other members of the executive branch. The governor's office and most other state government offices are located in Trenton.

The governor helps set goals for our state. He or she chooses many people who help run state departments, such as the Department of Transportation and the State Parks and Recreation Department. These two departments work to care for our state's highways and parks.

New Jersey citizens pay taxes that allow the state government to provide these services. The governor prepares a budget to plan how the money will be used. The state budget shows how much money New Jersey will spend on each service. Look at the chart on this page. It shows how New Jersey spent the money it received from taxes and other sources in the year 2001.

**CHART WORK: 1.** 38¢ of each dollar

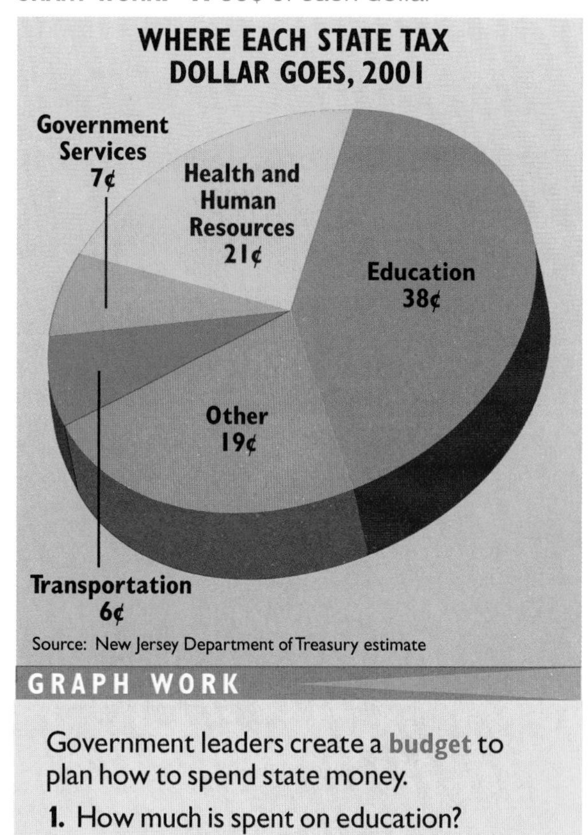


**GRAPH WORK**

Government leaders create a budget to plan how to spend state money.

1. How much is spent on education?

Governor Whitman signs the 1999 state budget.

## THE LEGISLATIVE BRANCH

The legislative branch of our state government is the branch that makes the laws. The legislative branch has two parts—the Senate and the General Assembly. New Jersey voters elect 40 senators and 80 members of the assembly. State senators serve for four years. Members of the assembly serve for two years.

These legislators create and vote on bills. A bill is a written idea for a law. The legislators also vote on whether to approve the budget created by the governor.

How does a bill become a law? Look at the chart on this page. Then read about one bill that made riding on school buses safer for students in our state.

### Taking Action

In 1998 many people in New Jersey were concerned that school buses in the state were not safe enough. Members of the legislative branch studied the issue. They decided that steps could be taken to keep school buses in better condition and to make sure buses are operated by safe drivers.

Assemblyman John S. Wisniewski from Middlesex County introduced a bill for the Senate and General Assembly to vote on. It called for school buses to get more careful checkups for safety. In addition, the drivers' licenses and driving records of bus drivers would also be looked at carefully. These checks would cost money. So the bill also asked for money to fund the new programs.

Both branches of the legislature had to vote on the school bus safety bill. On December 17, 1998, the bill passed the legislative branch. Then it went to the governor. The governor could choose to sign the bill, or she could veto, or reject, the bill. On January 21, 1999, Governor Whitman signed the School Bus Enhanced Safety Inspection Act. The hard work of citizens and lawmakers helped make school buses in our state safer for students like you!

***What is New Jersey's state song?***

**New Jersey has a state flower (the purple violet), a state insect (the honeybee), and even a state dinosaur (the hadrosaurus). However, New Jersey is one of only two states that does not have a state song. Over the years, citizens have suggested different state songs, but none has become a law. What words might you write in a state song for New Jersey?**

## You Can Make a Difference

You too, can help make a law in New Jersey. Suppose you want to help protect the environment and save natural resources. One way would be to start a program for recycling aluminum cans. First you could write to your state assembly person and senator. You would then ask them to write a bill to start a recycling program. Follow the arrows in the chart on the opposite page to find out how it might happen.

**A law passed in 1999 made school buses much safer.**

## THE JUDICIAL BRANCH

The **judicial** (joo DISH uhl) **branch** of state government interprets, or explains, our state's laws. This branch includes judges, who work in courts. The highest court in New Jersey is the Supreme Court. The governor chooses the Supreme Court judges, who are called justices. The State Senate can approve or reject the governor's choices. If approved, justices serve a seven-year term. In 1994 Justice **James H. Coleman, Jr.** was appointed by Governor Whitman. He became the first African American to serve on New Jersey's Supreme Court.

Read the following words of Chief Justice **Deborah Poritz**. She describes **Marie Garibaldi**, the first woman appointed to the New Jersey Supreme Court. What does she say about the challenge of being the "first"?

**Excerpt from an interview with Chief Justice Deborah Poritz, 1999.**

*Marie Garibaldi took the oath of office as an Associate Justice of the New Jersey Supreme Court and forever changed the way the Court works. Being 'first' inevitably made outside demands on her time, but she never let those demands interfere with the quality of her performance as a Justice.*

See p. T93 for Answers to Think About It.

## WHY IT MATTERS

New Jersey's state government is our government. Yet it cannot work without the involvement of citizens. Citizens take part in government by voting, paying taxes, and by attending meetings where laws are discussed and made. They also can help by telling their elected representatives what they think government should do. One day you will help elect leaders by voting. Perhaps one day you will be elected to office yourself.

### Reviewing Facts and Ideas

#### MAIN IDEAS

- Our state government's decisions affect our everyday lives.
- Our state government is made up of the executive, legislative, and judicial branches.
- The system of checks and balances makes sure that no single branch of government has too much power.

#### THINK ABOUT IT

1. What is the system of checks and balances?
2. How does a bill become a law in New Jersey?
3. **FOCUS** What is the job of each branch of our state government?
4. **THINKING SKILL** Make a <u>conclusion</u> about how our state government works. What facts did you use to support your conclusion?
5. **WRITE** Think of a bill you would like to see passed in New Jersey. Write a short paragraph stating why you think this bill would make a good law.

See p. T94 for Answers to
Building Citizenship.

CITIZENSHIP

# MAKING A DIFFERENCE

## Starting a Family Tradition

Ewing, New Jersey—Children in Ewing are helping their parents carry out one of their most important rights and duties—voting. These students are part of a statewide program called Kids Voting New Jersey.

On election day in 1999 about 570 Ewing students and their parents cast ballots for town council members and other government officials. Although student votes were "mock", or pretend, their ballots looked just like the real ones used by adults. "Their votes will count when they are 18. They are practicing for a lifetime habit," says Candace Mueller, the head of Kids Voting Ewing.

Before the election, students talk in class about the importance of voting. Sometimes, the talks continue at home with family members. "My Dad told me you shouldn't just vote for someone because you've heard their name on TV," said 10-year-old Ben Caiola. "You should know more about them before you go to the polls."

After the election, many young people came with their families to an Election Night Results party at a local ice cream parlor. The results from the Kids Voting election were posted so that students could see how others their age voted. In 1999 Ewing was one of only four municipalities in the state to have such a program. The others were Glen Ridge, Newark, and Clementon. Now the program includes many more places in our state.

Melysa Wilson explained why she thought Kids Voting is good for the schools and the community. "It brings families together to vote. It teaches us to dig deeper and make good decisions. Most of all, we have a privilege that people in some other countries don't have. We should take advantage of it."

"It teaches us to... make good decisions."

Benjamin Caiola Melysa Wilson

# LESSON 3

See p. T95 for Lesson Teaching Strategies.

# Our National Government

## Read Aloud

*"I pledge allegiance to the flag of the United States of America, and to the republic for which it stands, one nation under God, indivisible, with liberty and justice for all."*

## Focus Activity

**READ TO LEARN**

***What are the rights and responsibilities we have as United States citizens?***

**VOCABULARY**

- democratic republic
- candidate
- United States Congress
- United States Supreme Court

**PEOPLE**

- Grover Cleveland
- Woodrow Wilson
- William J. Brennan

**PLACES**

- Washington, D.C.

## THE BIG PICTURE

These words are probably very familiar to you. When you say the Pledge of Allegiance, you make a promise. You are promising to be loyal to the United States and to help our country's government.

Running a government is not easy. In 1776 our country's first leaders found out just how tough the job of governing is. In 1787 they wrote the United States Constitution, the plan for running our government.

The United States Constitution explains that our country is set up as a **democratic republic**. In our democratic republic, citizens elect representatives to run the government.

## THE UNITED STATES GOVERNMENT

The United States Constitution begins with the words, "We the people of the United States. . . ." These words remind us that we live in a democracy, with a government by the people. People in a democratic republic must care about choices that affect us all.

However, the United States is a big country. Not every citizen can take part directly in every decision. So citizens take part by voting to elect people to make decisions for them.

In an election, a person who runs for office is called a **candidate**. Usually candidates are members of a political party. As you have read, a political party is a group of people who share similar ideas about government. The Democratic and Republican parties are the largest political parties in the United States.

### Providing Services

Like our local and state governments, the United States government makes decisions and provides services. One of these services is defense. The United States government runs the Army and our other armed forces. Our government pays for the building of ships, airplanes, and weapons to protect our country.

Another service our government provides is help after natural disasters. The Federal Emergency Management Agency, or FEMA, helps people rebuild their lives after hurricanes, earthquakes, floods, and tornadoes. In Chapter 1 you read how Hurricane Floyd caused so much damage to our state in 1999. Afterward, FEMA provided shelter and supplies and helped rebuild roads and homes.

New Jerseyans pay for these and other services with their taxes. We pay taxes to our national and state government based on the amount of money we earn. As you read in Chapter 9, this tax is called an income tax. We also pay a sales tax to our state government on things we buy.

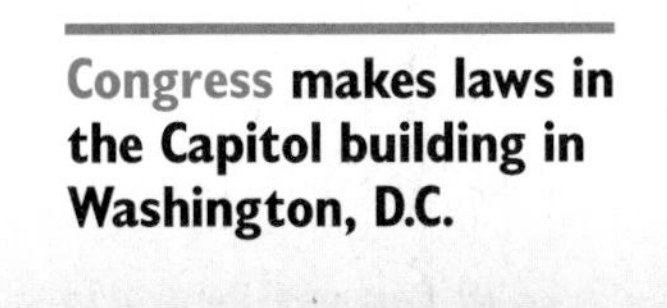

**Congress makes laws in the Capitol building in Washington, D.C.**

## THE THREE BRANCHES

Our national government is located in Washington, D.C. Like our state government, our country's government has three branches. Each branch has different duties. Find these branches on the chart below.

### Congress

The legislative branch of our national government is called the United States Congress. Congress makes laws for the whole country. Congress has two parts, the Senate and the House of Representatives.

The voters of each state elect two senators to the United States Senate. The number of representatives that voters elect depends on how many people live in their state. New Jersey elects 13 people to the United States House of Representatives. The state of California, which has a larger population than New Jersey, elects 52 representatives. Vermont only elects one. Senators are elected for six-year terms. Representatives are elected for two-year terms.

### The President

The President is elected every four years. As head of the executive branch of government, the President makes sure that laws passed by Congress are carried out. The President also meets with leaders of other countries and is the leader of our military forces.

Two presidents have come from New Jersey. Grover Cleveland was elected President of the United States in 1884 and again in 1892. Woodrow Wilson was elected President in 1912.

**OUR COUNTRY'S GOVERNMENT: Three Branches**

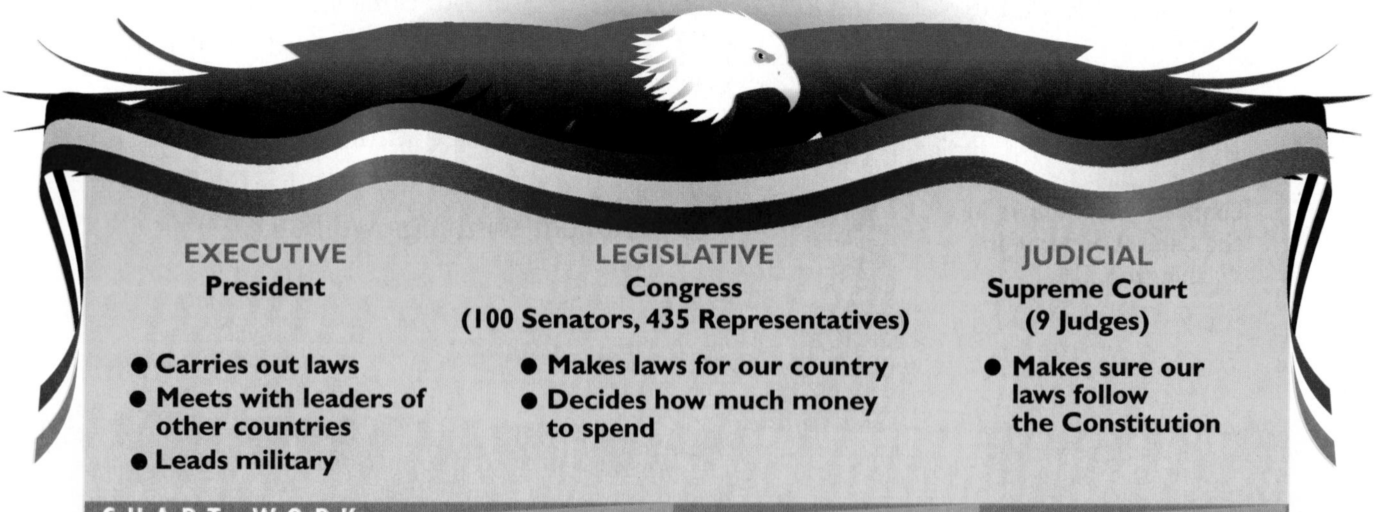

| EXECUTIVE<br>President | LEGISLATIVE<br>Congress<br>(100 Senators, 435 Representatives) | JUDICIAL<br>Supreme Court<br>(9 Judges) |
|---|---|---|
| • Carries out laws<br>• Meets with leaders of other countries<br>• Leads military | • Makes laws for our country<br>• Decides how much money to spend | • Makes sure our laws follow the Constitution |

**CHART WORK**

Our national government, located in Washington, D.C. has three branches.

1. How many senators does Congress have? How many representatives?
2. What branch does the President lead? What are the President's duties?
3. Who are the highest officials of the judicial branch of our government?

**CHART WORK: 1.** 100;435 **2.** executive; carry out laws, meet with leaders, lead military **3.** Supreme Court judges

See p. T95 for Answers to Think About It.

The United States Supreme Court decides if laws agree with our country's Constitution.

## The Courts

The President also selects the justices of the United States Supreme Court. The Supreme Court is the highest court in our country. Nine justices serve on the United States Supreme Court. Once chosen by the President and then approved by the Senate, they serve for the rest of their lives. These judges hear cases that come from the lower courts. They also decide whether laws that are passed by Congress agree with the United States Constitution. William J. Brennan from Newark first served as a justice of the New Jersey Supreme Court. In 1956 he was appointed to the United States Supreme Court, where he served until 1990.

## Rights and Responsibilities

Leaders in our national government work to protect the rights of American citizens. With rights come responsibilities. Citizens must pay taxes and obey our country's laws. As Americans, we are expected to learn about important issues and let our representatives know what we think. At election time, it is important for everyone to vote.

## WHY IT MATTERS

The United States is a democratic republic. Citizens elect leaders to serve in government. One way you can prepare for that responsibility is to know about your government—at the local, state, and national levels.

## Reviewing Facts and Ideas

### MAIN IDEAS

- The United States is a democratic republic.
- The United States government uses taxes to pay for services such as defense and disaster relief.
- The three branches of our national government are headed by Congress, the President, and the Supreme Court.

### THINK ABOUT IT

1. What is a democratic republic?
2. What is a political party?
3. **FOCUS** What are the rights and responsibilities that we have as United States citizens?
4. **THINKING SKILL** How can voters decide about which candidate to elect?
5. **WRITE** What qualities do you think are important in a citizen? Write a paragraph to explain your ideas.

See p. T96 for Answers to Chapter 11 Review.

# CHAPTER 11 REVIEW

## THINKING ABOUT VOCABULARY

**A.** Write a sentence for each pair of words below. Include details that give clues to the meaning of the first term in each pair.

1. elect, council
2. municipality, mayor
3. legislative branch, judicial branch
4. bill, veto
5. candidate, United States Congress

**B.** Number a sheet of paper from 1 to 10. Next to each number write the word or term from those in Part A that best completes the sentence.

1. The Senate and the General Assembly are the two parts of the ______ of the state government.
2. A ______ is a written idea for a law.
3. A person who runs for office is called a ______.
4. A ______ is the head of a municipal government.
5. Each of the 566 local governments in New Jersey is called a ______.
6. In our country, citizens ______ government leaders.
7. The ______ is the legislative branch of our national government.
8. Many municipalities have a group of people who make laws, called a ______.
9. To ______ a bill is to reject it.
10. Courts and judges are part of the ______ of our state government.

## THINKING ABOUT FACTS

1. How do the citizens of the United States take part in our government?
2. Who is the head of a municipal government?
3. What are two responsibilities of county government?
4. What are the three branches of our national and state governments? How does the system of checks and balances apply to them?
5. Who is the head of the executive branch of government in our state? For how long does this person serve?

## THINK AND WRITE

### WRITING A PLAN
Suppose a new law is passed that gives more money to your school. Write a plan for the best way to use that money.

### WRITING A POSTER
Write a poster showing the three branches of our state government. Label the responsibilities of each branch.

### WRITING AN ARTICLE
Suppose you are an editor of a newspaper. Write an editorial encouraging people to vote in the next election. Explain why it is an important responsibility for each citizen to vote.

## APPLYING THINKING SKILLS

### READING NEWSPAPERS

1. What five questions should a well-written news article answer?
2. Look at the news article about the soccer fields on page 275. Identify the headline, the byline, and the dateline.
3. What is an editorial? How does it differ from a news article?
4. Look again at the news article on page 275. How would you change the article if you wanted it to be an editorial?
5. What can you learn from reading newspapers?

## Summing Up the Chapter

Use the following table to organize information from the chapter. Copy the table on a sheet of paper. Then list the people and groups that run each level of government. When you have filled in the table, use it to help you write a paragraph that answers the question, "What do the local, state, and national governments have in common? How are they different?"

**LEVELS OF GOVERNMENT**

| LOCAL | STATE | NATIONAL |
|---|---|---|
| mayor | governor | President |
| council | New Jersey General Assembly, New Jersey Senate | United States Senate, United States House of Representatives |
| | New Jersey Supreme Court | United States Supreme Court |

CHAPTER 12

# New Jersey's People and Culture

## THINKING ABOUT PEOPLE AND CULTURE

What is your favorite way to enjoy your free time? Maybe you like to paint pictures, play baseball, or march in a local parade. In New Jersey, we have thousands of ways to enjoy and celebrate our special state and its many cultures. Read Chapter 12 to find out more about the people of our state and how they make it a great place to live.

See pT97 for Chapter Organizer.



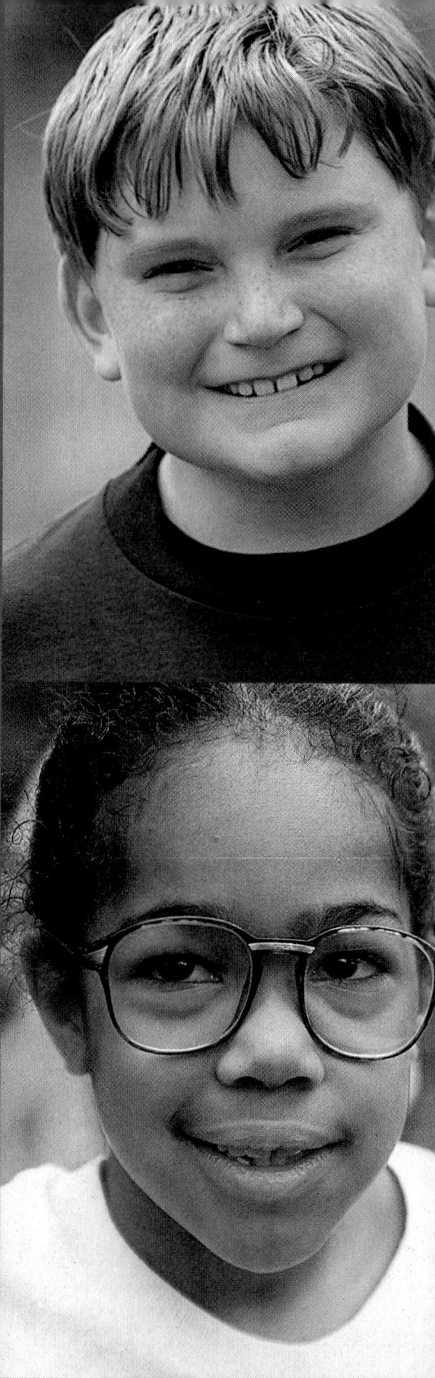

LESSON 1

See p. 98 for Lesson Teaching Strategies.

# The People of New Jersey

## Read Aloud

*Dasharath Chaudhari [dah shah RAH tuh CHOW dah ree] was born in India. Today he lives with his family in Dayton, New Jersey. "I have observed a very remarkable thing in New Jersey," Dasharath says. "Wherever I moved, my neighbors were eager to help."*

## Focus Activity

**READ TO LEARN**

***Who are New Jerseyans today?***

**VOCABULARY**

- ethnic group
- diversity
- festival
- megalopolis
- population density
- edge city

**PLACES**

- Mahwah
- Woodbridge
- Princeton
- Cherry Hill

## THE BIG PICTURE

Immigrants like Dasharath Chaudhari have been coming to New Jersey for more than 400 years. This immigration has made our state home to many different **ethnic groups**. An ethnic group is a group of people whose ancestors are from the same area. Today, almost one in three New Jerseyans was born in another country or has a parent who was.

Today's immigrants are more likely to arrive by plane than by boat. Still, they have much in common with the immigrants who came before. They come in search of freedom and a better life. They bring with them hope, determination, and new ideas.

**Festivals are one way that an ethnic group can celebrate its heritage and culture.**

# WHO ARE NEW JERSEYANS TODAY?

One of our state's strengths is the diversity, or many different kinds, of people who live here. This diversity helps make our state an interesting place to live. Take a look at the chart on this page. It shows just some of the many ethnic groups that make up our state's diverse population today.

## A World of Festivals

Festivals, or celebrations, are one way people in our state preserve their ethnic customs and share them with others. At the African American festivals in Newark or Montclair, for example, people of all cultures can enjoy music and sample foods with an African and Caribbean flavor. The Hungarian festival in New Brunswick every June features folk dancing and special foods like kolbasz (KOL baas) sandwiches and strudel.

CHART WORK: 1. African Americans

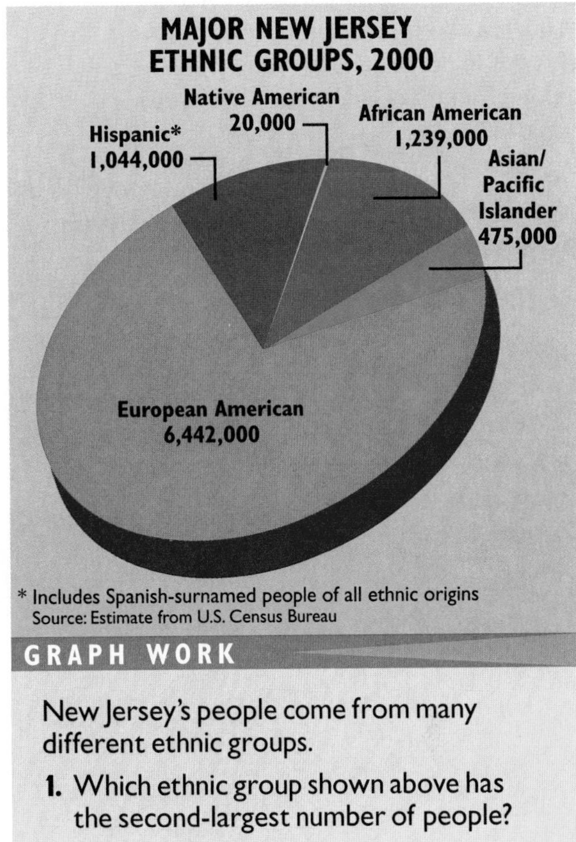


**GRAPH WORK**

New Jersey's people come from many different ethnic groups.

1. Which ethnic group shown above has the second-largest number of people?

Jersey City holds the annual American Day Parade and Festival every year. At the festival, many ethnic groups share the foods and music of their various cultures. One exciting part of this festival involves immigrants from around the world taking an oath to become new American citizens.

Many New Jerseyans live in suburbs like this one in Bergen County (below). Others enjoy life in cities like Jersey City (right).

## WHERE NEW JERSEYANS LIVE TODAY

New Jersey today is part of the **megalopolis**, or giant city, of the northeastern part of our country. The term *megalopolis* describes the chain of cities and suburbs that reaches from north of Boston to south of Washington, D.C. Most people in this megalopolis live in large cities or surrounding suburbs. New Jersey is located in the center of this megalopolis.

### Living Together

It is no surprise, then, that New Jersey has the highest **population density** of any state in the United States. Population density is the measure of how many people live in a certain place, usually a square mile. A square mile is an area of land, shaped like a square, that measures one mile on each side.

Our state has more than 1,050 people per square mile. Compare that to the rest of the country, which has only 25 people per square mile. If you traveled across our state from New York to Philadelphia, you would pass through most of our state's largest urban areas. In fact, more than half of our state's people live in one of the seven counties in this area.

Still, New Jersey offers a great variety of places to live, including small towns and villages and farms. Warren Albertson has lived in Bates Mill in Camden County for more than 70 years. He enjoys living in a rural community. "South Jersey . . . is a fine place. There is a lot of open space, so we can really enjoy our life."

## An Edge City

Recently, a new type of community has begun to grow in our state. Some people call these new communities edge cities. An edge city is a combination of a suburb and a city. Edge cities include the office parks, factory areas, and shopping malls of cities. Yet they also include the houses and apartment buildings of suburbs. Mahwah, Woodbridge, Princeton, and Cherry Hill are examples of New Jersey's new edge cities.

### WHY IT MATTERS

New Jersey has attracted immigrants for hundreds of years. Newcomers bring customs and ideas that add to our state's economy and culture. The diversity they contribute makes New Jersey an interesting place to live.

See p. T98 for Answers to Think About It.

### DID YOU KNOW?

***How do immigrants become citizens?***

**To become a United States citizen, an immigrant must live in the United States for five years. He or she must be at least 18 years old.**

**Immigrants who apply for citizenship have to prove that they can read, write, and speak English. They also take a test on United States history and government.**

**Once they meet these requirements, immigrants must then say a special Oath of Allegiance, or loyalty, to the United States. They swear to "support and defend the Constitution and laws of the United States of America against all enemies."**

## Reviewing Facts and Ideas

### MAIN IDEAS

- New Jersey's diverse population includes many different ethnic groups.
- Festivals are one way in which people celebrate and preserve their ethnic customs.
- New Jersey is located in the center of the megalopolis of the northeastern United States.
- Today most New Jerseyans live in cities, suburbs, or edge cities.

### THINK ABOUT IT

1. Give three examples of ethnic groups that settled in New Jersey.
2. What is a megalopolis?
3. **FOCUS** How does our state's diverse population help make it a special place?
4. **THINKING SKILL** *Compare* and *contrast* an edge city with a suburb.
5. **GEOGRAPHY** Look at the atlas map on page R12. Draw a line with your finger between Trenton and Jersey City. List five large New Jersey cities along that line.

# Study Skills

See p. T99 for Skill Teaching Strategies.

## Writing Notes and Outlines

**VOCABULARY**
outline

### WHY THE SKILL MATTERS

You have just read about some of the ethnic festivals held each year in our state. What if you were asked to write a report about a festival? How would you prepare? You might use an **outline**. An outline is a plan for organizing written information about a subject.

How do you create an outline? You start by collecting information. When you read, take notes in your own words. Write down the main ideas of what you are reading. You should also jot down the important facts that support each main idea.

To organize the information, place a roman numeral next to each main idea and a capital letter next to each fact. Then group under each of your main ideas the facts that support it. You have created an outline.

### USING THE SKILL

The following short article describes a festival held by one group of New Jerseyans to celebrate their heritage. Try taking notes. Then study the outline below the article to see how the information is organized.

**The Return to Beaver Creek Native American Indian Festival is an important New Jersey event. Each year Native American people of various groups gather in Belvidere, New Jersey. The festival lasts three days. It celebrates the common Native American culture, as well as the customs that are special to each group.**

**What happens at the festival? Native American performers share their stories, music, and dance. Craftspeople demonstrate their skills and offer handmade crafts for sale. Cooks prepare traditional Native American foods.**

**The festival has several purposes. It gives people from many backgrounds the opportunity to learn more about Native American cultures. The festival also helps keep important Native American traditions alive. Last but not least, the purpose of the festival is also to have fun!**

Beaver Creek Native American Indian Festival

I. An important New Jersey tradition
  A. celebrates common heritage
  B. teaches about the culture
II. What happens?
  A. stories, music, dance
  B. handmade crafts
  C. traditional foods
III. Purposes
  A. to help people from many backgrounds learn more about Native American cultures
  B. to keep traditions alive
  C. to have fun

*the festival celebrates traditional music; the festival has become a Labor Day tradition; there is a lot to see and do

**main ideas

See p. T99 for Answers to Reviewing the Skill.

## TRYING THE SKILL

Now read the article about the Delaware Valley Bluegrass Festival. Take notes as you read. Then write an outline. Use the Helping Yourself box for hints. What are the main ideas?* Be sure to use facts to support them. Do main ideas or supporting facts get roman numerals in your outline?**

### Helping yourself

- An **outline** is a way of organizing what you learn.
- Take notes in your own words.
- Identify and label each main idea. Then choose two or more facts that support each main idea.

## REVIEWING THE SKILL

1. How does writing an outline help you organize information?
2. How did you decide which statements were main ideas and which were supporting facts?
3. In your outline of the Bluegrass Festival, what are the supporting facts? How can you tell?
4. How can taking notes and writing an outline help you learn about history?

The Delaware Valley Bluegrass Festival celebrates and honors traditional American music. The bluegrass music played on the stage is only one of the ways that the festival celebrates folk music. Traditional music is also honored by the people who come from all over the country to listen to the musicians.

The festival has become a Labor Day tradition for fans of bluegrass music throughout our state. The festival began in the early 1970s, when two bluegrass pioneers, Bill Monroe and Ralph Stanley, decided to organize a bluegrass fair in Delaware. In 1989, the festival moved to its present location in New Jersey. It is now held each year at the Salem County Fair Grounds, about four miles west of Woodstown.

There is a lot to see and do during the two-day festival. For example, you can learn how to play the banjo or buy new guitar strings at one of the stands. Of course, there is lots of great music to be heard. To listen to the performers, you can sit under a large tent or have a picnic on the grass. But the stage is not the only place music is played. Many people bring their musical instruments with them to the festival. So if you take a walk around the campgrounds, you will hear more bluegrass.

LESSON 2

See p. T100 for Lesson Teaching Strategies.

# Sports and Recreation

## Read Aloud

*It was the last inning of the last game of the Little League World Series in August 1998. The team from Toms River led the team from Kashima, Japan, by three runs. When the Toms River pitcher struck out the last Kashima batter, the game was over. Toms River had won the world championship! Manager Mike Gaynor later said, "It was unbelievable!"*

## Focus Activity

**READ TO LEARN**

***What do New Jerseyans do for fun?***

**VOCABULARY**

- recreation
- professional
- Special Olympics

**PEOPLE**

- Carl Lewis
- Elaine Zayak

**PLACES**

- Paramus
- High Point State Park
- Liberty State Park
- Cape May Point State Park
- Vernon
- Jackson
- Washington Crossing State Park

## THE BIG PICTURE

New Jerseyans young and old love sports. Some people like playing. Others like watching. However, sports are just one type of **recreation** that people enjoy in our state. Recreation is activities that we do for fun. Perhaps you enjoy family picnics, sledding, or playing stickball with friends in your neighborhood. Or you might enjoy riding a speeding roller coaster, driving through a jungle habitat, balancing on ocean waves, or playing volleyball on the beach. Getting outside and having fun is an important part of life in New Jersey. No matter what you enjoy, there is always something fun to do in New Jersey!

## SPORTS GALORE

People have been enjoying sports in New Jersey for hundreds of years. The Lenape held foot races and wrestling matches. The Dutch and English settlers played games like bowling and soccer. In 1846, the first organized baseball game in the United States was played in Hoboken. The first college football game was played between Princeton and Rutgers in 1869.

Today, sports are a big business in New Jersey. Fans pay money to see and cheer the athletes of their favorite professional teams. Professional athletes play sports as a job, not just for fun.

Many of our state's professional sports teams play at the Meadowlands Sports Complex. The New Jersey Devils hockey team and the New Jersey Nets basketball team play indoors at the arena. The MetroStars soccer team and two football teams, the Jets and the Giants, play outdoors in the stadium.

In addition, there are now six minor league baseball teams in our state. They play in Atlantic City, Augusta, Montclair, Newark, Somerset, and Trenton.

### A State of Athletes

Over the years New Jersey has been home to many great athletes. Carl Lewis, from Willingboro, won nine gold medals in track and field during several Olympic Games. World Champion Olympic figure skater Elaine Zayak comes from Paramus.

Every year many New Jerseyans take part in the Special Olympics. In the Special Olympics children and adult athletes with disabilities compete in sports like swimming, figure skating, and volleyball.

**Sports fans in New Jersey can watch many different sports, including hockey (left), lacrosse (middle), and baseball (right).**

## OUTDOOR FUN IN NEW JERSEY

Every year, people from New Jersey and from all over the world enjoy outdoor recreation in our state. Many people think of the beach when they think of New Jersey. The beach is just one of many places to have fun!

Our state has 40 state parks and 11 state forests. You can camp out at High Point State Park in the northwest corner of our state. You can launch a boat at Liberty State Park in Jersey City. You can paddle a canoe down the Delaware and Raritan Canal. You might even try surf fishing at Cape May Point State Park.

At Mountain Creek in Vernon, you can snowboard in January or cool off in the water park in August. In Jackson, you can take a ride on the world's first floorless roller coaster! For people who like to keep their feet on the ground, New Jersey's historic sites offer a chance to have fun and learn something, too. For example, at Washington Crossing State Park you could follow in George Washington's footsteps and see where he crossed the Delaware River over 200 years ago.

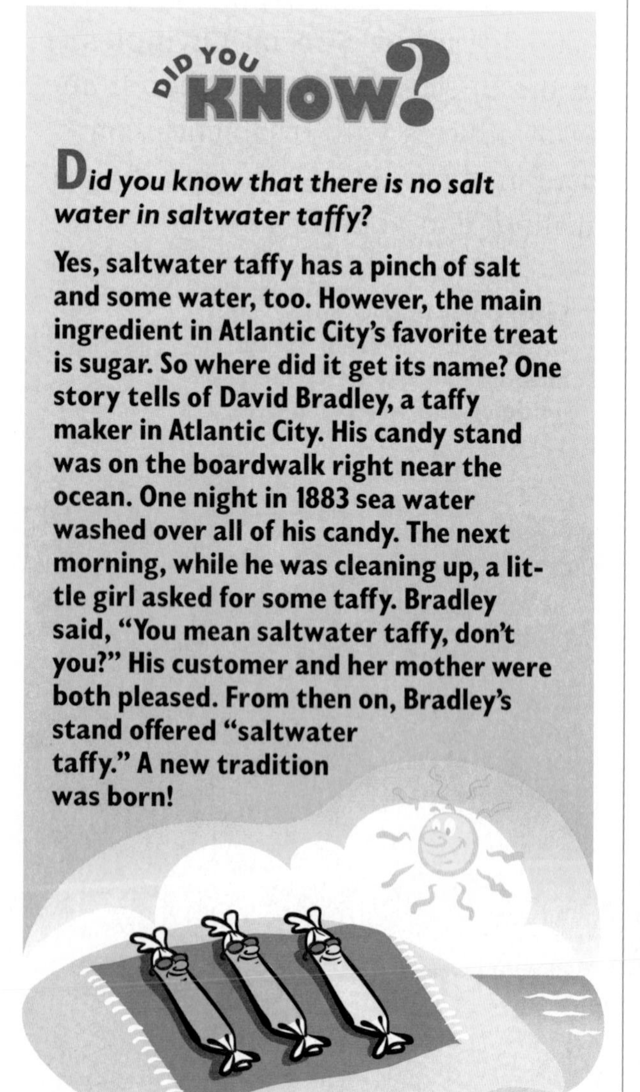

**DID YOU KNOW?**

***Did you know that there is no salt water in saltwater taffy?***

**Yes, saltwater taffy has a pinch of salt and some water, too. However, the main ingredient in Atlantic City's favorite treat is sugar. So where did it get its name? One story tells of David Bradley, a taffy maker in Atlantic City. His candy stand was on the boardwalk right near the ocean. One night in 1883 sea water washed over all of his candy. The next morning, while he was cleaning up, a little girl asked for some taffy. Bradley said, "You mean saltwater taffy, don't you?" His customer and her mother were both pleased. From then on, Bradley's stand offered "saltwater taffy." A new tradition was born!**

**Our state offers lots of ways to enjoy the outdoors. You can cruise the boardwalk in Spring Lake (above), enjoy the waterslides in Wildwood (middle), ski at Vernon (above, far right), or just play in the sand at any of New Jersey's many beaches (right).**

Sara Matthews of New Egypt loves being outdoors. "The only limit to the fun you can have in New Jersey is your imagination," she says. "If you can think of a way to enjoy the outdoors, you can find it in New Jersey!"

## WHY IT MATTERS

From sports to state parks to historic sites, New Jersey offers many kinds of recreation. Thanks to our state's many natural resources and rich history, you can always find something fun to do in the "Garden State."

See p. T100 for Answers to Think About It.

## Reviewing Facts and Ideas

### MAIN IDEAS

- New Jersey provides many opportunities to watch and play sports.
- New Jerseyans enjoy an exciting variety of outdoor recreation.

### THINK ABOUT IT

1. What sports did the Lenape play?
2. What are professional sports?
3. **FOCUS** List some of the things New Jerseyans can do for recreation.
4. **THINKING SKILL** *Classify* into three groups some different types of recreation available in New Jersey.
5. **GEOGRAPHY** What landforms and bodies of water make New Jersey a good place for recreation?

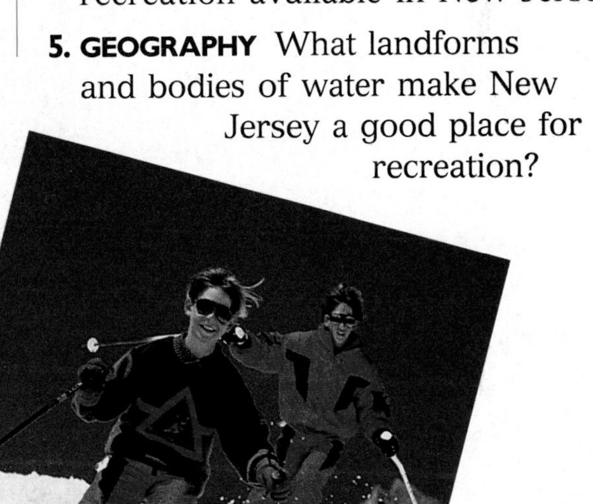

See p. T101 for Legacy Teaching Strategies.

Legacy

LINKING PAST AND PRESENT

# The Jersey Shore

The Jersey Shore has something for everyone! Its bays, marshes, and inlets are home to birds, fish, and other wildlife. Its sandy beaches and cool summer breezes offer fun and relaxation for countless visitors.

Many years ago, the Lenape used to come to the shore to catch fish and find relief from the summer heat. Today, visitors come to swim, shop, stroll the beaches and boardwalks, listen to music, and of course to eat saltwater taffy. The Jersey Shore continues to be a legacy that generations of people can enjoy!

**In the late 1800s, railroads began to bring tourists, like President Ulysses S. Grant (above, center), to the shore. Modern tourists can still stay in hotels from that time (right).**

Surfing (above) is a sport enjoyed by many people along the Jersey Shore. Seaside amusement parks, such as Ocean Pier (right), were a favorite place for visitors in the middle 1900s.

Lifeguards (above) protect swimmers at many Jersey Shore beaches. Saltwater taffy (right) is a favorite treat for boardwalk visitors.

LESSON 3

See p. T102 for Lesson Teaching Strategies.

# Education and Arts

## Focus Activity

**READ TO LEARN**

***In what ways is New Jersey a leader in education and the arts?***

**VOCABULARY**

- public

**PEOPLE**

- Walt Whitman
- Amiri Baraka
- William Carlos Williams
- Robert Smithson
- Sarah Vaughan
- Frank Sinatra
- Bruce Springsteen
- Lauryn Hill

**PLACES**

- East Orange
- Camden
- Rutherford
- Freehold
- South Orange

### Read Aloud

*Speaking to students at the Lenna Conrow School in Long Branch, Governor Christine Todd Whitman explained the value of education: "When I was in school, I liked to go to the library to read, and to borrow books. The library took me so many places. I still love to go to the library. I try to get there as often as I can. The library offers so much more now than when I was your age."*

### THE BIG PICTURE

Education in New Jersey has come a long way since the one-room schoolhouses of 300 years ago. Back then, most students went on to become farmers, homemakers, or craftworkers.

Today, more than one million students go to **public** schools in our state. Public means "for all the people of a state or country." Schools and teachers are busy preparing students for life and work in a fast-changing world. What would students from the 1700s think of today's schools, with computers, science labs, and art studios?

## AN EDUCATION LEADER

Education is important in our state. Each year, New Jersey's government spends a lot of money to make sure that students get an education. This effort has helped make our state a leader in fields like high technology, telecommunications, and research.

New Jersey is home to 28 public community colleges and universities. It also has more than 30 private colleges. One of the best-known of these schools is Princeton University. It is the fourth oldest university in the United States. Together, these schools—and the one you are in, too—help prepare today's students to be tomorrow's leaders.

### Making Dreams Come True

In 1986 Mark Barfield graduated from the Upward Bound Program at Mercer County Community College in Trenton. Upward Bound helps students from low income families prepare for college. Mark finished college at Upsala College in East Orange. Later he earned a Masters degree at Montclair State University.

Today Mark directs a similar program at a college in Boston. "I got my academic birth from the Upward Bound Program," says Mark. "Without it, I don't know where I would be or what I would be doing now. New Jersey offered me a lot of opportunity, and I was lucky to have some great teachers."

**Rutgers University in New Brunswick (below) is one of more than 50 colleges and universities in New Jersey that prepare graduates (right) for the future.**

## THE ARTS IN NEW JERSEY

New Jersey is also a leader in the arts. Over the years, it has been home to many great writers, singers, and artists. The poet Walt Whitman for example, lived in Camden in the 1800s. Many of his poems celebrate America and everyday life.

Amiri Baraka is a poet, playwright, and novelist from Newark. His writing focuses on the struggles and successes of African Americans. Another well-known New Jersey poet was William Carlos Williams. He lived in Rutherford. His most famous poem is about the city of Paterson. His poems use simple language to create beautiful images. What does the poem below make you think of?

**MANY VOICES**
**LITERATURE**

**"This Is Just To Say" by William Carlos Williams, written in 1934.**

*I have eaten*
*the plums*
*that were in*
*the icebox*
*and which*
*you were probably saving*
*for breakfast*

*Forgive me*
*they were delicious*
*so sweet*
*and so cold*

### Visual Arts

Many visual artists have also found inspiration in our state. The sculptor Robert Smithson grew up in Passaic. He created art about the Passaic River and other industrial areas. Many of his sculptures, called "earthworks," were created outdoors from natural resources like sand and stone.

### Sounds of New Jersey

New Jersey has produced some of America's most popular singers. Sarah Vaughan of Newark and Frank Sinatra of Hoboken were important jazz and popular music artists in the middle and later 1900s. Bruce Springsteen, a rock music songwriter and performer, grew up in Freehold. His songs often describe the hopes and fears of working people in New Jersey. Lauryn Hill, from South Orange, won five Grammy Awards for her first solo hip-hop album in 1999. Hill sings about her experiences growing up as a black woman in New Jersey.

### The Performing Arts

New Jersey is home to many important performing arts groups. The Crossroads Theater Company in New Brunswick is one of the best. It presents plays about African American life. In 1999 it won an award for being an outstanding theater group in the country. Since 1997 performers have had a new and exciting place to perform in our state. The New Jersey Performing Arts Center in Newark was

See p. T102 for Answers to Think About It.

Frank Sinatra (bottom) and Lauryn Hill (middle) were both born in New Jersey. The New Jersey Performing Arts Center (top) in Newark hosts performing artists from around the world.

designed to reflect the diversity of our state. "It is a celebration of people, community, and urban life," says Barton Myers, the center's designer.

The Performing Arts Center also provides opportunities for New Jersey's next generation of performers. Each year there are programs that give more than 2,500 students dance and theater training.

## WHY IT MATTERS

New Jersey's education system helps keeps our economy strong. Educated workers have more opportunities to succeed in the workplace. The arts make New Jersey an interesting place to live.

## Reviewing Facts and Ideas

### MAIN IDEAS

- Our state's many schools help to keep the state growing.
- Many important writers, artists, and performers are from our state.

### THINK ABOUT IT

1. Why is education more important than ever in New Jersey?
2. Name two famous artists from New Jersey.
3. **FOCUS** Why are education and the arts important in New Jersey?
4. **THINKING SKILL** What *effect* has New Jersey's system of public education had on our state's economy?
5. **WRITE** Write a poem describing your favorite kind of art.

See p. 103 for Answers to Chapter 12 Review.

# CHAPTER 12 REVIEW

## THINKING ABOUT VOCABULARY

Number a sheet of paper from 1 to 10. Next to each number write **C** if the underlined term is used correctly. If it is not, write the term that would correctly complete the sentence.

1. The rich mixture of people in our state is called ethnic group.
2. An edge city is a large city and the communities close to it.
3. Public schools are for all the people of the state.
4. A megalopolis is a giant city.
5. Population density is the measure of how many people live in a certain place, usually a square mile.
6. Professional athletes play a sport as a job, not just for fun.
7. A festival is one way people in our state keep their ethnic customs and share them with others.
8. A group of people whose ancestors are from the same country or area is known as a diversity.
9. Activities that we do for fun are called recreation.
10. The Special Olympics provide sports opportunities for people with disabilities.

## THINKING ABOUT FACTS

1. Why are festivals important?
2. Name two reasons immigrants come to New Jersey.
3. What are some of the major ethnic groups living in our state?
4. List three kinds of recreation that are popular in New Jersey today.
5. What is population density?
6. Who was William Carlos Williams? What is he known for?
7. List three examples of edge cities in New Jersey.
8. How does New Jersey's government help education in our state?
9. What is the name for the chain of cities and suburbs that stretches from above Boston to below Washington, D.C.?
10. Who is Carl Lewis? What is he known for?

## THINK AND WRITE

### WRITING A PARAGRAPH

Write a paragraph about the ways in which diversity helps to strengthen New Jersey.

### WRITING AN ARTICLE

Suppose you are a sports reporter for the local newspaper. Write an article about one of the sports mentioned in Lesson 2. Include a headline, byline, and dateline.

### WRITING A DESCRIPTION

Write a description of a recreation area in New Jersey. Include details about what you might see or do there.

## APPLYING STUDY SKILLS

### WRITING NOTES AND OUTLINES

1. What is an outline? How can writing outlines help you organize information?
2. What are the steps in writing an outline?
3. Read the section in Lesson 1 titled "Where New Jerseyans Live Today" on page 292. Take notes as you read, then write an outline of the section.
4. Read the section in Lesson 2 titled "Outdoor Fun in New Jersey" on page 298. Then write an outline of the section.
5. How can taking notes and writing an outline help you to write a research report about recreation in New Jersey?

## Summing Up the Chapter

Use the following main idea chart to organize information from the chapter. Copy the chart on a sheet of paper. Then fill in the blank spaces on the chart. When you have filled in the chart, use it to write a paragraph answering the question, "How have different cultures, recreation, and the arts contributed to making New Jersey a special state?"

| PEOPLE OF NEW JERSEY | SPORTS AND RECREATION | EDUCATION AND THE ARTS |
|---|---|---|
| diversity | recreation | public education |
| ethnic group | professional sports | writing |
| festivals | Special Olympics | visual arts |
| megalopolis | state parks | music |
| population density | historic sites | performing arts |

See p. T104 for Answers to Unit 5 Review.

# UNIT 5 REVIEW

## THINKING ABOUT VOCABULARY

Number a sheet of paper from 1 to 10. Beside each number write **C** if the underlined word is used correctly. If it is not, write the word that would correctly complete the sentence.

1. Free enterprise is the economic system that allows people to own and run their own businesses.
2. A person who buys goods or uses services is called an investor.
3. A written idea for a law is called a budget.
4. Population density is the measure of how many people live in a certain place, usually a square mile.
5. A group of people whose ancestors are from the same country or area form a diversity.
6. Checks and balances is the system in which each branch of government keeps watch over the other two branches.
7. Activities that we do for fun are called recreation.
8. The on-line world of computer networks is called software.
9. Tourism is the business of providing services for people who travel for fun or to learn about new places.
10. A program, or set of instructions, that tells a computer what to do is called cyberspace.

## THINK AND WRITE

### WRITING AN EXPLANATION
Write a paragraph that explains the different kinds of reference books you might use at your school library.

### WRITING A LETTER
Suppose you are vacationing somewhere in New Jersey. Write a letter to a friend describing some of the different activities you did for recreation.

### WRITING A REPORT
Choose one of the three branches of state government described in Chapter 11. Research one of the branches, then write a report and share it with the class.

## BUILDING SKILLS

1. **Reading newspapers** Why is it important to read newspapers?
2. **Reading newspapers** If you wanted to learn the editor's opinion about an issue, what kind of article would you read?
3. **Notes and outlines** How can writing outlines help you organize information?
4. **Reference sources** How are reference books different from other books?
5. **Reference sources** Which reference book would you use to find the meaning of the word *judicial*?

## YESTERDAY, TODAY & TOMORROW

**Through the years, new machinery has been invented to help farmers with their work. Today, fewer people and less land are needed to produce the food we need. What new machines or technologies do you think will improve farming in the future?**

## READING ON YOUR OWN

These are some of the books you might find at the library to help you learn more.

*GHOSTS OF THE WHITE HOUSE*
**by Cheryl Harness**
Go on a personal tour of the White House to learn the history of the presidents.

*CLASS PRESIDENT*
**by Johanna Hurwitz**
Julio must decide to keep a friendship or become a candidate for class president.

*MARVIN REDPOST, CLASS PRESIDENT*
**by Louis Sachar**
What if the President of the United States came to your school?

## UNIT 5 REVIEW PROJECT

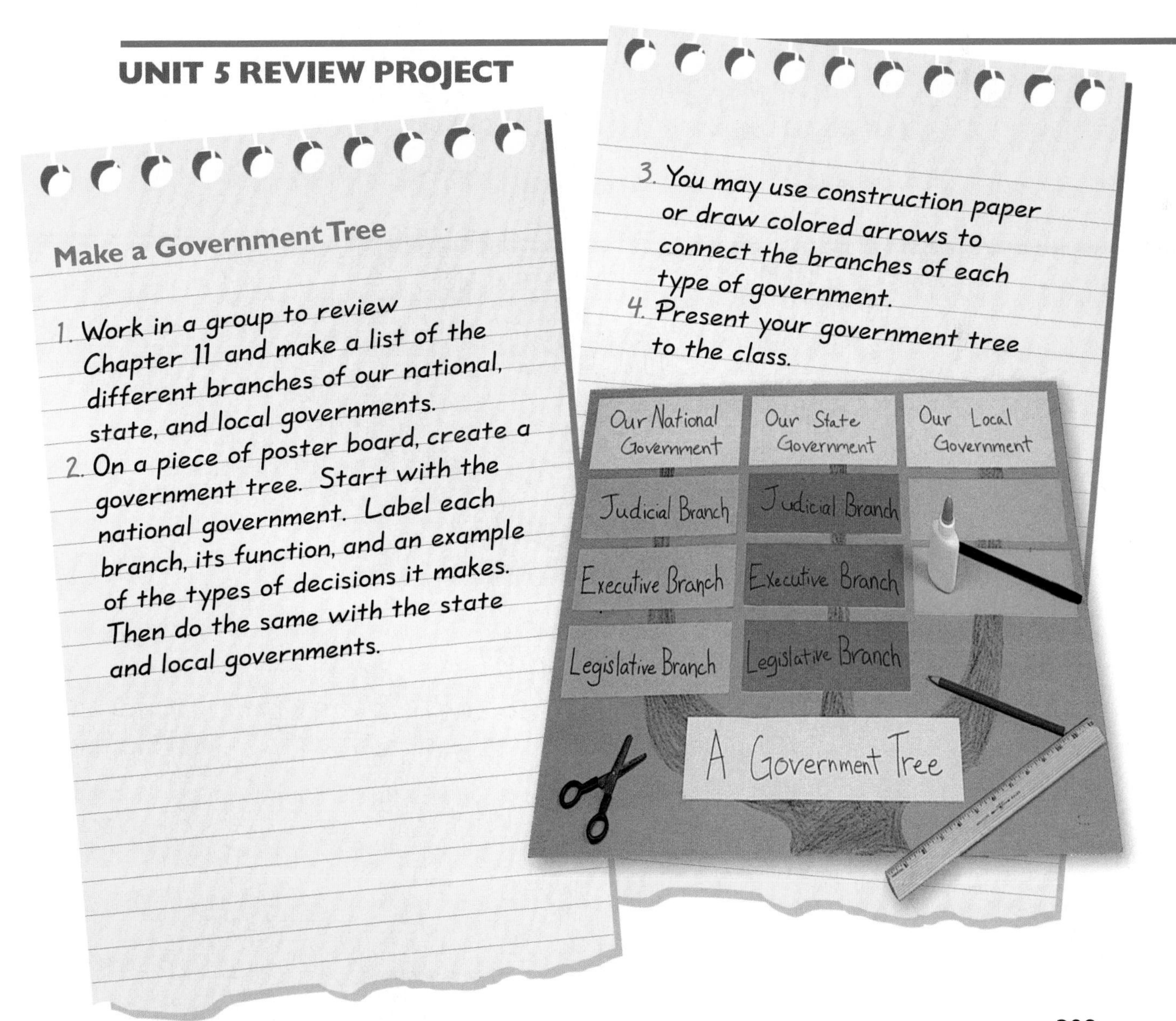

# REFERENCE SECTION

The Reference Section has many parts, each with a different type of information. Use this section to look up people, places, and events as you study.



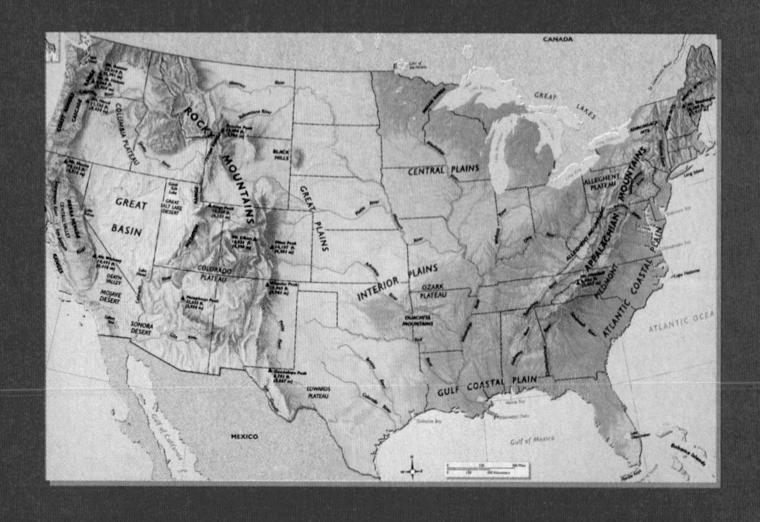

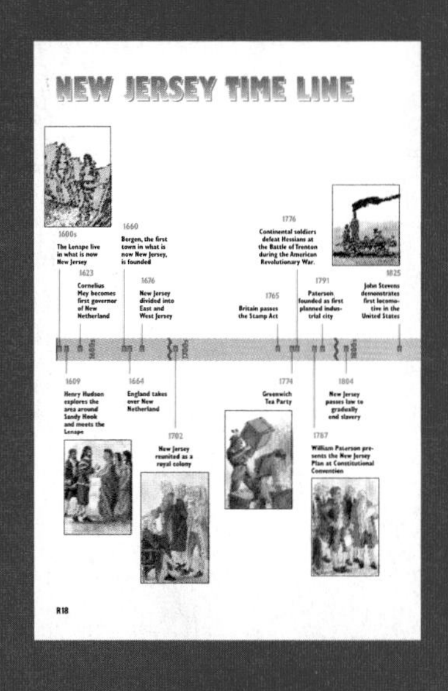

NEW JERSEY TIME LINE


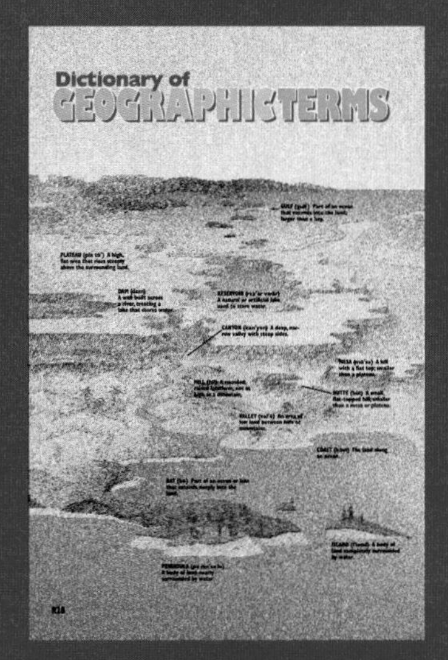

Dictionary of
GEOGRAPHIC TERMS

ARCTIC OCEAN
GREENLAND (DENMARK)
Arctic Circle
ALASKA (U.S.)
CANADA
NORTH AMERICA
UNITED STATES
BERMUDA (U.K.)
ATLANTIC OCEAN
MIDWAY ISLANDS (U.S.)
Tropic of Cancer
HAWAII (U.S.)
MEXICO
See inset below
Caribbean Sea
PACIFIC OCEAN
VENEZUELA
GUYANA
SURINAME
FRENCH GUIANA (FRANCE)
COLOMBIA
Equator
GALÁPAGOS ISLANDS (ECUADOR)
ECUADOR
SOUTH AMERICA
PERU
BRAZIL
SAMOA
AMERICAN SAMOA (U.S.)
FRENCH POLYNESIA (FRANCE)
TONGA
BOLIVIA
Tropic of Capricorn
PARAGUAY
URUGUAY
CHILE
ARGENTINA
FALKLAND ISLANDS (U.K.)
SOUTH GEORGIA (U.K.)
Antarctic Circle
ANTARCTICA
Central America and West Indies
Gulf of Mexico
FLORIDA (U.S.)
THE BAHAMAS
TURKS AND CAICOS IS. (U.K.)
ATLANTIC OCEAN
CUBA
CAYMAN ISLANDS (U.K.)
JAMAICA
HAITI
DOMINICAN REPUBLIC
VIRGIN ISLANDS (U.K.)
ST. KITTS AND NEVIS
ANTIGUA AND BARBUDA
PUERTO RICO (U.S.)
VIRGIN ISLANDS (U.S.)
GUADELOUPE (FRANCE)
DOMINICA
MARTINIQUE (FRANCE)
ST. LUCIA
ST. VINCENT AND THE GRENADINES
BARBADOS
GRENADA
TRINIDAD AND TOBAGO
MEXICO
BELIZE
GUATEMALA
HONDURAS
EL SALVADOR
NICARAGUA
Caribbean Sea
PACIFIC OCEAN
ARUBA (NETHERLANDS)
NETHERLANDS ANTILLES (NETHERLANDS)
COSTA RICA
PANAMA
COLOMBIA
VENEZUELA
GUYANA
0 250 500 Miles
0 250 500 Kilometers

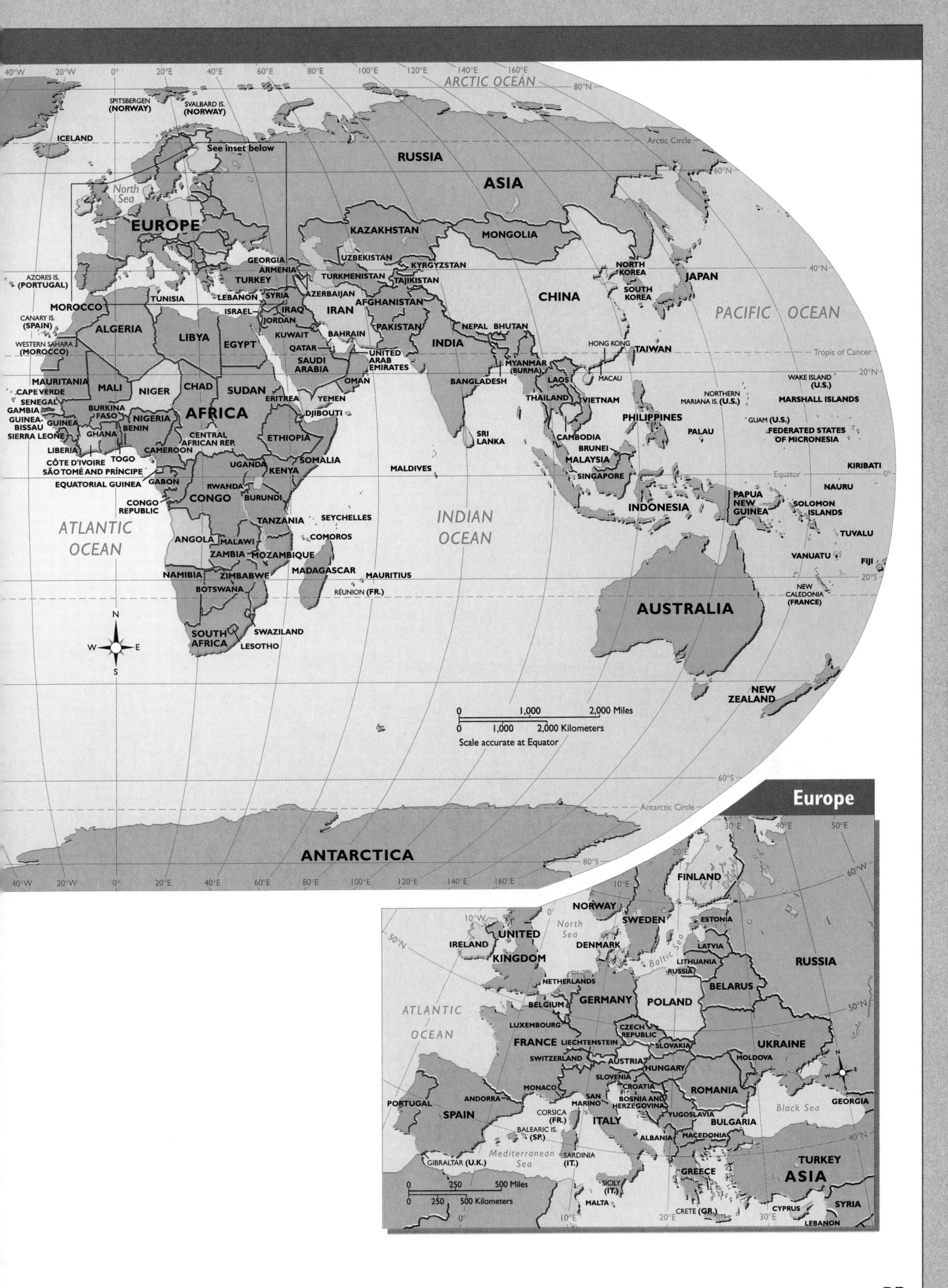
ARCTIC OCEAN
SPITSBERGEN (NORWAY)
SVALBARD IS. (NORWAY)
ICELAND
See inset below
RUSSIA
ASIA
North Sea
EUROPE
KAZAKHSTAN
MONGOLIA
GEORGIA
ARMENIA
TURKEY
UZBEKISTAN
KYRGYZSTAN
TURKMENISTAN
TAJIKISTAN
AZERBAIJAN
NORTH KOREA
SOUTH KOREA
JAPAN
AZORES IS. (PORTUGAL)
CANARY IS. (SPAIN)
MOROCCO
TUNISIA
LEBANON
SYRIA
ISRAEL
IRAQ
JORDAN
IRAN
AFGHANISTAN
CHINA
PACIFIC OCEAN
ALGERIA
LIBYA
EGYPT
KUWAIT
BAHRAIN
QATAR
PAKISTAN
NEPAL
BHUTAN
INDIA
HONG KONG
TAIWAN
WESTERN SAHARA (MOROCCO)
SAUDI ARABIA
UNITED ARAB EMIRATES
OMAN
MYANMAR (BURMA)
BANGLADESH
LAOS
MACAU
WAKE ISLAND (U.S.)
MAURITANIA
MALI
NIGER
CHAD
SUDAN
ERITREA
YEMEN
THAILAND
VIETNAM
NORTHERN MARIANA IS. (U.S.)
MARSHALL ISLANDS
CAPE VERDE
SENEGAL
GAMBIA
GUINEA-BISSAU
GUINEA
SIERRA LEONE
BURKINA FASO
NIGERIA
BENIN
AFRICA
DJIBOUTI
PHILIPPINES
GUAM (U.S.)
FEDERATED STATES OF MICRONESIA
PALAU
GHANA
CENTRAL AFRICAN REP.
ETHIOPIA
SRI LANKA
CAMBODIA
LIBERIA
TOGO
CAMEROON
BRUNEI
MALAYSIA
CÔTE D'IVOIRE
SÃO TOMÉ AND PRÍNCIPE
UGANDA
KENYA
SOMALIA
MALDIVES
KIRIBATI
EQUATORIAL GUINEA
GABON
RWANDA
SINGAPORE
Equator
CONGO
BURUNDI
NAURU
CONGO REPUBLIC
PAPUA NEW GUINEA
SOLOMON ISLANDS
INDONESIA
TANZANIA
SEYCHELLES
INDIAN OCEAN
ATLANTIC OCEAN
COMOROS
TUVALU
ANGOLA
MALAWI
ZAMBIA
MOZAMBIQUE
VANUATU
FIJI
NAMIBIA
ZIMBABWE
MADAGASCAR
MAURITIUS
RÉUNION (FR.)
BOTSWANA
NEW CALEDONIA (FRANCE)
AUSTRALIA
SWAZILAND
SOUTH AFRICA
LESOTHO
NEW ZEALAND
0 1,000 2,000 Miles
0 1,000 2,000 Kilometers
Scale accurate at Equator
Arctic Circle
Tropic of Cancer
Antarctic Circle
ANTARCTICA
Europe
FINLAND
NORWAY
SWEDEN
ESTONIA
North Sea
Baltic Sea
IRELAND
UNITED KINGDOM
DENMARK
LATVIA
LITHUANIA
RUSSIA
NETHERLANDS
BELARUS
ATLANTIC OCEAN
BELGIUM
GERMANY
POLAND
LUXEMBOURG
CZECH REPUBLIC
FRANCE
LIECHTENSTEIN
SLOVAKIA
UKRAINE
SWITZERLAND
AUSTRIA
MOLDOVA
HUNGARY
SLOVENIA
CROATIA
MONACO
ROMANIA
SAN MARINO
BOSNIA AND HERZEGOVINA
ANDORRA
PORTUGAL
SPAIN
Black Sea
GEORGIA
CORSICA (FR.)
ITALY
YUGOSLAVIA
BULGARIA
BALEARIC IS. (SP.)
ALBANIA
MACEDONIA
Mediterranean Sea
SARDINIA (IT.)
GIBRALTAR (U.K.)
TURKEY
ASIA
GREECE
0 250 500 Miles
0 250 500 Kilometers
SICILY (IT.)
MALTA
CRETE (GR.)
CYPRUS
SYRIA
LEBANON

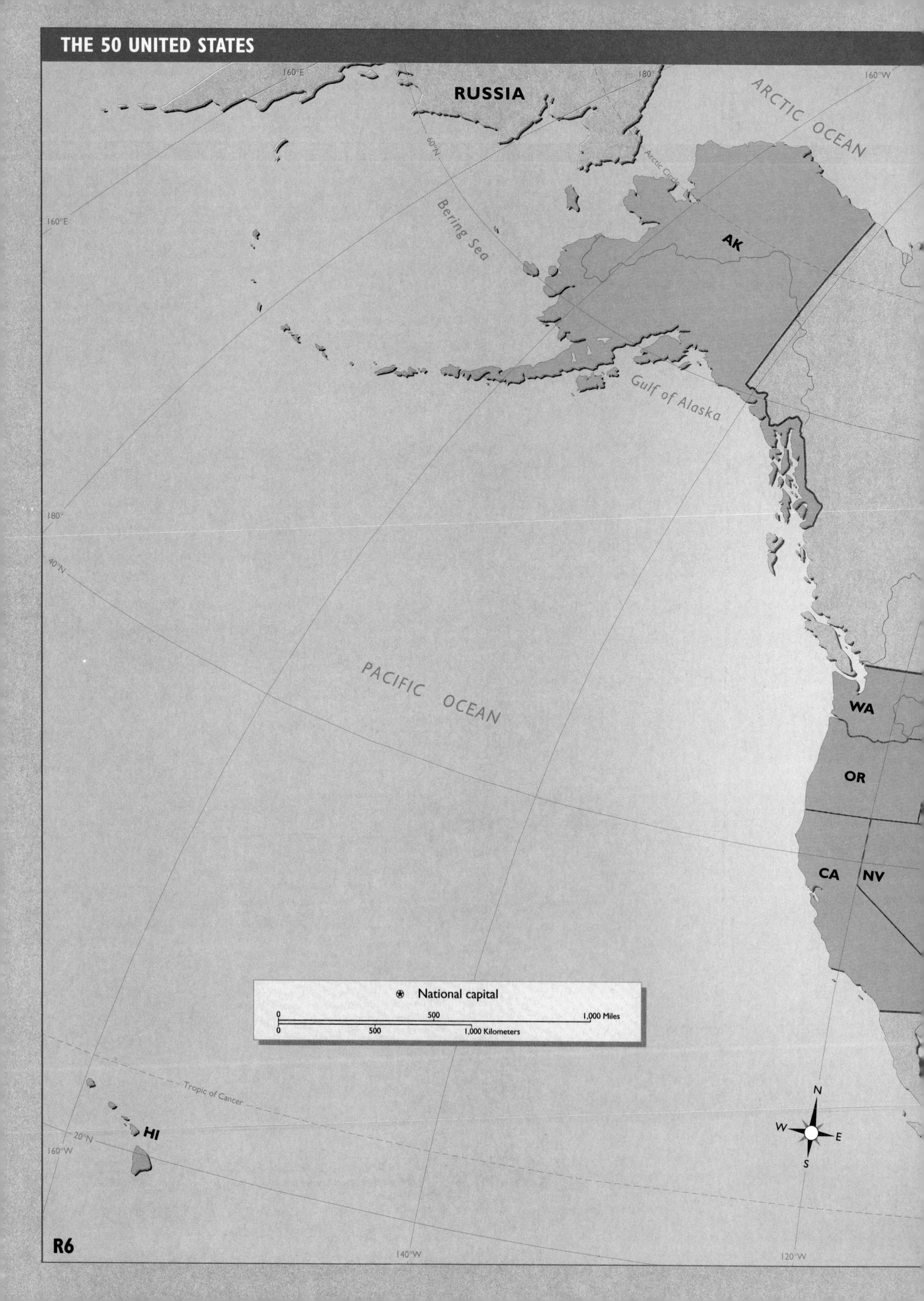
RUSSIA
ARCTIC OCEAN
Arctic Circle
Bering Sea
AK
Gulf of Alaska
PACIFIC OCEAN
WA
OR
CA
NV
HI
Tropic of Cancer
National capital
0
500
1,000 Miles
0
500
1,000 Kilometers
N
S
E
W
160°E
180°
160°W
60°N
40°N
20°N
140°W
120°W

140°W
80°N
120°W
100°W
80°W
60°W
40°W
20°W
Greenland
(DENMARK)
40°W
60°N
Hudson Bay
CANADA
Great Lakes
MT
ND
MN
MI
ME
VT
NH
ID
SD
WI
MI
NY
MA
WY
CT
RI
IA
NE
PA
NJ
IL
OH
Washington, D.C.
UT
CO
KS
IN
WV
MD
DE
MO
KY
VA
ATLANTIC OCEAN
TN
NC
OK
AR
AZ
NM
SC
MS
AL
GA
LA
TX
FL
Gulf of Mexico
60°W
40°N
MEXICO
80°W
CUBA
100°W

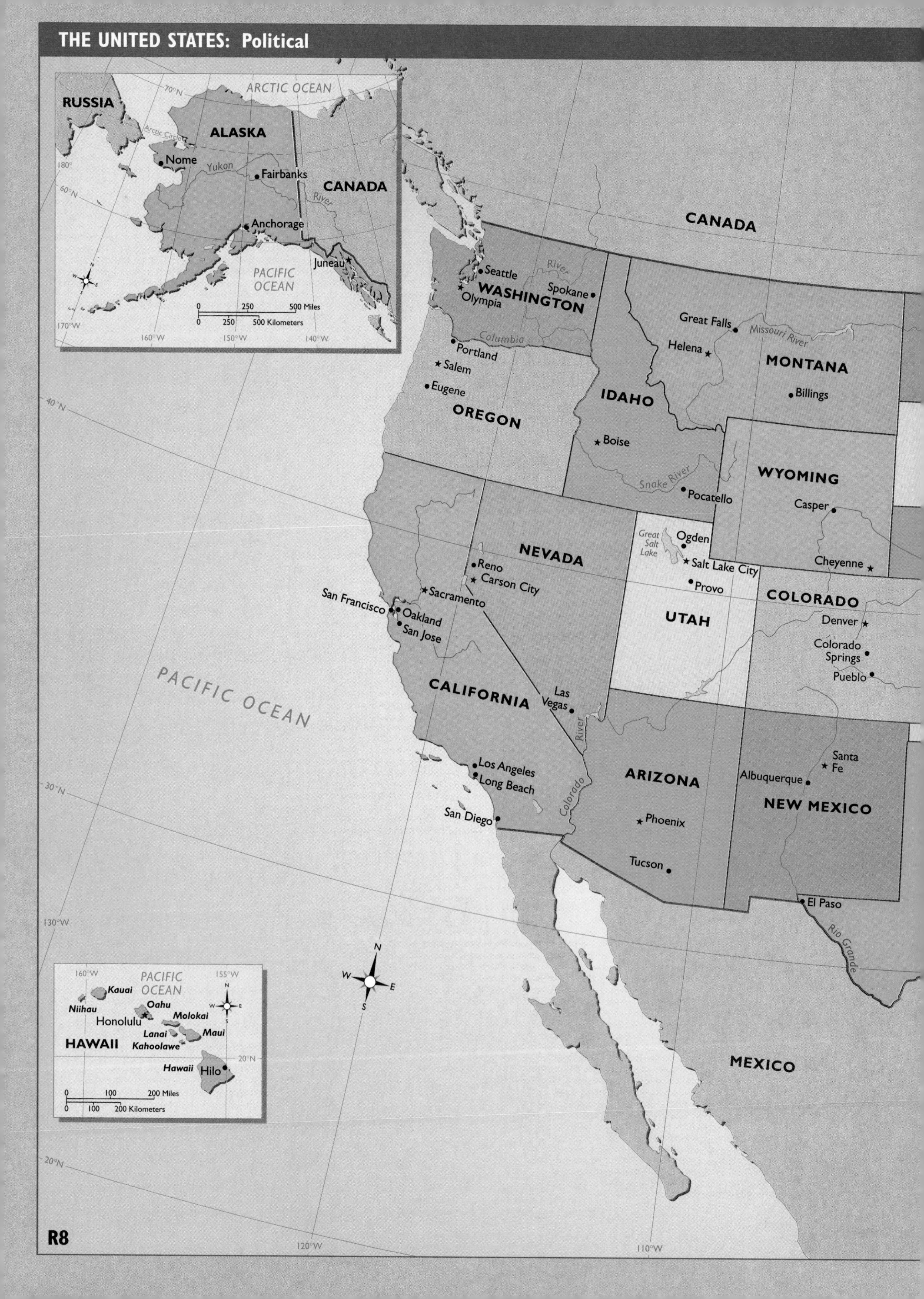
RUSSIA
ARCTIC OCEAN
70°N
Arctic Circle
ALASKA
Nome
Yukon
River
Fairbanks
CANADA
180°
60°N
Anchorage
Juneau
PACIFIC OCEAN
0 250 500 Miles
0 250 500 Kilometers
170°W
160°W
150°W
140°W
CANADA
WASHINGTON
Seattle
Olympia
Spokane
River
Columbia
Portland
Salem
Eugene
OREGON
IDAHO
Boise
Snake River
Pocatello
MONTANA
Great Falls
Missouri River
Helena
Billings
WYOMING
Casper
Cheyenne
NEVADA
Reno
Carson City
Las Vegas
Great Salt Lake
Ogden
Salt Lake City
Provo
UTAH
COLORADO
Denver
Colorado Springs
Pueblo
CALIFORNIA
Sacramento
San Francisco
Oakland
San Jose
Los Angeles
Long Beach
San Diego
Colorado
River
ARIZONA
Phoenix
Tucson
NEW MEXICO
Santa Fe
Albuquerque
El Paso
Rio Grande
MEXICO
PACIFIC OCEAN
40°N
30°N
20°N
130°W
120°W
110°W
N
S
E
W
160°W
155°W
PACIFIC OCEAN
Kauai
Niihau
Oahu
Honolulu
Molokai
Maui
Lanai
Kahoolawe
HAWAII
20°N
Hawaii
Hilo
0 100 200 Miles
0 100 200 Kilometers

CANADA
NORTH DAKOTA
Grand Forks
Bismarck
Fargo
MINNESOTA
Duluth
Minneapolis
St. Paul
SOUTH DAKOTA
Pierre
Sioux Falls
WISCONSIN
Green Bay
Madison
Milwaukee
MICHIGAN
Grand Rapids
Lansing
Detroit
Lake Superior
Lake Michigan
Lake Huron
Lake Ontario
Lake Erie
NEW YORK
Buffalo
Albany
New York
MAINE
Augusta
Portland
VERMONT
Burlington
Montpelier
NEW HAMPSHIRE
Concord
MASSACHUSETTS
Boston
Providence
RHODE ISLAND
CONNECTICUT
Hartford
PENNSYLVANIA
Pittsburgh
Harrisburg
Philadelphia
Newark
Trenton
NEW JERSEY
Dover
DELAWARE
Baltimore
Annapolis
MARYLAND
Washington, D.C.
IOWA
Cedar Rapids
Davenport
Des Moines
NEBRASKA
Omaha
Lincoln
Missouri River
Platte River
ILLINOIS
Rockford
Chicago
Peoria
Springfield
INDIANA
Gary
Fort Wayne
Indianapolis
Evansville
OHIO
Toledo
Cleveland
Columbus
Cincinnati
Wheeling
Ohio River
WEST VIRGINIA
Charleston
VIRGINIA
Richmond
Norfolk
KANSAS
Topeka
Wichita
Kansas City
Arkansas River
MISSOURI
Jefferson City
St. Louis
Mississippi River
KENTUCKY
Frankfort
Louisville
TENNESSEE
Nashville
Knoxville
Memphis
Tennessee River
NORTH CAROLINA
Raleigh
Charlotte
SOUTH CAROLINA
Columbia
Charleston
ATLANTIC OCEAN
OKLAHOMA
Tulsa
Oklahoma City
ARKANSAS
Fort Smith
Little Rock
Red River
MISSISSIPPI
Jackson
Biloxi
ALABAMA
Birmingham
Montgomery
Mobile
GEORGIA
Atlanta
Columbus
Savannah
TEXAS
Fort Worth
Dallas
Austin
Houston
San Antonio
Laredo
Corpus Christi
LOUISIANA
Shreveport
Baton Rouge
New Orleans
FLORIDA
Tallahassee
Jacksonville
Tampa
Miami
Gulf of Mexico
THE BAHAMAS
CUBA
National capital
State capital
Other city
0
150
300 Miles
0
150
300 Kilometers
50°N
40°N
30°N
70°W
100°W
90°W
80°W
R9

# THE UNITED STATES: Physical

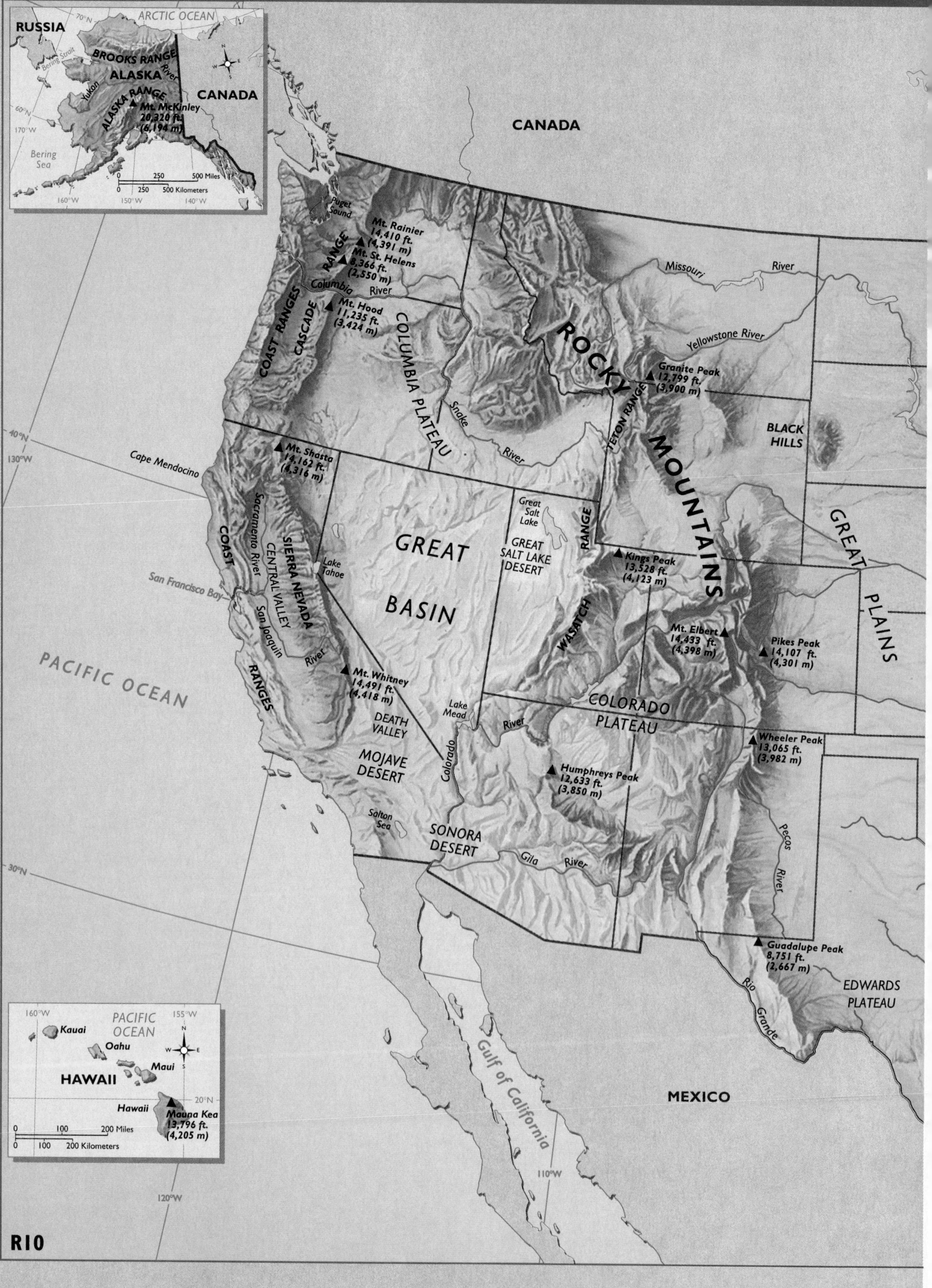

RUSSIA
ARCTIC OCEAN
70°N
Bering Strait
BROOKS RANGE
ALASKA
Yukon
River
ALASKA RANGE
Mt. McKinley
20,320 ft.
(6,194 m)
CANADA
60°N
170°W
Bering Sea
0 250 500 Miles
0 250 500 Kilometers
160°W
150°W
140°W

CANADA
Puget Sound
Mt. Rainier
14,410 ft.
(4,391 m)
Mt. St. Helens
8,366 ft.
(2,550 m)
CASCADE RANGE
Columbia River
Mt. Hood
11,235 ft.
(3,424 m)
COAST RANGES
COLUMBIA PLATEAU
Snake River
Missouri River
Yellowstone River
ROCKY MOUNTAINS
Granite Peak
12,799 ft.
(3,900 m)
TETON RANGE
BLACK HILLS
40°N
130°W
Cape Mendocino
Mt. Shasta
14,162 ft.
(4,316 m)
Sacramento River
COAST RANGES
SIERRA NEVADA
CENTRAL VALLEY
San Francisco Bay
San Joaquin River
Lake Tahoe
GREAT BASIN
Great Salt Lake
GREAT SALT LAKE DESERT
WASATCH RANGE
Kings Peak
13,528 ft.
(4,123 m)
GREAT PLAINS
Mt. Elbert
14,433 ft.
(4,398 m)
Pikes Peak
14,107 ft.
(4,301 m)
PACIFIC OCEAN
Mt. Whitney
14,491 ft.
(4,418 m)
DEATH VALLEY
Lake Mead
COLORADO PLATEAU
Colorado River
Wheeler Peak
13,065 ft.
(3,982 m)
MOJAVE DESERT
Humphreys Peak
12,633 ft.
(3,850 m)
Salton Sea
SONORA DESERT
Gila River
Pecos River
30°N
Guadalupe Peak
8,751 ft.
(2,667 m)
Rio Grande
EDWARDS PLATEAU
Gulf of California
MEXICO
110°W
120°W

160°W
155°W
PACIFIC OCEAN
Kauai
Oahu
Maui
HAWAII
Hawaii
20°N
Mauna Kea
13,796 ft.
(4,205 m)
0 100 200 Miles
0 100 200 Kilometers

CANADA
Lake of the Woods
Lake Superior
GREAT LAKES
Lake Huron
Lake Michigan
Lake Ontario
Lake Erie
St. Lawrence River
MESABI RANGE
WHITE MTS.
Mt. Washington 6,288 ft. (1,917 m)
GREEN MTS.
ADIRONDACK MTS.
Cape Cod
Hudson River
Long Island
CENTRAL PLAINS
Mississippi River
ALLEGHENY PLATEAU
MOUNTAINS
Susquehanna River
Potomac River
Delaware Bay
Platte River
Missouri River
Wabash River
Ohio River
ALLEGHENY MOUNTAINS
APPALACHIAN
Chesapeake Bay
PLAIN
Arkansas River
INTERIOR PLAINS
OZARK PLATEAU
Mt. Mitchell 6,684 ft. (2,037 m)
PIEDMONT
ATLANTIC COASTAL
Cape Hatteras
Tennessee River
OUACHITA MOUNTAINS
Savannah River
ATLANTIC OCEAN
Red River
Alabama River
Chattahoochee River
Brazos River
GULF COASTAL PLAIN
Colorado River
Mobile Bay
Mississippi Delta
Galveston Bay
Gulf of Mexico
Lake Okeechobee
Bahama Islands
Florida Keys
Straits of Florida
CUBA
50°N
40°N
30°N
70°W
80°W
90°W
N
S
E
W
0 150 300 Miles
0 150 300 Kilometers

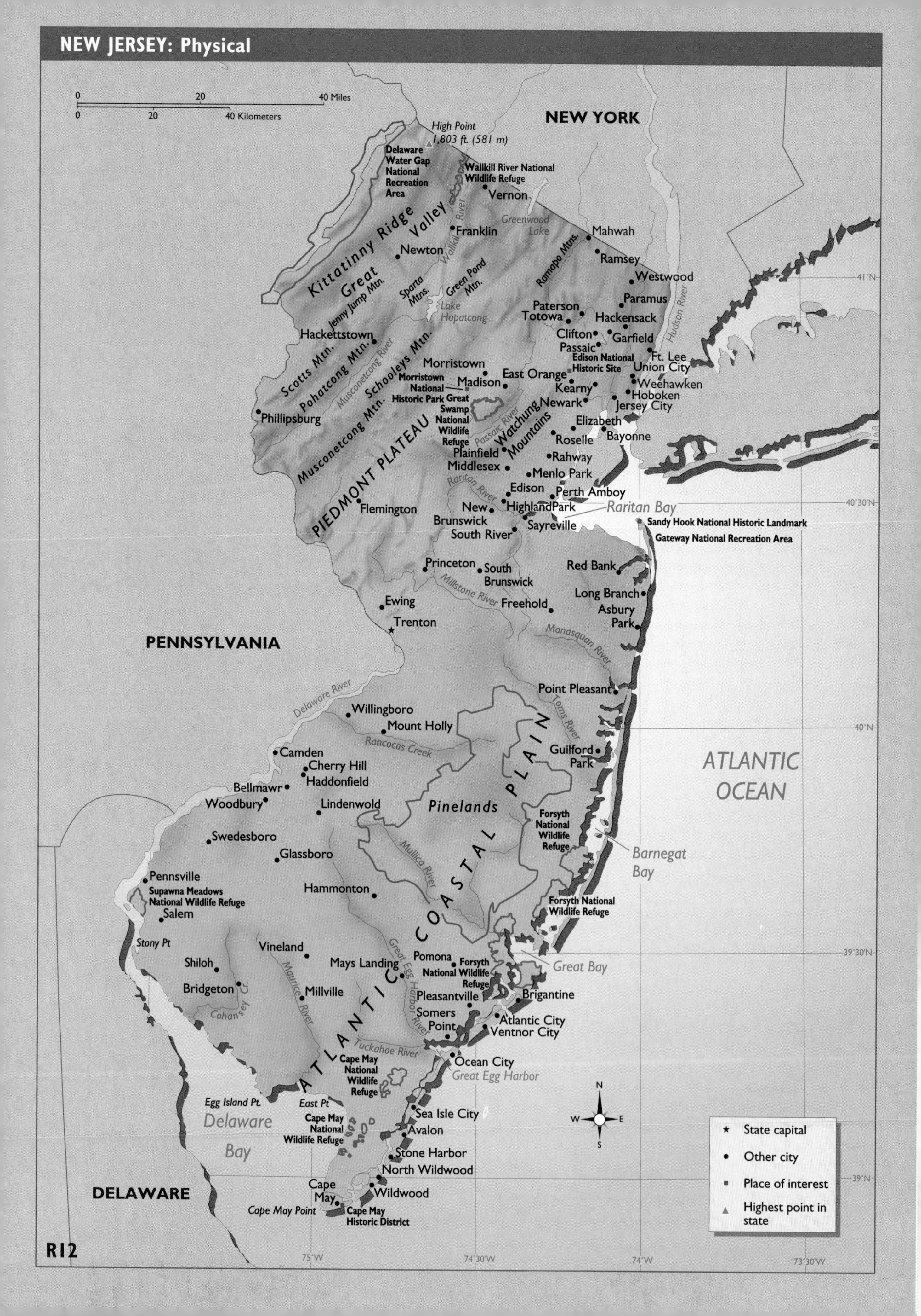

NEW JERSEY: Physical
0 20 40 Miles
0 20 40 Kilometers
NEW YORK
PENNSYLVANIA
DELAWARE
ATLANTIC OCEAN
High Point 1,803 ft. (581 m)
Delaware Water Gap National Recreation Area
Wallkill River National Wildlife Refuge
Vernon
Kittatinny Ridge
Great Valley
Franklin
Newton
Greenwood Lake
Mahwah
Ramsey
Westwood
Paramus
Ramapo Mtns.
Jenny Jump Mtn.
Sparta Mtns.
Green Pond Mtn.
Lake Hopatcong
Paterson
Totowa
Hackensack
Clifton
Garfield
Passaic
Hudson River
Hackettstown
Scotts Mtn.
Pohatcong Mtn.
Musconetcong River
Schooleys Mtn.
Morristown
Edison National Historic Site
Ft. Lee
Union City
Weehawken
Hoboken
Jersey City
Morristown National Historic Park
Madison
East Orange
Kearny
Newark
Great Swamp National Wildlife Refuge
Phillipsburg
Musconetcong Mtn.
Passaic River
Watchung Mountains
Elizabeth
Bayonne
Roselle
Rahway
PIEDMONT PLATEAU
Plainfield
Middlesex
Menlo Park
Raritan River
Edison
Perth Amboy
New Brunswick
Highland Park
Raritan Bay
Flemington
Sayreville
South River
Sandy Hook National Historic Landmark
Gateway National Recreation Area
Princeton
South Brunswick
Red Bank
Millstone River
Long Branch
Freehold
Asbury Park
Ewing
Trenton
Manasquan River
Point Pleasant
Delaware River
Willingboro
Mount Holly
Toms River
Rancocas Creek
Camden
Cherry Hill
Haddonfield
Guilford Park
Bellmawr
Woodbury
Lindenwold
Pinelands
Forsyth National Wildlife Refuge
Swedesboro
Glassboro
Mullica River
Barnegat Bay
Pennsville
Supawna Meadows National Wildlife Refuge
Salem
Hammonton
ATLANTIC COASTAL PLAIN
Forsyth National Wildlife Refuge
Stony Pt
Vineland
Mays Landing
Pomona
Forsyth National Wildlife Refuge
Great Bay
Shiloh
Great Egg Harbor River
Bridgeton
Cohansey Cr.
Millville
Maurice River
Pleasantville
Brigantine
Somers Point
Atlantic City
Ventnor City
Tuckahoe River
Cape May National Wildlife Refuge
Ocean City
Great Egg Harbor
Egg Island Pt.
East Pt
Delaware Bay
Cape May National Wildlife Refuge
Sea Isle City
Avalon
Stone Harbor
North Wildwood
Cape May
Wildwood
Cape May Point
Cape May Historic District
N
W
E
S
★ State capital
● Other city
■ Place of interest
▲ Highest point in state
41°N
40°30'N
40°N
39°30'N
39°N
75°W
74°30'W
74°W
73°30'W

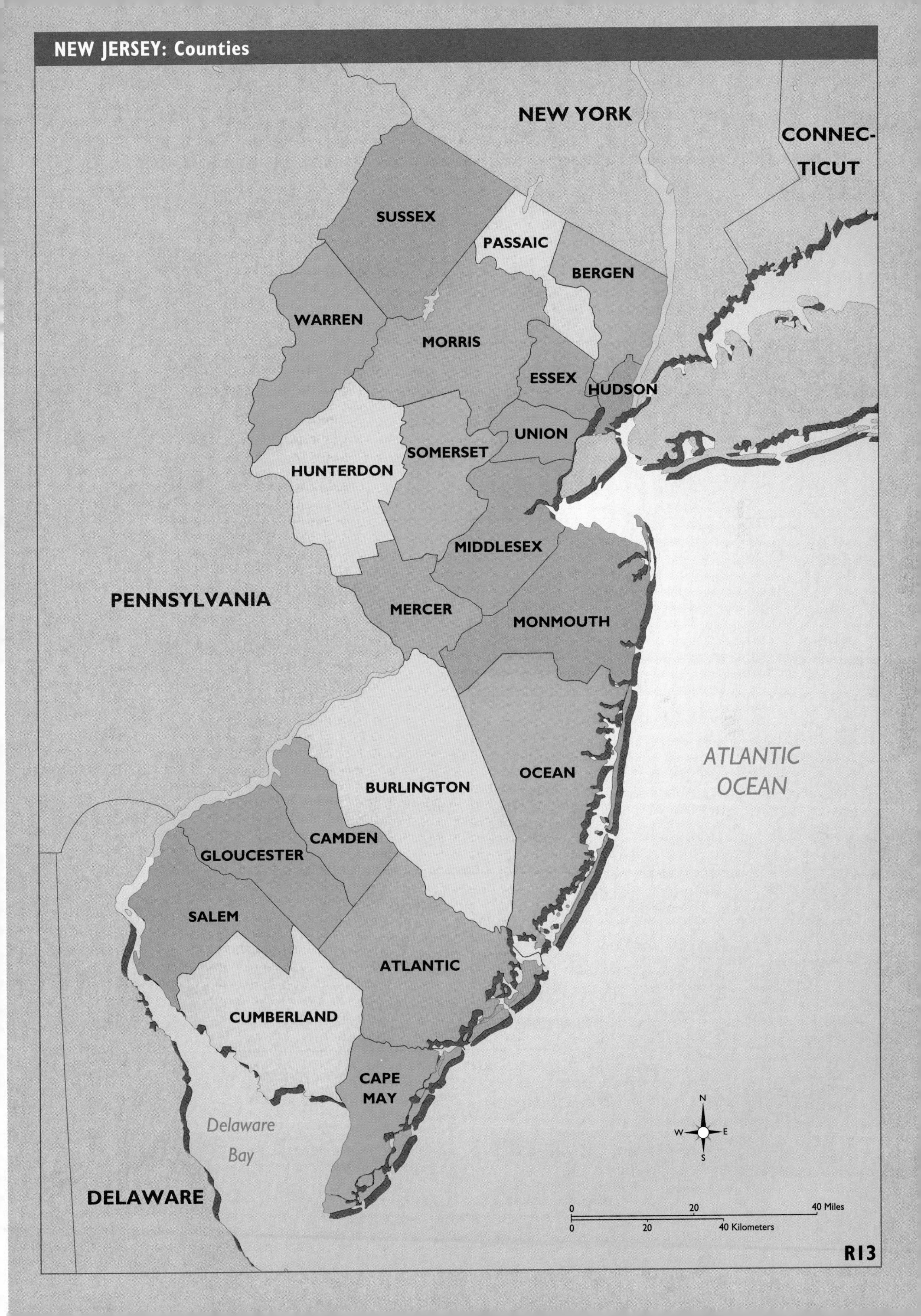
NEW JERSEY: Counties
NEW YORK
CONNEC-
TICUT
SUSSEX
PASSAIC
BERGEN
WARREN
MORRIS
ESSEX
HUDSON
UNION
SOMERSET
HUNTERDON
MIDDLESEX
PENNSYLVANIA
MERCER
MONMOUTH
ATLANTIC
OCEAN
OCEAN
BURLINGTON
CAMDEN
GLOUCESTER
SALEM
ATLANTIC
CUMBERLAND
CAPE
MAY
Delaware
Bay
DELAWARE
N
W
E
S
0
20
40 Miles
0
20
40 Kilometers
R13

# OUR FIFTY STATES

DATE OF STATEHOOD **1819**
NICKNAME **Heart of Dixie**
POPULATION **4,273,084**
AREA **52,423 sq mi; 135,776 sq km**
REGION **Southeast**

CONNECTICUT
Hartford

DATE OF STATEHOOD **1788**
NICKNAME **Constitution State**
POPULATION **3,274,238**
AREA **5,544 sq mi; 14,359 sq km**
REGION **Northeast**

DATE OF STATEHOOD **1959**
NICKNAME **The Last Frontier**
POPULATION **607,007**
AREA **656,424 sq mi; 1,700,138 sq km**
REGION **West**

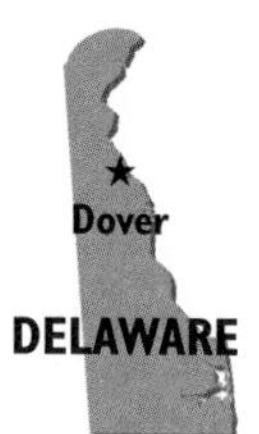


DATE OF STATEHOOD **1787**
NICKNAME **First State**
POPULATION **724,842**
AREA **2,489 sq mi; 6,447 sq km**
REGION **Northeast**

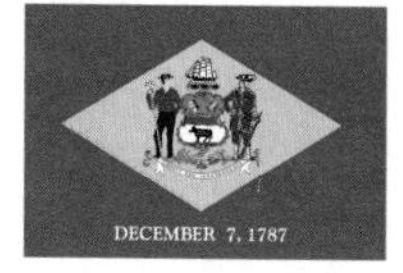


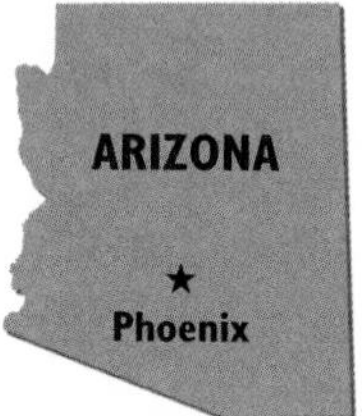


DATE OF STATEHOOD **1912**
NICKNAME **Grand Canyon State**
POPULATION **4,428,068**
AREA **114,006 sq mi; 295,276 sq km**
REGION **Southwest**

DATE OF STATEHOOD **1845**
NICKNAME **Sunshine State**
POPULATION **14,399,985**
AREA **65,758 sq mi; 170,313 sq km**
REGION **Southeast**

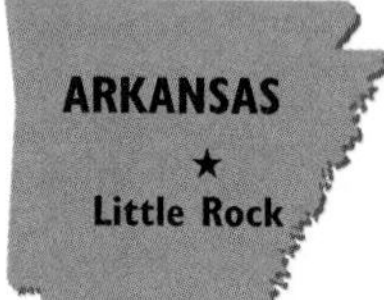


DATE OF STATEHOOD **1836**
NICKNAME **Land of Opportunity**
POPULATION **2,509,793**
AREA **53,182 sq mi; 137,741 sq km**
REGION **Southeast**

DATE OF STATEHOOD **1788**
NICKNAME **Peach State**
POPULATION **7,353,225**
AREA **59,441 sq mi; 153,952 sq km**
REGION **Southeast**

DATE OF STATEHOOD **1850**
NICKNAME **Golden State**
POPULATION **31,878,234**
AREA **163,707 sq mi; 424,001 sq km**
REGION **West**

HAWAII
Honolulu

DATE OF STATEHOOD **1959**
NICKNAME **The Aloha State**
POPULATION **1,183,723**
AREA **10,932 sq mi; 28,314 sq km**
REGION **West**

Denver
COLORADO

DATE OF STATEHOOD **1876**
NICKNAME **Centennial State**
POPULATION **3,822,676**
AREA **104,100 sq mi; 269,619 sq km**
REGION **West**

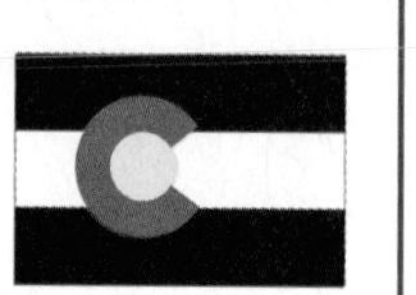

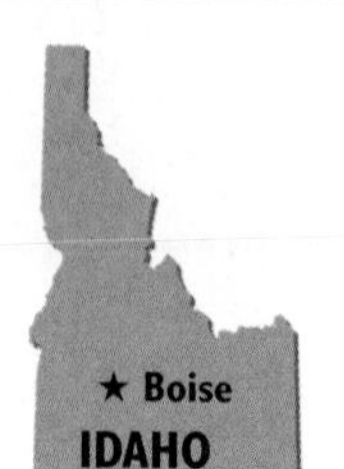


DATE OF STATEHOOD **1890**
NICKNAME **Gem State**
POPULATION **1,189,251**
AREA **83,574 sq mi; 216,457 sq km**
REGION **West**

## ILLINOIS

DATE OF STATEHOOD **1818**

NICKNAME **The Prairie State**

POPULATION **11,846,544**

AREA **57,918 sq mi; 150,008 sq km**

REGION **Middle West**

## MAINE

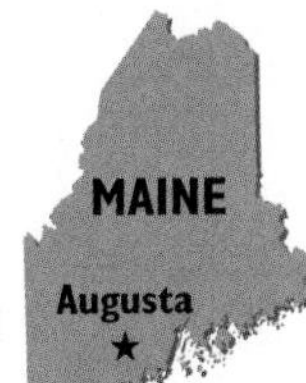


DATE OF STATEHOOD **1820**

NICKNAME **Pine Tree State**

POPULATION **1,243,316**

AREA **35,387 sq mi; 91,652 sq km**

REGION **Northeast**

## INDIANA

DATE OF STATEHOOD **1816**

NICKNAME **Hoosier State**

POPULATION **5,840,528**

AREA **36,420 sq mi; 94,328 sq km**

REGION **Middle West**

## MARYLAND

Annapolis

DATE OF STATEHOOD **1788**

NICKNAME **Free State**

POPULATION **5,071,604**

AREA **12,407 sq mi; 32,134 sq km**

REGION **Northeast**

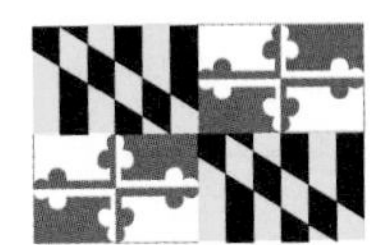

## IOWA

Des Moines

DATE OF STATEHOOD **1846**

NICKNAME **Hawkeye State**

POPULATION **2,851,792**

AREA **56,276 sq mi; 145,755 sq km**

REGION **Middle West**

## MASSACHUSETTS

Boston

DATE OF STATEHOOD **1788**

NICKNAME **Bay State**

POPULATION **6,092,352**

AREA **10,555 sq mi; 27,337 sq km**

REGION **Northeast**

## KANSAS

Topeka

DATE OF STATEHOOD **1861**

NICKNAME **Sunflower State**

POPULATION **2,572,150**

AREA **82,282 sq mi; 213,110 sq km**

REGION **Middle West**

## MICHIGAN

DATE OF STATEHOOD **1837**

NICKNAME **Wolverine State**

POPULATION **9,594,350**

AREA **96,810 sq mi; 250,738 sq km**

REGION **Middle West**

## KENTUCKY

Frankfort

DATE OF STATEHOOD **1792**

NICKNAME **Bluegrass State**

POPULATION **3,883,723**

AREA **40,411 sq mi; 104,664 sq km**

REGION **Southeast**

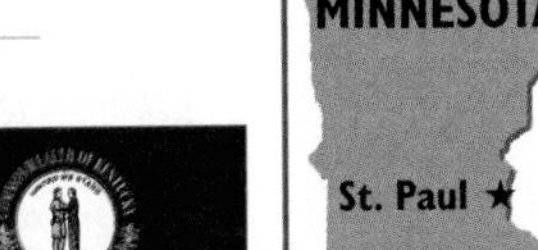

## MINNESOTA

DATE OF STATEHOOD **1858**

NICKNAME **North Star State**

POPULATION **4,657,758**

AREA **86,943 sq mi; 225,182 sq km**

REGION **Middle West**

## LOUISIANA

Baton Rouge

DATE OF STATEHOOD **1812**

NICKNAME **Pelican State**

POPULATION **4,350,579**

AREA **51,843 sq mi; 134,273 sq km**

REGION **Southeast**

## MISSISSIPPI

DATE OF STATEHOOD **1817**

NICKNAME **Magnolia State**

POPULATION **2,716,115**

AREA **48,434 sq mi; 125,444 sq km**

REGION **Southeast**

# OUR FIFTY STATES

DATE OF STATEHOOD 1821
NICKNAME Show Me State
POPULATION 5,358,692
AREA 69,709 sq mi; 180,546 sq km
REGION Middle West

MONTANA
★ Helena

DATE OF STATEHOOD 1889
NICKNAME Treasure State
POPULATION 879,372
AREA 147,046 sq mi; 380,849 sq km
REGION West

NEBRASKA
Lincoln ★

DATE OF STATEHOOD 1867
NICKNAME Cornhusker State
POPULATION 1,652,093
AREA 77,358 sq mi; 200,357 sq km
REGION Middle West

NEVADA
★ Carson City

DATE OF STATEHOOD 1864
NICKNAME Silver State
POPULATION 1,603,163
AREA 110,567 sq mi; 286,369 sq km
REGION West

NEW HAMPSHIRE
Concord ★

DATE OF STATEHOOD 1788
NICKNAME Granite State
POPULATION 1,162,481
AREA 9,351 sq mi; 24,219 sq km
REGION Northeast

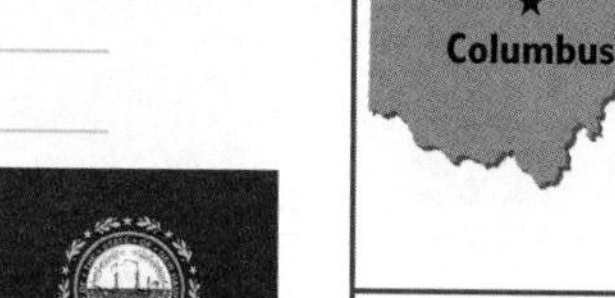

NEW JERSEY
★ Trenton

DATE OF STATEHOOD 1787
NICKNAME Garden State
POPULATION 7,987,933
AREA 8,722 sq mi; 22,590 sq km
REGION Northeast

DATE OF STATEHOOD 1912
NICKNAME Land of Enchantment
POPULATION 1,713,407
AREA 121,598 sq mi; 314,939 sq km
REGION Southwest

NEW YORK
Albany ★

DATE OF STATEHOOD 1788
NICKNAME Empire State
POPULATION 18,184,774
AREA 54,475 sq mi; 141,090 sq km
REGION Northeast

NORTH CAROLINA
Raleigh ★

DATE OF STATEHOOD 1789
NICKNAME Tar Heel State
POPULATION 7,322,870
AREA 53,821 sq mi; 139,396 sq km
REGION Southeast

NORTH DAKOTA
Bismarck ★

DATE OF STATEHOOD 1889
NICKNAME Peace Garden State
POPULATION 643,539
AREA 70,704 sq mi; 183,123 sq km
REGION Middle West

OHIO
★ Columbus

DATE OF STATEHOOD 1803
NICKNAME Buckeye State
POPULATION 11,172,782
AREA 44,828 sq mi; 116,105 sq km
REGION Middle West

OKLAHOMA
★ Oklahoma City

DATE OF STATEHOOD 1907
NICKNAME Sooner State
POPULATION 3,300,902
AREA 69,903 sq mi; 181,049 sq km
REGION Southwest

★ Salem
OREGON

DATE OF STATEHOOD 1859
NICKNAME Beaver State
POPULATION 3,203,735
AREA 98,386 sq mi; 254,820 sq km
REGION West

## PENNSYLVANIA

Harrisburg ★

DATE OF STATEHOOD **1787**

NICKNAME **Keystone State**

POPULATION **12,056,112**

AREA **46,058 sq mi; 119,290 sq km**

REGION **Northeast**

## RHODE ISLAND

Providence ★

DATE OF STATEHOOD **1790**

NICKNAME **Ocean State**

POPULATION **990,226**

AREA **1,545 sq mi; 4,002 sq km**

REGION **Northeast**

## SOUTH CAROLINA

★ Columbia

DATE OF STATEHOOD **1788**

NICKNAME **Palmetto State**

POPULATION **3,698,746**

AREA **32,007 sq mi; 82,898 sq km**

REGION **Southeast**

## SOUTH DAKOTA

Pierre ★

DATE OF STATEHOOD **1889**

NICKNAME **Mount Rushmore State**

POPULATION **732,405**

AREA **77,121 sq mi; 199,743 sq km**

REGION **Middle West**

## TENNESSEE

★Nashville

DATE OF STATEHOOD **1796**

NICKNAME **Volunteer State**

POPULATION **5,319,654**

AREA **42,146 sq mi; 109,158 sq km**

REGION **Southeast**

## TEXAS

Austin ★

DATE OF STATEHOOD **1845**

NICKNAME **Lone Star State**

POPULATION **19,128,261**

AREA **268,601 sq mi; 695,677 sq km**

REGION **Southwest**

## UTAH

★ Salt Lake City

DATE OF STATEHOOD **1896**

NICKNAME **Beehive State**

POPULATION **2,000,494**

AREA **84,904 sq mi; 219,901 sq km**

REGION **West**

## VERMONT

★ Montpelier

DATE OF STATEHOOD **1791**

NICKNAME **Green Mountain State**

POPULATION **588,654**

AREA **9,615 sq mi; 24,903 sq km**

REGION **Northeast**

## VIRGINIA

Richmond ★

DATE OF STATEHOOD **1788**

NICKNAME **Old Dominion**

POPULATION **6,675,451**

AREA **42,769 sq mi; 110,772 sq km**

REGION **Southeast**

## WASHINGTON

★ Olympia

DATE OF STATEHOOD **1889**

NICKNAME **Evergreen State**

POPULATION **5,532,939**

AREA **71,303 sq mi; 184,675 sq km**

REGION **West**

## WEST VIRGINIA

★ Charleston

DATE OF STATEHOOD **1863**

NICKNAME **Mountain State**

POPULATION **1,825,754**

AREA **24,231 sq mi; 62,758 sq km**

REGION **Southeast**

## WISCONSIN

Madison ★

DATE OF STATEHOOD **1848**

NICKNAME **Badger State**

POPULATION **5,159,795**

AREA **65,503 sq mi; 169,653 sq km**

REGION **Middle West**

## WYOMING

Cheyenne ★

DATE OF STATEHOOD **1890**

NICKNAME **Equality State**

POPULATION **481,400**

AREA **97,818 sq mi; 253,349 sq km**

REGION **West**

Sources: population—U.S. Bureau of Census; area—U.S. Bureau of Census, 1991; capital—*World Almanac*, 1995.

# NEW JERSEY TIME LINE

**1600s**
The Lenape live in what is now New Jersey

**1609**
Henry Hudson explores the area around Sandy Hook and meets the Lenape

**1623**
Cornelius Mey becomes first governor of New Netherland

**1660**
Bergen, the first town in what is now New Jersey, is founded

**1664**
England takes over New Netherland

**1676**
New Jersey divided into East and West Jersey

**1702**
New Jersey reunited as a royal colony

**1765**
Britain passes the Stamp Act

**1774**
Greenwich Tea Party

**1776**
Continental soldiers defeat Hessians at the Battle of Trenton during the American Revolutionary War.

**1787**
William Paterson presents the New Jersey Plan at Constitutional Convention

**1791**
Paterson founded as first planned industrial city

**1804**
New Jersey passes law to gradually end slavery

**1825**
John Stevens demonstrates first locomotive in the United States

1600s | 1700s | 1800s

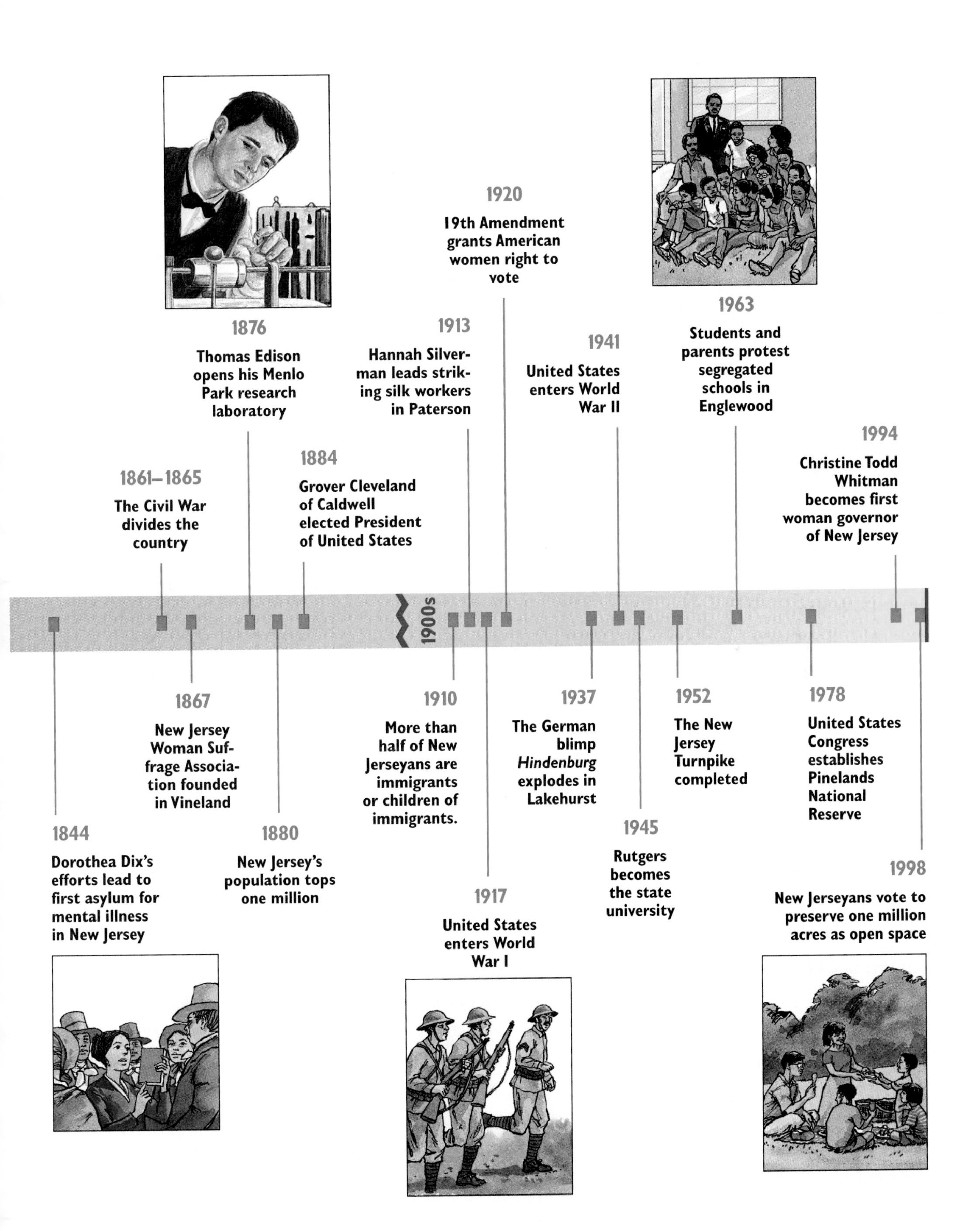
1844
Dorothea Dix's efforts lead to first asylum for mental illness in New Jersey
1861–1865
The Civil War divides the country
1867
New Jersey Woman Suffrage Association founded in Vineland
1876
Thomas Edison opens his Menlo Park research laboratory
1880
New Jersey's population tops one million
1884
Grover Cleveland of Caldwell elected President of United States
1900s
1910
More than half of New Jerseyans are immigrants or children of immigrants.
1913
Hannah Silverman leads striking silk workers in Paterson
1917
United States enters World War I
1920
19th Amendment grants American women right to vote
1937
The German blimp *Hindenburg* explodes in Lakehurst
1941
United States enters World War II
1945
Rutgers becomes the state university
1952
The New Jersey Turnpike completed
1963
Students and parents protest segregated schools in Englewood
1978
United States Congress establishes Pinelands National Reserve
1994
Christine Todd Whitman becomes first woman governor of New Jersey
1998
New Jerseyans vote to preserve one million acres as open space

# GOVERNORS of NEW JERSEY

| STATE GOVERNOR | TERM |
|---|---|
| William Livingston | 1776–1790 |
| Elisha Lawrence | 1790 |
| William Paterson | 1790–1793 |
| Elisha Lawrence | 1793 |
| Richard Howell | 1793–1801 |
| Joseph Bloomfield | 1801–1802 |
| John Lambert | 1802–1803 |
| Joseph Bloomfield | 1803–1812 |
| Charles Clark | 1812 |
| Aaron Ogden | 1812–1813 |
| William S. Pennington | 1813–1815 |
| William Kennedy | 1815 |
| Mahlon Dickerson | 1815–1817 |
| Jesse Upson | 1817 |
| Isaac H. Williamson | 1817–1829 |
| Garret D. Wall (declined) | 1829 |
| Peter D. Vroom | 1829–1832 |
| Samuel L. Southard | 1832–1833 |
| Elias P. Seeley | 1833 |
| Peter D. Vroom | 1833–1836 |
| Philemon Dickerson | 1836–1837 |
| William Pennington | 1837–1843 |
| Daniel Haines | 1843–1845 |
| Charles C. Stratton | 1845–1848 |
| Daniel Haines | 1848–1851 |
| George F. Fort | 1851–1854 |
| Rodman M. Price | 1854–1857 |
| William A. Newell | 1857–1860 |
| Charles S. Olden | 1860–1863 |
| Joel Parker | 1863–1866 |
| Marcus L. Ward | 1866–1869 |
| Theodore F. Randolph | 1869–1872 |
| Joel Parker | 1872–1875 |
| Joseph D. Bedle | 1875–1878 |
| George B. McClellan | 1878–1881 |
| George C. Ludlow | 1881–1884 |
| Leon Abbett | 1884–1887 |
| Robert S. Green | 1887–1890 |
| Leon Abbett | 1890–1893 |
| George T. Werts | 1893–1896 |
| John W. Griggs | 1896–1898 |
| Foster M. Voorhees | 1898 |
| David O. Watkins | 1898–1899 |
| Foster M. Voorhees | 1899–1902 |
| Franklin Murphy | 1902–1905 |
| Edward C. Stokes | 1905–1908 |
| John Franklin Fort | 1908–1911 |
| Woodrow Wilson | 1911–1913 |
| James F. Fielder | 1913 |
| Leon R. Taylor | 1913–1914 |
| James F. Fielder | 1914–1917 |
| Walter E. Edge | 1917–1919 |
| William N. Runyon | 1919–1920 |
| Clarence E. Case | 1920 |
| Edward I. Edwards | 1920–1923 |
| George S. Silzer | 1923–1926 |
| A. Harry Moore | 1926–1929 |
| Morgan F. Larson | 1929–1932 |
| A. Harry Moore | 1932–1935 |
| Clifford R. Powell | 1935 |
| Horace G. Prall | 1935 |
| Harold G. Hoffman | 1935–1938 |
| A. Harry Moore | 1938–1941 |
| Charles Edison | 1941–1944 |
| Walter E. Edge | 1944–1947 |
| Alfred E. Driscoll | 1947–1954 |
| Robert B. Meyner | 1954–1962 |
| Richard J. Hughes | 1962–1970 |
| William T. Cahill | 1970–1974 |
| Brendan T. Byrne | 1974–1982 |
| Thomas H. Kean | 1982–1990 |
| James J. Florio | 1990–1994 |
| Christine Todd Whitman | 1994– |

# NEW JERSEY CITIES

Note: Figures are based on 1998 estimates.

| CITY/TOWNSHIP NAME | CITY/TOWNSHIP POPULATION | COUNTY | POPULATION RANK |
|---|---|---|---|
| Bayonne (city) | 61,051 | Hudson | 16 |
| Brick (township) | 75,565 | Ocean | 12 |
| Camden (city) | 83,546 | Camden | 10 |
| Cherry Hill (township) | 69,117 | Camden | 14 |
| Clifton (city) | 76,180 | Passaic | 11 |
| Dover (township) | 86,700 | Ocean | 7 |
| East Orange (city) | 69,598 | Essex | 13 |
| Edison (township) | 95,705 | Middlesex | 5 |
| Elizabeth (city) | 110,661 | Union | 4 |
| Gloucester (township) | 58,839 | Camden | 19 |
| Hamilton (township) | 86,023 | Mercer | 8 |
| Irvington (township) | 57,752 | Essex | 20 |
| Jersey City (city) | 232,429 | Hudson | 2 |
| Lakewood (township) | 50,191 | Ocean | 26 |
| Middletown (township) | 68,378 | Monmouth | 15 |
| Newark (city) | 267,823 | Essex | 1 |
| Old Bridge (township) | 59,976 | Middlesex | 18 |
| Parsippany–Troy Hills (township) | 50,002 | Morris | 27 |
| Passaic (city) | 60,817 | Passaic | 17 |
| Paterson (city) | 148,212 | Passaic | 3 |
| Piscataway (township) | 51,911 | Middlesex | 24 |
| Trenton (city) | 84,494 | Mercer | 9 |
| Union (township) | 50,925 | Union | 25 |
| Union City (city) | 57,621 | Hudson | 21 |
| Vineland (city) | 55,484 | Cumberland | 22 |
| Wayne (township) | 54,577 | Passaic | 23 |
| Woodbridge (township) | 95,659 | Middlesex | 6 |

# FAMOUS NEW JERSEYANS

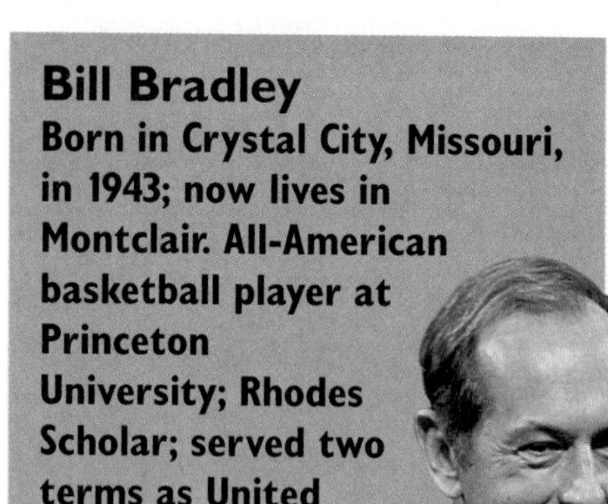

**Bill Bradley**
Born in Crystal City, Missouri, in 1943; now lives in Montclair. All-American basketball player at Princeton University; Rhodes Scholar; served two terms as United States Senator from New Jersey.

**Joyce Carol Oates**
Born in Lockport, New York, in 1938; now lives in Princeton; award-winning writer known for novels, short stories, and poems; professor of creative writing at Princeton University.

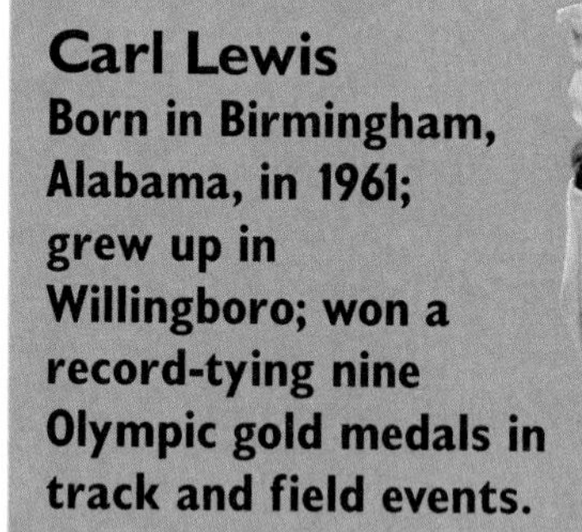

**Carl Lewis**
Born in Birmingham, Alabama, in 1961; grew up in Willingboro; won a record-tying nine Olympic gold medals in track and field events.

**Daisy Fuentes**
Born in Havana, Cuba, in 1966; grew up in Harrison; news reporter, host of MTV programs, restaurant owner, and model.

**Martha Stewart**
Born in Nutley in 1941; now lives in Westport, Connecticut; known for home decorating and cooking television show and magazine.

**Christopher Reeve**
Born in New York City in 1952; grew up in Princeton and attended Princeton Day School; actor and director known for role as Superman; works for spinal cord research funding.

**Connie Chung**
Born in Washington, D.C., in 1946; now lives in Rumson; investigative reporter and interviewer; won three Emmy Awards and a Peabody Award.

**Robert Menendez**
Born in New York City in 1954; now lives in Union City; served as mayor of Union City for 10 years; in 1993 became the first Hispanic member of the House of Representatives from New Jersey.

**Queen Latifah**
Born in Newark in 1970; rap recording artist and actress; won a Grammy Award in 1995 for the song *U.N.I.T.Y.*

**Robert Pinsky**
Born in Long Branch in 1940; now lives in Newton, Massachusetts; author of five books of poetry and four books of criticism; named United States Poet Laureate and Consultant in Poetry to the Library of Congress in 1997.

**Joetta Clark**
**Born in 1962 in East Orange; now lives in Gainesville, Florida; track star chosen as New Jersey Woman Athlete of the Century; now runs a motivational business.**

**Dave Thomas**
**Born in Atlantic City in 1932; adopted at 6 weeks old by a couple from Kalamazoo, Michigan; founder of Wendy's Old Fashioned Hamburgers and the Dave Thomas Foundation for adoption.**

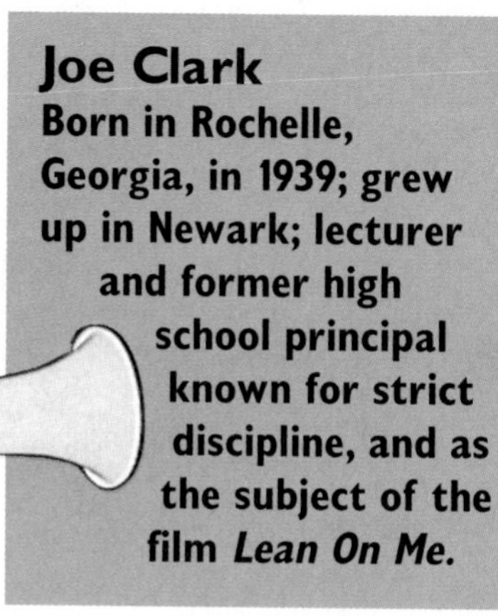

**Joe Clark**
**Born in Rochelle, Georgia, in 1939; grew up in Newark; lecturer and former high school principal known for strict discipline, and as the subject of the film *Lean On Me*.**

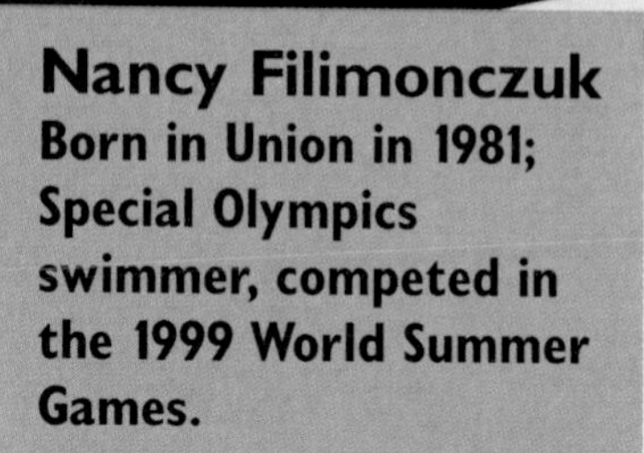

**Nancy Filimonczuk**
**Born in Union in 1981; Special Olympics swimmer, competed in the 1999 World Summer Games.**

**Christina Ricci**
**Born in Santa Monica, California, in 1980; grew up in Montclair; actress known for roles in *Addams Family, Casper,* and *Sleepy Hollow*.**

# Places to Visit

**Our state is filled with places that people find interesting and fun to visit. You can see why many New Jerseyans spend their vacations right in our own state. How many of these places have you visited?**

Visit the birthplace of American industry at the PATERSON MUSEUM

THOMAS ALVA EDISON HOUSE in West Orange

Delaware Water Gap National Recreation Area

Space Farms Zoo and Museum

Ringwood State Park

Paterson Museum

Waterloo Village

Wild West City

Morristown National Historic Park

Edison's House

Liberty Science Center

Duke Gardens

Washington Crossing State Park

New Jersey State Museum and Planetarium

Old Barracks Museum

Six Flags Great Adventure

Island Beach State Park

New Jersey State Aquarium

Popcorn Park Zoo

Edwin B. Forsythe National Wildlife Refuge

Thundering Surf Water Slide

Leaming's Run Gardens

American Museum of Glass

Maurice River Cove

Cape May Point State Park

At ISLAND BEACH STATE PARK, walk along the nature trail, or spend some time swimming and beachcombing.

Find out all about the mysteries of the deep at the NEW JERSEY STATE AQUARIUM in Camden.

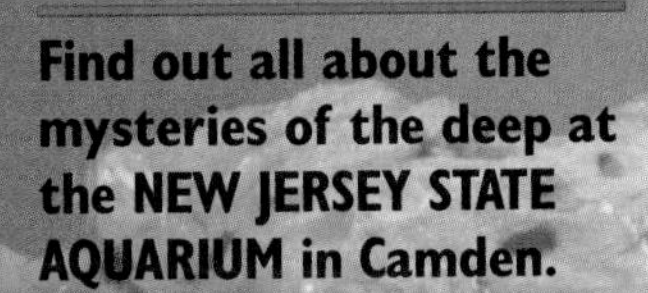

At the MUSEUM OF AMERICAN GLASS, you can see the almost 8-foot tall bottle as well as more than 6,500 other items.

At the OLD BARRACKS MUSEUM in Trenton, visit barracks that still stand since the French and Indian War.

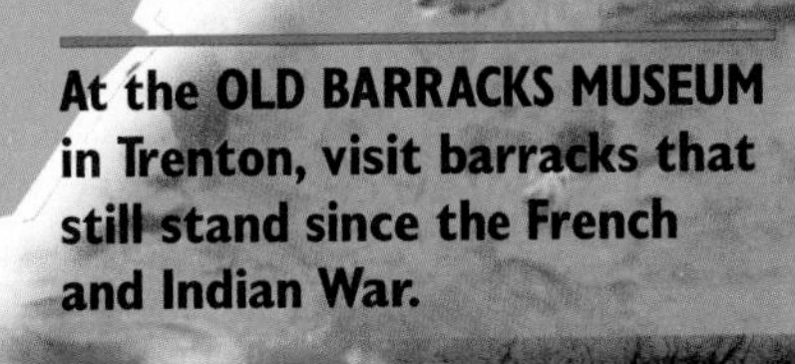

ANIMALS AND PLANTS OF NEW JERSEY
2
9
25
11
13
30
21
28
18
6
27
8
7
5
29
22
1
3
44
15
31

An (E) indicates an animal at risk (endangered).
1. Black Bear
2. Great Horned Owl
3. Copperhead (snake)
4. Wild turkey
5. May Apple
6. Mountain Laurel
7. Beaver
8. White-tailed deer
9. Red-shouldered hawk (E)
10. Pine Barrens Tree Frog (E)
11. Flying Squirrel
12. Red-Bellied Turtle
13. Eastern Bluebird
14. Black-Banded Sunfish
15. Pitcher Plant
16. White Water Lily
17. Black Jack Oak
18. White Cedar Trees
19. Dwarf Pine
20. Cranberry
21. Opossum
22. Wood Rat (E)
23. Blue Heron (E)
24. White Perch
25. Raccoon
26. Lady's Slipper
27. Red Fox
28. Skunk
29. Milk Snake
30. Gray Squirrel
31. Shad (fish)
32. Pheasant
33. Atlantic Surf clam
34. Bluefish
35. Laughing Gull
36. Blue Crab
37. Bayberry
38. Holly
39. Dune Grass
40. Bay Scallop
41. Glass Eel
42. Bald Eagle (E)
43. Bay Anchovy
44. Highbrush blueberry
35
19
32
17
38
37
39
40
23
4
26
20
10
36
34
12
42
43
14
16
41
24
33
40

# Dictionary of GEOGRAPHIC TERMS

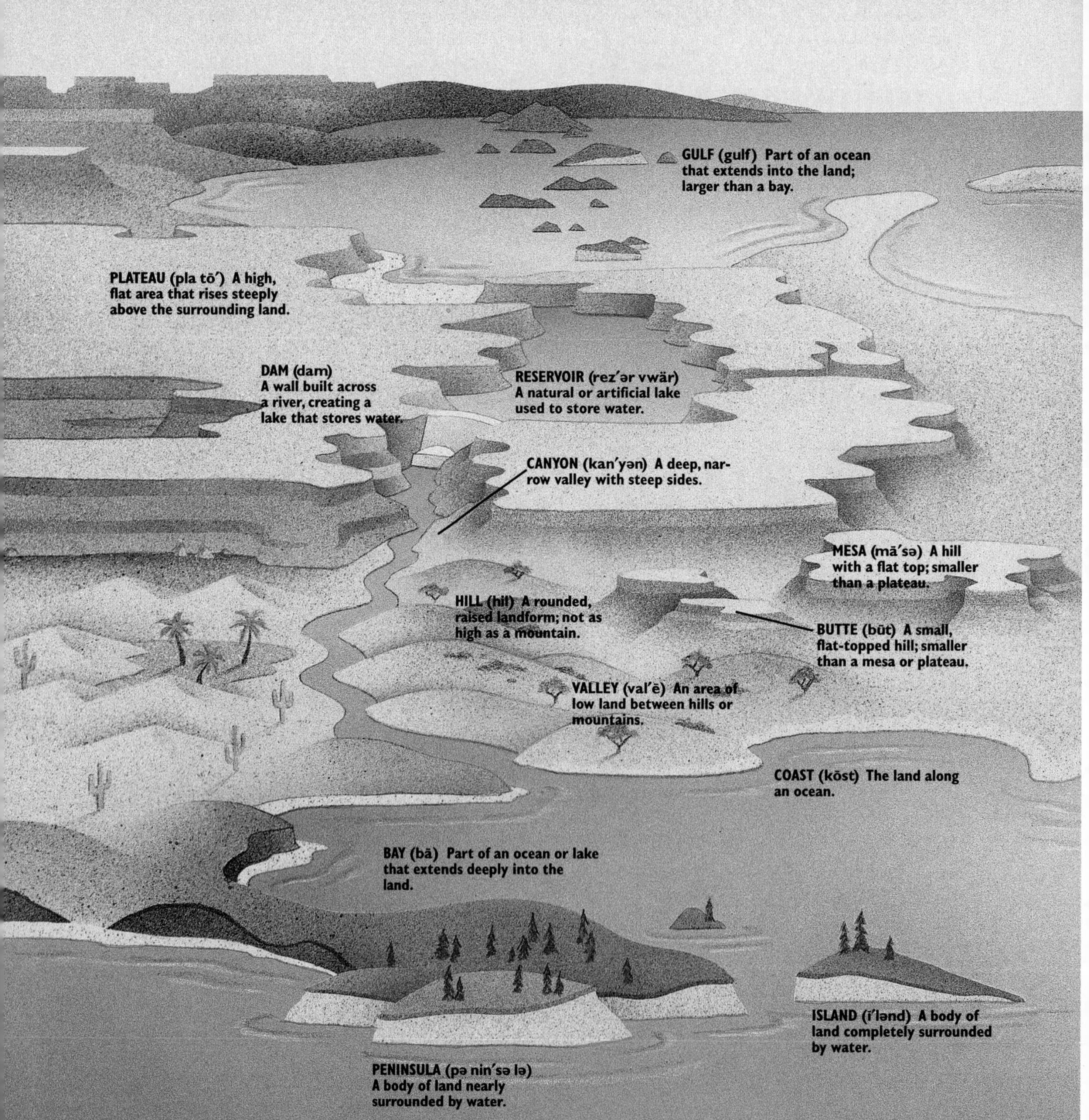

**VOLCANO** (vol kā′nō) An opening in Earth's surface through which hot rock and ash are forced out.

**MOUNTAIN** (moun′tən) A high landform with steep sides; higher than a hill.

**PEAK** (pēk) The top of a mountain.

**HARBOR** (här′bər) A sheltered place along a coast where boats dock safely.

**GLACIER** (glā′shər) A huge sheet of ice that moves slowly across the land.

**CANAL** (kə nal′) A channel built to carry water for irrigation or transportation.

**LAKE** (lāk) A body of water completely surrounded by land.

**TRIBUTARY** (trib′yə ter ē) A smaller river that flows into a larger river.

**PORT** (pôrt) A place where ships load and unload their goods.

**SOURCE** (sôrs) The starting point of a river.

**TIMBERLINE** (tim′bər līn) A line beyond which trees do not grow.

**RIVER BASIN** (riv′ər bā′sin) All the land that is drained by a river and its tributaries.

**WATERFALL** (wô′tər fôl) A flow of water falling vertically.

**MOUNTAIN RANGE** (moun′tən rānj) A row or chain of mountains.

**PLAIN** (plān) A large area of nearly flat land.

**RIVER** (riv′ər) A stream of water that flows across the land and empties into another body of water.

**BASIN** (bā′sin) A bowl-shaped landform surrounded by higher land.

**DELTA** (del′tə) Land made of soil left behind as a river drains into a larger body of water.

**MOUTH** (mouth) The place where a river empties into a larger body of water.

**OCEAN** (ō′shən) A large body of salt water; oceans cover much of Earth's surface.

# Gazetteer

This gazetteer is a geographic dictionary that will help you to pronounce and locate the places discussed in this book. Latitude and longitude are given for cities and some other places. The page numbers tell you where each place appears first on a map or in the text.

## A

**Abbott Farm** (a′but) Archaeological site containing prehistoric artifacts near Trenton. (t. 59)

**Appalachian Mountains** (a pe lā′chē ən moun′tenz) Chain of mountains stretching from Maine to Alabama; 41°N, 75°W. (m. G10, t. 29)

**Appomattox** (ap ə mat′əks) Town in Virginia where Robert E. Lee surrendered to Ulysses S. Grant; 37°N, 79°W. (t. 172)

**Asbury Park** (az′bə rē pärk) City in eastern New Jersey; 40°N, 74°W. (m. G7)

**Atlantic City** (at lan′tik si′tē) City in southeastern New Jersey; 39°N, 74°W. (m. G6, t. 21)

**Atlantic Coastal Plain** (at lan′tik kōs′təl plān) The largest region in New Jersey, extending inland from the Atlantic Ocean. (m. 35, t. 35)

## B

**Barnegat** (bär′nə get) Township in southeastern New Jersey; 40°N, 74°W. (m. G7, t. 41)

**Belvidere** (bel′və dēr) Town in northwestern New Jersey. The county seat of Warren County; 41°N, 75°W. (t. 294)

**Bergen** (bûr′gin) The first Dutch town in New Jersey, now a part of Jersey City; 41°N, 74°W. (m. 87, t. 89)

**Beringia** (bə rin′jē ə) A land bridge believed to have connected Asia with North America for about 2,000 years during the Ice Age. (m. 59, t. 58)

**Bering Strait** (bâ′ring strāt) Body of water that separates North America from Asia. (t. 58)

**Blairstown** (blârz′toun) Town in northwestern New Jersey; 41°N, 75°W. (m. 85)

**Bordentown** (bôrd′ən toun) Site where John Stevens's locomotive the *John Bull* was demonstrated in 1831; 40°N, 75°W. (t. 145)

**Bridgeton** (brij′tən) City in southwestern New Jersey. The county seat of Cumberland County; 39°N, 75°W. (m. R12)

**Burlington** (bûr′ling tən) The capital of the colony of West Jersey; 40°N, 75°W. (m. 92, t. 92)

## C

**Camden** (kam′dən) City in southwestern New Jersey; 40°N, 75°W. (m. G6, t. 22)

**Camp Dix** (kamp diks) Site built to train soldiers for World War I; 40°N, 75°W. (t. 207)

**Cape May** (kāp mā) City in southern New Jersey; 39°N, 75°W. (m. G6, t. 11)

**Cape May Point State Park** (kāp mā point stāt pärk) State park on the southern-most tip of New Jersey; 39°N, 75°W. (t. 298)

**Catskill Mountains** (kat′skil moun′tənz) Mountain range in southeastern New York. (m. 19, t. 19)

**Central Plains** (sen′trəl plānz) Eastern part of the Interior Plains, an area of gently rolling hills where much corn is grown. (m. R11, t. 31)

**Cherry Hill** (cher′rē hil) Town in southwestern New Jersey; 41°N, 75°W. (m. R12, t. 238)

## pronunciation key

| | | | | | | | |
|---|---|---|---|---|---|---|---|
| a | at | ī | ice | u | up | th | thin |
| ā | ape | îr | pierce | ū | use | th | this |
| ä | far | o | hot | ü | rule | zh | measure |
| âr | care | ō | old | u̇ | pull | ə | about, taken, pencil, lemon, circus |
| e | end | ô | fork | ûr | turn | | |
| ē | me | oi | oil | hw | white | | |
| i | it | ou | out | ng | song | | |

## D

**Davis Bayou** (dā′vəs bī′yū) Marshy, slow-moving stream in Mississippi. (t. 30)

**Delaware Bay** (de′lə wâr bā) Body of water that connects the Delaware River with the Atlantic Ocean; 39°N, 75°W. (m. 9, t. 15)

**Delaware River** (de′lə wâr ri′vûr) River that forms the border between New Jersey and Pennsylvania. (m. G6, t. 10)

**Delaware Water Gap** (de′lə wâr wät ər gap) Region in northwest New Jersey where the Delaware River passes through the Appalachian Mountains; 41°N, 75°W. (m. G8, t. 10)

## E

**East Jersey** (ēst jûr′zē) Colonial province made up of the eastern portion of the current state. (m. 92, t. 92)

**East Orange** (ēst ôr inj) City in northeast New Jersey; 41°N, 74°W. (m. R12, t. 303)

**Elizabeth** (ē liz′ə bəth) Major port city in northeastern New Jersey; 41°N, 74°W. (m. G6, t. 17)

**Ellis Island** (el′əs ī′lənd) Island in New York Bay, served as immigration center from 1892 to 1954; 41°N, 74°W. (t. 183)

**Englewood** (en′gul wůd) City in northern New Jersey where African Americans staged a sit-in in 1963; 41°N, 74°W. (t. 232)

**Ewing** (ū′hwing) Town in central New Jersey; 40°N, 75°W. (m. R12, t. 281)

## F

**Flemington** (flem′ing tən) Borough in central New Jersey. The county seat of Hunterdon County; 40°N, 75°W. (m. R12, t. 273)

**Fort Lee** (fôrt lē) City in northeastern New Jersey. Home of the abolitionist Grimké sisters; 41°N, 74°W. (m. R12, t. 163)

**Fort Nassau** (fôrt na′saw) Small Dutch settlement built in 1624. (m. 87, t. 87)

**Franklin** (frank′lən) City in northern New Jersey known for its deposits of rare minerals; 41°N, 75°W. (m. R12, t. 38)

**Freehold** (frē′hōld) City in central New Jersey. The county seat of Monmouth County; 40°N, 74°W. (m. 142, t. 304)

## G

**Gettysburg** (get′ēz bûrg) City in southern Pennsylvania. Site of a major Civil War battle; 40°N, 77°W. (t. 171)

**Grand Canyon** (grand kan′yən) Large canyon on the Colorado River in northwestern Arizona. (t. 32)

**Great Plains** (grāt plānz) Western part of the Interior Plains. (m. G10, t. 31)

**Great Swamp** (grāt swämp) Wetland area in north-central New Jersey; 41°N, 74°W. (m. R12, t. 10)

**Greenwich** (gren′ich) Site of 1774 protest in which colonists burned tea; 39°N, 75°W. 164, t. 109)

**Greenwood Lake** (grēn′wůd lāk) The largest lake in New Jersey; 41°N, 74°W. (m. 9)

## H

**Hackensack** (hak′ən sak) City in northeastern New Jersey. The county seat of Bergen County; 41°N, 74°W. (m. 87)

**Haddonfield** (had′ən fēld) Borough in southwestern New Jersey; 40°N, 75°W. (m. R12)

**Hammonton** (ham′ən tən) Town in southern New Jersey; 40°N, 75°W. (m. G6)

**Highlands** (hī′ləndz) Region of New Jersey bordered by the Piedmont and the Ridge and Valley regions. (m. 35, t. 38)

**High Point State Park** (hī point stāt pärk) State park that includes High Point, the state's highest peak; 41°N, 75°W. (t. 10)

**Hoboken** (hō′bō kən) City in northeastern New Jersey; 41°N, 74°W. (m. 142, t. 207)

**Hudson River** (hud′sən ri′vûr) River that flows into New York Bay. It forms part of the border between New Jersey and New York. (m. G6, t. 14)

## I

**Interior Plains** (in tîr′ē ûr plānz) Region in the central part of the United States that includes the Central Plains and the Great Plains. (m. R11, t. 31)

## J

**Jackson** (jax′un) Town in central New Jersey; 40°N, 74°W. (t. 298)

**Jersey City** (jûr′zē si′tē) City in northeastern New Jersey. The county seat of Hudson County; 41°N, 74°W. (m. G6, t. 40)

## K

**Kittatinny Ridge** (kit′ə tin ē rij) Chain of mountains in northwestern New Jersey. (m. 9, t. 10)

## L

**Lenapehoking** (luh nä pē′hâ king) Area where the Lenape lived, including parts of New Jersey, Delaware, New York, and Pennsylvania. (m. 65, t. 64)

**Levittown** (lev′ət toun) Suburb built in the 1950s and 1960s. Now known as Willingboro; 40°N, 75°W. (t. 223)

**Liberty State Park** (lib ərt ē stāt pärk) State park located in Jersey City, near the Statue of Liberty; 41°N, 74°W. (t. 298)

**Linden** (lin′dən) City in northeastern New Jersey; 41°N, 74°W. (m. 228, t. 44)

## M

**Mahwah** (mä′hwä) City in northern New Jersey. In 1955, site of the nation's largest automobile factory; 41°N, 74°W. (m. R12, t. 224)

**Maplewood** (mā′pul wüd) City in northern New Jersey; 41°N, 74°W. (t. 271)

**Mays Landing** (māz land′ing) The county seat of Atlantic County; 39°N, 75°W. (m. R12, t. 252)

**Meadowlands** (med′ō landz) Wetland area in northeastern New Jersey; 41°N, 74°W. (t. 238)

**Menlo Park** (mən′lō pärk) Town in northeastern New Jersey. Site of Thomas Edison's "invention factory"; 41°N, 74°W. (m. R12, t. 176)

**Middle Colonies** (mid′ul kol′ə nēz) England's North American colonies between New England and the Southern Colonies. (t. 98)

**Mississippi River** (mis ə sip′ē ri′vûr) The longest river in the United States. (m. G9, t. 30)

**Monmouth Courthouse** (mon′muth kôrt′hous) Town in central New Jersey. Site of 1778 Revolutionary War battle. Now known as Freehold; 40°N, 74°W. (m. 120, t. 119)

**Monroe** (mun rō′) Township in southern New Jersey; 40°N, 75°W. (t. 270)

**Morristown** (mär′əs toun) The county seat of Morris County. Site of the Continental Army's winter camp in 1778–1779; 41°N, 74°W. (m. G6, t. 47)

**Mount Holly** (mount hol′lē) The county seat of Burlington County; 40°N, 75°W. (m. 85)

**Mount Olive** (mount ol′iv) City in north-central New Jersey; 41°N, 75°W. (t. 250)

**Murray Hill** (mûr′ē hil) City in northern New Jersey that is home to many research laboratories; 41°N, 74°W. (t. 224)

**Musconetcong River** (məs kə′net käng ri′vûr) A tributary of the Delaware River; 41°N, 75°W. (m. 15, t. 14)

## N

**New Amsterdam** (nü am′stûr dam) Dutch settlement started in 1625 on Manhattan Island, which became New York City. (m. 87)

**Newark** (nü′ûrk) Major port city in northeastern New Jersey. The county seat of Essex County; 41°N, 74°W. (m. G6, t. 17)

**Newark Bay** (nü′ ûrk bā) Body of water linking the city of Newark to the Atlantic Ocean; 41°N, 74°W. (t. 80)

**New Brunswick** (nü brunz′wik) The county seat of Middlesex County; 40°N, 74°W. (m. 9, t. 141)

**New Netherland** (nü neth′ûr lənd) Dutch colony in North America (1624–1664) that includes parts of present-day New York, New Jersey, and Delaware. (m. 87)

**New Sweden** (nü swē′dən) Swedish colony in the Delaware Bay area, founded in 1636. (m. 87)

**Newton** (nü′tən) The county seat of Sussex County; 41°N, 75°W. (m. G6)

## P

**Paramus** (pə′ram əs) City in northeast New Jersey; 41°N, 74°W. (m. R12, t. 297)

**Paterson** (pa′tûr sən) Site of the first planned industrial city in the United States, and the county seat of Passaic County; 41°N, 74°W. (m. G6, t. 148)

**Perth Amboy** (pûrth am′boi) Capital city of the province of East Jersey that became an important transportation hub; 41°N, 74°W. (m. 92, t. 92)

**Piedmont** (pēd′mont) The narrow region in north-central New Jersey with many foothills. (m. 35, t. 35)

**Pinelands** (pīn′landz) A large area of pine forest and wetlands in the Atlantic Coastal Plain region; 40°N, 74°W. (m. 9, t. 10)

**Pomona** (pə mōn′ə) City in southern New Jersey; 39°N, 75°W. (m. R12)

**Princeton** (prins′tən) City in central New Jersey that served as the national capital for a short time in 1783; 40°N, 75°W. (m. 228, t. 40)

## R

**Raritan River** (rar ət ən ri′vûr) Longest river in New Jersey. (m. G6, t. 14)

**Ridge and Valley** (rij and val′lē) Region in the northwest corner of New Jersey that contains part of the Appalachian Mountains. (m. 35, t. 39)

**Rocky Mountains** (rok′ē moun′tənz) Mountain chain that stretches from Canada through the western United States into Mexico. (m. G10, t. 32)

**Roselle** (rō zel′) The first city in the United States to be lighted by electricity; 41°N, 74°W. (m. R12, t. 177)

**Rutherford** (ruth′ûr fûrd) City in northeastern New Jersey that was the home of poet William Carlos Williams; 41°N, 74°W. (t. 304)

## S

**Salem** (sā′ləm) City in southern New Jersey that was an important station on the Underground Railroad. The county seat of Salem County; 40°N, 75°W. (m. 92, t. 99)

**Sandy Hook** (san′dē hůk) Home to the oldest working lighthouse in the United States; 40°N, 74°W. (m. 9, t. 10)

**Secaucus** (sə kau′kus) City in northeastern New Jersey; 41°N, 74°W. (m. 228, t. 21)

**Short Hills** (shôrt hilz) Warning shots and fires here marked the last Revolutionary War battle in New Jersey; 41°N, 74°W. (t. 123)

**Shrewsbury** (shrüz′bûr ē) Town in central New Jersey; 40°N, 74°W. (m. 92)

**Somerville** (sum′ûr vil) Borough in central New Jersey. The county seat of Somerset County; 41°N, 75°W. (t. 227)

**South Brunswick** (south brunz′wik) Township in central New Jersey; 40°N, 74°W. (m. R12, t. 237)

**South Orange** (south ôr inj) City in northeast New Jersey; 41°N, 74°W. (t. 304)

**Sparta** (spär′tə) Town in north-central New Jersey; 41°N, 75°W. (t. 44)

## T

**Toms River** (tomz riv′ûr) The county seat of Ocean County; 40°N, 74°W. (m. G6, t. 296)

**Totowa** (tō′tə hwä) City in northern New Jersey; 41°N, 74°W. (m. R12, t. 264)

**Trenton** (tren′tən) The capital of New Jersey and the county seat of Mercer County; 40°N, 75°W. (m. G6, t. 37)

## V

**Vernon** (vûr′nən) City in northwestern New Jersey; 41°N, 74°W. (m. R12, t. 298)

**Vineland** (vīn′lənd) City in southern New Jersey; 39°N, 75°W. (m. G6)

## W

**Washington Crossing State Park** (wä′shing tən stāt pärk) State park on site where George Washington crossed the Delaware River; 40°N, 75°W. (t. 298)

**Washington, D.C.** (wä′shing tən dē sē) Capital of the United States; 39°N, 77°W. (m. G9, t. 284)

**Weehawken** (wē′haw kən) Site of duel between Aaron Burr and Alexander Hamilton in 1804; 41°N, 74°W. (m. R12, t. 149)

**West Jersey** (west jûr′zē) Colonial province made up of the western portion of the current state. (m. 92, t. 92)

**Willingboro** (wil′ing bûr ō) Farming village that grew into a suburb; 40°N, 75°W. (m. R12, t. 223)

**Woodbridge** (wůd′brij) Town in northeastern New Jersey; 41°N, 74°W. (t. 181)

**pronunciation key**

a **at**; ā **ape**; ä **far**; âr **care**; e **end**; ē **me**; i **it**; ī **ice**; îr **pierce**; o **hot**; ō **old**; ô **fork**; oi **oil**; ou **out**; u **up**; ū **use**; ü **rule**, ů **pull**; ûr **turn**; hw **white**; ng **song**; th **thin**; th **this**; zh **measure**; ə **about, taken, pencil, lemon, circus**

Biographical Dictionary

# Biographical Dictionary

The Biographical Dictionary tells you about the people you have learned about in this book. The Pronunciation Key tells you how to say their names. The page numbers tell you where each person first appears in the text.

## A

**Abbott, Charles C.** (a′bət), 1843–1919 One of New Jersey's first archaeologists; he found stone tools on his farm in 1867. (p. 59)

**Alexander, Walter G.** (a lex an′dûr), 1880–1953 First African American elected to the New Jersey State Legislature. (p. 209)

## B

**Baraka, Amiri** (bə rä′kə, ə mēr′ē), 1934– African American novelist, playwright, and poet from Newark. (p. 304)

**Berkeley, John, Lord** (bûrk′ə lē), d. 1678 One of the two first proprietors of New Jersey. (p. 91)

**Brennan, William J.** (bren′ən), 1906–1997 United States Supreme Court Justice 1956–1990; from Newark. (p. 285)

**Byrne, Brendan** (bûrn), 1924– Governor from 1974–1982; he passed the first state income tax for New Jersey in 1976. (p. 234)

## C

**Cabot, John** (kab′ət), 1450–1498 Italian explorer working for England who reached North America in 1497. (p. 79)

**Carteret, George, Sir** (kär tə ret′), c. 1610–1680 One of the two first proprietors of New Jersey. (p. 91)

**Carteret, Philip** (kär tə ret′), 1639–1682 First colonial governor of New Jersey; he was appointed by Lord Berkeley and Sir Carteret and arrived in 1665. (p. 91)

**Clark, Abraham** (klärk), 1725–1794 Signer of the Declaration of Independence. (p. 110)

**Cleveland, Grover** (klēv′lənd), 1837–1908 Born in Caldwell, died in Princeton, he served two nonconsecutive terms as 22nd and 24th president of the United States from 1885–1889 and 1893–1897. (p. 183)

**Coleman, James H., Jr.** (kōl′mən), 1933– In 1994 he became the first African American to serve on the New Jersey Supreme Court. (p. 280)

**Colt, John** (kōlt), 1786–1877 Paterson clothmaker who convinced the United States Navy to use cotton instead of linen for sails. (p. 150)

**Columbus, Christopher** (kə lum′bəs, kris′tə fûr), 1451–1506 Italian explorer working on behalf of Spain who arrived in the Americas in 1492. (p. 78)

## D

**Dix, Dorothea** (diks, dôr ō thē′ə), 1802–1887 Called for reforms in the treatment of the mentally ill in New Jersey and other states. (p. 156)

## E

**Edison, Thomas Alva** (ed′i sən), 1847–1931 Inventor of the light bulb in 1879, the phonograph, and more than 1,000 major inventions. (p. 176)

**Einstein, Albert** (īn′stīn), 1879–1955 Princeton University scientist from Germany who created the atomic bomb, which ended World War II. (p. 217)

## F

**Fagan, Mark** (fā′gən), 1869–1955 New Idea mayor of Jersey City, 1902–1907, 1913–1917. (p. 199)

**Fauset, Jesse Redmon** (faw′sət, jes′ē red′mən), 1882–1961 Harlem Renaissance-era African American writer. (p. 210)

## pronunciation key

| | | | | | | | |
|---|---|---|---|---|---|---|---|
| a | **at** | ī | **ice** | u | **up** | th | **thin** |
| ā | **ape** | îr | **pierce** | ū | **use** | t͟h | **this** |
| ä | **far** | o | **hot** | ü | **rule** | zh | **measure** |
| âr | **care** | ō | **old** | ů | **pull** | ə | **about, taken, pencil, lemon, circus** |
| e | **end** | ô | **fork** | ûr | **turn** | | |
| ē | **me** | oi | **oil** | hw | **white** | | |
| i | **it** | ou | **out** | ng | **song** | | |

**Fitch, John** (fitch), 1743–1798 Launched the nation's first steamboat in 1787. (p. 144)

**Franklin, William** (frank′lən), 1731–1813 New Jersey's last royal governor; he took office in 1763. (p. 109)

## G

**Garibaldi, Marie** (gär ə bawl′dē), 1934– In 1982 she became the first woman appointed to the New Jersey Supreme Court. (p. 280)

**Gibson, Kenneth** (gib′sən), 1932– In 1970 he became the first African American mayor of Newark. (p. 233)

**Grant, Ulysses S.** (grant, ü lis′ēz es), 1822–1885 Led the Union Army during the Civil War and later became the 18th president of the United States. (p. 172)

**Grimké, Angelina and Sarah** (grim′kē, anj ə lē′nə and sa′rə), 1805–1879, 1792–1873 Sisters from Fort Lee who were Quakers and abolitionists; they wrote *American Slavery as It Is: Testimony of a Thousand Witnesses* with Angelina's husband, Theodore Weld. (p. 163)

## H

**Hague, Frank** (hāg), 1876–1956 Jersey City mayor and political boss from 1917–1947. (p. 214)

**Hamilton, Alexander** (ham′əl tən), 1757–1804 First Secretary of the Treasury who developed the idea for America's first planned industrial city at Paterson in 1789. (p. 148)

**Hancock, Cornelia** (han′kok), 1840–1884 Volunteer nurse who served at the Battle of Gettysburg during the Civil War. (p. 171)

**Hays, Mary Ludwig** (hāz) 1752–1832 Known more commonly as Molly Pitcher, she reputedly carried water to the American soldiers in the Battle of Monmouth during the American Revolution. (p. 119)

**Hill, Lauryn** (hil), 1975– Grammy-winning hip-hop/soul singer from South Orange. (p. 304)

**Hudson, Henry** (hud′sən), 1565–1611 English explorer who came upon the Delaware Bay while looking for a Northwest Passage to Asia. He met the Lenape in 1609. (p. 80)

## J

**Jefferson, Thomas** (jef′ûr sən), 1743–1826 A principal writer of the Declaration of Independence and the third president of the United States. (p. 110)

## K

**Kearny, Philip** (kär′nē), 1814–1862 Leader of the First New Jersey Brigade during the Civil War. (p. 170)

**Kiersted, Sarah** (kier′sted) b. 1622?–? Dutch settler in New Netherland, she learned the Lenape language and helped the Dutch settlers and the Lenape work out peace treaties. (p. 88)

**King, Martin Luther, Jr.** (king) 1929–1968 Baptist minister and major civil rights leader during the 1950s and 1960s. (p. 232)

## L

**Lawrence, Jacob** (lär′əns) 1917–2000 African American artist from Atlantic City, famous for his series of paintings called "The Migration of the Negro." (p. 209)

**Levitt, William J.** (lev′ət), 1907–1994 Builder who mass-produced houses to create suburbs such as Willingboro. (p. 223)

**Lewis, Carl** (lü′is), 1961– Nine-time Olympic gold medalist in track and field events; from Willingboro. (p. 297)

**Lincoln, Abraham** (ling′kən), 1809–1865 Sixteenth president of the United States who led the country during the Civil War. (p. 168)

**Livingston, William** (liv′ing stən), 1723–1790 The first state governor of New Jersey after independence, 1776–1790. (p. 117)

## M

**McClellan, George B.** (mik klel′ən), 1826–1885 General-in-chief of the Union Army for one year during the Civil War. (p. 170)

**Mey, Cornelius** (mā), 1570?–1630? The first governor of New Netherland in 1623. (p. 87)

**Minuit, Peter** (min′ū ət), 1580–1638 Dutch colonial governor of New Netherland who obtained Manhattan Island from the Lenape. (p. 87)

**Murphy, Franklin** (mûr′ fē), 1846–1920 New Idea governor of New Jersey, 1902–1905. (p. 199)

## N

**Nicolls, Richard** (nik′əlz), 1624–1672 Sent by England to defeat the Dutch in New Netherland. (p. 90)

**Norton, Mary T.** (nôr′tən), 1875–1959 In 1924 she became one of the first women elected to the United States House of Representatives. (p. 203)

## P

**Paterson, William** (pa′tûr sən), 1745–1806 Drafted the New Jersey Plan for the 1787 Constitutional Convention in Philadelphia. (p. 128)

**Paul, Alice** (pawl), 1885–1977 Leader from Mount Laurel in the fight for women's suffrage. (p. 202)

**Penn, William** (pen), 1644–1718 He wrote the "Concessions and Agreements . . . of West New Jersey." (p. 93)

**Philbrook, Mary** (fil′brùk), 1872–1958 In 1895 she became the first female lawyer admitted to the New Jersey Bar Association. (p. 202)

**Poritz, Deborah** (pôr′itz), 1937– Chief Justice of the New Jersey Supreme Court since July 10, 1996. (p. 280)

## R

**Randolph, Oliver** (ran′dolf), 1881–1951 The only African American delegate to the 1947 state constitutional convention. (p. 231)

**Robeson, Paul** (rō′bə sən), 1898–1976 African American singer and actor from Princeton who was also a scholar-athlete at Rutgers University. (p. 210)

**Rock, John S.** (rok), 1825–1866 African American abolitionist from Salem. (p. 162)

**Roosevelt, Franklin D.** (rō′zə velt), 1882–1945 The thirty-second president of the United States, from 1933–1945. He created New Deal programs to fight the Great Depression and led the country during World War II. (p. 214)

## S

**Seabrook, Charles** (sē′brùk), 1881–1964 Founder of the frozen food business Seabrook Farms in the 1930s in Upper Deerfield Township, Cumberland County. (p. 224)

**Silverman, Hannah** (sil′vûr mən), 1896–1960 17-year-old leader during the 1913 Paterson silk workers' strike. (p. 201)

**Sinatra, Frank** (sə nä′trə), 1915–1998 Popular singer from Hoboken. (p. 304)

**Smithson, Robert** (smith′sən), 1938–1973 Sculptor from Passaic. (p. 304)

**Springsteen, Bruce** (spring′stēn), 1949– Popular rock singer and songwriter from Freehold known as "The Boss." (p. 304)

**Stevens, John** (stē′vənz), 1749–1838 In 1825 he ran the first locomotive in America on a track he built in Hoboken. (p. 144)

**Still, Charity** (stil), c. 1775–1857 A former slave who found freedom in New Jersey. (p. 165)

**Stockton, Richard** (stok′tən), 1730–1780 Signer of the Declaration of Independence. (p. 110)

**Stone, Lucy** (stōn), 1818–1893 Leader in the struggle for women's rights. She was opposed to women being taxed without being able to vote. (p. 155)

**Stuyvesant, Peter** (stī′və sənt), 1610–1672 Governor of New Netherland from 1647 until 1664, when the English took over. (p. 88)

## T

**Tubman, Harriet** (tub′mən), 1820–1913 A former slave who led others to freedom along the Underground Railroad; she worked in Cape May hotels to finance her efforts. (p. 164)

## V

**Vaughan, Sarah** (vawn), 1924–1990 Jazz singer from Newark. (p. 304)

**Verrazano, Giovanni da** (ver ə zän′ō, jō vä′nē də), 1485–1528 Italian explorer working for France who reached what is now Sandy Hook in 1524. (p. 79)

## W

**Washington, George** (wä′shing tən), 1732–1799 First president of the United States and general of the Continental Army during the American Revolution, as well as a general for the British during the French and Indian War. (p. 107)

**Whitman, Christine Todd** (hwit′mən), 1946– New Jersey's first female governor; she was elected in 1993 and reelected in 1997. (p. 42)

**Whitman, Walt** (hwit′mən), 1819–1892 Great American poet who spent the last 20 years of his life in Camden. (p. 304)

**Wiggins, Ulysses S.** (hwig′inz), d. 1969 A leader of the civil rights movement in New Jersey. (p. 232)

**Williams, William Carlos** (wil′yəmz), 1883–1963 Pulitzer Prize-winning poet from Rutherford who was also a doctor. (p. 304)

**Wilson, Woodrow** (wil′sən), 1856–1924 Former president of Princeton University and governor of New Jersey who served as the twenty-eighth president of the United States from 1913 to 1921. He led the United States during World War I. (p. 200)

**Witherspoon, John** (hwith′ûr spün), 1722–1794 Signer of the Declaration of Independence. (p. 110)

**Woodson, S. Howard, Jr.** (wůd′sən) 1916–1999 A leader of the civil rights movement in New Jersey. In 1975 he became the first African American leader of the state General Assembly. (p. 232)

**Wright, Marion Thompson** (rīt), 1902–1962 African American scholar from South Orange who studied New Jersey schools in the 1940s. (p. 231)

**Worthy Williams, Madeline** (wil′yəmz), 1894–1968 A leader of the civil rights movement in New Jersey. (p. 232)

## Z

**Zayak, Elaine** (zī′ak), 1965– World Champion Olympic figure skater from Paramus. (p. 297)

**pronunciation key**

a **at**; ā **ape**; ä **far**; âr **care**; e **end**; ē **me**; i **it**; ī **ice**; îr **pierce**; o **hot**; ō **old**; ô **fork**; oi **oil**; ou **out**; u **up**; ū **use**; ü **rule**, ů **pull**; ûr **turn**; hw **white**; ng **song**; th **thin**; th **this**; zh **measure**; ə **about**, **taken**, **pencil**, **lemon**, **circus**

# Glossary

This Glossary will help you to pronounce and understand the meanings of the vocabulary in this book. The page number at the end of the definition tells where the word first appears.

## A

**abolition** (ab ə lish′ən) Ending or doing away with completely; often used in reference to slavery. (p. 162)

**agriculture** (ag′ri kul chûr) The business of farming. (p. 43)

**Allied Powers** (al′līd pow′ûrz) The name given to the forces led by Great Britain, France, and Russia during World War I. The United States joined the Allied Powers in 1917. See **Central Powers**. (p. 206)

**Allies** (al′īz) The name given to the countries allied against the Axis Powers in World War II, including the United States, Britain, France, the Soviet Union, and China. *See* **Axis Powers**. (p. 216)

**ally** (al′ī) A friendly person or country that joins with another for a common purpose. (p. 107)

**American Revolution** (ə mer′i kən rev ə lü′ shən) The war between Great Britain and its 13 American colonies from 1775 to 1783 that led to the founding of the United States of America. (p. 110)

**ancestor** (an′ses tər) A relative who lived before you. (p. 60)

**apportionment** (ə′pôr shən mənt) Dividing according to a plan. (p. 234)

**aquifer** (ak′wə fər) A layer of rock or gravel that traps water underground. (p. 16)

**archaeologist** (är kē ol′ə jist) A scientist who looks for and studies artifacts. *See* **artifact**. (p. 59)

**artifact** (är′tə fakt) An object left behind by people who lived long ago. (p. 59)

**assembly** (ə sem′blē) A lawmaking body. (p. 93)

**Axis Powers** (ak′sis pow′ərz) The name given to the countries that fought the Allies in World War II, including Germany, Italy, and Japan. *See* **Allies**. (p. 216)

## B

**bayou** (bī′ü) A marshy, slow-moving stream, usually found in the southern United States. (p. 30)

**bill** (bil) A written proposal, or idea, for a law. (p. 278)

**Bill of Rights** (bil uv rītz) The first ten amendments to the United States Constitution, ratified in 1791. *See* **ratify**. (p. 129)

**biotechnology** (bī′ō tek nol ə gē) The combination of biology and technology to make scientific advances. (p. 263)

**blizzard** (bli′zərd) A snowstorm with very strong winds. (p. 22)

**Board of Chosen Freeholders** (bôrd uv chō′zən frē′ hōl dûrz) Elected officials who govern a county in New Jersey. (p. 273)

**border** (bôr′dər) A line that people agree on to separate one place from another. (p. 9)

**bribe** (brīb) Money paid to an official to do something. (p. 199)

**budget** (bu′jət) A plan for using an amount of money for specific purposes. (p. 277)

**byline** (bī′līn) A line at the beginning of a newspaper article that names the writer. (p. 274)

## C

**canal** (ke nal′) A human-built waterway. (p. 142)

**candidate** (can′də dāt) A person running for office in an election. (p. 283)

**cardinal direction** (kärd′nəl di rek′ shən) One of the four main points of the compass: north, south, east, and west. *See* **compass rose**. (p. G6)

**cause** (koz) An event that makes something else happen. *See* **effect**. (p. 62)

**CD-ROM** (sē dē rom′) A type of reference source used that is similar to a compact disc that is "read" by a computer. It combines text, sound, and even short films. *See* **reference source**. (p. 260)

**Central Powers** (sen′trəl pow′ərz) The forces led by Germany, Austria-Hungary, and Turkey in World War I. *See* **Allied Powers**. (p. 206)

## pronunciation key

| | | | | | | | |
|---|---|---|---|---|---|---|---|
| a | at | ī | ice | u | up | th | thin |
| ā | ape | îr | pierce | ū | use | <u>th</u> | this |
| ä | far | o | hot | ü | rule | zh | measure |
| âr | care | ō | old | u̇ | pull | ə | about, taken, |
| e | end | ô | fork | ûr | turn | | pencil, lemon, |
| ē | me | oi | oil | hw | white | | circus |
| i | it | ou | out | ng | song | | |

**charter** (chär′tər) An official document giving a person or company permission to do something, such as settle in an area. (p. 142)

**checks and balances** (cheks and bal′ən səz) The system in which the power of each branch of government is balanced by the powers of other branches. (p. 276)

**circle graph** (sûr′kəl graf) A kind of graph that shows how something can be divided into parts. (p. 152)

**civil rights** (siv′əl rīts) The individual rights of all citizens to be treated equally under the law. (p. 232)

**Civil War** (siv′əl wôr) In the United States, the war fought between the Union and the Confederacy from 1861 to 1865. (p. 169)

**climate** (klī′mit) The weather of an area over a number of years. (p. 20)

**coast** (kōst) The land next to an ocean. (p. 9)

**cold flat** (kōld flat) An apartment with only cold water. (p. 185)

**colony** (kol′ə nē) A settlement far away from the country that rules it. (p. 86)

**commute** (kə mūt) To travel back and forth to work. (p. 37)

**compass rose** (kum′pəs rōz) A drawing that indicates directions on a map, especially cardinal and intermediate directions. *See* **cardinal direction** *and* **intermediate direction**. (p. G6)

**competition** (kom′pə ti shən) Other businesses offering consumers a similar product. (p. 252)

**compromise** (kom′prə mīz) The settling of a dispute by each side agreeing to give up part of its demands. (p. 128)

**conclusion** (kən klū′zhən) A statement reached by considering all the information about something. (p. 174)

**Confederacy** (kən fed′ûr ə sē) The government formed by the 11 southern states that seceded from the Union during the Civil War. (p. 169)

**conscience** (kon′shəns) The feeling of right or wrong. (p. 93)

**consequence** (kon′si kwəns) Something produced by a cause. *See* **cause**. (p. 280)

**conservation** (kon sər vā′shən) The protection and careful use of natural resources. (p. 46)

**constitution** (kon sti tü′shən) A plan that explains the parts of a government and outlines the most important laws. (p. 93)

**consumer** (kon sü′mûr) A person who buys a product or uses a service. (p. 250)

**continent** (kon′tə nənt) One of Earth's seven large bodies of land, including Africa, Antarctica, Asia, Australia, Europe, North America, and South America. (p. G4)

**Continental Army** (kon′tə nen təl är′ mē) The army created by the Continental Congress in May 1775 with George Washington as commander-in-chief. *See* **Second Continental Congress**. (p. 110)

**convention** (kən ven′shən) A formal meeting held for a special purpose. (p. 128)

**council** (koun′səl) A group of people who meet to talk and make decisions. (p. 272)

**county** (koun′tē) One of the sections into which a state is divided. (p. 260)

**county seat** (koun′tē sēt) The municipality in which the government of the county is located. *See* **county**. (p. 273)

**culture** (kul′chûr) The entire way of life of a people, including their customs, beliefs, and language. (p. 34)

**current events** (kûr′ənt i vents′) The things that happen every day. (p. 274)

**cyberspace** (sī′bûr spās) The world or environment of computer networks in which on-line communication takes place. (p. 265)

## D

**dateline** (dāt′līn) A line at the beginning of a newspaper article that tells when and where the story was written. (p. 274)

**decision** (dē si′zhən) A choice made from a number of ways of doing something. (p. 40)

**Declaration of Independence** (dek lə rā′shən uv in də pen′dəns) The official document issued by the Second Continental Congress on July 4, 1776, explaining why the American colonies were breaking away from Great Britain. (p. 110)

**degree** (di grē′) A unit of measurement. It can be used for calculating latitude and longitude. *See* **latitude** *and* **longitude**. (p. 82)

**delegate** (del′i gət) A member of an elected assembly. *See* **assembly**. (p. 93)

**democratic republic** (dem ə krat′ik ri pub′lik) A government in which citizens elect representatives to run the government. (p. 282)

**desert** (de′zərt) A dry area that gets less than 10 inches of precipitation each year. (p. 32)

**dictionary** (dik′shə nâr ē) A book that explains the meanings of words and shows how to pronounce and spell them. (p. 260)

**discrimination** (dis kri mi nā′shən) An unfair difference in the treatment of people. (p. 186)

**diversity** (di vûr′si tē) Variety; differences. (p. 290)

**draft** (draft) A plan to select people and force them to serve in the military. (p. 171)

## E

**economy** (i kon′ə mē) The way a country's people use natural resources, money, and knowledge to produce goods and services. (p. 42)

**edge city** (edj si′ tē) A combination of a city and a suburb. (p. 293)

**editorial** (e di tôr′ē əl) A newspaper article or news report in which the editors give their opinions on important issues. (p. 274)

**effect** (i fekt′) Something that happens as a result of a cause. See **cause**. (p. 62)

**elect** (i lekt′) To choose by voting. (p. 270)

**elevation** (el ə vā′shən) The height of an area above sea level. (p. 18)

**e-mail** (ē′māl) Messages that are sent between computers connected through telephone lines by means of a modem. E-mail is a very fast means of communication. The longer name for it is *electronic mail*. (p. 265)

**Emancipation Proclamation** (i man sə pā′shən prok lə mā′shən) An official announcement issued by President Abraham Lincoln in 1862 that led to the end of slavery in the United States. (p. 172)

**encyclopedia** (en sī klə pē′dē ə) A book or set of books that gives information about people, places, things, and past events. (p. 260)

**entrepreneur** (on′trə prə nûr) A person who organizes and runs a business. (p. 250)

**environment** (en vī′rən mənt) All the surroundings in which people, plants, and animals live. (p. 42)

**equator** (i kwā′tûr) An imaginary line encircling Earth halfway between the North Pole and the South Pole, designated as 0° latitude. See **latitude**. (p. G5)

**ethnic group** (eth′nik grüp) People with the same customs and language, often having a common history. (p. 290)

**executive branch** (eg zek′yə tiv branch) The part of government, headed by the President, that carries out the laws. (p. 277)

**explore** (ek′splôr) To travel in unfamiliar places in order to find out and learn about them. (p. 79)

## F

**fact** (fakt) A statement that can be checked and proved true. (p. 114)

**fall line** (fawl līn) The boundary between an upland area and a lowland area. (p. 36)

**feature article** (fē′chûr är′ti kəl) A newspaper story that is a detailed report on a person, an issue, or an event. (p. 274)

**festival** (fes ti′vůl) A celebration. (p. 291)

**fiber optics** (fī′bər op′tiks) A technology that uses special glass cables to send light waves that carry information. (p. 263)

**First Continental Congress** (fûrst kon tə nen′təl kong′ris) The assembly of colonial delegates from every colony except Georgia that met in 1774 in Philadelphia to talk about their problems with Great Britain. See **Second Continental Congress**. (p. 109)

**free enterprise** (frē en′tər prīz) An economic system in which people can own property and businesses and are free to decide what to make, how much to produce, and what price to charge. (p. 250)

**French and Indian War** (french and in′dē ən wôr) A conflict between Great Britain and France in North America from 1756 to 1763. British colonists used this name to describe those they were fighting—the French and their Native American allies. (p. 106)

**fuel** (fū′əl) A substance burned as a source of heat and power, such as coal, wood, or oil. (p. 44)

**Fugitive Slave Act** (fū′jə tiv slāv akt) A law passed by Congress in 1850 that required police in free states to help secure escaping slaves. (p. 167)

## G

**geography** (jē og′rə fē) The study of Earth and the way people live on and use it. (p. 8)

**glacier** (glā′shər) A huge sheet of ice that moves slowly across the land. (p. 58)

**global economy** (glō′bəl i kon′ə mē) An economy in which people, products, and resources move from one country to another. (p. 237)

**global grid** (glō′bəl grid) The crisscrossing lines of latitude and longitude found on a map or globe. See **latitude** *and* **longitude**. (p. 84)

**government** (gu′vûrn mənt) The laws and people that run a country, state, county, city, or town. (p. 43)

**governor** (gu′vûrn ûr) An official appointed or elected to rule a colony or state. (p. 87)

**graph** (graf) A diagram that presents information in a way that makes it easy to detect patterns, trends, or changes over time. (p. 152)

**Great Depression** (grāt di pre′shən) The period of widespread economic hardship in the 1930s. (p. 212)

**Great Migration** (grāt mī grā′ shən) The journey of hundreds of thousands of African Americans from the South to such Northern cities as Chicago that peaked in the early 1900s. (p. 208)

**guide word** (gīd wûrd) One of the words at the top of each page of a reference book that shows the first and last entries on that page. (p. 260)

## H

**headline** (hed′līn) A sentence or phrase printed in large type across the top of a news article to get the reader's attention. (p. 274)

**hemisphere** (hem′i sfîr) One-half of a sphere or globe. Earth can be divided into four hemispheres. The equator divides Earth into the Northern and Southern Hemispheres. The prime meridian divides it into the Eastern and Western Hemispheres. See **equator** *and* **prime meridian**. (p. G5)

**heritage** (her′i tij) The history, beliefs, and way of life that a group of people shares. (p. 67)

**Hessians** (he′shənz) Soldiers from Germany paid to fight for England against the Continental Army in the American Revolution. (p. 118)

**historical map** (hi stôr′ik əl map) A map that shows information about the past or where past events took place. (p. G10)

**history** (his′tə rē) The story or record of what happened in the past. (p. 34)

**hunter-gatherer** (hun′tər gath′ər ər) A person who found food by both hunting animals and gathering plants, fruits, and nuts. (p. 60)

**hurricane** (hûr′i kān) A violent storm with winds above 75 miles per hour revolving around a calm center. It is accompanied by heavy rains, high tides, and flooding in coastal regions. (p. 22)

## I

**Ice Age** (īs āj) A period of time when glaciers covered much of Earth's surface. (p. 58)

**immigrant** (im′i grənt) A person who leaves one country to live in another. (p. 87)

**incidental** (in ci den′təl) By chance. (p. 280)

**income tax** (in′cum taks) A tax on a person's salary. (p. 235)

**indentured servant** (in den′chərd sûr′vənt) A person who agreed to work for someone in colonial America for a fixed amount of time in order to pay for the ocean voyage. (p. 100)

**industry** (in′də strē) All the businesses that make one kind of product or provide one kind of service. (p. 99)

**inlet** (in′let) A recess in the shore of an ocean or river. (p. 17)

**interdependent** (in′tûr dē pen dent) Depending on one another to meet needs and wants. (p. 237)

**intermediate direction** (in tûr mē′dē ət di rek′shən) A direction halfway between two cardinal directions: northeast, northwest, southwest, southeast. See **cardinal direction**. (p. G6)

**Internet** (in′tûr net) A computer network that connects various sources of information such as libraries to a person's home or office computer. (p. 260)

**interstate highway** (in′tûr stāt hī′wā) A road that connects cities in two or more states with at least two lanes of traffic flowing in each direction. (p. 228)

**investor** (in ves′tôr) A person who uses money to buy or make something in order to produce a profit. See **profit**. (p. 251)

## J

**Joint Companies** (joint kum′pə nēz) The combined businesses of the Delaware and Raritan Canal and the Camden and Amboy Railroad. (p. 145)

**judicial branch** (jū dish′ əl branch) The part of government that decides the meanings of the laws. See **United States Supreme Court**. (p. 280)

**jury** (jûr′ē) A group of citizens in a court of law that must decide if someone accused of a crime is innocent or guilty under the law. (p. 285)

## L

**labor union** (lā′bûr ūn′yən) A group of workers united to gain better wages and working conditions. (p. 178)

**landform** (land′fôrm) A shape on Earth's surface, such as a mountain or hill. (p. 8)

**landform map** (land′fôrm map) A map that shows the landforms of an area. See **landform**. (p. G10)

**latitude** (lat′i tūd) An imaginary line, or parallel, measuring distance north or south of the equator. See **equator** *and* **parallel**. (p. 82)

**legislative branch** (leg′is lā tiv branch) The lawmaking part of government, with the power to raise the money needed to run the government. (p. 278)

**Lenape** (le′nä pē) Native American tribe who lived throughout New Jersey and in parts of Delaware, Pennsylvania, and New York. (p. 64)

**line graph** (līn graf) A kind of graph that shows changes over time. (p. 152)

**locator** (lō′kā tûr) A small map inset in the corner of a larger map that helps you understand where the subject area of the larger map is located on Earth. (p. G8)

**longhouse** (long′hous) A long, covered building in a Native American village that housed several families together. (p. 72)

### pronunciation key

a **at**; ā **ape**; ä **far**; âr **care**; e **end**; ē **me**; i **it**; ī **ice**; îr **pierce**; o **hot**; ō **old**; ô **fork**; oi **oil**; ou **out**; u **up**; ū **use**; ü **rule**, ů **pull**; ûr **turn**; hw **white**; ng **song**; th **thin**; th **this**; zh **measure**; ə **about**, **taken**, **pencil**, **lemon**, **circus**

**longitude** (lon′ji tud) An imaginary line, or meridian, measuring distance east and west of the prime meridian. *See* **meridian** *and* **prime meridian**. (p. 83)

**Loyalist** (loi′əl ist) A colonist who supported Great Britain in the American Revolution. (p. 117)

## M

**manetu** (man′ə tu) The Lenape word for the many different spirit forces that they believed controlled the world. (p. 67)

**manufacturing** (man yə fak′chə ring) The making of goods by machinery. (p. 148)

**map key** (map kē) A guide telling you what each symbol on a map stands for. (p. G7)

**marsh** (märsh) An area of low, wet land covered mostly with tall grasses. (p. 30)

**mass production** (mas prō duk′shən) The manufacture of large numbers of goods using identical parts and assembly line methods. (p. 223)

**mayor** (mā′ûr) An elected head of government of a city. (p. 272)

**megalopolis** (me gə lop′ō lis) A group of cities that have grown so close together they seem to form one city. (p. 292)

**meridian** (mə rid′ē ən) Any line of longitude east or west of Earth's prime meridian. *See* **longitude** *and* **prime meridian**. (p. 83)

**militia** (mə lish′ə) A group of volunteers who fought in times of emergency during the colonial period and the American Revolution. (p. 109)

**mineral** (min′ûr əl) A substance found in Earth that is neither plant nor animal. (p. 44)

**monopoly** (mə no′pō lē) A company that controls an entire industry. (p. 144)

**mouth** (mouth) The place where a river empties into a larger body of water. (p. 15)

**municipality** (myū nis ə pal′i tē) A community with its own government: a borough, township, city, town, or village. (p. 272)

## N

**natural resource** (na′chər əl rē′sôrs) A material found in nature that people use to meet their needs and wants. (p. 42)

**New Deal** (nü dēl) Government programs started by President Franklin D. Roosevelt in the 1930s to aid business, farms, and the unemployed to recover from the Great Depression. (p. 214)

**New Idea** (nü ī dē′ə) A plan to reform government by defeating bosses, punishing businesses that bribed officials, and making businesses pay a fairer share of taxes. (p. 199)

**New Jersey Plan** (nü jûr′zē plan) The plan offered by the small states at the Constitutional Convention of 1787 that would have given all states an equal number of representatives in Congress. (p. 128)

**news article** (nūz är′ti kəl) A newspaper story that factually describes an important recent event. (p. 274)

**nonrenewable resources** (non ri nü′ə bəl rē′ sôr səz) Materials found in nature that cannot be replaced, such as coal, oil, or natural gas. (p. 44)

## O

**ocean** (ō′shən) One of Earth's four large bodies of water. They are the Arctic, Atlantic, Indian, and Pacific Oceans. (p. G4)

**opinion** (ə pin′yən) A personal view or belief. (p. 114)

**oral tradition** (ôr′əl tra di′ shən) A way of preserving a culture by passing information along through word of mouth and stories. (p. 73)

**outline** (out′līn) A plan for organizing written information about a subject. (p. 99)

## P

**parallel** (pâr′ə lel) A line of latitude. *See* **latitude**. (p. 82)

**patent** (pa′tənt) A document issued by the government that gives the inventor the right to make, use, or sell an invention. (p. 177)

**Patriot** (pā′trē ət) An American colonist who supported the fight for independence. (p. 117)

**patroon** (pa trün′) A landowner in New Netherland who had to bring 50 settlers to the colony to help settle his land. (p. 87)

**peninsula** (pə nin′sū lə) A piece of land nearly surrounded by water or sticking out into the water. (p. 10)

**physical map** (fiz′i kəl map) A map that highlights Earth's natural features. (p. G10)

**plain** (plān) An area of flat or nearly flat land. (p. 31)

**political map** (pə lit′i kəl map) A map that shows the boundaries of states and countries. (p. G9)

**political party** (pə lit′i kəl pär′tē) A group of people who share similar ideas about government. (p. 200)

**pollution** (pə lü′shən) Anything that dirties the air, soil, or water. (p. 46)

**population** (po pyə lā′shən) The total number of people who live in a particular area or place. (p. 35)

**population density** (po pyə lā′shən den′si tē) A measure of how many people live in a certain place, usually within a square mile. (p. 292)

**port** (pôrt) A place where ships load and unload their goods. (p. 17)

**precipitation** (pri sip i tā′shən) The moisture that falls to Earth as rain, snow, sleet, or hail. (p. 21)

**prehistory** (prē his′tə rē) The time before written records. (p. 59)

**primary** (prī′mə rē) An election in which all party members choose a candidate. (p. 200)

**primary source** (prī′mə rē sôrs) A firsthand account of an event or an artifact created during the period of history that is being studied. *See* **artifact** *and* **secondary source**. (p. 204)

**prime meridian** (prīm mə rid′ē ən) The line of longitude labeled 0° longitude. Any place east of the prime meridian is labeled E; any place west of it is labeled W. *See* **longitude**. (p. 83)

**professional** (prə fesh′nəl) Doing something, such as playing sports, as a job, and not just for fun. (p. 297)

**profit** (pro′fit) The money remaining after the costs of a business have been paid. (p. 250)

**proprietor** (prə prī′ət ûr) A person who owns a property or a business. (p. 91)

**public** (pub′lik) Anything that is partly or fully supported by taxes. (p. 302)

## R

**rain shadow** (rān sha′dō) The side of a mountain that is usually dry because the precipitation falls on the other side. (p. 33)

**ratify** (rat′i fī) To give official approval, for example, to the Constitution or amendments to it. (p. 129)

**recreation** (re krē ā′shən) What people do for relaxation and enjoyment. (p. 296)

**recycle** (rē sī′kəl) To save discarded items, such as cans or bottles, so that they can be used again. (p. 46)

**reference source** (re′fər ens sôrs) A book or other source that contains facts about many different subjects. (p. 260)

**reform** (ri fôrm′) A change to make government or business work better. (p. 154)

**region** (rē′jən) A large area with common features that set it apart from other areas. (p. 28)

**religion** (ri li′jən) The way people worship God, a god, or gods they believe in. (p. 67)

**renewable resource** (ri nü′ə bəl rē′sôrs) A natural resource that can be replaced, such as forests. (p. 43)

**research and development** (rē′sûrch and di vel′ əp mənt) The process of coming up with new ideas for the creation of new products. (p. 263)

**reservoir** (rez′ər vwär) A natural or human-built lake used to store water. (p. 38)

**road map** (rōd map) A map that indicates cities, highways, and points of interest and shows you how to get from one place to another. (p. 228)

**rural** (rûr′əl) Having to do with the countryside. (p. 35)

## S

**sakima** (sə kē′mə) A wise man or woman in a Lenape village whom the people turned to for advice and guidance. (p. 72)

**scale** (skāl) A guide that explains the relationship between real distances on Earth and distances on a map. (p. G8)

**secede** (sə sēd′) To break away from a group, such as the Southern states seceding from the Union in 1861. (p. 169)

**Second Continental Congress** (sek′ənd kon tə nen′təl kong′ris) A meeting in Philadelphia in 1775 of delegates from all 13 colonies that established a colonial army and declared American independence. *See* **Continental Army** *and* **Declaration of Independence**. (p. 110)

**secondary source** (sek′ən dər ē sôrs) An account of the past based on information from primary sources and written by someone who was not an eyewitness to those events. *See* **primary source**. (p. 204)

**segregation** (seg rə gā′shən) The separation of people, usually based on race or religion. (p. 231)

**service** (sûr′vis) A job in which a person's work is helping others, rather than making things. (p. 236)

**slavery** (slā′vrē) The practice of people owning other people and forcing them to work. (p. 87)

**software** (soft′wâr) A program or set of instructions that tells a computer what to do. (p. 265)

**source** (sôrs) The place where a river begins. (p. 15)

**special district** (spe′shůl dis′trikt) An area in which a particular service is provided for the people who live there. (p. 272)

**Special Olympics** (spe′shůl ə lim′piks) A nationwide organization that provides athletic training and competition for children and adults with disabilities. (p. 297)

**Stamp Act** (stamp akt) A law passed by the British Parliament in 1765 requiring colonists to pay a tax on newspapers, pamphlets, legal documents, and even playing cards. (p. 108)

**pronunciation key**

a **at**; ā **ape**; ä **far**; âr **care**; e **end**; ē **me**; i **it**; ī **ice**; îr **pierce**; o **hot**; ō **old**; ô **fork**; oi **oil**; ou **out**; u **up**; ū **use**; ü **rule**, ů **pull**; ûr **turn**; hw **white**; ng **song**; th **thin**; th **this**; zh **measure**; ə **about**, **taken**, **pencil**, **lemon**, **circus**

**states' rights** (stāts rīts) The belief that each state should be allowed to make its own decisions about issues affecting it. (p. 168)

**strike** (strīk) A refusal of all the workers in a business to work until the owners meet their demands. (p. 151)

**suburb** (sub'ûrb) A community just outside a large city. (p. 222)

**suffrage** (suf'frij) The right to vote. (p. 155)

**swamp** (swomp) A wetland with many trees. (p. 30)

**symbol** (sim'bəl) Something that stands for something else. (p. G7)

## T

**tax** (taks) Money people pay to a government so that it can perform public services. (p. 108)

**telecommunications** (te li kə myū nə kā'shənz) Sending information long distances by telephone and television. (p. 256)

**temperature** (tem'pûr chûr) The measurement of heat and cold. (p. 21)

**time line** (tīm līn) A diagram showing the order in which events happened. (p. 96)

**toll** (tōl) A small fee people pay to use a canal, bridge, or road. (p. 142)

**tourism** (tôr'iz em) The business of providing services for tourists, or people who travel for fun or to learn about new places. (p. 256)

**transistor** (tranz is'tôr) A very small electronic device that controls the electric current in television sets, radios, computers, and other equipment. (p. 224)

**transportation** (tranz pûr tā'shən) The moving of goods or people from one place to another. (p. 10)

**transportation map** (tranz pûr tā'shən map) A map that shows how to travel from one place to another. (p. G10)

**tributary** (tri'byə ter ē) Any river that flows into another, larger river. (p. 15)

**turnpike** (tûrn'pīk) A road on which a person must pay a toll to travel. (p. 142)

## U

**Underground Railroad** (un'dər ground rāl'rōd) A system of secret routes used by escaping slaves to reach freedom in the North or in Canada. (p. 164)

**Union** (ūn'yən) The states that make up the United States. Used during the Civil War to refer to the government of the Northern states. (p. 169)

**United States Congress** (ū nī'təd stāts kong'ris) The legislative branch of the United States government. (p. 284)

**United States Supreme Court** (ū nī'təd stāts sə prēm' kôrt) The highest court of the United States, which heads the judicial branch of the United States government. (p. 284)

**urban** (ûr'bən) Having to do with a city and the communities that surround it. (p. 35)

**veto** (vē'tō) To refuse to approve. (p. 266)

## W

**War of 1812** (wôr uv ā'tēn twelv) The war between the United States and Great Britain from 1812 to 1815. (p. 50)

**waterway** (wô'tûr wā) A system of streams and rivers that connect communities to one another. (p. 14)

**weather** (weth'ûr) The condition of the air at a certain time and place. (p. 20)

**wetland** (wet'land) An area such as a swamp or marsh where water is at or close to the surface of the ground. (p. 10)

**wigwam** (wig'wäm) A one-room Native American hut, usually round-shaped, made of poles covered with bark, skins, or woven grass. (p. 72)

**World War I** (wûrld wôr wun) A war that began in Europe in 1914 between the Central Powers and the Allied Powers, who were joined by the United States in 1917. *See* **Allied Powers** *and* **Central Powers**. (p. 206)

**World War II** (wûrld wôr tü) War between the Axis Powers and the Allies that involved most of the countries of the world. It was fought from 1939 to 1945. The United States joined the Allies on December 8, 1941. *See* **Allies** *and* **Axis Powers**. (p. 216)

# index

This index lists many topics that appear in the book, along with the pages on which they are found. Page numbers after an *m* refer you to a map. Page numbers after a *p* indicate photographs, artwork, or charts.

## A



## B

## C



## D

## S



## T

## U



## V



## W



## Y



## Z

**Cover:** MHSD

**Maps:** MapQuest.com, Inc.

**Electronic Production:** Visual Education Corporation

**Chapter Opener Globes:** Greg Wakabayashi

**Illustrations:** Moffitt Cecil: pp 16, 72, 143, 150; Max Crandall: pp 16, 37, 89, 144, 157, 224, 279, 298; Gershom Griffith: pp 160–161; Joe Lemonnier: p 69; Mike Maydak: pp R22–R23; Den Schofield: pp 56–57; Charles Shaw: pp 138–139, 196–197, 220–221; Steve Sullivan: pp 22, 36, 37, 38, 39, 45, 258–259; Mike Tofanelli: p 122; Robert Van Nutt: p 166; Stephen Wells: pp 76–77, 104–105

**Photography Credits:** All photographs are by the McGraw-Hill School Division except as noted below.

**Chapter 1:** 2: c.: Phil Deggenger/Bruce Coleman, Inc.; 2: b.: David Frazier/ Photo Researchers, Inc.; 2: t. inset: E. R. Degginger/Color–Pic, Inc.; 3: b.r.: E. R. Degginger/Color–Pic, Inc.; 4: m.l.: Kelly/Mooney Photography; 4: b.l.: Kelly/Mooney Photography; 4–5: 2 p. spread: David Muench; 5: t.l.: Joe McDonald/CORBIS; 5: b.l.: Bill Curtsinger; 7: t.: Walter Choroszewski; 7: m.l.: Walter Choroszewski; 7: m.r.: Walter Choroszewski; 7: b.: Nancy and Bill Erickson/New Wave Photography; 8: t.l.: John Henley/The Stock Market; 9: b.: G. Ahrens/H. Armstrong Roberts; 10: b.: G. Ahrens/H. Armstrong Roberts; 11: t.l.: E.R. Degginger/Color–Pic, Inc.; 11: m.: Walter Choroszewski; 11: t.c.: E.R. Degginger/Color–Pic, Inc.; 12: b.l.: E.R. Degginger/ Color–Pic, Inc.; 12–13: b.m.: G. Ahrens/H. Armstrong Roberts; 13: t.: E.R. Degginger/Color–Pic, Inc.; 13: b.r.: P. Degginger; 13: m.r.: E.R. Degginger/ Color–Pic, Inc.; 14: t.l.: E.R. Degginger/Color–Pic, Inc.; 14: m.: John T. Kraft, Waterloo Village; 14–15: b.: Nancy L. Erickson/New Wave Photography; 15: l.: Bettmann/CORBIS; 15: t.c.: American Labor Museum/Botto House National Landmark; 17: b.: Cliff Moore; 18: b.: Carr Clifton; 20: t.l.: R. Walker/H. Armstrong Roberts; 20–21: b.: H. Abernathy/H. Armstrong Roberts; 22: m.: WWOR-TV; 23: b.l.: Reuters New Media Inc./Corbis. **Chapter 2:** 27: b.: Scott Barrow Photography; 27: t.: Scott Barrow Photography; 27: c.t.: J. Nettis / H. Armstrong Roberts; 27: c.b.: Phil Degginger / Color–Pic, Inc.; 28: t.l.: Jim Simmern/Tony Stone Images; 30: b.l.: Philip Gould; 30: b.r.: Stephen Kirkpatrick; 31: t.l.: Felicia Martinez/PhotoEdit; 31: t.r.: Chuck Pefley/Tony Stone Images; 32: m.r.: Tom Till/Tony Stone Images; 32: b.: Tom Bean/Tony Stone Images; 33: t.l.: SuperStock; 34: t.l.: Richard Hutchings; 34: b.r.: Phil Degginger/Color–Pic, Inc.; 35: b.l.: Scott Barrow; 36: b.r.: Cape May County Department of Tourism; 36: b.l.: Cape May County Department of Tourism; 37: t.l.: Steve C. Healey; 38: b.r.: Michelle Goman; 38: b.: Jerry Irwin/Uniphoto Picture Agency; 39: t.l.: Walter Choroszewski; 39: t.m.: E.R. Degginger/Color–Pic, Inc.; 40–41: b.: Cliff Moore; 41: m.l.: William R. Wright/H. Armstrong Roberts; 42: t.l.: Ralph Krubner/H. Armstrong Roberts; 43: b.l.: SuperStock; 43: b.r.: Bob Daemmrich/Stock Boston; 44: b.: E.R. Degginger/Color–Pic, Inc.; 47: b.r.: Ruth Brennfleck; 47: b.l.: Ruth Brennfleck; 47: b.r.: Ruth Brennfleck; 47: b.m.: Ruth Brennfleck; 49: t.r.: AP Photo/Tina Markoe/Courier Post. **Chapter 3:** 51: b.r.: Cliff Moore; 52: r.: Lee Snider/Photo Images; 52: b.l.: MHSD Photo, Courtesy Bergen County Historical Society, River Edge, N.J.; 52: t.l.: Northwind Picture Archives; 53: b.l.: Rae Russel/Int'l. Stock Photo; 54: t.: Bergen County Historical Society; 54: b.: Lee Snider/CORBIS; 54–55: 2 pg spread: Kelly/Mooney Photography; 55: t.l.: Powhatan Renape Nation; 58: t.l.: Dr. Herbert C. Kraft, Seton Hall University; 58–59: b.: Courtesy Dept. of Library Services, American Museum of Natural History; 59: b.l.: New Jersey State Archives, Department of State; 60: b.: Corbis-Bettmann; 62–63: b.: Sean Reid/Alaska Stock; 64: t.l.: John T. Kraft, Waterloo Village; 65: b.r.: Walter Choroszewski; 66: very t.r.: Grant Heilman/Grant Heilman Photography; 66: b.r.: MHSD; 66: m.: Raymond Bial; 66: m.l.: Thaw Collection, Fenimore Art Museum, Cooperstown, NY. Photography by John Bigelow Taylor. ; 66: b.l.: Sara Matthews; 66: t.r.: John T. Kraft/Waterloo Village; 67: m.: Walter Choroszewski; 68: t.: Sara Matthews; 68–69: b.l.: Lee Snider/Photo Images; 68–69: b.m.: Michael S. Yamashita/CORBIS; 69: t.r.: Walter Choroszewski; 69: b.r.: Cliff Moore; 70: t.l.: John T. Kraft, Waterloo Village; 70–71: b.: John T. Kraft, Waterloo Village; 73: b.: Walter Choroszewski; 75: t.r.: Caddoan Mounds State Historical Park. **Chapter 4:** 78: t.l.: Vanni Genova/Art Resource, NY; 78–79: b.: National Geographic Society; 80: b.: The Granger Collection, New York; 81: t.l.: Lynda Richardson/Peter Arnold, Inc.; 86: t.l.: Jose Azel/Aurora/PictureQuest; 86: b.r.: Al Clayton/Stock South/PictureQuest; 86/87: b.l.: Superstock; 88: b.r.: Geoffrey Grossman; 88: b.m.: Courtesy, Bergen County Historical Society, River Edge, N.J.; 90: t.l.: The Granger Collection, New York; 91: b.: Delaware Art Museum, Howard Pyle Collection; 92: b.r.: The Granger Collection, New York; 93: m.r.: The Council of Proprietors of West New Jersey; 94: t.r.: The Granger Collection, New York; 94: m.l.: Richard T. Nowitz/CORBIS; 94: m.r.: The Granger Collection, New York; 94: b.l.: Newberry Library, Chicago/Superstock; 94: b.r.: Lee Snider/Photo Images; 95: m.: The Bridgeman Art Library; 98: t.l.: Walter Choroszewski; 99: m.: The Winterthur Museum; 100–101: b.: Scott Barrow; 101: b. inset: Landis Valley Museum, Lancaster, PA/Pennsylvania Historical & Museum Commission. **Chapter 5:** 106: t.l.: Lee Snider; 106–107: b.: Lee Snider; 108: t.r.: The Granger Collection; 109: t.l.: The Granger Collection; 109: b.l.: The Granger Collection; 109: b.r.: painting by Gertrude Albertson Huber courtesy Cumberland County Historical Society; 110: m.r.: Culver Pictures; 110: b.: H. Armstrong Roberts; 111: t.l.: New Jersey State Archives, Department of State; 112: t.: North Wind Pictures; 113: t.r.: National Geographic Image Collection; 113: b.r.: Brown Brothers; 114: b.r.: The Granger Collection, New York; 115: b.l.: The Granger Collection, New York; 116: t.l.: Kelly-Mooney Photography/Corbis; 117: b.r.: The Granger Collection, New York; 118–119: b.: Art Resource, NY; 119: t.r.: The Granger Collection, New York; 120: b.r.: Scott Barrow; 120: t.l.: Culver Pictures; 120–121: b.: The Granger Collection, New York; 121: m. inset: The Granger Collection, New York; 121: t.l.: The Granger Collection, New York; 121: b.l. inset: The Granger Collection, New York; 121: m.r. inset: E.R. Degginger/Color–Pic, Inc.; 123: b.l.: N. Carter/North Wind; 124: m.: Lawnside Historical Society; 124–125: b.: United States Navy Official File Photo (BB–62); 125: b.r.: Walter Choroszewski; 125: t.l.: Kelly/Mooney Photography; 125: t.l.: Walter Choroszewski; 125: m.l.: Lee Snider; 126: t.l.: The Granger Collection, New York; 127: b.l.: Nawrocki Stock Photo; 127: b.r.: The Granger Collection, New York; 128–129: b.r.: D. Degnan/H. Armstrong Roberts; 129: m.l.: Northwind Picture Archives; 133: b.r.: Cliff Moore. **Chapter 6:** 134: t.r.: Double Exposure Two, Ploughshare Press, By Permission of George Moss; 134: b.l.: MHSD Photo; 134–5: Andy Williwams/H. Armstrong Roberts; 135: r.: Corbis/Bettman; 136: m.l.: Bettman/CORBIS; 136: b.l.: Ellis Island Keystone-Mast Collection, UCR/California Museum of Photography, University of California at Riverside; 136–137: b.: Brown Brothers; 136–137: 2 full pages: CORBIS Sygma; 137: t.l.: Rick Friedman/Black Star/ PictureQuest; 140: t.l.: Anne Keiser/National Geographic Society; 141: b.: The Granger Collection, New York; 141: m.r.: Newark Public Library/Armen Photographers; 144–145: b.: Courtesy New Jersey Room, Fairleigh Dickinson University; 145: b. inset: Culver Pictures; 148: t.l.: Chromosohm/Joe Sohm/The Stock Market; 148–149: b.: Library of Congress; 149: m.: Library of Congress; 150: m.: The Passaic County Historical Society; 151: t.r.: Rudi Von Briel; 154: t.l.: Mark E. Gibson/Visuals Unlimited; 155: m.r.: Stock Montage, Inc.; 156: b.: Mary Evans Picture Library, London; 156: m.r.: The Granger Collection, New York. **Chapter 7:** 162: t.l.: The Granger Collection, New York; 163: m.l.: North Wind Pictures; 163: b.: Bettman Archive/CORBIS; 163: m.r.: North Wind Pictures; 165: t.r.: Louis Psihoyos/Matrix; 165: b.r.: The Granger Collection, New York; 167: t.r.: The Monmouth County Historical Association; 168: t.l.: Terence P. O'Leary; Copied by Alfreda Robinson; 170–171: b.r.: The Granger Collection, New York; 171: t.: Medford Historical Society Collection/CORBIS; 172: b.: Archive Photos; 172–173: t.: CORBIS; 174: t.r.: CORBIS-BETTMANN; 175: b.: Gettysburg National Military Park; 176: t.l.: The Granger Collection, New York; 176–177: b.: Culver Pictures; 178: b.: Courtesy Paterson Museum; 178–179: b.: Archive Photos; 180: b.m.: SEF/Art Resource, NY; 180: b.r.: Stock Montage; 180: t.l.: David Allen/CORBIS; 181: m.r.: Becky Luigart-Slayner; 181: m.l.: Courtesy of The Whitesbog Preservation Trust; 181: b.r.: Brown Brothers; 181: b.l.: UPI/CORBIS-BETTMAN; 181: t.r.: CORBIS-BETTMAN; 182: t.l.: Courtesy George Eastman House; 182–183: b.: The Granger Collection, New York; 184: b.l.: The Granger Collection, New York; 184: f.p.: Phil Degginger/Color–Pic, Inc.; 184: b.r.: Bettman/CORBIS; 184: m.r.: Museum of the City of New York; 184: t.r.: Underwood & Underwood/CORBIS; 185: b.: Culver Pictures; 186: t.l.: The Granger Collection, New York; 187: b.r.: Courtesy Latinas Unidas; 191: b.r.: Cliff Moore. **Chapter 8:** 192: b.l. inset: Superstock; 192: r.: Corbis Bettmann; 192: m.l. : Corbis/Bettmann; 192: t.l. inset: Ohio Historical Society; 193: l.: Stock Montage/Picture Quest; 194: t.: Forbert, Photri-Microstock; 194: m.l.: Brian Gordon Green; 194: b.l.: Walter Choroszewski; 194: b.r.: Brian Gordon Green; 195: t.l.: Kelly/Mooney Photography; 195: b.l.: Peter Genovese; 198: t.l.: Culver Pictures; 198: b.r.: McGraw-Hill School Division; 199: b.: CORBIS/BETTMANN; 201: b.: Bettmann/CORBIS; 201: m.r.: American Labor Museum/Botto House National Landmark; 202: b.: Newark Public Library; 203: t.l.: The Granger Collection, New York; 205: b.: The Granger Collection, New York; 206: t.l.: Brown Brothers; 206–207: b.: The Granger Collection, New York; 209: b.: The Phillips Collection, Washington, DC; 210: m.: Brown Brothers; 210: t.: The Granger Collection, New York; 210–211: b.: Walter Choroszewski; 212: t.l.: Bettmann/CORBIS; 212–213: b.: Brown Brothers; 214: b.: Culver Pictures; 215: b.: Ricardo Barros, Courtesy of the Roosevelt Arts Project; 215: m.l.: Newark Public Library; 215: t.: Millville Historical Society; 216: b.l.: Hulton-Deutsch Collection/CORBIS; 216: b.r.: Library of Congress. **Chapter 9:** 222: t.l.: Superstock; 223: b.l.: Superstock; 223: b.: Superstock; 224–225: b.: Roger Wood/CORBIS; 226: t.: R. Kord/H. Armstrong Roberts; 227: b.r.: Courtesy Lynn Wilkins; 227: t.r.: Courtesy Donna McDonough; 227: m.r.: Courtesy Pam Fischer; 229: b.: John Serafin for MHSD; 230: t.l.: Archive Photos; 231: b.l.:

Bettmann/CORBIS; 232: b.l.: Brown Brothers; 233: b.l.: CORBIS/Bettmann; 233: t.: CORBIS/BETTMANN-UPI; 233: b.r.: CORBIS; 235: t.l.: AP/Wide World Photos; 236: t.l.: Vince Streano; 238–239: b.: J. Nettis/H. Armstrong Roberts; 238–239: t.r.: Carol Kitman; 243: b.r.: Cliff Moore. **Chapter 10:** 244: m.l.: Stephen Frisch/Stock Boston/Picture Quest; 244: t.r.: Corbis/Bettmann; 244: b.l. inset: Jon Feingersh/The Stock Market; 244–245: c. spread: AP Photo/Frank Gunn; 245: r.: Lisa Quinones/Black Star/Picture Quest; 246: b.: Thomas Anthony DeFeo; 246: b.: Joseph Sohm; ChromoSohm Inc./CORBIS; 246: b.: Kelly/Mooney Photography; 246–247: 2 page spread: Kelly/Mooney Photography; 247: b.l.: Courtesy Lucent Technologies; 247: b.: Robert Maas/CORBIS; 249: c. t.: Associated Press AP Pool; 249: t.: Joseph Sohm/ChromoSohm/Corbis; 249: b.: Sheldan Collins/Corbis; 249: c.b.: Donald Sietz/Stock Boston/Picture Quest; 250: t.l.: McGraw-Hill School Division; 251: b.: McGraw-Hill School Division; 252: l.: McGraw-Hill School Division; 252: m.: McGraw-Hill School Division; 252: b.r.: McGraw-Hill School Division; 254: t.l.: Pete Saloutos; 254–255: b.: Mitch Kezar/Tony Stone Images; 256: m.r.: Larry Mulvehill/The Image Works; 256: m.l.: Bruce Ayres/Tony Stone Images; 256: b.l.: Michael S. Yamashita/CORBIS; 257: b. far l.: Medford Taylor/National Geographic; 257: b.r.: Mark E. Gibson; 257: m.: E.R. Degginger/Color–Pic, Inc.; 257: t.r.: Cliff Moore; 260: b.r.: Sara Matthews; 261: b.: McGraw-Hill School Division; 262: t.l.: CORBIS; 263: m.r.: Superstock; 263: N/A: Kit Kittle; 264: t.r.: McGraw-Hill School Division; 267: t.r.: Bob Daemmrich/The Image Works. **Chapter 11:** 268–69: r. spread: Andre Jenny/Focus Group/Picture Quest; 270: t.l.: Courtesy Karen Kurick, Mayor's Office, Monroe Township; 270: b.r.: John Serafin for McGraw-Hill School Division; 270–271: b.: John Serafin for McGraw-Hill School Division; 271: m.r.: Richard Hutchings/Photo Edit; 273: t.l.: McGraw-Hill School Division; 274: b.r.: McGraw-Hill School Division; 275: b.m.: Lori Adamski Peek/Stone; 276: t.l.: Associated Press AP; 277: b.l.: AP/Wide World Photos; 279: b.: Jerry Howard/ Stock, Boston/PictureQuest; 280: b.l.: AP/Wide World Photos; 281: b.: Ruth Brennfleck; 282: t.l.: Russell D. Curtis/Photo Researchers; 282–283: b.: Greg Pease/Panoramic Images; 285: t.l.: Photography by Richard Strauss, Smithsonian Institution, Courtesy the Supreme Court; 287: t.r.: McGraw-Hill School Division. **Chapter 12:** 288: t.r.: Mark Burnett/Stock Boston; 288: b.r.: Myrleen Ferguson/Photo Edit; 288: m.r.: MHSD; 289: b.r.: David Stover/Uniphoto; 289: m.l.: Myrleen Feruson/Photo Edit; 289: t.r.: MHSD; 289: b.l.: Myrleen Ferguson/Photo Edit; 289: t.l.: MHSD; 289: m.r.: David Young-Wolff/Photo Edit; 290: t.l.: Chuck Savage/ The Stock Market; 291: b.: Carol Kitman; 291: b.l.: David M. Grossman/Photo Researchers, Inc.; 292: t.l.: Superstock; 292: t.r.: Walter Choroszewski; 295: b.r.: Cathy Crawford/CORBIS; 296: t.l.: AP/Wide World Photos; 296–297: b.: Mark Lewis/Liaison International; 297: b.l.: Bruce Bennett Studios; 297: B C inset: Paul A. Souders/Corbis; 297: b.r.: Courtesy Trenton Thunder; 298: m.r.: Kelly-Mooney Photography/CORBIS; 298–299: b.: Julie Houck/Stock Boston; 299: m.r.: Mark Junak/Tony Stone Images; 299: m.: CORBIS; 300: b.: Pedrick/The Image Works; 300: m.l.: CORBIS; 300–301: : Sara Matthews; 301: m.r.: CORBIS; 301: b.l.: Steven Needham/Envision; 301: m.l.: Lee Snider/The Image Works; 301: t.l.: Louis Portnoy/Uniphoto Picture Agency/Pictor; 301: t.m.: CORBIS; 301: t. far l.: Sara Matthews; 302: t.l.: Courtesy University of California/San Diego; 303: b.: PictureQuest; 303: m.r.: Superstock; 304: m.l.: Archive Photo; 305: t.: Fred Charles/The Gamma Liason Network; 305: b.l.: George Campos/Liaison Agency; 305: b.l.: CORBIS/Bettmann; 307: t.r.: McGraw-Hill School Division; 309: b.r.: Cliff Moore. **Reference Section:** G2: b.l.: Carol Kitman; G2: b.r.: Kelly/Mooney Photography; G3: t.l.: Pete Souza; G3: b.l.: Bob Krist; G3: r.: Martha Cooper; G4: m.: MHSD; iii: b.m.: E.R. Degginger/Color–Pic, Inc.; iii: b.l.: Scott Barrow; iii: b.l.: Walter Choroszewski; iv: b.l.: Walter Choroszewski; iv: b.: Art Resource, NY; iv: t.l.: Caddoan Mounds State Historical Park; ix: m.: The Granger Collection, New York; R3: b.l.: The Granger Collection, New York; R22: b.r.: Wally McNamee/CORBIS; R22: t.l.: Reuters Newmedia Inc./CORBIS; R22: t.r.: Patrick McMullan/The Gamma Liaison Network; R22: b.l.: Mitchell Gerber/CORBIS; R23: t.r.: AFP/CORBIS; R23: b.r.: Diana Walker/The Gamma Liason Network; R23: t.l.: Martine Daniel/CORBIS; R23: b.m.: Neal Preston/CORBIS; R23: m.l.: Judi Wolford/Office of the Democratic Caucus Vice Chair; R23: t.m.: Mitchell Gerber/CORBIS; R24: b.r.: Reuters Newmedia Inc./CORBIS; R24: t.r.: AFP/CORBIS; R24: b.l.: Courtesy Special Olympics New Jersey, photo by Frank Gensheimer; R24: t.l.: Scott Cunningham/The Liaison Agency Network; R24: m.: R. Maiman/SYGMA; R25: t.r.: Walter Choroszewski; R25: t.l.: Joseph Sohm, ChromoSohm, Inc./CORBIS; R25: b.r.: CORBIS; R25: full page: CORBIS; R25: m.l.: David Frazier/Photo Researchers, Inc.; R25: b.m.: Lee Snider; R25: m.l.: CORBIS; v: b.l.: Courtesy George Eastman House; v: t.r.: Anne Keiser/ National Geographic Society; v: b.r.: CORBIS-BETTMANN; vi: t.l.: Bettmann/CORBIS; vi: b.l.: Brown Brothers; vi: b.l.: Superstock; vii: t.r.: Richard Hutchings/Photo Edit; vii: m.l.: AP/Wide World Photos; vii: b.: Julie Houck/Stock Boston; viii: b.r.: Steven Needham/Envision; xii: m.: Mark E. Gibson/Visuals Unlimited; xiii: m.: Stock Montage, Inc.

**ACKNOWLEDGMENTS (continued)**

Rutgers, The State University of New Jersey. From *The Lenape or Delaware Indians* by Herbert Kraft. Copyright © 1987, 1996 Herbert Kraft. From *The Indians of Lenapehoking.* Copyright © 1985 Lenape Books. From *I Columbus, My Journal 1492–93* by Peter and Connie Roop. Copyright © 1990 Walker and Co. From *New Jersey: America's Main Road* by John T. Cunningham, copyright © 1956, 1966. From *An Ecological History of New Jersey.* Copyright © 1996 New Jersey Historical Commission. From *U.S. Colonial History.* Copyright © 1966 by the Bobbs-Merrill Company, Inc. From *Colonial New Jersey* by John T. Cunningham, copyright © 1971 Thomas Nelson, Inc. From *Colonial America: A History, 1607–1760* by Richard Middleton. Copyright © 1992 Richard Middleton. Published by Blackwell of Cambridge. From *A New Jersey Anthology* edited by Maxine Lurie. Copyright © 1994 New Jersey Historical Society. From *Girls: A History of Growing Up Female* by Penny Coleman. Published by Scholastic Trade. Copyright © 2000. From *The American Tory* by Morten Borden and Penn Borden. Copyright © 1972 Prentice Hall. From *The Papers of William Livingston, Vol. 2, July 1777–December 1778* edited by Carl E. Prince and Dennis P. Ryan. Copyright © 1980 New Jersey Historical Commission. From *The Diary of the American Revolution 1775–1781* compiled by Frank Moore. Copyright © 1967 John Anthony Scott. Published by Washington Square Press. From *New Jersey and the Revolutionary War* by Alfred Hoyt Bill. Copyright © 1964 The New Jersey Tercentenary Commission. Published by D. Van Nostrand Company Ltd. From *New Jersey: A History.* Copyright © 1977, 1984 the American Association for State and Local History. Published by W. W. Norton and Co. From *Indian Trail to Iron Horse* by Wheaton Lane. Copyright © 1939 Princeton University Press. From *Women and the American Labor Movement* by Philip Foner. Published by the Free Press. Copyright © 1979. From *America Enters the World* by Page Smith. Copyright © 1985 Page Smith. Published by McGraw-Hill Book Company. From *Freedom Not Far Distant: A Document History of Afro-Americans in New Jersey* compiled and edited by Clement Alexander Price. Copyright © 1980 by The New Jersey Historical Society. From *Past and Promise: Lives of New Jersey Women,* Joan Burstyn, editor-in-chief. Copyright © 1990 Women's Project of New Jersey, Inc. From *The Underground Rail Road* by William Still. Published in 1872. From *Jersey Blue: Civil War Politics in New Jersey 1854–1865* by William Gillette. Copyright © 1995 William Gillette. "The True Jersey Blue" song lyrics by Theophilus Townsend Price in *Words That Make New Jersey History: A Primary Source Reader* by Howard L. Green. Reprinted by permission of the Department of Special Collections and University Archives, Rutgers University Libraries. From *South After Gettysburg: Letters of Cornelia Hancock 1863–1868* edited by Henrietta Stratton Jaquette. Copyright © 1937, 1956 Henrietta Stratton Jaquette. From *Edison's Electric Light: Biography of an Invention* by Robert Friedel and Paul Israel with Bernard S. Finn. Copyright 1986 by Rutgers, The State University of New Jersey. From *Edison: A Biography* by Matthew Josephson. Copyright © 1959 John Wiley and Sons, Inc. From *Up from the Cellar* by Lini De Vries in *Women in New Jersey History* edited by Mary R. Murrin. Copyright © 1985 New Jersey Historical Commission. From *America: The Dream of My Life* edited by David Steven Cohen. Copyright © 1990 Rutgers, The State University of New Jersey. From *The Uses of Abundance* by Paul G. E. Clemens. Copyright © 1992 New Jersey Historical Commission. From *Arrival and Settlement in a New Place* by Giles Wright. Copyright © 1986 New Jersey Historical Commission. From the New Deal Network web site launched by the Franklin and Eleanor Roosevelt Institute (FERI). From The Rutgers Oral History Archives of World War II web archive, Rutgers University. From *New Jersey Firsts* by Harry Armstrong and Tom Wilk. Copyright © 1999 Harry Armstrong and Tom Wilk. Published by Camino Books. From *The Modern Civil Rights Movement* by Clement Alexander Price. Copyright © 1980 New Jersey Historical Commission. From *The Meadowlands: Wilderness Adventures at the Edge of a City* by Robert Sullivan. Copyright © 1998. Published by Scribner's. From "Communities; No More Cherry Trees, And the Hill Is Leveled" by Robert Strauss in *The New York Times,* March 19, 2000. From "Family Business: A Sweet Sensation" by Claire Moore in *The Morris County Daily Record,* March 13, 2000. From the "Fall for New Jersey" Tourism Campaign Press Release, September 18, 1998, quoting Secretary Gualberto Medina of the NJ Commerce and Economic Growth Commission. From "Frequently Asked Questions" on the Sensar company's web site (sensar.com). From "Business Race to Be a Part of the Internet Revolution" on NJBIZ.com, March 22, 1999, quoting Edmund DePalma of World Internet Resources. From "In search of field of dreams . . ." by David M. Campbell in *Princeton Packet,* December 15, 1999. From "New Jersey State of the Senate 2000" address by Governor Christine Todd Whitman. From "State of New Jersey Judiciary Press Release," December 22, 1999, quoting Chief Justice Deborah T. Poritz. From "Town Celebrates Little League Win" by Wayne Parry on jrzshore.com, August 30, 1998. Copyright © 1998 The Associated Press. From *The Story of the Jersey Shore* by Harold F. Wilson. Copyright © 1964 The New Jersey Tercentenary Commission. Published by D. Van Nostrand Company Ltd. From "Office of the Governor News Release," April 12, 2000, quoting Governor Christine Todd Whitman. From "New Jersey's Plan for Higher Education: 1999 Update" adopted June 25, 1999. From "This Is Just to Say" by William Carlos Williams in *Collier's Encyclopedia,* Vol. 23. Copyright © 1989 Macmillan Educational Company, A Division of Macmillan, Inc.

TEACHER'S ANNOTATED EDITION

# Table of Contents

UNIT 1 ORGANIZER

# The Geography of New Jersey

**PAGES 2-51**

## UNIT OVERVIEW

New Jersey is part of the Northeast region of the United States and has four regions of its own. Our state has a variety of landforms, including mountains, hills, and plains. There are many waterways throughout New Jersey that are important for both transportation and recreation. New Jerseyans use our many natural resources in a wide variety of ways.

## UNIT PLANNING GUIDE

| CHAPTER | SUGGESTED PACING | CHAPTER OVERVIEW | CHAPTER RESOURCES |
|---|---|---|---|
| **1 New Jersey, Our Home** pages 6–25 | 13–14 days | New Jersey has many different landforms, plus a variety of waterways used for transportation and recreation. Our state's weather is varied and our climate is moderate. | ***Practice and Project Book*** pages 6–10 ***Transparencies:*** 1, 2 ***Technology:*** *Adventure Time CD-ROM* |
| **2 Regions and Resources** pages 26–49 | 14–15 days | The United States has five regions. Each has landforms that distinguish it from other regions. New Jersey has four regions with many natural resources that we must conserve. | ***Practice and Project Book*** pages 11–15 ***Transparencies:*** 1, 2 ***Technology:*** *Adventure Time CD-ROM* |

**Internet CONNECTION**

The Home Page at **http://www.mhschool.com** contains on-line student activities related to this unit.

**For Further Support**
- Handbook of Test-Taking Strategies

## ASSESSMENT OPPORTUNITIES

### UNIT ASSESSMENT

**Unit Review** pages 50–51
***Unit Project*** page 51, page T3

**Assessment Book**
***Unit Test*** Unit 1 Test
***Performance Assessment*** page T35

### CHAPTER ASSESSMENT

**Meeting Individual Needs** pages T5, T6, T8, T16, T17
**Write About It** pages T5, T7, T9, T12, T13, T16
**Chapter Review** pages 24–25, 48–49

**Assessment Book**
***Chapter 1 Test, Chapter 2 Test***
***Performance Assessment***
pp. T29–T31, T32–T34

## TECHNOLOGY CENTER

# Enriching with Multimedia

**RESOURCE:** *Internet*

- Look at McGraw-Hill School's home page on the World Wide Web at **http://www.mhschool.com** for activities related to this unit that your students can do on-line.

**RESOURCE: Adventure Time CD-ROM**

Enrich Unit 1 with *Explore, Build,* and *Paint* on the CD-ROM.

## SCHOOL-TO-HOME

# The Land We Call New Jersey

- Throughout the unit, students will have the opportunity to learn about the importance of preserving our natural resources. Discuss with students some ways of cutting down the amount of garbage that goes into our landfills.
- Encourage students to work with their families to set up home recycling centers. They should list items their families recycle in one week. This will help them become aware of the amount of garbage just one family can save from a landfill. The students can make diagrams of their home recycling center to share with the class.

## ONGOING UNIT PROJECT

# Create a New Jersey Tour Book

**CURRICULUM CONNECTION**
**Language Arts/Art**

Throughout the unit, students will work individually and cooperatively to produce a New Jersey tour book. Students will collect information about New Jersey's landforms, climate, waterways, and natural resources.

1. As a class, discuss topics and places to cover in the tour book. These ideas can be listed on the board.
2. Invite individuals to take responsibility for an article or illustration. This can be decided as a group to prevent overlapping of topics.
3. Encourage students doing illustrations to cut out photos from old magazines and glue them onto colored paper. Students can then write a caption under each picture.
4. As a group, decide what the cover of the tour book will look like. Assign one student to design and produce the cover.
5. When all articles and illustrations are complete, students may punch holes in the pages and assemble their tour book with string, ribbon, or fasteners.

Assessment suggestions for this activity appear on page T19.

CHAPTER 1 ORGANIZER

# New Jersey, Our Home

PAGES 6–25

## CHAPTER OVERVIEW

New Jersey has a rich variety of landforms within its borders, including mountains, hills, and plains. Many waterways throughout New Jersey provide pathways for transportation as well as recreational opportunities. New Jersey has a temperate climate that is influenced by its nearness to the Atlantic Ocean and distance from the equator.

## CHAPTER PLANNING GUIDE

**Suggested pacing: 13–14 days**

| LESSON | LESSON FOCUS | LESSON RESOURCES |
|---|---|---|
| **1 LANDSCAPE OF NEW JERSEY** pages 8–11 | The Geography of New Jersey | ***Practice and Project Book:*** page 6<br>***Technology:*** *Adventure Time CD-ROM* |
| **LEGACY STATE AND NATIONAL PARKS OF NEW JERSEY** pages 12–13 | New Jersey's Parks | ***Practice and Project Book:*** page 7<br>***Transparency:*** 1 |
| **2 WATERS OF NEW JERSEY** pages 14–17 | Use of Waterways | ***Practice and Project Book:*** page 8<br>***Technology:*** *Adventure Time CD-ROM* |
| **GEOGRAPHY SKILLS** pages 18–19 | Reading Elevation Maps | ***Practice and Project Book:*** page 9 |
| **3 OUR STATE'S CLIMATE** pages 20–23 | Weather Patterns and Climate | ***Practice and Project Book:*** page 10<br>***Assessment Book:*** Chapter 1 Test<br>***Performance Assessment*** pages T28–T30 |
| **CHAPTER REVIEW** pages 24–25 | Students' understanding of vocabulary, content, and skills is assessed. | ***Technology:*** *Adventure Time CD-ROM* |

### New Jersey Core Curriculum Content Standards for Social Studies

**Content Standards** These content standards and progress indicators for students completing Grade 4, correlated with Chapter 1, have been developed by the New Jersey Department of Education. A complete listing of the standards can be found on pages T110–T112.

**Standard 6.7** All students will acquire geographical understanding by studying the world in spatial terms.
1. pp. 9, 15, 18–19, 21–22

**Standard 6.8** All students will acquire geographical understanding by studying human systems in geography.
3. pp. 14–17
5. p. 22

**Standard 6.9** All students will acquire geographical understanding by studying the environment and society.
2. pp. 11, 16–17

CHAPTER 1

# LESSON 1

## LANDSCAPE OF NEW JERSEY

PAGES 8-11

### Lesson Overview

New Jersey has a rich variety of *landforms*, including mountains, hills, and plains.

Geography is the study of Earth and the way people, plants, and animals live on it and use it.

### Lesson Objectives

- ★ Define geography.
- ★ Define landforms.
- ★ Identify and describe the major landforms of New Jersey.

## Reading Strategies and LANGUAGE DEVELOPMENT AND DETAILS

**MAIN IDEAS** Remind students to look for main ideas and supporting details as they read. Have students read the second paragraph of The Big Picture on page 8 and discuss the main idea as a class *(the variety of landforms in New Jersey)*. Ask volunteers to identify supporting details in the paragraph.

**LANGUAGE HISTORY AND ETYMOLOGY** Explain to students that the word *geography* comes from two Greek words. Write the word on the board. Explain that *geo* means "Earth," while *graphia* means "writing." Tell students that *geography* means "writing about Earth." Encourage students to look in a dictionary for other words that begin with *geo*, such as *geology, geode*, and *geometry*.

## Second-Language SUPPORT

**USING VISUALS** Second-language learners may follow the lesson more easily if they make a poster on which they draw a picture of each landform discussed. Have them label each picture with the name of the landform. Display the poster at the front of the classroom.

## Technology CONNECTION

**ADVENTURE TIME CD-ROM**

Enrich this lesson with *New Jersey, Explore*, and *Investigate* on the CD-ROM.

## Meeting INDIVIDUAL NEEDS

**RETEACHING (Easy)** Have students label the major landforms of New Jersey on an outline map of the state.

**EXTENSION (Average)** Ask groups of students to prepare a wall map of New Jersey that details its borders with other states. Suggest that they label towns, cities, and rivers along the borders. Have them label the surrounding states and show parts of these states' borders.

**ENRICHMENT (Challenging)** Have students create a physical map of New Jersey using drawings or magazine clippings that show examples of New Jersey landforms. The map should include labels identifying each landform and telling elevations of the different areas included on the map.

## Background INFORMATION

**NEW JERSEY LANDFORMS** New Jersey contains parts of two major landforms in North America—the Appalachian Mountains in northwestern New Jersey, and the Atlantic Coastal Plain in southern New Jersey.

- The Appalachian Mountains are the second largest mountain system in North America—stretching about 1,500 miles from Alabama to Canada.
- The Atlantic Coastal Plain extends all the way from Cape Cod, Massachusetts, to Florida.

## ✓Answers to THINK ABOUT IT

1. an area that is covered by water at least part of the year
2. the shapes that make up Earth's surface
3. mountains, hills, plains, coast
4. Lake Hopatcong, the Passaic River, the Pinelands, Great Egg Harbor River
5. Answers should use the proper geographic terms to describe the major landforms of the local region.

**Write About It** Ask students to suppose that they went on the same trip as Sara and her grandmother. Have them create a postcard on unlined index cards. On one side have students draw a picture or paste a clipping of a place that they visited. On the other side, students should write a message including a detailed description of the place they visited.

### Resource REMINDER

**Practice and Project Book:** page 6

**Technology:** *Adventure Time CD-ROM*

**Transparency:** 1

# LEGACY

## LINKING PAST AND PRESENT STATE AND NATIONAL PARKS OF NEW JERSEY

PAGES 12-13

**Lesson Overview**

The state and national parks of New Jersey preserve the natural beauty, wildlife, and history of the state. People enjoy the parks in many ways.

**Lesson Objectives**

★ Explain how state and national parks preserve New Jersey's natural beauty, wildlife, and history.

★ Identify different natural environments protected in New Jersey parks.

## Understanding the CONCEPT OF A LEGACY

Help students understand why New Jersey's state and national parks are a *legacy.* Discuss with students the need to preserve natural sites such as wetlands and wildlife areas. Ask students to describe what might happen to such sites and the plants and animals that live there if they were not protected.

**EXAMINING THE PHOTOGRAPHS** Direct students to the photographs on pages 12–13. Have student volunteers read the captions aloud. Ask students if they have ever visited any of the places shown in the photographs or collected conch shells on New Jersey beaches. Have students describe their park visits, including what they did and what they saw. Then have students locate each park illustrated on a map of New Jersey.

## Thinking FURTHER

**COMPARING AND CONTRASTING** Have students point out similarities and differences in the photographs. Ask students what the photographs tell us about the geography of New Jersey.

## Meeting INDIVIDUAL NEEDS

**RETEACHING (Easy)** Write the following phrase on the board: "State and National Parks are a legacy because" Have students complete the sentence either orally or in writing.

**EXTENSION (Average)** Have students choose one New Jersey state park and use library resources to find out more about it. Each student should prepare a short report that includes information about the location of the park, its history, the types of plants and animals that live there, and its recreational facilities.

**ENRICHMENT (Challenging)** Ask students to plan a trip to visit three or more state and/or national parks in New Jersey. Students should create a map showing the location of each of the sites and trace a route using roads that connect each site. Routes should start and end at the students' community.

**FIELD TRIP** The best way to appreciate the beauty and value of New Jersey's state parks may be to visit them. Plan a trip to the closest state park or invite a park ranger to talk with students about the attractions of nearby parks. (Contact the New Jersey Division of Travel and Tourism at (800) Jersey-7 or (609) 292–2470 for information about the state's parks.) If taking a trip, divide the class into groups of 10 students with an adult chaperone to hike and explore the park's attractions. You might want to ask students to stop at a particular spot to write a poem or draw a picture that describes the park. If a ranger is visiting the class, have students take notes during the presentation and then write an essay about park attractions.

## Building CITIZENSHIP

**PRESERVING LOCAL LEGACIES** Ask students to identify places within their community that they would like to see preserved as legacies. Encourage students to think of places of natural beauty, of historical importance, or of artistic or architectural interest. Make a class list and write a letter as a class to the local historical society or municipal government asking if any of these places are in danger of development.

CHAPTER 1

# LESSON 2

## WATERS OF NEW JERSEY

PAGES 14-17

### Lesson Overview

New Jersey's many waterways are important pathways for transportation. Its shoreline on the Atlantic Ocean connects New Jersey to the rest of the world.

### Lesson Objectives

- ★ Explain how New Jersey's shoreline connects our state to the rest of the world.
- ★ Describe how people use New Jersey's waterways.
- ★ Analyze why caring for our state's waterways is important.

## Reading Strategies and LANGUAGE DEVELOPMENT

**COMPOUND WORDS** Tell students that compound words are words made from two smaller words. Point out that *waterways,* in the first sentence of the Big Picture, is a compound word. Challenge students to find two additional compound words in the Big Picture *(pathways, shoreline).* Discuss with students how analyzing the parts of a compound word will help them figure out its meaning.

## Background INFORMATION

**NAMES FOR WATERWAYS** The names given to New Jersey's waterways reflect the cultures of the people doing the naming. *Kill* is a Dutch word for stream or channel. The Walkill River in northwestern New Jersey owes its name to the Dutch, although the word *River* is really not necessary. In old East Jersey, some small streams are called *brooks,* reflecting the culture of the New Englanders who named them. In the Pinelands, a small stream may be called a *branch,* a term common from Maryland to West Virginia.

## Technology CONNECTION

**ADVENTURE TIME CD-ROM**
Enrich this lesson with *New Jersey, Explore,* and *Investigate* on the CD-ROM.

## Second-Language Support

**USING VISUALS** Help second-language learners follow this lesson by making a poster of a river, including its source, mouth, and tributaries. Label small cards with the words *river, source, mouth,* and *tributaries.* Ask students to attach the labels to the poster to identify the river and its parts.

## Curriculum CONNECTION

**LINKS TO MATH** Water is one of New Jersey's most important resources, and groundwater (water below the surface) provides much of the supply. In 1996, New Jerseyans used about 652 million gallons of groundwater a day. Of this groundwater, about 489 million gallons were potable water, or water that is safe for drinking. How much groundwater did New Jerseyans use each day in 1996 for purposes other than drinking? *(163 million gallons)*

**FIELD TRIP** Arrange a field trip to the nearest stream, creek, or river. Ask students to draw the waterway and its banks and to identify the direction in which it flows. Locate the waterway on a map of your county or community. Using a map, trace the route of the waterway as it flows to the ocean or joins a larger river. If a field trip is not practical, you may have students work from photographs of a local waterway for this activity.

## ✓Answers to THINK ABOUT IT

1. The source is where the river begins; the mouth is where the river flows into a larger body of water.
2. It flows into a larger river.
3. Waterways are used for transportation and provide water for drinking, farming, factories, and recreation.
4. Using the map on page 15; south on the Delaware River to Delaware Bay, southeast around Cape May to the Atlantic Ocean, and north up the coast to Atlantic City.
5. Letters should show knowledge of geographic terms and the body of water.

**Write About It** Have students write a poem or a story about their favorite way to have fun on or in the waters of New Jersey.

## Resource REMINDER

**Practice and Project Book:** page 7
**Technology:** *Adventure Time CD-ROM*
**Transparency:** 1

CHAPTER 1

# SKILLS LESSON

## READING ELEVATION MAPS

PAGES 18-19

**Lesson Overview**

Elevation maps provide important information about landforms and the height of land above sea level. They may be used to determine the direction in which a river flows.

**Lesson Objectives**

★ Read and interpret an elevation map.

★ Analyze the effect of elevation on waterways.

### Why the SKILL MATTERS

Discuss with students the different kinds of information presented by specialized maps. Have students list as many different kinds of specialized maps as they can, such as road maps, historical maps, and weather maps. Tell students that elevation maps present information about the height of various locations. Read with students the *Helping Yourself* box on page 19. Using the color key, help them identify areas within specific ranges of elevation on the map.

### Using the SKILL

Call on volunteers to read the text aloud as the rest of the class traces the path of the Delaware River on the map. Have students work in pairs to answer the questions on page 19.

### Trying the SKILL

Have students compare the courses of the Delaware and the Hudson Rivers on the map. Then have students tell the direction of flow of the Susquehanna River.

### Meeting INDIVIDUAL NEEDS

**RETEACHING (Easy)** Have students write a paragraph explaining how an elevation map can be used to show the direction in which a river flows.

**EXTENSION (Average)** Ask students to create a chart that includes the following information for three different rivers shown on the elevation map: beginning elevation, final elevation, and direction of flow.

**ENRICHMENT (Challenging)** Have students conduct research and write an essay about the methods used to create elevation maps. Encourage students to include historical approaches to surveying (land-based methods), as well as current methods, such as satellite imaging.

### Curriculum CONNECTION

**LINKS TO ART** Have students draw or paint a mountain, hills, a plain, and the ocean. Students should show elevation on their drawing by using the colors from the map for appropriate heights.

### √Answers to REVIEWING THE SKILL

1. the height of the land above sea level
2. 1,803 feet at High Point; along the coast, elevation is between 0 and 700 feet.
3. light green
4. An elevation map helps us to learn about geography by showing the heights of various landforms and by identifying the direction in which rivers flow.

### Technology CONNECTION

**ADVENTURE TIME CD-ROM**

Enrich this lesson with *United States, Explore, Build,* and *Paint* on the CD-ROM.

### Resource REMINDER

**Practice and Project Book:** page 8

**Technology:** *Adventure Time CD-ROM*

CHAPTER 1

# LESSON 3

## OUR STATE'S CLIMATE

PAGES 20-23

### Lesson Overview

The main influences on the climate of New Jersey are its nearness to the Atlantic Ocean and its distance from the equator.

### Lesson Objectives

★ Define *climate* and identify temperature and precipitation as key parts of climate.

★ Explain how New Jersey's nearness to the Atlantic Ocean and its distance from the equator affect its climate.

★ Recognize the forms of extreme weather that sometimes occur in New Jersey.

## Reading Strategies and LANGUAGE DEVELOPMENT

**REREADING** Remind students to preview the lesson before they read it and to ask themselves questions about the lesson's content. They will think of questions as they look at the lesson's visuals and main headings. If they find that all of their questions have not been answered when they finish reading the section, suggest that they reread parts of the lesson. Practice generating questions by previewing the Big Picture. Check with students to see that all of their questions have been answered.

## Background INFORMATION

**JEDIDIAH MORSE** Morse had some expertise to back up his comments on New Jersey's weather. He collected a great deal of information about geography and wrote *Geography Made Easy,* the first geography book published in the United States. Morse was called the "Father of American Geography." His son Samuel F. Morse is credited with the invention of the telegraph and Morse code.

## Technology CONNECTION

**ADVENTURE TIME CD-ROM**

Enrich this lesson with *New Jersey, Explore, Investigate, Charts,* and *New Jersey's Climate* on the CD-ROM.

## Curriculum CONNECTION

**LINKS TO SCIENCE** Although not common to New Jersey, tornadoes sometimes occur in our state. A tornado is a twisting funnel, and tornadoes are sometimes called "twisters." The wind speeds inside a tornado can reach more than 300 miles per hour. Tornadoes, which move in a straight line, can be enormously destructive. Ask students to research tornadoes using library resources. Ask them to present information to the class about the causes of tornadoes and what to do in case of a tornado.

## Global CONNECTIONS

**THE ORIGINS OF HURRICANES** Hurricanes are tropical storms that begin over warm seas. They occur in many different parts of the world, but they are called by different names in different regions. They are called hurricanes if they begin over the Atlantic Ocean, the Gulf of Mexico, or the Caribbean Sea. They are called typhoons if they begin in the Northwest Pacific Ocean. Near Australia and the Indian Ocean, these storms are known as tropical cyclones.

## ✓Answers to THINK ABOUT IT

1. Weather describes the condition of the air at a certain time and place. Climate is the pattern of weather for one place over many years.
2. It becomes cooler.
3. closeness to the Atlantic Ocean and distance from the equator
4. This answer should accurately reflect the current weather and the weather six months ago. Answers should note the temperate climate and seasonal changes in New Jersey.
5. Students should describe the type of climate where they live and demonstrate an understanding of the factors that affect climate in their area.

**Write About It** Have students write a descriptive paragraph about a day on which the weather was very stormy. Encourage students to use specific and vivid words in their descriptions. Have students note whether the stormy day was typical of New Jersey weather for the season in which it occurred.

Resource REMINDER

**Practice and Project Book:** page 9

**Technology:** *Adventure Time CD-ROM*

ANSWERS TO

# Chapter 1 REVIEW

PAGES 24-25

### THINKING ABOUT VOCABULARY

1. transportation
2. tributary
3. port
4. precipitation
5. geography
6. border
7. climate
8. hurricane
9. wetland
10. landform

### THINKING ABOUT FACTS

1. High Point
2. Delaware River
3. mouth
4. Any two: Raritan, Delaware, Hudson, Passaic, Great Egg Harbor, Mullica, and Musconetcong Rivers
5. because smaller rivers and streams called tributaries flow into it
6. Weather is the condition of the air at a certain time and place. Climate is the pattern of weather in a place over many years.
7. Temperature and precipitation are important. They tell us how warm or cold it will be and whether it will be raining or snowing.
8. It is neither too hot nor too cold.
9. Atlantic City is warmer because the ocean stays warmer than the land all winter, and ocean breezes warm the coast.
10. The water is cooler than the land, so the breezes blowing off the water are cooler.

## Suggestions for THINK AND WRITE

**SIGNS OF SUCCESS**

***Letter*** Students' letters should be descriptive and use several of the terms defined in Lesson 3, such as *temperature* and *precipitation.*

***Description*** Students' descriptions should demonstrate a knowledge of the variety of experiences available in New Jersey. They should also include some mention of the sounds, the feel, and the smells of our state as well as the sights.

***Explanation*** Students' explanations should show a knowledge of the term *tributaries* and how they flow into a larger body of water.

*For performance assessment, see* **Assessment Book,** *Chapter 1, pages T28-T30*

### APPLYING GEOGRAPHY SKILLS

**READING ELEVATION MAPS**

1. from the map title
2. the northwestern part of New Jersey
3. light green
4. 0–300 feet above sea level
5. southeast; it flows from higher to lower elevation

**Technology CONNECTION**

**ADVENTURE TIME CD-ROM**

Enrich Chapter 1 with *New Jersey, Explore,* and *Investigate* on the CD-ROM.

**Resource REMINDER**

**Practice and Project Book:** page 10

**Assessment Book:** Chapter 1 Test

**Performance Assessment,** pages T29–T31

 **Technology:** *Adventure Time CD-ROM*

CHAPTER 2 ORGANIZER

# Regions and Resources

PAGES 26–49

## CHAPTER OVERVIEW

The United States is divided into five regions: Northeast, Southeast, Southwest, Middle West, and West. New Jersey is divided into four different regions. Rich soil, thick forests, water, clay, sand, and gravel are a few of our state's many natural resources. The people and businesses of New Jersey work together to make sure these resources last well into the future.

## CHAPTER PLANNING GUIDE

**Suggested pacing: 14–15 days**

| LESSON | LESSON FOCUS | LESSON RESOURCES |
|---|---|---|
| **1 ONE COUNTRY, FIVE REGIONS** pages 28–33 | Landforms and Regions of the United States | ***Practice and Project Book:*** page 11<br>***Transparency:*** 2<br>***Technology:*** *Adventure Time CD-ROM* |
| **2 REGIONS OF NEW JERSEY** pages 34–39 | Features of New Jersey's Four Regions | ***Practice and Project Book:*** page 12<br>***Technology:*** *Adventure Time CD-ROM* |
| **THINKING SKILLS** pages 40-41 | Decision Making | ***Practice and Project Book:*** page 13<br>***Technology:*** *Adventure Time CD-ROM* |
| **3 OUR STATE'S RESOURCES** pages 42-46 | The Uses and Conservation of New Jersey's Resources | ***Practice and Project Book:*** page 14<br>***Technology:*** *Adventure Time CD-ROM* |
| **CITIZENSHIP** page 47 | Helping the Environment and the Community | ***Practice and Project Book:*** page 15<br>***Assessment Book:*** Chapter 2 Test, ***Performance Assessment*** pages T31–T33 |
| **CHAPTER REVIEW** pages 48–49 | Students' understanding of vocabulary, content, and skills is assessed. | ***Technology:*** *Adventure Time CD-ROM* |

### New Jersey Core Curriculum Content Standards for Social Studies

**Content Standards** These content standards and progress indicators for students completing Grade 4, correlated with Chapter 1, have been developed by the New Jersey Department of Education. A complete listing of the standards can be found on pages T110–T112.

**Standard 6.7** All students will acquire geographical understanding by studying the world in spatial terms.
1. pp. 29, 34–39, 45

**Standard 6.8** All students will acquire geographical understanding by studying human systems in geography.
2. pp. 35–39
3. pp. 35–39
5. pp. 28–33

**Standard 6.9** All students will acquire geographical understanding by studying the environment and society.
1. pp. 43–46
2. pp. 35–39, 43–46

CHAPTER 2

# LESSON 1

## ONE COUNTRY, FIVE REGIONS

PAGES 28–33

**Lesson Overview**

The United States is a large country of varied landforms and climates. Geographers divide it into five major regions.

**Lesson Objectives**

★ Identify the country's five regions.

★ Compare major landforms and other features of each region.

★ Locate the region in which New Jersey lies.

## Reading Strategies and LANGUAGE DEVELOPMENT

**COMPOUND WORDS** Remind students that compound words are formed by combining two smaller words. Point out these words in *The Big Picture: Northeast* and *landforms*. Discuss the meanings of the bases of the compound words. Note that compound words may appear as one word (*lowland* and *sunlight* on page 29), two words (*Middle West* on page 31), or with hyphens (*wind-driven* on page 33). Encourage students to look for others as they read the lesson.

## Background INFORMATION

**ABOUT THE APPALACHIAN TRAIL**

- The Appalachian Trail is the world's longest marked, continuous hiking trail. It stretches more than 2,000 miles along the crest of the Appalachian Mountains from northern Maine to northern Georgia.
- Construction of the trail began in 1921. It has been part of the National Park System since 1968.

## Technology CONNECTION

**ADVENTURE TIME CD-ROM**

Enrich this lesson with *United States, Explore, Investigate,* and *Our Country's Landforms* on the CD-ROM.

## Second-Language SUPPORT

**USING PROPS** Second-language students will have a better understanding of the seasons if you can demonstrate how they occur. Have one student be the sun holding a light. Have another student hold a ball as the earth. Paste a star on the earth to show the location of the northeastern region of the United States. As Earth revolves around the sun, tilts, and rotates on its axis, have other students describe seasonal changes.

## Curriculum CONNECTION

**LINKS TO SCIENCE**

- The Northeast's combination of trees produces the most brilliant autumn colors in the world. Cottonwoods, birches, hickories, and some ash varieties yield the golds and yellows. Red Maple, Sugar Maple, White Oak, Scarlet Oak, and Sassafras trees produce red and wine colors. Highlands, lakes, and rivers offer some of the best viewing locations.
- Direct students to field guides to North American trees and help them identify some of the trees of the Northeast. Have them create a booklet in which they draw outlines of the leaves and silhouettes of the trees, and indicate the fall colors of the varieties included.

## √Answers to THINK ABOUT IT

1. Possible answers: Coastal Plain, Appalachian Mountains, Interior Plains, Rocky Mountains
2. an area with common features that set it apart from other areas
3. The Northeast includes parts of the Coastal Plain and the Appalachian Mountains; the seasons of winter, spring, summer, and autumn, when the leaves turn bright colors, bring different kinds of weather.
4. Students' questions may relate to landforms, climate, economy, population, or lifestyle.
5. the Coastal Plain with the Southeast and Southwest, the Appalachian Mountains with the Southeast

**Write About It** Have students write a diary entry about a visit to another region of the United States. The entry should describe a natural feature and the writer's impressions of it.

## Resource REMINDER

**Practice and Project Book:** page 11

**Technology:** *Adventure Time CD-ROM*

**Transparency:** 2

CHAPTER 2

# LESSON 2

## REGIONS OF NEW JERSEY

PAGES 34–39

### Lesson Overview

New Jersey's four regions differ from one another because each has special landforms, history, and culture.

### Lesson Objectives

★ Identify our state's four regions.

★ Explain how the people who live in a region affect the land.

★ Distinguish between *urban* and *rural*.

## Reading Strategies and LANGUAGE DEVELOPMENT

**MAIN IDEAS AND DETAILS** Remind students that picking out details, or different points related to a main topic, helps them understand and remember what they read. Call attention to the last sentence in *The Big Picture*. Have students pick out details about each region as they read the lesson.

## Field Trip

**WILDLIFE AND NATURE AREAS** Help students appreciate our state's natural features by visiting a state nature preserve. In northern New Jersey, the Great Swamp National Wildlife Refuge offers swamp woodlands, forests, and marshes plus opportunities for wildlife observation. For information write to the Great Swamp National Wildlife Refuge; R.D. 1, Box 52; Basking Ridge 07920, or telephone (973) 425–1222. In southern New Jersey, The Wetlands Institute provides 34 acres of salt marsh plus a special children's exhibit. For information write to The Wetlands Institute, Stone Harbor Boulevard, Stone Harbor 08247, or telephone (609) 368–1211. As an alternative, share with students slides or video footage of a state nature preserve and ask them to draw a scene that appealed to them.

## Technology CONNECTION

**ADVENTURE TIME CD-ROM**

Enrich this lesson with *New Jersey, Explore and Investigate* on the CD-ROM.

## Curriculum CONNECTION

**LINKS TO SCIENCE** Some of the milk produced on New Jersey dairy farms is used to make ice cream. Students may be surprised to know that ice cream must be heated before it can be frozen. Once the milk and other basic ingredients such as sugar and dried egg yolk are combined, the mixture is heated to a temperature between 160°F (71°C) and 240°F (116°C). This process kills harmful germs and helps make the ice cream smooth and tasty. Invite students to further research the process of making ice cream or to research other products made from New Jersey milk.

## √Answers to THINK ABOUT IT

1. An urban area includes a city and the communities that surround it. A rural area has fewer people and includes farms, villages, or unsettled land.
2. The Piedmont region has the largest population in New Jersey.
3. Any one from each region: Atlantic Coastal Plain: low-lying plains, beaches, wetlands, farms, Pinelands, forests; Piedmont: low hills, large population, large cities, fall line; Highlands: Palisades, Hudson River, unique rocks, large lakes, rugged and beautiful; Ridge and Valley: mountainous, High Point State Park, rocky soil, grassy slopes with dairy farms, recreation
4. Atlantic Coastal Plain: large area, southern location, sloping land at low elevation with many farms; Ridge and Valley: small area, northwestern location, higher elevation with many dairy farms but soil too rocky to grow crops
5. Letters should accurately describe the region in which the student lives and give at least two reasons that region is special.

**Write About It** Have students write a poem about a favorite place in New Jersey. Ask them to include as many descriptive details as they can in their poem.

## Resource REMINDER

**Practice and Project Book:** page 12

**Technology:** *Adventure Time CD-ROM*

**Transparency:** 1

CHAPTER 2

# SKILLS LESSON

## DECISION MAKING

PAGES 40–41

**Lesson Overview**

Decision making involves two major skills: identifying your goal and predicting the possible results of each choice you have.

**Lesson Objectives**

★ Define *decision making.*

★ Practice the skill of decision making by first choosing a goal and then identifying and evaluating the choices.

### Why the SKILL MATTERS

Discuss choices students may have made since waking up this morning, such as what to wear or whether to ride a bicycle to school. Ask if the choices were easy or difficult to make. Ask students to define the word *goal* and describe goals they have or may have had in the past. Call on volunteers to describe the goals involved in choices they have made today. Tell students that their goals and choices were part of making decisions. Explain that in this lesson they will learn the steps in making good decisions. Point out that decision-making skills make it easier to make good choices, especially when making big decisions like choosing a place to live.

### Using the SKILL

Refer students to the *Helping Yourself* box. Call on volunteers to read the three steps involved in good decision making. Then ask students to identify the decision Deepa has to make. Discuss the choices she has and the possible results of each choice. Invite students to tell the class the decision they would make in Deepa's place and to explain the goal their choice would accomplish.

### Trying the SKILL

Ask students what goals they might have when choosing a place for a family vacation.

### Background INFORMATION

**USING A GRAPHIC ORGANIZER** This would be an appropriate lesson for using spider webbing to organize information. Draw the sample web shown here or another of your own choosing on the chalkboard for students to copy and complete.

MY GOAL:________________________

possible result

Choice #1

Choice #2

Choice #3

### Second-Language SUPPORT

**DIALOGUES** Invite second-language students to relate goals their family had when moving from their country of origin to the United States. Ask them how they reached the decision to settle in New Jersey. Remind students that someone at some time made the decision that brought them to New Jersey.

### ✓Answers to REVIEWING THE SKILL

1. Possible answers include making a choice and making up your mind to do something.
2. High Point State Park
3. Predicting possible results can help us avoid bad choices and give us a clearer idea of a good decision.
4. Answers may vary, but students should note that making a good decision allows us to meet our goals.

### Technology CONNECTION

**ADVENTURE TIME CD-ROM**

Enrich this lesson with *New Jersey, Explore, Investigate* and *Create* on the CD-ROM.

**Resource REMINDER**

**Practice and Project Book:** page 13

 **Technology:** *Adventure Time CD-ROM*

# LESSON 3
## OUR STATE'S RESOURCES
PAGES 42–46

**Lesson Overview**

New Jersey's natural resources include forests, soil, water, and minerals. Our resources help provide jobs, recreation, and products for the people of New Jersey.

**Lesson Objectives**

★ Identify major natural resources.

★ Recognize the importance of natural resources in New Jersey's economy.

★ Distinguish between renewable and nonrenewable resources and ways to conserve them.

### Reading Strategies and LANGUAGE DEVELOPMENT

**PROBLEM AND SOLUTION** Discuss the *Read to Learn* question, noting that in this lesson students can expect to learn what natural resources are and how people use them. Point out problems connected with the use of resources and have students discuss possible ways to solve them.

**QUOTATION MARKS** Remind students that quotation marks enclose the actual words a person has said or written, as with Governor Whitman's words in the *Read Aloud*. Quotes can also be used around a word or words to stress meaning ("renewed," page 43), or to indicate a nickname ("black gold," page 44). Have students look for different ways quotation marks are used in the lesson.

### Technology CONNECTION

**ADVENTURE TIME CD-ROM**

Enrich this lesson with *New Jersey, Explore* and *Investigate* on the CD-ROM.

### Second-Language SUPPORT

**DIALOGUES** Help second-language students grasp the concept of natural resources and how they are used by relating it to resources in students' countries of origin. Working in small groups, ask them to describe and possibly present visual information about the natural resources in their country of origin. Have the class discuss how New Jersey's resources are alike or different from these resources.

### Global CONNECTION

**GLOBAL OIL SUPPLY** Alaska, Texas, Louisiana, and some other states in the United States have rich oil reserves that supply part of the crude oil arriving in New Jersey refineries. Most of the crude oil, however, is imported from other countries, where it is cheaper to find and remove oil from underground reservoirs.

- Some of the world's largest known oil deposits lie in countries around the Persian Gulf, West and North Africa, Indonesia, Mexico, and Venezuela. These countries supply at least half of all the oil shipped to and refined in the United States.
- Some scientists predict that most of the world's oil supply may be used up during the 21st century. By then oil will probably be too valuable to burn in automobiles. Because of this, the world's auto manufacturers are exploring new technologies.

### Background INFORMATION

**THE ENDLESS WATER CYCLE** Falling moisture that refreshes the water supply results from recycling in nature. As the sun warms the earth's surface, water from land, lakes, rivers, and oceans constantly evaporates, or becomes vapor in the air. The water vapor rises, cools, and forms clouds. Eventually the clouds become cool enough to release the moisture as rain, snow, or other forms of precipitation, and the cycle begins again.

## Expanding the INFOGRAPHIC

**RESEARCH AND WRITING** Point out that *people* are New Jersey's most important natural resource. Explain to the class that the high number of college-trained workers suggests that a college education may be important to finding a job in New Jersey. Have students research and write a report on "Going to College." Suggest that they use such sources as encyclopedia articles under the headings "colleges and universities" or "college education." Encourage them to interview adults who have attended college. Their reports should discuss such topics as

- choosing a college
- college entrance exams
- campus life
- benefits of a college education

## Curriculum CONNECTION

**LINKS TO ART** Have students prepare posters illustrating one or more of New Jersey's natural resources. Students may use clippings from magazines or make their own sketches. The posters should be colorful and should show how the people of New Jersey use and conserve the natural resources of our state. Display the finished posters around the classroom.

## Meeting INDIVIDUAL NEEDS

**RETEACHING (Easy)** Have each student fold a sheet of paper in half. Tell them to head one side "Renewable" and the other "Nonrenewable." Have them illustrate an appropriate resource under each heading.

**EXTENSION (Average)** Have students write a research report on our state's nonrenewable sand and gravel resources. Ask them to include information such as where the deposits are located, how large the reserves are, how the minerals are removed from their sources, and interesting products made from them.

**ENRICHMENT (Challenging)** Ask students to research one of the renewable energy sources currently being developed, such as wind or solar power. Have them explain how the new source works, where it has been tried, and what advantages or disadvantages it offers.

## Building CITIZENSHIP

**DRAMATIZING CONSERVATION** Have small student groups select a resource and list ways individuals and/or organizations can help preserve and protect it. Then have each group plan and present a 60-second TV infomercial skit, including props, that encourages people to practice the conservation measures. Have the groups present their skits to the class.

## ✓Answers to THINK ABOUT IT

1. Any three: forests, soil, water, iron, sandstone, limestone, granite, petroleum, uranium, and people
2. Farmers can renew the soil by adding fertilizer or rotating crops.
3. New Jerseyans need to conserve resources because people need them to live and because they may be nonrenewable.
4. Using renewable resources helps conserve nonrenewable resources; renewable resources can be replaced and are often free.
5. Student answers should include a resource found in the area in which they live and should demonstrate an understanding of how people use the resource.

**Write About It** Have students write a newspaper story explaining why people in the community should practice conservation.

**Resource REMINDER**

**Practice and Project Book:** page 14

**Technology:** *Adventure Time CD-ROM*

# CITIZENSHIP

## Making a Difference

## HELPING THE ENVIRONMENT

PAGE 47

**Lesson Objective**

★ Describe how the Lafayette 4-H Club improved the environment by removing accumulated trash and "adopting" the Jersey Cottage Park in Morristown.

### Identifying the FOCUS

Discuss with students what it means "to volunteer." Ask students to think about how the Lafayette 4-H Club volunteered to work on their environment. Have them identify the improvements club members made in their community.

### Discussing WHY IT MATTERS

Discuss the condition of the environment in Morristown before the cleanup began. *(Furniture and other discarded items in the Whippany River, trash along the riverbank and in at least two parks)* Ask students how they think the litter affected not only the appearance but also the use of these areas. Ask volunteers to read aloud the statements of Matthew King and Jordan Anderson. Have students identify what these two volunteers believe they accomplished. Invite them to suggest other consequences of a littered environment and the benefits of a clean environment.

### Meeting INDIVIDUAL NEEDS

**RETEACHING (Easy)** Have students illustrate the work of the Lafayette 4-H Club with "before" and "after" drawings at each of the sites where they worked. Have them caption each illustration appropriately.

**EXTENSION (Average)** Have students use sources such as encyclopedia entries, magazine articles, and science books to prepare an oral report on landfill. Their reports should explain what landfill is, possible harm of landfill sites, and how some sites are converted to useful areas. After students have presented their reports, have the class brainstorm ideas for how we might reform our "throwaway" society in the future.

**ENRICHMENT (Challenging)** Have students research the causes and possible solutions for ocean pollution. Students will use the information they gather to present a press conference in which "reporters" interview "experts." Each interviewer-expert team might concentrate their research in one of these areas: industrial waste, solid waste, medical waste, pesticides (insect killers), crop fertilizers, sewage, oil spills, or thermal pollution.

### CITIZENSHIP

**LOCAL CLEANUP** Students might like to participate in a cleanup activity like that of the Lafayette 4-H Club.

- Help students identify local areas affected by litter, such as parks or playgrounds, parkways, vacant lots, or possibly the school grounds. With the assistance of several adult guardians, plan an afternoon of litter removal. Direct students to wear gloves and appropriate clothing and to bring trash collection bags. If necessary, obtain permission from the proper authorities to work on the property.
- If a community cleanup is impractical, have students plant a tree or shrub in the school yard or cultivate a potted plant to beautify the school entrance or classroom.

### Curriculum CONNECTION

**LINKS TO ART** Have students create illustrated advertising posters with slogans or other messages reminding people to avoid specific types of littering. Display the posters around the school.

ANSWERS TO
# Chapter 2 REVIEW
PAGES 48–49

### THINKING ABOUT VOCABULARY

1. C
2. C
3. C
4. C
5. C
6. rain shadow
7. conservation
8. C
9. bayou
10. C

### THINKING ABOUT FACTS

1. mountains, hills, plains
2. landforms, climate, bodies of water
3. The Central Plains, where corn is grown, are low with gently rolling hills. The Great Plains are mostly dry grassland with few trees; wheat is the major crop.
4. The number of people in a region makes up its population in both urban and rural areas. Different groups of people with different cultures also shape a region.
5. Atlantic Coastal Plain, Piedmont, Ridge and Valley, Highlands
6. In earlier times, people did not live there because the land was not good for farming. But when people were able to commute to work, they began living in this beautiful, rugged region.
7. Ridge and Valley
8. They cut down forests for wood, use soil to grow crops, and get drinking water from lakes and rivers. People feed their families, build their homes, and earn their livings from natural resources.
9. Atlantic Coastal Plain
10. newspapers, paper, glass, plastics, and aluminum and steel cans

## Think and Write

***Description*** Students' descriptions should reflect a knowledge of marshes *(wetlands covered with tall grasses)* and bayous *(marshy, slow-moving streams)* and distinguish between them. They should mention the location of marshes along rivers that flood regularly and bayous in Louisiana.

***Travel Brochure*** Students' travel brochures should describe their town or community and explain what makes it unique. Brochures should give information on what there is to see and do, and the various landforms, resources, and points of interest.

***Summary*** Students' summaries should reflect an understanding of why these resources are important and should show that soil and water help New Jersey farmers grow crops like corn, soybeans, and tomatoes.

*For performance assessment, see* **Assessment Book,** *Chapter 2 pages T32–T34*

### APPLYING GEOGRAPHY SKILLS
**DECISION MAKING**

1. to go to the aquarium and see lots of different fish and other sea creatures
2. Answers may include: choosing a time of year when I can spend time looking at the fish; choosing a time when my cousin is available; choosing a time when the fish are plentiful.
3. the number of fish I see; the amount of time I will have to see the fish and visit my cousin
4. Students' answers should explain their responses by predicting the results of their choices.
5. Students' answers will depend on whether their choices helped them reach their goal.

**Technology CONNECTION**

**ADVENTURE TIME CD-ROM**

Enrich Chapter 2 with *New Jersey, Explore, Investigate* and *Create* on the CD-ROM.

**Resource REMINDER**

**Practice and Project Book:** page 15

**Assessment Book:** Chapter 2 Test

**Performance Assessment,** pages T32–T34

 **Technology:** *Adventure Time CD-ROM*

ANSWERS TO

# Unit 1 REVIEW

PAGES 50–51

### THINKING ABOUT VOCABULARY

1. b
2. b
3. c
4. c
5. d

## Suggestions for THINK AND WRITE

### SIGNS OF SUCCESS

***Letter*** Encourage students to include their own impressions of life in New Jersey as well as information they have learned in Unit 1. They may want to include details about local climate, landforms, bodies of water, or natural resources. Review the elements that make up a good letter including date, greeting, body, and closing.

***Paragraph*** Students' paragraphs should be descriptive and will clearly identify which regions of the state they have selected. Material might focus on such topics as cultural heritage, history, landforms, cities, and possible points of interest.

***List*** Students' paragraphs should include five vocabulary words from Unit 1 and demonstrate an understanding of the correct definition and proper way to use the word in a sentence. Encourage students to choose vocabulary words that can be encompassed by a single topic.

## Building SKILLS

1. **Elevation Maps** Sample answers: An elevation map would show you where the hills were steep or where the ground is level and easier to travel. It could also show you which way the streams and rivers run.
2. **Elevation Maps** Students' answers should show a knowledge of their region of New Jersey and an ability to read the correct elevation on the map; Kittatinny Ridge's elevation is 1,000 feet above sea level.
3. **Decision Making** Students should indicate that the first step to making a decision is to determine their goal. Then they can identify their choices and predict the results of each choice.
4. **Decision Making** Students' answers should reflect an understanding of the decision-making process.
5. **Decision Making** Students' answers should indicate that they understand they will have to make important decisions throughout their life. Learning how to make good decisions will get them closer to their goal.

## Suggestions for YESTERDAY, TODAY, AND TOMORROW

As students speculate about the efforts being made to preserve our state's resources, remind them that pollution can be caused by individuals, businesses, and the community. Explain that conservation and preservation of natural resources is everyone's job. Encourage them to use the decision-making process in evaluating various conservation programs in New Jersey. Have students brainstorm other ways they can help conserve and protect precious New Jersey resources and the environment.

## ONGOING UNIT PROJECT

### OPTIONS FOR ASSESSMENT

The ongoing unit project begun on page T3 can be part of your assessment program, along with other forms of evaluation.

## UNIT PROJECT

### MAKE A NATURAL RESOURCES MOBILE

***Objective*** Designing their own natural resources mobile will help students identify the different resources in New Jersey.

***Materials*** cardboard, construction paper, crayons or markers, paper punch, scissors, string, tape

- Divide the class into groups. Suggest that revisiting the text to review the different resources may help groups decide which ones they want to include.
- Encourage students to do additional research, using an encyclopedia or other books to find out more about the resources of New Jersey they plan to include.
- Give each group a supply of construction paper, scissors, crayons, string, tape, and cardboard.
- Remind students to write a caption below each picture.

### OPTIONS FOR ASSESSMENT

*For performance assessment, see* **Assessment Book, *Unit 1, page T35.***

**FOR THE PORTFOLIO** Individual notes and sketches can be included in students' portfolios.

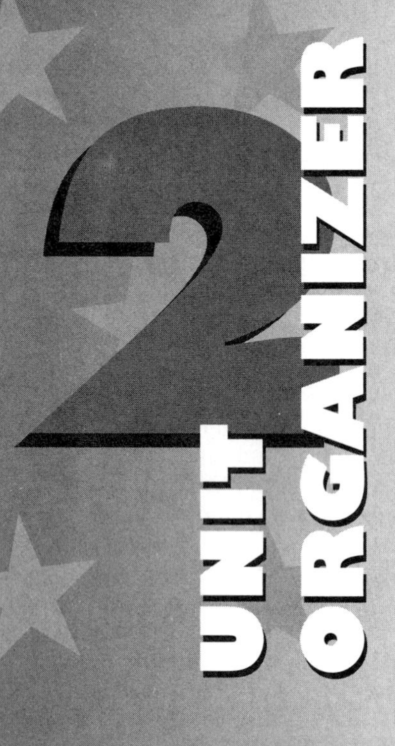


# The Settlement of a New Land

**PAGES 52–133**

## UNIT OVERVIEW

Bands of hunters following wild animals were the first people to come to New Jersey about 12,000 years ago. These Native Americans eventually developed societies. They were followed by explorers and settlers from Europe. Later the settlers won the American Revolution and made the United States a country. New Jersey was one of the first states in the new nation.

## UNIT PLANNING GUIDE

| CHAPTER | SUGGESTED PACING | CHAPTER OVERVIEW | CHAPTER RESOURCES |
|---|---|---|---|
| **3 The First People of New Jersey** pages 56–75 | 13–14 days | Descendants of Ice Age hunters from Asia first settled in New Jersey. They later formed the Lenape Native American groups. | ***Practice and Project Book*** pages 16–20 ***Transparency:*** 1 ***Technology:*** *Adventure Time CD-ROM* |
| **4 Colonial New Jersey** pages 76–103 | 17–18 days | Europeans began to explore North America. Colonists from the Netherlands and Great Britain began new lives in New Jersey. Enslaved Africans were brought to the new colonies. | ***Practice and Project Book*** pages 21–27 ***Transparencies:*** 1, 2 ***Technology:*** *Adventure Time CD-ROM* |
| **5 The American Revolution** pages 104–131 | 15–16 days | France and Britain were arguing over the North American colonies. In 1776, the 13 British colonies decided to break away from Great Britain. They fought and won the American Revolution. | ***Practice and Project Book*** pages 28–32 ***Transparency:*** 2 ***Technology:*** *Adventure Time CD-ROM* |

**Internet CONNECTION**

The Home Page at **http://www.mhschool.com** contains on-line student activities related to this unit.

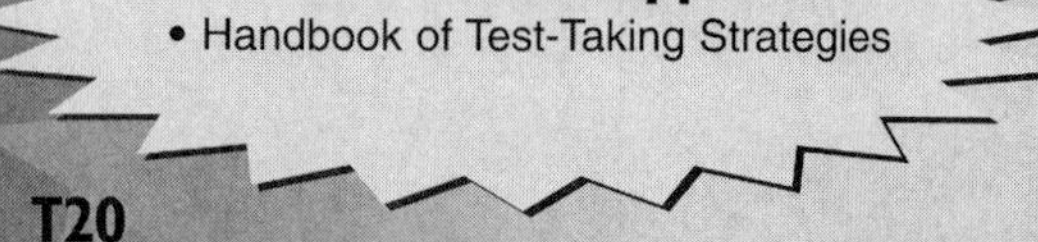

**For Further Support**

- Handbook of Test-Taking Strategies

## ASSESSMENT OPPORTUNITIES

### UNIT ASSESSMENT

**Unit Review** pages 132–133
***Unit Project*** page 133, page T21

**Assessment Book**
***Unit Test*** Unit Test 2
***Performance Assessment*** page T45

### CHAPTER ASSESSMENT

**Meeting Individual Needs** pages T23, T26, T30, T34, T35, T38, T40, T43
**Write About It** pages T23, T25, T26, T27, T30, T32, T33, T35, T38, T41, T42, T43
**Chapter Review** pages 74–75, 102–103, 130–131

**Assessment Book**
***Chapter 3 Test, Chapter 4 Test, Chapter 5 Test***
***Performance Assessment***
T36–T38, T39–T41, T42–T44

## TECHNOLOGY CENTER

# Enriching with Multimedia

**RESOURCE:** ***Internet***

- Look at McGraw-Hill School's home page on the World Wide Web at **http://www.mhschool.com** for activities related to this unit that your students can do on-line.

**RESOURCE: Adventure Time CD-ROM**

Enrich Unit 2 with ***Explore, Build,*** and ***Paint*** on the CD-ROM.

## SCHOOL-TO-HOME

# Settling New Jersey

- Throughout the unit, students will have the opportunity to learn more about early New Jersey. Discuss the information about daily life in the English colony on page 99 of this textbook with students. Ask them to think about how the ways we live are different from the ways early English settlers lived. For example, students should think about how clothing was made and how houses were built.
- Have students talk to their families about how food is grown, shipped, sold, and cooked. Ask them if any family members hunt, fish, or grow vegetables, and, if so, how they prepare the food for cooking. Have students compare modern methods of obtaining food with the description of mealtime in a Lenape village on page 71. Ask them how refrigeration has affected people's daily diet.

## ONGOING UNIT PROJECT

# Early New Jersey Environments

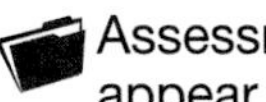

**CURRICULUM CONNECTION**
**Art/Math/Language Arts**

Throughout the unit, students will be working individually and cooperatively to design displays that show the varied environments of the early New Jerseyans.

1. After each chapter, have students write down information that will help them construct accurate displays.
2. At the end of the unit, divide the class into groups. Provide each group with materials such as grass, bark, oaktag, sticks, construction paper, and craft sticks.
3. Guide students to create their displays using notes taken at the end of each chapter.

Assessment suggestions for this activity appear on page T45.

# The First People of New Jersey

**PAGES 56–75**

## CHAPTER OVERVIEW

Many scientists believe that the first people in North America crossed over a land bridge from Asia during the Ice Age. Descendants of these Ice Age hunters, called hunter-gatherers, probably first lived in New Jersey about 12,000 years ago. By the 1600s, the Lenape settled into villages and were farming, hunting, and gathering to get what they needed to live.

## CHAPTER PLANNING GUIDE

**Suggested pacing: 13–14 days**

| LESSON | LESSON FOCUS | LESSON RESOURCES |
|---|---|---|
| **1 EARLY PEOPLES OF NEW JERSEY** pages 58–61 | New Jersey's First People | ***Practice and Project Book:*** page 16<br>***Technology:*** *Adventure Time CD-ROM* |
| **THINKING SKILLS** pages 62–63 | Identifying Cause and Effect | ***Practice and Project Book:*** page 17<br>***Technology:*** *Adventure Time CD-ROM* |
| **2 NATIVE AMERICANS OF NEW JERSEY** pages 64–67 | Lenape Use of Resources | ***Practice and Project Book:*** page 18<br>***Technology:*** *Adventure Time CD-ROM* |
| **LEGACY** pages 68–69 | New Jersey's Highways | |
| **3 DAILY LIFE OF THE LENAPE** pages 70–73 | The Pattern of Lenape Life | ***Practice and Project Book:*** page 19<br>***Technology:*** *Adventure Time CD-ROM* |
| **CHAPTER REVIEW** pages 74–75 | Students' understanding of vocabulary, content, and skills is assessed. | ***Practice and Project Book:*** page 20<br>***Assessment Book:*** Chapter 3 Test<br>***Performance Assessment*** pages T35–T37<br>***Technology:*** *Adventure Time CD-ROM* |

### New Jersey Core Curriculum Content Standards for Social Studies

**Content Standards** These content standards and progress indicators for students completing Grade 4, correlated with Chapter 3, have been developed by the New Jersey Department of Education. A complete listing of the standards can be found on pages T110–T112.

**Standard 6.3** All students will acquire historical understanding of political and diplomatic ideas, forces, and institutions throughout the history of New Jersey, the United States, and the world.
1. pp. 62–63

**Standard 6.4** All students will acquire historical understanding of societal ideas and forces throughout the history of New Jersey, the United States, and the world.
1. pp. 70–73
2. pp. 67, 70–73

**Standard 6.5** All students will acquire historical understanding of varying cultures throughout the history of New Jersey, the United States, and the world.
3. pp. 67, 70–73

CHAPTER 3

# LESSON 1

## EARLY PEOPLE OF NEW JERSEY

PAGES 58–61

### Lesson Overview

The first people to live in New Jersey were descendants of Ice Age hunting groups that came to America thousands of years earlier.

### Lesson Objectives

★ Indicate how and when early hunting groups may have entered the Americas and how archaeologists study them.

★ Describe the lives of early New Jerseyans.

★ Tell how New Jerseyans' lives changed after the Ice Age.

## Reading Strategies and LANGUAGE DEVELOPMENT

**SKIMMING** Tell students that this lesson is about the earliest known groups of people living in New Jersey. Have students read the headings and subheadings in this section and tell what they expect to be reading about early New Jerseyans in this lesson.

**COMPOUND WORDS** Write the word *arrowheads*, found on page 59, on the chalkboard. Have students identify the two words composing this one word and define it. Explain that single words made up of two other words form compound words. Note that some compound words are hyphenated. Have students look for a hyphenated compound word (*hunter-gatherers*) as they read.

## Second-Language SUPPORT

**USING VISUALS** Second-language students may benefit from visual-verbal reinforcement. On index cards, ask them to draw pictures or paste magazine clippings illustrating a term from the lesson on one side of each card and to write the term on the other side. Have students quiz each other with the cards.

## Technology CONNECTION

**ADVENTURE TIME CD-ROM**

Enrich this lesson with *The Northeast, Explore, Investigator, Charts,* and *Native Americans of the Northeast* on the CD-ROM.

## Global CONNECTION

**THE AGRICULTURAL REVOLUTION** Explain that after the Ice Age, people in various parts of the world tried to grow wild plants, changing some of them into field crops. People in Central America were the first to grow corn. The idea of growing corn spread to people living in North America and South America. Have students find Central America on a world map and trace with their fingers a route from Central America to New Jersey. Have students research the origins of another New Jersey crop, such as tomatoes.

## Meeting INDIVIDUAL NEEDS

**RETEACHING (Easy)** Have students draw a picture showing New Jersey in the Ice Age. Have them include artifacts and show the kinds of clothing people may have worn.

**EXTENSION (Average)** Have students do research to learn the extent of the glaciers in North America during the Ice Age. Ask them to draw a map showing the glaciers and Beringia.

**ENRICHMENT (Challenging)** Invite students to do research on the cycle of ice ages throughout Earth's history. Have them make a chart showing when ice ages occurred, how long they lasted, and the extent of the glaciers. Encourage students to learn what scientists predict about possible future ice ages.

## √Answers to THINK ABOUT IT

1. the time before people left written records
2. an object made by people in the past
3. Archaeologists have studied artifacts they found.
4. Hunter-gatherers and early farmers hunted animals and gathered plants and fish. But hunter-gatherers had to move around to find their food, while early farmers could stay in one area by storing some of their crops for winter food.
5. People often lived in caves and near rivers, leaving artifacts behind.

**Write About It** Have students write a short story about what a day in the life of an Ice Age hunter might have been like.

## Resource REMINDER

**Practice and Project Book:** page 16

 **Technology:** *Adventure Time CD-ROM*

CHAPTER 3

# SKILLS LESSON

## IDENTIFYING CAUSE AND EFFECT

PAGES 62-63

**Lesson Overview**

Students learn to recognize cause-and-effect relationships as they identify the connections among sets of facts and events.

**Lesson Objectives**

★ Recognize causes and effects in the migration of early hunters and apply the skill to other situations.

### Why the SKILL MATTERS

Explain to students that understanding cause-and-effect relationships is important in the study of both science and history and can help us understand current events. List some simple effects on the chalkboard, such as *The fourth graders were late for school.* Have students suggest possible reasons, or causes, such as *The school bus got stuck in the snow.* Then list some possible causes, such as *Vadhith lost his book bag,* and ask students to list some possible results, or effects, such as *Vadhith was unable to finish his homework.* Note that the effects of a cause can become the cause of other effects. Ask students to suggest some possible effects of Vadhith's unfinished homework.

### Using the SKILL

Help students understand that the glaciers and the appearance of the land bridge have an important cause-effect relationship for historians. Ask in what sense the cold weather might also be seen as a cause (*it kept the ice from melting*). Ask why scientists might be interested in learning causes for the cold weather (*to help them predict similar events in the future*).

### Trying the Skill

Have a student read the passage on page 63 aloud. Call on volunteers to answer the questions that follow it.

### Technology CONNECTION

**ADVENTURE TIME CD-ROM**

Enrich this lesson with *New Jersey, Explore, Investigate,* and *Create* on the CD-ROM.

### Background INFORMATION

**USES OF CAUSE-AND-EFFECT**

- Writers consider cause-and-effect when plotting stories. They may think first of a cause or an action and then choose what effect it has.
- Sometimes the idea for an effect comes first. When the popular movie director Steven Spielberg wanted to impress viewers with the enormity of dinosaurs *(effect)*, he filmed a close-up of a fake dinosaur foot stepping on a car and crushing it *(cause)*.

### Curriculum CONNECTION

**LINKS TO LANGUAGE ARTS** Write the following sentences on the chalkboard and demonstrate how to use the clue words such as *because, so,* and *as a result* to combine related thoughts.

Sammy, Maria's cat, ran away.
Maria ran an ad in the lost-and-found.
Our camping trip was a great success.
It stopped raining.

### Building CITIZENSHIP

**USING CURRENT EVENTS**

- Bring in newspapers and magazines. Have students choose articles about current events and identify causes and effects.
- Discuss with students how describing the events' causes and effects helps clarify the issues involved.

### ✓Answers to REVIEWING THE SKILL

1. A cause is an event that makes something else happen. An effect is what happens as a result of something else.
2. Melting glaciers returned water to the oceans, which then rose and covered the land bridge.
3. The land bridge was an effect of Ice Age glaciers and a cause of early migrations.
4. Any one: Icy waters returned to the oceans. The land bridge was flooded. People in America were cut off from Asia.
5. Answers will vary but should suggest that it helps explain how historical events are connected or why things happen.

**Resource REMINDER**

**Practice and Project Book:** page 17

**Technology:** *Adventure Time CD-ROM*

CHAPTER 3

# LESSON 2
## NATIVE AMERICANS OF NEW JERSEY

PAGES 64–67

**Lesson Overview**

The Lenape living in New Jersey used resources in their environment for food, clothing, and shelter.

**Lesson Objectives**

★ Identify the two main Lenape groups.

★ Summarize the role of the seasons and religion in Lenape life.

### Reading Strategies and LANGUAGE DEVELOPMENT

**MAKE AND SUPPORT GENERALIZATIONS** Tell students that a generalization is a conclusion based on supporting details. Highlight the following generalization in *The Big Picture*: "The Lenape used the resources in their environment for food, clothing, and shelter." As students read the lesson, ask them to point out details that support this generalization. Then have them organize these details in a three-column chart.

### Background INFORMATION

**SONG OF THE GRANDFATHERS**

- The Lenape are also known as the Delaware. Part of the Delaware heritage is a document called the Wallam Olum. The title is translated as "Red Record." Tradition holds that the symbols were first painted in red on wooden tablets. A manuscript version of the tablets is in a special collection at the University of Pennsylvania Library in Philadelphia.
- The story tells of the origin of the Lenape and their migration over the land bridge between Asia and Alaska and across North America.
- Today, groups of Delaware live in Oklahoma, Wisconsin, and Ontario.

### Technology CONNECTION

**ADVENTURE TIME CD-ROM**

Enrich this lesson with *The Northeast, Explore, Investigate, Charts, and Native American Cultural Areas* on the CD-ROM.

### Curriculum CONNECTION

**LINKS TO ART** Suggest that students produce a four-panel mural depicting Lenape life during the cycle of the seasons. Have them refer to the text to decide what things to include in each of the panels.

### Expanding the INFOGRAPHIC

**RESEARCHING AND WRITING** Ask students to choose one of the items shown in the infographic and use encyclopedias, library reference books, and texts on North American Native Americans to learn more about it. Have them record their findings in written reports. Remind students to focus their reports on how the Lenape interacted with their environment.

### √Answers to THINK ABOUT IT

1. any of the many spirits the Lenape believed were found throughout nature
2. Any five: the soil, clams, oysters, fish, water, trees, nuts, berries.
3. Traveling with the seasons allowed the Lenape to make sure there would be enough food for the year. In spring, they planted crops in the village. In summer, some Lenape traveled to the seashore to gather shellfish while village crops grew. In fall, they returned to help harvest the crops. Later in the fall, the men went on long hunting trips to get food for the winter.
4. Any one: stinging insects, thorns, illness
5. Munsee used Hudson, Delaware, and Raritan Rivers. Unami used Delaware and Raritan Rivers and Delaware Bay.

**Write About It** Invite students to write a short paragraph or poem that shows how the Lenape might show respect for a manetu.

### Resource REMINDER

**Practice and Project Book:** page 18

 **Technology:** *Adventure Time CD-ROM*

CHAPTER 3

# LEGACY

## LINKING PAST AND PRESENT IN THE FOOTSTEPS OF THE LENAPE

PAGES 68–69

**Lesson Overview**

The Lenape traveled by foot over well-defined trails. Due to geography, a number of New Jersey's modern roads and highways follow the same routes.

**Lesson Objective**

★ Trace some routes of Lenape trails and corresponding highways on a map.

★ Describe how modern roads evolved over time.

### Understanding the CONCEPT OF A LEGACY

Help students understand that a legacy is like a heritage—something passed on from one generation to the next. Discuss the "then and now" aspect of the routes. Why would both Lenape and modern land travelers choose to avoid hills, mountains, or large bodies of water? How did the Lenape trails gradually change from foot paths to paved highways?

### Examining the PHOTOGRAPHS

- Call on a volunteer to identify the highway pictured (Route 27), and have students locate it on the map. Ask them to name towns or cities auto travelers can reach by using Route 27. Discuss why the Lenape may have wanted to reach the Raritan River.
- Have a volunteer explain the meaning of the road signs pictured on the map borders. Invite students to relate experiences their families may have had with road signs when traveling.
- Have students identify the trail-highway route nearest their local community and trace its course.

### Technology CONNECTION

**ADVENTURE TIME CD-ROM**

Enrich this lesson with *Native Americans of the Northeast* and *Iroquois Longhouse* on the CD-ROM.

### Thinking FURTHER

**COMPARING AND CONTRASTING** Note that road signs like those pictured on page 69 are necessary for guiding modern travelers to their destination. Help students picture a footpath through a dense forest. Ask them what "road signs" they think the Lenape might have used. Invite students to compare the way the Lenape used roads with the way modern New Jerseyans use roads. How did the Lenape use the roads to make their living? How do modern New Jerseyans use the roads to make their living? What uses do modern New Jerseyans have for roads that the Lenape did not?

### Curriculum CONNECTION

**LINKS TO MATH** Tell students that the distance between Trenton and New Brunswick along Route 27 is approximately 25 miles. Have them calculate how long it would take a person walking at 3 miles per hour to cover the distance *(8 hours, 20 minutes)*. How long would it take a car traveling at 50 miles per hour *(half an hour)*?

### Meeting INDIVIDUAL NEEDS

**RETEACHING (Easy)** Have students construct "road signs" using symbols that show Lenape foot travelers which trail(s) and directions to take from different locations to planting, fishing, hunting, and camping grounds.

**EXTENSION (Average)** Ask groups of three or four students to prepare a five-minute presentation on a local highway, bridge, waterway, or other means of transportation. Their presentation should include pictures or maps and should tell why the route is important today.

**ENRICHMENT (Challenging)** Ask students to use a New Jersey road map and physical maps to identify natural features along the Minisink Trail between Metuchen and the Delaware River. Assuming a travel rate of 15 miles per day, have students prepare a detailed journal of what a Lenape would have seen while making such a trip.

**Write About It** Have students write a letter to a friend explaining why they would rather travel along a Native American trail than along a modern highway—or vice versa.

### Resource REMINDER

**Technology:** *Adventure Time CD-ROM*

**Transparency:** 3

CHAPTER 3

# LESSON 3

## DAILY LIFE OF THE LENAPE

PAGES 70–73

**Lesson Overview**

The village was the center of Lenape life. Men, women, and children fulfilled various roles, such as farming, hunting, preparing food, building homes, and governing.

**Lesson Objectives**

★ Discuss the tasks of Lenape girls and boys.

★ Describe Lenape village life, including meals, homes, tradition, and recreation.

## Reading Strategies and LANGUAGE DEVELOPMENT

**COMPARE AND CONTRAST** Tell students that relating a new idea to something familiar to them can help them remember information. As they prepare to read the lesson, tell them to look for and think about ways in which life among the Lenape was similar to and different from their own lives today. Draw two columns on the chalkboard titled "Similar" and "Different." Invite students to fill in the columns as they read.

## Second-Language SUPPORT

**USING TEXT HEADINGS** Understanding and using built-in text clues can help second-language students focus on the important content. Call attention to the five headings in the text following "The Big Picture." Help students rewrite each heading as a question and have them look for answers as they read.

## Technology CONNECTION

**ADVENTURE TIME CD-ROM**

Enrich this lesson with *United States, Explore, Investigate, Movies, and Powwow* on the CD-ROM.

## Building CITIZENSHIP

**RECOGNIZING ROLES AND RESPONSIBILITIES**

- Discuss the contributions and responsibilities of children, women, and men in Lenape society. Invite students to name various jobs or careers in modern society. How does each job help society as a whole? In what ways do people today have similar responsibilities as people in Lenape villages had?
- Ask students what responsibilities Lenape children had. Invite them to list their own responsibilities at home. Have students compare the completed lists. Conclude by discussing with them how doing their best in school is also a responsibility.

## Field Trip

**LIVING HISTORY** Students might enjoy visiting the Village of Waterloo in Allamuchy State Park, at Stanhope. Part of it is a reconstruction of a Lenape village, which re-creates the life of the Lenape 250 years ago. A bark longhouse and a garden are included at the site. Waterloo Village is open from mid-April through Mid-November. Information is available at (973) 347-0900 or by writing: Waterloo Village, Waterloo Road, Stanhope 07874. As an alternative, you might invite a member of the local historical society to speak to students about the Native Americans who lived in your area around or before 1600.

## √Answers to THINK ABOUT IT

1. Any three: corn, beans, squash, strawberries, raspberries, crab apples, onions, nuts, fish, meat from deer, elk, or bear
2. information passed on by word of mouth
3. Children learned by working with their parents and by listening to the stories of older members of their group.
4. Answers may vary but should focus on such areas as education, chores and tasks, diet, homes, and recreation.
5. Stories should focus on design and methods and materials used.

**Write About It** Ask students to prepare a menu for the two meals a Lenape family ate in a day.

## Resource REMINDER

**Practice and Project Book:** page 19

**Technology:** *Adventure Time CD-ROM*

ANSWERS TO

# Chapter 3 REVIEW

PAGES 74–75

### THINKING ABOUT VOCABULARY

1. oral tradition
2. prehistory
3. ancestor
4. archaeologist
5. hunter-gatherer
6. manetu
7. artifact
8. longhouse
9. heritage
10. sakima

### THINKING ABOUT FACTS

1. The Bering Strait is a body of water that separates North America and Asia. Beringia was a land bridge that connected North America and Asia during the Ice Age; it is now covered by the waters of the Bering Strait.
2. about 12,000 years ago; across Beringia
3. They hunted big animals like mastodons and caribou for meat, and they gathered fruits, nuts, and fish as well.
4. by about 1,000 years ago
5. the Munsee and the Unami
6. Girls helped women with cooking and caring for younger children; boys learned to hunt and fish.
7. a ceremony in which the Lenape gave thanks to the Creator, the most important manetu
8. by working with their parents and listening to the stories of older members of their group
9. corn
10. Men and women met in the longhouse to discuss important matters.

## Suggestions for THINK AND WRITE

**SIGNS OF SUCCESS**

***Summary*** Summaries should mention three or more of the following: food, clothing, shelter, tasks, tools, village leadership, and ceremonies.

***Journal*** Students' entries should give general descriptions of artifacts appropriate to Lenape culture and should be written in the first person.

***Comparison*** Students' comparisons should show an understanding of the progression from hunter-gatherer existence to farming and village living

### APPLYING GEOGRAPHY SKILLS

**CAUSE AND EFFECT**

1. A cause is something that makes something else happen; an effect is what happens as a result.
2. It was covered by water when glaciers melted at the end of the Ice Age.
3. cause
4. They learned more about New Jersey's early people.
5. Answers may vary but should suggest that studying cause and effect can help them put facts together in a meaningful way, make connections between one event and another, or explain why things happen.

**Technology CONNECTION**

**ADVENTURE TIME CD-ROM**

Enrich Chapter 3 with *New Jersey, Explore,* and *Investigate* on the CD-ROM.

**Resource REMINDER**

**Practice and Project Book:** page 20

**Assessment Book:** Chapter 3 Test

**Performance Assessment,** pages T36–T38

 **Technology:** *Adventure Time CD-ROM*

CHAPTER 4 ORGANIZER

# Colonial New Jersey

PAGES 76–103

## CHAPTER OVERVIEW

Columbus and other Europeans arrived in North America looking for a water route to Asia. Verrazano and Hudson explored present-day New Jersey for France and the Netherlands. Dutch settlers started farms, settlements grew into towns, and enslaved Africans were brought to the colony. The English took over the colony from the Dutch and it was later divided into East Jersey and West Jersey for a period before becoming a single royal colony of England.

## CHAPTER PLANNING GUIDE

**Suggested pacing: 17–18 days**

| LESSON | LESSON FOCUS | LESSON RESOURCES |
|---|---|---|
| 1 **THE ARRIVAL OF THE EUROPEANS** pages 78–81 | Why Europeans First came to New Jersey | ***Practice and Project Book:*** page 21<br>***Technology:*** *Adventure Time CD-ROM* |
| **GEOGRAPHY SKILLS** pages 82–85 | Using Latitude and Longitude | ***Practice and Project Book:*** page 22<br>***Technology:*** *Adventure Time CD-ROM* |
| 2 **NEW NETHERLAND** pages 86–89 | Dutch Settlers in New Jersey | ***Practice and Project Book:*** page 23<br>***Technology:*** *Adventure Time CD-ROM* |
| 3 **ENGLISH NEW JERSEY** pages 90–95 | New Jersey Under English Rule | ***Practice and Project Book:*** page 24<br>***Technology:*** *Adventure Time CD-ROM* |
| **STUDY SKILLS** pages 96–97 | Reading Time Lines | ***Practice and Project Book:*** page 25<br>***Technology:*** *Adventure Time CD-ROM* |
| 4 **LIFE IN THE NEW JERSEY COLONY** pages 98–101 | Farming and Industry in the Growing New Jersey Colonies | ***Practice and Project Book:*** page 26<br>***Technology:*** *Adventure Time CD-ROM* |
| **CHAPTER REVIEW** pages 102–103 | Students' understanding of vocabulary, content, and skills is assessed. | ***Practice and Project Book:*** page 27<br>***Assessment Book:*** Chapter 4 Test<br>***Performance Assessment*** pages T38–T40<br>***Technology:*** *Adventure Time CD-ROM* |

### New Jersey Core Curriculum Content Standards for Social Studies

**Content Standards** These content standards and progress indicators for students completing Grade 4, correlated with Chapter 4, have been developed by the New Jersey Department of Education. A complete listing of the standards can be found on pages T110–T112.

**Standard 6.3** All students will acquire historical understanding of political and diplomatic ideas, forces, and institutions throughout the history of New Jersey, the United States, and the world.

1. pp. 79–81, 90
3. pp. 92–93

**Standard 6.4** All students will acquire historical understanding of societal ideas and forces throughout the history of New Jersey, the United States, and the world.

1. pp. 88–89, 99–101
2. pp. 92–95

**Standard 6.7** All students will acquire geographical understanding by studying the world in spatial terms.

1. pp. 82–85

CHAPTER 4

# LESSON 1
## THE ARRIVAL OF THE EUROPEANS

PAGES 78–81

### Lesson Overview

The first Europeans to arrive in New Jersey were looking for a water route to Asia. They found no such route. Instead, they found a land rich in resources inhabited by many Native American groups who were eager to trade. As a result, many Europeans were drawn to this area.

### Lesson Objectives

★ Identify Columbus and his first voyage to the Americas.

★ Identify Cabot, Verrazano, and Hudson and describe their explorations of New Jersey and their interactions with Native Americans.

★ Explain the purpose for the first voyages of exploration in the New Jersey area.

## Reading Strategies and LANGUAGE DEVELOPMENT

**CONTRADICTIONS** Remind students that a *contradiction* occurs when a new development or discovery conflicts with what people believe to be true. Direct students' attention to *The Big Picture*. Explain that many Europeans believed that by sailing west they could reach Asia. Christopher Columbus believed that Japan and India were much closer than they actually were. When he found a land unknown to Europeans, it contradicted their beliefs about the world's size and lands to be found. Tell students that looking for contradictions as they read can help them remember facts and spot problems in arguments.

## Second-Language SUPPORT

**TAKING NOTES** Help second-language learners remember explorers introduced in this lesson by playing "Who Am I"? Tell students to write one statement about each of the people listed on page 78. Students can quiz a partner by reading a statement and then asking "Who am I?"

## Technology CONNECTION

**ADVENTURE TIME CD-ROM**

Enrich this lesson with *The Northeast, Explore, Investigate,* and *Key People* on the CD-ROM.

## Meeting INDIVIDUAL NEEDS

**RETEACHING (Easy)** Have students create a web organizer for either Verrazano or Hudson. Have students write the explorer's name in a center circle and dates and details about their explorations in smaller connecting circles.

**EXTENSION (Average)** Have students do research about one of the explorers discussed in the section. Ask students to create a poster with a picture of the explorer, a map showing the explorer's major voyages, and a short biography.

**ENRICHMENT (Challenging)** Have students research a recent space mission and write a report. Have them compare and contrast the explorers in this chapter with space explorers.

## Curriculum CONNECTION

**LINKS TO LANGUAGE ARTS** Discuss with students the characteristics required of explorers, such as courage and love of adventure. Ask students to write a paragraph explaining why they would or would not want to apply for a post on a voyage to a distant planet.

## Background INFORMATION

**EXPLORATION AND CHRISTIANITY**

- Europeans wanted to spread Christianity to other parts of the world.
- Spanish missionaries spread Catholicism in the American Southeast and the West.
- French missionaries were active in Canada and along the Mississippi.

## √Answers to THINK ABOUT IT

1. the explorer who set sail for Asia in 1492 and reached the Americas
2. to find a water route to Asia
3. John Cabot and Giovanni da Verrazano
4. Students may predict that another European explorer would have reached the Americas eventually.
5. They could have sailed around South America and across the Pacific Ocean.

**Write About It** Have students write a scene for a movie about trading among Hudson's sailors and the Lenape.

### Resource REMINDER

**Practice and Project Book:** page 21

**Technology:** *Adventure Time CD-ROM*

**Transparency:** 1

CHAPTER 4

# SKILLS LESSON

## USING LATITUDE AND LONGITUDE

PAGES 82–85

**Lesson Overview**

The grid of *latitude* and *longitude* lines helps us locate places on Earth.

**Lesson Objective**

★ Apply map-reading skills to locate places using the lines of latitude and longitude.

### Why the SKILL MATTERS

Ask students how they would explain their location to a pen pal planning to visit from Japan. Students may mention using a map, giving their address, or sending directions. Then direct students to the map on page 85 and describe the elements shown on it. Point out the lines and numbers on the map and have students trace them with their fingers. Ask which lines are straight and which lines curve. Tell students that these imaginary lines provide a very precise way to locate places, a way that is understood around the world.

### Using LATITUDE

Have volunteers point out lines of latitude on "The World: Political" map on page R4 of the textbook. Ask them to locate the equator and discuss the difference between north latitudes and south latitudes.

### Using LONGITUDE

Read the text aloud or allow student volunteers to read. Direct students to locate the prime meridian on the map. Answer the text questions as a class.

### Trying the SKILL

Have students locate and describe cities in New Jersey and the United States by their latitudinal and longitudinal "addresses." Remind students that they may use the information in the *Helping Yourself* box.

### Technology CONNECTION

**ADVENTURE TIME CD-ROM**

Enrich this lesson with *World, Explore, Investigate, Charts,* and *Lines of Latitude* on the CD-ROM.

### Curriculum CONNECTION

**LINKS TO MATH** Have students use the political map of the United States on page R6 to complete these math problems based on the lines of latitude and longitude.

- About how many degrees of longitude separate Los Angeles, California, from Raleigh, North Carolina? *(40)*
- About how many degrees of latitude separate Anchorage, Alaska, from Austin, Texas? *(30)*

### Global CONNECTIONS

**TIME ZONES**

- At an international conference held in 1884 in Washington, D.C., the Greenwich meridian became the prime meridian at zero (0) degrees. The prime meridian is the reference line for setting universal time.
- The International Date Line is located in the Pacific Ocean halfway around the world from the prime meridian (180° longitude).
- As Earth rotates each day, its rays pass through one degree of longitude every 4 minutes. Each international time zone covers 15 degrees of longitude in width *(15° X 24 hrs = 360°),* so that time changes are calculated on an hourly basis.

### √Answers to REVIEWING THE SKILL

1. Lines of latitude are imaginary parallel lines running east and west that measure how far north or south a place is from the equator; lines of longitude are imaginary lines running north and south that measure distance east or west of the prime meridian. Lines of latitude and longitude help us locate places on Earth.
2. Mount Holly; Palmyra; Normandy Beach
3. Butzville and Maple Shade (75°W)
4. Students may reply that they followed a line of longitude across the map to find two cities located on the line.

### Resource REMINDER

**Practice and Project Book:** page 22

**Technology:** *Adventure Time CD-ROM*

CHAPTER 4

# LESSON 2
## NEW NETHERLAND
PAGES 86–89

### Lesson Overview
The Dutch were the first Europeans to settle in New Jersey. They traded with the Lenape and started settlements to protect and support their trading. The Lenape taught the Dutch many skills before tensions brought on by cultural differences and disease eventually caused fighting between the two groups.

### Lesson Objectives
- ★ Explain why the Dutch first came to New Jersey.
- ★ Identify the Dutch West India Company and its role in forming New Netherland.
- ★ Examine the life of the colonists and their relationship with the Lenape.

## Reading Strategies and LANGUAGE DEVELOPMENT
**PREDICT** Direct students to read the Read Aloud at the beginning of the lesson. Have them make predictions about what might happen as they read on.

**SEQUENCE** Help students recognize that the events in this lesson happened in a specific sequence. Make a chronological list on the chalkboard of the events covered in this lesson. Remind students to pay attention to sequence as they read.

## Technology CONNECTION
**ADVENTURE TIME CD-ROM**
Enrich this lesson with the *United States, Explore, Investigate,* and *Pictures* on the CD-ROM.

## Field TRIP
Students who live in or near Hudson County may enjoy visiting Jersey City to see the outline of the original town square of Bergen. South of Journal Square, the area is now known as Bergen Square. It is bounded by Newkirk, Van Reypen, and Vroom Streets, and Tuers Avenue. As an alternative to a visit, ask students to draw the original town of Bergen as described in the text.

## Second-Language SUPPORT
**NATIONALITIES AND LANGUAGES** Second-language students may benefit from making a chart listing the countries discussed in the section (the Netherlands and Sweden), the words for people who come from these countries, and the languages that they speak. For example, *Dutch* settlers who came from *the Netherlands* spoke *Dutch.* Keep the chart and add the words pertaining to England in Lesson 3.

## Global CONNECTION
**DUTCH EAST INDIA COMPANY** At practically the same time that the Dutch West India Company was starting settlements in New Jersey, the Dutch East India Company, started in 1602, was at work in Asia. It quickly gained control of all of present-day Indonesia, which was called the Dutch East Indies. The spice trade with the East Indies made the Netherlands very wealthy.

## ✓Answers to THINK ABOUT IT
1. A colony is a place ruled by another country.
2. A patroon was a Dutch landowner in New Netherland who agreed to bring over 50 immigrants to farm the land.
3. The Dutch wanted to protect and support their trading interests in the area.
4. The Dutch settlers may have starved to death because they were not familiar with the environment.
5. the South River

**Write About It** Have students write a conversation between a Dutch settler and a Lenape acquaintance.

## Resource REMINDER
**Practice and Project Book:** page 23
**Technology:** *Adventure Time CD-ROM*
**Transparency:** 1

CHAPTER 4

# LESSON 3

## ENGLISH NEW JERSEY

PAGES 90-95

### Lesson Overview

English rule in New Jersey began in 1664. The colony was divided into two parts from 1676 until 1702, when it was reunited as a royal colony. English rule brought freedom of religion and a government of delegates of the people to New Jersey.

### Lesson Objectives

★ Describe how the English gained control of New Netherland.

★ Explain how the English attracted settlers to New Jersey.

★ Compare the development of East Jersey and West Jersey and explain how New Jersey became a unified royal colony.

## Reading Strategies and LANGUAGE DEVELOPMENT

**COMPARE AND CONTRAST** Help students compare and contrast East and West Jersey. Draw a large Venn diagram on the board. Label the two circles East Jersey and West Jersey. Ask students to write details about how the regions differed in the separate areas of the two circles. In the overlapping area, students should note how the regions were similar, for example, both were English.

**QUOTATION MARKS** Point out to students the quotation marks around Stuyvesant's words in the *Read Aloud.* Remind students that these quotation marks mean that these words were the exact words spoken by Stuyvesant. Ask students to find another example of quotation marks used in this way.

## Second-Language SUPPORT

**DIALOGUES** Second-language learners may better understand the changing rulers of New Jersey if they participate in a role-play about that period. Have students role play the following events: the English takeover of New Netherland; the granting of New Jersey to Carteret and Berkeley; and the unification of New Jersey as a royal colony.

## Technology CONNECTION

**ADVENTURE TIME CD-ROM**

Enrich this lesson with *New Jersey, Explore, Investigate,* and *Time Lines* on the CD-ROM.

## Expanding the INFOGRAPHIC

**RESEARCHING AND WRITING** Have students examine the photographs and discuss what the photographs and captions represent. Then have students research one of the items and write a paragraph that provides information in greater depth.

## Background INFORMATION

**ALBANIA** Before the Duke of York gave the territory of New Jersey to Carteret and Berkeley, Governor Nicolls had named the region "Albania," after the Duke's Scottish title. Nicolls also had arranged land grants in the region to two different groups of settlers. When the governor learned that the Duke had granted the same land to Berkeley and Carteret, he resigned, telling the Duke he had given away the best of his holdings.

## Building CITIZENSHIP

**UNDERSTANDING FREEDOM OF RELIGION** Have students consult a telephone directory to examine a list of the houses of worship in their community. Have them total the number of religions represented. Discuss with students the importance of religious freedom in the growth of the United States and of New Jersey. Ask them why they think religious freedom is important.

## ✓Answers to THINK ABOUT IT

1. The English believed they had a right to all of North America because John Cabot had sailed there 150 years before the Dutch.
2. freedom of religion
3. Any two: the English offered low rents and many freedoms; appointed a governor; appointed proprietors; divided New Jersey into 2 sections.
4. Settlers believed that they, not the proprietors, owned the land. Settlers did not want to pay rent to proprietors, and they wanted to govern themselves through elected representatives.
5. Letters should mention the small farms and towns of East Jersey and the variety of churches.

**Write About It** Have students research and write a short biography of Sir George Carteret or Lord John Berkeley.

## Resource REMINDER

**Practice and Project Book:** page 24

 **Technology:** *Adventure Time CD-ROM*

CHAPTER 4

# SKILLS LESSON
## READING TIME LINES
PAGES 96-97

**Lesson Overview**

*Time lines* show the order in which events took place.

**Lesson Objective**

★ Read and interpret time lines.

### Why the SKILL MATTERS
Explain to students that a time line provides a lot of information in a small space. A time line shows them at a glance the main events in a lesson and tells them when the events occurred.

### Using the SKILL
Ask volunteers to read the text aloud while the rest of the class finds each event mentioned in the time line of events in colonial New Jersey history. As a class, answer the questions posed in the text.

### Trying the SKILL
Remind students to look at the time line as a whole before they begin to answer questions about it. Point out that the two time lines on these pages cover the same time period. Ask volunteers to state the subject and purpose of each time line. Then divide students into pairs to answer the questions in this section. Remind them to refer to the time line and to the *Helping Yourself* box as needed.

### Building CITIZENSHIP
**LEARNING MORE ABOUT LOCAL HISTORY**

Ask students to make and illustrate a time line showing important events in their community in the past year. Direct students to the library for back issues of local newspapers and to the offices of community government for additional information. Ask if the class may display the completed time line at the library.

### Technology CONNECTION
**ADVENTURE TIME CD-ROM**

Enrich this lesson with *North America, Explore, Investigate,* and *Time Lines* on the CD-ROM.

### Meeting INDIVIDUAL NEEDS
**RETEACHING (Easy)** Help students make a simple time line of their own lives. Tell them to draw a horizontal line across the center of a piece of paper. Then have them add a short vertical line at the left side of the line and another at the right side. Have students label the left line *birth* and the right line with their current age. Tell them to draw a third vertical line in the middle of the horizontal line and label it with one half of their current age. Then direct students to enter four events they consider important in the proper places on their time line.

**EXTENSION (Average)** Have students create a time line of the school year to date. Using the school calendar and your lesson plan book, have each student write the name and date of a special event on an index card. You may include the first day of school, holidays, parties, and assemblies. If you cannot list as many events as you have students, use current events. Place a long strip of wide masking tape along the floor. With a marker, divide the strip into twelve time periods, one for every month of the year. As you name each event and date, have students place their event on the time line.

**ENRICHMENT (Challenging)** Ask students to refer to the New Jersey time line in the reference section of the book, pages R18–R19. Have students study the time line and then write a short report explaining how they might use this time line for their study of New Jersey.

### ✓Answers to REVIEWING THE SKILL
1. A time line shows you when events happened.
2. taking New Netherland from the Dutch
3. 74 years
4. Cornelius Mey became the first governor of New Netherland.
5. Answers may vary, but students should note that a time line is useful in any subject for which keeping track of key events and developments is important. Examples are science and art.

### Resource REMINDER
**Practice and Project Book:** page 25

 **Technology:** *Adventure Time CD-ROM*

CHAPTER 4

# LESSON 4

LESSON 4

## Life in the New Jersey Colony

PAGES 98–101

### Lesson Overview

The New Jersey colony grew quickly in the 1700s. Towns developed, industries got started, and farming thrived. While most people enjoyed freedom, other New Jerseyans were indentured servants or enslaved Africans. Colonists continued to treat the Lenape poorly, forcing many to leave.

### Lesson Objectives

- ★ Describe how men, women, and children lived and worked on colonial New Jersey farms.
- ★ Identify early New Jersey industries.
- ★ Explain New Jersey's early society and the differences in the lives of the people who lived there.

## Reading Strategies and LANGUAGE DEVELOPMENT

**SYNONYMS AND ANTONYMS** Remind students that an antonym is a word that means the opposite of another word. Direct students to these words in *The Big Picture* and have them supply antonyms: *important (unimportant), swell (shrink),* and *enslaved (free).* Ask students to find antonyms for other words in the section.

**CAUSE AND EFFECT** Draw students' attention to this statement on page 99: "The iron industry needed wood to produce this heat *(cause),* and so the lumber industry grew up as well *(effect).*" Ask volunteers to point out which part of the sentence shows cause and which shows effect. When students have finished reading page 101, ask them to identify the cause of the loss of land by the Lenape.

## Curriculum Connection

**LINKS TO MATH** Ask students to find New Jersey population figures for 1700, 1750, and 1800 in *The Big Picture.* Then ask them to calculate the increase in population in New Jersey between 1700 and 1750 *(57,000)*, between 1750 and 1800 *(140,000)*, and between 1700 and 1800 *(197,000).*

## Technology CONNECTION

**ADVENTURE TIME CD-ROM**

Enrich this lesson with *United States, Explore, Investigate,* and *Pictures* on the CD-ROM.

## Meeting Individual Needs

**RETEACHING (Easy)** Have students write a diary entry from the point of view of a child on a colonial New Jersey farm. Entries should mention chores and school time.

**EXTENSION (Average)** Have students work together to research and build a model of a colonial New Jersey farm with buildings, fields, and figures engaged in various activities. Provide students with posterboard, construction paper, modeling clay, markers, and poster paints.

**ENRICHMENT (Challenging)** Have students research and present reports on one of the following subjects: how to weave cloth on a loom, how make candles, how to make soap from animal fat, or how to make glass.

## Background INFORMATION

**SLAVERY IN NEW JERSEY**

- The Dutch settlers of New Jersey owned enslaved Africans. These people were most likely captured by the Spanish or the Portuguese.
- In 1680, about half of the 120 enslaved Africans in New Jersey worked making iron. Most of the others worked on one plantation in Shrewsbury.

## ✓Answers to THINK ABOUT IT

1. Women took care of the home, helped with farming, and made soap, candles, and cloth. Men farmed and hunted.
2. iron mining; sawmills; glass-making; whaling and fishing
3. New Jersey colonists had to provide their own food and clothing.
4. Colonial and Lenape children worked at chores that supported the household. Colonial children attended school. Lenape children learned everything by working with their parents and listening to older members of their group.
5. Letters may include an explanation of how long the indenture would last, the work, and hopes for the future.

**Write About It** Have students write a short essay on how mining iron ore in New Jersey helped industries.

## Resource REMINDER

**Practice and Project Book:** page 26

 **Technology:** *Adventure Time CD-ROM*

ANSWERS TO

# Chapter 4 REVIEW

PAGES 102-103

1. slavery
2. colony
3. proprietor
4. delegate
5. constitution

### THINKING ABOUT FACTS

1. They said the Lenape were friendly and eager to trade.
2. They came to trade for furs and other valuable items.
3. cultural differences; also, the Dutch brought diseases that killed many Lenape
4. the outlines of Bergen at Bergen Square in Jersey City
5. He did not want to surrender and said he would rather die.
6. The Duke of York named it after Sir George Carteret's birthplace, the island of Jersey.
7. They offered low rents and many freedoms, including religious freedom.
8. West Jersey
9. They spent a few weeks each year in school.
10. They had no rights; they could not vote or own property.

## Suggestions for THINK AND WRITE

**SIGNS OF SUCCESS**

***Journal*** Students' entries should give general descriptions of seeing America and meeting the Lenape and should be written in the first person.

***Menu*** Students' answers should describe a meal including foods such as hard-boiled eggs, fruits and vegetables, and meat.

***Chart*** Students' charts should show an understanding of the power structure, including information on rights of women, land owners, indentured servants, and enslaved Africans.

### APPLYING STUDY SKILLS

**TIME LINES**

1. 300
2. 1609
3. 5 years later
4. before
5. They help give a sense of order to history by showing when events happened and how much time passed between them.

**Technology CONNECTION**

**ADVENTURE TIME CD-ROM**

Enrich Chapter 4 with *New Jersey, Explore,* and *Investigate* on the CD-ROM.

**REMINDER**

**Practice and Project Book:** page 27

**Assessment Book:** Chapter 4 Test

**Performance Assessment,** pages T38-T40

 **Technology:** *Adventure Time CD-ROM*

# The American Revolution

PAGES 104–131

## CHAPTER OVERVIEW

In the middle of the 1700s, France and Britain were fighting over their North American colonies. In 1776, the 13 British colonies decided to break away from Great Britain. New Jersey played a major role in the American Revolution.

## CHAPTER PLANNING GUIDE

**Suggested pacing: 15–16 days**

| LESSON | LESSON FOCUS | LESSON RESOURCES |
|---|---|---|
| **1 UNREST IN THE COLONIES** pages 106–111 | The Beginning of the American Revolution | ***Practice and Project Book:*** page 28<br>***Technology:*** *Adventure Time CD-ROM* |
| **CITIZENSHIP VIEWPOINTS** pages 112–113 | 1776: What Did the People of New Jersey Think About Declaring Independence? | ***Practice and Project Book:*** page 29<br>***Technology:*** *Adventure Time CD-ROM* |
| **THINKING SKILL** pages 114–115 | Identifying Fact and Opinion | ***Practice and Project Book:*** page 30<br>***Technology:*** *Adventure Time CD-ROM* |
| **2 CROSSROADS OF THE REVOLUTION** pages 116–123 | New Jersey's Key Location and Role in the Revolution | ***Practice and Project Book:*** page 31<br>***Technology:*** *Adventure Time CD-ROM* |
| **LEGACY** pages 124–125 | Special Places in New Jersey History | |
| **3 A MORE PERFECT UNION** pages 126–129 | New Jersey and the Constitution | ***Technology:*** *Adventure Time CD-ROM* |
| **CHAPTER REVIEW** pages 130–131 | Students' understanding of vocabulary, content, and skills is assessed. | ***Practice and Project Book:*** page 32<br>***Assessment Book:*** Chapter 5 Test, ***Performance Assessment*** pages T41–T43 |

### New Jersey Core Curriculum Content Standards for Social Studies

**Content Standards** These content standards and progress indicators for students completing Grade 4, correlated with Chapter 5, have been developed by the New Jersey Department of Education. A complete listing of the standards can be found on pages T110–T112.

**Standard 6.3** All students will acquire historical understanding of political and diplomatic ideas, forces, and institutions throughout the history of New Jersey, the United States, and the world.
2. pp. 112–113, 117, 128
3. pp. 108–111, 118–119

**Standard 6.7** All students will acquire geographical understanding by studying the world in spatial terms.
1. p. 120

CHAPTER 5

# LESSON 1
## UNREST IN THE COLONIES
PAGES 106–111

### Lesson Overview
Britain's efforts to tax the colonies after the French and Indian War brought colonial protests. Fighting in Massachusetts convinced Americans to declare independence.

### Lesson Objectives
★ Summarize the French and Indian War.

★ Explain why colonists declared independence from Britain.

★ Explore the writing of the Declaration of Independence and New Jersey's constitution.

## Reading Strategies and LANGUAGE DEVELOPMENT

**MAKE AND SUPPORT GENERALIZATIONS** Write the following sentence on the chalkboard. "France and England wanted to control land in North America." Note that the statement is a generalization—a general statement that points out something common among different things. Tell students that valid generalizations need to be supported by facts. Ask what facts in the lesson make this generalization valid.

**PREFIXES AND SUFFIXES** Direct students to the word "unfair" found in the second paragraph under the heading "Important Meetings" on page 109. Call on a volunteer to define the word. Explain that "un" is a prefix meaning "not," which reverses the meaning of a root word.

## Second-Language SUPPORT

**DRAMATIZATION** To help second-language students understand events described in the lesson, arrange the class into three groups, each assigned one of the lesson's main headings. Have each group choose a narrator to set the scene. Then have other group members dramatize section events.

## Technology CONNECTION

**ADVENTURE TIME CD-ROM**

Enrich this lesson with *French Lands in North America, 1750, Signing the Declaration, Declaration of Independence,* and *Printing Press* on the CD-ROM.

## Meeting INDIVIDUAL NEEDS

**RETEACHING (Easy)** Ask students to review the lesson and write key events on sentence strips. Then have partners take turns scrambling and correctly reordering the strips.

**EXTENSION (Average)** Have students design and construct a cause-and-effect chart of events in the lesson. Tell them to include events that may be both effects and causes.

**ENRICHMENT (Challenging)** Direct students to American history books containing accounts of the French and Indian War. Have them research and prepare a short report on the Battle of Quebec, the last major battle of the war.

## Background INFORMATION

**SIGNERS OF THE DECLARATION OF INDEPENDENCE**

- Abraham Clark was a wealthy farmer who lived near present-day Elizabeth. He later refused to sign the new Constitution.
- Richard Stockton was a successful lawyer and firm Patriot living in Princeton. When he returned home from Philadelphia after the signing, Loyalists arrested him and put him in jail in New York City.
- John Witherspoon was a minister and college president. His student James Madison helped write the Constitution.

## ✓Answers to THINK ABOUT IT

1. Britain wanted the colonies to help pay for the French and Indian War.
2. People in Greenwich burned stored tea.
3. the Stamp Act of 1765; the British response to the Boston Tea Party; the fight between British troops and colonists at Lexington and Concord
4. French and Indian War, Stamp Act, Greenwich Tea Party, Declaration of Independence
5. Student letters should demonstrate an understanding of colonial taxation issues.

**WRITE ABOUT IT** Have students write a newspaper advertisement urging colonists not to pay the tea tax.

**Practice and Project Book:** page 28

 **Technology:** *Adventure Time CD-ROM*

CHAPTER 5

# CITIZENSHIP
## Viewpoints

### 1776: WHAT DID THE PEOPLE OF NEW JERSEY THINK ABOUT DECLARING INDEPENDENCE?

PAGES 112–113

**Lesson Objective**

★ Analyze colonists' different points of view concerning independence from Great Britain.

## Identifying the ISSUE

Help students see that the issue of independence was political and that political issues tend to involve many different opinions.

## Discussing THREE DIFFERENT VIEWPOINTS

Remind students that declaring independence from Great Britain was a very big step for American colonists. Discuss the long-standing ties the colonies had with Britain and have students suggest what the colonists hoped to gain by breaking those ties. Ask students to keep this information in mind as they read the viewpoints of Franklin, Elmer, and Livingston.

## CITIZENSHIP

**MAKING A COMPROMISE** The viewpoints expressed by Franklin, Elmer, and Livingston show how differently people can feel about the same issue. In many situations, people who disagree must compromise with each other.

- Challenge students to come up with a compromise that the three men could have made. Students should work in small groups to develop their compromise.
- Students will have to consider how the opinions of each person would have to change in order to bring about a compromise. Be sure that students' suggestions are reasonable.
- Have groups present their plans for compromise to the class. The class should then discuss or debate the proposed plans and vote on the single best plan.

## √Answers to BUILDING CITIZENSHIP

**THINKING ABOUT VIEWPOINTS**

1. **Franklin** opposes independence; **Livingston** supports it.
2. **Franklin** The colonies have been happy under British rule and a Patriot government will fail. **Elmer** Attractive and frightening as it is, Britain is now just another country to Americans. **Livingston** Making peace with Britain would only mean more trade restrictions, while independence would mean freedom to make our own laws and trade with whomever we want.
3. Possible answers: Native Americans might favor the British because the British had protected their western lands. Enslaved African Americans might favor independence, thinking they could seize a chance for freedom in wartime confusion.

## Sharing VIEWPOINTS

Discuss the validity of each point of view, considering who each person was and when his statements were made. Students' statements about the conflict over British rule may go beyond the basic thoughts expressed by Franklin, Elmer, and Livingston on page 113. Possible statements might include: 1. We agree that we have been happy under Great Britain's rule to this point. 2. We agree that we are free citizens, no longer tied to Great Britain or its people. 3. We agree that the United States should always be free to trade with whomever it wishes.

**DEBATING VIEWPOINTS** Encourage each student to take one of the viewpoints and prepare arguments to support it in a debate.

CHAPTER 5

# SKILLS LESSON

## IDENTIFYING FACT AND OPINION

PAGES 114–115

**Lesson Overview**

Identifying fact from opinion helps students distinguish statements that can be proven true from statements that cannot.

**Lesson Objective**

★ Distinguish facts from opinions in written materials.

## Why the SKILL MATTERS

Establish that facts can be proven true and that opinions—or a person's beliefs or feelings—cannot be proven. Tell students that people who read newspaper articles, view TV news reports, vote, or serve on juries need to be able to recognize facts versus opinions. Write the headings "facts" and "opinions" on the chalkboard and have students suggest examples of each. List their responses under the headings. Refer them to the *Helping Yourself* on page 115 for help in deciding which are facts and which are opinions. Remind students that they can check reference books to make sure a statement is a fact.

## Using the SKILL

Have a volunteer read the passage in the text. Ask other volunteers to explain how to tell whether the first three sentences are facts or opinions. Have them suppose the third sentence had not included the words "I believe." Would they have accepted it as fact? Why or why not?

## Trying the SKILL

Have a volunteer read the quoted passage about the colonist Jemima Condict Harrison. Answer the questions that follow it as a class.

## Technology CONNECTION

**ADVENTURE TIME CD-ROM**

Enrich this lesson with *New Jersey* and *Create* on the CD-ROM.

## Curriculum CONNECTION

**LINKS TO READING** Have students look for examples of fact and opinion in newspapers and newsmagazines.

- Distribute copies of newspapers and newsmagazines and have students find three or four examples of both facts and opinions. Note that news reports contain many facts while editorials and features contain more opinions.
- Have students record their examples of both facts and opinions. As a class, discuss student choices and clues used to distinguish facts from opinions.

## Meeting INDIVIDUAL NEEDS

**RETEACHING (Easy)** Have students select a paragraph from a magazine of their choosing and indicate which statements are facts and which are opinions.

**EXTENSION (Average)** Ask students to research newspaper and magazine articles on a current local issue, such as building new schools or parks. Have them write several facts and several opinions of their own about the issue, based on the articles they have read.

**ENRICHMENT (Challenging)** Ask students to research a controversial topic such as global warming or current political activities. Have them choose one side of the argument on the topic and write a persuasive paper that includes both facts and opinions.

## ✓Answers to REVIEWING THE SKILL

1. A fact can be proven true, but an opinion cannot.
2. People can disagree about what is best in a given instance but none of their opinions can be proven true.
3. If a statement agrees with information given in a reference book, the statement is most likely a fact.
4. Student answers should recognize that facts help people make sound, informed decisions.
5. Students' statements should include a provable fact and a belief or feeling about that fact.

Resource REMINDER

**Practice and Project Book:** page 29

 **Technology:** *Adventure Time CD-ROM*

CHAPTER 5

# LESSON 2

## CROSSROADS OF THE REVOLUTION

PAGES 116–123

### Lesson Overview

British control of New Jersey would have helped separate New England from the southern colonies. The war had been going poorly for the Americans, but victories at Trenton and Princeton showed Americans that victory was possible.

### Lesson Objectives

★ Explain the importance of New Jersey's location to the American Revolution.

★ Analyze the significance of the Battles of Trenton and Princeton.

★ Identify the contributions of Patriot Molly Pitcher.

## Reading Strategies and LANGUAGE DEVELOPMENT

**REREADING** Remind students that a good way to remember and understand what they read is to read the text more than once. Tell them they will often discover information on a second read that they did not see on the first. Have students practice rereading main sections of the lesson.

## Curriculum CONNECTION

**LINKS TO MUSIC**

- Tell students that the tune and words of "Yankee Doodle" originated with the British, whose soldiers first fifed, sang, and marched to it to mock the ragtag American soldiers. Patriot soldiers, however, including those under Washington's command, soon claimed the song for themselves. It was first published in sheet music in 1775.
- Invite students to write other lyrics for "Yankee Doodle"—perhaps lyrics aimed at British soldiers or policies.

## Technology CONNECTION

**ADVENTURE TIME CD-ROM**

Enrich this lesson with *Tough Times at Valley Forge* and *Lexington and Concord* on the CD-ROM.

## Expanding the INFOGRAPHIC

**RESEARCHING AND WRITING** Help students do further research on the Battle of Trenton in 1776. Have them write a newspaper editorial describing details of the battle and urging Patriots to take heart that their cause will succeed.

## Field Trip

**SITES OF THE REVOLUTION** Arrange a visit to a Revolutionary home, building, or field site in your local area. The remains of Fort Mercer and the Whithall House in Gloucester County at 100 Hessian Avenue, National Park 08063, offer special insights into the period, including a reenactment of the Battle of Fort Mercer. For information, call (856) 853–5120. As an alternative, have students research nearby sites and map out a road trip to one or more sites, starting from and finishing at their own community.

## Global CONNECTION

**HELP FROM ABROAD** Both America and France favored greater French aid. In 1778, after a Patriot victory at Saratoga. The French provided naval forces that supported the Patriot victory. Volunteers from various countries were already helping Patriot armies. Among them were France's Marquis de Lafayette, who served as an aide to Washington, and Prussia's Baron Von Steuben, who helped train Washington's army.

## ✓Answers to THINK ABOUT IT

1. a colonist loyal to Britain
2. people were divided in their beliefs, homes businesses, and crops were burned
3. the battles of Trenton, Princeton, and Monmouth
4. Possible answers: The patriots might have lost hope and given up. The British might have won the war.
5. New Jersey was a link between New England and the southern colonies, and between New York and Philadelphia.

**Write About It** Have students write a poem of victory and independence.

## Resource REMINDER

**Practice and Project Book:** page 30

**Technology:** *Adventure Time CD-ROM*

CHAPTER 5

# LEGACY

## LINKING PAST AND PRESENT
## SPECIAL PLACES IN NEW JERSEY HISTORY

PAGES 124–125

**Lesson Overview**

Parks, buildings, monuments, and other special places make up New Jersey's historic sites. These sites keep alive the memory of important historic events and the contributions of people in New Jersey's past.

**Lesson Objectives**

★ Explain what a historic site is.

★ Describe some specific historic sites in New Jersey and why they are preserved.

### Understanding the Concept OF A LEGACY

Ask students if they have ever been cleaning a drawer or closet and discovered a favorite toy or book they enjoyed when they were younger. What good memories did the discovery bring back? Then call on a volunteer to read aloud the closing paragraph in the introduction. Help students understand that historic sites remind us of parts of our past we do not want to forget. In this role, they represent a legacy.

### Examining the PHOTOGRAPHS

Call students' attention to the Ford Mansion. Ask why it is especially appropriate to picture this historic site in the winter. Have students speculate about what Washington might have thought or said while quartered in the building. Call on volunteers to tell what they may already know about the history of enslaved African Americans. Then ask what the photographs of Lawnside tell them about this part of New Jersey's past. Tell students they will learn more about the history of slavery in the next unit. Invite students who may have visited any of the sites pictured on these pages to share their experiences.

### Background INFORMATION

**A PROUD MILITARY PAST** Developed during the industrialization of the late 1800s, battleships were for a time the most important ships in a country's navy. Large, heavy, and armed with huge guns, a battleship was nearly unsinkable. During World War II, aircraft carriers replaced battleships in importance. After the war, many battleships were destroyed. Today the United States has only two, the *Missouri* and the *New Jersey*. Both battleships became historic sites in the late 1990s.

### Field Trip

Plan a visit to one of the historic sites shown here or to another in or near your community. As an alternative, call Howell Living History Farm, (609) 737–3299, for a free calendar describing the many events featured throughout the year. Then have students pick an event and make a drawing or model of a scene representing the event.

### Curriculum CONNECTION

**LINKS TO LANGUAGE ARTS** Remind students that in this textbook and in their language arts classes they have read passages from the journals of historic figures. Journals, which record daily life, can be an interesting way to learn about history firsthand. Ask students to choose a figure discussed in this legacy or elsewhere in Chapter 5. Suggest that they write a brief journal entry that the person might have written. For example, they might create a journal entry written by a participant in the Greenwich Tea Party or an entry written by George Washington at Morristown.

**Write About It** Have students draw up a proposal for submission to a government agency on historic site preservation. Their proposal should identify an important site in their community and explain why they think it should be preserved for future New Jerseyans.

CHAPTER 5

# LESSON 3
## A MORE PERFECT UNION

PAGES 126–129

**Lesson Overview**

New Jersey was the third state to ratify the Constitution, which replaced the weak Articles of Confederation.

**Lesson Objectives**

★ Explain why and how the Constitution was written.

★ Describe the New Jersey Plan and its role at the Constitutional Convention.

## Reading Strategies and LANGUAGE DEVELOPMENT

**CONTRADICTIONS** Write the word *contradiction* on the chalkboard and call on volunteers to help establish its meaning—something that denies another statement or expectation. Discuss reasonable American expectations that happy times were in store after the War, with the British gone. Note that actual events after the Revolution contradicted those expectations. Have students list the events that contradicted colonists' expectations as they read the lesson.

**PREFIXES AND SUFFIXES** Write the word *nation* on the chalkboard and have students define it. Add the suffix *-al* to *nation* and have students define the meaning of *national*. Note that *-al* means "pertaining to" and changes the word *nation* to a word that describes something. Have students look for a similar use of this suffix as they read *(constitutional)*. Follow the same steps for *govern*, noting that the suffix *-ment* changes an action word to a naming word, *government*.

## Building CITIZENSHIP

**DEFINING CONSTITUTIONAL RIGHTS** Have students research the Bill of Rights. Have them construct a bulletin board naming the rights and using drawings, photographs, and clippings to show how the rights are exercised today.

## Technology CONNECTION

**ADVENTURE TIME CD-ROM**

Enrich this lesson with *Explore* and *Investigate* on the CD-ROM.

## Second-Language SUPPORT

**DRAMATIZATION** Second-language students may better understand lesson events if the class dramatizes them. Assign groups of students sections of the text. Have students in each group take turns as narrators, reading the text as other class members dramatize events. Have each group create two questions to ask after the dramatization.

## Meeting INDIVIDUAL NEEDS

**RETEACHING (Easy)** Have students hold a mock meeting at the Constitutional Convention. They should discuss why a new constitution is needed, make plans for this constitution, and come to a final agreement.

**EXTENSION (Average)** Have students research the numbers of Representatives in New Jersey today. Have them compare their finding with the numbers of Representatives from surrounding states.

**ENRICHMENT (Challenging)** Have students research the debate over ratification and create "colonial" leaflets and/or handbills supporting some different points of view.

## √Answers to THINK ABOUT IT

1. New York taxed New Jersey goods that were shipped across New York.
2. Government under the Articles of Confederation was too weak to collect taxes or settle disputes among states.
3. New Jersey had a plan for a one-house legislature, which led to a compromise between large and small states.
4. The Virginia Plan called for a two-house legislature with larger states having greater representation in both houses. The New Jersey Plan called for a one-house legislature with equal representation for all states.
5. Student opinions should reflect an understanding of the small state's concerns about being dominated by large states in the national government.

**Write About It** Have students write a carriage "bumper sticker" expressing their opinion of the Articles of Confederation.

## Resource REMINDER

**Practice and Project Book:** page 31

 **Technology:** *Adventure Time CD-ROM*

ANSWERS TO

# Chapter 5 REVIEW

PAGES 130–131

### THINKING ABOUT VOCABULARY

1. During the American Revolution, Loyalists supported the British, while the Patriots supported the Revolution.
2. The British Stamp Act was a tax placed on colonial items such as newspapers.
3. People in the militia helped to fight the American Revolution.
4. The Battle of Trenton and the Battle of Princeton restored Americans' confidence in the Continental Army.
5. Supporters of the Virginia Plan and the New Jersey Plan reached an agreement known as the Great Compromise which insured that all states would get equal representation.

### THINKING ABOUT FACTS

1. They wanted the colonists to help pay for the costs of the war.
2. Patriots wanted independence; Loyalists stayed faithful to Great Britain.
3. They though it was unfair to be taxed by a government in which they had no representatives, and it made them angry.
4. Greenwich
5. unfair tax laws and disregard of the rights of the colonists as British citizens
6. because its location between New England and the southern colonies made it strategically important, and both armies marched, camped, and fought there often
7. They restored Americans' confidence in the Continental Army and the Patriot cause.
8. The winter was cold with much snow. The Continental Congress ran out of money. Soldiers had no money for food and spirits were low.
9. The states disagreed on the tax New York was placing on New Jersey goods that were shipped through New York.
10. The New Jersey plan insured equal representation for states with smaller population.

**Technology CONNECTION**

**ADVENTURE TIME CD-ROM**

Enrich Chapter 5 with *New Jersey, Explore,* and *Investigate* on the CD-ROM.

## Suggestions for THINK AND WRITE

### SIGNS OF SUCCESS

***Letter*** Students' letters should explain that it is unfair for Great Britain to tax the colonists to pay for the French and Indian War, since they have no representatives in the British government. Letters should also include all the elements of a letter: date, salutation, body, closing, and signature.

***Essay*** Students' essays should list several reasons for their position and back it up with facts from the lesson.

***Paragraph*** Students' paragraphs should explain each of the two plans, showing an understanding of the Great Compromise.

*For performance assessment, see* **Assessment Book,** *Chapter 5, pages T41-T43.*

### APPLYING GEOGRAPHY SKILLS
### IDENTIFYING FACT AND OPINION

1. A fact can be proven. An opinion cannot be proven—it expresses a belief or feeling.
2. think, should, believe
3. first sentence is fact, second sentence is opinion
4. Answers will vary, but should demonstrate an understanding of the difference between a fact and an opinion.
5. so that you can make decisions based on facts

**Resource REMINDER**

**Practice and Project Book:** page 32

**Assessment Book:** Chapter 5 Test

**Performance Assessment,** pages T42–T44

**Technology:** *Adventure Time CD-ROM*

ANSWERS TO

# Unit 2 REVIEW

PAGES 132–133

### THINKING ABOUT VOCABULARY

1. b
2. a
3. a
4. c
5. b

## Suggestions for THINK AND WRITE

### SIGNS OF SUCCESS

***Description*** Students' descriptions should include information about one artifact from Chapter 3 as well as the material it was made from and ideas of how the artifact was used.

***Interview*** Students' questions should reflect a knowledge of the crops grown by New Jersey farmers, the farmers' way of life, and how English rule affected farmers.

***Article*** Students' articles should demonstrate a knowledge of the event selected, including the date, location, and reason for the event.

## Building SKILLS

1. **Cause and Effect** because, since; so, therefore
2. **Cause and Effect** Britain's need to pay for the costs of keeping an army in the colonies; the colonists became angry with the British for imposing this tax
3. **Latitude and Longitude** Palmyra
4. **Time Lines** Responses will vary but may include any of the dates found in Unit 2. Make certain students have the dates in the correct order.
5. **Fact and Opinion** I think, I believe, the best, should

## Suggestions for YESTERDAY, TODAY, AND TOMORROW

Ask students to list places that have not been fully explored yet. Allow them to speculate as to what may remain to be explored. Ask them what is more important—exploration, or care for what we already have? Discuss with students how it costs a lot of money to explore new places, yet sometimes explorations give us new resources or solutions to current problems. You might discuss with students whether we should explore new places if life exists there.

## ONGOING UNIT PROJECT

The ongoing unit project begun on page T21 can be part of your assessment program, along with other forms of evaluation.

## UNIT PROJECT 

### WRITE A HISTORICAL DIARY

***Objective*** Writing a historical diary will help students better understand the people, their ways of life, and the time period in which they lived.

***Materials*** paper, pencil

- Suggest that rereading the text to review the groups of New Jerseyans they read about may help students decide which person to choose for their historical diary.
- Encourage students to do additional research using an encyclopedia or other books to find out more about the everyday lives of the various groups mentioned in Unit 2.

### OPTIONS FOR ASSESSMENT

*For performance assessment, see* **Assessment Book,** *Unit 2, page T45.*

**FOR THE PORTFOLIO** Individual notes and sketches can be included in students' portfolios.

# A Growing State

**PAGES 134–191**

## UNIT OVERVIEW

In the 1800s, New Jersey grew and changed. Transportation improved dramatically, industries developed, and reformers tried to better people's lives. The slavery issue led to the Civil War between the North and South. New Jerseyans fought for the Union. After the war, our state saw new industries and inventions change American life forever.

## UNIT PLANNING GUIDE

| CHAPTER | SUGGESTED PACING | CHAPTER OVERVIEW | CHAPTER RESOURCES |
|---|---|---|---|
| **6 Changes in a New State** pages 138–159 | 13–14 days | New Jersey industries grew as roads and waterways were developed and railroads were built. Reformers worked to help all New Jerseyans. | ***Practice and Project Book*** pages 33–38<br>***Transparencies:*** 1, 3<br>***Technology:*** *Adventure Time CD-ROM* |
| **7 Challenge and Growth** pages 160–189 | 18–19 days | The issue of slavery led to the Civil War. Many New Jerseyans fought on the side of the Union. Invention and new industries flourished after the war and immigrants flocked to our state. | ***Practice and Project Book*** pages 39–44<br>***Transparencies:*** 1, 2<br>***Technology:*** *Adventure Time CD-ROM* |

**Internet CONNECTION**

The Home Page at **http://www.mhschool.com** contains on-line student activities related to this unit.

**For Further Support**

• Handbook of Test-Taking Strategies

## ASSESSMENT OPPORTUNITIES

### UNIT ASSESSMENT

**Unit Review** pages 190–191
***Unit Project*** page 191, page T47

**Assessment Book**
***Unit Test*** Unit 3 Test
***Performance Assessment*** page T52

### CHAPTER ASSESSMENT

**Meeting Individual Needs** pages T49, T50, T52, T57, T58, T59, T60, T62
**Write About It** pages T49, T51, T53, T56, T57, T59, T60, T62
**Chapter Review** pages 158–159, 188–189

**Assessment Book**
***Chapter 6 Test, Chapter 7 Test***
***Performance Assessment*** pages T46–T48, T49–T51

## TECHNOLOGY CENTER

### Enriching with Multimedia

**RESOURCE:** *Internet*

- Look at McGraw-Hill School's home page on the World Wide Web at **http://www.mhschool.com** for activities related to this unit that your students can do on-line.

**RESOURCE: Adventure Time CD-ROM**

Enrich Unit 3 with *Explore, Build,* and *Paint* on the CD-ROM.

## SCHOOL-TO-HOME

### Building New Jersey

- Throughout the unit, students will have the opportunity to learn more about the long history and importance of industry in New Jersey. They will also learn that swift, reliable transportation has always been key to the success of industry, in addition to its convenience for travelers. Provide maps of New Jersey for students to take home. Have them use highlighters to identify major roadways, railroad lines, and waterways in their area.
- Have students talk to their families about how family members get to work, to school, and to homes of other relatives and friends in the state. On the back of their maps, students can list the destinations discussed, the routes and means of transportation used, and the approximate time for each trip, with the help of family members. Have students compare those trips with the travel described on page 141 of this textbook. Ask them how they think their family's weekly travelling would change if they had to deal with conditions like those described.

## ONGOING UNIT PROJECT

### Personality Skits

**CURRICULUM CONNECTION**
**Art/Drama/Music**

Throughout the unit, students will work individually and cooperatively to create and present skits illustrating New Jersey's challenges and growth during the 1800s.

1. After completing each chapter, students will list people they feel were important during this time. They should also note what each person did and identify where and when the action was done. Then have them think about ideas for skits.
2. When the unit is complete, tell students they will write and perform skits about the people they noted. Guide students working in groups to plan how they will perform their personality skits. Invite them to add songs, costumes, and props to portray each personality.
3. Encourage creative thinking for costume ideas and dialogue.
4. As skits are performed, guide the class in discussing the ideas portrayed in each one.

Assessment suggestions for this activity appear on page T65.

# Building the Garden State

PAGES 138–159

## CHAPTER OVERVIEW

In the 1800s, New Jersey grew and changed. Roads and waterways were developed and improved, and railroads were built. Industries took root and grew. New Jersey reformers fought to make life better for all.

## CHAPTER PLANNING GUIDE

**Suggested pacing: 13–14 days**

| LESSON | LESSON FOCUS | LESSON RESOURCES |
|---|---|---|
| **1 CHANGES IN A NEW STATE** pages 140–145 | Transportation in New Jersey | ***Practice and Project Book:*** page 33<br>***Transparencies:*** 1, 3<br>***Technology:*** *Adventure Time CD-ROM* |
| **GEOGRAPHY SKILLS** pages 146–147 | Using Map Scales | ***Practice and Project Book:*** page 34<br>***Technology:*** *Adventure Time CD-ROM* |
| **2 THE FIRST FACTORY TOWN** pages 148–151 | The Growth of Industry | ***Practice and Project Book:*** page 35<br>***Transparency:*** 1<br>***Technology:*** *Adventure Time CD-ROM* |
| **STUDY SKILLS** pages 152–153 | Reading Circle and Line Graphs | ***Practice and Project Book:*** page 36<br>***Technology:*** *Adventure Time CD-ROM* |
| **3 FIGHTING FOR A BETTER LIFE** pages 154–157 | New Jersey Reformers | ***Practice and Project Book:*** page 37<br>***Technology:*** *Adventure Time CD-ROM* |
| **CHAPTER REVIEW** pages 158–159 | Students' understanding of vocabulary, content, and skills is assessed. | ***Practice and Project Book:*** page 38<br>***Assessment Book:*** Chapter 6 Test<br>***Performance Assessment*** pages T45–T47<br>***Technology:*** *Adventure Time CD-ROM* |

### New Jersey Core Curriculum Content Standards for Social Studies

**Content Standards** These content standards and progress indicators for students completing Grade 4, correlated with Chapter 6, have been developed by the New Jersey Department of Education. A complete listing of the standards can be found on pages T110–T112.

**Standard 6.3** All students will acquire historical understanding of political and diplomatic ideas, forces, and institutions throughout the history of New Jersey, the United States, and the world.

1. pp. 142, 155–157
2. pp. 150–151, 154–157
3. pp. 140–145, 154–157
4. pp. 150–151, 154–157

**Standard 6.4** All students will acquire historical understanding of societal ideas and forces throughout the history of New Jersey, the United States, and the world.

3. pp. 150–151, 154–157

**Standard 6.7** All students will acquire geographical understanding by studying the world in spatial terms.

1. pp. 146–147, 152–153

CHAPTER 6

# LESSON 1

## CHANGES IN A NEW STATE

PAGES 140-145

### Lesson Overview

In the early 1800s, New Jersey was an important link between New York City and Philadelphia despite difficult travel. People improved transportation by building new roads and canals. Steamboats and railroads further improved transportation.

### Lesson Objectives

- ★ Describe how new bridges and turnpikes improved transportation in New Jersey.
- ★ Explain the importance of canals.
- ★ Identify John Fitch and his role in steamboat travel.
- ★ Trace the development of railroads.

## Reading Strategies and LANGUAGE DEVELOPMENT

**PROBLEM AND SOLUTION** Tell students that identifying problems and solutions will help them organize their reading. As students read ask them to explain why transportation was a problem for New Jersey. Then ask them to identify six solutions to this problem (repairing roads, building bridges, turnpikes, and so on). Draw a problem/solution chart on the chalkboard and invite students to add details about each solution.

**LANGUAGE HISTORY AND ETYMOLOGY** As students read page 142, have them list some of the things a charter could be used for: to build roads and bridges, to settle an area of land, to start up a business, and more.

You might note that the word *charter* comes from the Latin word *charta,* meaning "papyrus leaf." Papyrus is a plant that ancient Egyptians used to make paper.

## Field Trip

Plan a field trip to the Delaware and Raritan Canal State Park. Students may view the locks, bridges, and buildings. For more information, call the park at (732) 873–3050, or write 625 Canal Road, Somerset 08873.

As an alternate activity, have groups research canals and design and sketch a lock.

## Technology CONNECTION

**ADVENTURE TIME CD-ROM**

Enrich this lesson with *New Jersey, Explore,* and *Investigate* on the CD-ROM.

## Meeting INDIVIDUAL NEEDS

**RETEACHING (Easy)** Have students draw pictures of the new modes of transportation and add captions explaining their importance.

**EXTENSION (Average)** Have students write a paragraph, beginning each with a topic sentence, about the following changes in transportation: turnpikes, bridges, canals, steamboats, and railroads.

**ENRICHMENT (Challenging)** Ask students to prepare a detailed chart comparing the ways New Jerseyans traveled in the 1830s to means of transportation available today.

## Expanding the INFOGRAPHIC

**RESEARCHING AND WRITING** Divide the class into groups and have each one do further research on canals. Then tell each group to imagine that it is a canal-building committee in the late 1820s. They should study a physical map of New Jersey to select a site for a new canal and write a proposal designed to foster interest in the canal, explaining how the canal will work and what goods it might carry.

## Curriculum CONNECTION

**LINKS TO MATH** Pose mental math problems to students based on information in the section. For example, if the *John Bull* could travel at 30 miles per hour, how long would it take the train to travel 50 miles? *(1 hr. and 40 min.)* 100 miles? *(3 hrs. and 20 min.)* 150 miles *(5 hrs.)*?

## ✓Answers to THINK ABOUT IT

1. Some areas had no roads; roads that existed were poorly cared for.
2. a business that has total control of one kind of good or one kind of service
3. Any three: by foot, horse, carriage, boat
4. John Fitch launches his steamboat in Philadelphia; John Stevens builds the first American locomotive; the *John Bull* begins regular trips.
5. Traffic between New York City and Philadelphia traveled through New Jersey, making the state a crossroads.

**Write About It** Have students write a newspaper article reporting the opening of the Morris Canal.

## Resource REMINDER

**Practice and Project Book:** page 33

**Technology:** *Adventure Time CD-ROM*

**Transparencies:** 1, 3, 4

CHAPTER 6

# SKILLS LESSON

## USING MAP SCALES

PAGES 146-147

**Lesson Overview**

Map scales are used to measure real distances on a map.

**Lesson Objective**

★ Use a scale strip to accurately measure distances on a map.

### Why the SKILL MATTERS

Have students volunteer examples of times when people use maps. Ask them to identify a range of uses, from maps that tell how to get to a friend's house to historical maps in textbooks. Encouraging student contributions, draw a map of the school grounds. Then draw a second map of the same area, using a much larger scale. Help students see that the scales on the maps on the board and the scales on the maps in the book serve similar functions. Emphasize that a correct scale is important for a map to be useful. Direct students to the *Helping Yourself* box on page 147.

### Using the SKILL

Direct students' attention to the map on page 146. Then help them cut strips of paper to use as scale strips. After working through the examples, have students volunteer additional pairs of city names and, as a class, determine the distance between these cities. Ask students to think of times they would need a precise measurement of the distance between two places. Explain that an exact measurement would help them figure out the shortest possible route between two places.

### Trying the SKILL

Remind students to mark accurately when making a scale strip and to be careful to distinguish between two units of measurement: miles and kilometers.

### Technology CONNECTION

**ADVENTURE TIME CD-ROM**

Enrich this lesson with *New Jersey* and *Explore* on the CD-ROM.

### Curriculum CONNECTION

**LINKS TO LANGUAGE ARTS** Have students write a short story, set in the past, present, or future, about a quest for treasure, in which the characters travel from one place to another.

- Each student should create an illustrated map that includes the places mentioned in their story, as well as a map scale. Ask students to trace the route the characters travel in their story to determine the total distance traveled.
- As an example of stories that use maps, you might show students *They're Off! The Story of the Pony Express* by Cheryl Harness (New York: Simon and Schuster, 1996).

### Meeting INDIVIDUAL NEEDS

**RETEACHING (Easy)** Have partners practice using map scales to measure distances on other maps in this book and on maps in atlases.

**EXTENSION (Average)** Have students find two other maps of New Jersey with scales that are different from Map B. Have students show the class the details that are included on one map but not on the other.

**ENRICHMENT (Challenging)** Have students draw a map of the classroom on a scale of one inch to one foot. Using the maps as a guide, tour the room with students.

### ✓Answers to THINK ABOUT IT

A map scale shows the relationship between the distance on a map and the real distance on Earth.

2. A scale strip accurately copies the map scale over the distance that needs to be measured.
3. Map A; about 45 miles; 73 km
4. Many more New Jersey communities and railroad lines are shown on Map A. Map B is drawn to a larger scale and shows fewer details.
5. Answers will vary. Students should recognize that small-scale maps generally show a larger area and fewer details, while large-scale maps show a smaller area and more details.

### Resource REMINDER

**Practice and Project Book:** page 34

**Technology:** *Adventure Time CD-ROM*

**Transparency:** 1

# LESSON 2
## THE FIRST FACTORY TOWN

PAGES 148–151

### Lesson Overview

Alexander Hamilton helped to plan the town of Paterson as a factory town. After a shaky start, Paterson became a great textile center. Industry grew in other New Jersey towns as well. In the late 1890s, Paterson workers went on strike to gain better working conditions.

### Lesson Objectives

★ Describe the founding of Paterson.

★ Explain how the mills of Paterson were powered.

★ Identify the major products of Paterson's factories.

★ Describe how Paterson's workers fought for rights.

## Reading Strategies and LANGUAGE DEVELOPMENT

**MAKE AND SUPPORT GENERALIZATIONS** Tell students that a generalization is a judgment or conclusion based on supporting details. Write the following generalization on the chalkboard: "Industry grew in New Jersey in the 1800s." Ask students to skim pages 150–151 to find details that support this generalization. Then ask students to suggest one or more additional generalizations that could be made based on the lesson.

**SYNONYMS** Remind students that synonyms are words that have similar meanings. Divide the class into pairs. Have each pair look up the words *factory* and *worker* in a thesaurus. Tell students to make a list of the synonyms they find for each word. Have students use dictionaries and other reference sources to discover the variations in meaning among the synonyms. After pairs discuss these differences, have them choose three synonyms for each term and use each synonym in a sentence.

## Second-Language SUPPORT

**DRAMATIZATION** Second-language students may better understand the events of this section if the class dramatizes them. Assign one of the following events to a small group: Hamilton's visit to the Great Falls in 1778, the granting of a charter to the S.U.M., the Paterson strike of 1828. Each group should produce a short dramatization of the event.

## Technology CONNECTION

**ADVENTURE TIME CD-ROM**
Enrich this lesson with *New Jersey, Explore,* and *Investigate* on the CD-ROM.

## Global CONNECTION

**WORLDWIDE INDUSTRIAL GROWTH** The Industrial Revolution is the name given to a period of great change that occurred in the 1700s and 1800s in several parts of the world. It began in Great Britain in the 1700s. Natural resources, such as abundant coal and iron, as well as the markets for industrial goods provided by British colonies, spurred the Industrial Revolution in Britain. By the early 1800s it had reached the United States. Industry grew quickly, living standards rose, and populations grew—especially in the cities.

## Background INFORMATION

**THE HAMILTON-BURR DUEL** Alexander Hamilton and Aaron Burr were long-time enemies.

- Hamilton had used his influence against Burr in the presidential election of 1800 and in the race for governor of New York in 1804.
- Hamilton accepted Burr's challenge even though he did not believe in dueling.
- The duel was held in New Jersey because dueling was illegal in New York.

## √Answers to THINK ABOUT IT

1. Alexander Hamilton
2. making large amounts of goods in factories
3. People bought factory-made products; many people went to work in factories; some workers joined unions.
4. Possible answers: Factories were built in Paterson because of its waterpower and because the S.U.M. encouraged industry. As a result, businesses developed in the area and the population of the town grew.
5. The Great Falls of the Passaic River provided waterpower.

**Write About It** Have students write an advertisement that the S.U.M. might have written to attract workers to Paterson.

## Resource REMINDER

**Practice and Project Book:** page 35

**Technology:** *Adventure Time CD-ROM*

CHAPTER 6

# SKILLS LESSON
## READING CIRCLE AND LINE GRAPHS

PAGES 152–153

**Lesson Overview**

*Circle* and *line graphs* make comparing different facts and figures easier.

**Lesson Objective**

★ Use information on circle and line graphs to make comparisons and form conclusions.

### Why the SKILL MATTERS

Have a volunteer relate the information that is presented in the circle graph on page 152. Ask the class which method made the information easier to understand—hearing it described or looking at the graph. Discuss with students the reasons for comparing facts and figures in history.

### Using a CIRCLE GRAPH

Make a simple circle graph using data drawn from your class. Ask students how many of them walk to school, how many ride a bus, and how many ride in a car. Represent those numbers as a percent of a whole. Draw a circle on the board and form the three "slices." Make sure students understand that a circle graph shows how the parts make up the whole, or 100 percent.

### Using a LINE GRAPH

Continue collecting the data used in the circle graph above. Then use class data over a week's or a month's time to produce a simple line graph. Help students understand that line graphs are used to show changes over time.

### Trying the SKILL

Have volunteers answer the questions in this section. Remind students that the *Helping Yourself* box tells when to use each kind of graph.

### Technology CONNECTION

**ADVENTURE TIME CD-ROM**

Enrich this lesson with the *Build and Paint* segments of the *U.S. January Temperatures* on the CD-ROM.

### Background INFORMATION

**SOURCES OF DATA** Graphs are built using *data*. Data are facts that have been collected, often over a period of time. Historians use many sources to collect data. A major source of data about the United States is the Bureau of the Census.

### Meeting INDIVIDUAL NEEDS

**RETEACHING (Easy)** Ask students to explain (orally or in writing) the difference between a circle graph and a line graph and tell why each is useful.

**EXTENSION (Average)** Have students find examples of circle graphs and line graphs from newspapers or magazines. Ask students to write one or two questions about each graph they find. Have students exchange graphs and answer each other's questions.

**ENRICHMENT (Challenging)** Show students how to use almanacs to obtain data on subjects such as weather or population growth. Then have students work in groups to create line graphs. Tell students to include a title, key, and labels with their graphs.

### √Answers to REVIEWING THE SKILL

1. leather making; by looking at the graph and comparing the size of the part for carpentry to the part for leather making (also by reading the numbers)
2. The population of Newark grew by about 65,000 people.
3. Line graphs show changes over time; circle graphs show how the parts of something make up the whole. They show information in a clear way with just a few words.

### Resource REMINDER

**Practice and Project Book:** page 36

**Technology:** *Adventure Time CD-ROM*

CHAPTER 6

# LESSON 3

## FIGHTING FOR A BETTER LIFE

PAGES 154-157

### Lesson Overview

Between 1830 and 1860, many New Jerseyans worked for reforms, ways to make government or business work better. Some New Jerseyans worked to expand suffrage. Others worked to establish free public schools and to improve care for the mentally ill.

### Lesson Objectives

★ Explain why some New Jerseyans fought for suffrage in the 1800s.

★ Describe the efforts to provide New Jersey children with free public schools.

★ Identify Dorothea Dix and describe her work.

## Reading Strategies and LANGUAGE DEVELOPMENT

**REREADING** Explain to students that rereading material will increase their understanding of it and their ability to recall what they have read. Have all students read the first section of this lesson. Then ask pairs of students to write a summary of the section. Have students reread the section and work together to revise or add to their summaries.

**APOSTROPHES IN POSSESSIVES** Point out the phrase *New Jersey's* and the word *reformers'* in The Big Picture. Review the rules for using apostrophes to show possession, noting that the first example is a singular possessive and the second is a plural possessive. Ask students to find another possessive formed with an apostrophe in the lesson.

## Building CITIZENSHIP

**VOTING REQUIREMENTS** Have students find out the current requirements for voting in New Jersey. Then ask students to obtain a voter registration card from the local election board or the League of Women Voters. Show students how to complete the card.

## Technology CONNECTION

**ADVENTURE TIME CD-ROM**

Enrich this lesson with *New Jersey, Explore,* and *Investigate* on the CD-ROM.

## Second-Language SUPPORT

**GRAPHIC ORGANIZERS** Direct students in groups to write *Reforms* in the middle of a blank sheet of paper. Have them read the chapter and cluster the section headings around the center term. Then encourage students to add a main idea and supporting details for each section heading.

## Background INFORMATION

**NOTABLE NEW JERSEY SUFFRAGISTS**

- Antoinette Louisa Brown Blackwell was the first ordained woman minister in the United States. A founder of the American Woman Suffrage Association, Blackwell lived in New Jersey for much of her adult life.
- Florence Peshine Eagleton and Lillian Ford Feickert worked for New Jersey's ratification of the suffrage amendment in 1919 to 1920.

## √Answers to THINK ABOUT IT

1. the right to vote
2. While poor New Jersey children received some education in the 1820s and rich children attended private schools, the children in between the rich and poor often received little education at all.
3. Any two: voting reforms, to found public schools, to help the mentally ill
4. The New Jersey legislature immediately set aside money to build the New Jersey State Asylum.
5. Answers may include the right to representation in the government.

**Write About It** Have students list five questions that they would like to ask Lucy Stone or Dorothea Dix.

## Resource REMINDER

**Practice and Project Book:** page 37

**Technology:** *Adventure Time CD-ROM*

ANSWERS TO

# Chapter 6 REVIEW

PAGES 158-159

### THINKING ABOUT VOCABULARY

1. toll
2. reform
3. suffrage
4. canal
5. strike

### THINKING ABOUT FACTS

1. Morris Canal; Delaware and Raritan Canal
2. S.U.M. was created to develop industry in Paterson.
3. Any three: cotton, silk, iron, glass, hats, paper
4. Lucy Stone was a leader in seeking voting rights for women in the 1800s.
5. Legislators set aside money to build the New Jersey State Asylum.

## Suggestions for THINK AND WRITE SIGNS OF SUCCESS

***Summary*** The summaries should demonstrate knowledge of the lesson but include only the most important ideas. Each summary should also highlight the major changes that occurred in New Jersey in the 1800s: improvements in transportation, the growth of industry, and important reforms.

***Advertisement*** Look for advertisements that indicate students' understanding of the text. The ads should refer to attractive features in the town, such as new factories offering a number of jobs, plans for the development of industry, or the beauty and power of the Great Falls.

***Explanation*** Students' explanations should reflect an understanding of the conditions in which the mentally ill were kept and the way Dorothea Dix hoped to see the system changed.

*For performance assessment, see* **Assessment Book,** *Chapter 6, pages T46–T48*

### APPLYING GEOGRAPHY SKILLS
**USING MAP SCALES**

1. A map scale tells you about the relationship between the distance on a map and the real distance.
2. You can lay the scale strip on the map and find the distance between wo places.
3. about 48 miles; about 25 miles
4. they are about the same distance
5. Maps with different scales are useful in different ways. Maps in which an inch stands for a great distance show a large area. Maps in which an inch stands for a short distance show more detail.

### APPLYING GEOGRAPHY SKILLS
**READING CIRCLE AND LINE GRAPHS**

1. Circle graphs show how parts fit into a whole. Line graphs show how a piece of information changes over time.
2. shoe making
3. 6,507
4. line graph
5. Graphs make some information easier to understand because they allow you to see at a glance how parts relate to a whole or what trends occur over time.

**Technology CONNECTION**

**ADVENTURE TIME CD-ROM**

Enrich *this lesson* with *New Jersey, Explore,* and *Investigate* on the CD-ROM.

*Resource* **REMINDER**

**Practice and Project Book:** page 38

**Assessment Book:** Chapter 6 Test

**Performance Assessment,** pages T46–T48

 **Technology:** *Adventure Time CD-ROM*

7 CHAPTER ORGANIZER

# Challenge and Growth

Pages 160–189

## CHAPTER OVERVIEW

In the early 1800s, viewpoints on slavery caused division between slaveholders and abolitionists in New Jersey and across the nation. The slavery issue led the North and South into the Civil War. After the war, New Jersey saw the rapid growth of new industries and inventions that changed how Americans live and work. Immigrants flocked to New Jersey seeking a better life.

## CHAPTER PLANNING GUIDE

**Suggested pacing: 18–19 days**

| LESSON | LESSON FOCUS | LESSON RESOURCES |
|---|---|---|
| 1 **A DIVIDED COUNTRY** pages 162–167 | The Antislavery Movement in New Jersey | ***Practice and Project Book:*** page 39<br>***Technology:*** *Adventure Time CD-ROM* |
| 2 **NEW JERSEY AND THE CIVIL WAR** pages 168–173 | New Jersey's Role in the Civil War | ***Practice and Project Book:*** page 40<br>***Technology:*** *Adventure Time CD-ROM* |
| **THINKING SKILLS** pages 174–175 | Making Conclusions | ***Practice and Project Book:*** page 41<br>***Technology:*** *Adventure Time CD-ROM* |
| 3 **INVENTIONS AND INDUSTRY** pages 176–179 | New Industries and New Inventions in New Jersey | ***Practice and Project Book:*** page 42<br>***Technology:*** *Adventure Time CD-ROM* |
| **LEGACY** pages 180–181 | Innovations | |
| 4 **WELCOMING THE WORLD** pages 182–186 | Nineteenth-Century Immigrants and New Jersey | ***Practice and Project Book:*** page 43<br>***Technology:*** *Adventure Time CD-ROM* |
| **CITIZENSHIP MAKING A DIFFERENCE** page 187 | Immigrants Help One Another | |
| **CHAPTER REVIEW** pages 188–189 | Students' understanding of vocabulary, content, and skills is assessed. | ***Practice and Project Book:*** page 44<br>***Assessment Book:*** Chapter 7 Test<br>***Performance Assessment*** pages T49–T51<br>***Technology:*** *Adventure Time CD-ROM* |

**New Jersey Core Curriculum Content Standards for Social Studies**

**Content Standards** These content standards and progress indicators for students completing Grade 4, correlated with Chapter 7, have been developed by the New Jersey Department of Education. A complete listing of the standards can be found on pages T110–T112.

**Standard 6.3** All students will acquire historical understanding of political and diplomatic ideas, forces, and institutions throughout the history of New Jersey, the United States, and the world. 2. pages 168–173; 3. pages 168–173, 176–186; 4. pages 162–167

**Standard 6.4** All students will acquire historical understanding of societal ideas and forces throughout the history of New Jersey, the United States, and the world. 2. pages 185–187; 4. pages 162–167

# LESSON 1
## A DIVIDED COUNTRY

PAGES 162-167

### Lesson Overview

Beginning in the late 1700s, some people took steps to abolish slavery in New Jersey with antislavery laws. Many enslaved African Americans in the South escaped slavery along the Underground Railroad.

### Lesson Objectives

★ Explain how the slavery issue divided the people of New Jersey.

★ Explore the importance of the Underground Railroad.

★ Examine the ways that many New Jerseyans opposed slavery.

## Reading Strategies and LANGUAGE DEVELOPMENT

**PROBLEM AND SOLUTION** Point out to students that they may find it easier to comprehend ideas by identifying problems and solutions in the text. Explain that this lesson talks about the fact that abolitionists were opposed to slavery (problem). Ask students to write a paragraph about how abolitionists chose to solve this problem.

**PREFIXES** Call students' attention to the term *antislavery* in the discussion of the Grimké sisters on page 163. Help them identify the base word *slavery* and the prefix *anti-*. Establish that the prefix means "not" or "against." Call on volunteers to suggest other prefixes that could also mean "not," such as *non-, un-, in-,* or *il-*. Have them look for other words with a "not" prefix in the lesson. (*illegal, disagreement*)

## Second-Language SUPPORT

**SHARING HIGHLIGHTS** Second-language students may benefit from focusing on specific concepts. Arrange the class into three groups and assign each group one of the three main lesson headings. Have students choose an idea from their section and illustrate it with an original drawing. Ask students to share their work with the class, giving an oral explanation of their illustrations.

## Technology CONNECTION

**ADVENTURE TIME CD-ROM**

Enrich this lesson with *New Jersey, Explore, Investigate,* and *Underground Railroad* on the CD-ROM.

## Global CONNECTION

**SLAVERY IN OTHER PLACES** Tell students that slavery was practiced elsewhere in the Americas, such as on plantations in Cuba and in mines in Brazil. Most colonial rulers, however, abolished slavery earlier than the United States did. As early as 1787, British abolitionists spoke out. In the same year, Britain started a colony in West Africa that included formerly enslaved blacks and blacks who had fought for the British during the Revolution.

**EXAMINING THE PHOTOGRAPHS** Have students choose a lesson photo and role-play an on-the-scene reporter describing a site and its importance or interviewing an influential person from the lesson.

## √Answers to THINK ABOUT IT

1. Abolition means the complete ending of something, in this case slavery.
2. New Jersey sold factory goods to the South. Its mills used Southern cotton.
3. Several laws worked toward abolition: 1786—made it illegal to import more slaves; 1788—made it illegal for a slaveholder to move out of state with slaves against their will; and 1804—allowed for the gradual freeing of slaves. New Jerseyans also published an antislavery book and worked with the Underground Railroad.
4. Some New Jerseyans had strong business ties with the South and were not abolitionists; many others were firm abolitionists who acted to end slavery. Although slavery was outlawed in New Jersey, the state did not oppose the Fugitive Slave Act.
5. the Delaware River

**Write About It** Have students write a letter from an enslaved person who has escaped on the Underground Railroad to a relative still in the South. Letters should describe the route, dangers, and how freedom felt.

## Resource REMINDER

**Practice and Project Book:** page 39

**Technology:** *Adventure Time CD-ROM*

**Transparencies:** 1, 2

# LESSON 2
## NEW JERSEY AND THE CIVIL WAR
PAGES 168–173

### Lesson Overview
In 1861 disagreements between the North and the South over slavery and states' rights led to the Civil War. By the end of the war in 1865, about one of every ten New Jerseyans had served in the Union forces.

### Lesson Objectives
★ Identify the ways in which New Jersey supported the Union in the Civil War.
★ Cite the purpose of the Emancipation Proclamation.

## Reading Strategies and LANGUAGE DEVELOPMENT
**APOSTROPHES IN POSSESSIVES** Call students' attention to the term *world's* in *The Big Picture*. Remind students that "'s" after a word that names a person, place, or thing always indicates possession, or that something belongs to, that person, place, or thing. Ask what belongs to the world in this construction. Have students think about what belongs to the named item in other possessives they find in the lesson.

## Curriculum CONNECTION
**LINKS TO READING** Libraries have a number of books containing fictional stories with Civil War settings and heroes or heroines. Have students read one of these books and present oral book reports, explaining what they learned about the war and times.

## Building CITIZENSHIP
**CLAIMING ALLEGIANCE** Discuss the song lyrics in the *Read Aloud*, asking how the soldiers might have considered themselves patriots. Ask students how saving the Union and ending slavery were patriotic. Have students create a Civil War wall mural illustrating New Jersey's contributions to the Union.

## Technology CONNECTION
**ADVENTURE TIME CD-ROM**
Enrich this lesson with *The Northeast, Explore, Investigate, Infographics,* and *Major Battles of the Civil War* on the CD–ROM.

## Field TRIP
**CIVIL WAR MEMORABILIA** Arrange a visit to a local museum or other site displaying Civil War artifacts. If a field trip is impractical, ask students to research one of the New Jerseyans mentioned in the text and share with the class interesting new facts about the person or his or her Civil War experiences.

## Meeting INDIVIDUAL NEEDS
**RETEACHING (Easy)** Have students write a paragraph explaining why most people thought that the Union would win the Civil War in just a few months.

**EXTENSION (Average)** Have students write two accounts of an event they have read about in this chapter. Ask them to present the event first as a primary source and then as a secondary source. Ask volunteers to read their accounts to the class, and have students evaluate the reliability of each source.

**ENRICHMENT (Challenging)** Have students use encyclopedias and history books to research the Civil War photographer Mathew Brady and his work. Have them place photocopies of Brady's photographs around a map of the United States with pins and leaders indicating where the photo was taken.

## ✓Answers to THINK ABOUT IT
1. Many New Jerseyans were firmly antislavery, but others had strong ties to the South.
2. the attack by Confederate soldiers on Union troops at Fort Sumter
3. New Jersey manufactured war goods, provided crops, and sent soldiers and other volunteers.
4. The Union had more people, wealth, factories, and railroad tracks. The Confederacy, however, had many trained military leaders and good soldiers.
5. Student letters should demonstrate an understanding of what was at stake in the war and what a relief it would be for the fighting to end.

**Write About It** Have students write a note a young American boy might leave for his family in July of 1861, explaining why he is joining the army, and which one he is joining.

## Resource REMINDER
**Practice and Project Book:** page 40
**Technology:** *Adventure Time CD-ROM*
**Transparencies:** 1, 2

# SKILLS LESSON
## MAKING CONCLUSIONS
PAGES 174–175

**Lesson Overview**
Making *conclusions* allows students to connect and better understand separate pieces of information.

**Lesson Objective**
★ Use historical facts to draw conclusions.

### Why the SKILL MATTERS
Tell students that studies show that readers who make conclusions when they read are more likely to remember what they read. To help students understand the skill, have them read the steps in the Helping Yourself box on page 175. Then have them read these statements from Lesson 2.

- Lincoln asked New Jersey's governor to send about 3,000 soldiers to fight for the Union. In less than a week, almost 10,000 had signed up.
- However, by the end of 1861, factories were busy turning out rubber, gun barrels, woolen uniforms, locomotives, and rails for train tracks.
- By the end of the war more than 88,000 New Jersey men—about one of every ten people who lived in New Jersey—had served in the Union forces.

Help students see that from these facts they can draw the conclusion that New Jersey actively participated in the Civil War.

### Using the SKILL
Tell students that making conclusions is a skill that people must master to be successful in school and later in life. Discuss how people in different professions need to make conclusions, such as doctors, police, or firefighters.

### Technology CONNECTION
**ADVENTURE TIME CD-ROM**
Enrich this lesson with *New Jersey* and *Create* on the CD-ROM.

### Trying the SKILL
Read the statements in this section of the lesson aloud and call on volunteers to answer the questions that follow.

### Curriculum CONNECTION
Links to Math  After students have read the first step in Helping Yourself, ask which school subject comes to mind (math). Discuss how reaching conclusions is similar to solving math problems. Have students create word problems that use addition, subtraction, multiplication, and division. For example, if 180,000 African American soldiers joined the Union Army over the two years of war following the Emancipation Proclamation, how many on average joined each month (*7,500*)? Discuss how the solution to the problem is like making a conclusion.

### Meeting INDIVIDUAL NEEDS
**RETEACHING (Easy)** Have students volunteer examples of everyday conclusions they have made this week.

**EXTENSION (Average)** Have students read a page in Lesson 2 and make a conclusion about the information it contains.

**ENRICHMENT (Challenging)** Arrange students into groups of three or four. Provide each group with a different article from a recent edition of a local newspaper. Have students read the articles and make a conclusion. Bring the class together and have groups state their conclusions and describe how they made them.

### √Answers to REVIEWING THE SKILL
1. Responses should demonstrate a search for a common idea in the four statements.
2. Answers should recognize that Cornelia Hancock was an important nurse who helped many Civil War soldiers. Facts that she nursed hundreds, obtained needed supplies, and received a medal add up to an outstanding contribution.
3. Making conclusions can help connect many facts together into a single idea, which is easier to remember.
4. Possible answers include when reading a textbook, listening to guest speakers or oral reports, and researching a topic.

### Resource REMINDER
**Practice and Project Book:** page 41
**Technology:** *Adventure Time CD-ROM*

CHAPTER 7

# LESSON 3
## INVENTIONS AND INDUSTRY

PAGES 176–179

**Lesson Overview**

New Jersey industry grew rapidly in the period following the Civil War. New inventions, new industries, and the formation of labor unions changed the way Americans lived and worked.

**Lesson Objectives**

★ Explain how industry expanded after the Civil War.

★ Identify Edison's innovations and list some of his inventions.

★ Describe the early labor movement.

## Reading Strategies and LANGUAGE DEVELOPMENT

**MAKE AND SUPPORT GENERALIZATIONS** Write this sentence on the chalkboard: "Life in New Jersey became more modern after the Civil War." Call on volunteers to suggest what question(s) they might ask after reading that statement, establishing that the statement seems to call for supporting information. Remind students that such a statement is a generalization. Have them list supporting facts from the lesson. Invite them to try making other generalizations based on the lesson.

**SYNONYMS** Draw students' attention to the terms *producing* and *making* in *The Big Picture*. Help them understand that the words' similar meanings make them synonyms. Tell students to find other synonym pairs in the lesson as they read *(began, started; expanded, grew)*. Have them think about how using synonyms makes writing more interesting to read.

**FIELD TRIP** Visit the Edison National Historic Site in West Orange (973) 736–0550. As an alternative, ask a science teacher to come to class and discuss or demonstrate how Edison's light bulb worked.

## Technology CONNECTION

**ADVENTURE TIME CD-ROM**

Enrich this lesson with *Explore, Investigate, Pictures,* and *After the Civil War* on the CD-ROM.

## Background INFORMATION

**BANDING TOGETHER** The American labor movement took hold in the early 1800s. In the 1820s and 1830s printers, carpenters, and other workers began labor organizations within cities. Nationwide organizations developed a few decades later. In 1869, for example, the Noble Order of the Knights of Labor was established. This national group of labor unions worked for an 8-hour workday and an end to child labor.

## Meeting INDIVIDUAL NEEDS

**RETEACHING (Easy)** Have students present a television news release describing a new invention from this period and changes it might bring.

**EXTENSION (Average)** Have students do library research to discover more of Edison's inventions made by Edison or others. Help them create a mobile of coat hangers, string, and cardboard cutouts and objects representing a number of inventions or innovations.

**ENRICHMENT (Challenging)** Have students make a time line of nineteenth-century inventions. Suggest that they illustrate their time lines with photocopies or drawings.

## ✓Answers to THINK ABOUT IT

1. any three: phonograph, light bulb, electric dynamo, motion picture camera, vote recorder, printing telegraph, typewriting machine, speaking telegraph, moving picture film
2. an organization of workers fighting for fair working conditions, such as better pay and shorter hours
3. Possible answers: More people lived in cities. Many people worked in factories. Some people could live in suburbs.
4. Possible answer: Factory work was noisy, dangerous, hard, and unpleasant.
5. Paragraphs should point out how we still use Edison's inventions in some form.

**Write About It** Write a brief letter to a newspaper editor in 1885 explaining why you think labor unions are necessary.

## Resource REMINDER

**Practice and Project Book:** page 42

**Technology:** *Adventure Time CD-ROM*

CHAPTER 7

# LEGACY
## LINKING PAST AND PRESENT
### Innovations

PAGES 180–181

**Lesson Overview**

People today use many different inventions developed by innovative New Jerseyans.

**Lesson Objectives**

- ★ Explain why New Jersey can be considered a center for innovation.
- ★ List and describe some inventions introduced by New Jerseyans.

## Understanding the CONCEPT OF A LEGACY

Help students understand how the inventions of Thomas Edison and other New Jerseyans created a legacy. Ask them what sort of impact they think the inventions had on people's lives when they were introduced. Have students describe the effects these inventions have on their lives today.

## Examining the PHOTOGRAPHS

Have students examine the photographs and study the captions. Help them see that the telegraph revolutionized cross-country communications. Messages that may have arrived in days, weeks, or months carried by horseback riders, wagons, or ships could now be sent in a matter of minutes. Comment that such innovations also created jobs, such as stringing telegraph wires (in the case of the telegraph). Ask students what role they think the telegraph played in the Civil War. Invite students to write a paragraph on how a more recent invention, such as the personal computer, has changed their own lives. Then have volunteers share their paragraphs with the class.

## Global CONNECTION

Tell students that Morse's successful use of the telegraph opened the door to better communication with Europe as well as among states and regions. Laid in 1866, an underwater cable of wires allowed telegraph messages to be sent back and forth across the Atlantic Ocean.

## Curriculum CONNECTION

**LINKS TO SCIENCE** Explain that people have been experimenting with and improving plants ever since they began farming thousands of years ago. Have students use library references and science texts to research the topic of genetic engineering. Have them write a short report on the topic.

## Meeting Individual NEEDS

**RETEACHING (Easy)** Ask students to list all of the items in their kitchens at home that have a no-stick coating. If they do not have many of these items, have them list the items that could be coated in this way and explain the purpose of no-stick coating.

**EXTENSION (Average)** Have students prepare one or two questions they would like to ask each of the inventors in the Legacy lesson.

**ENRICHMENT (Challenging)** Have students obtain a copy of Morse Code symbols from the library. Have them practice sending simple messages in code, using written symbols. Allow them to take turns tapping out a symbol for listeners to identify.

**Write About It** Have students write a short essay describing an invention they would like to make, or wish someone else would make. Essays should explain the benefits of their new invention.

CHAPTER 7

# LESSON 4
## WELCOMING THE WORLD
PAGES 182–186

**Lesson Overview**

During the 1800s, thousands of people from Ireland, Germany, Italy, Hungary, Russia, Poland, and other countries came to New Jersey to find a new life.

**Lesson Objectives**

★ Note the reasons people had for immigration.

★ Summarize the Ellis Island experience.

★ Describe immigrant communities and discrimination immigrants faced.

## Reading Strategies and LANGUAGE DEVELOPMENT

**PREDICT** After students have read *The Big Picture*, call on volunteers to review what was learned about changing life in America from Lesson 3. Ask students to predict what they think life would be like for new immigrants in the late 1800s and early 1900s. Have them consider points such as first impressions and experiences, where workers would fit into the new industrial economy, and difficulties and rewards immigrants might expect. List student suggestions on the chalkboard. As they read the lesson, have students see which of their predictions were correct.

## Second-Language SUPPORT

**DIALOGUES** Invite second-language students to share their own, more recent immigrant experiences with small discussion groups. Ask them to compare the experiences of immigrants in the late 1800s and early 1900s with those of immigrants today. What things about their country of origin do they miss? Do they and their families meet with others from their native country? How important are these associations to them and to their parents?

## Technology CONNECTION

**ADVENTURE TIME CD-ROM**

Enrich this lesson with *Time Lines: New Jersey, Ellis Island,* and *Statue of Liberty* on the CD-ROM.

## Global CONNECTION

**THE BUSINESS OF IMMIGRATION** By the early 1900s, leading European nations competed to build bigger and better ships for carrying immigrants to America. The countries judged their power on the seas by the number of passengers they transported. They cut the passage time down to less than a month and lowered fare rates to $10. With wages two or three times higher than in Europe, workers could earn back their $10 in less than a week. As for American business, firms sent representatives abroad to recruit workers. American firms paid the passage for half of the new immigrants, guaranteeing them a job upon arrival.

**A GIFT FROM FRANCE** The Statue of Liberty is located on Liberty Island near Ellis Island. It was a gift to the United States from the people of France as a symbol of friendship. Americans built the pedestal on which the statue stands, but the "lady" herself was designed by the French sculptor Frederic Auguste Bartholdi and built in France. It was taken apart and arrived in 214 crates in 1885. The statue was assembled by October 1886, when President Grover Cleveland dedicated it. Standing more than 100 feet tall, the Statue of Liberty has greeted newcomers arriving in New York Harbor ever since.

## Curriculum CONNECTION

**LINKS TO LITERATURE** Take a moment to discuss the configuration of the Statue of Liberty—noting particularly the lighted crown and torch. Supply students with a copy of "The New Colossus," Emma Lazarus's famous poem engraved on the base. Explain that the original Colossus was a famous ancient statue that stood astride the entrance to the harbor at Rhodes, Greece. Help students define unfamiliar words in the poem. Call on volunteers to restate the poet's message in their own words. Discuss how the poem applies to the immigrants of the late 1800s and early 1900s. Have volunteers take turns reading their favorite lines.

## Expanding the INFOGRAPHIC

**RESEARCHING AND WRITING** Introduce the term *tenement* to students. Then direct their attention to photos of tenement buildings that housed immigrants in the cities. Have them use encyclopedias, history books, and other library references to learn more about tenement conditions around the turn of the century in New Jersey and New York. Have students write a fictional story about a youngster growing up in a tenement setting. Encourage them to project their own feelings but to remember that the child in their story had little with which to compare his or her life. Ask them to think of ways their character could find fun, hope, and the better life their family was looking for.

## Meeting INDIVIDUAL NEEDS

**RETEACHING (Easy)** Ask students to compare and contrast the voyage and arrival experiences of immigrants who traveled in first and second class with those of immigrants who traveled in third class.

**EXTENSION (Average)** Have students imagine they are planning a film on the immigrant experience. Ask them to describe five scenes they would include in the film.

**ENRICHMENT (Challenging)** Have groups of three or four students write one scene from the movie described in the extension activity. Suggest that they do research on immigrants of the late 1800s and early 1900s to add realistic details to the scene they write. Allow time for groups to present their scenes to the class.

## Field Trip

**ELLIS ISLAND** Ellis Island ceased to be an immigration station in 1954. It became a part of the Statue of Liberty National Monument in 1965 and reopened as a museum in 1990. The museum features photographs and documents, oral histories, artifacts, music, and dramatizations related to immigration over the past 200 years. In 1998, most of the island was declared part of New Jersey. Arrange a visit to the Ellis Island museum (212) 363–3200. As an alternative, invite a spokesperson from the museum or a person who has visited it to share information. Make sure that students have time to examine the museum's new American immigrant Wall of Honor, on which the names of immigrants are inscribed.

## ✓Answers to THINK ABOUT IT

1. Italy, Hungary, Russia, Poland, and other countries.
2. Ellis Island
3. People came for jobs, freedom, fair treatment, and the chance to own land. Many were escaping wars, famine, or harsh treatment in their homelands.
4. Generalizations should recognize such attributes as courage, hope, and a willingness to work hard.
5. Letters may mention various experiences, including the ocean trip and arrival at Ellis Island, living in tenement neighborhoods, jobs, and discrimination from native-born Americans.

**Write About It** Have students write a brief essay comparing and contrasting the positive and negative aspects of being an immigrant in New Jersey in the late 1800s and early 1900s.

### *Resource* REMINDER

**Practice and Project Book:** page 43

**Technology:** *Adventure Time CD-ROM*

**Transparencies:** 1, 2

CHAPTER 7

# CITIZENSHIP

## MAKING A DIFFERENCE

### Immigrants Help One Another

PAGE 187

**Lesson Objective**

★ Explain how today's immigrants can help one another adjust to their new life.

## Identifying the FOCUS

Sasa Olessi Montano recognized the difficult adjustments newly arrived Latin American women faced and decided she could help. Her group, *Latinas Unidas*, brought the women together to share their feelings and acquire skills and knowledge they needed. Ask students to think about how such an organization could help form friendships. Invite volunteers to tell how friendships can help them feel more courageous or sure of themselves.

## Discussing WHY IT MATTERS

Have students imagine that they have just moved to a new country where the culture differs greatly from that in the United States and English is not the official language. Ask them what fears they think they would have. What might they do to try to cope on their own? How might earlier immigrants from the United States be important to them? Help students recognize that *Latinas Unidas* represents what earlier U.S. immigrants might mean to them in a similar situation. Ask students to restate the goal of *Latinas Unidas*. Have volunteers list activities of the group on the chalkboard. Discuss the last paragraph in the lesson. Ask if *Latinas Unidas* is meeting its goals. In what ways might it have exceeded its goals? Help students appreciate how the support, encouragement, and examples set by others contribute to the success of group members.

## CITIZENSHIP

**A WELCOMING HANDBOOK** Obtain several Spanish-English dictionaries from the library. Have students make a list of English words they think would be important for a student newcomer in your class to know. Have them fold 8 1/2 X 11 sheets in half to create stapled booklets. Have them neatly print the Spanish and English equivalents of the words they have listed. They may want to include a map of the school with important rooms indicated. Keep copies on hand to offer to new Latin American students.

## Second-Language SUPPORT

**DIALOGUES** Invite second-language students to share their own or their families' experiences with support groups or other immigrants when they arrived in the United States.

## Curriculum CONNECTION

**LINKS TO HOME ECONOMICS** Students will probably be familiar with a number of Latin American foods, such as tortillas. Point out that immigrants from Asian countries such as India, Thailand, and Vietnam have also contributed to the foods now enjoyed in America. Some students may wish to try the following Indian recipe with an adult at home. *Chapatis* are a traditional food eaten daily by many Indians.

## Chapatis

2 cups whole wheat flour

3 teaspoons vegetable oil

1/2 cup water

pinch of salt

butter

- Mix flour, oil, and salt.
- Gradually add water to form thick dough.
- Knead dough well and divide into 6 equal portions.
- Roll each portion into circles about 1/8 inch thick.
- Cook in a frying pan over low heat. Turn to avoid burning. *Chapati* will puff while cooking.
- Place warm *chapati* on serving plate, spread with butter, and enjoy.

ANSWERS TO
# Chapter 7 REVIEW
PAGES 188–189

### THINKING ABOUT VOCABULARY

1. secede
2. labor union
3. abolition
4. Emancipation Proclamation
5. discrimination

### THINKING ABOUT FACTS

1. Any two: John S. Rock, Angelina and Sarah Grimké, Harriet Tubman, Charity Still, William Still
2. Any two: Men served as soldiers, women worked as nurses, factories and farms provided supplies for the army
3. 1804
4. the Confederate States of America, or the Confederacy
5. Fort Sumter
6. She cared for wounded soldiers.
7. Menlo Park
8. Any three: wartime production of rubber, gun barrels, woolen uniforms, locomotives, and rails for train tracks; potteries; jewelry shops; leather factories; silk mills; furniture making; cloth making; iron production; production of Edison's new products (for example, the light bulb, phonograph, motion picture camera, and dynamo); production of medical suplies; production of bottled and canned foods; insurance
9. Ellis Island was the site of an immigration station built by the United States government; it was the first stop for most immigrants.
10. Any two: to find better jobs, to escape persecution, to find freedom and fair treatment, to have the chance to own land

## Suggestions for THINK AND WRITE

**SIGNS OF SUCCESS**

***Speech Students'*** Speeches should be persuasive and should demonstrate an understanding of slavery and the issues surrounding it prior to the Civil War.

***Diary*** Journal entries should describe several days in one journey. Students should include some descriptions (hiding places, travel routes, people, or events).

***Opinion*** Students' writing should identify a problem in their community, explain its importance, and suggest ways to solve the problem.

### APPLYING THINKING SKILLS

1. Making a conclusion is putting together several pieces of information and deciding what they mean.
2. Ask yourself what the statements have in common, then state the theme in your own words.
3. Students might draw conclusions such as that the people were brave or determined or that they endured many hardships to reach their goal.
4. Students might draw the conclusion that New Jersey contributed much to the war effort.
5. It is important to make conclusions because it helps you to understand what you read and remember it.

**Technology CONNECTION**

**ADVENTURE TIME CD-ROM**

Enrich Chapter 7 with *Explore, Investigate, Infographics, Major Battles of the Civil War,* and *New Jersey Today* on the CD-ROM.

**Resource REMINDER**

**Practice and Project Book:** page 44

**Assessment Book:** Chapter 7 Test

**Performance Assessment,** pages T49–T51

**Technology:** *Adventure Time CD-ROM*

ANSWERS TO

# Unit 3 REVIEW

PAGES 190–191

### THINKING ABOUT VOCABULARY

1. states' rights
2. charter
3. immigrant
4. labor union
5. reform
6. suffrage
7. manufacturing
8. strike
9. canal
10. abolition

## Suggestions for THINK AND WRITE

### SIGNS OF SUCCESS

***Comparison*** Comparisons should mention early forms of transportation such as stagecoaches, steamboats, and horses, along with the benefits of modern transportation such as airplanes and automobiles.

***Song*** Encourage students to write about why they might join the army, their beliefs, and how they feel about war and peace. They may also include details about the hardships they encounter or about specific people, battles, and events.

***Advertisement*** Students' advertisements should show a knowledge of why people traveled on railroads or used them to ship goods.

## Building SKILLS

1. **Making Conclusions** Responses will vary but students may include the Civil War brought an end to slavery, many soldiers lost their lives in the war, and the war began when Southern states chose to secede from the Union.
2. **Circle and Line Graphs** It increased.
3. **Circle and Line Graphs** circle graph because it shows how the parts of something make up the whole
4. **Circle and Line Graphs** Yes, because the size of the slice represents the number in the slice. The larger the number, the larger the slice.
5. **Map Scale** Different scales provide different details of an area. The smaller the scale, the finer the level of detail.

## Suggestions for YESTERDAY, TODAY, AND TOMORROW

Ask students if they have witnessed population growth or expansion in their own communities. Are new homes being built? Are there buildings in an area that was once an empty lot? Ask students to think about how more people and businesses could benefit their community. Also have them discuss the possible drawbacks if people continue to build in wilderness areas. Have students develop a plan for the future that would allow communities to grow while preserving forests and wildlife.

## ONGOING UNIT PROJECT

The ongoing unit project, begun on page T47 can be part of your assessment program, along with other forms of evaluation.

## UNIT PROJECT

### WRITING AN HISTORICAL NEWSPAPER

***Objective*** Researching and writing an historical newspaper can help students learn more about the information in the unit and how reference materials can be used.

***Materials*** paper, pens, pencils

- Divide the class into groups. Suggest that revisiting the text will help students to decide which topic to write about.
- Encourage students to do additional research using an encyclopedia or other reference source to find out more about their topic.
- Before they write their articles, have students do a mock layout of their paper so they can determine where articles, comics, and illustrations will go on the page.
- Give each group a supply of paper, pens, and pencils and have them create their own historical newspaper.

### OPTIONS FOR ASSESSMENT

*For performance assessment, see* **Assessment Book,** *Unit 3, page T52.*

**FOR THE PORTFOLIO** Individual notes and sketches can be included in students' portfolios.

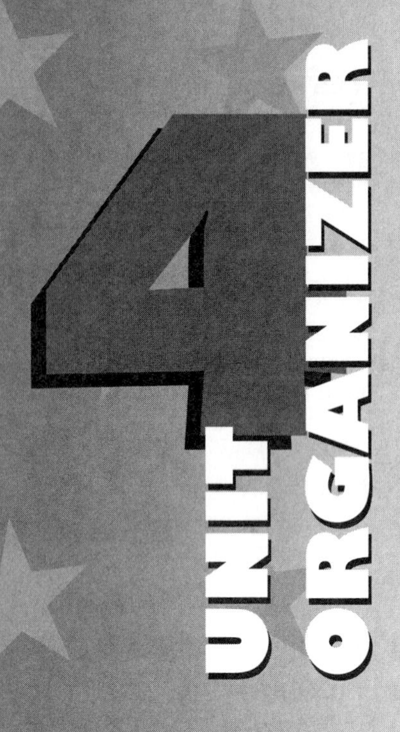


# New Jersey Comes of Age

**PAGES 192–243**

## Unit Overview

In the first half of the 20th century, many New Jerseyans worked for government reform and fought in two world wars. Rapid growth in New Jersey's population, housing, transportation, and industry occurred in the second half of the 20th century. The nature of New Jersey's jobs and workforce changed and New Jersey entered the global economy.

## UNIT PLANNING GUIDE

| CHAPTER | SUGGESTED PACING | CHAPTER OVERVIEW | CHAPTER RESOURCES |
|---|---|---|---|
| **8 A New Century** pages 196–219 | 12–13 days | The turn of the century brought change and hardship to the people of New Jersey. Our country fought in two world wars. Women won the right to vote. | ***Practice and Project Book*** pages 45–49<br>***Transparencies:*** 1, 2, 3, 4<br>***Technology:*** *Adventure Time CD-ROM* |
| **9 Growth and Change** pages 220–241 | 14–15 days | New Jersey experienced growth in many areas during the second half of the 20th century. African Americans struggled for civil rights. New Jersey's economy grew and changed. | ***Practice and Project Book*** pages 50–54<br>***Transparency:*** 3<br>***Technology:*** *Adventure Time CD-ROM* |

**Internet CONNECTION**

The Home Page at **http://www.mhschool.com** contains on-line student activities related to this unit.

**For Further Support**
- Handbook of Test-Taking Strategies

## ASSESSMENT OPPORTUNITIES

### UNIT ASSESSMENT

**Unit Review** pages 242–243
***Unit Project*** page 243, page T67

**Assessment Book**
***Unit Test*** Unit 4 Test
***Performance Assessment*** page T59

### CHAPTER ASSESSMENT

**Meeting Individual Needs** pages T70, T72, T77, T78, T79
**Write About It** pages T69, T71, T72, T75, T76, T78, T79
**Chapter Review** pages 218–219, 240–241

**Assessment Book**
***Chapter 8 Test, Chapter 9 Test***
***Performance Assessment*** pages T53–T55, T56–T58

## TECHNOLOGY CENTER

### Enriching with Multimedia

**RESOURCE:** *Internet*

- Look at McGraw-Hill School's home page on the World Wide Web at **http://www.mhschool.com** for activities related to this unit that your students can do on-line.

**RESOURCE: Adventure Time CD-ROM**

Enrich Unit 4 with *Explore, Build,* and *Paint* on the CD-ROM.

## SCHOOL-TO-HOME

### New Jersey Comes of Age

- Throughout the unit, students will learn about changes taking place in New Jersey in the 20th century. With the students, think of 12 questions for this time period. Have students cut a sheet of heavy-weight paper into 12 sections and write one question on each section. Have students take the questions home.
- Encourage students to share the questions with their families. Have students write the answer to each question on the back, so that the set can be used as flashcards. Invite families to add their own questions and send the completed set back to school for use in the classroom.

## ONGOING UNIT PROJECT

### New Jersey Melodies

**CURRICULUM CONNECTION**
**Music**

Throughout the unit, students will work individually to create songs about the people and places studied.

1. As each lesson or chapter is completed, students will each write a song based on some aspect of what they have learned. Well-known melodies can be used as well as music from old folk songs.
2. At the end of the unit, groups will work together to organize songs to be made into a song book. Sections of the book could be on different topics. For example, one section could be about people and another about places or important events that took place in New Jersey during this time.
3. Encourage the class to record some of the songs or to put on a performance.

Assessment suggestions for this activity appear on page T81.

8 CHAPTER ORGANIZER

# A New Century

Pages 196–219

## CHAPTER OVERVIEW

In the first half of the 20th century, many New Jerseyans worked to reform government. Our nation fought in two world wars and suffered a period of economic hardship known as the Great Depression. Women won the right to vote. Large numbers of African Americans left the rural South for the cities of the North and Middle West.

## CHAPTER PLANNING GUIDE

**Suggested pacing: 12–13 days**

| LESSON | LESSON FOCUS | LESSON RESOURCES |
|---|---|---|
| 1 **THE REFORM YEARS** pages 198–203 | The New Century Brings Many Changes to New Jersey | ***Practice and Project Book:*** page 45<br>***Transparency:*** 1<br>***Technology:*** *Adventure Time CD-ROM* |
| **STUDY SKILLS** pages 204–205 | Using Primary and Secondary Sources | ***Practice and Project Book:*** page 46<br>***Technology:*** *Adventure Time CD-ROM* |
| 2 **WORLD WAR I AND THE 1920S** pages 206–211 | Changes in New Jersey During and After World War I | ***Practice and Project Book:*** page 47<br>***Transparencies:*** 1, 2, 3<br>***Technology:*** *Adventure Time CD-ROM* |
| 3 **THE DEPRESSION AND WORLD WAR II** pages 212–217 | Effects of the Great Depression and World War II on New Jersey | ***Practice and Project Book:*** page 48<br>***Transparencies:*** 2, 3, 4<br>***Technology:*** *Adventure Time CD-ROM* |
| **CHAPTER REVIEW** pages 218–219 | Students' understanding of vocabulary, content, and skills is assessed. | ***Practice and Project Book:*** page 49<br>***Assessment Book:*** Chapter 8 Test<br>***Performance Assessment*** pages T53–T55<br>***Technology:*** *Adventure Time CD-ROM* |

### New Jersey Core Curriculum Content Standards for Social Studies

**Content Standards** These content standards and progress indicators for students completing Grade 4, correlated with Chapter 8, have been developed by the New Jersey Department of Education. A complete listing of the standards can be found on pages T110–T112.

**Standard 6.1** All students will learn democratic citizenship and how to participate in the constitutional system of government of the United States.
1. pages 202–203; 4. page 215

**Standard 6.2** All students will learn democratic citizenship through the humanities, by studying literature, art, history and philosophy, and related fields.
2. pages 208–209, 215

**Standard 6.3** All students will acquire historical understanding of political and diplomatic ideas, forces, and institutions throughout the history of New Jersey, the United States, and the world.
1. pages 198–201, 206, 212, 216–217
3. pages 207–209, 213–214, 216–217

**Standard 6.4** All students will acquire historical understanding of societal ideas and forces throughout the history of New Jersey, the United States, and the world.
3. pages 202–203; 4. pages 200–201, 205

CHAPTER 8

# LESSON 1

## THE REFORM YEARS

PAGES 198–203

### Lesson Overview

In the early 1900s, New Jerseyans worked to reform city and state government. Women won the right to vote with passage of the Nineteenth Amendment.

### Lesson Objectives

★ Describe the *New Idea* and its supporters.

★ Examine the Paterson silk strike of 1913.

★ Explain the provisions of the Nineteenth Amendment.

## Reading Strategies and LANGUAGE DEVELOPMENT

**PROBLEM AND SOLUTION** This lesson discusses the efforts of reformers to solve many problems confronting New Jersey. Help students identify the problems and write them on the chalkboard as headings for a chart (boss rule and corrupt government, poor working conditions, denial of the vote to women). Have students list the ways New Jerseyans tried to solve these problems under the headings. Then ask students to evaluate the success of each method.

**WORDS WITH MULTIPLE MEANINGS** As students read "Cleaning Up New Jersey" explain that the word *boss* has more than one meaning. They are probably familiar with the meaning "supervisor" or "employer." In this section, the word means a corrupt politician. Ask students how this kind of boss might have a negative effect on people.

## Second-Language SUPPORT

**DIALOGUES** Help second-language students remember important people discussed in this section through role plays. Ask student pairs to choose a historical figure listed on page 198. Have one student from each pair take the role of the historical figure; the other will play the role of a reporter interviewing the figure about his or her life and time.

## Technology CONNECTION

**ADVENTURE TIME CD-ROM**

Enrich this lesson with *New Jersey, Explore,* and *Investigate* on the CD-ROM.

## Building CITIZENSHIP

**UNDERSTANDING GOVERNMENT** Hold mock elections to help students see how a primary gives voters more control over government. In the first election, select two candidates for class president and allow students to choose between them. For a mock primary, divide the class into two parties. Let each party nominate a candidate for class president. Ask students to explain how the primary increases citizen control over government.

## Background INFORMATION

**WOODROW WILSON**

- Woodrow Wilson attended Princeton University as an undergraduate.
- In 1890, Wilson became a professor of political science at Princeton. He was a popular teacher and a recognized scholar.
- As president of Princeton University, Wilson raised academic standards and brought together the best young scholars to teach undergraduate students.

## ✓Answers to THINK ABOUT IT

1. Government should be honest; taxes and elections should be fair; children under 14 should not work.
2. Suffragists wrote newspaper articles, held meetings, gave speeches, took part in parades, and wrote letters.
3. any three: tougher punishments for cheating in elections; primary law; state government control of gas and electricity rates; compensation for workers' injuries caused by unsafe working conditions; laws limiting unfair business practices, such as forming monopolies; women's suffrage
4. Women's suffrage led to women's greater participation in government, including serving as elected leaders.
5. Letters should discuss specific reforms.

**Write About It** Have small groups of students write a scene for a movie about the Paterson Silk Strike of 1913.

## Resource REMINDER

**Practice and Project Book:** page 45

**Technology:** *Adventure Time CD-ROM*

**Transparency:** 1

CHAPTER 8

# SKILLS LESSON

## USING PRIMARY AND SECONDARY SOURCES

PAGES 204–205

**Lesson Overview**

Information about historical events may come from primary sources and secondary sources.

**Lesson Objective**

★ Define *primary sources* and *secondary sources* and distinguish between them.

### Why the SKILL MATTERS

Note that being able to use primary and secondary sources is helpful for examining a current issue as well as for studying history. Tell students to suppose that a newspaper prints an article written by an eyewitness about a stray dog and her puppies living in a park in your community. A second article gives estimated figures on stray dogs and cats in the community, what happens to many of these animals, and contact information for animal rescue groups. Ask students to identify the primary and the secondary source and to explain how each would help them understand the problem of stray animals.

### Using the SKILL

Provide students with several primary sources, such as old letters and journals. Allow them to examine the materials to see what they have in common. Tell students that historians use primary sources as evidence from a past time. Explain to students that when historians write books or articles about a historical period, they are producing *secondary sources*. Tell them that a good historian reads and analyzes many primary sources before producing a secondary source.

### Trying the SKILL

Work through the section, asking for volunteers to read the passages. Have students answer the questions, referring to *Helping Yourself* on this page as needed.

### Technology CONNECTION

**ADVENTURE TIME CD-ROM**

Enrich this lesson with *New Jersey* and *Create* on the CD-ROM.

### Curriculum CONNECTION

**LINKS TO LANGUAGE ARTS** Tell students that journals provide important information to historians. Ask students to start keeping a journal. Allow a few minutes once or twice a week for students to write in their journals. Mention current events or school events that would make good journal topics.

### Meeting INDIVIDUAL NEEDS

**RETEACHING (Easy)** Ask students to write definitions for *primary source* and *secondary source*. Then have them look through their textbook to find one or two primary sources.

**EXTENSION (Average)** Have students do library research to find examples of primary and secondary sources. Have them photocopy the sources and mount them on a poster. Students should write a caption for each source, explaining what it is and what information it provides.

**ENRICHMENT (Challenging)** Have students use library and Internet resources to produce a short booklet of primary and secondary sources about either the labor movement or women's suffrage in New Jersey. Tell students to photocopy or print out such materials as newspaper and magazine articles, journal entries, and interviews. Have students make a booklet by arranging their materials in chronological order and pasting them on construction paper. Students should write a caption for each source, giving additional information about it. Students should make a cover for their booklets.

### ✓Answers to REVIEWING THE SKILL

1. A primary source is a firsthand account from someone who saw or took part in the event being described. A secondary source is written by someone who was not present at the described event.
2. secondary; we were not alive in 1910, therefore could not have observed child labor
3. secondary
4. Primary sources make us feel a part of historical events and can help us understand how someone thought about events in history. Secondary sources help us see broader views of events and present more points of view on a subject.

### Resource REMINDER

**Practice and Project Book:** page 46

 **Technology:** *Adventure Time CD-ROM*

CHAPTER 8

# LESSON 2

## WORLD WAR I AND THE 1920S

PAGES 206–211

**Lesson Overview**

The United States entered World War I and many New Jerseyans aided the war effort. During the Great Migration, many African Americans came to New Jersey. The Jazz Age changed culture, industry, and technology.

**Lesson Objectives**

★ Explain why the United States entered World War I on the side of the Allies.

★ Analyze the Great Migration.

★ Describe some of the technological and cultural changes during the 1920s.

## Reading Strategies and LANGUAGE DEVELOPMENT

**CAUSE AND EFFECT** Help students identify cause-and-effect relations presented in *The Big Picture*. Have students look for the links between American and German actions and vice versa. Draw a chain with several large links on the chalkboard and ask students to fill the links with the causes and effects that led to Germany's decision to attack U.S. ships and to the United States' entry into the war.

**IDIOMS** Tell students that an *idiom* is a special expression that cannot be understood from the literal meaning of its words. Direct students to the subhead "The Home Front" on page 207. Tell students that in a war a "front" is a line of battle. Although there was no line of battle in the United States during World War I, the idiom "the home front" compares the work and sacrifices of people at home to a line of battle helping to win the war.

## Second-Language SUPPORT

**GRAPHIC ORGANIZERS** Second-language learners may benefit from plotting the events discussed in this lesson on a pictorial time line. Explain to students that some events occurred over many years and some events overlapped. For example the Great Migration continued through World War I and the Jazz Age. Have students work in groups to construct and illustrate a time line.

## Technology CONNECTION

**ADVENTURE TIME CD-ROM**

Enrich this lesson with *WWI: Trenches* and *New Jersey Today* on the CD-ROM.

## Global CONNECTION

**AMERICANS IN WORLD WAR I**

- General John J. Pershing commanded the American forces that went to France.
- American troops fought in important battles at Château-Thierry, Belleau Wood, Saint-Mihiel, and the Argonne Woods.
- 4.7 million Americans served, more than 100,000 were killed, and about 200,000 were wounded.

## Curriculum CONNECTION

**LINKS TO LANGUAGE ARTS** Have students research the life and work of Jessie Redmond Fauset, Paul Robeson, or another person from the time and prepare a short report. Have them share their reports with the class.

## ✓Answers to THINK ABOUT IT

1. by becoming soldiers; by making ammunition and other needed supplies; by sacrificing goods such as sugar, coal, and wheat
2. a movement of African Americans from the South to cities in the North and Middle West; to escape poverty and discrimination
3. During the war, factories produced war materials; soldiers came to camps in New Jersey; and many African Americans moved to New Jersey. After the war, the state prospered; automobiles and new inventions became plentiful in New Jersey; important transportation links were built.
4. Causes: poverty and discrimination; Effects: strong African American communities in New Jersey; political power for African Americans; discrimination
5. Articles should describe reasons the 1920s were called the "roaring twenties."

**Write About It** Have students suppose they are newspaper reporters in 1927. Ask them to write a story about driving through the new Holland Tunnel from New York to New Jersey.

## Resource REMINDER

**Practice and Project Book:** page 47

**Technology:** *Adventure Time CD-ROM*

**Transparencies:** 1, 2, 3

CHAPTER 8

# LESSON 3

## THE DEPRESSION AND WORLD WAR II

PAGES 212–217

### Lesson Overview

The Great Depression hit New Jersey hard: businesses closed, unemployment rose, banks failed. Recovery came as New Jerseyans found themselves taking part in another world war.

### Lesson Objectives

★ Describe the stock market crash of 1929 and the Great Depression that followed.

★ Explain how the New Deal helped New Jerseyans find work.

★ Describe how New Jerseyans contributed to the effort to win World War II.

## Reading Strategies and LANGUAGE DEVELOPMENT

**WORLDS WITH MULTIPLE MEANINGS** Point out the word *Depression* in the lesson title. Discuss the familiar meaning of the word—a feeling of extreme sadness. Tell students that in economics, *depression* has another meaning. Ask them to read *The Big Picture* and find this definition. Finally, ask students to explain how the two meanings are related.

**PREDICT** After reading *The Big Picture,* ask students to look at the headings and illustrations in the rest of the lesson. Then have them write predictions about how the Depression will affect Americans and about how it will end. When students have finished reading the section, have them check their predictions.

## Expanding the INFOGRAPHIC

**PAINT A MURAL** After students have read the first two sections of the lesson, ask them to study the Ben Shahn mural on page 215. Then have small groups of students paint a scene from the Depression on butcher paper. Assemble the paintings to form a mural.

**RESEARCHING AND WRITING** Have students research more about one of the New Jersey projects funded by New Deal programs. Divide the class into groups and have each group choose a particular program to research. Each group should prepare a written report on its program, including such information as when the program began, when it ended, people involved with its work, and an evaluation of the success of the program.

## Meeting INDIVIDUAL NEEDS

**RETEACHING (Easy)** Have students write a series of headlines that might have accompanied news stories about the events discussed in this lesson.

**EXTENSION (Average)** Ask students to choose an event from this lesson that they think is especially important or interesting. Have them design a commemorative stamp that honors the event. Students should also write a brief explanation for their choice.

**ENRICHMENT (Challenging)** Ask students to create an illustrated time line including at least ten major events of World War II. Have them write a caption for each illustration.

## ✓Answers to THINK ABOUT IT

1. The Great Depression was the period of widespread economic hardship in the 1930s following the stock market crash in 1929.
2. New Deal programs put people to work on projects that helped everyone.
3. Factories, stores, and businesses shut down and many New Jerseyans lost their jobs. Dozens of New Jersey banks failed and family life was disrupted.
4. the stock market crash; New Deal programs; the attack on Pearl Harbor; the end of World War II
5. Paragraphs should describe the landforms of the student's community.

**Write About It** Ask students to write a report to President Roosevelt about conditions in New Jersey in the spring of 1933. Reports should cover three areas of the state.

## Technology CONNECTION

**ADVENTURE TIME CD-ROM**

Enrich this lesson with *WWII* and *President Franklin D. Roosevelt* on the CD-ROM.

## Resource REMINDER

**Practice and Project Book:** page 48

 **Technology:** *Adventure Time CD-ROM*

ANSWERS TO

# Chapter 8 REVIEW

PAGES 218–219

### THINKING ABOUT VOCABULARY

1. C
2. C
3. C
4. World War I
5. Allied Powers
6. C
7. C
8. political party
9. C
10. C

### THINKING ABOUT FACTS

1. any two: New Deal reforms, election law reforms, voting rights for women
2. a movement, beginning in the 1890s, of African Americans from the rural areas of the South to the cities of the North and Middle West
3. Money was plentiful and more people were buying cars and traveling on the roads.
4. any three: factories that made machines and motors, resorts along the Jersey shore, fancy shops, banks
5. New Jerseyans fought in the war, worked in factories to support the war effort, and planted victory gardens. Children rolled bandages and saved needed items. New Jersey scientists helped developed powerful weapons.

## Suggestions for THINK AND WRITE

### SIGNS OF SUCCESS

***Speech*** Students' speeches should show an understanding of the power that bosses had and the damage that power could do to city and state government and government's responsiveness to citizens.

***Letter*** Students' letters should show an understanding of how World War I affected children in New Jersey, with sugar, coal, and meat in short supply.

***Description*** Students' descriptions should demonstrate an understanding of how the Depression affected New Jerseyans' work and quality of life.

*For performance assessment, see* **Assessment Book,** *Chapter 8, pages T53–T55.*

### APPLYING STUDY SKILLS

### USING PRIMARY AND SECONDARY SOURCES

1. A primary source is information that comes from someone who saw or took part in what he or she is describing. A secondary source is written by people who got their information secondhand.
2. any two: quotations from Woodrow Wilson, words about Paterson from a visitor, words about the silk factories from a worker, excerpt from the New Jersey Women's Suffrage Association, quotation from Teresa Cobianci, Mildred Arnold quotation, excerpt of the letter to Eleanor Roosevelt, quotation from a Maplewood woman, quotation from Eileen Witte Treash, quotation from Elizabeth Hawes, soldier's words
3. Students should give two examples from the chapter that are not primary sources.
4. Primary sources help give a feeling of what it was like to live in a particular period of history.
5. It is important because each kind of source provides a different kind of information and is useful for a different purpose.

## Technology CONNECTION

**ADVENTURE TIME CD-ROM**

Enrich Chapter 8 with *New Jersey, Explore,* and *Investigate* on the CD-ROM.

## Resource REMINDER

**Practice and Project Book:** page 49

**Assessment Book:** Chaper 8 Test

**Performance Assesment,** pages T53–T55

 **Technology:** *Adventure Time CD-ROM*

9 CHAPTER ORGANIZER

# Growth and Change

Pages 220–241

## CHAPTER OVERVIEW

New Jersey saw rapid growth in population, housing, transportation, and industry in the second half of the 20th century. African Americans worked hard to end segregation and discrimination. New Jersey jobs shifted from manufacturing to service industries, more women began working outside the home, and New Jersey entered the global economy.

## CHAPTER PLANNING GUIDE

**Suggested pacing: 14–15 days**

| LESSON | LESSON FOCUS | LESSON RESOURCES |
|---|---|---|
| 1 **BOOMING NEW JERSEY** pages 222–225 | Rapid Growth in New Jersey After World War II | ***Practice and Project Book:*** page 50<br>***Transparency:*** 3<br>***Technology:*** *Adventure Time CD-ROM* |
| **CITIZENSHIP VIEWPOINTS** pages 226–227 | How Can New Jersey Solve Its Traffic Problems? | |
| **GEOGRAPHY SKILLS** pages 228–229 | Reading Road Maps | ***Practice and Project Book:*** page 51<br>***Transparency:*** 3<br>***Technology:*** *Adventure Time CD-ROM* |
| 2 **TIMES OF CHANGE** pages 230–235 | The Struggle for Civil Rights | ***Practice and Project Book:*** page 52<br>***Technology:*** *Adventure Time CD-ROM* |
| 3 **A CHANGING ECONOMY** pages 236–239 | Growth and Change in New Jersey's Economy | ***Practice and Project Book:*** page 53<br>***Technology:*** *Adventure Time CD-ROM* |
| **CHAPTER REVIEW** pages 240–241 | Students' understanding of vocabulary, content, and skills is assessed. | ***Practice and Project Book:*** page 54<br>***Assessment Book:*** Chapter 9 Test<br>***Performance Assessment*** pages T56–T58<br>***Technology:*** *Adventure Time CD-ROM* |

### New Jersey Core Curriculum Content Standards for Social Studies

**Content Standards** These content standards and progress indicators for students completing Grade 4, correlated with Chapter 9, have been developed by the New Jersey Department of Education. A complete listing of the standards can be found on pages T110–T112.

**Standard 6.1** All students will learn democratic citizenship and how to participate in the constitutional system of government of the United States.
1. pages 232–233; 5. pages 230–231, 234–235

**Standard 6.3** All students will acquire historical understanding of political and diplomatic ideas, forces, and institutions throughout the history of New Jersey, the United States, and the world. 3. pages 222–225

**Standard 6.6** All students will acquire historical understanding of economic forces, ideas, and institutions throughout the history of New Jersey, the United States, and the world. 3. pages 236–237; 5. pages 238–239

**Standard 6.7** All students will acquire geographical understanding by studying the world in spatial terms.
1. pages 228–229

CHAPTER 9

# LESSON 1

## BOOMING NEW JERSEY

PAGES 222–225

**Lesson Overview**

After World War II, New Jersey experienced rapid growth in population, housing, industry, and transportation.

**Lesson Objectives**

★ Examine New Jersey's population growth and industrial expansion.

★ Describe new transportation routes built during the 1950s.

### Reading Strategies and LANGUAGE DEVELOPMENT

**COMPARATIVES AND SUPERLATIVES** Direct students to the words "bigger" and "biggest" in the opening paragraphs on page 224.

Remind students that "er" compares similar things, one having a greater value than the other, while "est" indicates the greatest value among all. Have students read for more comparatives and superlatives (*largest, closer, fairer*).

**CAUSE AND EFFECT** List the following terms as headings across the chalkboard and designate them as causes: *Growing Population, Growth of Suburbs*, and *Booming Economy*. Have volunteers list some effects under each heading (*need for housing; importance of automobile, more jobs*).

### Second-Language SUPPORT

**MAPPING DETAILS** Second-language students may benefit from visually sorting out the significant details in this lesson. Have students draw a circle enclosing the heading "New Jersey Boom Years." Tell them to draw smaller, outer circles in which they list factors contributing to the boom. Have them connect the outer circles to the inner circle in a web diagram.

### Global CONNECTIONS

**TELSTAR AROUND THE WORLD** Telestar, a satellite that was invented in New Jersey and launched on July 10, 1962, relayed the first television transmissions across the Atlantic Ocean. This satellite received messages from a ground station, amplified the signals, and relayed them back to other ground stations. On the day it was launched, it relayed television pictures sent from Andover, Maine, to stations in Britain and France. A new communications era was born.

### Technology CONNECTION

**ADVENTURE TIME CD-ROM**

Enrich this lesson with *New Jersey, Explore,* and *Investigate* on the CD-ROM.

### Curriculum CONNECTION

**LINKS TO SCIENCE** Note that radios were in use for many years before transistors were invented, but they depended on vacuum tubes for the flow of electricity. Invite a volunteer committee to do research in encyclopedias and science books to learn the basic principle on which vacuum tubes work, their size, and their disadvantages compared with transistors. Have the committee present their findings in an oral report.

**EXAMINING THE PHOTOGRAPHS** Invite students to compare the scenes pictured in this lesson with similar scenes from their experience. They may mention local construction of homes or businesses, suburban commuting or other highway travel, and workers in factories, on farms, or in fast-food restaurants.

### √Answers to THINK ABOUT IT

1. Soldiers returning to start families, African Americans migrating to New Jersey from the rural South, and new immigrants from abroad created a need for housing.
2. Transistors allowed electronic items such as radios and televisions to be made very small.
3. any two: mass-produced homes, frozen foods, plastics, television, rockets, transistors, communications satellites
4. New Jersey was close to New York and Philadelphia, offered lots of jobs, and had a tradition of innovation.
5. Suburbanites needed new and better roads for commuting to jobs in the cities.

**Write About It** Have students suppose that they were living in 1950s New Jersey. Have them write a letter to a friend trying to convince the friend to relocate by mentioning some of the advantages of living in New Jersey.

### Resource REMINDER

**Practice and Project Book:** page 50

**Technology:** *Adventure Time CD-ROM*

**Transparency:** 3

# CITIZENSHIP Viewpoints

## HOW CAN NEW JERSEY SOLVE ITS TRAFFIC PROBLEMS?

PAGES 226–227

**Lesson Objective**

★ Compare different points of view with regard to solving New Jersey's traffic problems.

### Identifying the ISSUE

Have students examine the traffic jam pictured in the lesson. Invite students to share their experiences with traffic congestion. Arrive at a class statement to summarize the state's traffic problems.

### Discussing Three DIFFERENT VIEWPOINTS

Have students read the three viewpoints on page 227. Ask volunteers to restate the viewpoints in their own words to make sure they clearly understand each.

### CITIZENSHIP

**PRACTICING ROAD COURTESY** Point out that driver patience often wears thin when highways are crowded and traffic tie-ups occur. Note that safe and courteous driving begins with knowing and following the rules of the road.

- Bring to class several copies of the state's driving codes that people seeking a driver's license must know in order to pass the driving test.
- Have small student groups look through the booklet, noting both familiar and unfamiliar rules. Then have each group compile a list of additional rules for safe, courteous drivers and passengers in heavy traffic situations.
- Bring the class together, vote on the five best suggestions, and create an illustrated "driving courtesy" chart for the bulletin board.

### ✓Answers to BUILDING CITIZENSHIP

1. Donna McDonough sees additional roads as only a temporary solution. She believes people should walk or bike for short trips and use car pooling and mass transit, at least some of the time, for longer trips. Pam Fischer believes that cars alone do not cause the problem. She suggests that business centers and housing developments be built near mass transit lines. Lynn Wilkins opposes the building of new or wider roads because it encourages auto use. She favors increased use of mass transit.
2. All of the speakers agree that mass transit is part of the solution. While McDonough sees new roads as only a temporary solution, Wilkins believes that new roads add to the problem. Fischer disagrees that cars are the main problem; she believes poor planning is the real problem.
3. Possible answers: More people could work at home, now that computers make it less necessary to be in an office. Office/factory hours might be changed in order to stagger rush hour traffic. New mass transit lines could be built to accommodate more people, or existing ones could be upgraded to make them more appealing. More people shop on the Internet to avoid shopping trips.

### Sharing VIEWPOINTS

Invite students to analyze the thinking of each person and discuss the workability of each viewpoint. Suggest that they consider the cost, for example, of building new highways. Would bike paths or improved sidewalks be needed if people biked or walked more often? Is it too late for better planning to resolve the traffic issue? How could more commuters be persuaded to carpool? Students' statements may go beyond the thinking expressed by the people on this page. Possible statements might include: 1. Solving New Jersey's traffic problems requires a variety of remedies. 2. Any new housing developments and business centers should be built near mass transit lines. 3. New buses and bus lines could be added without building new roads or rail lines.

**Write About It** Have students write bumper sticker slogans urging courteous driving.

CHAPTER 9

# SKILLS LESSON

## READING ROAD MAPS

PAGES 228–229

**Lesson Overview**

*Road maps* help travelers plan their trips by showing them how to get from one place to another.

**Lesson Objectives**

★ Identify the symbols used on a road map.

★ Use a road map to plan a route from one place to another.

★ Read a road map to obtain information.

### Why the SKILL MATTERS

Ask students if they have ever traveled to another town by car. Ask them how the driver knew the way and if there is a road map in their family's vehicle. Point out that New Jersey has so many roads, from city streets to six-lane highways, that no one could possibly know his or her way around without at least occasional help from a road map.

### Using the SKILL

Bring a state or national road atlas to class and allow students to examine it. Have them read aloud the *Helping Yourself* box to acquaint them with road maps.

### Trying the SKILL

Refer students to the New Jersey road map transparency (Transparency 3) Have them list some things they see on the map.

### Meeting INDIVIDUAL NEEDS

**RETEACHING (Easy)** Have students plan a route on a road map from their community to a large city in New Jersey.

**EXTENSION (Average)** Have students use a road map of New Jersey to find three places they would like to visit. Have them plot the route from their home to each of the places.

**ENRICHMENT (Challenging)** Ask students to bring in New Jersey road maps. Have them plan a scenic trip across the state, highlighting with colored markers the less traveled roads they would take to maximize their enjoyment. Have them identify the scenic places they would visit.

### Technology CONNECTION

**ADVENTURE TIME CD-ROM**

Enrich this lesson with *New Jersey, Explore,* and *Investigate* on the CD-ROM.

### Curriculum CONNECTION

**LINKS TO SOCIAL STUDIES** Discuss with students the differences between the road map on page 228 and a physical map. Explain that a physical map shows an area's natural features. Sometimes physical features are shown on other types of maps, such as political maps or road maps. Have students create for an imaginary place a road map that also shows physical features. Maps should include roads, rivers or other bodies of water, land formations (such as level plains or hilly areas), and other natural features, such as forests. Students should create map keys for their maps, with symbols or color codes for each feature.

### Building CITIZENSHIP

**CREATING A COMMUNITY ROAD MAP** Reinforce students' understanding of road maps and map keys by having them make a map showing the routes they take from home to school. First, have students make a list of the streets they take to school, noting directions in which they turn. Have them list landmarks such as hospitals or post offices that would help assure someone he or she is on the right road. Remind students they will need symbols for their map key. Then have them create a road map of their neighborhood using the information they put together.

### √Answers to REVIEWING THE SKILL

1. which roads to use to get from one place to another; types of roads; towns and cities; points of interest; scale; state names
2. interstate 95; found shield symbol, checked color on map key; state highway 36 and Garden State Parkway
3. a state highway
4. A road map helps us to get to places efficiently; it allows us to explore new places and see new things.

### Resource REMINDER

**Practice and Project Book:** page 51

**Technology:** *Adventure Time CD-ROM*

**Transparency:** 3

CHAPTER 9

# LESSON 2

## TIMES OF CHANGE

PAGES 230–235

**Lesson Overview**

African Americans in New Jersey struggled to end segregation and discrimination and to gain better jobs, housing, and schools.

**Lesson Objectives**

★ List the major changes to the New Jersey constitution in 1947.

★ Explain how the civil rights movement affected segregation and discrimination.

★ Describe changes in the apportionment of State Assembly seats and in education funding in the 1960s and 1970s.

## Reading Strategies and LANGUAGE DEVELOPMENT

**MAKE AND SUPPORT GENERALIZATIONS**

Remind students that a generalization is a statement based on several terms, ideas, or facts that shows how they are alike in one or more ways. Have students look at how the terms *discrimination, segregation,* and *unfair treatment* are used in this lesson. Then ask them to form a generalization about the Civil Rights movement.

## Field Trip

**CASE IN COURT** Arrange to visit a courtroom in a local courthouse. As an alternative, invite an attorney to tell students about the local courts—the kinds of cases tried there and the roles of lawyers, judges, and juries. Compare these details with those for the Supreme Court.

## Building CITIZENSHIP

**WRITING A CONSTITUTION** Help students draw up a classroom constitution describing laws, leaders, lawmakers, and ways to settle disputes. Discuss the constitution's goals and how it is each class member's duty to uphold them. Enforce the constitution for a week, then discuss its merits.

## Technology CONNECTION

**ADVENTURE TIME CD-ROM**

Enrich this lesson with *New Jersey, Explore,* and *Investigate* on the CD-ROM.

## Background INFORMATION

**EVOLUTION OF THE STATE CONSTITUTION**
Remind students that New Jersey wrote its first constitution in 1776. It gave the legislature most of the power. The governor was chosen by the legislature and served for one year. The courts had little authority to review or challenge the laws. The 1844 constitution strengthened the positions of the governor and the courts and made it possible to amend, or change, the constitution.

## Meeting INDIVIDUAL NEEDS

**RETEACHING (Easy)** Have students write a series of headlines that might have accompanied newspaper stories about the civil rights movement in New Jersey.

**EXTENSION (Average)** Have students write several journal entries as a New Jersey civil rights worker in the 1950s or 1960s. Have them list their goals and accomplishments.

**ENRICHMENT (Challenging)** Arrange students into three groups. Have each group research and present oral reports on Dr. Martin Luther King: his early life, philosophy, and contributions to the civil rights struggle. Have each group recite one of Dr. King's speeches. Close with a recording of a King speech.

## ✓Answers to THINK ABOUT IT

1. the rights of all citizens to be treated equally under the law
2. It outlawed discrimination, but did not end it.
3. any two: Dr. King's inspiring ideas and energy; sit-ins and other protests against segregation; work as elected representatives at the local level
4. New Jersey approves new constitution; African American students stage a sit-in; Kenneth Gibson becomes mayor of Newark; and New Jersey starts an income tax.
5. Student letters should recognize ways in which facilities and services for African Americans were kept separate from and unequal to those for whites.

**Write About It** Have students assume the role of Governor Byrne and write a brief press release explaining his position on a new state income tax.

**Resource REMINDER**

**Practice and Project Book:** page 52

**Technology:** *Adventure Time CD-ROM*

# LESSON 3
## A CHANGING ECONOMY
PAGES 236–239

**Lesson Overview**

Over a few decades, service jobs became far more numerous than manufacturing jobs, many more women began to work outside the home, and New Jersey entered the global economy.

**Lesson Objectives**

★ Describe the shift from manufacturing jobs to service jobs in New Jersey.

★ Explain why New Jersey is part of the global economy.

★ Describe the state's efforts to rebuild cities and preserve the environment.

## Reading Strategies and LANGUAGE DEVELOPMENT

**BASE WORDS AND ROOTS** Refer students to the words *worked, studying,* and *creates* in the first three paragraphs on page 237. Have volunteers identify and write the base words on the chalkboard. Also write the "ed," "ing," and "s" endings on the board and have students interchange them among the base words. Note that "ed" indicates a completed action while "s" and "ing" mean present and ongoing. Have students use these endings to identify completed and ongoing activities as they read the lesson.

**PROBLEM AND SOLUTION** Draw two columns labeled "Problem" and "Solution" on the chalkboard. Arrange students in pairs. Have each pair write a problem or a solution from the lesson under the appropriate heading. Across from each entry, have another student pair add the missing problem or solution.

## Meeting INDIVIDUAL NEEDS

**RETEACHING (Easy)** Have students use newspaper help wanted sections to identify and list service and manufacturing jobs available in the local community.

**EXTENSION (Average)** Ask students to select a subject discussed in the lesson. Have them draw "before" and "after" cartoons illustrating the need for change in that area and the results of a change that has been made.

**ENRICHMENT (Challenging)** Ask students to research information on the restoration of the Meadowlands. Suggest that they focus on the Richard DeKorte State Park, where a miniwilderness is now carefully preserved and managed. Have students present their information to the class in an oral report.

## Second-Language SUPPORT

**USING PROPS** The concept of a global economy may have special significance to second-language students. Distribute world outline maps, have students label second-language students' countries of origin, and draw arrows connecting the countries to New Jersey. Label the arrows with examples of products and resources exchanged between the two places. Import and export listings in almanacs may offer assistance if needed.

Help students remember to include immigrants and the human resources they represent.

## ✓Answers to THINK ABOUT IT

1. one that involves fixing things, helping people, and creating information rather than making things
2. Goods made in New Jersey may move from one country to another for manufacture or sale.
3. any two: cutting taxes to attract jobs and businesses, cleaning up the environment, preserving open space, renewing cities
4. Predictions should recognize efforts to keep cities clean, livable, and attractive to business.
5. Responses will vary but should refer to today's interdependent exchange of factory goods and raw materials with Britain and cite examples of colonial trade with other countries.

**Write About It** Have students write a poem about the changing workforce in New Jersey today.

## Technology CONNECTION

**ADVENTURE TIME CD-ROM**

Enrich this lesson with *New Jersey, Explore,* and *Investigate* on the CD-ROM.

*Resource* **REMINDER**

**Practice and Project Book:** page 53

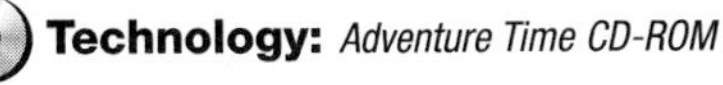

**Technology:** *Adventure Time CD-ROM*

ANSWERS TO
# Chapter 9 REVIEW
PAGES 240-241

### THINKING ABOUT VOCABULARY

1. C
2. Income tax
3. C
4. Service
5. C
6. apportionment
7. Mass production
8. C
9. C
10. global economy

### THINKING ABOUT FACTS

1. His company mass-produced houses, building many houses at once.
2. any two: automobiles, frozen foods, plastics, television, rockets, communications
3. Many new highways were built, including the New Jersey Turnpike and the Garden State Parkway.
4. The Constitution of 1947 forbade discrimination by race; the state Supreme Court ordered various towns to desegregate their schools.
5. Starting in the 1970s, the government began to spend millions of dollars to clean up the environment. In the Meadowlands, 16 city, county, and state government agencies have worked together to restore the wetland to its natural condition.

## Suggestions for THINK AND WRITE

### SIGNS OF SUCCESS

***Summary*** Answers should describe the Meadowlands before cleanup, signs of improvement, and the groups involved.

***Advertisement*** Advertisements should show knowledge of reasons people wanted to move to the suburbs.

***Editorial*** Editorials should demonstrate understanding of the constitution's stance on discrimination and should link discrimination to segregation.

*For performance assessment, see* **Assessment book,** *Chapter 9, pages T56–T58.*

### APPLYING GEOGRAPHY SKILLS
### READING ROAD MAPS

1. important places and the roads that connect these places
2. Interstate highway numbers are shown in white against a black background in the shape of a medallion or shield.
3. Interstate 78
4. Route 27
5. Road maps show people which roads to use to get from one place to another.

### Technology CONNECTION

**ADVENTURE TIME CD-ROM**

Enrich Chapter 9 with *New Jersey, Explore,* and *Investigate* on the CD-ROM.

### Resource REMINDER

**Practice and Project Book:** page 54

**Assessment Book:** Chapter 9 Test

**Performance Assessment,** page T56–T58

 **Technology:** *Adventure Time CD-ROM*

ANSWERS TO

# Unit 4 REVIEW

PAGES 242–243

### THINKING ABOUT VOCABULARY

1. political party
2. civil rights
3. mass production
4. transistor
5. primary
6. county
7. income tax
8. service
9. Great Depression
10. Great Migration

## Suggestions for THINK AND WRITE

#### SIGNS OF SUCCESS

***Report*** Students' reports should include at least two of the major industries in New Jersey in the early 1900s and two of today's major industries. Their reports should indicate that the large industries of the early 1900s were manufacturing-based, while today's industries are related to the service economy.

***Explanation*** Students' explanations should reflect an understanding of the extent of segregation in New Jersey in the early 1960s. They should also mention that some schools were segregated and students seeking civil rights started the sit-in.

***Speech*** Students' speeches should be descriptive and clearly identify the problems of the community. The speeches should also offer solutions to the problems cited.

## Building SKILLS

1. **Primary and Secondary Sources** primary source
2. **Primary and Secondary Sources** A primary source can make us feel as though we were there during a historical event. It can help us understand how one person thought about something. A secondary source may help us to see a broader view of events. It may give us more points of view on a subject.
3. **Reading Road Maps** Road maps show roads you can use to get from one place to another. Elevation maps show the height of land above sea level.
4. **Reading Road Maps** Students' answers should indicate an understanding of the different map symbols used to show state and interstate highways.
5. **Reading Road Maps** It helps us get to places easily and it allows us to explore new places and see new things.

## Suggestions for YESTERDAY, TODAY, AND TOMORROW

As students speculate about technological change in the future, review some of the changes from the past. Encourage students to think about how technology affects their lives, and what new technologies may appear in the future.

## ONGOING UNIT PROJECT

#### OPTIONS FOR ASSESSMENT

The ongoing unit project begun on page T67 can be part of your assessment program, along with other forms of evaluation.

## UNIT PROJECT

#### MAKE A NEW JERSEY HISTORY MURAL

***Objective*** Making a New Jersey history mural will help students better understand and remember the event or time period that they choose.

***Materials*** paper, pencils, crayons, markers, paints, paste, posterboard

- Have students review the work of the WPA artists during the Great Depression.
- Allow students time to plan their murals, choosing a time period and individual subjects for the sections of the mural. You may wish to hold a class discussion on the general history of New Jersey during the years mentioned.
- Encourage students to be creative and colorful as they draw the pictures for their mural. Also encourage them to be historically accurate.
- Students' murals should contain pictures related to their main topic.

#### OPTIONS FOR ASSESSMENT

*For performance assessment, see* **Assessment Book,** *Unit 4, page T59.*

**FOR THE PORTFOLIO** Individual notes and sketches can be included in students' portfolios.

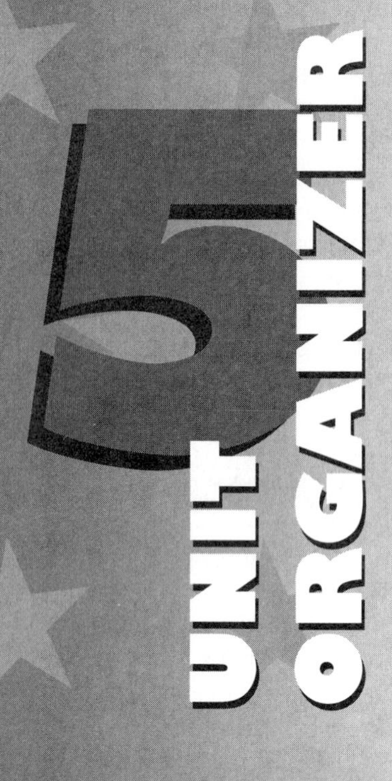


# New Jersey in the Twenty-first Century

**PAGES 244–309**

## Unit Overview

New Jersey's growing economy provides goods and services to consumers as well as jobs in a variety of industries. Citizens of a culturally rich and diverse state, New Jerseyans have rights and responsibilities to their local, state, and national governments.

## UNIT PLANNING GUIDE

| CHAPTER | SUGGESTED PACING | CHAPTER OVERVIEW | CHAPTER RESOURCES |
|---|---|---|---|
| **10 New Jersey's Economy Today** pages 248–267 | 12–13 days | The free enterprise system, service industries, and innovations in technology keep New Jersey's economy strong. | ***Practice and Project Book*** pages 55–59<br>***Technology:*** *Adventure Time CD-ROM* |
| **11 New Jersey's Government and You** pages 268–287 | 14–15 days | In a democracy, leaders serve and represent the people on the local, state, and national levels. Executive, legislative, and judicial branches provide a system of checks and balances. | ***Practice and Project Book*** pages 60–64<br>***Transparency:*** 4<br>***Technology:*** *Adventure Time CD-ROM* |
| **12 The People of New Jersey** pages 288–307 | 13–14 days | A mix of cultures calls New Jersey home. Sports, parks, and historic sites provide recreation. Great writers, singers, and artists have lived in our state. | ***Practice and Project Book*** pages 65–69<br>***Transparency:*** 1<br>***Technology:*** *Adventure Time CD-ROM* |

**Internet CONNECTION**

The Home Page at **http://www.mhschool.com** contains on-line student activities related to this unit.

**For Further Support**
- Handbook of Test-Taking Strategies

## ASSESSMENT OPPORTUNITIES

### UNIT ASSESSMENT

**Unit Review** pages 308–309
***Unit Project*** page 309, page T104

**Assessment Book**
***Unit Test*** Unit 5 Test
***Performance Assessment*** page T69

### CHAPTER ASSESSMENT

**Meeting Individual Needs** pages T85, T87, T88, T91, T92, T94, T98, T99, T100
**Write About It** pages T85, T86, T88, T91, T93, T95, T98, T100, T102
**Chapter Review** pages 266–267, 286–287, 306-307

**Assessment Book**
***Chapter Test 10, Chapter 11 Test, Chapter 12 Test***
***Performance Assessment*** pages T60–T62, T63–T65, T66–T68

## TECHNOLOGY CENTER

# Enriching with Multimedia

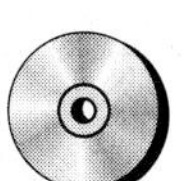

**RESOURCE:** *Internet*

- Look at McGraw-Hill School's home page on the World Wide Web at **http://www.mhschool.com** for activities related to this unit that your students can do on-line.

**RESOURCE: Adventure Time CD-ROM**

Enrich Unit 5 with ***Explore, Build,*** and ***Paint*** on the CD-ROM.

## SCHOOL-TO-HOME

# New Jersey's Artists

- The purpose of this project is to help students become better acquainted with past or present artists of New Jersey. Encourage students to find out about the life and work of a selected painter, writer, or musician. Their research might include the childhood, education, and professional development of the artist. Invite family members to take part in the research.
- In addition to a written report, have students present information from their research in another medium. Students can present drawings, photographs, a videotape, audiotape, or live reading of the artist's work.

## ONGOING UNIT PROJECT

# Design a Flag

**CURRICULUM CONNECTION**
**Art/Math/Language Arts**

Throughout this unit, students will be working individually and then in groups to design a flag.

1. After each chapter is completed, have students write their ideas on what is special about New Jersey's economy, government, people, and its arts, sports, and recreation. Have them draw a sketch of a state flag that reflects some of these features.
2. In groups, have students choose at least one idea from each group member to use as part of a group flag. Tell students their flags should reflect what is special about New Jersey today. They may want to compare their ideas with the symbols on the current state flag.
3. Provide each group with a large sheet of oaktag, markers, glitter, glue, and other available art materials. Have students decide the dimension of the flag, using a ruler to measure the rectangular shape. They should illustrate and label their flags. Students can then glue them to three paper towel tubes. Invite each group to share its flag with the class.

Assessment suggestions for this activity appear on page T104.

10 CHAPTER ORGANIZER

# New Jersey's Economy Today

Pages 248–267

## CHAPTER OVERVIEW

The economy of New Jersey is built on the free enterprise system. While manufacturing and farming remain important, service industries have become the largest contributors to our strong economy. New Jersey also remains a leader in new technology innovations.

## CHAPTER PLANNING GUIDE

**Suggested pacing: 12–13 days**

| LESSON | LESSON FOCUS | LESSON RESOURCES |
|---|---|---|
| 1 **THE FREE ENTERPRISE SYSTEM AT WORK** pages 250–253 | How the Free Enterprise System Works | ***Practice and Project Book:*** page 55<br>***Technology:*** *Adventure Time CD-ROM* |
| 2 **NEW JERSEY'S WORKERS** pages 254–259 | New Jersey's Service and Manufacturing Workers | ***Practice and Project Book:*** page 56<br>***Technology:*** *Adventure Time CD-ROM* |
| **STUDY SKILLS** pages 260–261 | Using References Sources | ***Practice and Project Book:*** page 57<br>***Technology:*** *Adventure Time CD-ROM* |
| 3 **CUTTING EDGE IN NEW JERSEY** pages 262–265 | New Technology and Innovation in New Jersey | ***Practice and Project Book:*** page 58<br>***Technology:*** *Adventure Time CD-ROM* |
| **CHAPTER REVIEW** pages 266–267 | Students' understanding of vocabulary, content, and skills is assessed. | ***Practice and Project Book:*** page 59<br>***Assessment Book:*** Chapter 10 Test<br>***Performance Assessment*** pages T60–T62<br>***Technology:*** *Adventure Time CD-ROM* |

**New Jersey Core Curriculum Content Standards for Social Studies**

**Content Standards** These content standards and progress indicators for students completing Grade 4, correlated with Chapter 10, have been developed by the New Jersey Department of Education. A complete listing of the standards can be found on pages T110–T112.

**Standard 6.6** All students will acquire historical understanding of economic forces, ideas, and institutions throughout the history of New Jersey, the United States, and the world.
2. pages 252–253
3. pages 250–251, 254–257, 263–264

CHAPTER 10

# LESSON 1

## THE FREE ENTERPRISE SYSTEM AT WORK

PAGES 250–253

**Lesson Overview**

The United States economy is based on a *free enterprise* system that allows individuals to decide for themselves what to sell and buy.

**Lesson Objectives**

★ Describe how free enterprise works.

★ Explain why consumers have a choice of goods and services in a free enterprise economy.

★ Explain how young people can take part in the free enterprise system by starting their own business.

## Reading Strategies and LANGUAGE DEVELOPMENT

**COMPARE AND CONTRAST** Ask students what advantages Jeanie Wilcox had in her office job and list responses on the chalkboard. Make a second list for her advantages as a shop owner. Note that her complaint that the job wasn't "going anywhere" probably meant that she wanted more money and responsibility. Help students use their lists to discuss why a worker might want to be an entrepreneur and why someone else might decide to work for an employer. Remind them that there is hard work as well as risks and advantages either way.

## Second-Language SUPPORT

**DRAMATIZATION** Arrange students into four teams. Assign one of the following scenarios from the story of Falcon Express to each team and have the students role-play the situations for the class. (1) Students hold a planning session to decide what to sell and their goal for the business; (2) Students meet with an investor and receive funds to set up shop; (3) Students set up their store, bringing in equipment and supplies; (4) Students open the store to great success.

## Technology CONNECTION

**ADVENTURE TIME CD-ROM**

Enrich this lesson with *New Jersey, Explore, Investigate, Symbols* and *New Jersey Today* on the CD-ROM.

## Building CITIZENSHIP

**HIGHLIGHTING ENTREPRENEURSHIP** Help students understand that entrepreneurs are valuable members of the community and society as a whole. They may introduce new inventions such as practical electric lighting or personal computers. Many, however, supply more everyday wants and needs. Have students create a community guide to small businesses in their area. In the guide, have them state each entrepreneur's contribution to the community.

## Meeting INDIVIDUAL NEEDS

**RETEACHING (Easy)** Have students make a poster advertising JJ's new list of offerings after the first winter.

**EXTENSION (Average)** Have a group of students script and act out a TV commercial to entice viewers to stop by JJ's Heavenly Delights.

**ENRICHMENT (Challenging)** Arrange for teams of two or three students to interview some local entrepreneurs. Help students plan such interview topics as why the owner started his or her business, what products or services are offered, what resources are needed, and what jobs were created. As a class, compare and contrast what interviewers learned about entrepreneurship.

## √Answers to THINK ABOUT IT

1. someone who takes risks in offering goods or services consumers might want to buy
2. Investors provide funds to buy equipment and materials.
3. Students own, operate, and make profits from the Falcon Express snack bar.
4. Sweets and baked goods keep the shop running in winter, when ice cream sales drop.
5. Responses will vary but should show an understanding of the choices consumers make and of competition in predicting success.

**Write About It** Have students list risks and rewards they think investing might involve.

## Resource REMINDER

**Practice and Project Book:** page 55

 **Technology:** *Adventure Time CD-ROM*

# LESSON 2
## NEW JERSEY'S WORKERS
PAGES 254–259

**Lesson Overview**

A wide range of service industries, plus manufacturing and agriculture, employ New Jersey's workers and form a strong base for our state's booming economy.

**Lesson Objectives**

★ Identify leading products manufactured in New Jersey.

★ Identify the type of industry that employs most of New Jersey's workers.

★ Examine the role of service industries such as tourism in New Jersey's economy.

### Reading Strategies and LANGUAGE DEVELOPMENT

**MAKE AND SUPPORT GENERALIZATIONS** Tell students that using this skill will help them remember what they read, even if they read a great deal of material. One generalization can address many details. To illustrate this skill, have students review the *Read Aloud*. Help students see that the first sentence is a generalization about New Jersey as a business leader. Have them identify the details that support the statement in the rest of the paragraph. Then have students find additional supporting details as they read the lesson.

### Expanding the INFOGRAPHIC

**RESEARCH AND WRITING** Explain to students that most of the fresh blueberries sold in supermarkets are highbush blueberries. Have students use encyclopedias to research highbush blueberries and write a report of their findings. Reports should focus on characteristics of the plants, their cultivation and yields, and how the fruit is harvested. Students might wish to include a drawing of blueberry flowers or fruit.

### Second-Language SUPPORT

**WORKING IN PAIRS** Team second-language students with native English-speaking students in a mock long-distance telephone conversation. The second-language student, considering emigration from his or her native land, asks about job opportunities in New Jersey.

### Technology CONNECTION

**ADVENTURE TIME CD-ROM**

Enrich this lesson with *New Jersey, Explore, Investigate, Symbols* and *New Jersey Today* on the CD-ROM.

### Global CONNECTION

**PORT OF ENTRY** The Port of Newark is part of the overall transportation system operated by the Port Authority of New York and New Jersey. A large percentage of foreign cars sold in the United States enter through the Port of Newark. Newark is also an important entry point for imported foods and lumber as well as a center for moving goods from cargo ships to the trains and trucks that bring them to the cities.

### Curriculum CONNECTION

**LINKS TO LANGUAGE ARTS** Have students write a letter to the New Jersey Department of Commerce and Economic Development, Division of Travel and Tourism, CN 826, Trenton, NJ, 08625, requesting brochures on one or two tourist sites illustrated or mentioned in this lesson. Display a copy of the letter and the information received on the class bulletin board.

### √Answers to THINK ABOUT IT

1. books, computers, soap, shampoo, medicine, food products, electronics
2. government, teaching, mail delivery, police and fire protection, banking, taxi driving, healthcare, restaurant service, telecommunications, tourist services
3. The service industry far outranks manufacturing and agriculture in size.
4. Possible predictions should recognize that current service industry growth, the educated workforce, and the demand for service suggest continued growth.
5. Paragraphs should note the attractions of the Jersey shore, parks and recreation areas, and historical sites.

**Write About It** Have students write a letter to a prospective New Jersey employer explaining why they would like a job in that business.

**Resource REMINDER**

**Practice and Project Book:** page 56

 **Technology:** *Adventure Time CD-ROM*

CHAPTER 10

# SKILLS LESSON

## USING REFERENCE SOURCES

PAGES 260–261

**Lesson Overview**

Reference sources are books and other sources that contain facts about many different subjects.

**Lesson Objective**

★ Apply research skills to locate information in a dictionary, an encyclopedia, and a CD-ROM.

### Why the SKILL MATTERS

Note that being able to use a dictionary and an encyclopedia is necessary when students are writing a report or conducting research on a particular subject. This skill is also helpful when students just want to know more about an interesting topic.

### Using the SKILL

**USING A DICTIONARY** Ask a volunteer to read the definition of the word *equipment* from a dictionary. Help students recognize that the dictionary also provides additional information. It tells how to spell and pronounce a word, how to break it into syllables, and what its origin is.

**USING AN ENCYCLOPEDIA, A CD-ROM, OR THE INTERNET** Note that an encyclopedia, a CD-ROM, or the Internet help students find more information on a specific topic, person, or place. These sources contain written data, photographs, and illustrations. CD-ROMs and the Internet often also present sounds and short movies.

### Trying the SKILL

Have students research the history of television. Stress the importance of choosing the correct type of reference sources. Because students are researching a particular topic, an encyclopedia, CD-ROM, and the Internet would be the best choices. Ask them how they would use an encyclopedia to find the information they are seeking.

### Technology CONNECTION

**ADVENTURE TIME CD-ROM**

Enrich this lesson with *New Jersey* and *Create* on the CD-ROM.

### Background INFORMATION

**THE REFERENCE SECTION** In addition to encyclopedias, dictionaries, and almanacs, the reference section in the library contains dozens of other more specialized references. Biographical and geographic dictionaries along with atlases can be especially useful to students. If there are CD-ROMs and on–line reference tools, these will also be found in the reference section.

Reference sections are staffed by reference librarians, who can help in locating appropriate sources. Researchers usually must use reference sources while at the library rather than checking them out.

### Meeting INDIVIDUAL NEEDS

**RETEACHING (Easy)** Review with students the purpose and use of a dictionary and an encyclopedia. Have students look up three or more words from the chapter that are not vocabulary terms, such as *loan, chemicals*, or *commerce*. Then have them write each word on the front of an index card and its definition on the back. They can quiz each other on the meanings.

**EXTENSION (Average)** Pair students and give each pair access to a dictionary or encyclopedia. Have partners take turns challenging each other to locate information on given words or subjects.

**ENRICHMENT (Challenging)** Have students write a one-page report on a New Jersey topic of their choice using an encyclopedia, CD-ROM, or the state web site **www.state.nj.us.**

### Field Trip

Arrange a visit to your school library or local public library with extra time spent in the reference section. Have students use the available resources to write a brief history of public libraries.

### √Answers to REVIEWING THE SKILL

1. a book or other source that contains facts about many different subjects
2. a dictionary
3. no
4. when they want to find the definition of a word or more information about a subject

### Resource REMINDER

**Practice and Project Book:** page 57

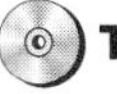 **Technology:** *Adventure Time CD-ROM*

CHAPTER 10

# LESSON 3

## CUTTING EDGE IN NEW JERSEY

PAGES 262–265

**Lesson Overview**

Innovations in technology have advanced medical care and changed the way people shop, communicate, and learn.

**Lesson Objectives**

★ Describe ways in which New Jersey leads in research and development in medicine and high technology.

★ Identify some of the new products created by New Jersey's scientists.

★ Explain the Internet's effect on business.

## Reading Strategies and LANGUAGE DEVELOPMENT

**LANGUAGE HISTORY AND ETYMOLOGY** Tell students that although the computer revolution is a modern one, the word *computer* dates back to the ancient Latin word *computare,* which means to count up, calculate, or reckon. Direct students' attention to "Links to Mathematics" on page 265 to see how numbers still apply to computer science.

## Field Trip

**COMPUTER STUDY** Arrange a class visit to a local computer store or community college computer lab. Ask a sales expert or computer instructor to explain and/or demonstrate some of the latest developments in computer science. As an alternative, invite a computer instructor or consultant to speak to class about future trends, such as computer interface with television.

## Meeting INDIVIDUAL NEEDS

**RETEACHING (Easy)** Have students create sequenced cartoon panels illustrating the steps in going on-line and possible Internet activities, such as shopping.

**EXTENSION (Average)** Have students create a glossary of terms useful to a new computer user. Have them include terms from the lesson, terms found in reference sources, and terms they remember learning when they first became computer users. They may wish to post a master list in the school library or computer lab.

**ENRICHMENT (Challenging)** Have students research the history of computers. Ask them to create a time line of important developments, including Blaise Pascal's calculator, early punched-card devices, ENIAC, UNIVAC, the introduction of transistors.

## Technology CONNECTION

**ADVENTURE TIME CD-ROM**

Enrich this lesson with *New Jersey, Explore,* and *Investigate* on the CD-ROM.

## Curriculum CONNECTION

**LINKS TO LANGUAGE ARTS** Tell students that Judy Blume is a popular writer from Elizabeth. Help students visit her web site at **www.judyblume.com/index.html** and have them read some of her tips for writers.

## Background INFORMATION

**NEW TECHNOLOGY MEDICINE** Tell students that fiber optics and biotechnology have special significance to medicine. Doctors can insert threadlike fiber-optic instruments called endoscopes into the body to see and treat diseases. They reflect light from the body tissue to produce images doctors work with to heal their patients. Through biotechnology, germs can be altered to produce useful medicines.

## √Answers to THINK ABOUT IT

1. creating new ideas and products
2. the combination of biology and technology to make scientific advances
3. New technology has expanded telephone capacity, improved the treatment of disease and injury, increased the exchange of information, and created Internet businesses.
4. Accept all reasonable predictions.
5. The Internet connects New Jersey–based companies with customers from across the country and around the world.

**Write About It** Have students compose a slogan for New Jersey's technology achievements.

## Resource REMINDER

**Practice and Project Book:** page 58

 **Technology:** *Adventure Time CD-ROM*

ANSWERS TO

# Chapter 10 REVIEW

PAGES 266–267

### THINKING ABOUT VOCABULARY

1. profit
2. C
3. C
4. entrepreneur
5. e-mail
6. C
7. C
8. investor
9. biotechnology
10. competition

### THINKING ABOUT FACTS

1. The free enterprise system is an economic system that allows people to own and run their own businesses.
2. Consumers are people who buy products or use services.
3. Investors contribute money that allows entrepreneurs to start businesses.
4. Any three: books, computers, soap, shampoo, medicine, food products, electronics equipment.
5. Telecommunications involves the sending of information over long distances by telephone and television.
6. Possible examples include hotels, amusement parks, casinos, and restaurants.
7. Research and development companies hire scientists to study and create new products and new technologies.
8. Fiber optics allow television, telephone, computer, and other cables to carry more information at higher speeds.
9. A company might create a web site and have an on-line catalog as well as a way for customers to order on-line.
10. The World Wide Web helps people from throughout the world to communicate.

## Suggestions for THINK AND WRITE

**SIGNS OF SUCCESS**

***Explanation*** Students' explanations should show an understanding of the fact that under the free enterprise system entrepreneurs can make choices about such things as what kind of business they will have, where to locate it, what supplies they will need, and how large they would like it to grow.

***List*** Students' lists should include manufactured items such as soap, shampoo, medicine, soup, cookies, tea, and electronics equipment. The lists should include services such as government, teaching, delivering mail, police protection, taxi driving, health care, banking, communicating information, and tourism services.

***Advertisement*** Students' advertisements should demonstrate an understanding of how features such as New Jersey's location, educated work force, and advances in technology make it a good place to start a business.

*For performance assessment, see* **Assessment Book,** *pages T60–T62*

### APPLYING STUDY SKILLS

**USING REFERENCE SOURCES**

1. sources that contain facts about many different subjects; any three: dictionary, encyclopedia, CD-ROM, Internet
2. encyclopedia, CD-ROM, Internet
3. yes
4. CD-ROM
5. They give you more information about people, places, things, and events. You can use them to better understand subjects and write reports.

### Technology CONNECTION

**ADVENTURE TIME CD-ROM**

Enrich Chapter 12 with *New Jersey, Explore,* and *Investigate* on the CD-ROM.

### Resource REMINDER

**Practice and Project Book:** page 59

**Assessment Book:** *Chapter 10 Test*

**Performance Assessment,** pages T60–T62

**Technology:** *Adventure Time CD-ROM*

11 CHAPTER ORGANIZER

# New Jersey's Government and You

Pages 268–287

## CHAPTER OVERVIEW

Municipal government in New Jersey provides services to our villages, towns, and cities. Both the state and national governments are divided into executive, legislative, and judicial branches.

## CHAPTER PLANNING GUIDE

**Suggested pacing: 14–15 days**

| LESSON | LESSON FOCUS | LESSON RESOURCES |
|---|---|---|
| **1 YOUR LOCAL GOVERNMENT** pages 270–273 | Municipal Government in New Jersey | ***Practice and Project Book:*** page 60<br>***Transparency:*** 4<br>***Technology:*** *Adventure Time CD-ROM* |
| **STUDY SKILLS** pages 274–275 | Reading Newspapers | ***Practice and Project Book:*** page 61<br>***Technology:*** *Adventure Time CD-ROM* |
| **2 OUR STATE GOVERNMENT** pages 276–280 | The Three Branches of State Government | ***Practice and Project Book:*** page 62<br>***Technology:*** *Adventure Time CD-ROM* |
| **CITIZENSHIP MAKING A DIFFERENCE** page 281 | Starting a Family Tradition | |
| **3 OUR NATIONAL GOVERNMENT** pages 282–285 | The Three Branches of National Government | ***Practice and Project Book:*** page 63<br>***Technology:*** *Adventure Time CD-ROM* |
| **CHAPTER REVIEW** pages 286–287 | Students' understanding of vocabulary, content, and skills is assessed. | ***Practice and Project Book:*** page 64<br>***Assessment Book:*** Chapter 11 Test<br>***Performance Assessment*** pages T63–T65<br>***Technology:*** *Adventure Time CD-ROM* |

### New Jersey Core Curriculum Content Standards for Social Studies

**Content Standards** These content standards and progress indicators for students completing Grade 4, correlated with Chapter 11, have been developed by the New Jersey Department of Education. A complete listing of the standards can be found on pages T110–T112.

**Standard 6.1** All students will learn democratic citizenship and how to participate in the constitutional system of government of the United States.

2. pages 270, 281, 285; 4. pages 271–273, 277–279; 5. pages 276, 282

**Standard 6.4** All students will acquire historical understanding of societal ideas and forces throughout the history of New Jersey, the United States, and the world.
2. pages 271–273, 276–280, 282–285

CHAPTER 11

# LESSON 1

## YOUR LOCAL GOVERNMENT

PAGES 270–273

### Lesson Overview

Local government makes decisions for the community. In New Jersey, local governments include five types of municipalities, special districts, and county governments.

### Lesson Objectives

★ Define local government and list some of the services local governments provide.

★ Identify the five kinds of municipalities in New Jersey.

★ Define special districts.

★ Explain how county government operates.

## Reading Strategies and LANGUAGE DEVELOPMENT

**COMPARE AND CONTRAST** As students read the lesson, have them fill in a chart on the chalkboard to compare and contrast municipal governments with county governments. They should consider the areas each serves, the services they perform, and the officials who head them.

**LANGUAGE HISTORY AND ETYMOLOGY** Tell students that the word *county* comes from the French word *conté* for the land owned by a count. It was adopted by the British after the French invaded in 1066.

## Background INFORMATION

**COUNTY GOVERNMENT**

- The county system of government was adopted by the colonies from the British system of government.
- All states except Connecticut and Rhode Island have county governments. In Louisiana, counties are called *parishes*. They are called *boroughs* in Alaska.
- In many states, county governments have taken on more tasks as people have moved from cities to suburbs and rural areas.

## Technology CONNECTION

**ADVENTURE TIME CD-ROM**

Enrich this lesson with *New Jersey, Explore,* and *Investigate* on the CD-ROM.

## Meeting INDIVIDUAL NEEDS

**RETEACHING (Easy)** Have students work together to draft a one-page letter to a local government official. They should write about an issue that interests them, such as improving schools, creating more parks, recycling, or repairing roads.

**EXTENSION (Average)** Have students work together to create a list of services provided by local government, such as public parks and sidewalks. Have students find out which local government agencies regulate and maintain the following: the public library, public street lights, and traffic signs.

**ENRICHMENT (Challenging)** Have students research, create, and display an organizational chart of their community's local government. Tell students to include the names of officials currently in office.

## Second-Language SUPPORT

**WORKING WITH A PEER** Have second-language learners work in pairs with native English speakers. Partners should write sentences on index cards that use each of the vocabulary words listed on page 270. Students can also black out the vocabulary word on each card, write it on the back, and use their flash cards to quiz one another.

## ✓Answers to THINK ABOUT IT

1. boroughs, townships, cities, towns, and villages
2. any two: keeps parks clean, runs the public library, pays for police and fire departments
3. any two: voting, paying taxes, serving on citizen committees
4. Both municipal governments and special districts provide services to residents and are funded by taxes; special districts may be run by a board; municipalities are usually governed by an elected council and mayor.
5. Answers should be complete, including all bordering counties.

**Write About It** Have students write a "public service message" about what local government does for their community.

### Resource REMINDER

**Practice and Project Book:** page 60

**Technology:** *Adventure Time CD-ROM*

**Transparency:** 4

CHAPTER 11

# SKILLS LESSON

## READING NEWSPAPERS

PAGES 274–275

**Lesson Overview**

Newspapers are a good source of information about current events.

**Lesson Objectives**

★ Identify the basic parts of a newspaper.

★ Explain how to read a newspaper article.

## Why the SKILL MATTERS

Newspapers are important sources of information. Newspaper stories cover events from around the world and close to home. Newspapers include different kinds of articles. They provide many facts, are easy to read, and are inexpensive.

## Using the SKILL

**USING A NEWSPAPER** If possible, provide one newspaper for each student. (Dates do not matter.) As you discuss each part of the newspaper, show an example of that part of a paper. Ask students to locate a news article, a feature article, and an editorial in their newspapers.

**USING A NEWS ARTICLE** Emphasize to students that most news articles follow the same format. Ask them to think about the "five questions" a well-written news article answers: who, what, when, where, and why.

## Trying the SKILL

Help students see how the article "In Search of Fields of Dreams" answers the five questions. Ask students to write the sentences or phrases from the story that answer the questions. Have students use the *Helping Yourself* box to aid them.

## Technology CONNECTION

**ADVENTURE TIME CD-ROM**

Enrich this lesson with *New Jersey, Explore,* and *Investigate* on the CD-ROM.

## Background INFORMATION

**NEW JERSEY NEWSPAPERS**

- Nine daily newspapers are published in New Jersey.
- Two African American weekly newspapers, the *City News* and the *Twin Visions Weekly*, are published in Newark.
- In 1972 *New Directions for Women*, the first statewide newspaper for the women's movement in the state and in the nation, began publishing. It was edited by Paula Kassel of Dover.

## Meeting INDIVIDUAL NEEDS

**RETEACHING (Easy)** Go through a newspaper page by page with students. Have them point out and differentiate among the major parts of the paper.

**EXTENSION (Average)** Have students scan a newspaper every day for three days. Ask them to log the articles and editorials that are about local government.

**ENRICHMENT (Challenging)** Have students write news articles about school or local events. Instruct them to follow correct news article form, including answering the five questions.

## Field Trip

Arrange for students to go on a guided tour of a local newspaper printing facility or invite a local reporter to speak to the class. After this activity, help students to produce a one-page class newspaper either by hand or on a computer.

## ✓Answers to REVIEWING THE SKILL

1. news articles, feature articles, and editorials
2. The article presents facts and not the writer's opinion.
3. so readers will know when and where the events took place
4. Students should note that a New Jersey paper will have many articles about events and people in our state.

## Resource REMINDER

**Practice and Project Book:** page 61

**Technology:** *Adventure Time CD-ROM*

# LESSON 2
## OUR STATE GOVERNMENT
PAGES 276–280

**Lesson Overview**

The New Jersey government is made up of the *executive, legislative,* and *judicial* branches.

**Lesson Objectives**

★ Explain why state government is important to the people of New Jersey.

★ Identify the three branches of state government.

★ Describe the checks and balances system and explain its importance.

### Reading Strategies and LANGUAGE DEVELOPMENT

**REREADING** Explain to students how rereading almost any material will increase their understanding of it and improve their ability to recall what they have read.

**SYNONYMS AND ANTONYMS** Remind students that synonyms are words with similar meanings. Explain that *legislator* is a synonym for the word *lawmaker*. Have students look up both words in the dictionary and then write a short paragraph using each of the terms.

### Field Trip

Make arrangements to visit the State House. Guided tours include part of the governor's office, legislative chambers, the rotunda, and a meeting room that once housed the state Supreme Court. To make arrangements, call 609-633-2709. As an alternate activity, invite a state representative to speak to the class.

### Second-Language SUPPORT

**GRAPHIC ORGANIZER** Second-language students may benefit from visually organizing the material in the lesson. Have students work in pairs to create a three-column chart with the following headings: Executive Branch, Legislative Branch, Judicial Branch. Tell students to write details from the lesson under each heading.

### Technology CONNECTION

**ADVENTURE TIME CD-ROM**

Enrich this lesson with *New Jersey, Explore,* and *Investigate* on the CD-ROM.

### Curriculum CONNECTION

**LINKS TO MATH** Use the chart on page 277 to pose some mental math questions for students. For example, how much of a state dollar is left after you subtract Education, Health and Human Resources, and Other expenses? *($.22)* Which two items equal $.40? *(Health and Human Resources and Other)*

### Background INFORMATION

**STATE GOVERNMENT**

- Out of the 50 states, only New Jersey and Maine do not elect a lieutenant governor.
- Thirteen states, including New Jersey, elect twice as many members to the assembly as they do state senators.
- In May 2000, the governor's cabinet had seventeen departments.

### ✓Answers to THINK ABOUT IT

1. the system in which each branch of government watches over the other two so that no branch, person, or group becomes too powerful
2. Citizens develop an idea for a bill. Legislators propose it. The General Assembly and Senate vote to approve it. It becomes law if the governor signs it. If the governor vetoes the bill, it may still become law if the Assembly has enough votes to override the veto.
3. The executive branch carries out laws; the legislative branch makes laws; the judicial branch interprets laws.
4. Students should support their conclusions with facts from the section.
5. Students should provide thoughtful suggestions and reasons for laws.

**Write About It** Have students create a bumper sticker saluting one branch of New Jersey's state government.

**REMINDER**

**Practice and Project Book:** page 62

**Technology:** *Adventure Time CD-ROM*

**Transparency:** 1

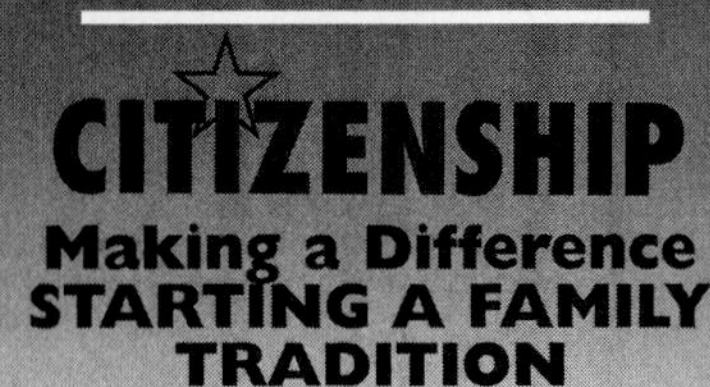

# CITIZENSHIP

## Making a Difference STARTING A FAMILY TRADITION

PAGE 281

**Lesson Overview**

A program called Kids Voting New Jersey lets students practice voting to help them establish a lifetime habit of exercising this important right and duty.

**Lesson Objectives**

★ Describe how Kids Voting New Jersey encourages voting.

★ Explain why voting is important.

## Identifying the FOCUS

Help students understand that the Ewing students who voted were part of a larger program called Kids Voting New Jersey. Make sure they realize that for the Ewing students to vote, they had to go to the polls. Most students probably voted while their parents were voting.

## Discussing WHY IT MATTERS

Discuss with students the importance of voting. Remind them that voting is the best way that citizens can influence or change their government. Ask them to speculate about what happens when only a few people vote in an election.

## Meeting INDIVIDUAL NEEDS

**RETEACHING (Easy)** Ask students to state the purpose of the Kids Voting New Jersey program in one or two sentences.

**EXTENSION (Average)** Have students pretend that they are running for a public office in their area. They should write a one-page campaign speech that explains why voters should choose them and what they will do while in office.

**ENRICHMENT (Challenging)** Have students research the program Kids Voting New Jersey to learn more about its sponsors and successes. Direct them to the organization's web site for details: **www.kvnj.org**

## CITIZENSHIP

**GETTING OUT THE VOTE** Have students find out when the next election will occur. Divide the class into committees to prepare a letter to the parents or guardians of children, reminding them of the importance of voting. Students may serve as writers, editors, photocopiers, and distributors of the letter.

## Field Trip

Arrange for students to visit the town or county clerk's office to see a voting machine and learn how it works. As an alternate activity, invite a representative of the League of Women Voters to visit your class to discuss the importance of voting and the work of the League.

## Curriculum CONNECTION

**LINKS TO LANGUAGE ARTS** Have students write a story about a child from their community going to vote with his or her parents. The story should include how the child decides for whom to vote, the voting process, the outcome of the election, and how the child feels about being a responsible citizen.

CHAPTER 11

# LESSON 3

## OUR NATIONAL GOVERNMENT

PAGES 282–285

### Lesson Overview

The United States is a democratic republic that operates under the Constitution. Like the state government, our national government is separated into three branches.

### Lesson Objectives

- ★ Define *democratic republic.*
- ★ Describe how the United States government pays for the services it provides.
- ★ Identify and describe the three branches of the national government.

### Reading Strategies and LANGUAGE DEVELOPMENT

**COMPARE AND CONTRAST** Draw a large Venn diagram, or two overlapping large circles, on the chalkboard. Label one circle "New Jersey state government" and one circle "United States national government." Label the overlapping area "both." As students work through the lesson, ask them to compare the national government with the state government by noting characteristics of, powers of, and services provided by each government in the appropriate area of the diagram.

### Second-Language SUPPORT

**WORKING WITH A PEER** Have second-language learners work in pairs with native English speakers. Partners should make a set of flash cards. On one side, each card should list a fact about one branch of the national government. On the other side, each card should name the relevant branch. Have students quiz each other using the cards.

### Technology CONNECTION

**ADVENTURE TIME CD-ROM**

Enrich this lesson with *United States, Explore, Investigate, Pictures* and *U.S. Congress* on the CD-ROM.

### Global CONNECTION

**THE UNITED NATIONS** The United Nations (UN) is an organization of countries dedicated to maintaining world peace. It began in 1945 with 51 countries. Today almost every nation in the world belongs to the UN. All members of the UN belong to the General Assembly and each member country has one vote. Fifteen nations belong to the UN's Security Council. The Security Council responds to threats to world peace. For example, it might decide to send a peacekeeping mission to a country on the verge of war.

### Building CITIZENSHIP

**SYMBOLS OF OUR COUNTRY** Challenge students to find as many symbols of our nation as they can. Symbols may include artifacts, such as flags and statues; pictures and photographs of symbols, such as the American eagle and the Capitol; musical selections, such as patriotic songs. Create a display of the symbols and invite another grade or class to visit it.

### √Answers to THINK ABOUT IT

1. a nation in which citizens elect representatives to run the government
2. a group of people who share similar ideas about government
3. to vote for representatives, to pay taxes, to obey the laws, to learn about important issues and let our representatives know our opinions on those issues
4. Voters can find out about a candidate's experience and opinions by reading newspapers.
5. Students should present several characteristics with a thoughtful discussion of their importance to the nation.

**Write About It** Have students write three questions that they would like to ask the President, their representative in Congress, and a Justice on the Supreme Court.

### Resource REMINDER

**Practice and Project Book:** page 63

 **Technology:** *Adventure Time CD-ROM*

ANSWERS TO

# Chapter 11 REVIEW

PAGES 286–287

### THINKING ABOUT VOCABULARY

**A.** Possible Answers:

1. Citizens usually have the right to elect a council.
2. This municipality has a very good mayor.
3. The legislative branch makes the laws and the judicial branch interprets them.
4. Even if the bill is passed, the President can still veto it.
5. Mr. Smith was a candidate for the United States Congress.

**B.**

1. legislative branch
2. bill
3. candidate
4. mayor
5. municipality
6. elect
7. United States Congress
8. council
9. veto
10. judicial branch

### THINKING ABOUT FACTS

1. Citizens elect government leaders, learn about important issues and let the leaders know what they think, pay taxes, obey our country's laws, and serve on juries.
2. the mayor
3. running the court system and keeping track of marriages, births, and deaths
4. executive, legislative, judicial; Each branch keeps watch over the other two branches.
5. the governor; for no more than two four-year terms

**Technology CONNECTION**

**ADVENTURE TIME CD-ROM**

Enrich Chapter 11 with *New Jersey, Explore,* and *Investigate* on the CD-ROM.

## Suggestions for THINK AND WRITE

**SIGNS OF SUCCESS**

***Plan*** Students' plans should suggest ways to use the money for specific educational programs or facilities.

***Poster*** Students' posters should accurately reflect the responsibilities of each branch of our state government.

***Article*** Students' articles should be presented in the form of an editorial, explaining that voting is a right as well as a responsibility.

*For performance assessment, see* **Assessment Book,** *Chapter 11, pages T63–T65.*

### APPLYING THINKING SKILLS

**READING NEWSPAPERS**

1. who, what, when, where, and why
2. In Search of Fields of Dreams; by David M. Campbell; West Windsor, December 15
3. An editorial is written by editors, sharing their ideas about an issue. It gives opinions rather than facts.
4. by saying that other communities should provide land for soccer fields.
5. what is happening in your area and the world

*Resource* **REMINDER**

**Practice and Project Book:** page 64

**Assessment Book:** Chapter 11 Test

***Performance Assessment,*** pages T63–T65

 **Technology:** *Adventure Time CD-ROM*

# New Jersey's People and Culture

Pages 288–307

## CHAPTER OVERVIEW

The culture of New Jersey has grown increasingly rich and diverse as it has become home to people from many different backgrounds. The people in our state live in big cities, suburbs, and small towns and enjoy many kinds of recreational activities.

## CHAPTER PLANNING GUIDE

**Suggested pacing: 13–14 days**

| LESSON | LESSON FOCUS | LESSON RESOURCES |
|---|---|---|
| **1 THE PEOPLE OF NEW JERSEY** pages 290–293 | The Diversity and Heritage of New Jerseyans | ***Practice and Project Book:*** page 65<br>***Technology:*** *Adventure Time CD-ROM* |
| **STUDY SKILLS** pages 294–295 | Writing Notes and Outlines | ***Practice and Project Book:*** page 66<br>***Technology:*** *Adventure Time CD-ROM* |
| **2 SPORTS AND RECREATION** pages 296–299 | What New Jerseyans Do for Fun | ***Practice and Project Book:*** page 67<br>***Transparency:*** 1<br>***Technology:*** *Adventure Time CD-ROM* |
| **LEGACY** pages 300–301 | The Jersey Shore | |
| **3 EDUCATION AND ARTS** pages 302–305 | New Jersey's Education System and Famous Creative Citizens | ***Practice and Project Book:*** page 68<br>***Technology:*** *Adventure Time CD-ROM* |
| **CHAPTER REVIEW** pages 306–307 | Students' understanding of vocabulary, content, and skills is assessed. | ***Practice and Project Book:*** page 69<br>***Assessment Book:*** Chapter 12 Test<br>***Performance Assessment*** pages T66–T68<br>***Technology:*** *Adventure Time CD-ROM* |

### New Jersey Core Curriculum Content Standards for Social Studies

**Content Standards** These content standards and progress indicators for students completing Grade 4, correlated with Chapter 12, have been developed by the New Jersey Department of Education. A complete listing of the standards can be found on pages T110–T112.

**Standard 6.1** All students will learn democratic citizenship and how to participate in the constitutional system of government of the United States.
2. page 291

**Standard 6.5** All students will acquire historical understanding of varying cultures throughout the history of New Jersey, the United States, and the world.
3. page 291; 4. pages 302–303

**Standard 6.8** All students will acquire geographical understanding by studying human systems in geography.
1. page 290; 2. pages 292–293;
5. pages 292–293, 298–301

CHAPTER 12

# LESSON 1

## THE PEOPLE OF NEW JERSEY

PAGES 290–293

**Lesson Overview**

A rich diversity of ethnic backgrounds characterizes New Jersey's people, who live in a variety of environments.

**Lesson Objectives**

★ Identify some of the ethnic groups that make up New Jersey's population.

★ Locate the northeastern megalopolis.

★ Describe the urban settings in which most New Jerseyans live.

### Reading Strategies and LANGUAGE DEVELOPMENT

**USE VISUALS** Ask a volunteer to read aloud the first heading on page 291. Then have students examine the photographs, chart, and captions in the lesson. Ask them how they would answer the question in the heading on the basis of the visuals. Have them expand their answers as they read the text.

### Second-Language SUPPORT

**DIALOGUES** In small group settings, ask second-language students to describe favorite celebrations from their countries of origin. Encourage them to bring photographs or other mementos to share with the class.

### Meeting INDIVIDUAL NEEDS

**RETEACHING (Easy)** Have students list the things they would choose to leave in a time capsule to be opened on our country's 500th birthday (2276). Give them opportunities to explain each choice and what they think it would imply about our culture today.

**EXTENSION (Average)** Have students work together to set up a class multicultural museum. Invite students to bring from home objects that show some aspect of their heritage as New Jerseyans or members of specific ethnic groups. Help students group and label the items to be displayed. Then allow students time to browse through the museum and ask questions of the donors.

**ENRICHMENT (Challenging)** Have students create a shadow box scene or diorama of an ethnic festival or holiday celebration. Students should research appropriate costumes and activities for their chosen festival.

### Building CITIZENSHIP

**CELEBRATING DIVERSITY** Have students select an ethnic group and stage their own ethnic fair. Form committees to research such areas as crafts, costumes, music, literature, foods, and drama. Each committee will create an appropriate presentation, such as singing and dancing, craft demonstrations, wearing native dress, and preparing ethnic foods. Invite other classes to attend the fair.

### Background INFORMATION

**THE OLD AND NEW OF WOODBRIDGE** Settled in 1664, Woodbridge is the oldest original township in New Jersey. Long known for brick making, it recently renovated its downtown with brick sidewalks. Its two-level enclosed shopping center is one of the largest in the East. One of New Jersey's edge cities, it includes access to high-speed train service that runs between Boston and Washington.

### ✓Answers to THINK ABOUT IT

1. any three: African American, Asian/Pacific Islander, European American, Hispanic, Native American
2. a giant city made of a chain of cities
3. Responses should reflect the many ethnic groups and types of places to live.
4. Responses should recognize that edge cities and suburbs have lots of housing, but edge cities also include office parks, factory areas, and shopping malls.
5. any five: Princeton, New Brunswick, Highland Park, Edison, Menlo Park, Rahway, Elizabeth

**Write About It** Have students write a poem about the New Jersey community or area where they live.

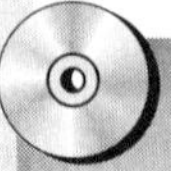

### Technology CONNECTION

**ADVENTURE TIME CD-ROM**

Enrich this lesson with *New Jersey, Explore,* and *Investigate,* on the CD-ROM.

### Resource REMINDER

**Practice and Project Book:** page 65

**Technology:** *Adventure Time CD-ROM*

CHAPTER 12

# SKILLS LESSON

## WRITING NOTES AND OUTLINES

PAGES 294–295

**Lesson Overview**

Taking notes and outlining are ways to organize information.

**Lesson Objectives**

★ Take notes while reading.

★ Organize notes into an *outline*.

### Why the SKILL MATTERS

Discuss how organizing information can save time and aid understanding. Explain that notes and outlines will help students write well-organized reports that are easy to understand. Also suggest that notes and outlines made while reading the text can be very useful when reviewing for tests.

### Using the SKILL

Have students cover up the outline on the Native American festival and then take notes on the article. Direct them to the *Helping Yourself* box. Guide them through the outlining process by asking for main ideas and details; write appropriate answers on the chalkboard in outline form. Then have students compare the class outline to the one in the text.

### Trying the SKILL

Have a volunteer read the article aloud. Then have students work in groups to take notes and make an outline.

### Technology CONNECTION

**ADVENTURE TIME CD-ROM**

Enrich this lesson with *Notebook* on the CD-ROM.

### Meeting INDIVIDUAL NEEDS

**RETEACHING (Easy)** Duplicate two- or three-paragraph sections from any textbook. Have students highlight the main idea of each paragraph with a colored highlighter. Then ask them to underline the supporting facts. As students master the process, have them transfer their work to their own paper as notes.

**EXTENSION (Average)** Have students take notes on and outline sections of the previous lesson. Remind them to take notes in their own words.

**ENRICHMENT (Challenging)** Ask students to find an article related to a topic in the previous lesson. Have them take notes on and outline the article. Ask them to use color coding to show how each idea transfers from article to notes to outline.

### Background INFORMATION

**ABOUT INFORMAL AND FORMAL OUTLINES**

Many writers consider any format that organizes information under main idea headings and supporting idea subheadings to be an outline.

- An outline with a loose form is considered informal.
- A formal outline has strict requirements: Roman numerals for main ideas, capital letters for supporting ideas, and Arabic numerals and small letters for further subclasses of ideas. A formal outline usually follows certain rules of form, such as never using one letter or numeral alone and beginning each subentry with a capital letter.
- The outline introduced in the text combines formal and informal elements.

### ✓Answers to REVIEWING THE SKILL

1. It helps to focus on main ideas, and it groups the facts that support them.
2. A main idea is general; supporting facts add more specific information about the main idea.
3. Responses should demonstrate an understanding of how main ideas differ from supporting facts.
4. Organizing ideas on paper makes them easier to understand and review.

**Resource REMINDER**

**Practice and Project Book:** page 66

**Technology:** *Adventure Time CD-ROM*

CHAPTER 12

# LESSON 2

## SPORTS AND RECREATION

PAGES 296–299

**Lesson Overview**

New Jersey has a wide variety of sporting events and recreational opportunities for its residents to enjoy.

**Lesson Objectives**

★ Identify some of the sports activities New Jerseyans can enjoy as participants and spectators.

★ Describe opportunities for outdoor fun involving New Jersey's parks, forests, and beaches.

### Reading Strategies and LANGUAGE DEVELOPMENT

**LANGUAGE HISTORY AND ETYMOLOGY** Tell students that athletes have a long history in human society, as illustrated by the Greek word *athlein*, from which the English word *athlete* is derived. *Athlein* means to compete, which is what ancient Greek athletes did in contests staged probably as early as the 1200s B.C. The first known Olympic competition took place in 776 B.C. in Greece.

### Second-Language SUPPORT

**TAKING NOTES** Second-language students may find it difficult to keep in mind the many examples included in this lesson. Help them use the headings in the text to devise main categories under which to list examples as they read. Headings might include *Kinds of Sports, Famous Athletes, Places for Outdoor Fun*. Encourage them to note details about the examples, such as what fun things there are to do at some of the places for outdoor fun.

### Field Trip

**VISITING A STATE PARK** Arrange to visit the state park nearest your community for a class picnic or nature walk. Before the visit, have the class research the history of the area where the state park is now located, when it became a state park, and what some of its special characteristics are. As an alternative, invite a park ranger to come to the school to discuss the parks in your community.

### Meeting INDIVIDUAL NEEDS

**RETEACHING (Easy)** Have students create postcards to send to a friend from a sports arena or place for outdoor fun in New Jersey. One side of the card should have an appropriate drawing or photo, the other a message the student writes about his or her activities at the site.

**EXTENSION (Average)** Have students plan a two-week vacation of sports and outdoor recreation activities in New Jersey. Have them create pocket-size booklets, with each page containing a date of arrival, the place they will visit, and what they plan to do there.

**ENRICHMENT (Challenging)** Have students research the physical setting and activities of a favorite recreational spot in New Jersey, such as the shore or a public park. Have them create a site model using various materials to make props and features.

### ✓Answers to THINK ABOUT IT

1. foot races; wrestling matches
2. sports in which players are paid
3. Possible responses include: winter—cross-country skiing, snowboarding; spring—visit historic sites; summer—swimming, boating, surf fishing, visit a water or amusement park; fall—visit historic sites.
4. Possible responses include: (1) sports—football, basketball, soccer, baseball, Special Olympics; (2) outdoor fun—visiting parks and beaches; (3) historic sites—visiting places George Washington slept.
5. highlands, rivers, canals, ocean

**Write About It** Have students write a personal experience story about a fun outing in New Jersey.

### Technology CONNECTION

**ADVENTURE TIME CD-ROM**

Enrich this lesson with *New Jersey, Explore,* and *Investigate* on the CD-ROM.

### Resource REMINDER

**Practice and Project Book:** page 67

**Technology:** *Adventure Time CD-ROM*

**Transparency:** 1

CHAPTER 12

# LEGACY

## LINKING PAST AND PRESENT THE JERSEY SHORE

PAGES 300–301

**Lesson Overview**

New Jerseyans and people from other areas have long enjoyed the sandy beaches and wildlife marshes of the Jersey Shore.

**Lesson Objectives**

★ Describe the features and activities to be enjoyed at the Jersey Shore.

★ Summarize the history of the Jersey Shore.

## Understanding the CONCEPT OF A LEGACY

Point out to students that the Jersey Shore has been enjoyed by people since the Lenape traveled there in the summer to harvest shellfish, making this area of New Jersey a legacy. Discuss why it is important to preserve the Jersey Shore for today and tomorrow.

## Examining the PHOTOGRAPHS

Have students examine the photographs on pages 300–301. Call on volunteers to read the photo captions. Ask students if they can add any further information about the images. Do some of the photos suggest their own experiences at the Jersey Shore? Invite students to relate their experiences.

## Thinking FURTHER

**COMPARING AND CONTRASTING** Have students identify each photo as either past or present. Ask what a photo of the Lenape might show. Have students list as many terms as they can to describe a common theme for all the photos, such as having fun, relaxing, and enjoying nature.

## Background INFORMATION

**SHIFTING SHORELINE** A number of lighthouses add to the shore scenery. The Sandy Hook lighthouse, opened in 1764, is the oldest operating lighthouse in New Jersey. In 1764, it was 500 feet from the tip of Sandy Hook. Since then ocean currents and waves have resculpted the sands so that today the lighthouse stands $1\frac{1}{4}$ miles from the tip.

## Curriculum CONNECTION

**LINKS TO HOME ECONOMICS** Invite students to conclude their study of New Jersey with a special treat—salt water taffy. Make sure that students understand that this recipe must be prepared under the close supervision of an adult. A candy thermometer is needed unless the adult has extensive candy-making experience.

**Ingredients:**

2 cups sugar

1 cup light corn syrup

1 cup cold water

$1\frac{1}{2}$ teaspoon salt

2 tablespoons butter (plus butter to grease pans)

$\frac{1}{8}$–$\frac{1}{4}$ teaspoon vanilla, chocolate, peppermint, or other flavoring

**Directions:**

- Butter the sides of a heavy 2-quart saucepan.
- Add all ingredients except butter and flavoring.
- Cook over medium heat, stirring constantly until sugar is dissolved.
- Continue to cook, without stirring, to the hard-ball stage. (The mixture reaches 248°F–254°F, as indicated on a candy thermometer, and a few drops form a hard ball when dropped in cold water.)
- Remove from heat and stir in butter and flavoring.
- Pour into a buttered 10 X 10 X 1 inch pan.
- Cool 15–30 minutes, or until candy can easily be picked up.
- Butter hands and pull taffy until it becomes stiff and difficult to pull.
- Divide into four or five parts.
- Pull each part into a long strip, about half an inch thick.
- Cut candy into small pieces and wrap each piece in cellophane.

CHAPTER 12

# LESSON 3

## EDUCATION AND ARTS

PAGES 302–305

**Lesson Overview**

New Jersey's strong public school system is supplemented by more than 50 institutions of higher learning. Many famous singers, artists, and poets come from New Jersey.

**Lesson Objectives**

- ★ Recognize the role New Jersey's schools play in the growth and success of its citizens.
- ★ Identify some well-known writers, visual artists, and performers from New Jersey.

### Reading Strategies and LANGUAGE DEVELOPMENT

**COMPOUND WORDS** Tell students that compound words are formed by combining two smaller words. Point out the word *schoolhouses* from page 302 and write it on the chalkboard. Have volunteers identify the two words that form *schoolhouses*, define its meaning in their own words, and then read aloud the dictionary meaning. Some compound words, like *schoolhouses*, are easily defined by the shorter words that form them. Have students find the compound words *icebox* and *earthworks* on page 304. Ask them if these words are easily defined this way. Have students give definitions in their own words, then consult the dictionary.

### Global CONNECTION

**SPRINGSTEEN ON TOUR** Bruce Springsteen has played throughout the United States and around the world. In 1999 alone, Springsteen and The E Street Band gave 87 shows in 44 cities in the United States and Europe for 1,800,000 fans. From early April to late June, they gave 35 shows in 26 cities in 13 European countries. In the United States, Springsteen and his band gave 52 shows in 18 cities from mid-July to late November. There were 15 shows at New Jersey's Continental Airlines Arena. All 15 sold out

### Technology CONNECTION

**ADVENTURE TIME CD-ROM**

Enrich this lesson with *New Jersey, Explore,* and *Investigate* on the CD-ROM.

### Background INFORMATION

**DOLLARS FOR SCHOLARS** New Jersey has many programs to help students continue their education beyond high school. Scholarship funds are awarded to high-achieving high school students. Tuition funds are also available to students with financial need.

### Curriculum CONNECTION

**LINKS TO LITERATURE** Write these lines from the beginning of William Carlos Williams's poem *Paterson* on the chalkboard:

> To make a start,
> out of particulars
> and make them general.

Help students understand that Williams is advising artists to start with something small or common and make something beautiful or meaningful from it. Invite students to try following the poet's advice in an original poem, painting, or sculpture. Some might make a miniature earthworks sculpture from sand, earth, water, and salt (designed to be viewed from above) in the manner of Robert Smithson. A large box with low sides could contain the sculpture.

### √Answers to THINK ABOUT IT

1. New Jersey's schools prepare young people for a world that is changing fast.
2. Any two: Walt Whitman, William Carlos Williams, Amiri Baraka, Robert Smithson, Sarah Vaughan, Frank Sinatra, Bruce Springsteen, Lauryn Hill
3. New Jersey's schools keep New Jersey at the forefront of fields like high technology, telecommunications, and research. The work of people in the arts enriches the lives of people everywhere.
4. New Jersey's public schools provide educated workers who help the economy grow.
5. Encourage students to be imaginative, but check their descriptions for accuracy.

**Write About It** Have students write a brief essay entitled "Going to School in New Jersey." Invite them to draw on their own experience as well as points in the lesson for ideas.

### Resource REMINDER

**Practice and Project Book:** page 68

 **Technology:** *Adventure Time CD-ROM*

ANSWERS TO

# Chapter 12 REVIEW

PAGES 306–307

### THINKING ABOUT VOCABULARY

1. diversity
2. C
3. C
4. C
5. C
6. C
7. C
8. ethnic group
9. C
10. C

### THINKING ABOUT FACTS

1. Festivals help people preserve their ethnic customs and share them with others.
2. They come in search of freedom and a better life.
3. African American, Asian/Pacific Islander, European American, Hispanic, Native American
4. Answers may include sports, outdoor activities, family gatherings, celebrations, and festivals.
5. the measure of how many people live in a certain place, usually a square mile
6. He was a Pulitzer Prize-winning poet; he used simple language to create beautiful images.
7. any three: Mahwah, Woodbridge, Princeton, Cherry Hill
8. New Jersey's government provides money for schools and teachers.
9. megalopolis
10. He is an Olympic athlete from Willingboro; he won 9 gold medals over a 16-year career in the Olympic Games.

## Suggestions for THINK AND WRITE

### SIGNS OF SUCCESS

***Paragraph*** Students' paragraphs should include a discussion of several ethnic groups and their contributions to the state. They should mention festivals and customs and note how diversity helps to make the state an interesting place to live.

***Article*** The headline should be short and catchy. Students might conduct imaginary interviews with the players involved in the sport they select and/or with fans of the sport. They might want to "cover" a sporting event and describe the mood of the crowd.

***Description*** The opening sentence should name the area and list recreational events and activities available there. The piece should include details that appeal to the five senses in order to provide a vivid picture of the area.

*For performance assessment, see* **Assessment Book,** *Chapter 12, pages T66–T68*

### APPLYING STUDY SKILLS

#### WRITING NOTES AND OUTLINES

1. An outline is a plan for organizing written information about a subject. It helps you identify the main ideas and the supporting details of the information you have gathered.
2. First, take notes in your own words as you read. Place a roman numeral beside each main idea. Write down facts that support each main idea. Write a capital letter beside each of these facts.
3. I. New Jersey is part of a megalopolis.
   - A. This megalopolis reaches from Boston to Washington, D.C.
   - B. New Jersey has the highest population density of any state.

   II. New Jersey provides a variety of places to live.
   - A. urban
   - B. rural

   III. Edge cities have grown up in our state.
   - A. Edge cities combine suburbs and cities.
   - B. They include office parks, factory areas, and shopping malls.
4. I. Many people enjoy outdoor recreation in New Jersey.
   - A. The shore is just one of many fun destinations.
   - B. State parks and forests offer great recreation.
   - C. Some places offer both winter and summer recreation.
5. Taking notes and writing an outline will help you organize information that you have taken from reference sources and provide a framework for your report.

**Practice and Project Book:** page 69

**Assessment Book:** Chapter 12 Test

**Performance Assessment,** pages T66–T68

**Technology:** *Adventure Time CD-ROM*

ANSWERS TO

# Unit 5 REVIEW

PAGES 308–309

### THINKING ABOUT VOCABULARY

1. C
2. consumer
3. bill
4. C
5. ethnic group
6. C
7. C
8. cyberspace
9. C
10. software

## Suggestions for THINK AND WRITE

### SIGNS OF SUCCESS

***Explanation*** Students' responses should include information about how to use dictionaries, encyclopedias, and CD-ROMs.

***Letter*** Students' letters should include as many details as possible about the types of recreational or cultural activities available in their chosen location, as well as a description of what they have seen and done.

***Report*** Students' reports should be accompanied by the notes they took while doing research. Have them organize the research notes into an outline and then write their reports in the same order as the outline.

## Building SKILLS

1. **Reading Newspapers** It is important to read newspapers to learn about current events.
2. **Reading Newspapers** To learn about an editor's opinion on an issue, you would read an editorial.
3. **Notes and Outlines** Taking notes and writing an outline can help you organize information because main ideas and supporting details are grouped together.
4. **Reference Sources** They contain information about many different subjects.
5. **Reference Sources** You would find the meaning of the word *judicial* in a dictionary.

## Suggestions for YESTERDAY, TODAY, AND TOMORROW

As students speculate about agricultural machinery of the future, remind them of the various changes in farming they have read about. Tell students to make predictions of new ways to accomplish old tasks that might appear on farms in New Jersey. Ask students what sort of inventions or advances might change the way farming is done. Students should understand and demonstrate how jobs change over time.

## ONGOING UNIT PROJECT

### OPTIONS FOR ASSESSMENT

The ongoing unit project, beginning on page T83, can be part of your assessment program, along with other forms of evaluation.

## UNIT PROJECT

### MAKE A GOVERNMENT TREE 

***Objective*** Designing a government tree will help students understand the functions and responsibilities of each of the different branches of local, state, and national governments.

***Materials*** posterboard, crayons or markers, construction paper, scissors, glue or tape

- Divide the class into groups. Suggest that students revisit the text to review the different branches of our national, state, and local governments.
- Encourage students to do additional research using an encyclopedia or other books to find out more about government.
- Give each group a supply of posterboard, crayons or markers, construction paper, scissors, and glue or tape.

### OPTIONS FOR ASSESSMENT

*For performance assessment, see* **Assessment Book,** *Unit 5, page T69.*

**FOR THE PORTFOLIO** Individual notes and sketches can be included in students' portfolios.

# UNIT 1 ANNOTATED BIBLIOGRAPHY


## Student Books

Aylesworth, Thomas G. ***Upper Atlantic: New Jersey, New York.*** New York: Chelsea House, 1987. An overview of geography, history, people, and sites of interest. **(Average)**

Barrow, Scott. ***Extraordinary New Jersey.*** Dublin, NH: Foremost Publishers, Inc./ Yankee Publishing Inc., 1988. Photographs of the beauty of the state's shore, woodlands, rivers, universities, communities. **(Easy)**

Fredeen, Charles. ***New Jersey***. Minneapolis: Lerner Publications, 1993. An introduction to geography, people, history, and industries. **(Average)**

■ Gibbons, Gail. ***Weather Forecasting.*** New York: Four Winds Press, 1987. This book explains how weather forecasters predict the weather and why weather forecasting is important. **(Easy)**

■ Knapp, Brian. ***Resources.*** Danbury, CT: Grolier Educational Corp., 1995. A study of natural resources such as coal and water, and our use of these resources. **(Average)**

***National Geographic United States Atlas for Young Explorers.*** Washington, DC: National Geographic Society, 1999. Maps, photo-essays, articles on regions of United States. **(Average)**

Parker, Steve. ***Pond and River***. New York: Alfred A. Knopf, 1988. This is a photo-essay about the range of freshwater plants, birds, fish, insects, mammals, amphibians. It includes brief mention of saltmarshes. **(Average)**

■ Rauzon, Mark J. and Cynthia Overbeck Bix. ***Water, Water Everywhere***. San Francisco: Sierra Club Books for Children, 1994. Read about the movement of water on the Earth's surface changing the geography and movement of people on the planet. **(Average)**

Sauvain, Philip. ***Rivers and Valleys.*** Minneapolis: Carolrhoda Books, Inc., 1995. The texts and illustrations demonstrate the sources, terrain, waterfalls, dams, reservoirs, wildlife, and flooding of rivers. Includes activities and questions to enhance understanding of impact of rivers' geography in shaping the land. **(Challenging)**

Taylor, Barbara. ***River Life.*** New York: Dorling Kindersley, Inc., 1992. A photo-essay about the plants, amphibians, birds, fish, insects, mammals, and reptiles that live in or along the banks of rivers. **(Average)**

## Teacher Books

Brown, Michael P. ***New Jersey Parks, Forests, and Natural Areas: A Guide.*** New Brunswick, NJ: Rutgers University Press, 1992. Includes national, state, county, and some municipal parks. It is divided into six regions by counties and includes practical information about locations, phone numbers, fees, hiking sites, hours, special activities, picnic sites.

DiIonno, Mark. ***New Jersey's Coastal Heritage: A Guide.*** New Brunswick, NJ: Rutgers University Press, 1997. Jersey Shore and Delaware Bay. This lists museums, buildings, and landmarks that highlight life along Jersey's shore, marsh, and Delaware Bay. Practical information about locations, phone numbers, fees.

## Read-Alouds

Livingston, Myra Cohn. ***Earth Songs.*** New York: Holiday House, 1986. This book contains poems that celebrate the continents, glaciers, mountains, lowlands, forests, waterways, and oceans.

Luenn, Nancy. ***Squish! A Wetland Walk.*** New York: Atheneum Books for Young Readers, 1994. Simple, poetic language and watercolor paintings convey the smell, sight, sound, and feel of marshes, swamps, bogs, and estuaries.

## Technology Multimedia

***Road Adventures U.S.A.*** CD-ROM. While learning geography, history, and math, students can map a road trip across the country. The Learning Company, 1999. 1-800-685-6322

## Free or Inexpensive Materials

Information about national parks in New Jersey, including the Delaware Water gap National Recreation Area, can be obtained from the U.S. government on the Internet at http://www.nps.gov/parklists/nj.html


■ *Book featured in the student bibliography of the Unit Review.*

# UNIT 2 ANNOTATED BIBLIOGRAPHY

## Student Books

Bierhorst, John. ***The White Deer and Other Stories Told by the Lenape.*** New York: William Morrow, 1995. This book contains origin tales, tales of heroic children, trickster tales, and amusing or poignant dog stories. **(Challenging)**

Cunningham, John T. ***This is New Jersey**, 4th ed.* New Brunswick, NJ: Rutgers University Press, 1994. Reference tool with descriptions of travel, industry, and history in each county. **(Challenging)**

Davis, Burke. ***Black Heroes of the American Revolution.*** New York: Harcourt Brace, 1976. An account of African American participants in the struggle for independence. **(Challenging)**

Fradin, Dennis Brindell. ***The New Jersey Colony.*** Chicago: Children's Press, 1991. Examines the history of the New Jersey colony from its beginnings to statehood after the Revolutionary War. **(Average)**

McPhillips, Martin. ***The Battle of Trenton.*** Morristown, NJ: Silver Burdett, 1985. This book presents the events in the Revolutionary War leading up to the Battle of Trenton and describes the clash and its aftermath. **(Average)**

■ Rinaldi, Ann. ***A Ride into Morning: the Story of Tempe Wick.*** San Diego: Harcourt Brace Jovanovich, 1991. When unrest spreads at the Revolutionary War camp in Morristown, NJ, a young woman cleverly hides her horse from the mutinous soldiers who have need of it. **(Average)**

■ Topper, Frank. ***A Historical Album of New Jersey.*** Brookfield, CT: Millbrook Press, 1995. This book gives a history of New Jersey from its earliest settlement by Native Americans to modern times. **(Average)**

Van Laan, Nancy. ***Rainbow Crow: A Lenape Tale.*** New York: Alfred A. Knopf, 1989. Tale of Crow, who flies up to receive the gift of fire from the Great Sky Spirit when the weather changes and heavy snows fall. **(Easy)**

■ Walker, Sally M. and Ellen Beier. ***The 18 Penny Goose.*** New York: HarperCollins Publishers, 1998. Eight-year-old Letty attempts to save her pet goose from marauding British soldiers. **(Average)**

Wilker, Josh. ***The Lenape Indians***. Broomall, PA: Chelsea House, 1994. This book examines the history, culture, and future prospects of the Lenape Indians. **(Challenging)**

## Teacher Books

Cohen, David Steven. ***The Folklore and Folklife of New Jersey.*** New Brunswick, NJ: Rutgers University Press, 1983. Oral traditions including legends, jokes, names, medicines, music, and dance; non-spoken traditions such as food, architecture, painting, games, and festivals.

McCormick, Richard P. ***New Jersey From Colony to State, 1609-1789.*** Newark: New Jersey Historical Society, 1981. A general survey of the state's history from Hudson's voyage through ratification of the U.S. Constitution.

## Read-Alouds

Avi. ***The Fighting Ground.*** New York: Lippincott, 1984. The story of thirteen-year-old Jonathan who goes off to fight in the Revolutionary War and discovers the real war is being fought within himself.

Osborne, Mary Pope. ***Standing in the Light: The Captive Diary of Catharine Carey Logan, Delaware Valley, Pennsylvania.*** New York: Scholastic, 1998. A Quaker girl's diary of growing up in the Delaware Valley, and her capture by the Lenape in 1763.

## Technology Multimedia

***The Lenape.*** (videocassette) Shows traditional Lenape life, first contacts with white settlers, the impact of white civilization on the Lenape, and current attempts to preserve the culture. Bala Cynwyd, PA: Schlessinger Video Productions, 1994. 1-800-843-3620

## Free or Inexpensive Materials

Information on the Lenape can be obtained from the Lenni Lenape Historical Society on the internet at http://www.lenape.org/

---

■ *Book featured in the student bibliography of the Unit Review.*

# UNIT 3 ANNOTATED BIBLIOGRAPHY

## Student Books

Bial, Raymond. ***The Underground Railroad.*** Boston: Houghton Mifflin, 1995. This book discusses the slave trade, daily life of slaves, and flight of fugitives to freedom, with photographs of slave quarters, chains, and hiding places. **(Average)**

■ Duffey, Betsy. ***The Gadget War***. New York: Puffin Books, 1991. Kelly Sparks has forty-three inventions to her credit, but with Albert Einstein Jones in the gadget war, which child has more imagination? **(Average)**

■ Hesse, Karen. ***Letters from Rifka***. New York: Henry Holt, 1992. In letters to her cousin at the turn of the twentieth century, a young Jewish girl describes her family's flight from Russia and her own experiences as she emigrates to America. **(Average)**

Mitchell, Barbara. ***The Wizard of Sound: A Story about Thomas Edison.*** Minneapolis: Carolrhoda Books, Inc., 1991. Chronicles the life and inventions of Edison, from his sickly childhood to creation of the phonograph. **(Average)**

■ Murphy, Jim. ***The Journal of James Edmond Pease: a Civil War Union Soldier, Virginia, 1863***. New York: Scholastic, 1998. James Edmond Pease, a sixteen-year-old orphan, keeps a journal of his experiences and those of "G" Company in the Union Army. **(Average)**

Ransom, Candice F. ***Children of the Civil War.*** Minneapolis: Carolrhoda Books, Inc., 1998. Explores the lives of children during the Civil War–those who joined armies, others who stayed home, and the large numbers who were left homeless due to the war. **(Average)**

Wallner, Alexandra. ***The First Air Voyage in the United States: the Story of Jean-Pierre Blanchard.*** New York: Holiday House, 1996. The voyage of an eighteenth-century French aeronaut by hot air balloon from Philadelphia to Woodbury, New Jersey, in 1793. **(Easy)**

Wulffson, Don L. ***The Kid Who Invented the Popsicle: and Other Surprising Stories about Inventions.*** New York: Cobblehill Books/Dutton, 1997. Stories about how various familiar things were invented, many by accident, from animal crackers to the zipper. **(Average)**

■ *Book featured in the student bibliography of the Unit Review.*

## Teacher Books

Sandler, Martin W. ***Civil War***. New York: HarperCollins, 1996. An overview of the Civil War from the causes and issues to the surrender at Appomattox, with photographs from the collection of the Library of Congress.

Sandler, Martin W. ***Inventors.*** New York: Harper Collins, 1996. This book draws upon photographs, documents, and illustrations from the Library of Congress to present information on some of the great inventions of history and discusses how they led the way to new industries and discoveries.

## Read-Alouds

Hamilton, Virginia. ***Many Thousand Gone: African Americans from Slavery to Freedom.*** New York: Alfred A. Knopf, 1993. This anthology of stories details hardships, escapes, courageous moments, and tragic episodes. The introductory notes enhance student understanding of issues.

Polacco, Patricia. ***Pink and Say.*** New York: Philomel Books, 1994. Picture book for older students. Say Curtis describes his meeting with Pinkus Aylee, a black soldier, during the Civil War, and their capture and imprisonment in Andersonville.

## Technology Multimedia

***Inventors and Inventions.*** (videocassette) Surveys a variety of inventions, from compact discs and cellular telephones to better milk jugs, that help people live longer, learn better, be more productive, and enjoy leisure time. Washington, D.C.: National Geographic Society, 1995. (202) 857-7215

## Free or Inexpensive Materials

A Civil War re-enactment with 14th Regiment New Jersey Volunteers Company H, presented by the New Jersey Civil War History Association Inc., can be accessed on the Internet at http://www.webcom.com/14njcoh/

# UNIT 4 ANNOTATED BIBLIOGRAPHY

## Student Books

■ Curtis, Christopher Paul. ***Bud, Not Buddy***. New York: Delacorte Press, 1999. Read about tough times during the Great Depression by reading about ten-year-old Bud, a motherless boy living in Flint, Michigan, who escapes a bad foster home and sets out in search of the man he believes to be his father, the renowned band leader H.E. Calloway of Grand Rapids. **(Average)**

Freedman, Russell. ***Kids at Work: Lewis Hine and the Crusade against Child Labor.*** New York: Clarion Books/Houghton Mifflin, 1994. This book closely examines the role of children in the industrial age and the subsequent changes in legislation. **(Challenging)**

George, Linda and Charles George. ***Civil Rights Marches.*** Chicago: Children's Press, 1999. Witnesses describe the Civil Rights protests. **(Average)**

■ Hesse, Karen. ***Out of the Dust***. New York: Scholastic, 1997. Experience the gritty times of the Dust Bowl through an unusual novel written as a cycle of poetry. **(Average)**

Lawrence, Jacob. ***The Great Migration: An American Story.*** New York: Harper Collins, 1993. Using paintings and narration, Lawrence chronicles the journey of African American migrants from the South. **(Easy)**

Stein, R. Conrad. ***The Great Depression.*** Chicago: Children's Press, 1993. An overview of the bleak period in American life after the Stock Market Crash. **(Average)**

■ Sullivan, George. ***The Day Women Got the Vote: a Photo History of the Women's Rights Movement***. New York: Scholastic, 1994. Learn more about the history of Women's Suffrage by reading fascinating information and examining dramatic photos in magazine-style format. **(Challenging)**

Wright, David K. ***Paul Robeson: Actor, Singer, Political Activist.*** Springfield, NJ: Enslow, 1998. A biography of the famous African American who played football for Rutgers and later became a noted actor, singer, and political activist. Includes primary sources. **(Challenging)**

■ *Book featured in the student bibliography of the Unit Review.*

## Teacher Books

Cohen, David Steven, ed. ***America, the Dream of My Life: Selections from the Federal Writers' Project's New Jersey Ethnic Survey.*** Piscataway, NJ: Rutgers University Press, 1990. Poignant personal histories of the immigrant experience in the Garden State, recorded in the 1930s.

Colman, Penny. ***Strike: The Bitter Struggle of American Workers from Colonial Times to the Present,*** Brookfield, CT: Millbrook Press, 1995. First-hand reports, contemporary songs, and vivid descriptions chronicle the battles that workers fought for better working conditions.

## Read-Alouds

McKissack, Patricia. ***Color Me Dark: The Diary of Nellie Lee Love, The Great Migration North, Chicago, Illinois, 1919.*** New York: Scholastic, 2000. A novel about an African American girl is presented through her diary of her experiences leaving the rural South to move North for a better life.

## Technology Multimedia

***World War II Era PictureShow.*** CD-ROM. Washington, D.C.: National Geographic Society, 1998. This book discusses the rise of dictators, the blitzkrieg, and the Allied victory. Includes class activities. English or Spanish narration and text. 1-800-368-2728.

***Civil Rights PictureShow*** CD-ROM. Washington, D.C.: National Geographic Society, 1998. This book discusses Martin Luther King, Jr., the change in lives of African Americans from slavery to full citizenship, and the influence of the Civil Rights Movement on Native Americans and women. Includes class activities. English or Spanish narration and text. 1-800-368-2728.

## Free or Inexpensive Materials

Information about Paul Robeson, with pictures and text, can be obtained from Rutgers University on the Internet at: http://www.rutgers.edu/robeson/main.html

# UNIT 5 ANNOTATED BIBLIOGRAPHY


## Student Books

Halperin, Wendy Anderson. ***Once Upon a Company: A True Story.*** New York: Orchard Books, 1998. The story of a seven-year-old boy and his sisters who started a wreath-making business that grew to include other businesses, marketing, wholesaling, and investing. **(Average)**

■ Harness, Cheryl. ***Ghosts of the White House***. New York: Simon and Schuster Books for Young Readers, 1998. Let George Washington's ghost pull you out of a school White House tour and take you on a personal tour of the building, introducing you to the ghosts of previous presidents and to the history of the White House and of the United States. **(Average)**

■ Hurwitz, Johanna. ***Class President***. New York: Morrow Junior Books, 1990. Have you ever run for class office? When Julio's interest shifts from managing his best friend's election campaign to becoming a candidate himself, Julio has to figure out how to enter the contest and keep his friendship. **(Average)**

McElroy, Lisa Tucker. ***Meet My Grandmother, She's a Supreme Court Justice.*** Brookfield, CT: Millbrook Press, 1999. A photo-essay about one day in the life of Sandra Day O'Connor is written from her grandchild's perspective. **(Easy)**

Prolman, Marilyn. ***The Constitution.*** Chicago: Children's Press, 1995. Explanations are provided about the significance of the Constitution and how it functions. **(Average)**

■ Sachar, Louis. ***Marvin Redpost, Class President***. New York: Random House, 1999. What if the President of the United States came to your school? Laugh with Marvin when his class has a special visitor. **(Average)**

Stein, R. Conrad. ***The Bill of Rights.*** Chicago: Children's Press, 1992. This book explains the Bill of Rights and the significance of the amendments to the Constitution. **(Average)**

Stein, R. Conrad. ***The Powers of the Supreme Court.*** Chicago: Children's Press, 1995. Explanations are provided of the role of the Judicial Branch of government. **(Average)**


■ *Book featured in the student bibliography of the Unit Review.*


## Teacher Books

Maestro, Betsy and Giulio Maestro. ***The Voice of the People: American Democracy in Action.*** New York: Lothrop, Lee & Shepard Books, 1996. Explains how democracy depends on the participation of the citizens through the election process.

Prabhu, Barbara Williams, ed. ***Spotlight on New Jersey Government**, 6th ed.* Piscataway, NJ: Rutgers University Press, 1992. This book provides a detailed explanation of state government and services. 1-800-446-9323

## Read-Alouds

Fritz, Jean. ***Shh! We're writing the Constitution.*** New York: Putnam Group Publishing, 1998. Explores the complex issue of the Constitutional Convention, from which emerged the basis of our government.

Herold, Maggie. ***A Very Important Day.*** New York: Morrow Junior Books, 1995. This picture book makes the perfect introduction to a civics unit. 219 people from 32 different countries make their way to downtown New York in a snowstorm to be sworn in as citizens of the United States.

## Technology Multimedia

***Trumpet Video Visits Donald Crews.*** (videocassette) A fast-paced video about a Newark-born African American award-winning author and illustrator of children's books. The Trumpet Club, Scholastic, 1992. (212) 343-6100

***20th Century Day by Day.*** CD-ROM. Tracks events day by day, month by month. Includes video clips, news stories, and archival sound clips. DK Multimedia, 1999. (877) 884-1600

## Free or Inexpensive Materials

Sports information of interest children can be obtained from the State of New Jersey on the Internet at http://www.state.nj.us/hangout/njsports.html

# New Jersey Core Curriculum Content Standards for Social Studies:

## Grade 4 Progress Indicators

**Standard 6.1** All students will learn democratic citizenship and how to participate in the constitutional system of government of the United States.

**Descriptive Statement:** Social studies must promote civic and democratic principles so that students become informed and active citizens. Before students can make informed decisions, they must have a knowledge of the United States Constitution and the constitutional system of the United States Government. Students should participate actively in constructive public action, including registering to vote, and should seek ways to contribute based on the rights and privileges afforded all citizens.

**Cumulative Progress Indicators** By the end of Grade 4, students:

1. Identify key principles embodied in the United States Constitution, and discuss their application in specific situations.
2. Identify examples of the rights and responsibilities of citizens.
3. Assess information about a public issue.
4. Give examples of the impact of government policy on their lives.
5. Identify key documents which represent democratic principles and beliefs, such as the Declaration of Independence, the United States Constitution, the Bill of Rights, the New Jersey Constitution, and the Pledge of Allegiance.
6. Identify symbols of American principles and beliefs, such as the flag and the blindfolded Statue of Justice.

**Standard 6.2** All students will learn democratic citizenship through the humanities, by studying literature, art, history and philosophy, and related fields.

**Descriptive Statement:** The humanities, history, literature, the arts, philosophy, law and related fields of study, enrich students' understanding of the human experience. They form a body of knowledge about human experience that is indispensable to informed civic participation in our democratic society. They enable students to recognize the moral and ethical dilemmas which have brought us to the present, and to project where our choices may lead in the future.

Through reading, writing, viewing and discussing humanities materials, students develop a knowledge base for understanding the complexities of American and world cultures. The humanities also equip students with a set of conceptual tools needed to engage in informed civic discourse about how to resolve conflicts between diverse cultures within our democratic society.

**Cumulative Progress Indicators** By the end of Grade 4, students:

1. Recognize human experiences through time, as depicted in works of history, and literature and in the fine arts.
2. Identify social history represented in works of literature and the fine arts.
3. Understand how works of aesthetic expression serve as cultural representations.
4. Evaluate works, such as personal creations, which communicate a human condition or question.

**Standard 6.3** All students will acquire historical understanding of political and diplomatic ideas, forces, and institutions throughout the history of New Jersey, the United States, and the world.

**Descriptive Statement:** History is the study of the human past: society's memory of where it has been, what it values, and how decisions of the past have contributed to present conditions. History deals with chronological sequences, continuity and change, the multiple causes and effects of historical phenomena, and changing interpretations of the past. Historical inquiry enables students to evaluate evidence and analyze events, fostering informed decision-making and thoughtful reflection.

In order to ensure that students share a common core of knowledge, by the end of their school experience students of United States history should have studied all five of the following major periods in history:

- The Colonial Period (to 1763)
- The Revolution and Early National Period (to 1820)
- The Age of Civil War and Reconstruction (to 1870)
- Industrial America and the Era of World Wars (to 1945)
- The Modern Age

In addition, students of World History should have studied all seven of the following World History Periods:

- Prehistory (to 2000 BC)
- The Ancient World (to 500 BC)
- The World of Hemispheric Interactions and the "Middle Ages" (to 1400)
- The Age of Global Encounters (to 1700)
- The Age of Revolutions (to 1850)
- The Age of Imperialism and World War (to 1950)
- The Modern World

School districts are encouraged to define the balance among materials from Western, Asian, African, and other world cultures in each of these periods. Furthermore, several suggested themes are included among the history standards to enhance and enrich the study of history.

**Cumulative Progress Indicators** By the end of Grade 4, students:

1. Apply the concepts of cause, effect, and consequences to historical events.
2. Analyze varying viewpoints of individuals and groups at turning points throughout history.
3. Identify and explain how events and changes occurred in significant historical periods.
4. Explain issues, standards, and conflicts related to universal human rights.

**Themes** By the end of their school years, students should have studied, within the periods outlined above, a designated number of the following specific themes:

The history of different political systems, with special attention to democracy; the history of relations among different political groups and entities; the history of warfare; the history of political leadership.

**Standard 6.4** All students will acquire historical understanding of societal ideas and forces throughout the history of New Jersey, the United States, and the world.

**Descriptive Statement:** The present can only be understood in the context of understanding how and why people acted in the past. History studies human behavior and motivation, since people have created governments and institutions based on their needs. Students should have opportunities to study the impact of various societal forces on the history of New Jersey, the United States, and the world.

In order to ensure that students share a common core of knowledge, by the end of their school experience students should have studied all five of the major periods in United States history cited in Social Studies Standard 6.3. In addition, students should have studied all seven of the World History periods cited in Social Studies Standard 6.3. School districts are encouraged to define the balance among materials from Western, Asian, African, and other world cultures in each of these periods. Furthermore, several suggested themes are included among the history standards to enhance and enrich the study of history.

**Cumulative Progress Indicators** By the end of Grade 4, students:

1. Compare and contrast similarities and differences in daily life over time.
2. Identify social institutions, such as family, religion, and government, that function to meet individual and group needs.
3. Identify instances when the needs of an individual or group are not met by their social institutions.
4. Identify events when people have engaged in cruel and inhumane behavior.

**Themes** By the end of their school years, students should have studied, within the periods outlined above, a designated number of the following specific themes:

The history of social classes and relations; the history of gender differentiation; the history of slavery; the history of agriculture; the history of population movements; the history of cities and city life.

**Standard 6.5** All students will acquire historical understanding of varying cultures throughout the history of New Jersey, the United States, and the world.

**Descriptive Statement:** Because we live in an interdependent world, students should be aware of the variety of approaches used by different cultures to define and meet their basic needs. Students should understand the impact of different cultures and civilizations at specific times and over time, and be aware of cultural similarities as well as differences. As students become more aware of varying cultures, they are more likely to understand themselves, the diversity and cultural values of others, and people in their own communities and in other parts of the world.

In order to ensure that students share a common core of knowledge, by the end of their school experience students should have studied all five of the major periods in United States history cited in Social Studies Standard 6.3. In addition, students should have studied all seven of the World History periods cited in Social Studies Standard 6.3. School districts are encouraged to define the balance among materials from Western, Asian, African, and other world cultures in each of these periods. Furthermore, several suggested themes are included among the history standards to enhance and enrich the study of history.

**Cumulative Progress Indicators** By the end of Grade 4, students:

1. Identify common elements found in different cultures.
2. Describe ways that family members, teachers, and community groups influence students' daily lives.
3. Describe the customs of people from different geographic, cultural, racial, religious, and ethnic backgrounds.
4. Describe the influence of technology in daily life.
5. Understand material artifacts of a culture.
6. Examine particular events, and identify reasons why individuals from different cultures might respond to them in different ways.

**Themes** By the end of their school years, students should have studied, within the periods outlined above, a designated number of the following specific themes:

The history of religion; the history of literature; the history of the arts; the history of education; the history of law; the history of popular culture; the history of philosophy and political and social thought.

**Standard 6.6** All students will acquire historical understanding of economic forces, ideas, and institutions throughout the history of New Jersey, the United States, and the world.

**Descriptive Statement:** Economic systems develop as individuals and societies employ resources to produce and distribute goods and services, while government policies develop to aid, control, and improve these activities. Whether economic decisions and policies are personal, institutional, or governmental, they are made in an interconnected context. Students should have the knowledge and skills to understand the economic forces which influence their lives, and to make decisions which maximize their own economic well-being and that of the larger society.

In order to ensure that students share a common core of knowledge, by the end of their school experience students should have studied all five of the major periods in United States history cited in Social Studies Standard 6.3. In addition, students should have studied all seven of the World History periods cited in Social Studies Standard 6.3. School districts are encouraged to define the balance among materials from Western, Asian, African, and other world cultures in each of these periods. Furthermore, several suggested themes are included among the history standards to enhance and enrich the study of history.

**Cumulative Progress Indicators** By the end of Grade 4, students:

1. Explain and demonstrate the role of money in everyday life.
2. Describe the relationship of price to supply and demand.
3. Describe work that people perform in our economic system.
4. Distinguish between wants and needs.
5. Illustrate the balance between economic growth and environmental preservation.

**Themes** By the end of their school years, students should have studied, within the periods outlined above, a designated number of the following specific themes:

Early agriculture; the history of travel and communications; the role of cities; the history of economic regulation; industrial revolutions; the history of banking and international finance; the history of the corporation.

**Standard 6.7** All students will acquire geographical understanding by studying the world in spatial terms.

**Descriptive Statement:** Thinking in spatial terms is essential to knowing and applying geography. It enables students to take an active, questioning approach to the world around them and to ask what, where, when, and why questions about people, places and environments and to formulate answers to critical questions about past, present, and future patterns of spatial organization, and to anticipate the results of events in different locations. Thinking spatially, students learn to devise their own mental maps, which relationships and students' perceptions and attitudes about the area. Thinking spatially enables students to predict what might happen given specific conditions. Spatial concepts and generalizations are powerful tools for explaining the world at all levels, from local to global. They are the foundation for geographical understanding.

**Cumulative Progress Indicators** By the end of Grade 4, students:

1. Use maps, globes, graphs, diagrams, and computer-based references and information systems to generate and interpret information.
2. Use mental maps to identify the location of places within the local community and in nearby communities.
3. Use mental maps to identify the locations of the earth's continents and oceans in relation to each other and in relation to principal parallels and meridians.
4. Use mental maps to identify the locations of major physical and human characteristics in the United States and on earth.
5. Demonstrate understanding of the spatial concepts of location, distance, direction, scale, region, and movement.

**Standard 6.8** All students will acquire geographical understanding by studying human systems in geography.

**Descriptive Statement:** Students need to understand the interaction of human and environmental factors. The study of human systems includes the characteristics, distribution, and migration of human populations on the earth's surface; the characteristics, distribution, and complexity of the earth's cultures; patterns and networks of economic interdependence; processes, patterns, and functions of human settlement; and how cooperation and conflict influence the division and control of the earth's surface.

**Cumulative Progress Indicators** By the end of Grade 4, students:

1. Identify the distribution and characteristics of populations at different scales, and understand the causes and effects of human migration.
2. Discuss the similarities, differences, and interdependencies among rural, suburban, and urban communities.
3. Compare the effects of geography on economic activities locally and in New Jersey, the United States, and different parts of the world.
4. Explain how improvements in transportation and communication have resulted in global interdependence.
5. Compare the physical characteristics of places and regions.

**Standard 6.9** All students will acquire geographical understanding by studying the environment and society.

**Descriptive Statement:** Students should learn how people are able to live in various kinds of physical environments by developing patterns of spatial organization that take advantage of opportunities and avoid or minimize limitations.

**Cumulative Progress Indicators** By the end of Grade 4, students:

1. Explain the characteristics of renewable and nonrenewable resources and their distribution, and the role of resources in daily life.
2. Explain how people depend on the physical environment and how they modify the environment.
3. Identify the consequences of natural environmental changes and crises and human modifications of the environment, and explain how an event in one location can have an impact upon another location.

STANDARDIZED TEST SUPPORT

# New Jersey

## ADVENTURES IN TIME AND PLACE



Throughout the school year, students have been learning and practicing many new skills. These skills are often assessed in a standardized test format. This section offers helpful tips and strategies for you to familiarize students with standardized test-taking.

It is suggested that you periodically review these strategies with your students to prepare them for the standardized tests they will be taking. During this time tell students that by working hard and paying attention to what you say, they will be ready for success on these standardized tests. Also remind students that you will help them prepare for these tests so that they won't be nervous or anxious.

Ensuring success for all students is a major goal of McGraw-Hill's *Adventures in Time and Place*. We hope these strategies will make all your students more successful learners.

# READ QUESTIONS CAREFULLY

The most common mistake students make when they take a test is to answer the questions too quickly. Rushing through a test causes careless mistakes. Don't rush. Read each question carefully. Make sure you understand the question BEFORE you try to answer it.

**Use the map to answer questions 1 through 3.**

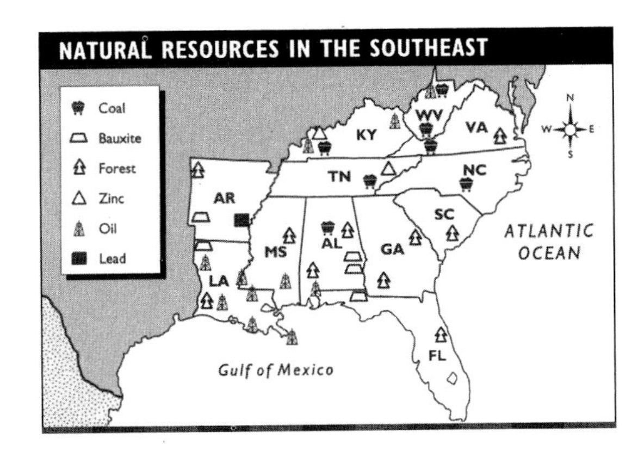


**1** In which state is oil an important natural resource?

- **A** Georgia
- **B** North Carolina
- **C** Louisiana
- **D** Tennessee

**2** South Carolina's natural resources include

- **F** bauxite
- **G** zinc
- **H** coal
- **J** forest

**3** In which state would a lead miner be most likely to find a job?

- **A** Arkansas
- **B** West Virginia
- **C** Florida
- **D** Alabama

**Remember: Do not write in your textbook.**



*Remind students not to write in their textbooks before beginning this section. Students will have a separate answer sheet when taking standardized tests. For the exercises that follow, they should respond aloud or on a separate piece of paper.*

## READ QUESTIONS CAREFULLY

**OBJECTIVES:**

- To reinforce good test-taking skills by directing students to pay careful attention to test questions.
- To make students aware of the fact that careless errors are the most common errors on standardized tests.

**Teaching suggestions:** Explain to students that good test-taking skills require students to take a careful look at questions BEFORE attempting to answer them. Students must also get in the habit of looking over the accompanying data before they begin answering the accompanying questions.

Have students read the questions and choose the correct answers.

1. **C** Louisiana. Oil—symbolized by an oil well—is not indicated in Georgia (forests only), North Carolina (coal only), or Tennessee (coal and zinc). Other states have oil, but they are not given as answer choices.

2. **J** Forests are the only natural resources indicated on the map for South Carolina.

3. **A** Arkansas. This question requires an additional level of reasoning from students. Students must infer that a lead miner would most likely find a job in a state in which lead is an important natural resource. Arkansas is the only state on the map that fits this description.

# TIME LINES

**OBJECTIVES:**

- To reinforce time line reading skills learned in class.
- To familiarize students with one type of time line question that they are likely to see on nationally administered standardized tests.

**Teaching suggestions:** Have students practice using their fingers to locate information on a time line. Direct them to find several years during which significant events occurred in Hawaiian history. Ask them which groups started to arrive in Hawaii in 1870. Ask them what happened in Hawaii during the 1890s.

Have students read the questions and choose the correct answers.

1. **D** According to the time line, Polynesians arrived in Hawaii around the year 500.

2. **F** According to the time line, European and American traders reached the Hawaiian islands during the years 1800 to 1860. Because 1845 falls within that time span, answer choice F is the best answer.

To wrap up the activity, direct students to find years during which NO significant event occurred. Ask them to find where 1790 falls on the time line, then ask them to find the event in Hawaiian history that occurred closest in time to 1790.

# TIME LINES

Historical information is sometimes presented in the form of a time line. A time line shows events in the order in which they happened. Time lines are usually read from left to right, like a sentence. If the time line is drawn vertically, it is usually read from top to bottom.

If you read carefully, you should do very well on time line questions.

**Look at the time line below. Then answer questions 1 and 2.**

**Groups Arrive in Hawaii, 500–1900**

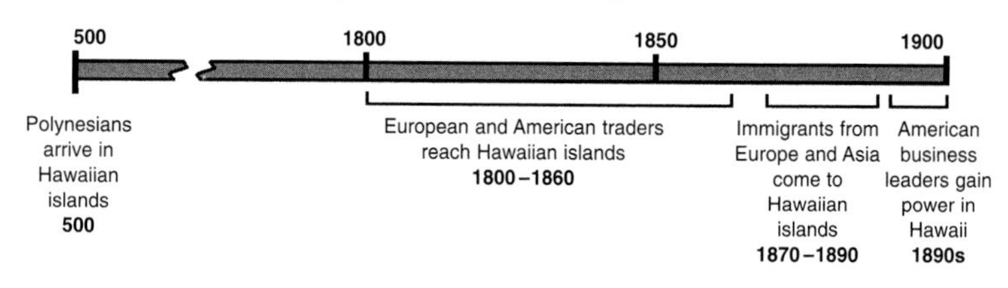


**1** Which group was the first to reach the Hawaiian islands?

- **A** Europeans
- **B** Americans
- **C** Asians
- **D** Polynesians

**2** Which of the following most likely occurred in 1845?

- **F** Traders from Europe and America came to the Hawaiian islands.
- **G** The first Polynesians arrived in the Hawaiian islands.
- **H** American business leaders gained power in Hawaii.
- **J** Asian immigrants came to the Hawaiian islands.



**Remember: Do not write in your textbook**

# LOOK AT THE DETAILS BEFORE YOU START

Some test questions contain lots of details. These questions may use:

- charts
- graphs
- flow charts
- time lines
- word webs
- maps

Before you try to answer questions like these, take a few moments to study the information that the charts, graphs, maps, or other visuals contain. The questions will be much easier to answer, because you will know exactly where to look for information!

**Study the bar graph. Then do questions 1 and 2.**

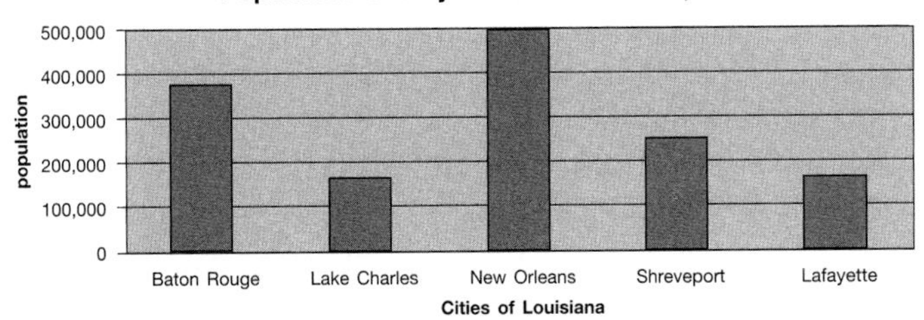


**1** In 1990, which Louisiana city had a population of about 380,000?

**A** Lake Charles
**B** New Orleans
**C** Shreveport
**D** Baton Rouge

**2** In 1990, which two Louisiana cities had approximately the same population?

**F** Baton Rouge and New Orleans
**G** Lake Charles and Lafayette
**H** Shreveport and Baton Rouge
**J** New Orleans and Lake Charles

**Remember: Do not write in your textbook.**



## LOOK AT THE DETAILS BEFORE YOU START

**OBJECTIVE:**

- To reinforce good test-taking skills by directing students to pay careful attention to the visuals accompanying questions.

**Teaching suggestions:** Read out loud the list of types of visuals that might accompany standardized test questions. Ask students to suggest some of the details that might accompany each type of visual. Prompt students with examples: charts might include titles, bar graphs include labels that tell you what each bar represents, etc.

Ask students to identify the information presented in the bar graph accompanying this question. Ask: **Which cities are represented?** (Baton Rouge, Lake Charles, New Orleans, Shreveport, Lafayette) **Which city has the smallest population?** (Lake Charles) **What is its population?** (about 170,000 or 180,000) **Which city has the largest population?** (New Orleans) **What is its population?** (about 500,000)

Have students read the questions and choose the correct answers.

1. **D** The graph indicates that the population of Lake Charles is approximately 180,000; New Orleans, 500,000; Shreveport, 250,000; Baton Rouge, 380,000.

2. **G** According to the graph, both have populations of approximately 180,000. If students are not sure what "approximately" means, let them know that it is the same as "about" or "around."

# DIFFERENT TYPES OF GRAPHS

**OBJECTIVES:**

- To reinforce students' knowledge of different types of graphs.
- To familiarize students with two types of graph questions that they are likely to see on nationally administered standardized tests.

**Teaching suggestions:** Read the first two paragraphs of the page aloud to the class. As you read paragraph one, ask students to think of examples of the different types of graphs discussed. Perhaps some are displayed in the classroom. Or, you might ask students to point out examples of the different types of graphs in their textbooks.

Have students read the questions and choose the correct answers.

1. **C** The line graph indicates this information. Ask students to explain what words in the question indicated to them that the answer would be found in the line graph (population, 380,000).

2. **F** The pie graph indicates this information. Ask students to explain what words in the question indicated to them that the answer would be found in the line graph ("working", "professionals"). Students do not need to actually know the meanings of the words "professionals" or "manufacturers," as long as they know how to read the rest of the graph.

# DIFFERENT TYPES OF GRAPHS

Different types of graphs are used to present numerical information. A **line graph** shows how something changes over time. A line graph might be used to show how the population of the United States has grown over the years. A **bar graph** compares amounts. A bar graph might show the population of different United States cities. A **circle graph** shows how a whole is divided into smaller parts. For example, a circle graph might show how the government divides its budget to pay for roads, education, and other services.

Sometimes you will see a set of questions accompanied by more than one graph. Each question will contain clues to tell you which graph you should read to find the answer. Take the extra time to make sure you are looking at the correct graph. This will help you avoid careless mistakes.

**Use the graphs below to answer questions 1 and 2.**

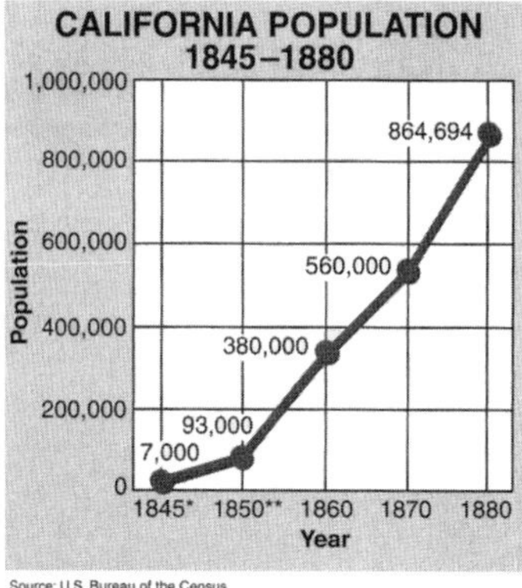


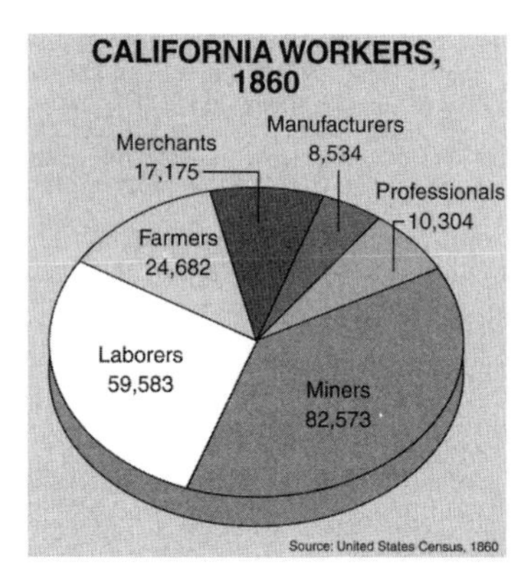


**1** In what year did the population of California reach 380,000?

- **A** 1840
- **B** 1850
- **C** 1860
- **D** 1870

**2** How many people were working as professionals in California in 1860?

- **F** 10,304
- **G** 17,175
- **H** 59,583
- **J** 82,573



**Remember: Do not write in your textbook.**

# PROCESS OF ELIMINATION

Sometimes when you read a test question, you will not know the answer right away. If you don't know the answer, don't give up. You may be able to find the correct answer another way.

On a multiple-choice test, you can look at the answer choices. One of the answers will be the best answer. The others will be wrong, or not as good. Look at the choices and see if there are any that you know are definitely wrong. If there are, you can ELIMINATE, or ignore, those answers.

Sometimes you will be able to eliminate all of the answers except one. When that happens, it means that you have found the best answer by the PROCESS OF ELIMINATION.

Try using the process of elimination to answer this question:

**1** The largest city in South Dakota is

**A** Los Angeles
**B** Dallas
**C** Sioux Falls
**D** Mexico City

Were you able to eliminate any *wrong* answers? How many?

Now try using the process of elimination to answer this question:

**2** The section of the United States Constitution that protects the freedom of Americans is called the

**F** Declaration of Independence
**G** Bill of Rights
**H** Civil War
**J** Star Spangled Banner

**Remember: Do not write in your textbook.**



## PROCESS OF ELIMINATION

**OBJECTIVES:**

- To make students aware of valid alternate strategies to problem solving.
- To teach students to use process of elimination on multiple-choice tests when they are unsure of the correct answer.

**Teaching suggestions:** Read the introductory material aloud to students. Then read the questions aloud, and ask students to use process of elimination to eliminate answers that cannot be correct. Ask them: **Could Los Angeles be the largest city in South Dakota? How about Dallas?** Persuade students to consider all answer choices, even when they believe they have found the correct answer before considering all choices. Say: **Let's look at the other answers to make sure that we have selected the best one.**

This skill will serve students well throughout their standardized test-taking careers.

1. **C** Sioux Falls. Most important here is that students recognize that Los Angeles, Dallas, and Mexico City are large cities NOT located in South Dakota. This is enough information to eliminate them as incorrect. What the student should realize is that s/he has found the correct answer even if s/he did not initially know that Sioux Falls was the largest city in South Dakota.

2. **G** Have students identify each of the incorrect answers and explain why they CANNOT be the correct answer. The Declaration of Independence is not part of the Constitution, but is instead the document that pronounced the colonies' separation from England. The Civil War is an historical event; the Star Spangled Banner is the United States' national anthem.

# OUTSIDE KNOWLEDGE

**OBJECTIVES:**

- To familiarize students with one type of question that they are likely to see on nationally administered standardized tests.
- To alert students to the fact that some questions will require students to remember information they have learned in class.

**Teaching suggestions:** Read the first three paragraphs aloud to students. Then have students answer the two sample questions on their own.

1. **B** This question tests students' familiarity with reference sources. It is a commonly tested area of information on nationally administered standardized tests for fourth grade.

2. **J** This question tests students' familiarity with basic characteristics of U.S. regions. This also is a commonly tested area of knowledge on nationally administered standardized tests for fourth grade.

# OUTSIDE KNOWLEDGE

Many questions on multiple-choice tests ask you to look at a map, a chart, a graph, or a drawing. Then you are asked to choose the correct answer based on what you see. On these questions, the information you need to answer the question will be in the map, chart, graph, or drawing.

Sometimes, however, multiple-choice tests will ask you to remember a fact that you learned in social studies class. You won't be able to find the correct answer on a map, chart, graph, or drawing; the correct answer will be in your memory. We call these OUTSIDE KNOWLEDGE questions.

If you are sure you know the answer to an OUTSIDE KNOWLEDGE question, choose the correct answer. It's that simple! When you're NOT sure what the correct answer is, use the PROCESS OF ELIMINATION to answer the question.

**1** Which of these books would probably provide the most information about the life of Martin Luther King, Jr.?

- **A** an atlas
- **B** an encyclopedia
- **C** a novel about the South during the Civil War
- **D** a collection of poetry

**2** Which of the following statements about the southern portion of the United States is true?

- **F** The South does not have many farms.
- **G** The South is home to the largest cities in the United States.
- **H** The South is the most mountainous region in the United States.
- **J** The South has a warmer climate than the northern United States.



**Remember: Do not write in your textbook.**

# FLOW CHARTS

A flow chart shows the sequence of steps used to complete an activity. It shows the steps in the order they happen. A flow chart usually uses arrows to show which step happens next.

The first thing to do when you look at a flow chart is to see if it has a title. The title will tell you what the flow chart is about. The next thing you should do is find the arrows. The arrows tell you the order in which to read the chart.

Read flow charts carefully. Don't just look at the illustrations. Make sure to read any text beneath the illustrations.

**Study the flow chart. Then do questions 1 and 2.**

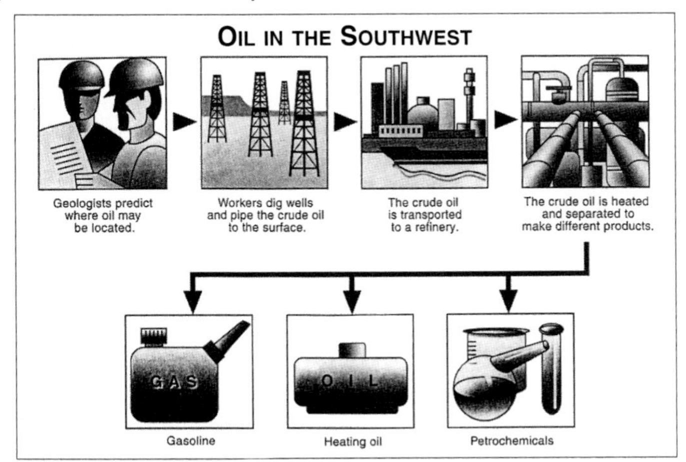


1 Which of these questions is answered by the flow chart?

- A What are some of the products that can be made from crude oil?
- B How much does it cost to produce heating oil?
- C Where in the United States is the most crude oil found?
- D How many automobiles are there in the United States?

2 The crude oil is probably transported to the oil refinery in

- F automobiles
- G large ships
- H helicopters
- J tractors

**Remember: Do not write in your textbook.**



# FLOW CHARTS

**OBJECTIVES:**

- To reinforce flow chart reading skills learned in class.
- To familiarize students with one type of flow chart question that they are likely to see on nationally administered standardized tests.

**Teaching suggestions:** Read the first three paragraphs of this page aloud to students. Have students identify the title of the accompanying flow chart ("Oil in the Southwest") at the appropriate time. Ask students to identify which step is the first in the petroleum production process described by the flow chart.

Have students read the questions and choose the correct answers.

1. **A** The flow chart indicates that gasoline, heating oil, and petrochemicals are all petroleum end products.

2. **G** Students may take any of several approaches to this question. The illustration in the flow chart provides a clue to the answer; above the entry "The crude oil is transported to the refinery," the illustration shows an oil tanker delivering crude oil. Students can also use process of elimination by reasoning that automobiles, helicopters, and tractors are all too small to deliver crude oil to a refinery.

# MAPS

**OBJECTIVES:**

- To reinforce map skills learned in class.
- To familiarize students with one type of map-reading question that they are likely to see on nationally administered standardized tests.

**Teaching suggestions:** Have the class read the first half of the page out loud. Call on students to read each of the questions concerning the features of a map, and review the terms "map key," "compass rose," and "scale." Then have students apply these questions to the map of Pennsylvania.

Remind students that careless errors are easy to make on standardized tests. Reinforce the idea that students should look at the map and all its parts BEFORE trying to answer the question.

Have students read the questions and choose the correct answers.

1. **B** Students should use process of elimination on this question, eliminating all resources that are found in eastern Pennsylvania. Coal, zinc, and iron ore can all be found in the region between Harrisburg and Philadelphia. Natural gas is found only in the western portion of the map. If students answer "coal," they probably looked for the western-most symbol on the map, instead of the resource found only in the western part of Pennsylvania. Remind students to read each question carefully.

2. **G** Scranton is surrounded by symbols for coal. Of all the workers mentioned in the answer choices, a coal miner would have the best chance of finding work near Scranton.



# MAPS

The ability to read and understand maps is an important skill in social studies. Many of the multiple-choice tests you take will require you to read a map.

Look carefully at all the parts of a map. Maps contain a lot of information. Whenever you see a map, you should ask yourself questions like these:

- What does the title of the map tell you?
- Where is the map key?
- What symbols are on the map key? What do they stand for?
- Where is the compass rose?
- What does the compass rose tell you?
- Is there a map scale?

**Use the map of Pennsylvania to answer questions 1 and 2.**

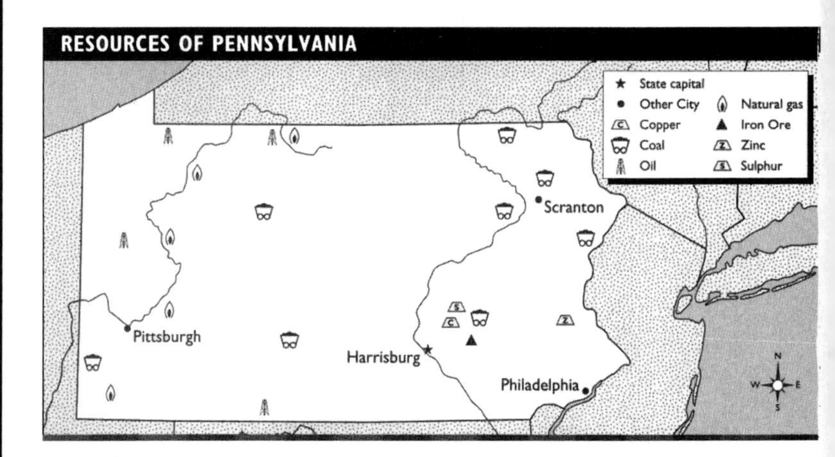


**1** Which natural resource is found only in the western part of Pennsylvania?

- **A** zinc
- **B** natural gas
- **C** coal
- **D** iron ore

**2** Which of these people would be most likely to find a job near Scranton?

- **F** a driller of oil wells
- **G** a coal miner
- **H** a miner of iron ore
- **J** a zinc miner



**Remember: Do not write in your textbook**

CIRCVLVS ARCTICVS
ANIAN regnum
AMERICA SIVE IN DIA NOVA. Ao 1492. a Christophoro Colombo nomine regis Castelle primum detecta.
Tolm
Chilaga
Noua Francia
Estotilant
Groclant
QVIVIRA regnu
Totonteac
Marata
Calicuas
Tagil
Florida
La Bermuda
TROPICVS CANCRI
Hispania noua
MAR DEL NORT
Archipelago di
CIRCVLVS AEQVINOCTIALIS
Caribana
Tisnada
Peru
Amazones
Brasil
MAR DEL ZVR
TROPICVS CAPRICORNI
Hanc continentem Australem, nonnulli Magellanicam regionem ab eius inventore nuncupant.
EL MAR PACIFICO
Chile
Chica
Rio de la Plata
Archipelago
Terra del Fuego
CIRCVLVS ANTARCTICVS
190 200 210 220 230 240 250 260 270 280 290 300 310 320 330
TERRA AVSTRA